THE PRACTICAL MAN'S
BOOK OF
THINGS TO MAKE AND DO

THE HANDYMAN AT WORK

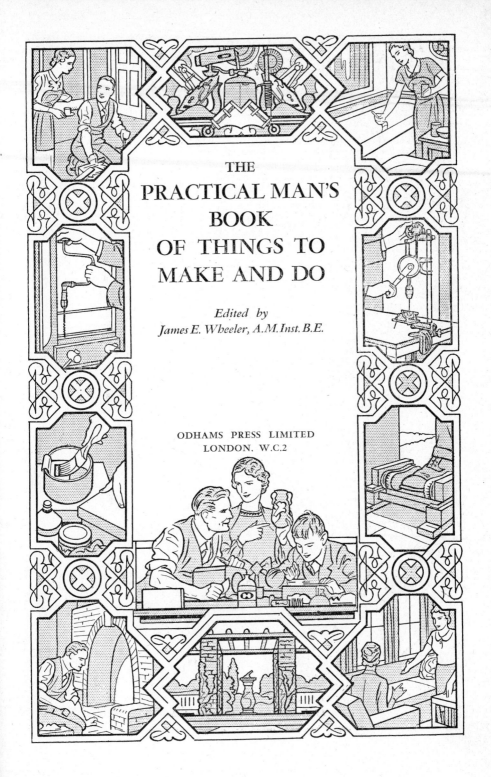

THE
PRACTICAL MAN'S
BOOK
OF THINGS TO
MAKE AND DO

Edited by
James E. Wheeler, A.M.Inst.B.E.

ODHAMS PRESS LIMITED
LONDON. W.C.2

Made and Printed in Great Britain by
Odhams (Watford) Limited, St. Albans Road, Watford.

INTRODUCTION

IT does not matter very much what particular form the pastime may take—whether it be woodworking, metalworking, household decoration, gardening or any other of the numerous spare-time occupations—the man with a hobby is generally far happier, more resourceful and better able to think things out for himself than one who has no interest in anything other than his usual routine of work, meals and sleep.

The man who can use tools properly is to be envied, for the field in which he can exercise his ability and skill is practically unlimited. He need never be bored for lack of something to do. There are hundreds of useful things to be made out of doors during the summer months and innumerable articles which can be constructed in the shelter of a room or workshop during the long evenings of winter.

And not only does such employment occupy spare time in a pleasant manner and satisfy the natural instinct to create something with one's own hands, but it is possible to make such recreations pay for themselves. Numerous cases can be instanced where new tools and equipment have been procured out of small commissions—such as making or repairing articles of furniture, decorating rooms, cycle repairing and what not; and many an amateur has looked to his tools as a temporary means of earning a livelihood when other ways have failed.

The man who selects carpentry as a means of occupying his spare time is to be congratulated on his choice, for few crafts involving the use of tools offer more variety. Moreover, working in wood has the advantage of promoting much healthy physical exercise. Each kind of handiwork, however, has its own peculiar charm and usefulness; and it would be useless further to stress their relative merits.

Before starting on work of a practical nature it may be as well to acquaint yourself with the following hints.

First you must be familiar with, and know how to use the numerous tools employed and the properties of materials used. Remember that no amount of description will teach you half so much as the actual work.

Make up your mind at the outset to be methodical in your work, otherwise your efforts may become a bore rather than an interesting and pleasant pastime. In woodwork, for example, if you have several parts to be glued, do all the gluing at one operation, as it is a waste of time and energy to continue to re-heat and prepare glue. The same thing applies, of course, to metalwork as instanced in the process of soldering. First prepare all the parts to be soldered and then carry on with the soldering.

Make a point of being accurate in your measurements and marking out, and always check such dimensions before starting any mechanical operations, bearing in mind that it is easier to reduce the size of a piece of work than to increase it. A little forethought bestowed upon the work in hand will often be the means of saving much unnecessary labour and will tend towards economy in material. It is extremely annoying to find a piece of work, which may have taken hours of patient labour to execute, condemned to the scrap-heap on account of a small error in measurement having been made at the start. Such errors are generally the result of being in too much of a hurry and of not paying attention to detail. Take things steadily and do not rush at the task. The old adage "more haste less speed" applies truly to work of a mechanical nature.

An important preliminary is the preparation of working drawings. Before starting on any work, always make a sketch or working drawing of the object you intend to construct. It may happen that you wish to make a certain article or piece of apparatus of your own design, in which case a working drawing is almost a necessity. It is much easier to alter a drawing if some detail or other does not suit than to alter or make fresh parts during construction.

If you are faced with a difficult problem, do not let it get the better of you, but make up your mind to master it and never hesitate to seek advice from a skilled worker. Much can be learned by watching skilled men at work; therefore, always make a point of keeping your eyes open and of making a mental note of what you see.

An example of how easily information can be gained if sought is instanced in the following: A keen amateur who found much pleasure in "tinkering" with small organs of the reed type wished to add a number of wooden pipes and thus enlarge the capacity of his instrument. Thinking over the proposition, he realised that there must be a snag somewhere, otherwise professional builders of organs would adopt this simple combination of harmonium, reed and pipes in their large instruments. He made it his business to find out by paying a visit to an organ factory. Here, the proprietor at once informed him that the idea was impracticable as it would be necessary to retune the pipes to the reeds practically every time the instrument was played. He also gave his reasons.

The moral to be learned from the above is obvious. Do not go ahead with a scheme if you have any misgiving, when a little extra knowledge may make all the difference.

Here are a further two suggestions worth following: Always keep your tools under lock and key and do not make a habit of lending them. You will then have only yourself to blame if tools are missing, and they will not be damaged by inexperienced hands.

Do not start on a difficult piece of work until you can make a perfect job of a simple one. Furthermore, do not begrudge the little extra time expended in finishing off work neatly. A few minutes extra labour generally determines the dividing line between good and bad craftsmanship. Get into the habit of always completing the work in hand before starting upon anything new, because one completed object is of more use than a dozen unfinished.

Keep a couple of junk boxes, one for odd pieces of hardwood and the other for scraps of metal and miscellaneous items such as nuts and bolts. You will be surprised how useful such odds and ends can be at times.

CONTENTS

THINGS FOR THE WOOD-WORKER TO DO

THE BEST WAY TO PURCHASE WOODWORKING TOOLS

HIGH-GRADE tools are essential. Hence it is wise to obtain your kit from a dealer who specialises in tools, and not be tempted in purchasing tools from a store where low prices are the chief consideration and quality an after-thought.

Although you yourself may be able to afford a full equipment of tools at the outset, there are hosts of others who cannot. In this case, there is no better plan than to purchase a few of the essentials and then acquire the remainder singly as the necessity arises. This method fosters economy inasmuch as it prevents the purchase of superfluous tools; that is to say, those which are required only on very rare occasions.

Second-hand tools are sometimes offered for sale at bargain prices, but it is unwise to purchase such articles unless you are competent to judge good tools.

A Beginner's Outfit.—Here is a list of the most important tools to enable you to make a good start in simple woodwork. The outlay is just over £4.

	s.	d.
Hand Saw, 20 in.	7	6
Tenon Saw, 10 in.	6	0
Jack Plane, in metal, 2 in. double iron	15	6
Smoothing Plane, metal, with adjustable iron	12	0
Pad Saw and Blade	1	6
Brace, ratchet type, 8 in. sweep ball bearings	7	6

½ doz. Bits	2	6
5 Fimer Chisels, $\frac{1}{8}, \frac{1}{4}, \frac{3}{8}, \frac{1}{2}, \frac{3}{4}$ in.	5	0
Gouge, ½ in. externally ground	1	0
Spokeshave	2	0
Screwdrivers, 4 in. and 9 in. blades	2	6
Try Square	2	3
Marking Gauge	1	3
Hammer, Warrington pattern	1	3
Nail Punch		3
Pincers	1	6
Oilstone, 8 × 2 × 1 in.	5	3
Mallet	1	6
Gimlets, small and medium sizes	1	6
Bradawls, small and medium sizes		8
Rule, 2 ft. four-fold type	2	0
£4	0	5

The figures given in the above list are for tools of really good quality, which, if properly looked after, should give years of service. This amount could be cut down by about 15s. if wooden planes were substituted for metal ones, but this would be false economy.

Tools for Advanced Work.—In due course, as progress is made, the following items will be found of great assistance:

	£	s.	d.
⅜ in. Jointer Plane	1	0	0
Combination Plane, Metal	1	10	0
Small Block Plane, double ended		6	0

Hand Drill-stock and Twist-drills	.. .. ..	7	6
Wing Compasses	.. ..	2	6
Rip Saw	.. .. ..	7	6
Set of Jennings' pattern Twist-bits in Canvas Roll	.. 1	0	0
Cutting Pliers	.. ..	1	6
Light Hammer	.. ..	1	0
Adjustable Bevel	.. ..	3	0
Mortice Gauge	.. ..	3	0
Spirit Level ..	.. ..	3	6
Fretsaw	.. ..	3	6
Grindstone ..	 1	5	0

£6 14 0

A strong work bench fitted with an adjustable vice in front for gripping material and an adjustable stop on top for work to butt against are essential items of the woodworker's equipment. Such a bench can be purchased ready made for approximately 30s., or it could be made at home if desired. As the construction of a work bench is simple and does not entail extreme accuracy, the beginner should make a point of starting his woodworking career by making one. Care must be taken not to make it too light and flimsy. A work bench should be rigid and of sufficient weight to keep it in place when in use.

Other accessories such as mitre block, shooting board, winding strips, straight-edge, and cramps can all be home constructed.

HINTS ON TOOLS, MATERIALS AND PROCESSES

THE following short articles on tools, materials, processes and items of interest to the amateur woodworker, metalworker, electrician and others have been arranged alphabetically for easy reference and should be read by the

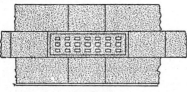

Air Brick

novice before making or proceeding with any of the useful things contained in this volume.

Air Brick.—A cast iron grating of the same size of a brick (see figure) has replaced the old-fashioned air brick with holes for ventilation purposes. Its chief use is to allow a current of air to pass from the outside into the space under the ground floors of buildings. Stagnant air in such spaces is conducive to dry rot. For this reason it is all important to see that such bricks are not allowed to become blocked up either with old leaves or soil. Broken grids should be replaced, as large apertures are likely to entice vermin.

Aluminium.—A whitish coloured metal produced in the electric furnace. It is the lightest metal in common use, being only about one-third the weight of iron. Non-corrodable, soft and easy to work. Aluminium cannot be soldered unless a proper flux is used, owing to a film of oxide which forms on the surface. The metal is easy to turn in the lathe, but unless the turning tool is very keen, particles of metal adhere to the cutting edge of the tool.

Turpentine is good to use when turning, drilling and screwing. Paraffin can be used, but is not so effective.

American Whitewood. — Often called canary wood, is of a yellowish-white colour. Although classified as a hardwood is really soft. It is of even texture, straight grained and fairly easy to work. Excellent for cabinet and other interior work. Can be stained and polished to imitate other more expensive woods and is used largely in cheap cabinet making, shopfitting, etc. Can be obtained in wide boards.

Bass wood resembles whitewood but is lighter in colour and softer.

Annealing.—Annealing or softening metals is sometimes required to make them workable. To anneal steel, heat it to a cherry red and allow to cool slowly in ashes or similar material. Copper and silver is softened by heating it up to a dull red heat and then plunging it in clean cold water. Brass can be annealed by heating it up to a dull red colour and then immersing it in warm water and allowing it to remain there until cold. On no account should brass

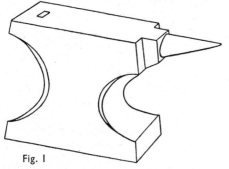

Fig. I

or copper be heated to above the stage given, otherwise it may be burned.

Anvil.—A shaped iron block having a hardened steel face (see Fig. 1) used principally by smiths for hammering upon. Such a tool will be found extremely useful in amateurs' workshops for such purposes as straightening out dents in sheet metal, straightening bars, and for giving a solid foundation when clinching nails. Anvils are rather expensive to buy, and one of a good quality measuring $8\frac{1}{2}$ in. by $2\frac{1}{2}$ in.

and weighing 15 lb. costs about 26s.

As an anvil requires a solid foundation it should be mounted upon a tree butt, but an oil drum filled with sand makes a good substitute.

For light work a domestic iron held in the vice (Fig. 2) is useful as a makeshift.

Fig. 2

Asbestos. — An incombustible mineral of great importance owing to its heat-resisting qualities. Its chief use from the practical man's point of view is perhaps in the form of asbestos-cement sheets which make a highly satisfactory cladding for garages, sheds and even bungalows. Such sheets are to be obtained in two standard sizes, 8 × 4 ft. and 6 × 4 ft. respectively and in thickness of $\frac{3}{16}$, $\frac{1}{4}$, $\frac{3}{8}$ in.

In fixing asbestos-cement sheets to framework it is important to see that the uprights are not spaced too far apart. A maximum of 2 ft. should not be exceeded. An allowance of about $\frac{1}{16}$ in. should be made between the joints to enable the nails of a covering batten to pass into the framework. New sheets are comparatively soft and nails may be driven into them with ease, but they become brittle with age and it is therefore necessary to drill nail holes before fixing. Galvanised wire nails about $1\frac{1}{2}$ in. long driven in at intervals of about 8 in. will make a sound job.

To cut new sheets use an old cross-cutting saw; for old material score it deeply with the corner of a triangular file guided by a straight-edge. A great saving of material will be effected if window openings, etc., are arranged to come between joints. Where this is not possible it is a good plan to cover such apertures and then remove the waste with the aid of a pad saw.

A pleasing finish can be obtained by allowing the rough side of the sheets to be painted and face the outside of the structure instead of erecting the sheets smooth side out, which is more usual.

Corrugated sheeting for roofing is also to be had which allows of a more

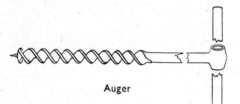

Auger

even temperature within the structure than does galvanised iron.

Asbestos cement slates are also excellent for covering roofs, while ridge tiles of the same material are to be obtained at most builders' merchants.

Owing to the heat-resisting qualities of asbestos, it is used extensively for lagging or jacketing boilers, hot-water pipes, domestic cylinders, etc. A hot-water system can very often be much improved by its use. For this, asbestos is mixed with water to make a thick paste. It is then put on with a trowel. To ensure a good job, three applications giving a total thickness of $2\frac{1}{2}$ in. should be made and should be put on while the apparatus is hot. The first one should be about $\frac{1}{2}$ in. thick and can be rough and allowed to dry. Then the second layer can be given, and when dry narrow wire mesh netting should be securely bound on to prevent the finishing layer

from peeling off. The final coat should be smooth and painted black when dry. Asbestos mats can be obtained for lagging purposes.

Ash.—A hardwood of light brown colour, straight grained and very tough. Durable if kept dry and very elastic. Owing to this latter feature it is not used for constructional work, but is excellent for such articles as oars, shafts of tools, spokes of wheels and other things where elasticity is needed.

Arris.—The edge of wood forming the angle between two exterior faces. This sharp edge should always be removed to prevent cut fingers. This can be done either by a plane held at an angle to chamfer the edge slightly or by a special tool called a cornering tool.

Auger.—A woodwork tool resembling a twist-bit used for boring long holes, as indicated in the figure. A hole is provided at the top of the shank through which a piece of round hardwood or a metal bar is inserted to obtain leverage. In use, augers in good condition do not require pressure after the screw point has entered the wood, the cone-shaped screw point drawing the tool into the material as the handle is rotated. These tools can be obtained for cutting holes from $\frac{3}{8}$ in. to 2 in. in diameter.

Batten.—A term given to lengths of timber varying in width from $1\frac{1}{2}$ in. to 3 in. and from $\frac{1}{2}$ in. to $1\frac{1}{4}$ in. in thickness. Used largely as a fixing for roofing tiles. Can be obtained sawn or prepared, i.e., planed. Battens are extremely useful for making light framework. Lengths of prepared batten, spaced at equal distances apart on horizontal rails, make excellent palings for fences.

Beech.—A hardwood of yellowish-white to brown colour, most of which is produced in Great Britain. Very tough and splits easily, hard and has a compact grain. Excellent for wood-turning and wooden parts of tools, chairs, cabinet work. Durable if permanently wet or dry; otherwise it is subject to rot.

Bells, Electric. —An electric bell is one of the most useful devices in the home, and provided it is kept in proper adjustment and installed in a dry place uncontaminated by steam or gas fumes, will give good service for years.

The principle upon which an electric bell works can be readily understood by referring to Fig. 1, which shows diagrammatically a bell connected to a battery and push.

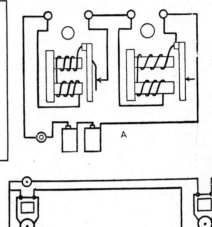

Fig. 1

When the button of the push A is pressed a current flows through the coils and magnetises the soft iron pole pieces of the electro-magnet B and attracts the armature C. The armature carries a spring contact D resting normally against a pointed contact screw E held in position by a metal pillar F. The movement of the armature towards the magnet automatically breaks the circuit at the contacts and causes the armature C to which the hammer is attached to fly back to its original position, and it continues to vibrate as long as the button is pressed.

In the course of time the bell will possibly fail, and this is usually caused by the contacts becoming pitted owing to a minute spark which takes place at these points when the circuit is broken by the armature.

To remedy this defect remove the contact screw and give the point a rub with a piece of fine glass-paper and treat the armature contact in the same way. Corroded terminals will often cause a failure, so the preventative is to keep them clean.

Fig. 2 shows three diagrams of useful circuits in connection with electric bells.

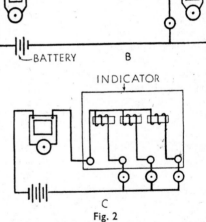

Fig. 2

That illustrated at A shows an additional bell to ring simultaneously. Note that there is no connection with the contact breaker of bell 2 as the impulses from the coils of the first bell cause similar impulses in the coils of the second.

That at B is a diagram of connection of two bells fed from a single battery and each operated by a distant push.

The connections of an indicator and bell as commonly used in a house installation is represented at c.

Bench.—A substantial and serviceable bench is essential for woodworking

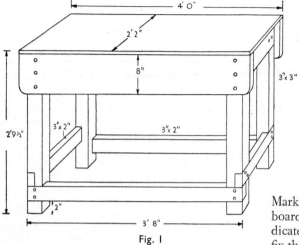

Fig. 1

and metalworking. The simple one illustrated at Fig. 1 will serve all ordinary requirements. Such a bench would cost about 30s. if ready made, but by making it yourself you will save more than half the cost. It consists of two end frames formed by the legs and top and bottom cross rails, two long rails, one at the back and one at the front, fixed to the lower ends of the legs at the proper distance apart and a back and front board fixed to the legs and the bench top to give strength and stability.

The timber required which should be best quality yellow deal is as follows. A 9 ft. length of 3 × 3 in. for the legs, a 10 ft. and a 9 ft. of 3 × 2 in. for the front and back rails and side rails respectively, three boards each 9 in. wide × 1½ in. thick for the top and two boards 8 × 1 in. for the front and back boards.

It is advisable to get prepared stuff; that is wood already planed by machines.

This will save a lot of planing, but the sizes will be ⅛ in. smaller in the thickness and width other than those specified owing to waste. Thus the legs only "hold up" 2⅞ in. square and the top boards 1⅜ in. thick × 8⅞ in. wide. These smaller dimensions, however, are of little consequence as accuracy is not essential.

Mark and cut the legs, side and bottom rails to true length, making sure that the ends are perfectly square, then mark the two end frames. Note that the rails are halved into the legs and fixed by screws in the manner shown in Fig. 2. Mark and cut the front and back boards, round the ends as indicated to give a finish, and then fix them to the end frames, using countersunk-headed screws driven well below the surface. Now measure the overall width and plane the outside edges

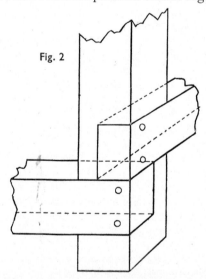

Fig. 2

of the top boards to correspond and screw them down to the tops of the end frames and the front and back boards, sinking

Bench Hook.—This almost indispensable woodworking device is used for steadying the work on the bench when sawing across the grain of wood. It is easily constructed by fixing a batten at the edge of the top face and a similar batten underneath the bottom edge of a piece of planed board in the position shown in the figure. The work is held

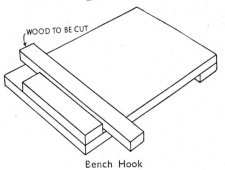

Bench Hook

against the top stop while the lower battens rest against the front edge of the bench.

Bevel.—An adjustable bevel (see figure) is a useful woodworking tool employed for marking and setting out angles. It consists of a slotted steel

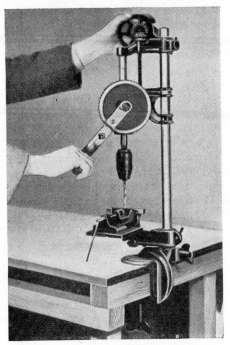

Bench Drill

the screws well below the surface. These come flush with the outside of the front and back boards. The top should then be skimmed over with a smoothing plane. The final operation consists of fitting a bench vice to the front board and a stop near the front and about 6 in. from the left-hand end of the top.

Bench Drill.—To drill holes accurately in metal by hand-operated tools is a difficult job, especially when the tool has to be kept perfectly upright when drilling. This obstacle is easily got over by using a bench drill such as the one illustrated in the figure. This type of machine is a handy tool for the amateur, as the swivelling vice below the drill chuck enables the work to be held in any desired position. The chuck holds drills up to $\frac{3}{8}$ in. in diameter and is fed down to the work by a wheel-operated screw.

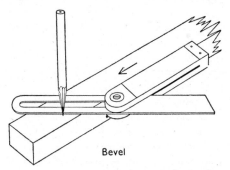

Bevel

blade held in position by a bolt passing through the top of the stock or body of the tool, and a lock-nut which keeps it in position. The inner face of the stock is lined with brass to prevent wear. After having been set to the desired angle the tool is used in very much the same way as a try square;

that is, the stock, held in the left hand, is run along the edge of the wood until it touches the point of the pencil which is held in the right hand and resting on the face edge of the work in the position required. The figure shows the method and how the tool is held, the arrows indicating the direction in which it is moved towards the pencil point.

Binder

lamp of half-pint capacity burns for about one and a quarter hours and costs about 8s., while a larger one holding pint, sufficient to burn two hours, costs nearly half as much again.

The lamp consists of a container holding the liquid, upon which is mounted a bunsen burner and a regulating valve.

To operate the lamp, first unscrew the filler cap, nearly fill the container, and replace the cap. Then partially fill the recess at the top of the container with methylated spirit and ignite it,

Binder.—A length of wood generally 3 × 2 in. fixed across and above the top floor joists and sometimes suspended from the rafters by ties to prevent the ceiling to which they are attached from sagging. The Diagram shows the arrangement.

Blocks, Glue.—Glue blocks are simply short lengths of wood cut from hardwood moulding of triangular section. They are used for strengthening the joints at the internal angles of woodwork.

Glue blocks can be obtained at most shops which cater for woodworkers. Stock sizes are $\frac{1}{2}$, $\frac{3}{4}$, and $1\frac{1}{2}$ in.

Blow-lamps.—The practical man will find that the money spent on a blow-lamp is not misspent. It will prove handy for numerous jobs and is invaluable for heating a soldering iron, burning off paint, plumbing, and other purposes where a hot clear flame is required. Fig. 1 shows a typical blow-lamp of good make, and such a lamp burning petrol can be obtained in several sizes. A small petrol blow-

taking care to see that the adjusting valve is closed; that is, the valve knob cannot be screwed up any farther when rotated in a clockwise direction. Just before the methylated spirit burns out, unscrew the valve a trifle. The

Fig. 1

vapourised petrol will ignite and burn with a bluish flame. If a long white flame appears it indicates that the burner is not sufficiently hot and the process of reheating must be repeated. When the burner has got sufficiently hot, the air-regulating sleeve should be adjusted to take the maximum amount of air.

The paraffin blow lamp is somewhat different from the petrol-fed lamp owing

Fig. 2

length from about 8 ft. to 24 ft., either sawn or prepared, with plain edges. Floorboards are to be procured with either plain or tongued and grooved edges as represented at A in the figure. Matched boards B, sometimes called matching, are provided with tongued and grooved edges and are useful for cladding sheds and making partitions, while weatherboards, as indicated at C, are used for outside work, principally in shed construction.

Bolts and Nuts.—Bolts and nuts are useful to the woodworker as well as the metalworker and form a convenient means of fastening which allows the parts joined to be taken apart. The bolt and nut shown at A in Fig. 1 is the type of steel bolt with a hexagonal head, used by engineers, and provided with a standard Whitworth thread. That shown at B is the type frequently used by woodworkers. It will be seen that the bolt is provided with a square

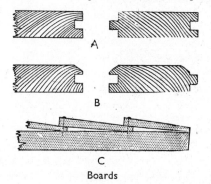

Boards

to the fact that paraffin is so much less volatile than petrol. This necessitates the use of an air pump to force the oil round the coiled pipe within the burner which, when heated by the flame, volatilises the oil and forms gas which issues from the jet. The filler cap is provided with a screw-operated valve which, when opened, reduces the pressure within the container. From this it will be seen that the amount of heat is regulated by the pump and valve. If the heat is too intense, the valve can be opened a trifle to reduce the pressure. On the other hand, if greater heat is needed, a few strokes of the pump will give the desired effect. An illustration showing a paraffin blow-lamp appears in Fig. 2.

To enable a blow-lamp to work efficiently, the minute hole in the nipple must be kept scrupulously clean. For this purpose a piece of thin steel wire fixed in a holder, called a pricker, is usually included with the lamp.

Boards.—The term board is generally applied to sizes of wood less than 2 in. thick and of any width. The usual stock thicknesses are $\frac{5}{8}$, $\frac{3}{4}$, 1, $1\frac{1}{4}$ and $1\frac{1}{2}$ ins., while the widths are 6, 7, 8, 9 and 11 in. Boards can be obtained in any

shoulder immediately below the rounded head and that the nut is of square section. The shoulder prevents the bolt from turning in the work when tightening up the nut. In using a bolt for fastening wood, it is important that a fairly large washer be placed under the head as well as between the nut and the wood, to prevent both bolt head and nut from being pulled into the work when tightened.

Bolts provided with wing nuts, such as that shown at c, come in handy for many purposes where great pressure is not required between the parts to be joined. The use of a spanner is unnecessary with this type of nut as

The rag bolt E is also a useful type of bolt for holding down purposes in stonework. The jagged holding portion of its body is tapered, and the hole into which it fits is filled with molten lead.

Rag bolts can be effectively used in concrete, the hole being filled with liquid portland cement.

When ordinary round-headed, square-shouldered bolts are to be fitted in concrete—as, for instance, for holding down the bottom sills or plates of a portable shed—it is necessary to fit a large iron plate with a square hole to fit the shoulder of the bolt to prevent it revolving. Fig. 2 shows the method, while Fig. 3 shows a useful method of securing a horizontal and vertical member of a frame.

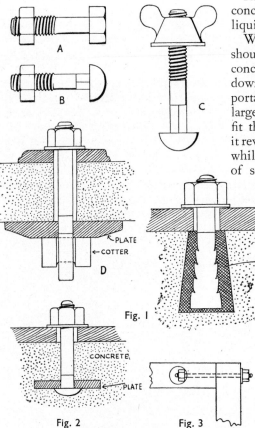

Fig. 1

Fig. 2   Fig. 3

Boxwood.—An exceedingly hardwood of yellowish colour and has a very close, even grain. Takes a good polish, and is used principally by the wood turner for making small ornamental articles.

Brackets. — Brackets are useful for a great variety of purposes. That shown in Fig. 1 can be constructed of planed batten $2\frac{1}{2}$ in. wide and 1 in. thick and is useful for supporting fairly wide shelves. Suitable dimensions for a shelf 15 in. wide would be as follows : Length of A, 12 in.; that of B, 16 in.; and C, 15 in. The parts should be screwed together in preference to nailing as the former makes a stronger job. The ends of the diagonal support should be cut to form a sharp angle and let into recesses made in the top batten and back plate.

the wing shape enables it to be screwed up or unscrewed by the fingers.

The bolt illustrated at D is useful for holding down engines, electric motors, and other comparatively heavy machines on a concrete foundation. The lower end of the bolt. has a rectangular hole through which a cotter passes. This keeps the bottom plate in position and prevents the bolt revolving when the nut is loosened or tightened.

A solid wooden bracket suitable for light shelves and having a back board is shown at B in Fig 2. Such brackets should be so arranged that the grain of the wood comes at the top, as indicated by the arrows. The brackets are kept in position by screws driven through the board above and by screws passing through the back board.

A bracket of more artistic design and suitable for supporting a plate-glass shelf in a bathroom is illustrated at c in Fig. 3. The top is cut out as shown to prevent the shelf slipping forward. An alternative to this arrangement is to use a small piece of sheet brass $\frac{1}{16}$ in. thick, as wide as the thickness of the shelf and of a length equal to the front vertical edge plus the thickness of the glass. Two small holes to clear the shanks of $\frac{1}{2}$ in. No. 4 round-headed brass screws should be drilled in the plate. The latter can then be screwed into position. The brackets should be well glass-papered and enamelled white. The arrangement is shown at D in Fig. 3.

Fig. 2 at A shows a patent stamped metal bracket for supporting shelves. This bracket is exceptionally strong and the peculiar formation of the stamping does away with a diagonal supporting piece. They are also very cheap and, being japanned, do not rust easily.

Brackets for supporting a pelmet board and fixing curtain rods can be made at B in Fig. 4. The part A consists of a piece of iron or brass, preferably the latter, $\frac{1}{2}$ in. wide, $\frac{1}{8}$ in. thick and $6\frac{1}{4}$ in. long, bent to form two right angles, and drilled to take wood screws. The lower projection is also drilled to take either a 1 in. No. 4 B.A. brass round-headed screw or a $\frac{1}{8}$ in. Whitworth. The screw is passed

through the hole and locked in position with a nut and forms a projection or peg over which the drilled end of the curtain rod fits, the rod being kept in position by the nut on the top of the peg.

Bradawl.—A small but useful wood-working tool used for boring small holes. In bradawls of good quality a

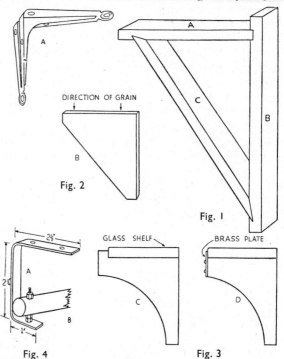

DIRECTION OF GRAIN

Fig. 2

Fig. 1

GLASS SHELF

BRASS PLATE

Fig. 3

Fig. 4

pin is inserted in the tang-end which fits into the handle, as illustrated in the figure. This feature prevents the handle and the blade coming adrift in

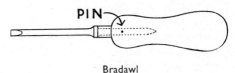

PIN

Bradawl

use as usually happens with cheap bradawls. The blade is wedge shaped, and for good cutting it must be very keen. To use the bradawl press it into the wood, blade across the grain to prevent splitting, giving the handle a slight twisting movement, and withdraw it in a similar manner. Give the cutting edge an occasional rub on the side of an oilstone to keep it in working condition.

Brass.—An extremely useful alloy from the practical man's point of view. Brass is easy to turn, file, screw and

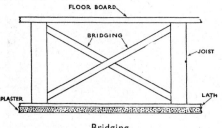

Bridging

solder, and is comparatively soft and ductile. It can be obtained in bars, sheet, tubes and in various angular sections. Brass consists of zinc and copper, the ordinary quality containing about 65 copper and 35 zinc.

Bridging.—Short lengths of wood about $1\frac{1}{2} \times 1\frac{1}{2}$ in. fixed crosswise between floor joists in the manner shown in the figure to keep them at the proper distance apart and to prevent them twisting, thus ensuring a rigid floor and a good ceiling below. In an endeavour to get work done quickly and without trouble, unthinking gasfitters, plumbers and electricians sometimes remove the bridging, thus defeating the object for which it is intended.

Bronze.—Ordinary bronze or gunmetal is an alloy principally used for bearings of machines. It is of a reddish colour and consists of nine parts copper and one part tin. Phosphor bronze is also used for bearings and its tensile strength is greater than gunmetal. It is composed of bronze with an addition of

2 per cent. to 4 per cent. of phosphorus.

Manganese bronze is about as tough and strong as mild steel and can be forged and rolled. It resists the erosion of sea water and is therefore used extensively for ships' propellers. Manganese bronze is composed of ordinary bronze and ferro-manganese.

Brace and Bits.—One of the most important tools in woodwork, used principally for boring. The brace is the device for holding and driving the bits which do the work. The woodworker has the choice of two types, namely, the plain and the ratchet. The former is rapidly becoming obsolete

Fig. 1

and is being superseded by the latter. By means of a ratchet device, the crank can operate either in a clockwise or anti-clockwise direction, in one circular sweep or part of a sweep. This consideration makes it particularly useful for work in awkward situations such as in corners as shown in Fig. 1, where a plain brace could not be operated.

A brace having a sweep of 8 in. is a handy size to have, and one fitted with ball bearings is better than one with plain ones. An occasional spot of oil on the screwed portion of the chuck, the ratchet and the top bearing will keep the tool in good condition.

The types of bit most used by the woodworker are those for forming shallow holes and those for making deep ones. The former are known as centre-bits, shown at A in Fig. 2 and the latter twist-bits, illustrated at B.

The cutting end of a centre-bit has the following parts. The centre consists of a three-sided prong and is called the centre-pin, as this enters the wood first and forms a centre round which the outside nicker revolves and severs the fibres of the wood, while the cutter follows the action of the nicker and removes the waste core of wood. The other end of the bit has a square tapered shank to enable it to be held in the jaw-chuck of the brace.

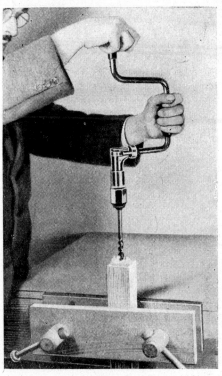

Fig. 4

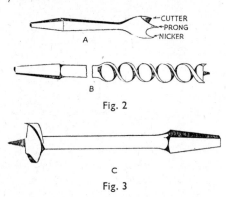

Fig. 2

Fig. 3

In boring a hole in a board with a centre-bit, it is important that the operation be stopped as soon as the point appears at the other side, and then to finish the hole from that side. If boring is continued right through in one operation the bit will tear the fibres at the bottom and produce an imperfect hole.

It is useless to attempt to bore a hole in the end grain of wood with a centre-bit. Firstly, the point will follow the direction of the grain; secondly, the nicker will be working parallel with the fibres of the wood instead of at right-angles to them and, lastly, the cutter will be cutting at right-angles to the fibres instead of parallel to them.

The proper bit for boring wood in the end grain is a Gedge's pattern twist-bit which has a curved cutter. Even this tool, with its gimlet point, will sometimes tend to follow the grain. Fig. 4 shows the process of boring wood in the end grain.

Fig. 3 shows a screw-nose centre-bit which is taking the place of ordinary centre-bits, except for making holes in very thin wood.

Such a bit cuts very quickly, does not require pressure by virtue of the screw end and leaves a very clean hole true to size. Its disadvantage is that if used

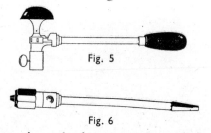

Fig. 5

Fig. 6

near the end of a piece of wood the screw point is likely to split it.

For boring long holes, the standard length twist-bit is the correct tool to use. These bits, like the screw-nose centre-bits previously mentioned, draw themselves into the wood and the helical body brings the waste material to the top of the hole. It is advisable, however, in boring deep holes, to draw the bit out from time to time as the hole sometimes get choked, which retards cutting.

Twist-bits about half the length of the standard type are to be obtained. Such bits are particularly useful for boring holes for dowels.

The illustration appearing at Fig. 5 is a special form of ratchet-brace for corners, while that pictured in Fig. 6 represents an extension bit-holder, useful for many awkward boring jobs.

The chief thing to observe in boring wood is to keep the tool upright. This applies especially to twist-bits. A try square set up against the work is a useful aid in this direction, which can be dispensed with after a little practice.

To sharpen a centre-bit, proceed as follows: If the corners of the prong are rounded and the point blunt treat it with a small smooth file, holding the shank of the tool in the vice. Be careful

not to remove too much metal, otherwise the point will be level with or even below the level of the nicker and this condemns the tool to the scrap heap. If the nicker needs attention, file it from the inside and not the outside, and if the top edge requires touching up, avoid altering the clearance angle. Take care to see that the cutting edge of the nicker does not come below the level of the outer edge of the inclined waste-cutter. Treat the inclined cutter with a smooth flat file, lifting the file after each successive cut, working from the front of the cutter. As this operation cannot be conveniently done with the tool supported in the vice, hold the shank at an angle, with the prong and nicker resting on the bench. Any wire edges remaining after treatment with a file should be removed by means of an oilstone.

Treat the cutting edges of twist-bits

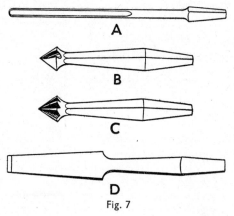

Fig. 7

from the inside as any interference with the outside will reduce its cutting diameter. Note carefully how the cutting edge is formed and use either a rat-tail file or a flat file as the case may be.

A shell bit shown at A in Fig. 7 is used principally for boring screw holes, while the countersink-bit B, called a snail-horn, and the rose bit C, which can be used either for wood or metal, are for recessing the tops of holes in wood to allow the heads of screws to be either flush or below the surface. The screwdriver-bit represented at D is for driving in or withdrawing large screws where a powerful leverage is required.

Burning Off.—Burning off is a process for removing old paint. A petrol blow-lamp and scraper is necessary. The blow-lamp is held in the left hand and the flame played on the paint, which is softened. The scraper, held at an angle in the right hand, should follow the flame and with an up and down scraping movement.

The chief points to observe when burning off are not to allow the flame to become too intense and not to keep it in one spot too long, otherwise it is liable to scorch the woodwork. Only a small area should be treated at a time.

Butt-joints.—A butt-joint is often required in woodwork for joining narrow boards together to obtain the required width, and joining parts of framework, etc. The glued butt-joint shown at A in Fig. 1 is a common method of joining boards for obtaining width. To make a satisfactory joint of this type, proceed as follows: True up the top and bottom of the boards to be joined so that they are flat and out of winding as tested by winding strips and a straight-edge, and carefully plane the long edges so that they are quite parallel and square. Place one board in the vice and apply very hot glue to the edges to be joined in both boards. Then rub the edges together in a longitudinal direction to squeeze out as much glue as possible. Carefully remove the work from the vice and place them long edge upwards against a support and leave for at least twenty-four hours to enable the glue to harden. Fig. 2 shows the process of rubbing

out glue from between the edges of two long boards, with the aid of a helper.

Another method is by means of dowels or wooden pins which are spaced at intervals along the edges to be joined as illustrated at B in Fig. 1. This joint is much stronger than the plain glued butt-joint. Before the holes can be

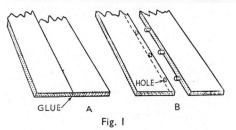

HOLE

GLUE A B

Fig. 1

bored the positions must be marked out accurately. After having planed up the faces and edges, place the two boards in the vice and accurately mark them together with the aid of a square and pencil as represented at Fig. 3, C, then bore the holes. For boards $\frac{1}{2}$ in. thick, use $\frac{1}{4}$ in. diametered dowels; for $\frac{3}{4}$ in.

Fig. 2

and 1 in. wood, $\frac{3}{8}$ in. diameter pins are required.

The holes should be 1 in. deep and bored with a sharp twist-bit. Hold the brace perfectly upright and square and remove the sharp edges from the top of each hole.

The dowels are made from prepared rods obtained from most hardwood stores. Cut them to length, round the ends slightly and make a slot along the length of each one. The best way to make the slots is to fix the tenon saw, teeth upwards, in the vice and rub the pins along the teeth.

Apply hot glue to half the length of the pins and drive them carefully into the holes in one board. Then apply glue to the edges, the projecting parts

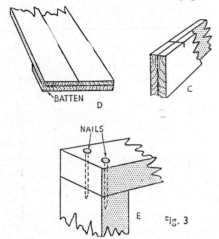

of the pins and the edge of the other board and gently tap the top of the upper board until the joint is closed.

A simple form of butt-joint is shown at D in Fig. 3 where two boards are fastened together by a couple of battens. They should be planed and trimmed squarely at the ends, while the top can be smoothed with a plane after fixing. Fix them by driving in nails or screws from the underside.

The joint shown at E is a simple butt-joint for joining rough framework. The ends to be joined should be sawn perfectly square and to prevent splitting, the top piece should be drilled slightly smaller than the diameter of the nail.

Callipers.—Callipers are used principally for gauging the size of work turned in a lathe. There are several types of callipers, but the usual ones are those employed for measuring the

diameters of external work such as bars and spindles, and known as external callipers. Internal callipers, as the name suggests, are used for gauging internal diameters of work.

The most important point to observe when using these instruments is to allow the points only just to touch the work to be measured; if forced over a bar or into a hole in a bar inaccuracy will result due to the springiness of the tool. External and internal callipers are illustrated at A and B respectively in the illustration.

Cast Iron.—Cast iron is impure iron and has an appreciable amount of carbon in its composition. It is crystalline in texture, brittle and non-ductile, strong in compression, but weak in tension and is useless for objects subject to bending. Cast iron is usually cast into various shapes in moulds and is largely used for supporting columns, beds for machinery and objects subject to compression. There are two common kinds

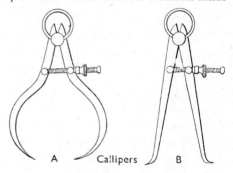

A   Callipers   B

of cast iron—white and grey. The former is smooth and white, while the latter is comparatively rough and soft which renders it easy to work. If small castings are required, it is advisable to get them made in the grey variety.

Cellulose Lacquer.—An excellent finishing medium similar to enamel for wooden and metal articles. The basic ingredient is cellulose and can be obtained in a large variety of colours at most oil and colour merchants. It is quick drying and produces a hard glossy surface. Two kinds of cellulose lacquer are made under various trade names, one for application with a brush and the other for spraying on. It is thinned by means of a special medium sold for the purpose. Turpentine and linseed oil cannot be used for thinning.

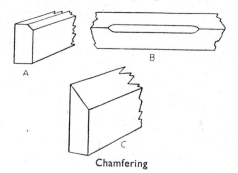

Chamfering

Chamfering.—Chamfering is the operation of forming a narrow flat face on the edge of wood to improve the appearance of the work, examples of which are illustrated at A and B in the figure. That shown at A represents a through chamfer, so called because the chamfer is carried through from one end of the work to the other. The example at B is a stopped chamfer and does not run through.

The through chamfer is carried out by first marking the desired distance from the face and side of the wood—equal distances giving an angle of 45 is the usual angle employed—and then formed by planing the edge down to the marked lines.

A stopped chamfer is marked out in a similar way, but as the cutting iron of a jack-plane cannot reach the end of the chamfer, a bull-nosed plane, having its cutting iron near the front of the tool, is the proper tool to use. If such a plane is not available, use a jack-plane and remove the remaining wood with a sharp chisel. The ends of a stopped

chamfer should be gradually sloped off in the manner shown. A bevelled edge is illustrated at C.

Chisels, Wood and Metal Cutting.—Although there are three types of chisels used by the professional, the firmer chisel as shown at A in Fig. 1 will generally satisfy the needs of most amateur woodworkers, and five chisels with blades $\frac{1}{8}$, $\frac{1}{4}$, $\frac{3}{8}$, $\frac{1}{2}$ and $\frac{3}{4}$ in. wide will be found the most useful sizes to have. Those having hexagonal handles have the advantage of not rolling off the bench like chisels with round handles.

The chisel with its hardened steel wedge-shaped cutting end is used principally for removing waste from grooves in wood, making square holes or mortices in forming joints.

Chisels are useless unless kept very sharp, as blunt edges merely break the fibres of the wood instead of severing them. It should be noted that new chisels always require sharpening on an oilstone before being put into service as they leave the works only roughly finished on a grindstone.

The illustration appearing at B in

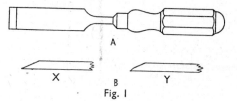

Fig. 1

Fig. 1 shows how a chisel should be sharpened. Note the difference between that indicated at X which shows the cutting edge of a chisel as bought and that at Y which illustrates an additional bevelled cutting edge produced after it has been treated on an oilstone. This small bevelled cutting edge must not be made too acute, otherwise the edge will be weakened. It is a good plan to get into the habit of rubbing down the main bevel every time the cutting edge is sharpened. If this is done it will prevent the angle of the bevel becoming too obtuse or thick. The angle of the bevel should be 30 degrees as shown.

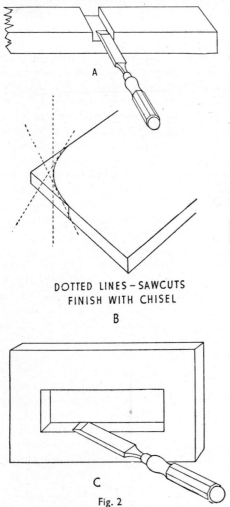

DOTTED LINES — SAWCUTS
FINISH WITH CHISEL

B

C

Fig. 2

Small chisels are best sharpened on the long edge of an oilstone.

At A, B and C in Fig. 2 are shown three practical applications of the wood chisel. That represented at A shows how a chisel is held in removing the waste from a channel, B illustrates the operation of trimming off the corner of

a piece of work where the use of a plane would be impossible.

On no account should a hammer be used upon the handle when it is necessary to strike the tool. The proper implement to use is a hardwood mallet. A hammer ruins the handle and the roughness produced makes it unpleasant to work with when used as a hand-operated tool.

Circuits, Electrical. — Electrical circuits, so far as the handyman is

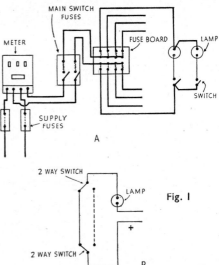

Fig. 1

concerned, are generally confined to those applicable to electric bells, light, heating and wireless. The circuits for electric bells have already been dealt with under the heading of Bells, Electric.

The circuit shown diagrammatically at A in Fig. 1 shows how an ordinary house lighting circuit is arranged. Here, it will be observed that the main supply cable terminates in a sealed fuse-box which is usually fixed near to where the supply cable enters the premises. From this point the consumer's main cable, which is of a larger size than the sub-circuit wires as it has to carry the total current, enters the meter. From this point the wires connect the main switch and fuses which control the lighting system.

From the main switch the cable feeds on to a distribution fuse-board where sub-circuits, each carrying about eight lighting points, radiate to different parts of the building.

The diagram at B shows a common method of controlling two points, two two-way switches being necessary.

A typical power circuit for supplying electro radiation and other domestic

immersion heater in the tank of a domestic hot water supply.

A common method for a wireless loud speaker is illustrated at D in Fig. 2.

Copper.—Copper is a soft metal of reddish colour and extremely ductile. It can easily be hammered to shape when cold, and is an excellent conductor of heat, hence a copper kettle is to be preferred to a tinplate one. It is also an excellent conductor of electricity and for this reason it is used extensively for electrical apparatus of all kinds.

Conduits, Electrical.—In order to protect the wires of a domestic electrical installation from damage, enamelled steel tubes or conduits are generally

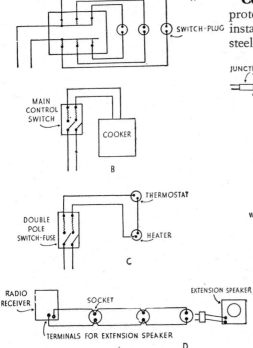

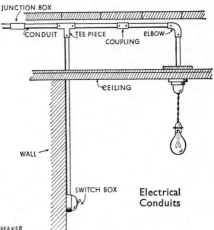

Fig. 2

employed. The tubes are used in conjunction with elbows, tee-pieces, connection and junction boxes as shown in the figure. There are several qualities of conduits. The cheapest kind has a close joint and is quite suitable for use in perfectly dry situations. The next quality is of the same gauge as the close joint variety, but has a brazed joint at the seam, while the best quality conduit is sufficiently thick to enable screw-threads to be cut at the ends to fit into screw-threaded fittings.

electrical apparatus is illustrated at A in Fig. 2. Note that each plug forms a separate sub-circuit protected by fuses in the fuse-board. This method of connecting power plugs is compulsory. At B are seen the connections for an electric cooker, while that illustrated at C represents the connection for an

This kind of conduit is employed in the best classes of electrical installation work as it forms practically a watertight system and by virtue of the screwed junctions is continuous throughout and can therefore be properly earthed. Where conduits are exposed to the weather, heavy-gauge screwed, galvanised conduit should be used, as the zinc coating protects the steel pipe from rust.

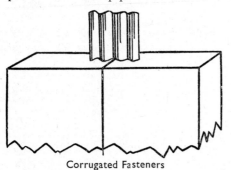

Corrugated Fasteners

Concrete and Cement.—Concrete and cement are invaluable for making floors for garages, garden paths and garden ponds and a host of other purposes.

Concrete is made of a mixture of portland cement, aggregate, sand and clean water and a good mixture for general purposes is composed of one part cement, two parts sharp clean sand, and four parts aggregate which may consist of washed ballast, small pieces of broken brick or small stones. It is essential that the sand be free from dirt and other foreign matter as their presence greatly reduces the strength of the concrete.

The rough concrete surface is generally faced with a layer of cement and sand to give it a smooth face.

To estimate the amount of concrete for a given job, first find the cubic capacity of the part to be treated. For instance in making a path 54 ft. long, 3 ft. wide and 5 in. thick (that is 4 in. of concrete plus 1 in. facing of cement

and sand), the amount of concrete required would be $54 \times 3 \times \frac{1}{3}$ ft. = 54 cu. ft. or 2 cu. yd. On the basis that 1 cu. yd. of a 1 : 2 : 4 : mixture requires 5 cwt. cement, 12 cu. ft. sand and 1 cu. yd. aggregate, it follows that $2 \times 5 = 10$ cwt. cement, $2 \times 12 = 24$ cu. ft. sand and $2 \times 1 = 2$ cu. yd. of aggregate will be required for the path.

Success in making concrete depends, to a very great extent, upon the mixing, which is first done in the dry state. This is done on a mixing board consisting of smooth boards held together at the back by battens, a handy size being about 4 ft. square. Procure a strong bucket and place 2 measures of sand in the centre of the board and add 1 measure of cement. Mix these together thoroughly with a spade or shovel and add 4 measures of aggregate. Turn the mixture over and over—the more times the better—until the whole is thoroughly incorporated. Then add from time to time as the mixing proceeds, sufficient water to form a plastic mass. Too much water will make the concrete sloppy and the aggregate will sink to the bottom when laid.

Corrugated Fasteners. — Short pieces of thin corrugated steel with sharp edges to enable them to be driven into wood in joining boards together (see diagram).

Corrugated Iron.—Corrugated galvanised iron is useful for covering sheds, garages and other structures and does not require boarding underneath as composition roofing materials do. Stock sizes run from 4 ft. to 10 ft. in length and from 2 ft. to 4 ft. wide. A useful size is 26 in. wide which covers 24 in. including a 2 in. overlap. In some cases it may be advisable to allow 4 in. overlap.

When used for roofing purposes, the sheets should overlap the ends 6 in. in their length, but, when used vertically, a lap of 3 in. will usually suffice.

Corrugated iron is obtainable in several thicknesses, No. 20 gauge being

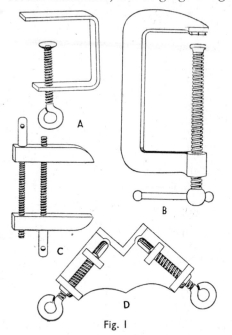

Fig. 1

recommended where very strong work is required. For ordinary purposes, a No. 24 gauge will generally answer requirements.

Galvanised iron screws and washers are used for attaching the sheets to the framework, etc., and these should be driven in holes punched in the top of a ridge not in a valley.

Cramps.—There are many wood-working jobs that call for the use of a cramp in some form or other. The small, light cramp consisting of a piece of iron bent twice at right angles and provided with a screw as illustrated at A in Fig. 1 costs but a few pence. When using such cramps it is advisable to interpose thin pieces of wood between the work and the cramp.

The cramp shown at B is for holding layer material, while that shown at C is a wooden cramp fitted with beech jaws and hornbeam screws.

Another useful type of cramp for cramped framework is represented at Fig. 2, where two are shown in position on a frame after having been glued.

These cramps consist of adjustable heads fitted to long hardwood members, preferably oak, drilled with a number of holes through which pegs pass and keep the heads in position. Cramp-heads of this description cost 2s. 9d. a pair, and such cramps are a good substitute for the tradesman's all steel cramps costing from 7s. 6d. upwards.

Fig. 3 shows a piece of work cramped up by means of a home-made cramp and wedges. Such a device is easily made with a piece of board about $\frac{3}{4}$ in. thick and 3 or 4 in. wide and two cross-battens screwed near the ends of the face, to the base.

The mitre cramps at D in Fig. 1 are useful for picture framing as they hold the moulding securely together whilst

Fig. 2

the nails are being driven in, and ensure the parts being put together squarely.

Damp-course.—The damp-course,

or what might be better termed the damp-preventing course, of the walls of a house is one of the most important items in building construction and its inclusion is insisted upon by all local authorities.

It consists of a layer of slate or other water resisting material such as specially prepared bitumen felt, and is used as a prevention against moisture

Fig. 3

working up by capillary attraction from the foundations and rendering the walls damp. The course is always made above ground level, otherwise its object is defeated. For this reason it is imperative that flower beds, paths and soil, etc., be kept well below the level of the damp-course.

A piece of slate or bitumen felt placed on the top of bricks, which are commonly used for supporting the floor joists of sheds and structures of a similar nature, will prevent moisture from the soil rising to the timber and prevent the timber from rotting.

Deal.—Wood, obtained from the northern pine of the Baltic regions and elsewhere, most frequently used by the amateur. There are two kinds of deal, one known as yellow deal and the other called white deal. The former is used for all kinds of joining work.

It is easy to work and, in the best quality, has but few knots. The white variety, sometimes called spruce, as it is the product of the spruce fir, is unsuitable for joinery but is handy for making shelves and the like. It is rather difficult to plane owing to the presence of numerous hard knots.

Distempering.—Before distempering a ceiling clean off the old distemper, using an old brush, a sponge and clean warm water. Start at one end of the room, mount a pair of steps and rest the bucket on a high box or better still, stand on a trestle formed by a scaffold board supported between two pairs of household steps. Apply a small quantity of water to about a square yard of the ceiling to soften the old whitewash. Then go over it again, this time rubbing vigorously. Repeat the operation as often as necessary, rinsing the brush well after each application. Then clean off thoroughly with a damp sponge. Continue in this way until the whole of the ceiling is thoroughly clean. Next, remove any loose plaster remaining in cracks and fill with a mixture of plaster-of-paris or Keen's cement and water, not too sloppy, applying it with the point of a plasterer's trowel. Before stopping the cracks, wet them with a brush as plaster will not adhere to a dry surface.

When the ceiling is dry, give it a coat of size to fill the pores. A six-penny packet of dry size mixed with warm water will be ample for a ceiling of average dimensions. Put it on with a distemper brush and take care not to miss any part, otherwise the ceiling will look patchy when finished.

As there are many excellent and inexpensive proprietary brands of distemper which only need the addition of water it is a waste of time to make it yourself. Some are supplied in paste form and others in powder, but, no matter what kind is chosen, follow the makers instructions as to the quantity of water required and the method of mixing. Allow 1 lb. for every 60 sq. ft. to be covered.

Put a small quantity of the mixed distemper in a clean bucket, dip the brush into it, taking care not to overload the brush, and apply it to the ceiling, starting from the window and working to the back of the room. Work the brush

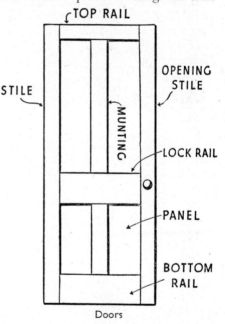

A   Dividers   B

unhesitatingly in all directions and cover a small section at a time, joining the parts when wet.

In distempering walls of important rooms, an oil-bound washable water-paint should be used. Such a distemper can be applied successfully to wall paper provided that the paper is firmly attached to the wall. If the paper is dark and the pattern bold two coats should be given, allowing the first coat to dry thoroughly before applying the second. Remove all dust from the paper and if the paper is thick apply a coat of size. Start at the top of a convenient corner and work downwards in strips about 3 ft. wide, joining each strip when wet.

Dividers, Wood and Metal.—The diagram A shows a divider suitable for

woodworkers. It is used principally for transferring measurements from the ruler to the work, drawing out equal distances on work and striking curves. The quadrant at the top of one leg and wing nut at the other enable the legs, after being set, to be locked.

Dividers suitable for metalworking are illustrated at B. The tool has a spring head and side adjusting screw by which accurate adjustment is obtained.

Doors.—There are numerous types of doors; the one shown in the diagram is one commonly used for rooms. Such a door is made up of components bearing different names as the illustration shows. The vertical pieces forming the sides

Doors

are known as the stiles, the top and bottom horizontal components, the rails and the middle horizontal piece is termed the lock rail. The centre vertical portions are the muntings, while all these parts endorse the panels. The frame supporting the door is built up of the following parts: the two vertical sides are jambs and the top horizontal is the lintel or head. Narrow strips of wood fastened to these and preventing the door from swinging beyond its closed position are the door stops, and the finishing bead is termed the architrave. Constructional details are given in subsequent articles.

Dowels.—Dowels are short pieces of hardwood of round section. They are of inestimable value to the woodworker

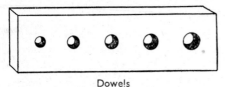

Dowels

as a means of joining framework and boards together, and very often eliminate a more complicated joint. Dowels are formed from dowel rods which can be bought quite cheaply or they may be made by driving a length of roughly shaped hardwood through a dowel plate as illustrated above. Such a plate with $\frac{1}{4}$, $\frac{5}{16}$, $\frac{3}{8}$, $\frac{7}{16}$ and $\frac{1}{2}$ in. holes can be bought for about half a crown. When the dowel pins are glued they should be slotted along their length to allow surplus glue to escape from the holes into which they fit.

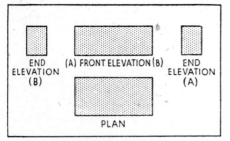

Working Drawings

Dowel rods make excellent curtain rods if enamelled, and they are useful in the construction of towel rails and other articles where strong, light, circular, wooden rods are required.

Drawings, Working. — Elaborate instruments are not necessary for amateur

work. A plain drawing-board, consisting of a piece of $\frac{1}{2}$ in. plywood with battens at the back, tee square, 60 deg. and 45 deg. set square, a pair of combination compasses and dividers, a protractor for setting out angles and a set of cardboard scales, will generally answer requirements. The cost of such an outfit should not exceed 15s.

The usual procedure is to give three views of the object, with additional drawings of details. Thus it is possible to show the length, width and depth. In the diagram the top centre figure shows a front elevation or view, that on the right is a side elevation or view of the end A (front elevation) while the drawing on the left-hand side is a similar view of the end B. Immediately

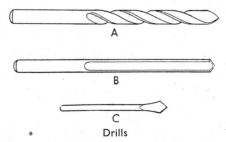

Drills

below the front elevation is the plan, or bird's-eye view, of the top. From this it will be seen that the front elevation gives the length and height, the end elevation the width and height and the plan the width and length.

Objects such as cigarette boxes may be drawn full size, but drawings of larger articles should be made to a scale such as 6 in. to the foot or half-full size, 3 in. to the foot or quarter-full size, 1 in. to the foot or $\frac{1}{12}$ full size and so on.

Drills.—For drilling clean holes in metal, except sheet stuff, twist-drills, varying from $\frac{1}{16}$ in. to $\frac{3}{8}$ in. in diameter, should be in every kit. Such drills, illustrated at A, above, can be used for drilling wood. This applies to boring holes for screws near the end of a piece of wood where a bradawl or gimlet might split it.

Twist-drills are often operated by a geared, hand-drill stock, the advantage of such a tool being that it can be operated in awkward places and the tool can be taken to the job whereas a drilling machine cannot.

The latter tool, however, is capable of producing holes absolutely at right angles to the face, a somewhat difficult operation where a hand-drill is employed.

For accurate work twist-drills must be sharp and, when in good condition, they will do their work with little pressure. On the other hand, a blunt drill rubs the metal instead of cutting it and, in the smaller sizes, abnormal pressure means a broken drill. As soon as a drill gets blunt, give it a rub on an oilstone, holding the tool at an angle and giving it a twisting motion. If this does not have the desired effect, the cutting edge should be re-ground on a grindstone and then finished on an oilstone.

Twist-drills are unsuitable for drilling thin metal as the cutting edge is likely to jam as it breaks through the hole. Fluted drills having parallel flutes as illustrated at B in the figure are the proper tools to use for this purpose, and the metal should be supported on a piece of wood to keep it flat.

Very small holes can be effectively drilled in sheet metal with diamond-pointed drills, worked with an Archimedian drill-stock.

Such drills are to be obtained in wooden cartons containing a dozen bits in assorted sizes for about sixpence.

When drilling large holes in metal, it is advisable first to drill a small pilot hole and then to proceed with a larger drill.

Dry Rot.—Dry rot is the result of the spores of a fungoid growth feeding on the substance of the wood. Its presence can usually be detected by a musty odour, and in some cases the wood has red and black streaks, while in others black and white spots appear on the surface. The timber is sometimes cracked and shrunken, and so soft that the blade of a penknife can be inserted with little effort. Dry rot generally occurs in the timbers of the ground floor of a building and usually can be traced to bad ventilation, damp, stagnant air being favourable to the growth of fungus.

If dry rot is present, it must be arrested without delay. The only satisfactory way of stopping the ravages is entirely to remove the woodwork and to treat supporting walls with a blow-lamp. New woodwork should be thoroughly treated with creosote before being installed, and it is of the utmost importance not to allow joists or boards to touch the walls. To prevent dry rot, see that the ventilating air-bricks which are spaced at intervals just below the ground-floor level in the outside walls are kept perfectly clear of leaves, dirt and other obstructions, and do not lay linoleum on a floor that shows dampness.

Earthing.—All electrical domestic appliances, whether permanent or portable, such as irons, heaters, washers, motors and garage lamps, should be efficiently earthed to prevent the danger of shocks, in case the device becomes alive through leakage or other defects. In the case of fixtures, this can easily be done by fitting a copper earth clip to the metallic sheathing or the conduit in which the conductors are enclosed, provided such protective material is continuous throughout and efficiently connected to earth, and connecting the conduit to the apparatus by means of either a bare or insulated copper wire of less than 7/22 S.W.G. wire. This method is represented at A in the figure.

Portable apparatus should be connected to the main wires through a 3 pin plug and socket and a three-core flexible lead as shown at B.

Elm.—A useful hardwood for use in damp situations and under water, but difficult to work owing to the presence of cross-grain. It is much used for the outside cladding of half-timbered buildings, barns, wheelbarrows and articles subjected to damp.

flowed on and not laid and brushed as paint is applied. The temperature of the room should be at least 65 deg. F. to enable it to flow without drag. Dust, which is fatal to enamelling, must be excluded at all costs. Avoid putting on too much enamel, as this will probably result in the formation of blobs or " tears." On the other hand, too little enamel will cause the brush to drag and a satisfactory finish cannot be expected.

It sometimes happens that, although

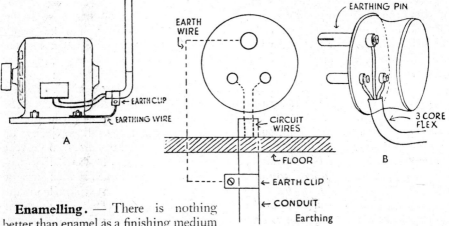

Earthing

Enamelling. — There is nothing better than enamel as a finishing medium for wood, for its hard, glass-like surface can be washed and washed again, provided a clean damp chamois leather be used, and the extra outlay of providing such a coat is money well spent.

As enamel is a finishing medium, two or more undercoats of flat oil paint should be given to the work, each being dried and lightly glass-papered before the next is applied. The last coat of paint must be approximately of the same colour as the enamel as the latter has very little body in it.

There are numerous proprietary brands of enamel supplied in various tints, and only the best should be used.

Enamel should be applied with a proper soft-bristled brush which should be clean and without dust. It should be

the room where the enamelling is being done is of the correct temperature, the enamel itself is cold and will not flow easily. When this happens, it is a good plan to put the container in a vessel of warm water.

Felt Roofing (Materials). — The old-fashioned tarred felt for covering boarded roofs is now rapidly becoming a thing of the past and flexible, inexpensive roofing materials, sold under various trade names, are taking its place.

There are two grades of such material, light and heavy, and it is usually supplied in rolls containing 108 sq. ft., 1 yd. wide and 12 yd. in length.

In fixing this material, start at the eaves or lower edge of the roof and lay the felt lengthways, allowing two or three inches at the ends and front for overlap. Fix the next piece so that the lower edge overlaps the top edge of the first strip by at least 2 in. The lower the

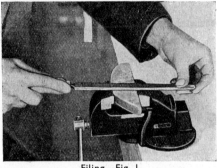

Filing—Fig. I

pitch of the roof, the greater the overlap required. Use galvanised clout nails, as ordinary clouts will rust rapidly, and drive them in at intervals of about 2 to 3 in. The light-quality material can be cut with a pair of strong scissors, but the heavy grade requires a sharp pointed knife. Place the material on a flat surface and use a straight-edge for guiding the knife.

Filing.—The process of filing accurately is acquired only with practice and does not consist merely of pushing the tool over the work and drawing it back again in a haphazard manner. Before attempting to use a file, see that you have got the proper tool for the job. Apart from the shape, which may be a hand or parallel, flat with bellied sides, square, round or half-round, the question of cut and coarseness of the cutting teeth is important. A single-cut file has parallel rows of teeth made at an angle across the face, and a double-cut file has extra rows crossing the others forming a series of cutting points.

For filing copper, brass, aluminium, lead and other soft metals, use a single-cut file. A double-cut file is for wrought iron, mild steel, hard steel (annealed). The degree of coarseness of the teeth will depend upon the nature of the work. In cases where a comparatively large amount of metal is to be removed, a coarse-toothed file can be used for taking off the majority, followed by a smooth file for finishing.

In filing wide metal, use the file obliquely and keep it perfectly flat. This is a difficult task, as the tendency is to produce a rounded surface. Hold the tool in the manner shown in Fig. 1 and push it gently forward to the end of the stroke, then relieve the pressure and draw the file back, continuing in this way and keeping the surface level and square along its entire length.

In taking the finishing cut it is usually advisable to drawfile the work. This is done by grasping the tool in both hands,

Filing—Fig. 2

placing it across and drawing it and pushing it back and forth the while along the work, standing in position at the head of the work as illustrated in Fig. 2.

Never use a file without a handle and always use an old file for removing the scale on castings, for a new one will be ruined. Keep a piece of file card, consisting of fine steel wires on a cloth backing, for removing any metal that may clog the teeth.

Flashing.—A piece of metal, usually

lead but sometimes zinc, cut to a suitable shape for making a waterproof joint between angles in brick walls, etc.

Fig. 1 shows an illustration of a flashing suitable for covering the gap between a wall and the back plate of a lean-to conservatory, while that shown

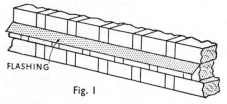

FLASHING

Fig. 1

at Fig. 2 represents the side flashing between a roof and chimney stack. The ends are tucked in the joints of the brickwork, secured with lead wedges and pointed with cement.

Fretwork.—Fretwork is an interesting branch of light woodwork which fills the gap where circumstances do not permit heavier kinds of constructed woodwork.

Briefly stated, the process consists of tracing the outline of a design, made

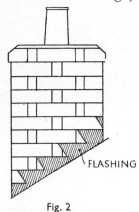

FLASHING

Fig. 2

either on the wood itself or on a printed paper pattern stuck on the surface, with the aid of a small saw-blade held in a hand frame. Very little practice is needed before proficiency in fret-cutting is attained, and such articles as photo frames, artistic boxes, clock cases and many other ornamental and useful objects can be made with little effort.

Besides a hand frame, costing about 4s., including a dozen saw-blades, a small Archimedian drill-stock with a few small diamond-pointed drills, a sawing table, glass-paper, tube glue and a supply of thin hardwood such as satin walnut, oak or mahogany, complete the outfit. Fretwork designs are to be obtained at numerous woodcraft shops.

Stick the pattern on with paste, not glue, taking care to smooth all wrinkles, and drill small holes in the interior part that has to be removed, to enable the saw blade to be threaded through. Support the work on the cutting table, which should be clamped to a corner of an ordinary table or other suitable flat surface, and start by cutting away the waste from the interior, using the saw in an upright position and giving it a

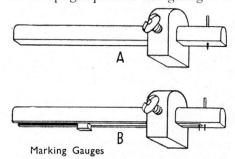

Marking Gauges

gentle up and down motion. Then remove the exterior waste and glass-paper the surface to get rid of the pattern. The latter is better done by pinning the work down to a flat surface and applying fine glass-paper held on either a wood or cork block. Do not use water or the work will swell and the grain be raised. Any rough parts in the interior can be removed by a piece of glass-paper wrapped round a small stick or by a fine file. The parts can then be assembled and fixed with tube glue and left to harden.

Gauges, Marking.—A m a r k i n g gauge is a simple yet important tool for the accurate marking of a line parallel to the edges of wood. As the illustration shows at A, the instrument consists of a hardwood bar or stock and an adjustable fence kept in position by a screw. At one end of the bar is a steel point which marks the wood when the tool is drawn along the surface.

A mortice gauge B, by which two parallel lines can be marked in one operation, is similar to the ordinary marking gauge but has an extra point which is adjustable. As its name suggests, it is used principally for marking out mortices and tenons and is used in the same way as the single-pointed tool.

Gimlets.—Gimlets are used for boring small holes in wood. They fulfil these requirements admirably, provided that such holes are not bored near the edges of the work, when there is great risk of splitting the wood. Gimlets are becoming obsolete and their place is being taken by the hand drill-stock and metal twist-drills, which not only obviate the risk of splitting the wood but cut a cleaner hole.

Glass-paper.—Glass-paper is a useful material for producing a perfectly smooth surface on wood, but it must not be used in a haphazard fashion or it is likely to spoil the work.

Glass-paper is to be obtained in several grades of coarseness, No. 2 being the coarsest, 1 a medium grade, while 0 is fine, and the one to use will naturally depend upon the work. If the surface left by the plane is rough, use the coarse grade followed by the medium and finish with the fine, while if the surface is comparatively smooth, omit the coarse and use the medium and fine.

In glass-papering a flat surface, never hold the material in the hand, as illustrated but employ a cork block and use it in the direction of the grain, otherwise deep scratches are likely

to result which are difficult to obliterate. Concave and convex mouldings can be treated with glass-paper wrapped round a piece of wood shaped to correspond

Glass-papering; incorrect method

with the depression and projection of the moulding.

Glazing.—Every handyman should acquire knowledge of the process of fitting glass, for he will find plenty of scope for exercising his ability in such instances as glazing a greenhouse, sashes, cabinet doors or picture frames.

To explain the methods involved, it is assumed that a simple sash is to be fitted with glass. Such a sash is provided with a rebate or recess along one side

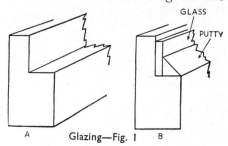

Glazing—Fig. 1

of its inner edges as represented at A in Fig. 1 for supporting the glass on one side. On the other, the glass is held in position with putty, as indicated at B in Fig. 1.

The first thing to do is to ascertain

the size of glass. To do this, measure the length and width of the rebate and deduct ⅛ in. from both dimensions, as the glass must not fit tightly otherwise

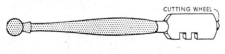

Glazing—Fig. 2

it may crack while being fitted, or the wood may swell with the same result. It may be that you have an odd piece of glass which could be cut to the desired dimensions, in which case a glass cutter will be required. If such a piece of glass is not available, purchase the glass cut to size.

Glass is sold at so much per square foot and the thickness is represented by the number of ounces contained in a

Glazing—Fig. 3

square foot. For instance, 16 oz. glass is thin and suitable for glazing light cabinets, while 22 oz. stuff is about ⅛ in. thick and is the thickness generally used for glazing window sashes.

If you decide to cut the glass yourself, get a good quality cutter with a hardened steel cutting wheel. The tradesman uses a glazier's diamond for cutting

purposes, but these are expensive and, for occasional use, the wheel cutter will answer the purpose quite well. Fig. 2 shows such a tool.

Clean the glass and place it on a perfectly flat surface. To enable the glass to be supported equally over its entire area a folded cloth should be interposed between the glass and the supporting surface, as any inequalities in the surface will probably cause the glass to crack when pressure is applied to the cutter.

Mark the desired dimensions on the glass and use a straight-edge for guiding the cutter. The tool is held between the forefinger and the second finger of the right hand and kept in a sloping position as shown in Fig. 3. Start at the top and gradually draw the cutter towards the bottom in one stroke. If the cutting has been successful, a clearly-defined scratch will be seen. A rough, uneven, more or less wide depression indicates bad cutting. Assuming that the cut is good, move the glass to the edge of the supporting surface so that the cut coincides with the edge. Hold the waste loosely with one hand and, with the tool, gently tap the underside of the unwanted piece near the cut, tapping from left to right. As this proceeds, the waste will break away, leaving a perfectly straight edge.

The next step consists of fixing the glass to the sash. Putty will not stick to bare wood as wood absorbs the oil. Paint the rebate with red lead paint and when dry apply a bed of putty in the recess for the glass to rest against. This is best done with the frame placed flat on a table. Place the glass in position and press it near the edges to exclude the surplus putty. Then drive one or two thin panel pins into the rebate to keep the glass in position. Work some putty into the remaining portion of the rebate and trim off the waste with a putty knife. Finally, level the puttied surface so that it forms a neat angle joint.

In glazing cabinet doors, the puttying operation is generally omitted. The glass is simply butted up to the shoulder of the rebate and kept in position by nailing on a narrow bead as indicated in Fig. 4.

Gluing.—Gluing is one of the most important processes in woodworking, and unless glue is made and applied in a proper manner, satisfactory results cannot be expected.

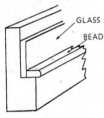

GLASS

BEAD

Glazing. Fig. 4

For joining the parts of small work, liquid glue, sold in tubes, can be used; but in large work such glue is uneconomical unless purchased in tins.

Many woodworkers, however, prefer to prepare their own glue. For ordinary glue, use only the best Scotch glue and, when purchasing it, see that it is hard, brittle and transparent. Prepare only sufficient glue for the job in hand as reheated glue loses its adhesive properties. Break a cake or part of a cake into fragments, place it in the inner container of a glue-pot having an inner and outer vessel, add clean cold water and allow to swell into a jelly. This will take twelve hours or more. Pour off the surplus water, fill the outer container with clean water and allow the glue to simmer gently for an hour or two, giving it an occasional stir. Then remove the scum which forms on the surface. The consistency should be that of thin treacle.

Use the glue very hot and apply it quickly with a good brush and, if necessary, heat the parts to be joined— chilled glue is useless—then rub the parts together to exclude as much glue as possible, and put the work aside for at least twenty-four hours in a dry place to allow the glue to harden.

The chief points to observe in gluing are that only a small quantity of glue is required to make a strong joint, that glue must be very hot and that large work should be cramped after gluing.

Gouges.—Gouges (see below) are really wood chisels provided with a circular cutting edge and are used for making circular-shaped grooves in wood. The cutting edge is either external-ground or internal-ground; that is, the bevel is formed at the end of the convex face of the tool or the concave portion. A gouge is used in very much the same way as a chisel and, in cutting a groove in a length of wood, is worked in the direction of the grain.

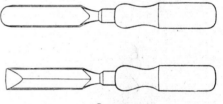

Gouges

Like chisels, gouges are useless unless very sharp. To sharpen an internal-ground tool use an oilstone slip either held edgeways in the bench vice or in the hand. An external-ground gouge is sharpened by rubbing it back and forth on a flat oilstone, holding the tool at an angle and giving it a twisting motion.

Graining.—Graining is a method of painting deal woodwork such as doors or window frames to imitate ash, maple and other better woods. Special tools in the shape of steel combs, each having teeth of different width, are drawn in zig-zag fashion along the finishing coat of paint, or graining coat, as it is called, before it is allowed to dry, and in this way producing the grain marks of the wood it is intended to imitate. When dry, the surface is usually given a coat of varnish. Graining requires exceptional skill and is rarely attempted by the amateur decorator. Owing to the time it takes, and the use of inexpensive, washable, hard-gloss paint, graining is rapidly becoming a thing of the past.

Grinding. — A suitable grinding wheel should be included in every

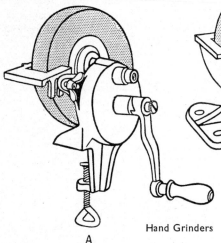
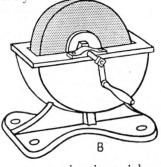

Hand Grinders

A

B

handyman's kit, as it is invaluable for sharpening tools, knives, taking off small quantities of surplus metal and other useful purposes.

A hand-operated, geared, high-speed grinding machine for fixing to the bench as that shown at A in the figure can now be obtained quite cheaply while abrasive wheels such as emery and carborundum are to be procured in various degrees of coarseness.

For grinding edge-tools there is nothing better than the old-fashioned grindstone B, and the amateur woodworker will find that this machine is better adapted for grinding his tools than the high-speed emery type which is likely to draw the temper.

The grindstone should be used in a wet condition and it is better to allow the water to trickle on the surface from a container fitted with a tap to regulate the an ou ıt of water, than to rely on that drawn up from a trough. It is also advisable to draw off water from the trough when not in use as a partial wetness is detrimental to the life of the stone.

The stone should revolve towards the tool and not away from it, and if the surface becomes worn, it should be ground level. This can be done effectively by applying the end of a piece of gas piping near the edge and gradually moving it straight across from side to side while the stone is revolving.

Grooving and Rebating Wood. — For making a groove in the narrow edge, in the direction of the grain, a grooving plane with an adjustable fence is used, as illustrated at A in Fig. 1, page 41. Such a plane, with three steel cutters for making grooves, $\frac{1}{8}$, $\frac{3}{16}$ and $\frac{1}{4}$ in. respectively, costs about 6s. 6d. and is a useful tool to have when grooving frames to take plywood panels. For preparing grooves at some distance from the edge of the face of a wide board, a plough plane is necessary as indicated at C, which illustrates a metal plough plane with three cutters, obtainable for 6s. 6d. In both cases planing is started from the farther end of the work and gradually worked back towards the near end.

In cutting grooves across the grain, a tenon saw is sometimes used for cutting down the sides to the required depth and the waste removed with a chisel, working the latter from one edge to the centre and then reversing the work,

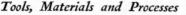

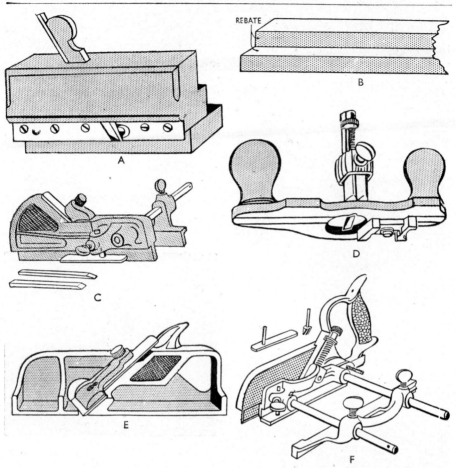

Fig. 1

and repeating the operation. A better method would be to make the saw cuts and remove the waste with a router as illustrated at D.

Rebating is the term used when forming a recess in the edge of a piece of wood as illustrated at B. The usual method is to use a rebate plane as shown at E.

All these operations, except routing, can be done with a single plane known as an improved combination plane. This plane, represented at F in Fig. 1, is supplied with no fewer than seventeen tungsten steel cutters, and the amateur

B*

woodworker who takes his work seriously is advised to invest in one.

Fig. 2 shows a groove being formed by means of a combination plane.

Hacksaw.—The proper tool for sawing metal is the hacksaw. Such a saw is shown in action on page 42. The tool consists of an adjustable metal frame with suitable pegs at the top and bottom which fit into corresponding holes in the saw blades and hold it in position, while a wing nut at the top of the frame allows the tension of the blade to be adjusted. A handle at the lower end is provided for operating the tool.

In using the hacksaw, the blade should be inserted so that the teeth are away from the operator as the saw cuts only on the outward stroke. Fix the work

Fig. 2

securely in an engineer's vice, which should be rigidly attached to a strong bench to prevent vibration, and file a nick at the desired position in the metal. Hold the hacksaw as shown and start the cut at the nick which was

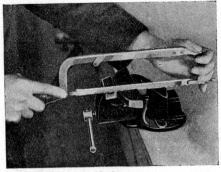

Hacksaw

made to prevent the blade from slipping during the first stroke. Keep the saw square to the work and apply a little pressure to the outward or cutting stroke only, then relieve the pressure and draw the blade back. Continue in this way until near the end of the cutting when

the pressure must be almost entirely relieved.

If a finished piece of work has to be sawn, place a piece of sheet lead over each jaw of the vice before tightening up to prevent the work being marked.

For cutting mild steel, wrought iron and cast iron, use a blade having about twenty-four teeth, while for sawing brass and other soft metals a blade having eighteen teeth will give good results.

When sawing sheet metal edgeways, place the work between two pieces of hardwood in the vice and saw both wood and metal. Do not oil the saw.

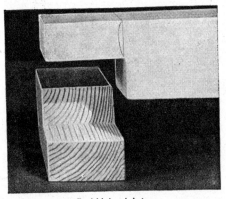

End Halved Joint

Halved Joints.—A simple joint illustrated above is known as an end halved joint.

In making the joint, a tenon saw is required for cutting the wood down to the proper depth and a chisel for removing the waste. Care should be taken when sawing to make the cut in the waste side of the guide lines and not to saw too deep. Another form of halved joint, known as the tee halved joint, is shown on page 43.

Hammers. — The woodworker's hammer, known as a Warrington hammer, is shown at A, in the figure, while a claw hammer B is also a handy implement for woodwork. The head

Tee Halved Joint

has a claw for withdrawing nails in addition to a striking face. The tool

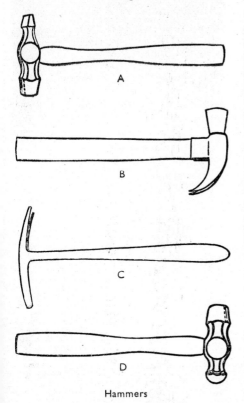

Hammers

shown at c is an upholsterer's hammer used for driving in tacks. It is also useful for light cabinet work, for driving in panel pins and similar work. The essential difference between the engineer's hammer D and the others represented in the figure is the ball pane or the hemispherical reverse end of the head. This feature enables the ends of rivets to be hammered over.

In using these hammers, the blow should be imparted from the wrist and not from the whole of the arm as in using a sledge hammer, and, in driving nails, it is essential to reduce the power of the blows as the nail head approaches the surface of the work to prevent the hammer from bruising the wood.

Hand Drill.—A tool for rotating drills and exceedingly useful in woodworking as well as metalworking. It consists essentially of a steel, adjustable chuck for holding the drills, driven at high speed by means of gear wheels as the illustration shows. The one shown will suffice for most amateur requirements, and will hold drills up to $\frac{1}{4}$ in. diameter. It costs about 3s. 9d.

Hand Drill

Hardening and Tempering Steel. The cutting edges of wood and metalworking tools sometimes need rehardening and tempering. The process of hardening is simple enough as the material only requires to be heated up to a bright red and then plunged into clean cold water. This treatment, however, renders the steel very hard and brittle; so brittle in fact that the tool

Fig. I

Fig. 3

Fig. 2

proceed in the following way: Heat the nose, not directly upon the cutting edge or you may burn it, to a bright red, then plunge it vertically into clean cold water for a few seconds to make it dead hard. Rub the edge immediately with a piece of emery cloth to enable the changing colours to be observed as the heat turns from the body of the tool to the point. As soon as the surface assumes a light straw colour plunge it

would be of little use. To give the body of the tool toughness and strength and, at the same time, impart sufficient hardness to the cutting edge to prevent it becoming blunt, tempering is necessary. This reduces hardness and increases

into cold water, keeping the tool swirling about until cold.

Fig. I shows the nose of the tool being heated in the flame of a blowlamp, the operator is seen watching the colour-change in Fig. 2, while Fig. 3 illustrates the final quenching.

The following table will enable you to judge when to quench a particular tool:

Centre punches, scrapers, lathe tools	Light straw
Drills	Dark straw
Plane-irons, wood-cutting chisels, gouges, cold chisels, etc.	Brown
Knives	Light blue
Springs, screwdrivers ..	Dark blue

High speed steel requires special treatment and makers' instructions for tempering should always be followed.

strength, and the amount of tempering depends on the particular tool.

When dealing with edge-tools, it is usual to combine hardening and tempering in one process. Thus, in dealing with a lathe tool, it is necessary only to heat up the nose as the body is already sufficiently tough.

To harden and temper such a tool

Mild steel and wrought iron, which are comparatively soft metals, cannot be hardened by heating them up and plunging them into cold water, as cast or hard steel can, owing to the lack of sufficient carbon in their composition. These metals, however, can be case-hardened; that is, their surfaces can be rendered hard by heating the metal to a high degree of temperature and allowing it to absorb carbon. This treatment produces a hard-steel case or steel, hence the name case-hardening.

A common method of case-hardening is to enclose the work to be treated in a thick, iron, air-tight container, packed with either bone dust or scraps of leather and then heat it up to a cherry-red colour. The heat treatment is continued until the desired thickness of the case is obtained, four or five hours generally being necessary to produce a thickness of $\frac{1}{16}$ in. The glowing metal is swirled about and then removed from the container and plunged vertically into cold water, or, better still, cold water to which has been added a handful of salt. This hardens the outside case, leaving the interior soft. The kitchen fire may be used for case-hardening small articles.

In cases where only a thin hardened surface is required, the container method can be dispensed with and a prepared compound in powder form known as Kasenit can be applied to red-hot metal. The powder is sprinkled on the work and more is added from time to time as the compound melts. After about thirty minutes' treatment, which is generally sufficient for case-hardening small screws, the work is plunged into a bucket of cold salt water.

Hinges.—Fig. 1 shows a number of useful hinges designed for numerous woodworking purposes. That shown at A is an ordinary butt used for hinging heavy doors, while that represented at B is a loose butt which enables a door to be detached from its frame. A wide brass hinge suitable for attaching the desk board to a writing bureau is illus-

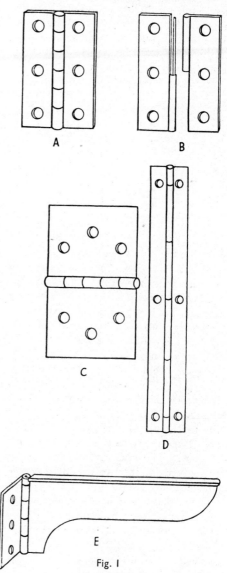

Fig. 1

trated at C, and that at D is a long brass hinge as used for attaching the rising cover of a radiogram. A novel hinge in the shape of a bracket is shown at E.

This is useful for supporting the flaps of tables, etc., and is fitted simply by screwing it to the rail of the table.

In fitting ordinary butt hinges it is usual to sink the leaves of flaps into the member forming the joint, as shown at A in Fig. 2, although in some cases, as in B, it may be advisable to sink both leaves into one member only.

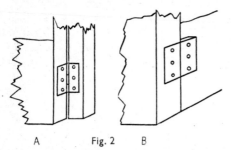

A   Fig. 2   B

Before fitting hinges, always mark their position on the work and pay special attention that the pinned joints are parallel with the edges of the work.

Housing Joint.—Fig. 1 shows a through housing-joint. Grooves equal in width to the thickness of the shelves are cut in the uprights with the aid of a tenon saw and chisel. The uprights are of thicker material than the shelves, as shown. The depth of the grooves is generally one-third the thickness of the wood and allowance for the depth of the grooves must be added to the effective length of the shelves. The ends of the shelves are then glued and inserted into the grooves.

A neater form is shown in Fig. 2. The grooves terminate at a short distance from the edges, while the ends of the shelves are cut away to enable them to butt up against the front inside faces.

Lead.—A dull bluish-grey coloured common metal, very soft, heavy and ductile. Used extensively in the form of sheets for covering flat roofs, thin strips for making flashings (see flashings), pipes for cold water, electric

storage batteries and sheathing for electric cables. It can be cast easily as it melts at a temperature of only 620 deg. F. An old tenon saw is

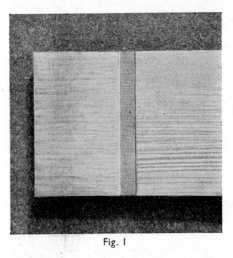

Fig. I

excellent for cutting lead pipes. A square foot of sheet lead $\frac{1}{8}$ in. thick weighs 7.4 lb. It can be worked into

Fig. 2

all shapes by beating it with hardwood tools obtainable for the purpose.

Ledged Joint.—A common wood-working joint used principally at the ends of boards to prevent twisting. The ends of the boards have ledges; that is, they are cut to form a tongue which fits into a corresponding groove in the end pieces as illustrated at A in the figure, while the sketch at B shows the ledged buttons as applied to a table for fixing the top to the rails.

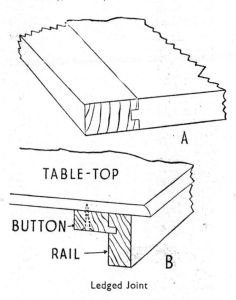

TABLE-TOP

BUTTON

RAIL

B

Ledged Joint

Locks, Bolts and Fastenings.— The fitting of locks, bolts and other woodwork fastenings calls for neat and accurate work. Fig. 1 shows a number of locks. For common doors, such as those used for sheds, greenhouses and house doors where appearance is not of importance, the ordinary rim lock as illustrated at A may be used. To fit, first mark the position, usually in the middle rail or lock-rail, and cut a shallow recess on the front edge of the door to take the front plate or flange. This enables it to be flush with the edge of the door. Then hold the lock in position and mark the centres for the spindle and keyhole. With a sharp twist-bit, a trifle larger than the diagonal thickness of the spindle, bore the spindle

hole, taking care to make it square with the face of the door. Next, cut the keyhole by boring two holes, one at the top and one at the bottom. Remove the waste between them, as represented by the dotted lines, with a pad saw. Before making screw holes, place the lock temporarily in position, insert the spindle and key from the outside to see that they work satisfactorily. If everything is as it should be, the lock can be fixed permanently. The final operation consists of fitting the box staple that receives the latch to the frame.

The lock shown at B is known as a mortice lock because the body is housed in a mortice cut into the edge of the door.

The fitting of this type of lock calls for careful workmanship. Mark the position in the edge of the door where the lock is to go and make the recess by boring a series of holes with a twist-bit a little smaller than the width of the recess, and removing the remaining waste with a chisel. The depth of the mortice should be a trifle longer than the length of the body of the lock plus the fixing plate. Next, accurately mark the

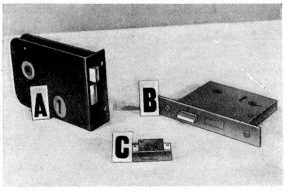

Fig. 1

positions for the spindle on both sides of the door. First bore these holes on one side only, insert the lock into the mortice to verify that the bored holes correspond with those in the lock and, if such is the case, repeat the operation on the other side, finally removing the waste between the holes of the keyhole.

Insert the lock temporarily in position, put in the key and spindle to see that they work freely, and if correct, fix the lock permanently by driving in the fixing screws. Fix the handles, not forgetting the escutcheon plates that cover the keyholes and the spindle plates.

bore a smaller hole below it slightly larger than the thickness of the ward or rectangular part of the key and remove the waste between the holes. Next, mark and accurately cut the recesses for the top and back plates and then chop out the recess for the box or body containing the mechanism of the lock. Then fix the lock by means of countersunk-headed screws.

Finally, locate, mark and prepare the mortice and recess for the catch plate

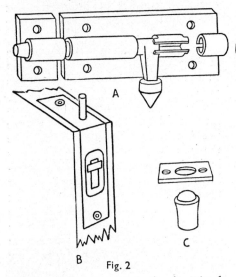

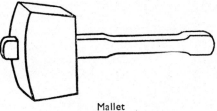

Mallet

Fig. 2

and fix the plate with screws so that it is quite flush with the face

Little difficulty should be experienced in fitting any of the fastenings shown in Fig. 2. The door bolt shown at A is simply screwed to the face of the door first. To ensure the catch being in line with the bolt it is advisable to shoot the bolt, place the catch into the projecting end and drive in the fixing screws.

Finally, cut a recess in the door jamb to take the cover or fixing plate for housing the latches. This plate lies flush with the face of the jamb, and is fixed, as with the lock itself, by means of countersunk-headed screws.

In fitting a drawer lock, c in Fig. 1, the first thing to do is to locate the exact position of the keyhole.

This will come in the centre of the front and at a distance from the top edge equal to that of the top plate of the lock and the pin over which the barrel of the key fits, when the plate lies flush with the top edge. Having marked the position, bore a hole a trifle larger than the barrel of the key and

The blind bolt illustrated at B is usually fitted to the closing edges of the top and bottom rails of the left-hand door. The bolt shoots into a hole bored in the top and bottom of the woodwork.

The ball-catch fastener illustrated at c costs only a few pence. The ball fitment is let tightly into a hole bored in the top of the opening stile of the door so that only the ball portion projects. The ball fits in a corresponding plate which is recessed into the woodwork and secured by screws.

Mallet.—A woodworker's striking tool made of beech or other hardwood and used principally for striking chisels, gouges and other tools where the use of a hammer would injure the wooden handles. The illustration shows a serviceable mallet weighing about a pound. Note that the shaft projects beyond the top of the head. The shaft is tapered and fits into a corresponding tapered hole in the head. This feature acts as a wedge and tends to tighten the head on the shaft when in use.

Mahogany.—Mahogany is an ideal wood for cabinet-making and other purposes where a strong, durable hardwood is required.

There are many kinds of mahogany and that known as Spanish mahogany is the best and most expensive. It is beautifully marked, of a deep red-brown colour and has a whitish, chalky substance which fills the pores. Spanish mahogany is almost entirely free from knots and other imperfections and does not warp or shrink to any appreciable extent. It can be obtained in very wide boards. For this reason, furniture of the highest class, organ sound-boards tee-squares, and similar articles are made from this wood.

Mahogany from Central America, known as Honduras mahogany, or bay wood, as it is sometimes called, is inferior to Spanish mahogany and is lighter in colour. It is difficult to plane owing to inequality of the texture.

Mahogany takes glue well and an exceptionally brilliant polish can be imparted to it.

Measuring and Marking Wood.— The fate of a piece of constructional woodwork depends almost entirely upon the accuracy exercised in measuring and marking out. Slipshod methods and inaccurate marking out lead to failure.

A good 2 ft. four-fold rule with plainly marked inches and sub-divisions, try square, bevel, marking-gauge, dividers, a sharp-pointed pencil and the ability to use them are necessary for marking out.

In marking a dimension on a board, the rule should be placed on edge and a mark made exactly opposite the figure required as indicated in Fig. 1. This method obviates the possibility of an

Fig. 1

error in judging the exact spot as often happens when the rule is used flat.

When measuring a long board with a 2 ft. rule, mark each individual 2 ft. length with a pencil and do not rely upon the accuracy of marking wood with the brass end of the rule, as is

Fig. 2

often done. The latter method answers the purpose only for rough work.

Various methods are used for marking lines parallel to a planed edge of wood. The usual way, however, is to use a marking-gauge as illustrated in Fig. 2. To use the tool, set the adjustable fence at the desired distance from the point with the aid of a rule. Press the fence tightly against the prepared edge of the work to be marked and draw or push the tool along the

Fig. 3

work so that the point scores the wood lightly. Then repeat the process in order to obtain a more definite line. The tool should be held so that the point slopes in the opposite direction of motion as indicated in Fig. 2, otherwise the point will score the wood too deeply. Avoid using a marking - gauge having a blunt point ; if necessary remove the pin and sharpen it with a fine file. The point should not project more than ⅛ in. from the bar.

A quick method of drawing a line parallel to the planed edge of a board, is to hold the rule flatly in the left hand and bring it up to a pencil point resting on a previously marked spot on the board indicating the desired width. The rule and pencil is

then run along the board using the forefinger of the left hand as a guide (Fig. 3).

A try square (Fig. 4 A) is used as a guide when it is desired to mark lines at right angles to an edge. The proper way to use it is first to hold the pencil so that its point rests on the exact spot where the line is to be made and then to slide the square along the work until the blade touches the pencil point as

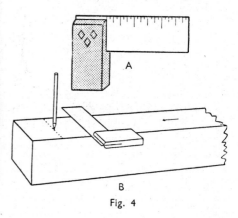

Fig. 4

shown at B in Fig. 4. The pencil is then drawn along the edge of the blade as indicated by the dotted lines.

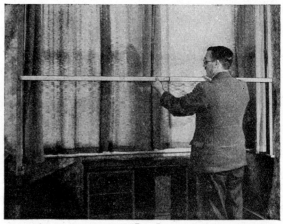

Fig. 5

Fig. 5 shows a pinch rod made out of two thin battens. Such an accessory is useful for gauging the width of recesses

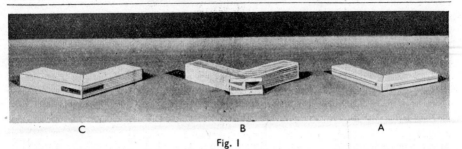

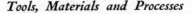

C   B   A

Fig. 1

between walls and similar purposes.

Mitre Joints.—For joining wood at right angles a mitre joint is often employed. As will be seen from the

of the joint as illustrated in Fig. 1B, while a still stronger joint is that shown in Fig. 1C which represents a mitre with a false tenon joint. A slot is

Fig. 2

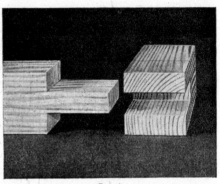

Fig. 1

illustrations at A in Fig. 1 the ends of the members to be joined are cut to an angle of 45 deg. so that the joined pieces form a right angle.

In forming an ordinary mitre, the ends are first marked out and sawn on a mitre block or in a mitre box (Fig. 2) which guides the saw, and then planed smooth on a mitre shooting-board (see Shooting-board). The ends are then glued and nailed with lost-headed nails, the heads of which are generally punched below the surface, and the small depressions filled with a filler such as plastic wood.

Such a joint is considerably strengthened by the insertion of keys or slips of hardwood that are fitted and glued into saw-kerfs made on the outside edge

made in each end of the parts to be joined as shown, and a slip of wood inserted and glued into the slots.

Fig. 2

Mortice and Tenon Joints.—One of the most if not the most important series of joints in woodwork. The joint consists essentially of a tenon or projection on one member that fits into a corresponding rectangular hole, called a mortice, in the part to be joined. A few of the common joints suitable for most amateur work are represented here. That illustrated at Fig. 1 shows a simple, open mortice and tenon, while that at Fig. 2 is a through, closed mortice and tenon, so called because the tenon goes right through the mortice. A stub

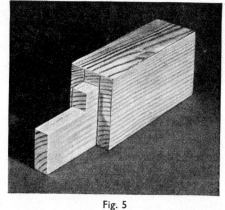

Fig. 5

The success of these joints lies in accurate marking out. Where the joint comes near the end of a piece of work, allow about an inch for waste.

In ordinary work, it is usual to make the tenons one-third the woodthickness.

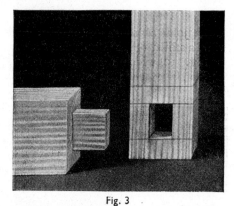

Fig. 3

or stopped tenon (Fig. 3) goes only part way through and so does not show. In Fig. 4 is seen a bare-faced tenon, having only one shoulder, which may

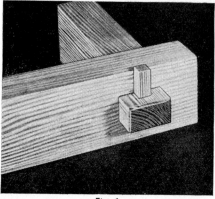

Fig. 6

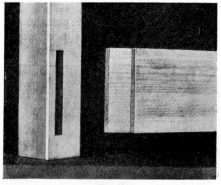

Fig. 4

be stopped or through. That shown at Fig. 5 is a square-haunched or shouldered tenon, while the tenon illustrated at Fig. 6 is a keyed tenon that projects beyond the mortice and is held in position by means of a wedge or key.

To make the open mortice and tenon joint, proceed in the following way. With a tenon saw, cut out the depth across the shoulder lines, keeping the saw teeth in the waste part of the wood. Next place the work in a sloping position in the vice and saw down to the shoulder and, if necessary, trim the wide faces of the tenon with a sharp chisel, working in the direction of the grain.

Having marked out the mortice, place

the work in the vice and make two saw cuts down to the depth of the line and remove the waste with a chisel.

In dealing with a through closed mortice and tenon joint, cut the tenon as previously explained and then proceed with the mortice after having marked out on the top and bottom faces. Fix the work in a vice and bore a number of holes close together with

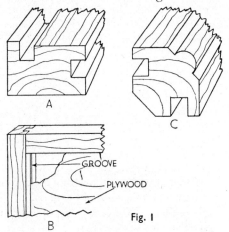

A

C

GROOVE

PLYWOOD

Fig. I

B

a brace and twist-bit a trifle smaller in diameter than the width of the mortice. Bore first from one face to the centre, reverse the work, and continue boring. Then remove the remaining waste with a chisel, taking care to keep the sides and ends of the mortice perfectly square.

The same procedure is followed in forming the stub or stopped tenon and mortice except that the mortice is made more or less shallow according to the length of the tenon.

To make the haunched or shouldered through tenon and mortice, make a full tenon first and then mark and saw it down to form the shoulder. Proceed with the mortice as in the through joint, but do not bore right through the mortice in that portion that is to receive the shoulder of the tenon. The depth of the recess is of course equal to the length of the haunch.

The keyed tenon is made longer than the ordinary tenon and must be provided with a rectangular hole into which the key or wedge is inserted.

Mouldings.—Decorative mouldings and grooved mouldings for constructional work are now obtainable at prices little above that of the raw material.

For constructing the framework of cabinets, doors and small carcase work generally, the example given at A in Fig. I will be found invaluable. The moulding is made of hardwood which can be stained and the grooves are of a width to take plywood of standard thicknesses. The illustration at B shows the use of grooved mouldings in the construction of a door. A short stub tenon is cut in one member which fits into the groove of the other and when glued forms a substantial joint.

A corner moulding grooved as in

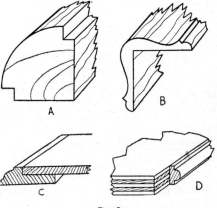

A

B

C

D

Fig. 2

the plain type is shown at C in Fig. I.

A flush corner moulding, one of many types, is represented at A in Fig. 2 and is handy for radio cabinets. The use of edge-moulding (B) hides unsightly joints.

A rebated moulding as seen at C is for edging thin plywood.

It enables a thin piece of wood to be used instead of a thick piece and yet retains ,the appearance of the latter.

The use of small mouldings, either plain or ornamental, is an ideal method of giving a finish to the unsightly edges of plywood as in the illustration at D.

Picture rail mouldings, moulded skirting boards and other soft wood mouldings are obtainable at most timber merchants.

Nails.—Always use a nail suitable for the job. For common woodwork, where appearance is not of much con-

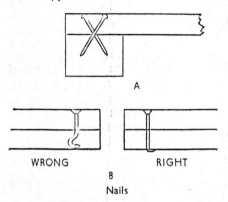

WRONG   RIGHT

B

Nails

sequence, the ordinary wire nail with its comparatively large circular head is generally employed. Such a nail has strong gripping power and does not split the wood. If a large head is not wanted, use an oval wire nail which has a small head enabling it to be punched below the surface of the wood. When using this type of nail, see that the widest part of the body is driven in parallel to the direction of the grain to obviate splitting.

For fixing floorboards, floor-brads having a projection on one side of the head should be employed. The taper faces of these, as well as cut clasp nails and other nails having wedge-shaped bodies, must follow the direction of the grain.

Large-headed, galvanised clout nails should always be used for outside work such as fixing roofing felt and other

purposes where an untreated nail would rust. Copper nails should be used for fixing copper and lead, but should not be used for iron or zinc.

Lost-head wire nails are circular in shape, thin, and have an almost imperceptible head which makes them extremely useful for cabinet work where it is particularly necessary that they should not show. Iron panel pins, not much thicker than ordinary pins, are handy for fretwork purposes, fixing small mouldings and small work in general.

Nails driven in at angles, as indicated in Fig. 1 A, are more effective than nails driven in straight.

Do not drive nails into hardwood without first boring holes for their reception, otherwise the wood is liable to split. The same applies when using large nails in soft wood.

The figure shows the wrong and right way to clinch the ends of the nails.

Nogging.—Nogging is the term given to the short horizontal pieces of

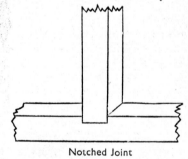

Notched Joint

wood between and about the middle of studs and uprights in a hollow partition and the like.

Notched Joint.—The illustration shows a common form of notched joint, such as could be formed in the top and bottom plates to accommodate the ends of studs or uprights in the framework of partitions and sheds. Such a joint gives greater stability than a nailed butt-joint and keeps the uprights at the correct distance apart. The joint is formed by first marking out on the face of the plate two guide lines representing the thickness of the part to be joined, and two depth lines, usually about $\frac{1}{2}$ in., on the front and back faces. The waste is then removed with the aid of a tenon saw and chisel.

Oak.—One of the most useful hardwoods in existence, of which there are many varieties. All have the same general characteristics and vary in colour from light brown to dark brown. Hard British oak, known as pedunculate oak, is suitable for outside purposes such as fences but is liable to twist and warp and is therefore generally unsuitable for furniture and cabinet making. Sessel-flora oak, another British product, is softer than pedunculate oak and has a straight grain. It is easy to work but difficult to obtain.

For all ordinary work such as furniture making, Japanese oak is recommended. It is straight-grained and mild and can be obtained in boards up to 11 in. wide and about 8 ft. in length, and is cheaper than oak imported from Austria.

Oilstones.—It is impossible to turn out good work with blunt tools. The cutting edge of a tool, such as a plane-iron, after being ground is too coarse to be of practical use. To produce a keen edge, the tool must have further treatment and this is done by honing it on an oilstone. This has a cutting action like a grindstone, but it cuts more slowly and produces a keener edge. There is no need to re-grind the tool every time it becomes blunt; a few rubs on an oilstone will soon restore a keen edge.

There are numerous kinds of oilstones, some of which are natural stone while others are manufactured. The best kind for carpenters' tools is one of medium coarseness and a Washita stone will generally give good results. Where an extremely keen edge is required, the

work should be finished on a fine stone. Some workers prefer a manufactured stone such as the India stone. This may be obtained with two sides, one face of medium grit and the other fine.

For honing plane-irons or chisels, a stone measuring from 6 in. to 8 in. long and 2 in. wide will serve.

An oilstone should be protected by sinking it partially into a block of wood or box and, when not in use, the exposed part should be covered with a dustproof lid. The stone should be a hand-tight

Using an Oilstone

fit in the block so that it can be removed easily. To prevent the stone from slipping about when in use on the bench it is a good plan to drive in a couple of nails minus their heads in the bottom of the block. The pegs should project about $\frac{1}{16}$ in.

Before putting a new stone into service, soak it in oil for a few days. This does not apply to India stones as they are oil-treated already.

The process of whetting or honing is very simple. In the case of plane-irons and chisels, it is simply a matter of rubbing the bevelled edge of the blade in a correct manner on the surface of the stone. As an example, let us assume that the cutting-iron of a plane has to be treated.

Put a few spots of oil on the stone and wipe it thoroughly clean with a fluffless rag to ensure that no grit is on the surface. Next put a little more oil on the stone and place the bevel of the blade on the stone, holding it in the manner indicated in the illustration. Now raise the back a trifle so that only the cutting edge remains on the stone and rub the blade to and fro along the surface, applying moderate pressure. If

Painting

the stone is not sufficiently wide to accommodate the entire width of the blade, hold it in an oblique position as shown, without altering the cutting angle. It is essential to avoid rocking the blade, otherwise a curved edge will result.

Having given the blade about a dozen strokes, turn it over perfectly flat on the stone and give two or three light rubs to remove the wire edge. Failure to keep the blade flat will spoil the cutting edge.

Do not use thick oil to lubricate the stone. A mixture of machine oil and paraffin will serve, or cycle oil.

After much use the stone may become glazed so that the edge of the tool being honed does not bite, but tends to slide along it. When this occurs, wash the stone well with paraffin.

Do not use a stone that has become hollow from wear, but true it up by rubbing its surface on a flagstone moistened with a paste of silver sand and water.

Painting. — Painting requires as much care and forethought as any other mechanical process. Slipshod methods are never successful.

The kind of paint used for a particular job depends on the surface to be covered, whether it be wood, metal or stone, but they are all applied in much the same way.

Before attempting to paint new woodwork, see that it is perfectly dry and rub over the surface with glass-paper as it is impossible to obtain a good finish if the groundwork is rough. Then treat all knots with knotting, which is a solution of shellac in methylated spirit obtainable at most oil stores. On no account must the knotting process be omitted, or the knots will absorb the paint and mar the finished work.

Remove all dust from the work, using a brush for the purpose. An ordinary duster should not be used as it leaves fluff behind.

The next operation consists of applying the first, or priming, coat of paint. Priming paint is composed of red and white lead mixed with linseed oil and is sold ready made. Use a good brush as a cheap one generally casts its bristles. Before use, thoroughly stir the paint with a stick, not a brush, so that no solid ingredients remain in the bottom of the container. Use a well-known and reliable brand of paint.

When applying the paint, work first in one direction and then in the other and lay off in the direction of the grain, as indicated. When dry, stop up holes and other imperfections with putty, lightly glass-paper the surface and remove all dust.

The next coat should be of undercoating; that is, a flat paint without gloss specially prepared for the purpose. This is applied in exactly the same way as the priming and, when dry, glass-papered and dusted, followed either by a further undercoat or by the finishing coat. To make a good job, two undercoats should be given, for the purpose of paint is to give a pleasing finish and to preserve the wood.

Where a rich, glossy finish is desired, a good hard-gloss paint should be used; but for a duller surface ordinary oil paint may be employed. The former is usually sold by the pint, half a pint generally being sufficient to cover about 50 sq. ft., while the latter is sold by the pound, which is usually enough to cover about 25 sq. ft.

Ordinary oil paint is applied in the same way as the undercoat, but a slightly different treatment is necessary when using gloss paint as it contains a proportion of varnish. During cold weather it is better to work with gloss paint in a warm room, and if the paint is thick and difficult to work the container should be placed in a bowl of warm water. Turpentine, or other thinners, should not be used with gloss paint as interference with the proportions will reduce durability and brilliance. Apply the paint first in one direction and then the other and finish off with long gentle sweeps with the tip of the brush, making sure that the whole of the surface is covered. Any attempt at painting an untreated spot when the paint is nearly set will result in an unsightly patch. If the work is well done the brush marks will fade away, leaving a surface which, when dry, will be hard and mirror-like.

In painting over old paintwork, which must be in fairly good condition, dust, glass-paper and wash the surface thoroughly with clean warm water and sugar soap to remove all grease and dirt. When quite dry, apply an undercoat and finish either with ordinary or gloss paint.

Paper-hanging. — Hanging wallpaper requires the following simple tools: A stripping tool costing about sixpence for removing the old paper, a brush for applying the paste, a rule, a pair of large scissors, a plumb-bob and line, a brush such as a fairly stiff clothes brush for smoothing the paper when being hung, a bucket of water for soaking the old paper, an old distemper brush for applying the water, a small quantity of Keene's cement for stopping up cracks and holes in the plaster, some glue-size for sizing the walls, a supply of special cold water paste flour (obtainable with the size and Keene's cement at wallpaper shops), a pair of steps, and a table upon which to paste the paper.

Although new wallpaper can be hung on the old if the latter is in good condition, it is better to remove it and start afresh.

Stripping old unvarnished paper off the walls is a simple operation. First soak the paper thoroughly with plenty of water applied with an old distemper brush or sponge. Allow sufficient time for the water to penetrate the paper and remove the latter with the stripper. This tool should be held at an angle so that the working edge lifts the paper from the wall, and care must be taken not to allow the blade to dig into the plaster.

Having removed every particle of paper, stop up all holes and cracks in the plaster with Keene's cement (see Distempering) and apply a coat of glue-size to fill the pores.

As a beginner you are advised to start operations on a small and unimportant room before attempting work on, say, a lounge or staircase. Choose a paper of medium thickness and with a small pattern. Large patterns look well in a large room, but are out of place in a small one. Also, select a predominating tint which harmonises with the paintwork and hangings.

English wallpapers are sold by the roll or piece containing about 12 yd. The width is 22 in., including a $\frac{1}{2}$ in.

margin on each side for trimming.

The number of pieces required is easily calculated, but it is wise to obtain an extra piece to make up for waste.

Before trimming off a margin, a decision must be made as to the method to be adopted in joining the edges when hanging the paper. Either a butt-joint or a lap can be employed. The former

Fig. 1

involves the trimming of both margins as the trimmed edges butt close together on the wall, while the latter requires the removal of only one, as the trimmed edge of one section laps over the margin of the other.

Butt-joints are to be preferred to lap-joints, but the edges must be perfectly true. Lap-joints are apt to show a ridge where one piece overlaps the other and, in hanging, the lap must be so arranged that the edge of the joint does not show when entering the room.

Wallpaper may be conveniently purchased at shops dealing in home-decoration goods, who usually trim, free of cost, one or both edges as required, on a machine.

If you prefer to trim the paper yourself it can be done on the table as indicated in Fig. 1, but it is better to sit on a chair and proceed as shown in Fig. 2. Here, the worker is seen operating the scissors with his right hand and, as the work proceeds, he rolls up the trimmed

portion at the same time pulling the paper with his left hand and thus unrolling the remainder at his feet.

The next operation consists of cutting the paper from the roll into sections. Measure the distance between the ceiling or picture rail if there is a frieze, and the top of the skirting board and allow 3 in. at each end for trimming. In cutting the sections of patterned paper be careful to see that the pattern of one piece coincides with the next.

Then follows the pasting. Mix the powder and water in a large bowl or bucket, taking care to see that it is free from lumps. Use a brush at least 4 in. wide and apply the paste evenly over the back of the paper, except for an inch at each end. Do not allow the paste to come in contact with the table top as this will spoil the next piece to be pasted. To avoid this it is a good plan to spread sheets of newspaper over the table top.

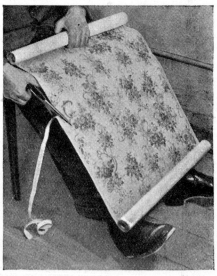

Fig. 2

Those at the front and back can be pulled so as to expose a clean surface at the long edges of the wallpaper after each successive pasting. Now loosely fold the pasted paper so that the ends meet about 6 in. or so from the centre and, holding it at this point between the finger and thumb of each hand, carry it with arms outstretched to where it is to be hung.

Unfold the top section of the folded sheet and place it in position, allowing 3 in. overlap at the top which must be cut away afterwards for trimming purposes and taking care to see that the piece is absolutely vertical. Now brush out the creases by working the brush upwards and downwards and then unfold the lower portion and continue brushing. Trim off the waste from the top and bottom by first scoring the paper with the point of the scissors, pulling the paper away a few inches from the wall and cutting along the guide lines. Replace the paper with the aid of the brush. Carry on as before.

A good place to hang the first piece is at a window, as indicated at A in Fig. 3, where the edge of the frame is vertical. As it is essential that the edge x of the first piece be quite upright, the edge of the frame should be tested with a plumb-bob. If correct, proceed in the direction shown by the arrow, towards B which represents an upright of a door frame. Then start from the opposite side of the window C and follow round the room to the other door-frame edge D, the surface under the window and over the door being the last pieces to hang.

Picture Rails.—The appearance of a room is sometimes enhanced by a picture rail. Apart from the primary object of such a rail, a light frieze between rail and ceiling has great reflecting power and therefore tends to make the room lighter.

The fitting of a picture rail is only a matter of a few hours' work.

Select a narrow moulding if the room is small as a deep one would look out of place, and remember that mouldings of elaborate design are a thing of the past, comparatively plain rails having taken their place.

Having acquired the necessary amount of material, with an extra 10 per cent. for waste, stop the knots with knotting and give the moulding a primary coat of paint; the finishing coats may be given when the rail is in position.

Saw the pieces to length and make either internal or external mortice joints to suit the angles of the walls.

In fixing the rail, it will usually be found better to keep the picture rail at the same height as the top of the door

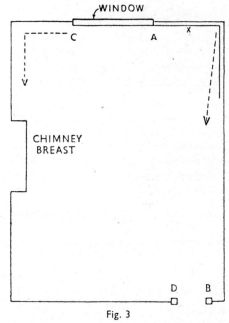

Fig. 3

frame or a little below rather than above it. This, however, will depend upon whether the horizontal mortar joint between the bricks into which the fixing nails are driven happens to come in line or below the level of the frames.

To find the course, measure on the wall a distance of $2\frac{1}{2}$ in. below the ceiling, as this is about the usual point under the ceiling where the first course comes. Below this position, longitudinal courses will be found at intervals of 3 in. Locate the course by driving a fine bradawl into the plaster. If it goes in deeply it may be taken that the course has been found, but it is wise to verify this by inserting the bradawl at other positions in line with the original one.

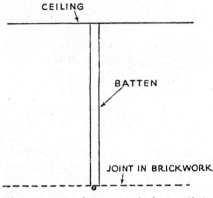

Then trace a line round the wall by first marking a piece of batten indicating the distance from the ceiling to the course and using this for measuring, as indicated above.

Use 2 in. cut-nails and drive them in at intervals of about 18 in. Sink the nail heads below the surface with a nail punch, stop up the holes with putty, give the rails one or two undercoats of paint and finish with ordinary or hard-gloss paint.

In fixing the picture rails to cokebreeze walls there is no need to find the mortar joints as nails can be driven in quite easily.

If the rail is to be fixed to a lath and plaster partition, find the vertical wooden studs and fix to these.

Pincers.—A woodworker's tool for withdrawing nails. Its power is derived from the leverage obtained between the jaws that grip the nail and the handles, the jaw forming the fulcrum of the lever. The figure shows the correct way to withdraw a nail. Note that a piece of

wood is inserted between the jaw of the tool and the work to prevent damage to the latter. An overall length of 6 in. is a serviceable size to have.

Pine, Yellow.—A useful, soft,

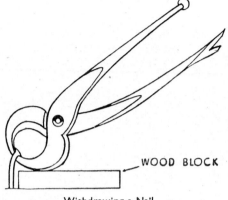

Withdrawing a Nail

straight-grained wood obtained from North America. It is very easy to work, remarkably free from knots and does not shrink and twist to any appreciable extent. It is softer but less durable than deal and liable to rot if exposed to moisture. Excellent for joinery work, panelling, backs of cabinets, parts of musical instruments and cupboards. It is more expensive than deal and can be obtained in boards up to 36 in. in width. Yellow pine is now scarce.

Pipes, Burst Water.—If a water pipe bursts inside the house, proceed

A Temporary Measure

as follows: Should it be a serious burst in the main supply pipe that feeds the cistern, cut off the supply at the stopcock to be found either inside the premises or below ground near the front entrance, and call in a plumber to effect the repair.

A small puncture in such a pipe can generally be sealed temporarily by lightly tapping the lead round the defective spot, or adhesive tape bound round the pipe may be applied as a temporary measure.

If a bad burst occurs in a pipe fed from a cistern, tie up the floating ball which operates the main water inlet valve and plug the outlet with a piece of wood if the tank is not provided with an outlet stop-cock. Empty the pipes of water, saw across the faulty pipe using an old tenon saw, turn up the live end and hammer it flat. See illustration.

The water can be allowed then to circulate to other taps by removing the stopper and releasing the ball valve of the tank, until a permanent repair can be effected.

Planes.—The three principal planes used by the joiner for smoothing and truing up wood are the jack, trying and smoothing plane, but his equipment is supplemented by a number of others for special purposes including a rebate plane for making rectangular cuts or rebates on the edges of wood, the plough for cutting grooves in or near the edges of wood, and others. Planes may be of wood or metal.

For amateur use, the metal plane is advisable for several reasons. First, the cutting edge of the plane-iron is very much easier to adjust. Wooden planes have wedges to keep the cutters in position. Second, metal planes keep their shape and do not wear on the sole or bottom face as wooden ones do.

Although the initial cost of metal planes is greater, such tools will give many years of service provided they are properly looked after.

The home carpenter should pay a reasonable price for a good plane as he cannot expect to get good service from cheap tools.

Fig. 1

Fig. 2

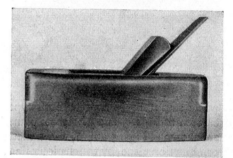

Fig. 3

Fig. 4

Figs. 1-4 show a representative group of planes, both of wood and metal. That illustrated at Fig. 1 is a jack plane, the most frequently used plane in the joiner's outfit, with wooden stock or body, with its metal counterpart Fig. 2,

Fig. 5

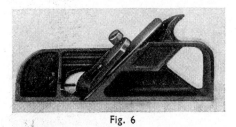

Fig. 6

while smoothing planes of both types are seen at Figs. 3 and 4. Rebate planes are shown at Figs. 5 and 6, and a metal combination plane, by which ploughing, beading, tonguing and grooving, rebating can be done, is illustrated at Fig. 7. The last obviates the purchase of separate rebate and plough planes.

In planing a rough sawn piece of wood to size, the joiner uses the jack plane roughly to trim the wood and follows with a trying plane to obtain a flat surface. Finally, the surface is finished with the smoothing plane.

For amateur work the trying plane can be omitted, as the jack plane will produce a flat surface.

The jack plane is held in the manner shown in Fig. 8. Try to avoid producing a rounded surface as

illustrated in Fig. 9. This is caused by pressure being applied at the wrong places when planing. The pressure should be greater at the front of the plane when beginning the stroke and be transferred to the back towards the end. Another important point is not to set the cutter too deep. It is far less laborious to take off several thin shavings by a number of strokes than to remove a single thick shaving by one stroke and it tends to more accurate work.

In planing the faces of a piece of timber, the tool must be used in the same direction as that of the grain, otherwise the cutter will simply tear up the wood, choke the mouth of the tool and perhaps ruin the work. The cutting edge of a smoothing plane should be set to produce a shaving of only tissue paper thickness as its function is not so much to remove waste as to produce a perfectly smooth surface.

To square up a flat piece of wood such as a board, examine and choose the best side upon which to commence operations. Test this side by applying a straight-edge in all directions. This is best done by laying the edge along the wood and holding it up to the light. If no light appears between the straight-edge and the board it can be taken that

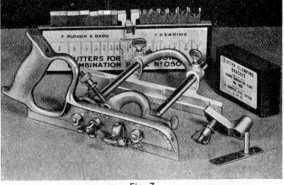

Fig. 7

it is true. If light shows, the work is twisted or " in winding," as the joiner

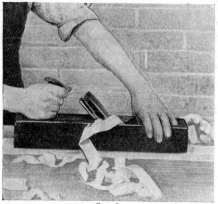

Fig. 8

working face, perfectly flat, plane the edge level along its length and square to the face, then mark the desired depth on both sides from the face and plane to depth. Finally, mark the true width from face to edge and plane to size.

Fig. 11

calls it. To verify whether the wood is in winding or not, apply two strips of hardwood of equal width, having their edges " dead " parallel—called winding strips—in the manner shown at A in Fig. 10, and take a sight over their tops. If the wood is in winding the strips will appear as at B. First plane the high parts down until the edges of the strips appear to coincide and then carry on in

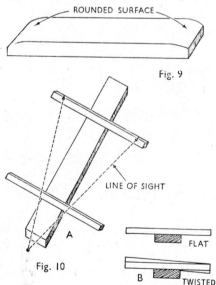

ROUNDED SURFACE

Fig. 9

LINE OF SIGHT

A

Fig. 10

FLAT

B

TWISTED

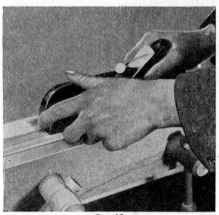

Fig. 12

the usual manner, using a straight-edge from time to time for guidance.

Having planed this face, called the

Fig. 13

To prevent ends splitting when planing on end grain, plane from one end towards the centre and then from the other. Use a very keen tool and hold it obliquely so that the cutter has a slicing action. A small block plane, as illustrated in Fig. 11, is handy for this.

A rebating plane has a cutter as wide as the body to enable it to cut into the corner of the rebate at the sides and to allow shavings to escape. The plough plane is fitted with an adjustable fence which keeps the tool at the desired distance from the edge of the work.

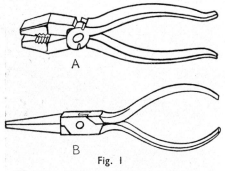

Fig. 1

Fig. 12 shows a metal rebate plane in action, while Fig. 13 illustrates the use of a combination plane used as a plough.

Blunt cutters mean hard labour and are liable to roughen the work. To keep them in working condition, they should be given a rub on an oilstone as soon as any symptoms of dullness appear. The method of sharpening a plane-iron is dealt with under oilstones.

The following hints will enable you to get the best out of your planes. Place a plane on its side when temporarily out of commission to prevent the cutting edge from damage. Hammer heads and other metal are likely to come in contact with the cutting edge and chip it and if this happens it means re-grinding. Withdraw the cutter a trifle into the body before putting away. Remember that a smoothing plane is not for rough work. For easy working, smear a spot or two of lubricating oil on the sole.

Pliers.—A useful tool for many purposes for the metalworker as well as the woodworker. Those with side cutters are preferred to the plain type as they may be used for cutting wire. Pliers measuring 6 in. overall, as illustrated at A in Fig. 1, are suitable for general purposes, while those at B are the correct size for wireless and similar work. Do not use pliers for withdrawing nails, or you will strain the jaws.

Plugging Walls.—It is often necessary to plug a brick wall to obtain a firm fixing for a fitment of some kind.

Small hollow fibre plugs known as rawlplugs are the most modern method.

These involve the use of a special tool consisting of a hardened steel bit to suit the size of the plug and a metal holder (see illustration).

Mark the position where the plug is

Plugging Walls

required, apply the point of the tool at that position and give the end of the holder a series of light blows until the hole is sufficiently deep to allow the end of the plug to lie flush with the surface. The plug is inserted, and the fixing screw driven into the plug which expands and grips it firmly.

Plywood.—The advent of plywood has reduced the cost of constructing wooden articles to a minimum. This useful material is sold in the form of sheets consisting of a number of layers or plys of thin wood cemented together under pressure. The grain of one layer of wood crosses that of the next, a feature which gives great strength to the finished material and prevents it shrinking.

Plywood is obtainable in standard size sheets measuring as much as 7×5 ft. wide, but smaller panels 24×24 in., 48×24 in., and 48×48 in. are the usual stock sizes. The thickness ranges from 8 millimetres, equivalent to approximately $\frac{1}{32}$ in., to 25 millimetres or 1 in. Plywood is faced with either common wood, birch, alder or deal, or more expensive woods such as oak, mahogany, walnut and all of these may be obtained in several qualities.

Common plywood is useful for many purposes, including the backs of cabinets, cladding unimportant cupboards where utility and cheapness are of more consequence than looks. Plywood faced with a better class wood is ideal for making panels, table tops and other parts of furniture where a good appearance is necessary and the cost of ordinary wood prohibitive. Metal-faced plywood is also obtainable and is admirable for making the chassis of radio sets.

Posts.—It is a great mistake to use wooden posts where they are subject to the weather without treating them to delay rot. This applies particularly to the portion of the post which is buried in the ground. Tar applied hot is effective, but boiling creosote is better. As the process of boiling the creosote is a rather dangerous operation, the ends of the posts may be stood upright in a suitable container such as an old milk churn or an upright barrel holding the cold liquid. The depth of creosote

should be such as to cover the portion of the post sunk in the ground plus 6 or 7 in. It is at ground level, as shown in Fig. 1, that most rotting usually takes place. Two or three hours' treatment in this way, adding more liquid to make up for that absorbed by the wood, will add greatly to the life of the post.

Another method is to char the end of the post, but the best method of all is to set the post in concrete.

Prepared Wood.—Prepared stuff, in woodworker's parlance, means rough sawn timber that has been machine-planed and therefore requires little smoothing, a desirable feature as it saves a lot of planing. In purchasing ready planed wood, note that the finished sizes are $\frac{1}{8}$ in. under in width and thickness owing to waste in machining. Thus, 2×2 in. prepared stuff measures only $1\frac{7}{8} \times 1\frac{7}{8}$ in., and a $7 \times \frac{3}{4}$ in. prepared board is $6\frac{7}{8} \times \frac{5}{8}$ in. thick.

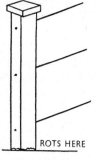

Fig. 1

Pulpwood.—A useful material made from wood pulp and compressed into sheets. It is used principally for cladding partitions, ceilings and for similar purposes. It is sold under various trade names and in different thicknesses and qualities. Standard size sheets measure from 6 to 16 ft. in length and 3 ft. and 4 ft. in width. Some kinds are soft and spongy while others are hard and close-grained, which renders them practically moisture-proof and fireproof. They can be sawn and the edges can be planed, provided a sharp tool is used. Pulpwood can be nailed without fear of splitting.

Punches.—The woodworker's punch is used principally for sinking the heads

C

of nails below the surface of wood. In important work the holes are afterwards filled up. The heads of large nails are usually sunk with a rectangular punch having a smooth working end; punches for sinking small-headed nails such as panel pins are generally round in section with a fine cup-shaped end to prevent the tool from slipping off.

A similar tool but larger is used by the metalworker for forming the

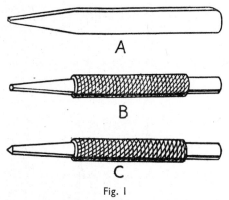

Fig. I

bottoms of rivets, while a pointed punch is used for marking the positions of holes in preparation to drilling. The depressions left by such a punch are known as pop holes. Fig. I shows the three types of punches mentioned.

Putty.—Putty is a plastic material composed of whiting and linseed oil. It is extremely useful for such purposes as fixing glass in rebates or recesses of sash frames, stopping up holes, cracks and other imperfections in wood, natural or otherwise.

Putty can be bought cheaply or it can be made by mixing a quantity of whiting and linseed oil and kneading it well with the hands to form a semi-solid paste. For outside work, the addition of a small quantity of white lead is an advantage. Putty can be coloured by adding red-ochre, lamp black, or other colours with the whiting.

It is useless to apply putty to bare wood as it will not stick. Before starting the puttying process, give the work a coat of priming paint and then apply the putty.

Putty can be kept indefinitely if kept

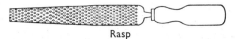

Rasp

under water. When using putty, place it on a non-absorbent material such as a piece of glass or the oil will be absorbed, to the detriment of the putty.

Quartering.—A term applied to timber of square section varying in size from 2 × 2 in. to 6 × 6 in.

Rasp.—A tool for smoothing metal, wood and other material. For rasping or filing wood a half-round medium-smooth tool should be chosen. The rounded face of the tool is particularly useful for smoothing inside curved work after working with a pad saw or bow saw.

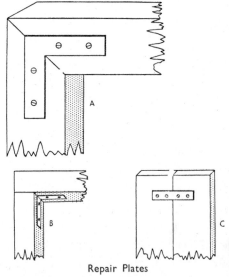

Repair Plates

Repair Plates.—The home worker may not be aware that a number of plates of various shapes and sizes are available for repair purposes. These plates, a few are illustrated above, can be obtained in several sizes either in brass or iron, and can be put to many useful purposes other than repairs. As they are thin they may be either let in flush with the surface of the wood or they may be fixed on the face.

The illustration A depicts a flat angle plate used at the back of a mitre frame to reinforce the joint; that shown at B is a right-angled bracket used in a support, and that at C is a flat plate which may be used for joining boards together and for similar purposes.

Rebating.—See grooving and rebating.

Riveting.—Riveting is a method of joining metal where a permanent joint of great strength is required.

There are two common methods of riveting—the hot and the cold. The former is seldom used by the amateur, while the latter is simple and within the scope of the novice.

The essential tools include a ball-pane engineer's hammer for striking the

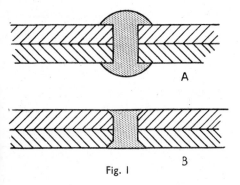

Fig. I

rivets, a drill for boring holes, a file and an anvil or a substitute for an anvil in the shape of a block of hard metal.

In riveting two pieces of metal together with snaphead or dome-shaped rivets, as shown at A in Fig. 1, proceed in the following way:

First drill a hole at each end of the pieces to be joined and fasten them

together by means of small bolts and nuts in the manner shown in Fig. 2, taking care to see that the edge of one piece overlaps at the correct distance and is parallel to the edge of the other. Then mark, centre-pop and drill the holes through both pieces to fit the rivets and slightly countersink the edges of the holes in both sides.

Having completed the drilling, undo the temporary fastenings and remove

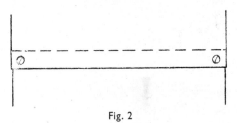

Fig. 2

any burrs round the holes which may have been thrown up between the plates by the drill. Replace the bolts and nuts and proceed with the riveting. To do this, slip a rivet in a hole and place it head downwards on either the anvil or block and give the end of the rivet a smart blow dead in line with the axis of the rivet, using the flat face of the hammer. This preliminary blow spreads the rivet in the hole. Then, using the ball face of the hammer, gently tap all round the edge of the rivet, striking at an angle of 45 deg. so that the end of the rivet assumes a neat dome-shaped appearance. Continue in this manner until the work is completed.

When using countersunk-headed rivets (B in Fig. 1) which lie flush with the surface of the work, much the same procedure is followed as for the snap-headed type. After drilling, well countersink the top and bottom of the holes and, in closing the rivet, first use the ball face of the hammer until the end of the rivet has spread to the outer edges of the hole and finish off with the flat face of the hammer.

Router.—A special kind of woodworking tool of the plane species for removing the waste in grooves, etc. The tool shown below is the modern edition in metal of its wooden predecessor known as an " old woman's tooth."

Rules.—An indispensable measuring tool for the woodworker and metal-

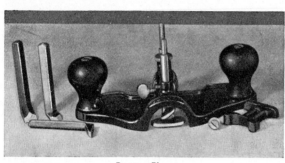

Router Plane

worker. Wooden rules are used principally by the former while metal ones are employed by the latter. The home carpenter is advised to use a fourfold two-foot rule, and one having bold figures marked upon its faces is to be preferred. Steel rules a foot long will serve most amateur engineers' requirements.

A carpenter's rule and an engineer's rule are shown at A and B respectively in Fig. 1.

Saws, Wood.—The saws commonly used for cutting wood are the rip saw, with comparatively wide teeth for sawing timber along the grain; the cross cutting saw having narrower teeth than the rip saw for sawing across the grain; the fine-toothed tenon saw, generally used as a bench tool for cutting tenons, and saws for special

purposes such as the pad saw for cutting curved work, both internal and external. To these may be added the bow saw, also used for sawing curved work in thickish timber, and its smaller contemporary the fretsaw, used for a similar purpose on thin wood. These tools are all represented at Fig. 1, page 69.

For amateur purposes, a panel saw will answer the purpose for ripping and cross cutting and thus obviates the necessity of buying two saws, while a tenon saw having a blade 10 in. long, which has a stiffened back of brass or steel in order to keep the blade rigid, will generally suffice for all ordinary bench work, although a smaller one will be an advantage when dealing with thin material.

In using a hand saw and saws of the tenon type, grip the handle with the forefinger extended towards the end of the blade and saw with long, even strokes. Little pressure is needed when

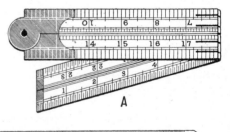

A

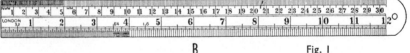

B

Fig. 1

sawing if the tool is sharp, and, even if slight pressure is required on the down or forward stroke, the pressure should be entirely relieved on the return or upstroke. Try to avoid the natural

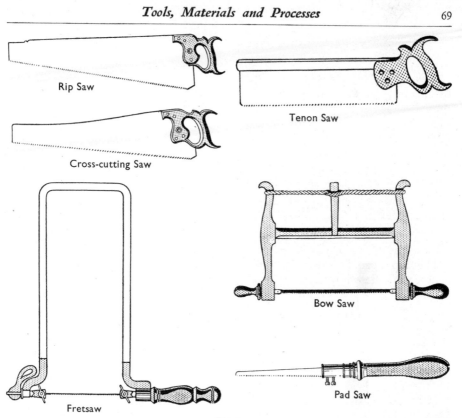

Rip Saw

Cross-cutting Saw

Tenon Saw

Bow Saw

Fretsaw

Pad Saw

Fig. 1

tendency of tilting the saw; the blade should be kept square with the work.

A tenon saw is generally used for wood held in a vice, but there are times when a piece of work has to be cut on the bench. For this purpose a bench-hook should be used to support the work. Such a device is shown in Fig. 2.

A pad saw is a small tool having a separate blade which is held in the handle by set screws when in use; when not required the blade is housed in the handle.

In using the pad saw, the work is placed in the vice and the handle of the tool gripped with both hands. This saw must be operated carefully as the thin tapered blade is easily buckled. A pad saw in action is depicted in Fig. 3.

A bow saw consists of a handled wooden frame at the ends of which is held a thin and narrow blade. The blade is kept at the correct tension by means of a twisted cord at the opposite end, the cord being kept taught by a thin piece of wood, one end of which is inserted between the cord and the other by the vertical member of the frame.

In use the bow saw is operated in a horizontal position on work held in a vice, while its smaller companion, the steel-framed fretsaw with its delicate fragile blade, is used vertically upon work supported horizontally.

Sawing Stool.—The sawing stool illustrated on page 70 is a great convenience in sawing lengths of wood and should be included in every amateur's workshop. Such a stool can

Fig. 2

be constructed within an hour or so.

The top board consists of a piece of 4 × 2 in. planed timber 3 ft. long, while the legs are of 2½ in. square section material about 18 in. high and should be splayed as shown.

Scantlings.—Scantlings are rectan-

Fig. 3

gular pieces of timber with sides anything between 2 and 5 in., as, for example, 3 × 2 in., 4 × 3 in., etc.

Scarfed Joints, Wood. — Scarfed joints are used for lengthening timber. That shown at A in Fig. 1 is a simple scarfed joint formed by cutting away one half of the ends to be joined, as shown. Such a joint is useful in joining the plates of horizontal members of

framework. The use of a joint of this type allows two or more short lengths of wood to be used instead of a single one of equivalent length. The joint should always be supported by a stud or vertical member.

The joint shown at B is a good form to use when the members are subject to tensional stresses, and, to render them as strong as the uncut portion, fish-plates are invariably used.

Sawing Stool

Scrapers, Wood and Metal. — A wood scraper is a cabinet maker's tool which acts like a very finely set plane and is used principally for smoothing

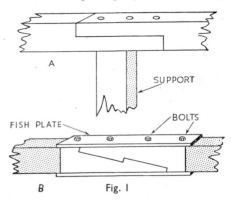

A

SUPPORT

FISH PLATE

BOLTS

B   Fig. I

hardwoods. For flat work it consists of nothing more than a thin piece of steel about 5 in. long by 3 in. wide and $\frac{1}{16}$ in. thick, having a burr on its long edges for cutting purposes. The burr is formed by supporting the scraper on a bench or other flat surface, allowing its cutting edge to project a trifle beyond the edge of support, and rubbing the edge to be treated back and forth with a piece of hard steel rod held at an angle

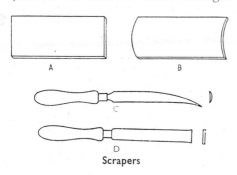

Scrapers

so as to turn up the edge. Both edges are so treated and then finished on an oilstone. Such a tool is shown at A above.

In use, the tool is held at an angle of about 60 deg. and is gripped in both hands. Some workers prefer to push

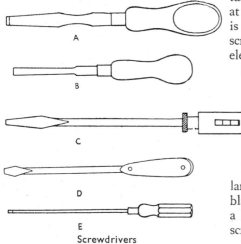

Screwdrivers

the tool along the work while others like to pull it. It is imperative that the scraper be held at the correct angle and be perfectly true and sharp.

If only a comparatively small surface is to be smoothed, a piece of glass may answer the same purpose.

For curved work, scrapers having convex, B, and concave-shaped cutting edges are to be obtained.

The illustration at c and D show two metal scrapers made of hardened steel used for removing minute quantities of metal to obtain an accurate finish. That shown at c has a curved blade and is a handy tool for treating machine bearings, while it can also be used for flat surfaces. The tool illustrated at D is the correct tool for scraping flat surfaces.

Screwdrivers.—These useful tools are in frequent use by the woodworker, metalworker, electrician and mechanic in general for driving or extracting screws. The illustration shows screwdrivers for various purposes. That illustrated at A is a carpenter's screwdriver, while that seen at B is the tool favoured by the cabinet maker. A general purpose ratchet screwdriver for turning screws of medium size is shown at c, and the type used by the mechanic is represented at D. The long-bladed screwdriver depicted at E is used by the electrician.

Several screwdrivers should be included in a woodworker's kit, proportioned to suit the size of the screws on which they are used. If an attempt is made to turn a large screw with a small screwdriver the blade will probably be ruined, while if a large screwdriver is used on a small screw the surrounding wood will suffer.

Keep the ends of the blades at the correct shape and do not allow them to become blunt as tools in this condition will invariably spoil the screw head.

Screw threads, Cutting. — Screw threads may be cut in metal either by the use of hand-operated tools or by means of a lathe. For ordinary purposes the former method, involving the use of taps and dies, is employed, while the latter is generally confined to making threads on special work where hand-operated tools could not be used.

Happily, most screw threads are standardised to suit the particular work for which they are to be used. For instance, the Whitworth thread is the standard thread for engineering work in general,

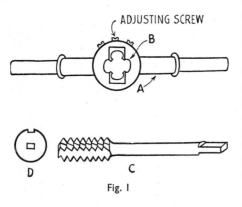

ADJUSTING SCREW

Fig. I

while the B.A. (British Association) thread is employed for small screws used in electrical instruments, wireless devices and similar objects. Standardised gas threads are used at the ends of gas pipes, and conduit threads are used at the junctions of electrical conduits.

Fig. 1 shows the tools for making small external and internal threads. The set consists of stock A for holding and turning the die B that is used for cutting external threads, and a tap C for forming internal threads. The tap has a square shoulder at the upper end which engages in a corresponding hole in the centre of a circular piece of metal D which fits into the stock.

In cutting an external thread, the work is usually placed in a vice, and having removed the sharp edge of the rod the die is simply placed over the work and rotated. In doing this a few threads only should be cut at a time by

first rotating the tool in a clockwise direction then reversing the action for a distance of a few threads and then going forward again and so on until the full length of thread has been cut.

Two operations are generally necessary when cutting an internal thread. The first one involves the use of a tapered tap which has only a few full-sized threads at the top cutting portion of the tool, and this is followed by a second tap having only a few tapered threads at the starting end. The tool is used like a die.

When drilling holes which have to be threaded, a tapping size drill—that is, a drill of the same diameter as that of the bottom or root of the thread—must be used. When cutting threads on iron and steel, lubricate with machine oil and use paraffin or turpentine for aluminium. Copper, brass and cast iron are threaded dry.

Scriber.—A thin steel rod with a sharp pointed end used for marking metal in lieu of a pencil, the marks of which are quickly obliterated.

A hardened steel knitting needle

Metal Cutting Shears

ground at the end to a fine point makes an excellent scriber.

Shears, Metal Cutting.—A pair of hand shears, such as that illustrated above, is useful for cutting sheet metal. The action is similar to that of a pair of scissors, but they are very much stronger and have plain handles.

A pair of straight tinman's snips, 8 in. long and costing about 2s., is a handy size to have.

Shooting Boards.—Two useful planing accessories are illustrated at

A and B below. The former is an ordinary shooting board, and is used for shooting or trimming the edges of wood, while the latter, called a mitre shooting board, is handy for finishing off mitres.

In using the ordinary shooting board, the work is placed so that its edge

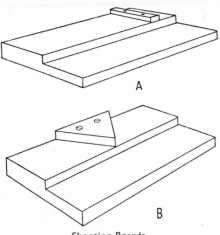

A

B

Shooting Boards

projects slightly beyond that of the top board and is held tightly against the stop with one hand while the plane is operated on its side with the other.

A similar procedure is followed with the mitre shooting board. To prevent these from slipping on the bench, the end butts against the bench-stop.

Soldering, Soft.—Soft soldering is a simple method of uniting such metals as brass, copper, tinplate and zinc by means of an alloy of lead and tin made molten by a copper soldering bit or a blow-pipe, as shown at A in Fig. 1. The tools for simple soldering comprise a soldering bit, a heater, a file and some-times a pair of pliers. In addition, a flux is needed to prevent oxidization of the surfaces to be joined, a piece of emery cloth for cleaning the surfaces and a supply of solder, obtainable in sticks.

Soldering comprises several simple

c*

operations. The first consists of pre-paring the work by thoroughly cleaning the parts to be joined, as solder will not adhere to dirty surfaces. This operation is important and requires the use of either a file or emery cloth or both. The next consists of tinning the bit, which is accomplished by heating the pointed end of the copper to a full black heat, not red heat, and rubbing the nose on a blob of solder and flux placed on a piece of clean tin-plate.

Then follows the fluxing process which consists of applying a suitable ready-made flux to the surfaces to be joined.

The final operation is to apply the solder with the aid of the heated bit. Before applying the tool to the work, insert the end of the nose in the flux for a moment to clean it, and then melt a little solder by applying it to the bit.

A

Fig 1.

If the work is small, apply the bit to the work and hold it there until the metal has be-come sufficiently hot to enable the solder to run.

In soldering seams, it is a good plan to tack the two parts together at the ends and then to draw the hot bit along the seams, feeding the bit with solder from a stick held in the left hand as the work proceeds.

When soldering zinc, use a flux of spirits of salts (hydrochloric acid) and wash the parts directly after soldering.

Killed spirit made by adding zinc cuttings to spirits of salts and allow-ing the zinc to dissolve is a good flux for brass, while powdered resin or

sal ammoniac may be used for copper.
Fig. 2 shows a soldering bit in use,

Fig. 2

while Fig. 3 illustrates the method of using a small methylated spirit blow-lamp for soldering.

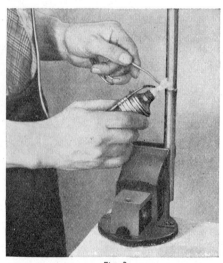

Fig. 3

Spanners and Wrenches.—Spanners are used for tightening or loosening nuts. The ordinary double-ended spanner is shown at A in Fig. 1.

The box or tubular spanner seen at B is for dealing with nuts in corners and places where an ordinary spanner cannot be used. It is turned by a rod passing through holes in the body or shank.

An adjustable spanner, as shown at C, is useful for turning small nuts, and is handy for making cycle adjustments and for turning coach screws in wood.

A pair of grips, known as a footprint wrench, is used for gasfitting, gripping electrical conduits, iron water pipes and the like is depicted at D.

In using a spanner, see that the jaws

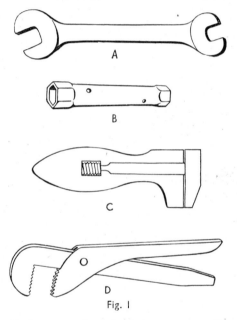

Fig. 1

fit the nuts; a loosely fitting spanner will ruin the edges of the nut and may slip off and damage the hand.

Spirit Levels.—A spirit level is necessary when a true level has to be ascertained as, for example, when fitting shelves in woodwork, levelling ground for concrete foundations or for brick-work in the building of walls. It consists of a sealed tube nearly filled with tinted methylated spirit, set in a perfectly true block of wood or metal.

A slot in the top plate exposes a short length of tube and allows a small bubble to be seen. Level is attained when the centre of the bubble coincides with a centre mark on the top plate.

Spirit levels can be had in various shapes and sizes ranging from about 3 in. to 4 ft. The instrument shown at A is a combined plumb and level, having two tubes. The vertical one near the end is for testing verticality. Such a level, 12 in. long, will answer most amateurs' requirements and costs about 3s. 6d.

The illustration at B shows the method of using a level when levelling between two pegs driven into the ground. The top and bottom edges of the intervening straight-edge must be quite parallel and dead true.

Spokeshaves.—A spokeshave is a woodworking tool of the plane category, used for smoothing the edges of curved

it along the work in the same direction as the grain.

In smoothing the rounded edge as that shown at C in the figure, use a flat faced tool and work in the direction indicated by the arrows—that is, first from 1 to 2 and then from 3 to 2. A

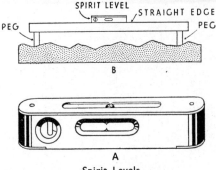

Spirit Levels

round-faced spokeshave should be used in smoothing a concave surface as at D.

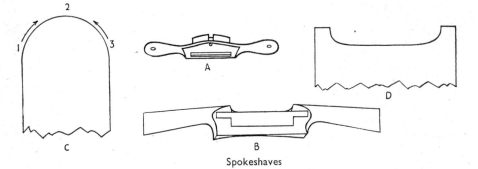

Spokeshaves

work. The figure shows two kinds of spokeshave.

That at A is a modern type of tool having a metal stock, while that at B has a wooden one. Both are fitted with an adjustable steel cutter. Owing to the narrow sole of the wooden type it soon wears, a drawback which is eliminated in the metal spokeshave.

The tool is used by gripping the handles with both hands and either drawing or pushing, usually the latter,

Squares.—A woodworker's square is called a try square and this important tool is illustrated at A on page 76. It is used principally for testing the squareness of wood and as a guide for marking lines at right-angles to the edge of the work. Two types are available, one having a wooden stock, the working face of which is faced with brass, and the other is an all-metal tool.

The square shown at B is an all-metal square of extreme accuracy used by engineers. Such a tool is used in the same way as the woodworker's square, but it is, of course, for metal.

A tee-square is a draughtsman's tool. Cheap squares of this description are generally made of pearwood, while

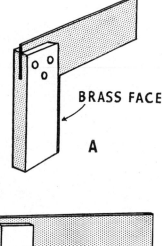

BRASS FACE

A

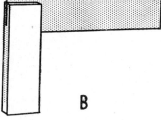

B

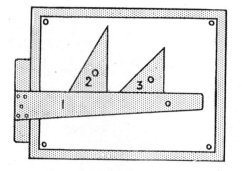

C

Squares

those of better quality are constructed of mahogany. The working faces are

sometimes faced with ebony to reduce wear. It is used principally as a guide when making or projecting horizontal lines, the stock being held tightly against the left-hand edge of the drawing board. A tee-square is illustrated at c (1).

The squares (2 and 3) seen in the same illustration are set squares also used by the draughtsman for setting out common angles and as a guide in conjunction with a tee-square for making vertical lines.

Staining Wood.—Staining is a process for colouring wood, either to give it a finish or to give common wood the appearance of a better one. The amateur is well catered for in the way of stains. The cheapest kinds are water stains which may be obtained in powder form and simply mixed with water, or they may be had ready mixed in suitable portions by the maker.

Spirit stains having the pigment or colouring matter dissolved in spirit are more expensive than water stains but they have the great advantage of not raising the grain and do not penetrate the grain very quickly.

Oil stains, in which the colouring matter is mixed with linseed oil and turpentine like spirit stains, do not raise the grain and are useful for colouring porous wood.

In treating finished woodwork of importance, all nail holes and other imperfections should be filled with a suitable stopping. Plaster-of-paris and whiting mixed with a small quantity of water to form a putty is quite suitable. When dry, the surfaces should be glass-papered down perfectly smooth.

Any end-grain surfaces should receive a coat of glue-size to prevent excessive absorption of the stain. If this is omitted these parts will appear darker than the rest of the finished work.

Before staining wood with water

stain, it is advisable to damp the wood all over in order to roughen it. The roughened surface is rubbed down when dry with fine glass-paper, and it is better to repeat the process especially if the wood is soft, as the stain will then have less tendency to raise the grain.

The next process is to fill the pores of the wood with a mixture of plaster-of-paris, whiting and water and, when dry, to glass-paper the surface, rubbing in the direction of the grain.

Apply the stain with a brush, and, when dealing with large surfaces, go over the work afterwards with a rag moistened with stain. Do not put on too much stain. If the shade is not dark enough after the first application apply another after the first one has been allowed to dry thoroughly. Then rub the surfaces with ordinary paper, coat them with thin size, allow to dry and repeat the process, allowing the work to stand for a day or two for the water to evaporate. The work is then ready to receive varnish, wax polish or any other finish desired.

Straight-edge.—An important yet simple tool used principally for testing the truth of wood surfaces. It consists of a strip of hardwood such as well seasoned mahogany which does not twist or warp to any appreciable amount, and has one edge planed perfectly straight. The figure shows a straight-edge in use.

Steel.—Steel is an alloy of iron and carbon and the amount of carbon in its composition determines its hardness. Soft steel, better known as mild steel, has a carbon content of less than o.5 per cent. and is easy to file, drill and turn. Hard steel, known as high-carbon or tool steel, containing between .75 per cent. and 2 per cent. of carbon, is used for tools and, unlike mild steel, can be hardened or softened. By heating it up to redness

and quenching it in water, it becomes extremely hard and brittle while by heating it up, and allowing it to cool very slowly, it is rendered soft. In this condition it is fairly easy to work.

Tools made of high-speed steel, which is an alloy of steel with some other

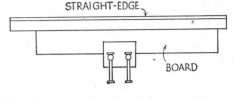

Straight-edge

metal such as tungsten or chromium are capable of cutting at a higher speed than an ordinary steel tool.

The difference between high-speed steel and carbon steel is easily detected by applying it to an emery wheel. Carbon steel emits bluish-white sparks while the sparks from high-speed steel are minute and of a reddish tint.

Stripwood.—Stripwood is the name given to ready planed strips of hard-wood. Such wood is of inestimable value to the amateur cabinet maker, and can be obtained at most dealers. Strip-wood is made in a variety of square sections ranging from $\frac{1}{8} \times \frac{1}{8}$ in. to $1\frac{1}{8} \times 1\frac{1}{8}$in., and rectangular sections from $\frac{1}{4} \times \frac{1}{16}$ in. to $2 \times \frac{7}{8}$ in. This material can be used for all sorts of purposes including framework for doors, panelling, false rebates, and many other things.

Studs, Wooden.—Studs, or stud-ding, is the technical term for the vertical intermediate members of frame-work such as that used in a lath and plaster partition and similar timber-framed structures.

Studs in lath and plaster partitions are usually spaced about 18 in. apart and they can generally be located by the more solid sound when tapped with a hammer.

If asbestos or other sheet material is to be fixed to studded framework, the studs should be so spaced that the edges of adjoining sheets come in the centre of a stud to enable them to be fixed, and a suitable number of studs should be fixed in the intervening space adequately to support the material. Thus, in using ¼ in. thick asbestos sheets 4 ft.

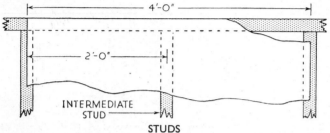

STUDS

wide, one intermediate stud would be sufficient. The illustration above shows the arrangement.

Surface Plates.—A surface plate is essentially an engineer's device and consists of a suitably designed cast-iron plate, the upper surface of which is scraped perfectly true. It is used in conjunction with a surface-gauge for marking out purposes, and is also employed for testing the accuracy of small flat surfaces such as a slide valve face of an engine cylinder. A hard scraped surface plate as shown at A in the illustration measuring 9 × 6 in. costs about 35s., while a similar tool, planed only, can be had for about a guinea. A piece of plate glass fixed in a stout wooden frame as seen at B, however, will generally

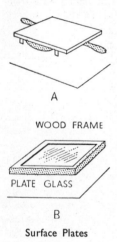

be quite sufficient for most amateur requirements.

Surface-gauge.—A surface-gauge or scribing block, as it is sometimes termed, is used principally in conjunction with a surface plate for marking out machine parts. In its simplest form it consists of a circular cast-iron base, the under-side of which is perfectly flat and square with the post. Sliding on the post is a swivelling clamping device which holds a thin steel scriber in any desired position.

In marking, the work is generally chalked to enable the lines made by the scriber to be seen distinctly.

Taps: Notes on Water and Gas.—It is a punishable offence to allow a water tap to leak indefinitely. A tap that drips when shut off shows that either the soft leather or fibre valve-washer requires renewing or the seating upon which the washer rests needs attention. To replace a tap-washer, proceed in the following manner. If the tap is fed directly from the main, shut off the supply by turning the stop-cock, which may be inside the premises or below ground somewhere outside, generally near the main entrance. When the tap is supplied from a cistern, turn off the stop-cock, usually fitted at the outlet, and drain off the water in the pipe by turning the tap on.

Unscrew the top portion of the tap carrying the spindle. This, in some instances, has a left-hand thread and will therefore have to be turned in the same direction as in tightening up a normal screw-thread.

As cold water taps are usually connected to lead pipes it is as well to support the tap with the other hand when unscrewing, and thus relieve the strain between tap and joint.

The valve, or jumper as it is called, to the underside of which the washer is attached, will be found at the lower end of the spindle, or, if of the loose type, it may be resting on the valve seating. Unscrew the small nut which keeps the washer in place, remove the worn washer and fit another of the same diameter.

While the tap is dissembled, examine the seating. If it is ridged or pitted the seating will need treatment to make it perfectly flat. If only slightly uneven, the surface may be trued by grinding it with emery powder and oil, applying the mixture to the perfectly flat end of a round metal rod and twisting it back and forth with a circular motion. In the event of the seating being badly damaged it will be as well perhaps to take it to the local ironmonger's who will have a special tool for dealing with it.

In re-washering hot water taps always use a fibre washer.

Leaking gas taps are a source of danger and should be looked to as soon as they show signs of looseness. It may be that all that is necessary to stop a leak is to screw up the small screw at the bottom of the plug. On the other hand, the trouble may arise from an ill-fitting plug. This can generally be remedied by the application of a mixture of emery powder and oil and grinding the plug into the socket. Before dismantling the taps, the gas supply must be turned off at the main.

Teak.—Teak, often referred to as Indian oak, is a strong hardwood, the better qualities of which are produced in Burma and Siam, while an inferior kind comes from Java. It is straight-grained and fairly easy to work and does not shrink and warp to any appreciable extent. Teak contains an oil which renders it impervious to woodworm and also prevents corrosion.

Teak is durable, even if alternately wet and dry, and it is for this reason that it is used extensively for garden furniture, window sills, draining boards.

Templates.—Templates are great time savers when it is necessary to mark out several pieces of work of the same design, and can be used with equal effect on wood or metal. Templates are really a solid pattern of the outline of the parts it is desired to make, the edges of the template being used as a guide for marking the work.

Using a template

Templates made either of cardboard or plywood can be used for wood, but tinplate, sheet brass or any sheet metal should be employed for metal.

In preparing a template for carved work, it is a good plan first to draw the pattern on a piece of squared paper then to stick it on the material used for the template and then shape the template accordingly.

The illustration depicts a template for marking out a number of wooden brackets and also shows the method employed in using it with a view to economy of material.

Timber, Selecting. — In selecting timber the following points should be carefully noted. The timber should be

(1) Of bright appearance and should have characteristic odour.

(2) Free from shakes, knots, waney edges and other imperfections and be of uniform colour as any sudden change of colour such as red patches usually denotes some form of decay.

(3) Dry and well seasoned. Unseasoned or green timber is useless for constructional work.

Tin.—Tin is a whitish, expensive metal used principally for mixing with other metals to form alloys. It has a

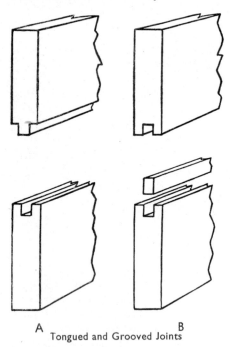

A   **B**
Tongued and Grooved Joints

low melting point and is one of the constituents of soft solder. Tin is employed for coating sheets of iron, in which form it is known as tinplate. Tinplate is extensively used for making household articles such as kettles, and commercial articles including boxes and containers.

Tongued and Grooved Joints.—A tongued and grooved joint is used in fastening a number of boards together to obtain width and greater strength than that given by the plain glued butt-joint. There are several types of such joints, two of which will be seen in the figure. The one shown at A is made by planing one edge of a board to form a tongue and the corresponding edge of the next board is grooved to receive it.

That shown at B requires a groove in adjacent edges the loose tongue being a strip of wood of the same thickness as the width of the groove. Where an extra strong joint is required the tongue can be formed with a number of pieces cut across the grain, or plywood could be used.

In making tongued and grooved joints, it is essential first carefully to plane the face sides and then accurately to mark and prepare the edges. Very hot glue should be used in gluing up, and the work should be cramped after gluing.

Varnishing Wood.—Varnish imparts a hard glossy and washable surface on both bare and painted wood, but before an attempt to apply it is made by a novice the following points should be noted.

Varnishes may be classified under two headings: those composed of various resins such as copal, shellac and others dissolved in methylated spirit, turpentine and volatile oils. The former, although they take longer to harden than the latter, should always be used for high-class work.

Spirit varnishes are generally confined to common work and they have the disadvantage that, when hard, they are extremely brittle and, if accidently scratched, produce a definite white mark.

Oil varnishes can be obtained to produce a transparent finish or they can be had in various shades of brown, in qualities suitable for inside work and for work exposed to the weather.

Before applying varnish, bare wood should be glass-papered thoroughly to produce a perfect finish as any number of coats will not hide defects but tend to emphasise them. The same applies to painted woodwork. In dealing with old paint, all gloss should be entirely removed with glass - paper and dusted thoroughly. Newly-painted surfaces must be absolutely dry before varnishing.

Use a special varnish brush; the bristles of an ordinary paint brush are generally too stiff for varnishing. See that the brush is free from dust as this is fatal to successful varnishing. This applies equally to the room in which the varnishing is to be done. Also do not attempt to varnish if the temperature is below 60 deg. F.

Having prepared the surface to be treated, flow the varnish on, not too much and not too little, and see that the entire surface is perfectly covered before the varnish starts to harden; an unsightly patch is likely to result if touched up afterwards. Do not over load the brush as this is conducive to the formation of "tears" on the wood. If properly done, the finished surface should be quite smooth and devoid of brush marks.

If it is desirable to give the work a further coat, the first one should be allowed to harden for at least a week. The surface should then be rubbed down quite smooth to remove the gloss with very fine pumice powder applied with a moist felt pad. The prepared surface should then be wiped with a perfectly clean sponge and clean water and allowed twenty-four hours to dry.

The final coat can then be applied.

Vices, Wood and Metal Workers'—Vices for gripping and supporting work are indispensable items in the equipment of the woodworker as well

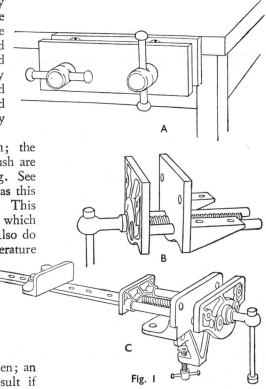

Fig. 1

as the metalworker. Fig. 1 shows three handy types of vices for holding wood. That shown at A, fitted with two wooden screws, is a cheap type suitable only for light woodwork.

A better type of vice for general woodwork is that illustrated at B. The vice is of iron and the advantage of such a tool is that even after being subjected to rough usage and hard wear the jaws remain parallel, a feature not attained in the old-fashioned vices of the wooden-screw type. A vice of this description having 6 in. jaws which open to $4\frac{1}{2}$ in. costs but 6s.

Before use, the inside faces of the

jaws must be fitted with wood, preferably hardwood, which is held in position by countersunk-headed screws driven through holes provided for the purpose.

In fitting the facings it is advisable to fasten the wood so that the grain runs vertically, and it is recommended that the top ends project a trifle above

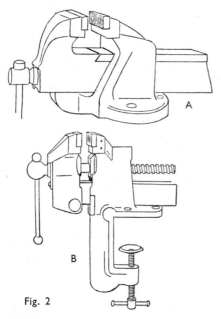

Fig. 2

the top of the jaws, especially if the worker is inexperienced.

To keep the vice in good order, an occasional drop of oil on the screw and guides is all that is necessary.

Another inexpensive vice is shown at c. This patent vice combines a cramp.

Metalworkers' vices are of a different construction from those used by woodworkers, as Fig. 2 shows. That illustrated at A is the type generally favoured by the expert craftsman, while that at B is a patent table vice having jaws $2\frac{1}{2}$ in. wide that open $2\frac{1}{2}$ in.

Such a vice is the best for model engineers, wireless fans, amateur electricians and others where a means of

holding small work is a necessity.

Winding Strips.—Winding strips are used in conjunction with the straight-edge in the preparation of timber for joinery as a test for accuracy when forming plane surfaces. They can be made of two pieces of straight grained mahogany about 2 ft. in length, 2 in. wide and $\frac{1}{2}$ in. thick. The long edges must be planed quite parallel and it is advisable to chamfer the top edges. They are placed across the wood to be tested, near each end, and then sighted over the tops. If the surface of the work is true, the two edges of the strips will appear to coincide. In the event of the surface of the work being twisted or in winding the edges of the winding strips will not lie in the same plane.

The illustration shows the method of using the strips.

Winding Strips

Workshop.—An outside structure is better than an attic or spare room where sawdust and shavings are likely to upset the general cleanliness of the house.

In constructing such a building, it is wise to make it of sufficient size at the outset as it is a nuisance to work in cramped space. A workshop about 10 ft. long by 7 ft. wide is large enough, but a couple of feet longer would be better.

Before constructing a workshop, one or two points must be considered. The question of whether to make it a permanent or a portable structure must be decided. A portable building is as simple to construct as a permanent one and adds little to the cost of making. Another query to be settled is whether to have a boarded or a concrete floor. The latter is better but more expensive, while a boarded floor is quite suitable provided tongued and grooved boards are used and kept at least 9 in. above the ground level to allow air to circulate and ensure dryness.

A structure walled with asbestos-cement sheets and roofed with the same material has the advantage of being heat-resisting and weatherproof. Galvanised iron, unless insulated with boards, is hot during summer and cold in winter, and the boarding adds considerably to the cost.

Tongued and grooved V matching is suitable for cladding the walls provided it is sufficiently thick. Nothing less than $\frac{5}{8}$ in. (finished) should be employed, and the joints should be arranged vertically.

The question of light is important. To obtain the maximum amount of light, it is advisable to make a window extending the whole length of the workshop and to fix an opening skylight towards the front of the roof.

Electric light, if available, is the safest artificial illuminant and, if installed in the house, it is not a difficult matter to run wires. In districts where neither gas nor electricity is available, a paraffin-gas lamp of good make will satisfy requirements.

The bench should be fixed as close as possible to the front walls and under the window, and cupboards and shelves should be provided for the convenient housing of tools and materials.

Wrought Iron.—Wrought iron is a greyish metal made from cast iron from which all impurities have been extracted. It is tenacious, soft, easy to file, turn and drill and can be welded and forged. Obtainable in sheets and bars, it is used largely in ornamental work such as gates.

Walnut.—This admirable hardwood, of which there are several varieties, is a favourite for cabinet making. American walnut, produced in eastern North America is of a dark brown colour and is hard, tough, strong and straighter in grain than that obtained in Europe. It takes a high polish. A lighter coloured wood also imported from America has a straighter grain and is used largely for manufacturing furniture.

Satin walnut is of a light reddish-brown colour, soft, fairly tough, but liable to warp and twist.

Weather Boards.—Weather boards are useful for cladding sheds and other outside structures. There are several types of board to be had, which are wedge shaped in the section the cheapest having plain edges. Weather boards are fixed horizontally, the wide edge of the upper board overlapping the narrow edge of the lower one, and it is usual to start fixing from the bottom of a framework and work upwards.

Rebated weather boards are a little more expensive than plain ones and have a rebate in the wide edge which allows the corresponding narrow edge of the board to lie flush with the frame.

Zinc.—Pure zinc is a bluish-white element of lustrous surface. It is used extensively in alloys such as brass, which is an alloy of copper and zinc. Zinc is also employed in galvanising iron. The iron is immersed in a bath of molten zinc leaving a protective coat which protects the iron from rust and corrosion.

Sheet zinc is useful for making roofing, kitchen utensils and lining the interiors of cases.

It is soft, easy to work and can be soft soldered.

WOOD TURNING

THE practice of wood-turning consists essentially of revolving pieces of wood at a high speed in a lathe and shaping the material while spinning with suitable cutting tools.

The wood is fixed into the lathe and is made to revolve quickly by a belt passing over a pulley. As the wood spins round, a sharp cutting tool held in a proper manner against the material removes the waste wood.

The lathe required for simple wood-turning is not complicated; it is in fact extremely simple. The power required to drive it is obtained from a treadle.

Parts of the Lathe.—Fig. 1 shows a simple lathe suitable for the purpose. The machine consists of the following principal parts: The bed, sometimes constructed of wood, which is mounted upon the stand and legs, A; the headstock, B; the tee-rest, C; the tailstock, D.

The headstock is fixed down to the bed and consists of a coned-stepped pulley, over which the driving belt runs, mounted on a shaft or spindle and suspended between two bearings.

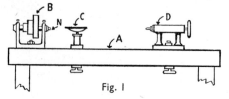

Fig. 1

A spur-centre as illustrated at A in Fig. 2 is screwed into the nose of the spindle (N in Fig. 1) which digs into the wood and holds it firmly in position when the lathe is in use.

The tee-rest, so called because it resembles the letter T, is used for keeping the cutting tools in position. This rest has two adjustments, one of which allows it to be moved along the bed of the lathe and to be clamped down in a suitable position, and the other allows the height of the rest to be altered at will to suit the height of the tool used on the work.

The tailstock is fixed to the opposite end to the headstock on the lathe bed and carries the back centre which consists of a short sharp-pointed piece of hard steel. Like the tee-rest the tailstock can be moved along the bed and clamped down.

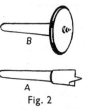

Fig. 2

A screwed spindle which runs through the body of the tailstock allows a further adjustment to be made to the back centre, the latter being housed in the end of the spindle.

Power is transmitted to the coned pulley on the headstock by the belt through the medium of a treadle driving wheel and connecting rod, all of which are contained in the stand of the lathe.

Turning Tools.—The principal tools required for simple wood-turning are gouges and chisels. These are, of course, different from those used in carpentry and joinery.

Fig. 3 shows both these tools. You will notice that they are longer than those used by the carpenter, and that the cutting edge of the gouge is more or less rounded instead of being straight across. This curvature allows only one edge at a time to cut.

The cutting edge of the chisel slants, the reason for this being that as only a portion of the cutting edge is used, it allows the tool to be held at the correct angle and prevents the point of the tool from digging in the work. The cutting edge is also bevelled on both sides which enables the chisel to be used in either direction.

The best woods for turning are hard woods such as beech, mahogany and oak, as they are easier to work than soft woods like pine and deal.

You should practise with hard woods until you have learned how to handle the tools properly and can turn out fair work before attempting to work with soft woods.

A Preliminary Experiment.—A good thing to make for a start, and one which will enable you to get the feel of wood-turning tools, is a plain wooden cylinder.

Get a piece of hard wood, round or square in section and a trifle larger than the required finished size of the cylinder. Saw the ends so that they are square and find the centre of each.

Now make a saw cut as indicated in Fig. 4, about ⅛ in. or so deep, across one end and in the centre, to allow the prong to sink well into the wood. This is necessary for driving purposes. Next, make a small centre hole about ⅛ in. deep at the opposite end, using a centre punch for the purpose, and trim off the long edges of the wood with a chisel or plane as shown in Fig. 5.

Place the slotted end of the wood against the points of the prong chuck (A in Fig. 2), so that the prongs enter the cut and be careful to see that the centre point of the chuck comes in the exact centre of the wood. Drive the wood well home with a mallet.

When you have put a drop of oil on the point of the back centre and fed the centre up to the work so that the point enters and is fairly tight in the hole provided, the chucking process, as it is termed, is complete.

The next thing to do is to adjust the tee-rest so that the top is slightly lower than the centre of the work and far enough back from the work to give a clearance of not more than ¼ in.

Now start spinning the work round by working your foot up and down on the

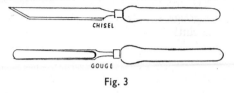

Fig. 3

treadle. When the work is revolving at a fairly high speed in a direction towards you, you are ready to commence operations.

Roughing Out.—Hold the handle of the gouge firmly with the right hand, keeping the knuckles downwards and the concave or hollow surface of the tool to the top. With your left hand, grasp the tool near its cutting edge and bring it to rest on the top of the tee-rest, keeping the cutting edge tilted a trifle upwards.

Push the gouge gently forward towards the work until the cutting edge begins to remove the waste in the manner shown in Fig. 6, then slide the gouge steadily along the rest for a short distance, being careful that you do not push the tool forward in so doing. When you have traversed the tool along the work for about an inch or so, make

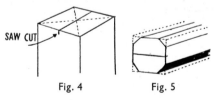

Fig. 4   Fig. 5

a little deeper cut by pushing the gouge slightly forward and then move it back along the work.

Repeat this process until sufficient material has been removed all along the work, and its size is reduced to a diameter slightly larger than the finished size.

This completes the roughing out. Finishing consists of smoothing the uneven surface resulting from the roughing out.

To produce a smooth surface, turn the gouge slightly on its side to bring one cutting edge against the work, and take a slight skim along the material.

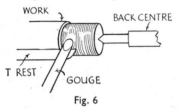

Fig. 6

If the resulting surface is not quite as smooth as you desire, take the chisel—which is held in practically the same way as the gouge, except that it should be tilted so that only the middle portion of the cutting edge touches the work—and traverse the tool along the work, reversing the chisel with each alteration in direction of traverse.

An excellent surface may be obtained by holding a piece of fine glass-paper against the work while it is revolving.

A Warning.—A very important point which you should carefully observe when using the chisel is to see that the point of the tool is not allowed to come in contact with the work, otherwise the point will dig in and probably ruin it, to say nothing of

minor injuries inflicted on the operator.

The gouge is not only useful for turning the outside surface of wood, but can also be used for hollowing out such things as egg-cups or wooden bowls.

In this case the gouge is held in position with its face downwards.

To hollow out a piece of wood you must first of all screw the material on to a taper screw chuck as that illustrated at B in Fig. 2, and then work from the centre, gradually raising the cutting point of the tool above the centre until the desired diameter of the recess is cut out.

By repeating the process it is possible to get the correct depth of hole.

If the work is a circular box or an article of similar nature, where the inner corners are usually square, the chisel can

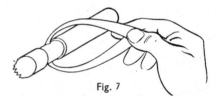

Fig. 7

be used to remove the small amount of waste left in by the gouge, owing to the rounded shape of its cutting edge.

When you wish to turn a piece of wood down to a definite size, you should use a pair of callipers for measuring. This operation is shown in Fig. 7.

VENEERING

THE quality of the ground-work upon which the veneer is applied is important. Resinous and knotty woods

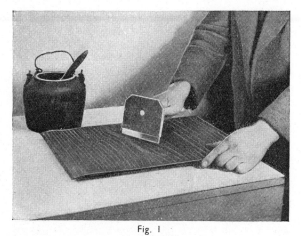

Fig. 1

should not be used. Such woods are prone to unequal shrinkage and cause blisters and other imperfections. Yellow pine, whitewood and most straight grained woods make good foundations for veneer. Plywood and laminated boards are excellent as they are not liable to shrink and split.

Veneers are either saw-cut or knife-cut. The former is thicker and therefore more expensive and has a rougher surface than the latter, while knife-cut veneer is smooth and easier for the amateur to manipulate. Some knife-cut veneers are not much thicker than stout brown paper.

Different Methods.—There are two methods of hand veneering. One involves the use of a caul which is a perfectly flat block of wood. This block is heated and then cramped down to press the veneer to the groundwork and squeeze out superfluous glue. The other method, known as hammer veneer-

ing, necessitates the use of a tool of special shape called a veneering hammer, as shown in Fig. 1.

To make the tool, procure a piece of hardwood $4\frac{1}{2}$ in. long × $3\frac{1}{2}$ in. wide and $\frac{1}{2}$ in. thick for the stock and a strip of brass $4\frac{1}{4}$ in. in length × 1 in. wide and $\frac{3}{32}$ in. thick for the blade. Saw off the top corners of the wood, cut a slot $\frac{1}{2}$ in. deep and $\frac{3}{32}$ in. wide in the lower narrow face and bore a $\frac{1}{2}$ in. hole for taking the end of the handle. File off the sharp edges of the metal and drill a hole 1 in. from each end, large enough to clear a thin wood screw. Insert the blade into the slot in the stock and fix it with screws driven through the holes provided. Then prepare a handle about 4 in. long and glue it into the hole already prepared to receive it.

As hammer veneering is the process more likely to appeal to the amateur,

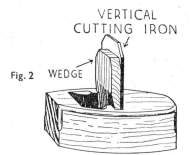

VERTICAL CUTTING IRON

Fig. 2 WEDGE

owing to its simplicity, a simple piece of work by this method will be described step by step.

In addition to the veneering hammer, a heavy domestic iron, toothing plane, straight-edge, rule, sharp wood-chisel, glue, hot water and a clean rag will be required, together with a supply of knife-cut veneer and a suitable groundwork.

The toothing plane (Fig. 2) referred to is similar in shape to an ordinary smoothing plane. It is fitted with a cutting iron, held vertically in the stock,

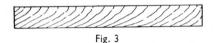

Fig. 3

while the back of the iron has a number of fine grooves which produce a serrated cutting edge, their object being to produce a slightly rough surface on the groundwork, and to remove any marks left by the previous planing. If such a tool is not available, a piece of coarse glass-paper, wrapped round a block of wood makes a good substitute.

First Steps.—The first thing to do is to prepare the groundwork. If this is of soft wood, such as yellow pine,

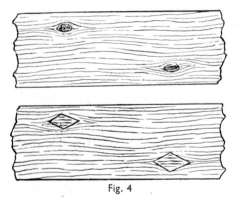

Fig. 4

examine the end grain, as the veneer should be placed on the heart side, as indicated in Fig. 3. Cut out any knots to a depth of at least $\frac{3}{16}$ in. and fill the recess by gluing in a piece of sound wood cut diamond-shaped if possible as this will hold the glue better than a square piece. This is illustrated in Fig. 4. Smooth the inlay down level and fill in any inequalities with a mixture of glue and plaster-of-paris. This treatment of

knots is essential, otherwise blisters will occur at these points and spoil the work.

Then apply the toothing plane or the glass-paper block as the case may be. In using a toothing plane, work it diagonally across the groundwork, first in one direction and then in the other. Remove all dust and brush some size composed of glue thinned with water over the entire surface to stop up the pores in the wood. Allow the work to dry.

Cut the veneer about $\frac{1}{2}$ in. wider and longer than the groundwork. Do not attempt to use a saw for cutting otherwise the veneer will break, but use a very sharp chisel and a straight-edge as a guide, in the manner shown in Fig. 5. Take great care in the cutting, as the veneer is very brittle and liable to break.

Preparing Glue.—Now prepare the glue. This must be free from lumps

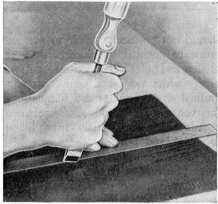

Fig. 5

and perfectly clean. Bring the glue nearly to the boil and test it by dipping the brush into the pot. If the glue trickles off the brush in a continuous stream it is ready.

Before placing the prepared ground on a flat surface such as a bench top, drive a couple of thin nails minus their heads partially into the bench, allowing the pointed ends to project about $\frac{1}{16}$ in. above the surface and place the work over the nail heads to prevent it from slipping when using the veneering hammer, as considerable pressure is needed when manipulating the tool.

Place the flat iron on a gas ring and heat it so that, when held a few inches from the back of the hand, it feels comfortably warm and no more. An extremely hot iron will probably scorch the veneer, while one insufficiently heated is useless.

Examine the veneer to see which side should be placed uppermost. Minute projections will be noticed on one side, corresponding depressions on the other. The veneer should be laid with the projections to the top so that they can be removed during the cleaning process.

Apply a thin coating of glue to the groundwork and the veneer and place the latter in position. Damp the surface of the veneer with a cloth moistened with warm water and at the same time brush a little glue here and there to seal the pores and so prevent the water from soaking through the veneer and reaching the glue underneath.

Ironing.—The next procedure is to apply the hot iron as if ironing clothes. The object of the process is to keep the glue in a melted condition so that it can easily be squeezed out with the hammer. Fig. 6 shows the method.

Now grasp the hammer as indicated in Fig. 1, apply pressure and work it in a zig-zag fashion from the centre towards the edge, taking care not to press on the overlapping part. This presses out the glue, which may be removed with a damp cloth.

Now tap the surface with the fingernails. If it feels solid, all is well. A hollow feeling, however, means that the veneer has not adhered to the groundwork at that point. If such is the case, apply heat with the iron and go over the work again with the hammer.

Turn the work face downwards on a

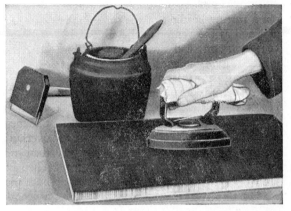

Fig. 6

flat surface and trim off the surplus veneer at the edges, using a sharp chisel.

Allow the glue to dry for at least twenty-four hours—the longer the better —then test the surface again. If a blister shows, make an incision in the centre with a sharp penknife in the direction of the grain, as indicated in Fig. 7, to release the air. Then apply the hot

Fig. 7

iron and hammer, and glue a thinnish piece of paper over the cut to prevent it from opening as the glue dries.

If the piece of work happens to be, say, a small table-top or the top of a chest of drawers, it is not advisable to veneer the narrow edges, especially those on end grain, as the latter absorb a great deal of glue and make adhesion difficult. In place of veneer, glue and pin a narrow beading of the same kind of wood as the veneer to the edges. If veneering on end grain cannot be avoided, give the ends several applications of glue size and allow each coat to dry before attempting to apply the veneer.

To complete the work, the veneered surface should be levelled with a scraper or a piece of glass, and then smoothed with fine glass-paper, rubbed in the direction of the grain.

Large Veneers.—When veneering a comparatively large surface it may be easier to use two pieces of veneer instead of a single sheet. This means that a joint will have to be made. To do this, fix the first sheet of veneer as already described and then lay the second sheet so that it overlaps by about 1 in. where the joint is to be. With a very sharp

Fig. 8

chisel, preferably of the paring type, and a straight-edge as a guide, sever the two thicknesses of veneer at the centre of the overlap by taking several light cuts and then removing the unwanted pieces. Then use the hot iron and hammer on both pieces forming the joint, and stick a length of paper along the joint as indicated in Fig. 8 to prevent it from opening as the glue sets.

Do not attempt to cover pronounced joints such as ordinary dovetails with thin veneer as they are bound to show through in time. If less obtrusive joints cannot be employed in making the carcase, thick veneer should be used.

WOOD FINISHING

WHEN finishing wood, you should always endeavour to bring out its character and grain and not disguise the natural beauties which help you to produce a lovely piece of woodwork. The modern methods of wood finishing dealt with here are designed to do this.

Red Deal.—Take any piece, plane it and finish with fine Nos. 2, 1½, 1 and 0 glass-paper. Wipe it with hot water on both sides, leave to dry, then rub again with No. 0 glass-paper. Purchase threepennyworth of vandyke brown powder (dry) and sixpennyworth of .880 spirits of ammonia. Mix some

of each in the form of a paste and thin out to the required colour with water.

Then, with a brush, put the stain on evenly, working with the grain, wipe off and leave to dry. Now rub with a piece of old calico to take down the grain, and prepare some wet wax in the following manner. Purchase one shillingsworth of real beeswax and half a pint of turpentine. Melt these together in a tin and add a small piece of resin about the size of a marble. Allow the mixture to get cold and rub it lightly on the deal. Leave for one hour and then polish with a soft cloth.

White Deal.—Plane and finish the wood as described for red deal. Buy a reliable grey dye and mix it in half a pint of hot water and apply with a brush, leave the wood to dry, then rub with hessian, pressing hard and working with the grain. Apply wet wax as before, leave it for an hour and polish with a piece of silk.

The result will be a beautiful purple-grey. (This is now named purple wood.)

Mahogany.—Plane up and finish the wood as usual, but omitting the fine No. 2 glass-paper. Purchase sixpenny-worth of bicromate of potash, mix well in half a pint of boiling water and apply with a brush. When dry, apply raw linseed oil and turpentine (mixed together in equal parts) and wipe off.

The wood should be left for a couple of days in a warm room. Then wet wax it, leave for an hour or so, and polish with coarse canvas. The result will be Chippendale colour without any of the common, unpleasant reddish tone.

Satin Walnut.—This wood, when french polished, is a yellow colour. Treated in the way described here, you get that lovely colour of bronzed satin walnut. Plane and finish the wood. If the article is small, such as a clock case, place it in a box (a packing case will do if you paste up the cracks with paper to make it air tight). Half fill a tea saucer with .880 spirits of ammonia, place it quickly in the box and shut down the lid and paste paper round the edges. Then oil and wax as described before.

Oak.—This wood is so much in fashion that it will be necessary to describe how to obtain all the different effects and colours. Note that Austrian wainscot oak and English oak respond better to the following treatments than American and Japanese varieties.

Weathered Austrian Wainscot Oak.—First wipe over the finished article with hot grey dye (see treatment for white deal) but, in this case, wash off the dye at once with a clean cloth and cold water. Then, when quite dry, rub with canvas and burnish with a chain burnisher. These burnishers are like a small piece of bright chain armour. An old cavalry epaulette will do quite well. Failing this, any piece of smooth bright steel, a flat-iron, the shaft of a screwdriver or the face of a hammer will do. Burnishing takes time and considerable pressure is necessary.

Bleached Austrian Wainscot Oak.—Wash over with hot water in which you have placed some oxalic acid ($\frac{1}{2}$ oz. to 1 pint of hot water), then use canvas and burnish as before.

Weathered Oak, Showing Flecks of White in the Grain.—It is best to wipe the finished work first with warm water and castile soap, and when dry, rub down the grain with No. 0 glass-paper and coarse canvas. The best way is to purchase a tin of light oak polish (in the form of a white paste). Apply this across the grain with a soft cloth and polish as you go with a piece of linen or clean calico.

Fumed Austrian Wainscot Oak.—Place the finished work in an air-tight box and fumigate the work as for bronzed satin walnut, but, in this case, do not oil and wax it. Simply burnish it. If a deeper colour is required, it may be oiled and waxed instead of burnishing it. Another shade of brown may be obtained by fumigating and dry-wax polishing. (Chippendale used this method on Cuban mahogany.) The method is simple. Rub a block of real beeswax vigorously with a nail brush. A certain amount of the wax will adhere to the brush. Then rub the wood with the brush. In some cases a piece of coarse canvas is better than a nail brush.

American Whitewood and Basswood.—Proceed in the same way as for red deal or white deal and, if you require a purple-brown, mix the hot dye with the vandyke brown mixture to the required shade.

American Black Walnut.—This wood is of such a beautiful colour (violet-brown) that it is best merely to rub it with coarse canvas and burnish it.

A browner shade may be obtained by rubbing with dry beeswax and a still darker tone by wet wax polishing.

Silver-grey Sycamore.—See that the wood is clean, then mix hot grey dye and put it on with a clean brush; a painter's sash tool is just the thing. Then quickly wash off with clean warm water, allow the wood to dry, and rub with canvas. Polish with dry beeswax.

Silver-grey Holly.—This colour effect may be obtained in the same way as for silver-grey sycamore, but as holly is only obtainable in small pieces it will be best to use it for small articles such as clock cases or cigarette caskets. It should be noted that these silver-greys do not fade or show dirt if done by the method described.

The following hints may be of further service:

Burnishing brings out the medullary rays of the wood (oak) as the burnisher slightly takes down the soft fibres.

Oil always intensifies colour. The strength of solutions may be varied according to the shade required.

Always experiment first on a spare piece of wood.

CHINA CABINET

THE china cabinet shown in Fig. 1 is of neat and modern design without elaborate mouldings, and is of simple construction as the major part of the work consists of making accurate frames.

The Fitment.—The fitment consists of two units, the upper portion or cabinet proper and the lower section containing the legs upon which the cabinet rests.

There is much to recommend this method of construction, primarily because the units can be separated, thus making the task of removal simpler and safer and, secondly, because it reduces the amount of headroom required when it is desired to take the structure through a doorway.

Position of the Cabinet's Legs.—Reference to the dimensioned drawings (Fig. 2) will show that the back legs of the lower unit are not flush with the back of the upper one. This is to allow the back of the cabinet to be flat against the wall, which it could not do if the legs were in line, owing to the skirting.

A cabinet of this description would look well made in oak, mahogany or walnut, or the frames could be made from a cheaper hardwood. Whatever wood is selected, it should be finished to harmonise with the other furniture in the room.

It matters little whether the upper or the lower unit is constructed first.

Construction.—The upper section consists of two side frames, two doors, a plywood back, a base, a top and a pediment, as the triangular-shaped ornament at the top is called.

Before starting on the work, choose a method to be adopted in forming the rebates or recesses against which the glass rests in the frames, and also the type of joint to be used for joining the stiles (uprights) and rails (cross-pieces) together. The professional cabinet maker forms the rebate in the solid wood with a rebate plane and it is a wise method. On the other hand, a rebate plane may not be available, in which case a narrow bead could be fixed to the inside edges of the frames after they have been put together, thus forming a false rebate for the glass to butt against.

With reference to the joints, dowel pins may be used for the side frames, but it is better to use mortice and tenon joints for the doors as the major portion of these frames is not supported when open.

To reinforce further the joints in the door frames, small brass flat angle-plates could be let into the back faces.

Illustrations of the rebates and the joints are shown in Fig. 3. That represented at A is a ploughed rebate and dowelled joint for the side frames ; that at B is a false rebate and dowelled joint which may be used

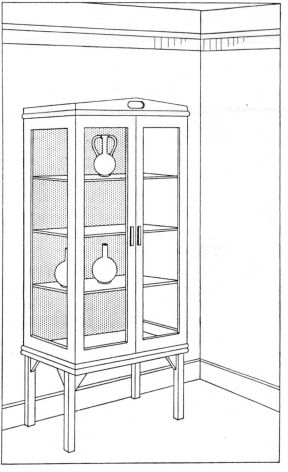

Fig. I

as a substitute for that at A; C illustrates a ploughed rebate and mortice and tenon joint for the door frames, while that appearing at D is the alternative to C. A reinforcing metal plate *in situ* is seen at E.

The Side Frames.—Start with the construction of the side frames. Saw all the stiles 2 in. longer than the dimensions given and plane them true and square, and then mark them out in pairs. Bore the holes at the ends for the dowels and plough the rebate if this method is adopted. Follow in the same

fashion with the rails and then glue and cramp the parts together. Improvised cramps made of battens (F in Fig. 3) and wedges will answer the purpose if ordinary cramps are not available. When the glue is hard, trim off the waste at the ends of the stiles with the aid of a tenon saw and plane, and if false rebates are to be used, cut and mitre the ends of the moulding and fix them with $\frac{1}{2}$ in. panel pins.

Then proceed in the same way with the doors.

The Top.—The top is made of two

$8 \times \frac{7}{8}$ in. prepared ($7\frac{7}{8} \times \frac{3}{4}$ in. finished) deal boards butted together and glued to form a glued butt-joint. When dry, the piece is sawn and planed square to a finished size of 2 ft. long × 1 ft. 2 in. wide. When the cabinet is assembled, a

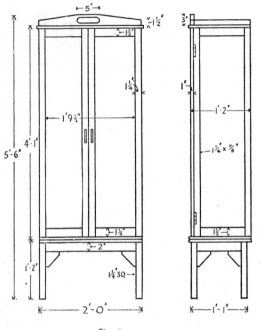

Fig. 2

narrow beading of the same kind of wood as the main structure is fixed round the edges to give them a neat appearance.

The Base.—The base is an exact replica of the top member, while the pediment is a simple frame with a sloping front as shown. The sides and back are $1\frac{1}{2}$ in. high.

It should be noted that it is necessary that the top and bottom members be square, for any deviation from squareness will put the whole structure out of alignment when assembled and difficulty will be experienced in fitting the doors.

The Back.—The back is a piece of $\frac{3}{16}$ in. plywood of the same length as, but $\frac{1}{4}$ in. less in width than that of the

cabinet. This, too, must be square.

The next operation consists of assembling the parts. This is simple, as the top and bottom are fastened to the side frames by means of countersunk-headed screws, and the plywood back is glued and pinned to the narrow back faces of the frames as well as to the backs of the top and bottom members. The long edges of the plywood are set back $\frac{1}{8}$ in. from the outer edges of the uprights.

Screws and Screw-holes.—The screw-holes in the top and bottom should be bored before assembly. Six screws should be used along each edge. The end ones, where they are driven into the end grain of the uprights, should be 2 in. long, while the intermediate ones need be only $1\frac{1}{2}$ in. in length. The screw-holes should be bored $\frac{7}{16}$ in. from the edges.

The pediment is glued to the top member and, to give additional strength, triangular glue blocks about 3 in. in length are used. The ornamental overlay is a piece of hardwood $\frac{1}{4}$ in. thick which is glued to the front of the pediment.

The Doors.—The cabinet is now ready to receive the doors. Mark the positions for the hinges and let them into shallow recesses so that the leaves of the hinges lie flush with the surfaces. Then test the doors to see whether they require easing. If so, remove the doors and skim off where necessary. Next, shape and fit the handles by screwing them from the inside.

As the interior should be as dustproof as possible, pin a length of $\frac{1}{4}$ in. square stripwood along the top and bottom, keeping it 1 in. from the outer edges to allow the doors to butt against when closed.

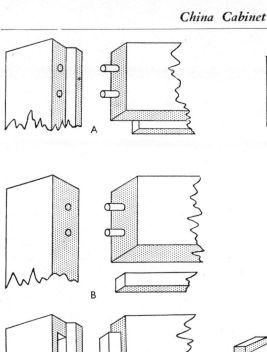

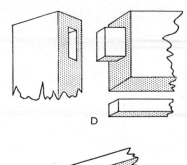

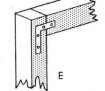

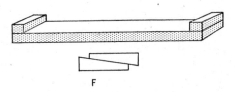

Fig. 3

For the same purpose, a strip of astragal moulding $\frac{3}{8}$ in. should be glued to the closing face of the right-hand door as indicated at A in Fig. 4.

To keep the doors closed, use ball catches as illustrated at B (Fig. 4) at the ends of the closing stiles as these are inconspicuous and effective.

Glaze the frames with 21 oz. glass and use $\frac{1}{4}$ in. plate glass for the shelves, the number of which must be left to the constructor's decision.

Shelf Support.—Small brass brackets screwed to the side frames may be used for supporting the shelves. To prevent the shelves slipping forward when the doors are open, a piece of brass should be cut, drilled and bent to shape to form a lip. To keep it in place, it is fixed between the wooden frame

and the bracket, as indicated at C in Fig. 4.

Fastening.—For fixing the cabinet to the lower unit, two $\frac{1}{4}$ in. shouldered bolts and wing-nuts are used. For each of these a hole should be bored in the bottom at a distance of about 6 in. from the outer edges and in the centre. The heads of the bolts should be sunk into the bottom member so that their heads are flush with the surface and, to prevent them turning when screwing up the nut from underneath, the diameter of the bolt-holes should not exceed those of the bolts. The square shoulder of the bolt will draw itself into the wood when the nut is tightened up.

Finishing.—To give the interior a proper finish, the back, top and bottom

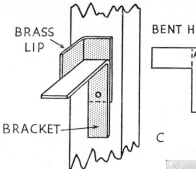

are housed and glued in recesses cut in the legs. The top is a facsimile of the bottom of the cabinet and is fixed to the top of the rails by screws.

Fig. 5 shows an illustration of a china cabinet made from an old-fashioned bookcase. The glazed upper portion of the cabinet was removed from an enclosed lower section, and a low pedestal with feet was fitted in its place, as shown.

Fig. 5

Fig. 4

may be covered with silk or other fabric.

The lower unit is really a low table. The ends of the rails are tenoned to fit into mortices cut in the legs, while the small strengthening brackets, $\frac{1}{4}$ in. thick,

OVERMANTEL

THE overmantel shown in Fig. 1 can be made of any even grained wood; oak or walnut are good or first quality pine. If the latter is varnished, it will make an attractive finish. To suit some rooms, an enamel finish in art tones will be found suitable. For a drawing-room,

a pale blue or green with a gilded stripmoulding around the glass and a gilt back behind the fretwork pattern below the shelf will be attractive and can be made to tone with any decorative scheme.

Frame Members.—The framing

(an end view is shown in Fig. 1A) is all in 1 in. stuff and the outside members are 2 in. wide, while the two inner vertical members are of 1½ in. wood, as are the two top rails. The bottom rail is of 6 in. stuff at the ends and carved out, as shown at the bottom. These three rails are cut into the side members, as shown in the side view. They fit in ⅜ in. deep slots cut across the vertical members and are of the same width as the rails, while the rails themselves are cut in ⅝ in. from the front of a length to fit the width of the vertical members. All are screwed together with two brass screws in each joint driven in from the back; the screws being ¾ in. long and well countersunk in the rails at the back.

The two inner vertical members are similarly let in from the back into the

All the frame members should be prepared first and assembled with the screws lightly driven. Then they should be taken apart and all the joint surfaces treated with hot thin glue, at once replaced and the screws tightened up. At the bottom of the side uprights are feet made of 1 in. stuff which should be 4 in. long and 2 in. wide, and have rounded corners. These will be glued to the bottom of the side members and, in addition, have two long thin screws with their heads well countersunk.

Mirrors and Mirror Panels.—The panel openings for the mirrors are 17 × 8¼ in. for the two side mirrors and 1 ft. 4½ in. × 17 in. for the central one. These can be had from the glass silverers plain or with bevelled edges, and they should be to the exact size ascertained after the framing has been made.

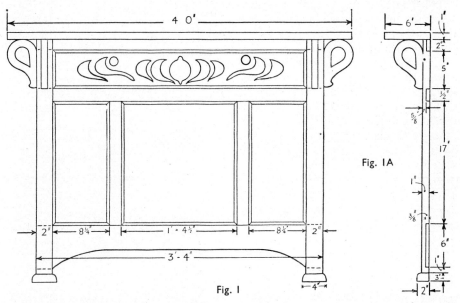

Fig. 1A

Fig. 1

bottom rail and the lower of the two top rails. This framing is then flush in front and should be well planed all over to clean off the tops of the joints which, when fitted, will be sure to be a little proud at places.

The glasses are held in position by beads at the back bradded to the sides of the frames, and in front by gilt beads if desired, or wood strip beads of contrasting colours which are mitred in firmly and sprung in after the glass has

D

been introduced. A sheet of thin ply-wood should go at the back of the glass and the front bead should be of a width to project just beyond the front surface of the framing.

This will be the last job in fitting it up, but it is important to see that the glass panels fit before finishing the framing. The top panel is fitted with beads like the mirror panels, but it

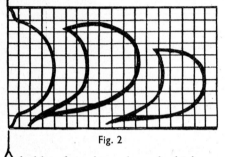

Fig. 2

holds a fretted wood panel which can be made of plywood and stained, varnished or enamelled according to the general finish of the piece.

The pattern shown is one example, and it can be copied by setting out in $\frac{1}{2}$ in. squares from the squares half shown in Figs. 2 and 3. The top shelf is of 1 in. stuff and is screwed down on the top rail (flush with the back) by four $2\frac{1}{2}$ in. screws. It is 4 ft. long and 6 in. wide with a square edge.

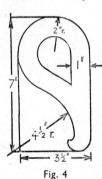

Fig. 4

The Brackets.—

The brackets which support it are fret-cut out of $\frac{3}{4}$ in. hard-wood such as oak. There are four of them alike. They can be cut in pairs (bradded together) with a fretsaw and cleaned with a half-round rasp and sand-paper. Keep the corners sharp. Rounded corners show amateurish work. The shape and dimen-

sions of the brackets are shown in Fig. 4. The height of the corner bracket, as shown in Fig. 4, is 7 in. and the width $3\frac{1}{2}$ in. The brackets in front are screwed up from the back and are the important ones. The top shelf is screwed down to the brackets by thin screws. The brackets at the side can be glued and bradded to the side of the framing and screwed from the top by one screw.

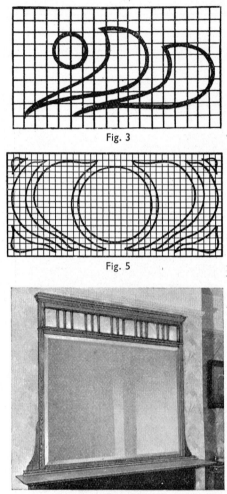

Fig. 3

Fig. 5

Fig. 6

They are merely ornamental and support no weight, but they balance the design and should not be omitted.

An alternative arrangement is to omit the two centre uprights and leave a full centre panel and to incorporate a fretted design on thin wood panelling and mount the glass behind this, thus leaving the mirror showing as a series of shaped panels. The fretted stuff can be held behind the beads as in the case of the glass panels, and backed up by a single sheet of mirror, the latter backed by plywood and securing beads at the back.

This can be made to conform with any particular feature in the decoration of the room. The design shown in Fig. 5 blends with that on the top panel. It is well to remember that any design of this kind which divides the glass into panels connected in design with each other should not be attempted if it is intended to place a clock, heavy vases or other ornaments in front of the mirror. It is suitable only to stand by itself with perhaps a slender vase or two before it, but with nothing to break up the design.

Fig. 6 shows an example of a plain framed overmantel which can be constructed on similar lines.

A USEFUL AFTERNOON TEA WAGON

A N afternoon tea wagon, shown in Fig. 1, is one of those useful labour-saving devices which can be constructed at little cost by any handyman.

As will be seen by referring to Figs. 2, 3 and 4, this piece of furniture consists of nothing more complicated than a couple of trays supported on four legs fitted with large castors.

Mahogany, walnut or oak may be used for the frame, while plywood $\frac{3}{8}$ in. thick faced to match the wood of the frame can be employed to advantage for the trays.

Materials Required.—To make the fitment the following materials (finished sizes) will be required:

4 legs, each 2 ft. 3 in. long, of wood $1\frac{1}{2}$ in. square section.

2 long rails, 2 ft. long, plus tenon, × 2 in. wide and $\frac{3}{4}$ in. thick.

2 side rails, 1 ft. $3\frac{1}{2}$ in., plus tenon, in length, 2 in. wide × $\frac{3}{4}$ in. thick.

2 pieces $\frac{3}{8}$ in. faced plywood.

1 set of 4 castors, having 3 in. wheels.

A supply of glue, screws and panel pins.

Start the construction by preparing the legs. The material for these is a stock size and can be obtained ready planed and sandpapered in lengths of $2\frac{1}{2}$ ft.; prime oak costing ninepence per length; beach and whitewood can be obtained to resemble mahogany at sevenpence per length. The material

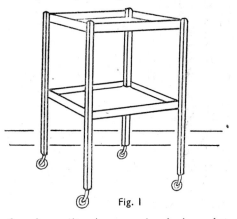

Fig. 1

for the rails also can be had ready prepared and costing about threepence per foot in hardwood and $3\frac{1}{4}$d. in oak.

Mark the legs to true length and set out the positions of the mortices, as mortice and tenon joints are used for joining the rails to the legs. The mortices are cut in two adjacent faces and are $\frac{1}{4}$ in. wide, 1 in. long and $\frac{7}{8}$ in. deep and communicate with each other as the dimensioned, sectional drawing of the joint appearing at A in Fig. 5 shows. The ends of the tenons are mitred as indicated. This joint is exceptionally

sawn and the edges should be shot so that each piece forms a perfect rectangle. The corners will have to be cut away slightly to allow room for the corners of the legs.

The bottom members are supported on

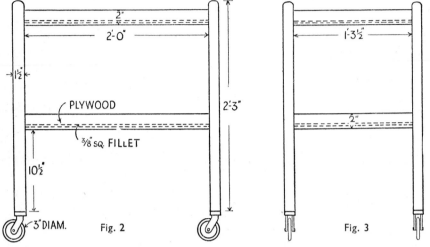

Fig. 2

Fig. 3

strong owing to the extra gluing surface at the mitre.

Having accurately marked the position, the majority of the waste may be taken out with a brace and twist-bit and the remainder removed with a sharp firmer chisel.

This done, mark the rails to length and prepare the tenons. These are $\frac{7}{8}$ in. long, $\frac{1}{4}$ in. thick and 1 in. wide, as illustrated at B in Fig. 5. These are mitred at the ends, as mentioned above and shown in the drawing.

Chamfer the edges of the legs, and, to give them a finish, rounded tops can be formed, if desired. Bore holes at the bottoms to take the shanks of the castors. The latter should be a tight fit in the holes, but they are not fitted permanently at this stage of construction. Then remove the arris, or sharp edges, at the corners.

Now prepare the bottom of the trays. These should be accurately marked and

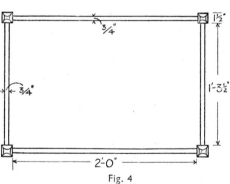

Fig. 4

$\frac{3}{8}$ in. square stripwood fillets screwed to the inside faces of the rails, the lower faces of the former being kept flush with the lower edges of the latter. This detail is represented at C in Fig. 5. Brass countersunk-headed screws $\frac{7}{8}$ in. long are advised, especially if the rails are of oak, as iron screws will corrode.

Gluing the Framework.—Gluing up the carcase is the next process. This is best done by forming the end frames first and then joining the long rails to those members. Place one leg on the floor, applying plenty of glue into the mortice and brush some of the adhesive on the tenon and its shoulder and insert it into the mortice. If necessary, give the free end of the rail several taps with a hammer to ensure that the shoulder butts closely to the leg. Do not strike the bare tenon, however, but use a piece of wood to strike upon, otherwise

holes have been countersunk, drive the screws through the bottoms into the fillets.

The whole assembly can now be finished with either stain and dull polish or stain and wax polish according to taste.

The final operation consists of fixing the castors. The holes have already been drilled, so all that remains to do is to insert the shanks and hammer the

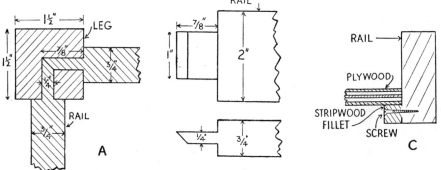

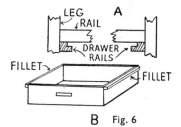

Fig. 5

the tenon will be damaged. Repeat the gluing operation with the lower rail and then fix on the other leg. It is now best to place the unit flat on the floor to enable the frame to be squared up with a try-square. To reinforce the joints, a 1 in. panel pin can be driven through the leg into the tenon. If this is inserted from the inside face it will not show as the end of a long rail will cover the tiny head.

Assemble the other frame in the same way and then fix the two long rails. See to it that the whole assembly is perfectly square, and allow the glue to harden before fitting the tray-bottoms.

Drill about half a dozen screw-holes spaced at equi-distant intervals $\frac{3}{16}$ in. from the long edges of the plywood tray bottoms and four similar holes at the same distance from the narrow edges. These should be of sufficient size to clear $\frac{3}{4}$ in. No. 5 brass countersunk-headed screws. When the tops of the

fixing prongs into the ends of the legs.

If desired, a drawer for holding cutlery could easily be added to the tea wagon. All that is necessary is a neat drawer of similar hardwood to that used

Fig. 6

for the main construction suspended from two rebated rails fixed on the under-side to the lower rails of the fitment. The rebates in the rails can either be formed with a rebate plane or built up to give the same effect. Fillets are screwed to the sides of the drawers at the top which slide in the rebates. The method of doing this is shown diagrammatically at A and B, in Fig. 6.

A WOODEN FIRESCREEN

THE folding firescreen consisting of a couple of hinged frames and stretched silk has now been replaced by a type of less ornate design, yet nevertheless as effective.

The screen shown in Fig. 1 consists of a single panel of ⅜ in. thick plywood

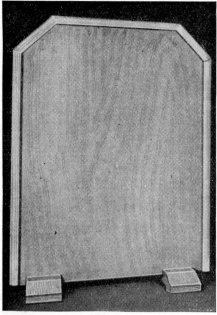

Fig. 1

supported on two shaped feet, and could be covered with tapestry finished in art colours, or a picture could be let into the panel, as shown in Fig. 2.

Frame Members.—The framework is simple, as Fig. 2 shows, and consists of grooved wood 1 in. wide and ¾ in. thick, mitred at the angles. An alternative method would be to use a panel of larger size and ½ in. thick and, when cut to shape, to fix facing strips of wood 1 in. wide round the edges. The former method is best, as the frame keeps

the panel rigid and prevents twisting.

To save grooving, it is wise to use ready-grooved moulding specially prepared for amateur woodworkers. The nearest stock size to that required is 1½ in. wide and ¾ in. thick and costs about half a crown per dozen feet, or three pence per foot if a smaller quantity is required. As the stock material is ½ in. wider than is necessary for the job, it is an easy matter to rip off the surplus with a saw and trim the rough edge with a sharp plane. It may also be necessary to widen the groove a trifle to obtain the requisite width, namely ⅜ in. This may be effected by the judicious use of a chisel worked in the direction of the grain.

Having cut the frame members a trifle longer than their finished sizes, the ends must be marked out, cut to form mitre joints and the mitred faces shot perfectly true with the aid of a mitre shooting-board and plane. The cutting of the mitre demands extreme accuracy as this is the most difficult part of the construction.

The panel should now be cut square and have nicely planed edges. At this juncture, the frame members should be fitted temporarily to the panel to see that the joints fit. Assuming they are correct, number the pieces to save confusion when gluing.

Apply thin glue to the edges of the plywood, grooves and at the joints, scrape off the surplus, cramp the parts and leave them cramped until the glue is dry.

In the interim, fashion the feet as shown in Fig. 3. These parts are cut from a piece of hardwood, the ends being bevelled and a slot ½ in. deep × ¾ in. wide cut across each top to accommodate those portions of the lower frame member to which they are fixed with glue.

The screen should now be smoothed with fine glass-paper and finished as required.

As a Picture Frame.— If a picture is desired in the panel, the aperture should be cut with a pad saw before the gluing process is put in hand. The edges should be smoothed with a rasp. An overlay of thin hardwood is then cut to size to overlap the edges by about $\frac{1}{4}$ in. This and the edges of the aperture form a rebate against which the glass rests. The water-colour, photograph, or whatever is deemed to be a suitable subject is then inserted against an appropriate mount and backed with a piece of thin plywood, held in position by sprigs.

The whole of the space is then covered with a further piece of plywood with nicely trimmed edges to keep out the dust and give it a finish.

It may be mentioned that, whether the picture is placed horizontally or vertically, it is advisable not to cut the

aperture in the exact centre of the panel but to allow a narrower margin at the top than at the bottom. Where tapestry is chosen, the alternative method of

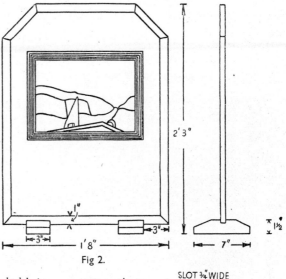

Fig 2.

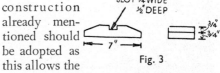

Fig. 3.

construction already mentioned should be adopted as this allows the fabric to be stretched across the panel and held down by means of the facing strips. The strips can be kept in position by means of small brass screws driven in from the back of the screen.

A GRAMOPHONE RECORD CABINET

THE cabinet shown in Fig. 1, and the working drawings, Fig. 2, is of sufficient size to accommodate fifty 12 in. and fifty 10 in. records, and forms a piece of furniture suitable for any room or home.

As gramophone records are heavy, the cabinet must be substantial. It is for this reason that the cabinet shown rests

on a low plinth and is made of material $\frac{3}{4}$ in. thick.

The interior of the cabinet is divided into two sections by a shelf; the upper one for taking 10 in. records and the lower for the heavier 12 in. ones.

Access to these compartments is obtained by opening the front flaps which form useful projecting shelves when selecting records. The upper flap is hinged to the shelf while the lower one is hinged to the bottom board; both are supported by hinged stays.

The records stand in grooves made of $\frac{1}{4} \times \frac{1}{8}$ in. stripwood, narrow edge up, pinned on to bases, four of which

Fig. I

will be required, a pair for each compartment. The grooved units are fixed to the cabinet by means of screws.

Hardwood Substitutes.—If cost is not important, a good hardwood such as oak or mahogany may be used for those parts which show. If this material is too expensive, American whitewood could be stained and finished to resemble a better class timber, or hazel walnut, similar in grain to satin walnut, could be employed as it takes stain well and can be given a high finish.

It is useful to know that American

whitewood, 14 in. wide, costs about $10\frac{1}{2}$d. per square foot, hazel walnut, 11d., oak and mahogany 1s. 3d. and 1s. 5d. respectively. Do not overlook the fact that a foot run of 14 in. stuff contains 14×12 in. $= 168$ sq. in. or a little more than a square foot which contains 144 sq. in. This is mentioned because, in purchasing the material, you may think that you are being overcharged.

To eliminate unnecessary expense, the back is a $\frac{1}{4}$ in. sheet of plywood, the middle shelf of good quality yellow deal and the bases of the grooved units of the same material.

As the wood for the carcase will be already planed, the first thing to do in the constructional work is to mark out, saw and trim up the ends of the sides with a sharp plane, paying attention to the squareness of the pieces. A groove is then formed in each inside face to house the ends of the shelf. The groove will be, of course, $\frac{3}{4}$ in. wide to correspond with the thickness of the shelf, and, as the depth of the channel of such a joint is generally made approximately $\frac{1}{3}$ the thickness of the wood, the grooves will be $\frac{1}{4}$ in. deep. The channels should not be cut right across the face but stopped about $\frac{3}{4}$ in. from the front edge. This kind of joint, known as stopped housing, is to be preferred to the ordinary through housing, as it eliminates the unsightly joint at the edges of the uprights.

The next part to put in hand is the top which measures 1 ft. 9 in. long $\times$ 1 ft. 3 in. wide including a $\frac{3}{4}$ in. overlap all round.

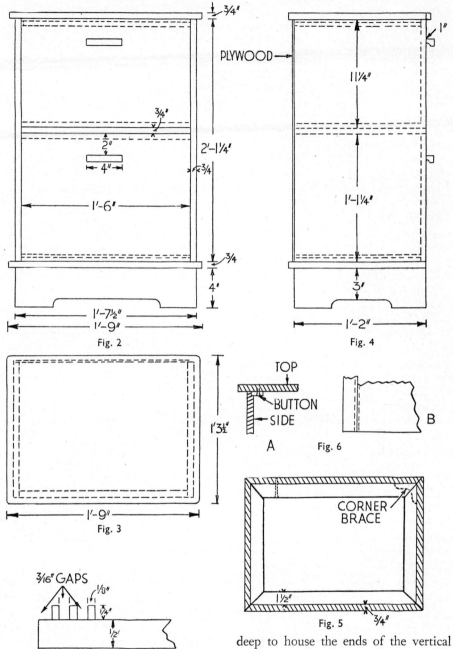

3/4"

PLYWOOD→

3/4"

2"

4"

2'-1¼'

⟵3/4

1'-6'

3/4

4'

1'-7½"

1'-9"

Fig. 2

1"

11¼"

1'-1¼'

3'

1'-2'

Fig. 4

1'3½"

1'-9"

Fig. 3

TOP

BUTTON

SIDE

A

Fig. 6

B

CORNER BRACE

1½"

3/4"

Fig. 5

3/16" GAPS

1/8"

1/4"

1/2'

Fig. 7

The underside of this member is trenched or grooved ¾ in. wide and ¼ in.

deep to house the ends of the vertical members. The edges of the top can be either left plain with just the sharp arris removed with a plane, or they can be rounded, chamfered at the top edges only, or chamfered at the top and bottom edges, according to the wishes of the worker.

The bottom board is a replica of the top, except that there is no overlap at the front.

Mitred joints are used at the ends of the plinth members which support the bottom board of the cabinet. An inner frame of $1\frac{1}{2} \times 1$ in. deal is screwed to the inner faces of the plinth as indicated in Fig. 5 and the corners are reinforced by means of corner braces.

Before assembling the parts together, three stopped mortices or slots are cut near the top edges of each vertical member. These are to accommodate the ends of fixing buttons screwed to the underside of the top, for further securing the top to the sides. This detail is shown at A in Fig. 6.

The front flaps now require consideration. The ends of these should be ledgered, that is to say, tongues should be formed in the ends which fit into corresponding grooves of cross-pieces as indicated at B in Fig. 6. This procedure prevents the flaps twisting.

Grooving to Hold Records.—Now construct the grooved units (Fig. 7) for holding the records. The two bases of these are of $\frac{1}{2}$ in. deal and measure 18 in. long and a shade under 12 in. wide, while the corresponding boards at the top are of the same dimensions but only $\frac{3}{8}$ in. thick. To obtain the necessary width, two boards 7 in. wide will be required. These are butt-jointed with glue, and the edges planed to size and squared up after the glue is dry.

Each piece is then marked out to indicate the position of the stripwood fillets. To mark out, start by drawing a line $\frac{3}{16}$ in. from and parallel to the left-hand edge and then pencil another line $\frac{1}{8}$ in. to the right of the original line. Then another line $\frac{3}{16}$ in. from the last followed by a gap of $\frac{1}{8}$ in. and

so on to the right-hand edge. Next, with $\frac{3}{4}$ in. thin panel pins fix lengths of $\frac{1}{4} \times \frac{1}{8}$ in. stripwood, narrow edge up, between the $\frac{1}{8}$ in. wide guide lines. This forms a groove $\frac{3}{16}$ in. wide which will accommodate a record with its cardboard wrapper. The parts can now be assembled. Start with the plinth. Apply glue to the inner edges of the frame members and screw them into the inner faces of the boards forming the plinth, keeping the tops of the former flush with the top edges of the latter. Brush glue on the mitred ends and the back of the braces and screw them up tight. When completed, put this part aside for the time being and begin assembling the body.

Screw on the fixing buttons at the correct positions on the underside of the top board but do not drive the screws right home at present as the ends will have to be turned to engage in the mortices after the top has been glued to the sides.

Apply the glue to the lower ends of the sides as well as the channels in the bottom boards, and drive in countersunk-headed screws from the undersides into each end. No. 8 gauge screws of not less than $1\frac{1}{2}$ in. long should be used as they have to grip the end grain of the vertical members.

Brush glue into the trench of the top board and also on the upper ends of the sides; place a piece of waste wood on the top and tap it gently with a hammer so that the ends of the vertical members bed down on the bottom of the grooves. Insert the ends of the buttons into their respective mortices and tighten up the fixing screws.

The shelf can now be fitted. It is advisable to place the cabinet face downwards on the floor, apply glue to the ends of the shelves and in the housings, insert the shelf from the back and gently tap it home, making sure that the front edge is flush with the front edges of the side members. Now square the cabinet up with a try square. To keep it square, tack on strips of wood diagonally across the corners at the front as the next procedure is to screw the plywood to the back. Before doing the latter, however, screw a strip of $\frac{1}{2}$ in. square hardwood to the underside of the top member and a similar piece to the top surface of the bottom, keeping the outer faces flush with the sides at the back to form horizontal fixing fillets for the upper and lower edges of the plywood sheet.

Place the cabinet face downwards and fix the back by driving in $\frac{3}{4}$ in. No. 6 screws, spaced about 6 in. apart.

Final Details.—The carcase has now to be fixed to the plinth. This is only a few minutes' work as it is kept in position by driving the screws through the plinth frame into the underside of the bottom member of the cabinet.

Before proceeding further, it is advisable to stain the interior and the grooved units to the desired colour, and when dry, to fix the units to the top and bottom of the compartments. The uppermost one will need a piece of $\frac{1}{2}$ in. thick deal between the fixing buttons to give it a solid fixing, while the gaps at the ends may be hidden from view by gluing or pinning on a strip of wood $\frac{1}{8}$ in. thick by 1 in. wide.

The fitment is now ready to receive the front flaps, which is merely a question of fitting the hinges, handles of hardwood, side supports and fasteners for keeping the flaps closed. Ball type fasteners are recommended because they are easy to fit to the opening edges and are hidden from view. The cabinet is now ready to be finished in any style the constructor may choose.

As it is wise to protect the surfaces of records, a number of containers should be made. These can be of thick manila paper, the edges of which are fastened together with adhesive linen.

A WINDOW SEAT

THE problem of a bay-window recess is easily solved by making a window seat on the lines shown in Fig. 1.

This seat is designed to fit a square bay measuring 7 ft. long by 2 ft. 4 in. wide or deep, the distance between floor level and window ledge being 2 ft. 5 in.

The structure is totally enclosed and the top is made in two sections and hinged at the back, thus enabling the space within to be utilised for storing magazines, books and articles which are only used occasionally. Such a fitment can be made in a few hours at quite a nominal cost.

Good yellow deal is used for the framework, and plywood for enclosing the front as this material can be purchased in one piece and presents a neat unbroken surface when fixed.

Simple Screwed Joints.—As simplicity is the keynote of the construction, the majority of the parts are screwed together which, in this instance, is as satisfactory as more complicated joints. The overall size of the window seat is 7 ft. long, 2 ft. wide and $15\frac{7}{8}$ in. high, which is a little lower than the average chair. Full dimensions of the framework can be obtained from Fig. 4.

Here is a list of the finished sizes of the parts in inches:

3 legs	.. ..	.. $15 \times 2 \times 2$
1 back support	..	.. $84 \times 5 \times 1$
1 front rail ..	..	.. $84 \times 3 \times 1$
3 cross-pieces (frame)	..	.. $22 \times 2 \times 2$
3 cross-pieces (top)	..	.. $24 \times 4 \times \frac{7}{8}$
1 piece plywood	..	.. $84 \times 15 \times \frac{1}{4}$
4 pieces batten	..	.. $36 \times 2 \times \frac{7}{8}$
Half round moulding	..	$72 \times \frac{7}{8}$

Four 3 in. plain iron angle-brackets, two pairs of $2 \times \frac{7}{8}$ in. iron butt-hinges and a supply of screws and oval brads are also needed.

Start work by cutting the backboard and planing the front face and top edge; the back face and bottom edge can be left in their natural state as they are

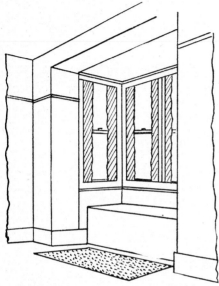

Fig. 1

them with a plane and cut the tops 3 in. down and 1 in. deep as illustrated in Fig. 3, to allow the front rail to lie flush with the front faces of the legs. Cut recesses in the outer legs for clearing the skirting, after which the legs can be fastened to the rail by driving in two 2 in. No. 8 screws at each joint.

Put this aside for the time being, as the next procedure is to fix the back support to the wall. As the latter nearly always consists of brickwork, the walls will have to be plugged in order to obtain a substantial fixing. This is not a difficult task provided the modern method of using small fibre plugs and a special tool for making the holes is used. The plugs and tool can be obtained cheaply at most iron-mongers. Half a dozen fixings will give ample strength, and the support is fixed by driving screws through the wood into the centre of the plugs.

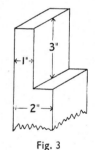

Fig. 3

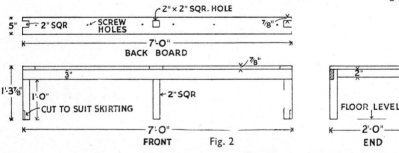

Fig. 2

not seen. As the top edge of this component should be unbroken by joints, cut recesses in the ends and a 2 in. square hole $\frac{7}{8}$ in. below the top edge to house the ends of the 2×2 in. cross-pieces, as illustrated in Fig. 2.

Then saw the legs to length, smooth

To obtain the correct position of the wall fixings, the screw holes should be drilled as shown in the back support and the latter held against a previously marked guide line when a bradawl or other sharp-pointed tool can be inserted in the holes and pressed into the plaster.

After fixing the back support, the two

ends and intermediate cross pieces can be inserted into the recesses in the back support and fixed by driving screws through the top edge of the board—one 2 in. No. 8 screw will be sufficient at each joint.

Attaching the Legs.—The legs attached to the front rail may now be fixed to the free ends of the cross-pieces by means of 4 in. No. 8 screws driven in from the front in the centre of each cross-piece. Clearing holes should be drilled and the edges countersunk in the front rail before driving in the screws. As these screws are large, it is useless to attempt to drive them with a small screwdriver.

To give additional support to the cross-pieces at these points, 3 in. iron brackets may be used, or small blocks of wood can be drilled and screwed to the back faces of the legs and into the cross members.

Iron brackets are used for fixing the lower ends of the legs to the floor. When fixing these it is important that the legs should be upright.

The next item is to fix the 4 in. wide top cross-pieces over the corresponding pieces of the framework. Oval brads 2½ in. long may be used for fixing them, but screws are better. It is essential that these parts be square and fixed squarely to enable the lids to fit. A try square will enable you to effect this result.

The lids are comprised of 1 in. tongued and grooved floorboards, which measure only ⅞ in. thick. The boards run parallel with the length of the fitment. In sawing the boards it is wise

to cut them 1 in. longer at each end as the surplus can then be removed and trimmed square after assembly. Greater accuracy is assured by doing it this way than by cutting each individual piece to the length first and then assembling the parts.

The tongued and grooved edges of the boards must be glued together at the joints and fixed to short cross-battens on the bottom by driving in screws from the underside. Having removed the surplus wood with a saw

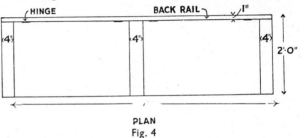

PLAN
Fig. 4

and plane, place the lids in position and ease them if necessary. Then give the top surfaces a skim over with a sharp, finely-set smoothing plane.

In fitting the hinges, shallow recesses should be cut both in the back edges of the lids and the face of the back support so that the leaves of the hinges lie flush with the surfaces.

The concluding items consist of fitting and fixing the plywood to the front, and fastening the half-round bead to the edge of the top. Recesses must be cut in the former just to clear the skirting board while the latter is fixed with glue and oval brads.

The fixture will look well if finished in the same colour as the window-frames, and the cushions covered with material to harmonize in shade and texture with the curtains.

A WIRELESS BOOKCASE

THIS cabinet is designed to suit both the wireless enthusiast and the book-lover.

As can be seen from Fig. 1 the ends of the cabinet are bookcases, and the shelf capacity is considerable. The

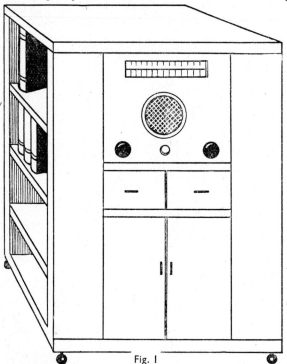

Fig. 1

centre division which carries in the upper part the wireless set, has room below for a drawer to take wireless periodicals as well as cupboard space for any accessory equipment.

The cabinet could be carried out in oak, relying entirely on the grain appearance. If desired, the drawer and doors could be veneered, although pieces of figured oak carefully chosen in both cases give the same attractive and pleasing appearance. The handles could be either wood or metal.

With regard to the finish, the natural colour of the wood (or one shade darker) might be preserved in the course of polishing, although many prefer the dark colouring of the Jacobean style.

Should you want to make this cabinet in walnut or mahogany you will find that it entails little or no alteration to the design.

Measurements and Joints.—A glance at Fig. 3 will show that the over-all sizes of the cabinet are 3 ft. 3¾ in. high, 2 ft. 7½ in. wide and 9½ in. deep. These measurements may seem odd, but they are determined by the size of the wireless set, 18 × 17 × 9½ in. and an allowance of 9 in. between the shelves for books. Fig. 2 gives a general idea of the construction. The sides C and the partitions E are tongued into the top and bottom A. Alternatively they may be fixed by dowels, as shown at A in Fig. 4. In any case the sides must fit flush with the partitions, and the top and bottom to ensure that the carcase is square. The shelves B, B1 and D will be stopped-housed into the partitions as shown at C in Fig. 4. It will be noticed from Fig. 2 that the shelves B and B1 tie the two end carcases together, and that the fixing on of the top and bottom assembles the whole carcase as one. This gives the method of working.

Having planed up the wood to the correct width and thickness and cut it

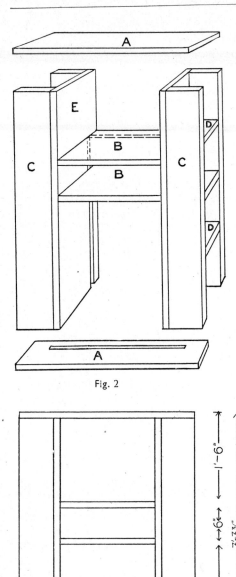

Fig. 2

to length, pair up the four sides c for setting out the grooves for shelves, as shown diagrammatically at F in Fig. 4. Having set out the groove (width $\frac{3}{4}$ in. depth $\frac{1}{4}$ in.) and stopped it $\frac{1}{2}$ in. from the front, saw and chisel out the waste matter. The six shelves D can be paired up in a similar manner and fitted to the grooves, as shown at H in Fig. 4. In a similar way, pair up the partitions, set out the stopped housings for B and BI and work these the same as in c and D. Note that the shelf BI is not the same width as B; this is to allow for the plough-groove—whose width is determined by the thickness of the plywood back—which is run in the partitions, and to shelf B, in the underside near the back of the latter (dotted line) and in the bottom A (Fig. 2). This completes the construction of the carcase.

Now for gluing. First have the glue hot and not too thick. Remove all the tools from the bench except a hammer, a mallet and some pieces of odd wood, and, most important of all—cramps.

Assembling the Carcase.—On the

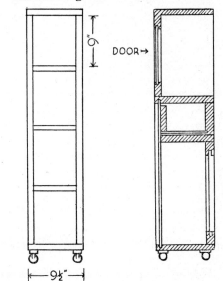

Fig. 3

bench have the two sides c and the three shelves D of one end carcase. Quickly glue all the grooves first, then the shelves, and slide the latter into their respective housings from the back and push forward. The shelves can be tapped into position with the hammer or mallet, using an odd piece of wood to take the blow and so prevent damage to the shelf. Cramp temporarily. Sight the top and bottom to see that they are square as indicated at I in Fig. 4, also the backs to see that they are not in winding. When you are satisfied, tighten the cramps and leave the glue to set. Repeat this process with the other end carcase. Before the glue chills, test for squareness by measuring the diagonals as suggested at J in Fig. 4. After twenty-four hours the cramps may be removed and the ends of c trimmed up ready for rub-jointing to the partitions E. Then glue the partitions to the end carcases. Whether the carcase is to be dowelled, or tongued and grooved to the top, sight very carefully the tops of c and E to verify that they are in line and square.

One advantage of dowelling is that the tops and bottoms of the end carcases can be planed square after gluing and then the dowel-pins can be fixed in position. Cramp into position and leave to set.

Now is the time to assemble the whole carcase. The shelves B and B1 can be slid into position in their respective housings and driven home and the top A fixed and tapped home, but before fixing the bottom A, remember to slide in the plywood back.

With the bottom driven home in position, test for squareness and cramp. Later, the whole carcase can be trimmed up flush and square.

The next problem is the drawer. If the front is to be veneered, the drawer should be made of mahogany, if not, oak. The thickness of the sides and back is to be $\frac{3}{8}$ in. and that of the front $\frac{3}{4}$ in.

The drawer is made in the usual way, the sides being lap-dovetailed to the front, and through dovetailed to the backs G in Fig. 4. The back should be at least $\frac{5}{8}$ in. less in width than the sides or front to allow for the plywood bottom to slide in easily. The bottoms are run in slips or beads glued to the sides.

Cutting Dovetails.—The method usually adopted for preparing the dovetails is to pair the sides, mark out the dovetails back and front and cut them. Place the sides in the required position on the front, mark round the dovetails with a sharp point pen-knife, leg of a compass, or a saw, and then remove the waste and fit the joints.

A plough-groove must also be run in the front to take the bottom. The drawer can be glued together and later fitted into position in the carcase. It is as well to leave $\frac{1}{8}$ in. on the width of the front and sides for fitting.

If the cabinet is made in mahogany or walnut, the drawer front can be veneered.

The doors can be made as suggested at D in Fig. 4, i.e., framed up with $\frac{1}{2}$ in. thick panels which are flush with the frames on the face. The frames should be morticed and tenoned together in the usual way, the panels being tongued and grooved in; D in Fig. 4 gives all the details for this work. Make the doors slightly full in size to allow for fitting.

After thoroughly smoothing the face surfaces, $\frac{5}{16}$ in. wide flat rounded edge beads are glued and pinned on to cover the joints, mitring them at the corners. Rebate the meeting stiles, and work a small bead down the stile of the right-hand door. Alternatively, for veneering purposes, the frames may be mitred

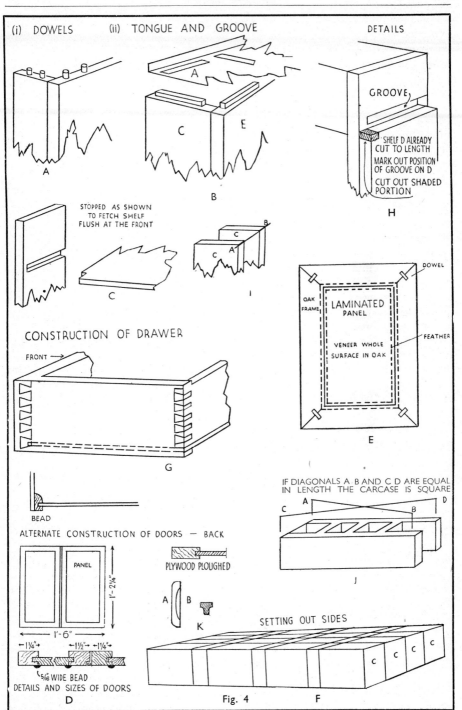

(i) DOWELS   (ii) TONGUE AND GROOVE   DETAILS

A

B

C   E

GROOVE

SHELF D ALREADY CUT TO LENGTH
MARK OUT POSITION OF GROOVE ON D
CUT OUT SHADED PORTION

H

STOPPED AS SHOWN TO FETCH SHELF FLUSH AT THE FRONT

C

I

DOWEL

OAK FRAME

LAMINATED PANEL

VENEER WHOLE SURFACE IN OAK

FEATHER

E

CONSTRUCTION OF DRAWER

FRONT

G

BEAD

IF DIAGONALS A B AND C D ARE EQUAL IN LENGTH THE CARCASE IS SQUARE

C   A   D
     B

J

ALTERNATE CONSTRUCTION OF DOORS — BACK

PANEL

1'-2¼"

PLYWOOD PLOUGHED

A   B

K

SETTING OUT SIDES

1'-6"

1¼"   1½"   1¼"

5/16" WIDE BEAD
DETAILS AND SIZES OF DOORS

D

Fig. 4   F

C C C C

together with the panels flush with the frames. The mitred frames should be fitted to solid panels, or panels of laminated board by means of feathers or keys. Details of this are shown at E in Fig. 4. The frames will be of the wood desired, i.e., oak, mahogany or walnut.

Applying Veneer.—Before veneering, thoroughly smooth the face surfaces, and then tooth these with a toothing plane (special tool) to provide a better surface for gluing. The veneer should be carefully chosen for figure, the face side damped, the other side and the frame (or ground) glued, the veneer placed into position on the frame and pressed down either by a caul or veneering hammer. In any case the centre will be pressed down first and the excessive glue squeezed out as the outside is gradually reached. The veneer should be held flat in a press until the glue has set, when careful scraping will reveal the natural beauty of the wood.

Each door (which includes the door at the back of the wireless set, should be hung with a pair of 1½ in. brass butt hinges. A small stop behind the left-hand door should be fixed on shelf B1 (Fig. 2) where it will not be seen, and either a small cupboard lock or a ball catch fitted to the right-hand door. Wooden or metal handles may be used; a suggestion for a wooden handle is made at K in Fig. 4. If metal is preferred, select a simple pattern. The toes to which the castors are fitted should stand in ¼ in. from the corners. Castors with 1 in. or 1½ in. wheels should serve the purpose.

A natural colour finish emphasises the beauty of oak and would suit the design. For those who desire a darker oak, there are many water stains that can be used with good effect. A fumed oak appearance can be obtained by the application of fumed oak stain, and also there are the various shades of lime finish. Wax polish is recommended, as a dull polish suits the nature of the wood. The wax polish is vigorously rubbed on to the work and into the pores of the wood with suitably open woven rag; the surplus wax is rubbed away with a clean rag, then the surface is polished with a clean cloth or piece of felt.

For mahogany or walnut, a high gloss finish is necessary, i.e., french polish.

AN OAK MUSIC STOOL

THE design for a music stool shown here, Fig. 1, possesses many advantages. The sides of the box for music and the top of the stool are flush, making it pleasant to handle and easy to dust. The lid is hinged, and the music can easily be taken out and replaced. This is better than a fall front, owing to the difficulty of pushing in the music exactly level.

Preparing the Legs.—Cut out and plane up the oak to the following sizes: Square up four legs each 1 ft. 8¼ in. × 1¼ in. × 1¼ in., 1 front and back piece each 1 ft. 5⅜ in. (plus tenons) × ¾ in. Then mark out the mortice and tenon, as shown in Fig. 2, taking care to use the mortice gauge from the face sides, alike of the legs, front and back and end pieces. Carefully saw the tenons and cut out the mortices and assemble the whole together so as to get the exact overall size of the music stool, as this will be the size to which you square up the bottom of the box (½ in. stuff).

Having done this, saw out the four

corners of the bottom $1\frac{1}{4} \times 1\frac{1}{4}$ in. and leave your gauge lines in for final fitting later on. Note the bottom is screwed up from underneath.

Now square up some oak strips about $1 \times \frac{3}{8} \times \frac{3}{8}$ in. from which to make the dowels. Plane and file them to $\frac{1}{4}$ in. diameter. This is best done by holding the strip in one hand and planing it round with a smoothing plane held in the other hand. Finish the dowels with glass-paper.

Then saw out two oak handles each $5\frac{1}{2} \times 1 \times 1$ in. to the shape shown in Fig. 3. Take the stool apart, finish all pieces with a finely set iron plane and then glue up. It is best to glue up the ends first and cramp them, test with try square, then with a $\frac{1}{4}$ in. twist-drill bore the holes and knock in and saw off the dowels. Take off the cramps and glue up the front and back pieces in the same way. The four sides and legs are now complete.

Now mark the positions of the handles. The top edges of these should be 2 in. down from the top of the stool. Bore and countersink the screw holes in the ends of the stool, fix the handles with glue and screw them from the inside of the music box.

Fit in the bottom and screw it up from underneath.

Wash the whole stool with hot water and wipe it as dry as possible, taking care to wipe off surplus glue. Leave the

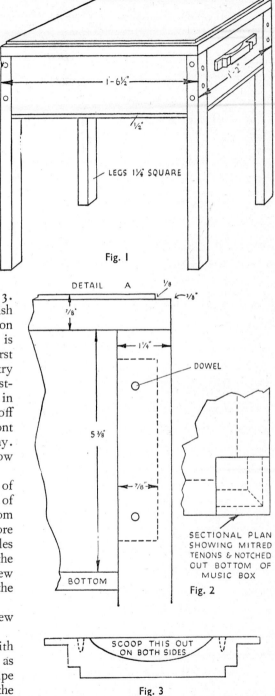

Fig. 1

DETAIL A

DOWEL

SECTIONAL PLAN SHOWING MITRED TENONS & NOTCHED OUT BOTTOM OF MUSIC BOX

Fig. 2

SCOOP THIS OUT ON BOTH SIDES

Fig. 3

stool twelve hours to dry. The reason for washing the stool with hot water, apart from taking off the surplus glue, is to raise the grain. If you stain the stool afterwards the grain does not come up so much.

Now square up the top to 1 ft. $6\frac{1}{2}$ in. × 1 ft. 2 in. × $\frac{7}{8}$ in., gauge a line all round the face-side of the top $\frac{3}{8}$ in. in from the edges, then gauge a line all round $\frac{1}{8}$ in. down from the face-side on all edges and take out the rebates with a rebate plane, plough plane, or chisel, as shown in detail at A in Fig. 2.

Lid Hinges.—Now square up and hinge the lid. One long brass piano hinge will be best. Failing that, use three 2 in. brass butts. The total thickness of the hinge or hinges may be let into the sides, but it will be better to let in one half of the thickness of the hinge in the top and the sides. This presents a neater appearance when the lid is open, as the hinges are flush with the wood. Finish your screwing so that the screw-slots finish one way, i.e., either in line or parallel to each other.

Clean off the edges of the lid so that they finish flush with all four sides of the stool. Now take off the lid, plane the underside slightly hollow and then wipe over the underside first with hot water. Then wipe over the face side. Leave for twelve hours to dry.

The construction of the stool is now finished and the next thing to do is to take off all sharp edges of legs and top so that the stool is smooth to the touch. This is done with an iron plane or file. Then go over the whole stool with fine Nos. 2, $1\frac{1}{2}$, 1 and 0 glass-paper. When glass-papering, use a small softwood or cork block and work with the grain (not across), pressing on the forward stroke. When using the finest grade glass-paper, rub lightly.

The next thing to do is to rub over the stool with hessian, pressing hard on the wood with the heel of the hand.

Polishing the Stool.—The stool is ready now for polishing, but thought and care are necessary before doing this. First of all you must consider the colouring of the stool—it must tone with the rest of the furniture, particularly the piano. If it is of light oak, the music stool may be polished with light oak polish, which is procurable anywhere in tins. The method of applying is simple, and a lasting polish is obtained. First turn the music stool upside down (on a cloth to prevent scratching the lid) and polish the four legs and underside of the box this way: With a soft cloth wipe the polish on the underside and the fore legs quickly, then with a piece of coarse calico polish each part, first slightly pressing and finishing with a light stroke. Then polish the inside of the box, the outside, and finally the top.

This stool would look equally well made in American walnut or mahogany.

NEST OF DWARF TABLES

A NEST of four small tables, as illustrated in Fig. 1, is useful in any home. Those shown in Fig. 2 are made of mahogany and french polished, but any good hardwood may be used. The table-tops, as well as the top rails, are $\frac{5}{8}$ in. thick and the legs of $1\frac{1}{4}$ in. square section material.

Fig. 1

Fig. 2

Glued dowelled joints are used through-out for joining the legs to the rails and the table-tops to the frames.

As the tops of tables 2, 3 and 4 are

legs, thus allowing runners $\frac{9}{16}$ in. thick to lie flush with the inner side faces of the legs, as shown in Fig. 5.

Full dimensions are given in Fig. 4.

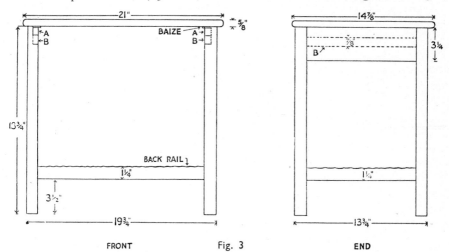

FRONT   Fig. 3   END

housed under those of 1, 2 and 3 respec-tively, no front rails are required; but as no table-top lies beneath the smallest unit, 4, front rails are provided.

The front faces of all top rails are set back $\frac{1}{16}$ in. from the front faces of the

It is only necessary to give construc-tion details of the largest one.

The Largest Table.—The top of this table measures 21 in. long × 14$\frac{7}{8}$ in. wide and projects $\frac{5}{8}$ in. beyond the outside faces of the legs. The top, side and back rails are 3¼ in. wide, while the legs are 18¾ in. in length. The bottom rails are 1¼ in. in width.

First prepare the legs. 1⅜ in. square-section stuff will be required and this will have to be gauged and planed to size. This process may be omitted if stock-size, prepared wood be obtained.

When the legs are ready, mark them to length, allowing ½ in. or so at each end for waste, which can be sawn off after having marked and bored holes for the dowel-pins. Two pins of ¼ in.

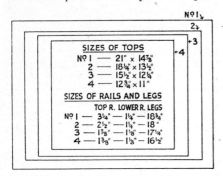

Fig. 4

diameter will be required at each joint. These may be home-made by driving a length of hardwood slightly larger than ¼ in. diameter in section through a ¼ in. hole drilled in a piece of steel if a ready-made dowel plate is not to hand. Alternatively, dowel-rods of exact diameter can be bought and cut to length.

The length of the pins is 1 in. One will be required at each joint at the legs and rails, and, allowing six for each table-top, this gives a total of eighteen for each large table, an extra eight must be added for the small one, thus giving a grand total of eighty.

The tedium of measuring and marking each pin, preparatory to sawing off from the length can be eliminated by screwing a bench-hook down to the bench and fixing a stop at a distance of 1 in. from the right-hand edge as indicated in Fig. 6. The end of the

rod to be cut is butted up to the stop, and the edge of the top member of the bench-hook used as a guide for the saw. Remove the sharp edges from the pins and make a saw kerf in the length of each one.

Next prepare the rails, the ends of which must be quite square to the faces and long edges. Mark the ends for the dowel pins and bore the holes a trifle deeper than ½ in., using a twist-bit ¼ in. in diameter for the purpose. Bore corresponding holes in the legs, remove the waste at each end and saw the top of each leg in the manner indicated at A in Fig. 3 to form a recess into which the table-top of No. 2 unit slides.

Prepare and fix a couple of runners ⅞ in. wide × 9/16 in. thick and of the same length as the side rails. These can be made of yellow deal as they are hidden from view. They are indicated by the dotted lines B in Fig. 3.

The Top.—The next procedure is to prepare the table-top. This should be made from a single piece of board if possible, but may be built up to width by gluing together two narrower boards. Mark, saw and plane to length and

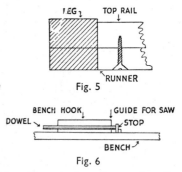

Fig. 5

Fig. 6

width. Round the edges, chamfer or finish them to whatever shape desired.

Smooth the parts with glass-paper not coarser than No. 00, and make preparations for assembly, not forgetting a supply of tube glue which saves the bother of preparing ordinary glue.

Assemble each side frame member using glue. See that the wood at the joints butts closely together and that all is square. When dry, fasten the runners to the inside faces of the side top rails, keeping the upper edges flush with the bottom of the recesses in the legs. Add the back rails, and in order to keep the assembly square, fix a batten across the front and another near the bottom for the time being, to act as front rails.

Having satisfied yourself that the assembly is square, place the table-top in position and mark the places for the dowel-pins on both the underside of the top member and the edges of the rails. Drill the holes and insert the pins. Apply glue to the top edges of the rails and legs and also on the underside of

the table-top where it joins the rails.

Place the table-top in position and force it down so that it beds evenly.

To prevent the top of each lower table from being scratched, a strip of baize is glued to the underside of the table above in the positions shown in Fig. 3.

The final process is to finish the tables by any method deemed desirable.

In constructing the tables, note that the width of the top rails is smaller in each instance and that the inner and outer edges of all bottom rails are slightly curved as in Fig. 3, to give them a little more ornate finish than plain edges. A spokeshave will come in handy for this.

If oak is the chosen wood, use brass screws for fixing the runners in lieu of iron ones to prevent corrosion.

A PORTABLE CAKE STAND

THIS light, portable cake stand, Fig. 1, can be closed up as indicated in Fig. 2 when not in use. It consists of a framed upright between which are suspended three circular pieces for holding cake dishes. The backs of the dish holders or supports are connected by means of hinges to a length of narrow wood which forms an extra leg when in use as indicated in Fig. 1.

Figs. 1 and 2 gives fully dimensioned drawings, and from these it will be seen that the circular dish holders are made from $\frac{3}{4}$ in. mahogany measuring $9\frac{1}{2}$ in. across. The same kind of wood of $\frac{5}{8}$ in. square section is used for the frame, while curved feet are of mahogany $\frac{1}{2}$ in. in thickness.

First prepare the two side frame members, A and B, Fig. 1, and then the curved top. The latter is cut from a piece of board $\frac{5}{8}$ in. thick, 3 in. wide and about a foot long. Make a paper

pattern of the outline, stick it on the face of the wood and cut round the outline with a pad saw. Finish off with

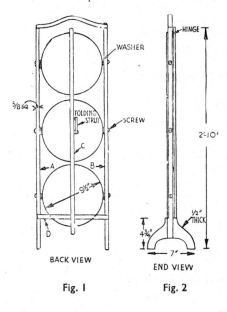

BACK VIEW

Fig. 1

END VIEW

Fig. 2

a spokeshave and glass-paper. The edges of the curved part of the member should be slightly rounded to form a handle.

A pad saw may also be used in cutting out the circular pieces, each piece first being marked by a pair of compasses. In order to prevent the dishes from slipping off the supports, an overlay of $\frac{1}{8}$ in. mahogany is glued to the tops. The overlays may be cut carefully with a fretsaw.

The extra leg at the back C is of wood $\frac{3}{8}$ in. thick and $\frac{1}{2}$ in. wide.

Joining the Parts.—The next step is to assemble the parts. Glue the feet to the uprights and reinforce the joints by driving in thin round-headed iron screws and then fix the handle at the top by means of screws and glue.

The circular plate supports are also secured by screws, but as they have to revolve between the uprights it is as well to insert washers between the uprights and the discs.

Three back flap hinges $\frac{3}{8}$ in. wide will be necessary for connecting the dish supports to the back leg. These should be of brass, as should be the folding strut which keeps the leg from slipping.

A strip of mahogany D, $1\frac{1}{2}$ in. wide $\times \frac{1}{4}$ in. thick, is fixed by screws to the back at a position just above the top of the feet of the upright frame. This keeps the plate supported in a vertical position when not in use.

A comparatively dull polish should be applied to the fitment in preference to a high gloss by applying a couple of coats of brush polish.

RADIO TABLE

A SUBSTANTIAL table to support a radio set is illustrated in Fig. 1. Satin walnut is used and is stained and finished dull to correspond with the receiver.

As satin walnut can be obtained in wide boards, nothing is gained by building up the table-top from narrow ones. Boards 14 in. wide cost about 11d. per square foot, so the wood for the top can be purchased for about a couple of shillings.

The dimensioned drawings appearing at Fig. 2 show a drawer provided for housing spare valves, odd bits of insulated wire, screwdrivers, a pair of pliers and other odds and ends.

Measurements.—The top is $20\frac{1}{4}$ in. long $\times 13$ in. wide and $\frac{5}{8}$ in. thick and this is supported by legs $25\frac{1}{2}$ in. in length of $1\frac{1}{4}$ in. square stuff. The top back and side rails are $4\frac{1}{2}$ in. wide, while the top front and drawer rails are $1\frac{1}{4}$ in.

wide fixed to the legs, with the narrower edge to the front.

The legs can be obtained ready planed to size, but if sawn wood is employed the faces must be accurately planed.

The bottom rails are $1\frac{1}{4}$ in. wide, $\frac{1}{4}$ in. thick, and the top edges have a series of wavy curves. Before cutting the legs to length they should be carefully marked for the joints. The ends of the side rails and back rails at the top are tongued and fit into corresponding grooves in the faces of the legs. The tongues extend the entire length of the end—that is, $4\frac{1}{2}$ in.—and are $\frac{1}{2}$ in. deep and $\frac{1}{4}$ in. wide. The grooves in the legs are, of course, of the same dimensions.

These joints are illustrated at A in Fig. 3.

The front rail immediately under the table-top is dovetailed into the top of the two front legs as indicated at B in

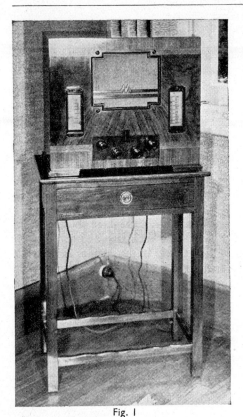

Fig. 1

after having ascertained that they are square. When dry, add the back rails and the three front ones, and allow the glue to harden before attempting to do more work on it. The whole assembly must be square.

The Drawer.—Details of the drawer are shown at c in Fig. 3. The overall width of the drawer is 1 ft. 4½ in. and 10 in. from front to back. The sides and back are of oak ⅜ in. thick, but the front is of walnut ¾ in. in thickness. Plywood 3/16 in. thick is used for the bottom and is held in position by means of lengths of ⅜ in. square rebated hardwoods fixed round the bottom of the inner faces of the sides and front. The piece forming the back does not extend right down to the bottom edges of the sides but is stopped ⅜ in. above as indicated at D in Fig. 3. The back edges of the plywood are attached to the lower edges of the back member of the drawer by means of ½ in. brass screws.

A strip of thin wood, hardwood for preference, to act as a drawer guide, is glued to each inner face of the side rails.

Fig. 3, while the ends of the drawer rails are stub tenoned and fit into mortices in the legs. The lower rails are all joined to the legs by simple mortice and tenon joints. In assembling the parts it is a good plan first to build up the two pairs of legs forming the ends, using strong glue for the purpose. These parts should then be fixed in suitable cramps

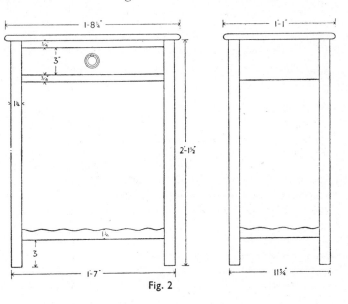

Fig. 2

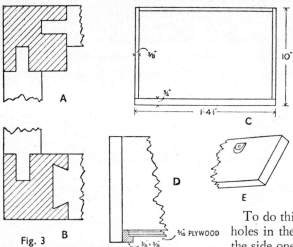

Fig. 3

The strips should be of a thickness to bring the face that butts up to the sides of the drawer flush with the inner side faces of the legs. The drawer runner is 2 in. wide and $\frac{3}{4}$ in. thick and is fixed by means of screws driven into the guides. The top of the runner must, of course, be dead flush with the top face of the drawer rail.

The underside of the drawer rails is covered in $\frac{3}{16}$ in. plywood to exclude dust.

Construction is completed when the top has been fixed to the top rails. To do this, make three oblique screwholes in the back rails and two each in the side ones in the manner indicated at E in Fig. 3. Also make three straight holes in the top front rail and fix the top by means of $1\frac{1}{2}$ in. No. 8 countersunk-headed screws.

SELF-CONTAINED BOOKSHELVES AND BOOK REST

SOLID oak is used in the construction of the self-contained book shelves and rest illustrated in Fig. 1, and its cost should not exceed 12s. 6d.

All wood used is $\frac{1}{2}$ in. in thickness except the ornamental beading along the front edges of the sides and the plywood at the back.

Procure 14 ft. of plain oak 7 in. wide for the sides, base and shelves, one piece 2 ft. long × 13 in. wide for the rest at the top, and 7 ft. of narrow edge beading of any pattern to choice.

See that the timber is in suitable lengths for the job, thus one piece measuring 5 ft. would be sufficient for the three shelves including $\frac{1}{2}$ in. for waste at each end, while another piece 9 ft. in length would be enough for the sides, the curved piece across the base and the two small projecting pieces at the bottom of the side members.

A sheet of $\frac{3}{16}$ in. alder or birch plywood will also be necessary for filling in the back, a few panel pins for fixing it and a supply of $1\frac{1}{2}$ in. No. 6 countersunk headed brass screws.

All dimensions can be seen by referring to Fig. 2.

Start by marking out and cutting the side members, retaining the waste pieces obtained after having sawn across the top to form the angles. From the waste, cut two feet to the shape shown and glue them to the front edge of the sides, and when the glue has set, form the curve at the lower ends of the sides with the aid of a pad saw and spokeshave.

The Shelves.—Attention may now be given to the shelves. These should

Fig. I

clearing holes for the screws by which the shelves are fixed.

Having bored the holes, countersink the edges to enable the heads of the screws to lie below the surface.

Then fix the ledge to the book rest by driving three screws through the ledge into the bottom edge of the wide board and fix this member to the sides also by screws.

The curved rail at the front of the base, B in Fig. 2, is now cut to length, the curve marked and sawn with a pad saw and smoothed with a spokeshave.

The top edge of this piece slopes back and another narrow strip indicated at A in Fig. 2 lies on the top and fills in the gap between the bottom rail and the lower edge of the shelf. These parts are fixed with glue as is also the beading along the front edges of the side members.

The Back.—Before fixing the plywood back, make sure that the fitment is perfectly square as well as the backing, and having satisfied yourself on this point, mark and cut the sheet and fasten it to the back with panel pins.

be sawn to length and the ends shot perfectly square with a plane.

Now saw the 2 ft. length of 13 in. wide wood along its length to produce, when planed, one piece $10\frac{3}{4}$ in. wide forming the book rest and the other $1\frac{3}{4}$ in. wide for the ledge. Cut and trim to length and slightly round the top and side edges of the wide piece and also the ends and front of the narrow one.

Mark the side members for the shelves and drill

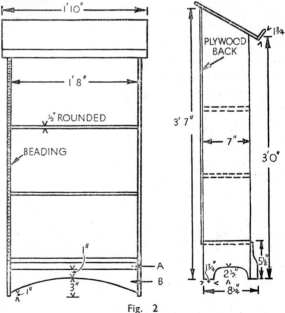

Fig. 2

In order to hide the long edges of the plywood, the piece is cut ½ in. narrower than the overall width of the fitment, giving a bearing surface of only ¼ in. on the back edges of the side members.

All screw holes should be filled with plastic wood and the whole glass-papered, stained and finished with two or three coats of french polish applied with a very soft camel-hair brush.

A FLOOR LAMP STANDARD

THE illustration, Fig. 1, shows a simple standard with a square tapered shaft and a solid base.

The height of the standard lamp shown is 5 ft. 6 in. but this may be varied and the shade could, of course, be of any shape. The wood may be oak, walnut, sycamore or mahogany.

Details of Standard.— The shaft is made of two pieces of 1 in. stuff, each piece being plough grooved ⅛ in. full deep for the flex and then glued together. See details, Fig. 2.

Square two lengths of wood each 5 ft. 3 in. × 3 in. × 1 in. The shaft is not tapered until after the square shaft is morticed into the base. Put them face to face to test the join and plough a groove $\frac{5}{16}$ × ⅛ in. full down the centre of each face side. Glue these together and clamp them with plenty of hand screws or G cramps. Plug up the hole at the bottom of the shaft with a piece of the same wood size 2 × $\frac{5}{16}$ × $\frac{5}{16}$ in. but do not glue this in as it has finally to be drilled out.

Now cut out and square up the base to size 11 × 11 × 2 in. Find the centre

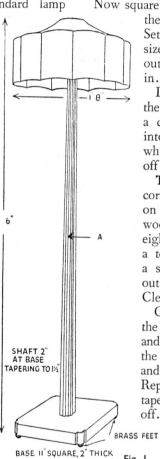

SHAFT 2"
AT BASE
TAPERING TO 1½"

5' 6"

—1 8—

A

BRASS FEET

BASE 11" SQUARE, 2" THICK

Fig. 1

of it, on both sides, and set out the mortice (with a gauge) 1⅜ × 1⅜ in., as shown in detail at Fig. 2.

Now square a line round the base of the shaft 2¼ in. from the end. Set out the tenon to the same size as the mortice and saw it out, keeping the gauge lines in.

Drill out the mortice in the base and cut square with a chisel, then fit the shaft into the base. The tenon which projects ¼ in. is sawn off after the shaft is glued in.

The Base.—Mark out the corners of the base as shown on both sides of the piece of wood and saw down the eight fillets $\frac{3}{16}$ in. deep with a tenon saw. Then, with a sharp ½ in. chisel, pare out to the circular lines. Clean up the base and edges.

Clean off surplus glue from the shaft and, with pencil and straight-edge, mark out the taper on front and back and plane to the pencil lines. Repeat by marking out the taper on the sides and plane off.

Now cut out and square four lengths each 5 ft. × ⅝ in. × ⅛ in. for the long fillets, A in Fig. 1. These fillets, are decorative and hide the two joins.

Cut out and square up a piece of wood for the collar—12 × ⅝ × ½ in.

Mitre or butt-join this and glue and pin it in position. When dry, clean both collar and shaft with glass-paper Nos. 1½, 1.

Then fit a brass nipple and base for a ½ in. electric lampholder. Cut two wedges and pare down the two sides of the mortice in the base as shown, then glue the shaft into the base.

Assembling.—Place the stand on the floor with two pieces of ¼ in. wood underneath each side of the projecting tenon and see that the stand is vertical. Leave it a few minutes before knocking in the wedges then turn the stand over and carefully tap them in with a hammer. Give one tap on each wedge alternately, or the shaft will be fixed out of square. Allow the work to dry, then saw off the wedges and clean up the base. Bore a ⁵⁄₁₆ in. hole from underneath in the centre of the tenon. The position of this hole is shown by the plugged up hole at the bottom of the shaft.

The four fillets should now be glued and pinned on with ⅜ in. veneer pins. Bore very fine holes with the cutting edge of a bradawl held across the grain. This may only be necessary at ends of the fillets.

Screw on domes of silence or four brass knobs, size 1 × 1 in.

Now clean up the whole stand again with Nos. 1½, 1, and 0 glass-paper. Take off the sharp edges, especially from the angles of the square shaft.

Another way to make the shaft is to square it out of one solid piece of wood and plough a ⁵⁄₁₆ in. wide by 1⅛ in. deep groove the whole way down on one side only while it is in square form. Then fill in with a ⁵⁄₁₆ × ⁵⁄₁₆ in. strip

and keep this flush with the face of the shaft, thus leaving a ⁵⁄₁₆ in. hole down the centre. Cover over the join with fillets.

If the stand is of mahogany or walnut,

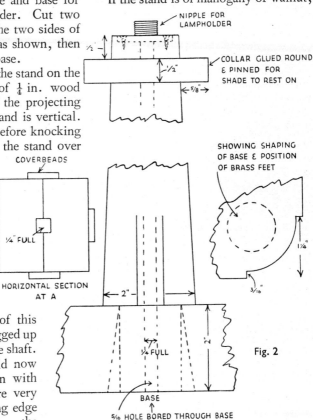

HORIZONTAL SECTION AT A

Fig. 2

it should be polished with wax polish and rubbed with a soft cloth. If in oak and a brown colour is required, it can be had by brushing it over with .880 liquid ammonia (this is best done out of doors), allowing time to dry and then glass-papering down the grain with Nos. 1½ and 0 glass-paper and polishing with brown wax polish.

Sycamore could be dyed silver grey by mixing one twopenny tube of grey dye in a half-pint of hot water. Apply with a brush, then wash off with clean water and polish with dry beeswax.

SMOKER'S COMPANION

A SMOKER'S companion should provide accommodation inside the cabinet for boxes and packets of cigarettes, tobacco pouch, tobacco jar and cigar box besides odds and ends like pipe-cleaners.

Pipes would be in a rack outside to keep the interior from getting foul.

smoker's companion of modern design. Every part of the cabinet is square, including the mouldings and handle.

The wooden handle is a pleasing feature and forms an integral part of the cabinet if it is cut out of the solid stile. Even if screwed on, it is still in sympathy with the rest.

The companion here shown may be in oak, walnut, mahogany or whatever wood is in keeping with the room. The example given is made in Austrian wainscot oak.

Cut out and square up two pieces for the sides, each 2ft. $1\frac{1}{2}$ in. $\times 5\frac{1}{2} \times \frac{1}{2}$ in. and two pieces for the top and bottom of the cabinet, 11 $\times$ $5\frac{1}{2} \times \frac{1}{2}$ in. Shape them as shown in the detail c in Fig. 2. Bore ($\frac{1}{8}$ in. twist-drill), countersink and screw these four pieces together. The top and bottom pieces are screwed in the clear, i.e., inside the sides. The bottom is screwed in position 1 ft. $6\frac{3}{4}$ in. in the clear, measuring down from inside the top.

The box now has projecting ends, but no top or back.

The Back.—Cut a piece of plywood ($\frac{5}{16}$ in. thick) to the required size for the back, square this up and pin it in position to the sides with $\frac{1}{2}$ in. veneer pins. It will be advisable to bore the sides first with a fine bradawl, holding its cutting edge across the grain and slowly rotating it.

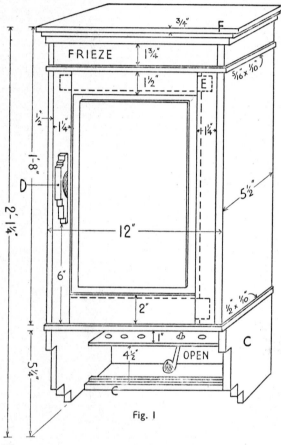

Fig. I

The rack itself must hold the pipes bowls downward to prevent nicotine running down the mouthpiece.

Up-to-date Design.—The illustration appearing in Fig. 1 shows a

Then cut out and square a piece of wood, size $11 \times 3 \times \frac{3}{8}$ in., for the top of the pipe rack and bore with a $\frac{1}{2}$ in. centre-bit equidistant holes for the pipe stems. The back edge of these holes should be 1 in. from the back edge of this piece of wood. Clean it up with Nos. $1\frac{1}{2}$, 1 glass-paper, and pin it in from the sides. It will be necessary to square pencil lines on the outer and inner surfaces of the sides to find the exact position for pinning.

Now cut out a piece $11 \times 3\frac{7}{8} \times \frac{3}{8}$ in. for the bottom shelf of the rack, square up and pin on it, just inside the front edge, a small fillet $\frac{3}{8} \times \frac{1}{4}$ in. This is to prevent the pipes from slipping. Then pin in the shelf from the sides of the cabinet.

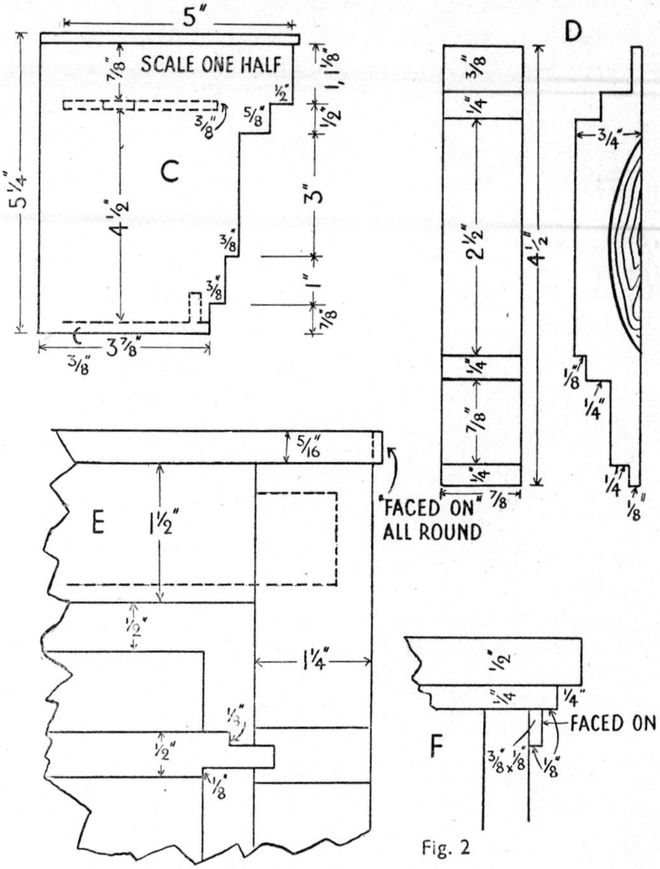

Fig. 2

Next cut and square up a piece for the frieze, size $11 \times 2\frac{7}{16} \times \frac{1}{2}$ in., and pin this in from the sides also. Cut and square a piece for the top, size $13 \times 6 \times \frac{3}{4}$ in., and rebate as shown in detail F, Fig. 2. Screw this from the inside of the top end of the box (carcase) so as to form the moulded top of the cabinet. Now glue and pin a $\frac{3}{8} \times \frac{1}{8}$ in. slip immediately under the top (faced on as shown in detail F) and pin the other mouldings on with $\frac{3}{8}$ in. veneer pins. This completes the outside of the cabinet.

Now cut three shelves $11 \times 4\frac{3}{8} \times \frac{1}{4}$ in. and fix them in convenient positions by means of $\frac{1}{4} \times \frac{1}{4}$ in. battens, pinned underneath for them to rest on so that they may be taken out and re-arranged if necessary.

The Door and Handle.—Measure the opening for the door exactly, cut out and square up the framework to sizes shown, mortice tenon and groove for panels, rebate the panel and glue up.

If the handle is to be cut from the solid stile, cut it out of a piece of stuff $1\frac{1}{4} \times 1\frac{3}{8}$ in., and, before morticing, saw down from each end, leaving a $4\frac{3}{4} \times \frac{3}{4}$ in. block standing up in position as shown in the illustration Fig. 1. Shape to design (see detail D in Fig. 2) and then frame up the panels and fit the framed door. If the handle is separate, square up and carefully saw out and chisel the little steps. Scoop pieces out of the sides, let in the handles $\frac{1}{8}$ in. deep, glue, screw from the back, countersink the screw heads below the surface and plug up with oak pegs.

Screw on two $1\frac{1}{2} \times \frac{1}{2}$ in. brass butts, the whole of the hinge thickness to be taken out of the door if preferred, and hinge the door. Take it off and put on its top and bottom edges two $\frac{5}{16}$ in. ball catches. Clean up the door with Nos. $1\frac{1}{2}$ and 1 glass-paper.

Punch all veneer pins down and fill up with beeswax or stopping.

Clean the whole of the companion. Rehinge the door.

The finishing may be done in any one of the following ways:

(1) Leave it natural colour.

(2) Light oak polish, rubbed on and off with soft cloth.

(3) Polish with wet beeswax, rubbed on and off with soft cloth.

(4) Polish with dry beeswax, rubbed on and off with canvas.

(5) Fumigating. Place the companion in an airtight box. Pour in a saucer sixpennyworth of .880 liquid ammonia, place this quickly in the box, shut down the lid, paste up any cracks in the box, leave for twelve hours and then polish as above.

For other methods, see the chapter on methods of wood finishing.

AN ADJUSTABLE ARMCHAIR

THE armchair shown in Fig. 1 and detailed in Fig. 2 has solid sides, back and seat instead of numerous dust-collecting rails.

Labour-saving.—The loose uphol-stered cushions are easily recovered without having the chair re-upholstered, and are more hygienic.

When the cushions are taken out, the inside of the chair has a smooth plain surface.

The chair may be made in oak, Aus-tralian walnut or Honduras mahogany. Plane and square up the two sides, each 1 ft. $7\frac{1}{2}$ in. $\times 2$ ft. $\times \frac{5}{8}$ in. Mahogany or Australian walnut boards may be bought 2 ft. wide. If oak is used, the wood must be joined.

Now square up the seat, size 1 ft. $7\frac{5}{8}$ in. $\times 1$ ft. 7 in. $\times \frac{5}{8}$ in. and dove-tail groove it in 11 in. from the ground, as shown. Slide the seat in from the front.

Then lap dovetail the top back rail in; size 1 ft. 8 in. bare $\times 3$ in. $\times \frac{5}{8}$ in. Knock it apart and shape the ends as shown with the bow saw and files.

Square up the two centre rails, each 1 ft. $7\frac{5}{8}$ in. $\times 4$ in. $\times \frac{5}{8}$ in. and dove-tail groove them in, in the same way as the seat. These rails are pushed in from underneath.

Dovetail Grooving.—A few hints may be useful. Set out the joint in the same way as for a housing joint, the lines being squared across first with a pencil.

Set the gauge to $\frac{5}{16}$ in. and gauge lines across the grain on the pieces that form the dovetail.

Now cut over these gauge lines deeply with a chisel then chisel down $\frac{1}{16}$ in. towards these shoulder lines.

On the pieces that are to be grooved, square lines $\frac{1}{16}$ in. inside the pencil lines and saw down $\frac{1}{16}$ in. outwards

instead of a vertical saw cut.
(See detail A in Fig. 2.)

When dovetail grooving in
the seat, it will be necessary
to use the front teeth of the
tenon saw and finish cutting
with a chisel as these grooves
do not go right through the
sides. These dove-tail grooves
resist both tension and compression.

Cut out the front rail 1 ft.
$7\frac{1}{2}$ in. $\times$ 2 in. $\times\frac{3}{4}$ in. Set it
back $\frac{1}{4}$ in. from the edge of
the seat and house this in
$\frac{1}{4}$ in. deep.

A Test Assembly.—When
gluing up, this rail must be
glued in first. Then assemble
the work to see that everything is correct. Take it apart
and clean up all the parts with

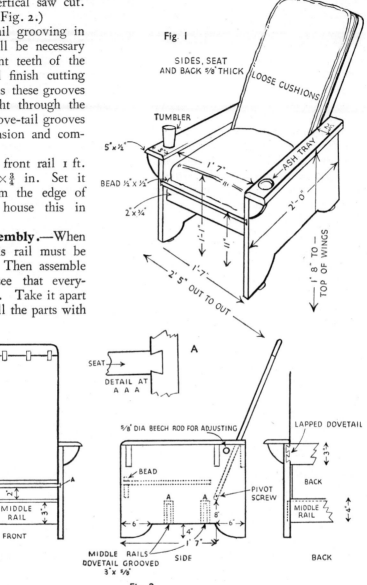

Fig. I

Fig. 2

Nos. $1\frac{1}{2}$, 1 and 0 glass-paper. Then
glue in the front rail, followed by the
seat and back rail and finally the two
centre low rails.

Put the cramps on and wipe over the
whole structure with hot water, getting
off surplus glue at the same time.
Allow twelve hours to dry. Next, cut
out two wings or arm rests each 2 ft.
$\times 5$ in. $\times\frac{1}{2}$ in. These may be tapered
to $2\frac{1}{2}$ in. wide at the back ends.

About 2 in. inside the edges of the

wings, bore a hole to fit the base of a tumbler and scoop out a circle 4 in. diameter by $\frac{1}{4}$ in. deep for the ash-tray, which is made as follows. Cut out a piece of 24 B.W.G. copper to 4 in. diameter. Strike upon it with pencil and compass a number of concentric circles $\frac{1}{4}$ in. apart. Starting from the centre, with a round-headed hammer, tap a chain of hammer marks between the lines and turn the copper over. Now and then give a few taps with a flat-headed hammer to spread the edges out flat. Round the edges with a file and emery paper.

Now glue and pin on the wings with $1\frac{1}{2}$ in. panel pins, allow time to dry and then cut out the four little brackets $\frac{5}{8}$ in. thick. Glue and pin these on and leave them to dry. Punch in the heads of the panel pins below the surface of the wings and round the latter over with a metal smoothing plane.

Measure 8 in. up from the ground and 1 ft. 7 in. from the front and bore two holes to take the pivot screws. Then bore the $\frac{5}{8}$ in. holes to take the ends of the adjuster rod. This rod is made of beech and turned or otherwise formed to $\frac{5}{8}$ in. diameter, with a button on one end. The length of the rod is 1 ft. 10 in.

The Back Panel.—Make the back out of one panel cramped at each end. Square up the panel to 2 ft. 6 in. × 1 ft. 7 in. bare × $\frac{5}{8}$ in. Cut two pieces each 1 ft. 7 in. × 2 in. × $\frac{5}{8}$ in. and cramp them on the ends.

Square pencil lines across the edges of the panel and the edges of the 2 in.

pieces about 6 in. apart and gauge a centre line. Where the lines cross will be the centres for boring, which is done with a $\frac{1}{4}$ in. twist-drill. Bore the holes $\frac{3}{4}$ in. deep and glue $\frac{1}{4}$ in. dowels in the panel first, sawing and bevelling them off as you go. (Note: They should project $\frac{5}{8}$ in. only, to allow room for glue which becomes imprisoned in the bottom of the holes.)

Knock on the 2 in. ends, cramp up and allow twelve hours for the glue to dry.

Then clean and glass-paper the panel and fit it in between the sides so that it just clears them.

Before pivoting the back, make the little bead $\frac{3}{4} \times \frac{1}{2}$ in. that is pinned on the front edge of the seat to stop the cushion from slipping forward. Pin this on and finish off.

Next punch in and fill up all the nail holes with stopping coloured to the finish of the armchair, and put on domes of silence.

Give the whole work a final glass-papering and polish before you pivot in the back.

If the wood is Australian walnut, which is a violet-brown colour, just rub it with dry beeswax and canvas.

If mahogany is used go over it with hot oxalic acid, wash off and put on hot grey dye and polish as before. This eliminates the unpleasant red colour of the wood.

If made of oak, it will be best just to polish it with light oak polish and rub up with canvas (hessian).

TWO EASILY CONSTRUCTED FOOT STOOLS

Footstools may be used as low tables, as fireside seats, and as foot rests.

Instructions are given here for making two low stools, one to harmonise with weathered oak furniture and the other with dark oak. The dark stool is dealt with first, in Fig. 1.

should be done with a marking gauge and the waste removed with a sharp chisel and mallet. Then mould the edges of the top of the stool as shown in the sketch, or round them if preferred.

Prepare the end pieces by sawing to length and planing to width, cutting the lower ends and sides to shape with pad saw and spokeshave. Cut a mortice in each end member for accommodating the ends of the $2 \times \frac{7}{8}$ in. rail. The bottom edge of the mortice should be 5 in. from the foot. Use a sharp twist bit for taking out the majority of the waste from the mortices and finish them squarely with a chisel.

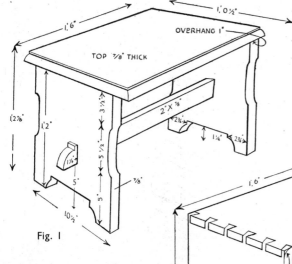

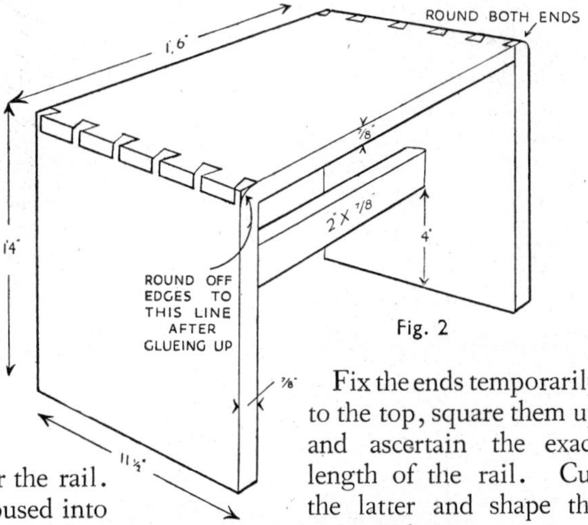

Fig. I

Fig. 2

First Steps.—Cut and square up the following pieces of Austrian wainscot oak: One piece, 1 ft. 6 in. × 1 ft. $\frac{1}{2}$ in. × $\frac{7}{8}$ in., for the top; two pieces, 1 ft. $2\frac{1}{2}$ in. × $10\frac{1}{2}$ in. × $\frac{7}{8}$ in., for the ends; one piece, 1 ft. $6\frac{1}{2}$ in. × 2 in. × $\frac{7}{8}$ in., for the rail.

As the two ends are to be housed into the top of the stool, place the top piece bottom face upwards on the bench and mark two grooves each $10\frac{1}{2}$ in. long × $\frac{7}{8}$ in. wide and $\frac{1}{2}$ in. deep, 1 in. from the ends, as the top of the stool overhangs 1 in. all round. The marking

Fix the ends temporarily to the top, square them up and ascertain the exact length of the rail. Cut the latter and shape the ends as shown.

Joining and Gluing.—With an iron plane, clean up each piece, taking care not to plane off any wood where it fits into another piece. Then glue the stool together, testing it each way with a try square. Wash it quickly with hot water, take off all surplus glue and wipe the stool dry.

Leave for twelve hours to dry.

Then smooth in the direction of the grain, first with No. 2 followed by $1\frac{1}{2}$, 1 glass-paper, to remove all sharp edges.

Mix vandyke brown powder with a small quantity of .880 spirits of ammonia, making a paste as in making cocoa, and then dilute it with water until the required colour is obtained. Stain the stool with this mixture.

Again leave the stool to dry, then rub it with coarse canvas (hessian) and polish with beeswax and turpentine.

Weathered Oak Stool.—To construct the stool shown at Fig. 2, plane and square up the following pieces of Austrian wainscot oak: One piece, 1 ft. 6 in. $\times$ $11\frac{1}{2}$ in. $\times$ $\frac{7}{8}$ in., for the top ; two pieces, 1 ft. 4 in. $\times$ $11\frac{1}{2}$ in. $\times$ $\frac{7}{8}$ in., for the ends; one piece, 1 ft. 5 in. $\times$ 2 in. $\times$ $\frac{7}{8}$ in., for the rail.

With a marking gauge set to $\frac{7}{8}$ in., gauge a faint line all round both ends of the top member and all round one end of each of the end pieces. The sockets of the dovetails are on the top of the stool and the pins on the ends. Therefore, it is necessary carefully to mark out and saw, with a small dovetail saw, down the sockets on the top first, leaving the pencil lines in.

Place the top on the two ends, one at a time, and mark the positions of the pins. Saw them down and chisel the waste out between the pins so as to leave the pins sticking up.

Chisel out the sockets on the top and assemble the stool to see that all fits well.

Take the stool apart, mark out the position of the rail on each end, and chisel out the slot to a depth of $\frac{1}{2}$ in.,

leaving the marked lines in to ensure a tight fit.

Now fit the rail into the ends. This is best done by placing the stool top upside down on the bench.

Take the stool to pieces again and glass-paper the whole of it with fine Nos. 2, $1\frac{1}{2}$, 1 and 0 glass-paper, avoiding the parts that actually fit into other pieces.

Now glue the parts together and test with a try square to ensure that the ends are square with the top. Wash the stool with hot water and wipe off the glue. Leave it for twelve hours to dry. Next, round off the edges at the ends as indicated in the drawing and again glass-paper the stool, using fine 2 glass-paper, taking care to take off sharp edges. Follow with the other grades of glass-paper. Finally, rub the stool with coarse canvas.

Finishing.—Everything is now ready for weathering and polishing. Purchase a sixpenny tin of light oak polish. This is in the form of a white paste and, if liberally applied across the grain, it leaves little specks of white in the pores of the grain. If these flecks are not required, the polish may be brushed out with a stiff brush and the wood polished afterwards with a cloth.

The white flecks give, however, a pleasing appearance. The polish should be liberally applied with a soft cloth. Start on the underneath of the stool and pass to the outsides of the ends and top, polishing with a piece of old washed calico as you go.

This will give a lasting polish, which will neither hide the beauty of the grain nor alter the colour.

These stools can be made of American black walnut or mahogany and either would look equally well. It is not advisable to make them of soft woods as they generally come in for rough usage.

HOME-MADE FRAMES FOR MIRRORS

THERE are many ways of mounting or framing a mirror. The newest vogue is to mount the glass on a laminated board, showing an inch or two of margin all round, which forms a setting. These margins are coloured to harmonise with the room.

The frame illustrated in Fig. 1 is made by halving the wood together. First square up the wood, oak, walnut or mahogany, to the following sizes.

Now measure $1\frac{1}{2}$ in. from the ends of the long pieces and square lines across the faces and down the edges. Gauge as before, chisel out the slots from the back of the short pieces and saw away the face halves of the long pieces.

Fit the frame together, take apart and with a small dovetail saw cut out and clean up the little steps as shown in Fig. 2.

Clean up the frame with Nos. $1\frac{1}{2}$ and

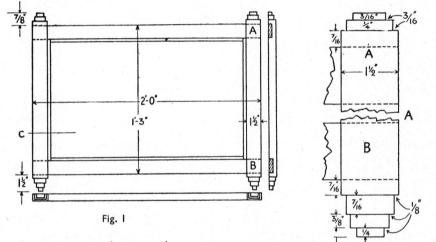

Fig. 1

Two pieces for the top and base, each 2 ft. $\times 1\frac{1}{2}$ in. $\times \frac{3}{4}$ in.; two pieces for the sides, each 1 ft. $5\frac{3}{8}$ in. $\times 1\frac{1}{2}$ in. $\times \frac{3}{4}$ in. Mark these " face side " and " face edge " and remember that the face edges are the inside edges.

Marking Chisel Lines.—On the backs of the two short pieces, square cross chisel lines at $1\frac{1}{2}$ in. from the bottom ends, then $1\frac{1}{2}$ in. again and from the top ends $\frac{7}{8}$ in. and $1\frac{1}{2}$ in. Carry these lines down the edges on both sides and gauge between the lines to half the thickness of the wood, i.e., $\frac{3}{8}$ in.

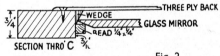

Fig. 2

1 glass-paper and glue it up, allow twelve hours to dry and then re-glass-paper it smooth.

Make four little $\frac{1}{4} \times \frac{1}{4}$ in. slips of wood and pin them in $\frac{3}{16}$ in. from the face sides to form the rebate, and prepare twenty-four little wedges size $\frac{3}{8}$ in. bare $\times \frac{1}{4} \times \frac{1}{2}$ in.

Square up the three-ply back, stain and polish the frame to the required colour, as explained in the chapter on modern methods of wood finishing.

Purchase a mirror $\frac{1}{16}$ in. less in size all round than the rebate measurement.

Turn the frame face down, put in the glass and, gluing on the outsides only

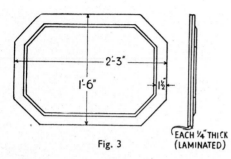

Fig. 3

EACH ¼″ THICK (LAMINATED)

of the little wedges, press them in and allow twelve hours to dry. Details of fixing the wedges are shown at c in Fig. 2.

Then screw on a three-ply back and suitable brass plates for fixing to the wall.

Choosing Wood.—Before starting to make the back panels for the mirrors shown in Figs. 3 and 4, consider the finished colour of the wood. If they are to be silvered or black, the best wood is mahogany. If the wood is to be left unstained, oak, Australian or American walnut will be suitable.

To make the mirror illustrated in Fig. 3, square up two panels, one 2 ft. 3 in. × 1 ft. 6 in. × ¼ in. for the front and one 1 ft. 6 in. × 2 ft. 3 in. × ¼ in. for the back.

The grain of these pieces go different ways and the two pieces are glued together to keep the panel from warping.

To do this, have ready a pot of hot, thin, clean glue and, working in a warm room, place the 1 ft. 6 in. × 2 ft. 3 in. piece of wood on an old table or bench, secure it by putting in some ½ in. veneer pins close to but outside the edges of the panel, knock these pins in so that they

stand up $\frac{3}{16}$ in. only from the table top.

Correct Gluing.—Rapidly spread the glue on the panel and on the underside of the top 2 ft. 3 in. × 1 ft. 6 in. panel. Put the top panel on and with a circular motion rub round and round,

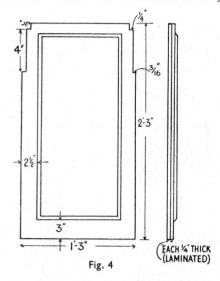

Fig. 4

EACH ¼″ THICK (LAMINATED)

so as to work out the glue. Wipe the face of the top panel with hot water to keep it from kicking up.

Then put in some ⅜ in. veneer pins. Knock them where they will not show. Take care pins are not in the way of the lines when sawing off the corners.

Put a heavy box on the panel to keep it flat, or cramp down with a piece of 1 in. stuff placed on top of it, then allow twenty-four hours to dry.

Mark out the corners and carefully saw them off with a dovetail saw. File and glass-paper the edges smooth with fine Nos. 2 and 1½ glass-paper, and clean up the front.

If the margin is to be silvered, purchase some liquid silver paint (not aluminium), put this on in the direction of the grain about 2 in. wide all round. Do not fill up before putting on the silver as the grain itself gives a pleasant effect.

The same applies if you stain with ebony or any other stain. Let the grain show up. If the wood is to be left unstained, polish it with light oak polish, which is put on and rubbed off with a soft cloth.

Allow the panel to stand for a week to become quite dry before fixing the mirror. There are several ways of doing the latter.

You can have eight ⅛ in. holes bored through the glass as shown and screw it on with tiny chromium-plated screws. Or it may be fixed by means of chromium-plated clips.

The mirror panel pictured in Fig. 4 can be made in the same way except that, instead of cutting off the corners, measure 4 in. down from the top and gauge a line ³⁄₁₆ in. in from the edges and saw this out first. Then measure down from the top ½ in. and ¼ in. from the edges and saw out the top corners. Then clean up and polish as before.

TEA TRAY AND COFFEE TRAY

THE trays shown in Figs. 1 and 2 have the edges and corners rounded and the inner corners reinforced and hollowed out so that they may be easily cleaned.

Lay out the cups, saucers and jugs.

fore to make the trays of American walnut or oak stained brown.

The Tea Tray.—To make a tray of the size shown in Fig. 1 square up two pieces of wood each 1 ft. 10 in × 1½ in. × ⅜ in.

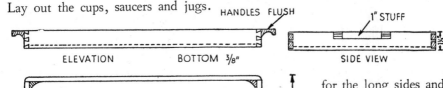

ELEVATION   BOTTOM ⅜″   SIDE VIEW

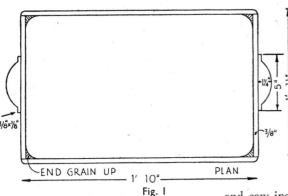

END GRAIN UP   1′ 10″   PLAN

Fig. 1

for the long sides and two pieces each 1 ft. ¾ in. × 1½ in. × ⅜ in. for the short sides or ends.

Set the marking gauge to ⅜ in. and gauge mark round the ends of all four pieces. Then set out the sockets of the dovetails on the long pieces and saw inside the lines with a 6 in. tenon saw.

Turn the saucers upside down and draw a circle round them, repeating with the coffee pot or tea pot and milk jug. The required sizes can thus be ascertained.

The colour of the wood should be as near as possible to unavoidable tea and coffee stains. It will be best there-

Place the long ends one by one over the short ends, which should be fixed in the vice. Place the tenon saw in the cuts and pull it towards you with the point of the saw, so as to get a scratched replica of the saw cuts on the short pieces. Square lines down the edges of these and saw down the outside lines.

Chisel out the necessary parts on all four pieces, working half from the back and half from the front.

Fit this framework together, glue the joints, test for squareness and leave for twelve hours to dry.

Meanwhile, cut out and square the the exact height of the rim, i.e., $1\frac{1}{8}$ in., and square round a line with pencil.

Saw down one of the diagonals, then saw off to the $1\frac{1}{8}$ in. line—thus you have two triangular pieces. Repeat the process until you have four triangular pieces.

With hot glue, press them securely in

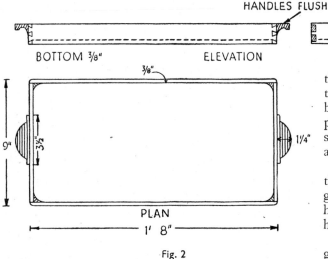

HANDLES FLUSH   1" STUFF

BOTTOM ⅜"   ELEVATION   SIDE VIEW

9"   3½"   ⅜"   1¼"

PLAN

1' 8"

Fig. 2

the four corners of the tray. These corners can be held in until dry by putting tight diagonal strips of 1×1 in. stuff across the tray.

When dry pare down these corners with a gouge until they are hollow and die the hollows into the sides. This is easy as the grain is vertical. Clean the corners carefully with a file and glass-paper, Nos. 2, $1\frac{1}{2}$ and 1, and level off the tops. Cut and square up the two handles $5 \times 1\frac{1}{4} \times 1$ in.

bottom of the tray to the exact inside measurement of the frame.

Fit in the bottom of the tray and secure it by veneer pins tapped in from the outside.

Filling Nail Holes.—Punch the veneer pins below the surface and fill in with brown stopping. This can be made of vandyke brown powder and a small piece of resin about the size of a marble. Drop this mixture in the holes while it is hot, and glass-paper it off smooth.

Now cut out the four reinforcing corners as follows:

Square up a piece of wood size $4 \times 1 \times 1$ in. Draw in pencil, diagonal lines at one end. Place the wood upright on a corner of the tray to get

The Handles.—Make the two handles out of one piece of wood size $10 \times 1\frac{1}{2} \times 1$ in. this way: mark the profiles of the handles on both edges of the wood and saw down the necessary lines across the grain to a depth of 1 in. only. Saw out the two ends and chisel down the centre groove ($1\frac{1}{16} \times 1$ in. deep). Then with a 1 in. chisel round off the handles and smooth them with file and glass-paper.

Turn the shaped piece of wood over in the vice and plane off the back to reduce it to $1\frac{1}{4}$ in., as shown. The extra $\frac{1}{4}$ in. was for fixing in the vice.

Now cut the two handles in halves and clean up the end grain. Next find the centres of the ends of the tray and glue and screw on the handles from inside, taking care to countersink and fill the screwheads with stopping. Hollow out the handles as shown.

Fix the tray in the vice and round off the corners with file and glass-paper. Also round over all the other edges, including the top, bottom and sides, so that the tray is smooth to handle.

If the tray is of American walnut, finish by rubbing with a soft cloth moistened with raw linseed oil and turpentine in equal parts. This will prevent the tea leaving marks upon it.

The Coffee Tray.—To make the tray shown in Fig. 2 proceed in the same way. The only difference is size.

A FLAT TOP PORTABLE DESK

THE novel feature about the writing desk in the accompanying illustration in Fig. 1 is that the top is removable from the two-drawer sections which form separate cabinets. This enables the desk to be taken apart when not required and the cabinets placed in a convenient recess.

The main dimensions are as follows : The top is 4 ft. long × 1 ft. 6 in. wide and the overall height 2 ft. 5 in., minus the thickness of the plywood. The width of the drawer sections is 1 ft. 3 in.

The top is constructed of plain boards $\frac{1}{2}$ in. thick glued together to obtain the width. The top surface of these boards is covered with thin plywood faced with Oregon pine.

Fig. I

To keep the drawer sections at the proper distance apart, the underside of the top is provided with a $\frac{1}{2}$ in. square fillet fixed all round near the edge and cross fillets at suitable positions as shown in Fig. 4, thus forming an inverted tray with two divisions.

Each drawer section or cabinet has four drawers and consists of two plywood panelled sides and back, a top and bottom of the same material, and is built up from a framework as shown in detail in Figs. 2 and 3 from which dimensions can be taken.

Beginning Construction.—To construct the desk, start with the drawer sections. Plane up sufficient $1\frac{3}{4} \times \frac{7}{8}$ in. yellow deal batten for the side panel frames and mark out the position for the dowel pins which form the joints. Then bore the holes for the dowels and plough a groove $\frac{1}{4}$ in. deep and $\frac{3}{16}$ in. wide in the centre of the inner edges to take the panels. Mark and cut the panels to size, not forgetting to add an extra amount to both dimensions for fitting into the grooves.

Next, assemble and glue each panel unit, cramp each one separately and

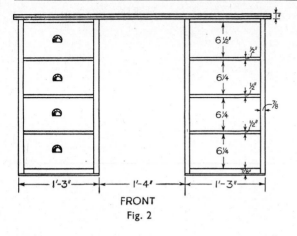

FRONT

Fig. 2

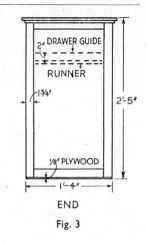

END

Fig. 3

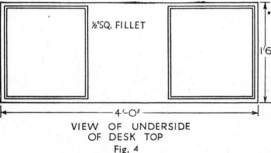

VIEW OF UNDERSIDE
OF DESK TOP

Fig. 4

allow sufficient time for the glue to dry.

Now mark on the front edges of the four panelled frames the positions of the drawer supporting rails. The latter are $1\frac{1}{4}$ in. wide $\times \frac{1}{2}$ in. thick and are tenoned into mortices cut in the inner side faces of the frames. Having cut the mortices, glue 2 in. wood strips of sufficient thickness to form the sides of the drawer runners and fix the runners themselves to the inner side faces of the frames and the side strips by means of countersunk-headed iron screws.

Prepare the top and bottom cross rails. These are of the same width and thickness as the panel frames and are tenoned into open mortices in the top and bottom edges of the frames. Glue in the front drawer supporting rails and the cross rails and cover the tops and bottoms with $\frac{3}{16}$ in. plywood. The top

pieces should be of the same material as that of the panels, but the bottom sheets can be of a cheaper quality as they are not seen.

The back panels are glued to $\frac{3}{8}$ in. square section fillets fastened $\frac{1}{2}$ in. from the outside edges of the frame members and kept in position by means of $\frac{3}{8} \times \frac{1}{8}$ in. bead fixed with thin, lost-headed nails.

This completes the carcase of the drawer section.

The next procedure is to make the drawers. They are all of the same type and of simple construction.

Preparing the Top.—It remains to make the top. Plane up the edges of the boards and glue them together, forming glued butt-joints. Cramp them together and allow the glue to dry. Then trim up the edges, making sure that all is square; round off the corners either with a chisel or spokeshave to give a neat appearance.

Cut the plywood top slightly larger than the finished size of the top foundation board and then, with plenty of hot thin glue applied to the surface of the foundation board and the underside of the plywood, fix the sheet in position and reinforce with a few $\frac{3}{4}$ in. panel pins, partially driven in here and there. This member should be put on a perfectly flat surface, heavily weighted and allowed to dry. The panel pins are withdrawn and the edges of the plywood trimmed up flush with the edges of the underpart. If the laminated edges of the plywood are not thought objectionable, they can remain in their natural state; but, if desired, they may be hidden by fixing strips of $\frac{1}{8}$ in. thick yellow deal to cover the edges of the plywood and the bottom board. The strips should be glued and pinned.

Before applying any finishing medium it is wise to place the drawers in position to see whether they are an easy fit. If at all tight, they should be eased with a sharp plane where necessary.

A good finish can be obtained by first sandpapering down the parts and giving the whole a coat of size which must be allowed to dry before applying an oil stain of the desired colour. This also must be allowed to dry, and a coat of french polish applied with a camel-hair mop will give an excellent result.

This piece of furniture is complete when suitable handles have been fitted to the drawers and furniture gliders fixed at the eight corners of the undersides of the drawer sections. Oxidized copper handles are cheap and effective, while the furniture gliders are simply dome-shaped pieces of plated metal having projections which are hammered into the wood.

Where a desk with a single set of drawers is preferred, the same procedure could be followed as already explained, but omitting one of the sections. In place of the section, a single frame panel could be used as a support provided it is hinged to the top member and held in position by a folding strut.

NEEDLEWORK TABLE

THE needlework table illustrated in the drawings, Figs. 1, 2 and 3 has several features not usually incorporated in a ready-made fitment which, more often than not, consists of nothing more than a simple box supported on four legs.

As will be seen from the illustrations, the top is not hinged in the customary way at the back, but is divided into two sections which slide along to allow access to a partitioned tray which lies immediately below. The front is hinged to the top of the middle rail and drops down to a horizontal position thus forming a shelf or support at low level which is easy to reach when the user is sitting down. The provision of a drawer also adds usefulness to the fitment.

Choosing the Wood.—With regard to the kind of wood to use for its construction much depends on how much the builder is prepared to spend. Where cost is the primary consideration, the framework could be of good yellow deal and the panels and the top made from one of the common kinds of plywood, which could be stained and waxed when completed to give it a finish. On the other hand there are those who believe that it is a pity to spoil the ship for a ha'porth of tar, in which case oak, mahogany or walnut framework and plywood faced with any of these beautiful woods for the panels, would give dignity of appearance. Those parts which do not show could be made of cheaper wood.

The following is a list of the finished sizes of the main parts:

Description	No.	Sizes in inches	Material
Legs	4	24 × $1\frac{1}{4}$ × $1\frac{1}{4}$	Oak.
Front Rails	3	$17\frac{1}{2}$ × $1\frac{1}{2}$ × $\frac{3}{4}$	,,
Back Rails	2	$17\frac{1}{2}$ × $1\frac{1}{2}$ × $\frac{3}{4}$	,,
Side Rails	4	$11\frac{1}{2}$ × $1\frac{1}{2}$ × $\frac{3}{4}$	,,
Top Runners ..	2	20 × $1\frac{3}{8}$ × $\frac{3}{8}$	,,
Table-top Pieces ..	2	11 × 16 × $\frac{1}{2}$	Oak-faced plywood.
Front	1	$17\frac{1}{2}$ × $10\frac{1}{2}$ × $\frac{1}{2}$	,, ,, ,,
Side Panels	2	$16\frac{1}{2}$ × 12 × $\frac{1}{4}$	,, ,, ,,
Back Panel	1	18 × $16\frac{1}{2}$ × $\frac{1}{4}$	,, ,, ,,
Bottom	1	$18\frac{1}{2}$ × $12\frac{1}{2}$ × $\frac{1}{4}$	Birch-faced plywood.
Drawer Front	1	$17\frac{1}{2}$ × 4 × $\frac{3}{4}$	Oak.
Drawer Back	1	$16\frac{1}{2}$ × $3\frac{7}{16}$ × $\frac{3}{4}$	Deal.
Drawer Sides	2	$11\frac{3}{4}$ × 4 × $\frac{1}{2}$	,,
Drawer Bottom	1	$11\frac{3}{4}$ × $16\frac{3}{4}$ × $\frac{3}{16}$	Birch-faced plywood.
Tray Sides	2	$17\frac{1}{2}$ × 3 × $\frac{3}{8}$	Deal.
Tray Ends	2	$12\frac{1}{2}$ × 3 × $\frac{3}{8}$	,,
Tray Bottom	1	$17\frac{1}{2}$ × $12\frac{1}{2}$ × $\frac{3}{16}$	Birch-faced plywood.

To the above list must be added about 7 ft. each of $\frac{3}{8}$ in. square and $\frac{7}{8} \times \frac{1}{4}$ in. deal for forming the groove under the divided table top, and the same quantity of $1\frac{1}{8} \times \frac{1}{8}$ in. oak strip for covering these edges and those of the plywood; two pieces of deal $12\frac{1}{2}$ in. long, 3 in. wide and $\frac{1}{2}$ in. thick and two similar pieces 1 in. wide with which to form the drawer runners; a foot of 1 in. square oak for shaping the handles, about 6 ft. of $\frac{3}{8} \times \frac{3}{8}$ in. deal upon which to fasten the bottom and sufficient $\frac{1}{4}$ in. diameter dowel-rod to make the pins which form the joints.

A supply of glue, $\frac{1}{2}$ in. panel pins, screws, a pair of brass butt-hinges, and two adjustable stays for keeping the front in position when open, and two ball fasteners for keeping it shut complete the list.

Start with the legs. Mark them to length and then saw them to size. If prepared stuff has been obtained for the framework, there will be no necessity to plane it, but if sawn material is to be used it must be planed to the dimensions given in Figs. 1 and 2.

Next mark out, with the aid of a try square, rule and pencil, on the front pair, the positions where the back and front rails join the legs. These will come on the inner and back faces of the legs. These must be true to length and the ends square, otherwise the joints will be imperfect and the structure out of true when finished.

It will be found better to clamp the three front ones and the back pair together for marking purposes, as this method is more conducive to accuracy than marking each individual rail. The same applies to the side rails.

Boring for Dowels.—The next procedure consists of marking the positions and boring the holes for the dowel-pins which form the joints. Details of such a joint are shown in Fig. 4. This operation also calls for careful workmanship as the holes in the legs must be bored to line up with those in the rails.

Having completed the boring, which is perhaps the most difficult part of the job, plough the grooves in the legs into which the edges of the panels fit. These will come in the back faces only of the

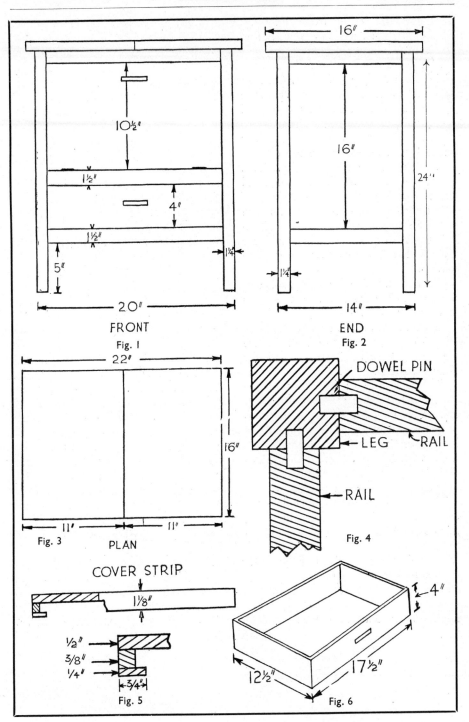

10½"

1½"

4"

1½"

5"

1¼"

20"

FRONT

Fig. 1

16"

16"

24"

1¼"

14"

END

Fig. 2

22"

16"

11'

11"

Fig. 3

PLAN

DOWEL PIN

LEG

RAIL

RAIL

Fig. 4

COVER STRIP

1⅛"

½"

3/8"

¼"

3/4"

Fig. 5

4"

12½"

17½"

Fig. 6

front pair and in the front and inner faces of the back pair, as viewed from the front.

As the grooves require to be stopped $1\frac{1}{4}$ in. from the top and $6\frac{1}{4}$ in. from the bottom, as much waste as possible should be removed by the plough and the remainder taken out with a sharp chisel. The rails are grooved their entire length on either the top or bottom faces, as the case may be. This done, the panels should be marked and squarely cut.

Gluing.—Cramp both frames and test for squareness before finally tightening up. Put these aside in a dry place for about a day to allow the glue to harden.

Then fit and glue the side panels and the rails to the front and back portions and leave to dry.

In the meantime the drawer, tray and sliding tops can be put in hand. These are straightforward jobs and call for little comment.

The back face of the front of the drawer is rebated at the ends to a depth and width of $\frac{1}{2}$ in. to house the ends of the side members. These latter pieces have a groove $\frac{3}{16}$ in. wide and $\frac{1}{8}$ in. deep, $\frac{3}{8}$ in. from the bottom edges, into which the plywood bottom fits. Details of the drawer are seen in Fig. 6.

The tray is made by mitreing the corners of the sides and ends, bradding them together and fixing the bottom so that its edges are flush with the sides. The number and positions of the partitions must be left to the maker's discretion. In any case, either thin slats of wood or plywood may be used and the sides and ends of the tray should be slightly recessed to house them.

Reference to the drawing at Fig. 5 will show the construction of the two sliding tops and the method of forming the groove.

The carcase is yet to be completed. Fix the two pieces of $\frac{3}{8}$ in. thick strips by which the top members are kept in position, using countersunk-headed screws for the purpose. Then fix the sides of the drawer runners by gluing and pinning the pieces to the inner faces of the end panels and complete this part of the work by fixing the pieces upon which the drawer runs, keeping the top faces level with the top edges of the side rails.

All that remains to be done as far as the constructional work is concerned is to glue and pin suitable lengths of $\frac{3}{8}$ in. square-section wood round the inner faces of the panels to form a fixing for the bottom; pin the bottom to the projections; hinge and fit the stays and the ball fasteners to the front; make and fit the handles, which are wedge-shaped and fixed by screws driven in from the inner face of the front and drawer front respectively; fix the tray by driving screws through the front and back members into the front and back rails; and, finally, slide the tops into position and glue a small piece of wood at a distance of about 3 in. from the closing edges to prevent them from coming out when opening.

The structure should then be sandpapered thoroughly, the interior stained and the exterior finished according to taste. Wax polish is suggested as this is simple to apply and very effective.

HAT AND COAT RACK

THE easily-constructed hat and coat rack, suitable for a small cloak room, shown in Fig. 1, makes an excellent present.

To construct this piece of furniture, details of which are illustrated in Fig. 2, obtain two 2 ft. 6 in., two 2 ft. and two 1 ft. 6 in. lengths of $\frac{3}{4} \times 2$ in. prepared oak (planed). This material is a stock size and may be obtained at most dealers. It costs about $4\frac{1}{2}$d. per foot. At the same time, purchase a piece of $\frac{3}{8}$ in. oak-faced plywood 15 in. long and 5 in. wide, two $\frac{3}{8}$ in. $\times$ 2 ft. long dowel-rods, two back plates, 4 ft. $\frac{1}{4}$ in. quarter-round moulding and a mirror 16$\times$8 in. (stock size) costing 2s. 3d., half a dozen double clothes-hooks finished in steel bronze or oxidized copper, if the fitment is to be stained dark, or chromium-plated ones if it is to be of a light colour, with round-headed screws for fixing. All parts are fitted together by means of glued dowel-joints which not only form a good substitute for mortices and tenons but have the advantage of being easy to make.

Dowelled Joints.—Cut the pieces to length and mark out the ornamental ends. It is advisable to make a cardboard template of the design and trace round the outline with a pencil. A pad saw will cut out the design.

The next procedure is to bore holes for the dowel-pins. To save time and labour, the top and bottom horizontal members can be marked out at the same time, as the centres of the dowel-holes

come in the same relative positions. This operation is best done by clamping the two pieces together and then placing them between the jaws of the vice. The same thing applies to the end and central pieces.

Keep the brace vertical while boring the holes, or the parts will not lie flush and square when they are assembled. The holes should be bored $\frac{1}{4}$ in. deep.

Fig. I

Having completed the boring, cut sixteen dowel-pins, each $1\frac{1}{2}$ in. long, and make a shallow channel along them as shown in Fig. 3. A tenon saw may be used for this. The channel allows air to escape from the holes during the gluing process.

Then with really hot glue at hand fix the pins and parts together. Do not use too much glue. The frame should now be cramped to ensure satisfactory joints. This can be done by laying the frame flat on the bench top and using pieces of batten and wedges as indicated in the diagram, Fig. 4, unless of course you possess joiner's cramps. The frame should be left in the cramps for about twenty-four hours for the glue to harden.

In the meantime the two ornamental fretted pieces can be put in hand and cut with a fretsaw.

After removing the cramps, the mould-

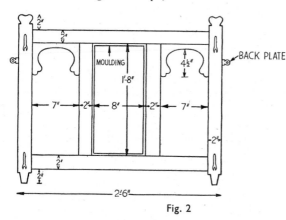

Fig. 2

ing for supporting the mirror can be cut to size and fixed in position with tube glue or panel pins or both.

The ornamental pieces can now be fitted with tube glue and allowed to dry.

Run a finely-set plane over the wide surface and take off one or two shavings unless you have made such accurate

joints that the surfaces are all flush.

Fitting Mirror and Pegs.—After having glass-papered the work, apply a light or dark oak stain to suit, and when dry, a good wax polish properly applied will impart an excellent finish.

The final step is to fit the mirror and

coat pegs. The mirror is fitted against the moulding, a thin piece of plywood or card-board fitted at the back and held in position by means of sprigs, and finally covered with stout brown paper, glued to the back of the frame, to exclude dust.

UMBRELLA STAND

THE umbrella stand illustrated in Fig. 1 is of the corner type, measures 2 ft. 6 in. high with sides 12 in. long and is constructed of oak.

Details of construction are shown in Fig. 2. Obtain three lengths of 1 in. square oak 2 ft. 9 in. long for the uprights, four 1 ft. lengths of the same material for the side rails and two pieces of oak 1 ft. 6 in. long × 5 in. wide and 1 in. thick from which to cut the curved front rails. A piece of $\frac{1}{4}$ in. plywood will also be needed to

support the zinc tray, which is 1 in. deep.

Cut the uprights to length and mark them out for the mortices into which the tenoned ends of the side rails fit. The ends of the curved front rails are not tenoned, but the joints with the uprights are formed with dowel-pins. The position of these should also be marked.

The mortices are $\frac{3}{4}$ in. long, $\frac{3}{8}$ in. wide and $\frac{3}{8}$ in. deep as shown at A in Fig. 2, while the tenons at the ends of the side rails are of the same dimensions.

Fig. I

so that they are square, and mark and drill the holes for the dowel-pins.

The parts may now be assembled. Use a good liquid glue and fasten the parts together by applying a film to all joints. Bind stout string round the fitment to cramp the parts together, but do not let the cord touch the bare wood or the corners will, in all probability, be marred. To prevent this, pieces of thick cardboard should be placed between the string and wood. When the glue is dry, shape a piece of ¼ in.

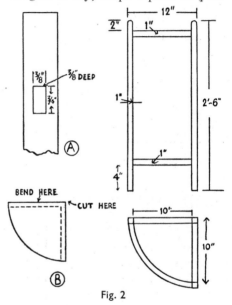

Fig. 2

Making Curved Rails.—To make the front curved rails, two paper patterns will be needed. To make the pattern, procure a sheet of thin paper about 14 in. square and on it draw two lines at right-angles to each other. From the corner where the two lines meet, mark a distance 12 in. and 11 in. respectively on one line and with a pair of compasses set at the 12 in. mark, join the two lines. The arc thus struck represents the outer edge of the rail. Repeat the process with the compass set at the 11 in. mark and join the lines as before. This curve is the outline of the inner edge of the front rail. Cut round the outlines with a pair of scissors and paste the paper on the piece of wood, and repeat the process with the other piece.

When the paste is dry, fix the wood between the jaws of the vice and cut near the outline with a pad saw and finish the rail with a spokeshave, taking care to work in the direction of the grain.

Cut the waste off the ends of the rails

plywood and fix it with brass screws to the underside of the bottom rail thus forming a shallow tray into which the zinc container fits.

Cutting and Soldering Zinc.—The zinc drip-tray is made a ½ in. smaller than the recess at the lower rails. To make the tray get a piece of zinc, not too thick, 10½ in. square and mark and cut it to the shape shown at B in Fig. 2, and bend up the two straight sides to form right-angles. This is best done by placing the zinc on the edge of a rectangular block of wood and gently tapping the zinc at the bend. A strip of the same material will be required for forming the curved front of the tray. When this has been cut the soldering materials can be got ready for fastening the joints and fixing the front strip.

In soldering zinc, ordinary spirits of salts is used as a flux; but, as this attacks zinc and eats it away, it is of the utmost importance that the receptacle should be thoroughly washed in water after soldering, to get rid of surplus flux.

Start by soldering the right-angled corner joint and then the front, putting a blob of solder here and there where two edges meet to tack the strip in place, and then running the hot soldering bit along the seam, finally soldering the joints.

As the zinc tray will look unsightly if left in its natural state, it is advisable to give it a couple of coats of paint, either green or brown, to suit the colour of the finished stand.

The completed stand may be stained to the desired depth of colour and varnished, or it may be simply varnished. A pleasing finish can be obtained by applying a few spots of linseed oil to a soft rag and then polishing the surface. If varnish is used, be sure to use a good oil varnish as spirit varnish shows the slightest scratch.

SIMPLE CLOCK CASES

THE solid oak case illustrated in Fig. 1 shows how effectively a cheap alarm clock can be cased. This clock

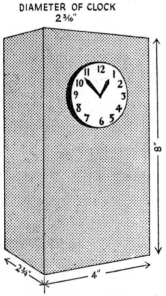

DIAMETER OF CLOCK
2 ³⁄₁₆"

8"

2¾"

4"

Fig. 1

was of $2\frac{3}{16}$ in. diameter and the alarm and feet were taken off.

Measure the exact diameter of the

clock for which you intend to make a case, as it may be necessary to alter the size of the block given here.

Square up a piece of oak, size $8 \times 4 \times 2\frac{3}{4}$ in.

Measure down from the top edge of the block $2\frac{1}{2}$ in. This will give the centre from which a circle of $2\frac{3}{16}$ in. diameter is struck, the exact size of the clock.

Boring the Block.—This circle has to be cut right through the block, which should be done by drilling a circular chain of $\frac{3}{4}$ in. holes close to the circle, but not quite touching it, so that the centre block will drop out. Pare off the little ridges that are left with a gouge, working half-way through from the front and back. Clean off with a coarse half-round file and then glass-paper (middle and fine 2), fitting the clock from time to time to ensure a hand-tight fit. This is important, as such clocks have to be wound from the back, and, unless it is a tight fit, it will move while being wound.

Turn the case over and, on the back, gouge out (or bevel) a $\frac{3}{4}$ in. hollow all round the edge of the circle to admit the hand for winding without taking out the clock.

Glass-paper the block with fine 2, $1\frac{1}{2}$ and 1 glass-paper and fumigate it. To do this, take a cardboard or wood box large enough to take the case and stand it in the box on four corks so that fumes may get all round it. Place a saucer in the box and pour into it 3 oz. of .880 liquid ammonia. Quickly shut the lid and paste strips of paper over all cracks to make it air-tight. Leave for twelve hours. Then brush with raw linseed oil and turpentine in equal parts.

back. The instructions show how to make the case for one that winds from the back.

Square up a piece of sycamore, size $13\frac{1}{4} \times 5\frac{3}{4} \times \frac{3}{8}$ in. for the front and ends. Measure carefully from the left, $2\frac{7}{8}$ in. Square a line across and saw this piece off with a small dovetail saw, keeping the squared line in. Repeat this a second time, thus leaving a piece measuring $7\frac{1}{2}$ in. wide. Shoot the ends of these three pieces to exact sizes. With the fretsaw, cut out a circular hole the exact size of the cylinder of the clock and fit it in so that the square face stands

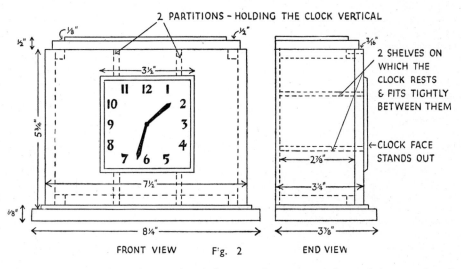

FRONT VIEW   Fig. 2   END VIEW

Leave for two or three days and polish with dark oak polish, applied and polished with a soft cloth.

This case can also be made of deal, mahogany or walnut. For methods of polishing these woods, see the chapter on Wood Finishing.

A Square Case.—Fig. 2 shows a silver-grey sycamore clock case of modern design to take a silver-faced clock with a face $3\frac{1}{2}$ in. square.

These square clocks are cylindrical at the back of the square face. Some wind from the front, others from the

out from the surface of the wood and rests upon it. Take out the clock and pin the three pieces together with $\frac{5}{8}$ in. veneer pins. Place the front piece of the clock case over the end pieces and glue and pin from the front. This needs care as sycamore easily splits. The holes should first be bored on the front piece with a very fine bradawl, taking care that the cutting edge is placed across the grain and rotated lightly.

Test with a try square to see that the ends are vertical. Cut out the top of the case and square to size, $7\frac{1}{8} \times 3\frac{1}{16} \times \frac{1}{2}$ in., and the bottom of the case to $8\frac{1}{4}\times3\frac{7}{8}\times\frac{5}{8}$ in. Rebate the three sides of each piece as shown (the back of the case is flush) and glue and pin them on as before. Wash off all glue with hot soap and water; allow to dry. . Plane up some strips of any wood, $\frac{1}{4}\times\frac{1}{4}$ in., and glue them into the four internal angles of the case for strength, stopping them $\frac{1}{4}$ in. short of the width of the sides of the case, so that the back, also cut from any wood $\frac{1}{4}$ in. thick, may be fitted in the

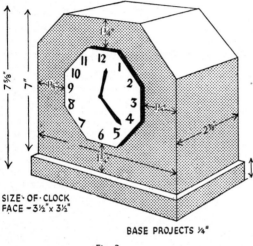

SIZE·OF·CLOCK
FACE – 3½"x 3½"

BASE PROJECTS ¼"

Fig. 3

clear. A little brass knob can be screwed to the back to facilitate its removal for winding. Pin in from the sides, top and bottom, the $\frac{1}{4}$ in. partitions which hold the cylinder of the clock tightly in place. Punch the veneer pins below the surfaces and fill up the holes with beeswax melted in a tin on a gas-stove with a pinch of dry grey dye to get the required colour.

Now glass-paper with $1\frac{1}{2}$, 1, 0 and flour. Mix one tube of grey dye in hot water and apply with a clean brush. Allow to dry and then polish with dry beeswax, rubbing wax vigorously with a piece of canvas and then rubbing and polishing the wood with the canvas.

The clock then can be put in from the front. This case could equally well be made of holly, but the colour would then be a lighter silver-grey.

A Walnut Case.—The illustration at Fig. 3 shows a modern case for an octagonal clock (face $3\frac{1}{2}$ in. across). This would look well in American walnut, as the violet-brown of this wood would make an effective contrast to a silver-faced dial.

Cut out and square up a solid block of American walnut, size $7\times7\frac{5}{8}\times 2\frac{7}{8}$ in. and bore the hole for the clock as described for the case illustrated in Fig. 1. Then saw off bevels. Next, cut out and square up a piece for the base, size $7\frac{1}{2}\times3\frac{1}{8}\times\frac{5}{8}$ in. Plane a $\frac{1}{4}$ in. bevel on three sides (not the back edge) and screw the base on from underneath. Finish with glass-paper as before, and burnish with a steel-chain burnisher. (See the chapter elsewhere on Wood Finishes.) This case could also be boxed up in the same way as the case illustrated in Fig. 2, except that it would be necessary to make a full-size elevation drawing of the front to get the exact angles of the mitres. Then plane up a strip of walnut sufficiently long to make the sides, bevels and top. Mark off the several pieces on the strip and draw on both edges the correct angles. Saw them down to the angles marked and finish off in a mitre block with a small metal smoothing plane.

When the case is glued up it will be necessary to reinforce the internal angles with small strips of wood.

All the cases mentioned could be made of red or white deal or American whitewood. Deal is a beautiful wood if its character and grain are brought out and not disguised by stains that clog the grain.

REVOLVING BOOKCASE WITH ELECTRIC STANDARD LAMP

THE revolving bookcase and standard lamp shown in Figs. 1 and 2 constitutes two pieces of furniture in one.

The standard lamp is 6 ft. 1 in. high. This may be reduced, but it is not recommended unless the bookcase is reduced also.

The elevation shown in Fig. 1 is divided into two-thirds of the height for the standard lamp and one-third for the bookcase.

Choose wood in keeping with the colour of the room—oak, walnut, mahogany or American whitewood. Begin with the construction of the book section.

Plane and square up two pieces of wood, each 1 ft. 9 in. × 1 ft. 9 in. × ¾ in. This may mean joining wood in the following way. As most of the woods mentioned are 11 in. wide, only one join will be necessary.

Joining Wood.—Planing two true edges, one on each piece of wood, place one piece of wood in the vice. Stand the other piece on it and see if you can observe any light between the edges to be joined.

When faults have been corrected, brush each of the edges to be joined with thin, hot glue. Stand the top piece on the lower one and rub out all the glue by working the top piece forwards and backwards, then leave the work in the vice for at least twelve hours to dry. Afterwards, plane and square up to 1 ft. 9 in. × 1 ft. 9 in. Plane up the four vertical divisions and square them each to 1 ft. 11¼ in. × 10½ in. × ½ in. Also plane and square up the four pilasters or end pieces marked x in the sectional plan in Fig. 2.

Saw out from all four corners of each pilaster a small piece ⅜ × ⅜ in. and house

them into the top and base of the bookcase as shown in Fig. 1, and fit together.

Now take the four vertical divisions and glue and pin them securely together

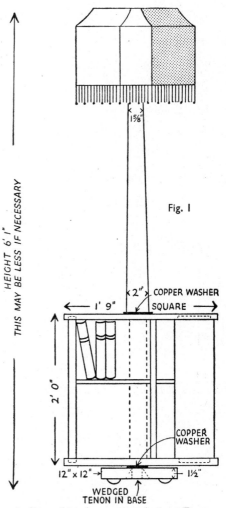

Fig. I

as indicated in the sectional plan, Fig. 2. Allow twelve hours for the work to dry.

Then push them in position as shown and correct any faults. Now clean everything up with Nos. 1½ and 1 glass-paper, glue in the pilasters and pin them with 1 in. veneer pins, from the top and base, slide in the vertical partitions and pin them in also. Bore accurate holes, 1⅝ in. in diameter, in the top and base to take the round stem of standard. This completes the bookcase, except for

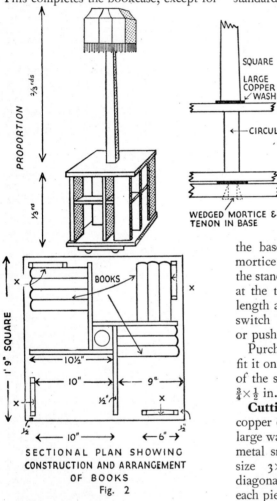

SQUARE

LARGE COPPER WASHERS

CIRCULAR

WEDGED MORTICE & TENON IN BASE

1' 9" SQUARE

BOOKS

10½"

10"

9"

½"

½"

10"

6"

SECTIONAL PLAN SHOWING
CONSTRUCTION AND ARRANGEMENT
OF BOOKS
Fig. 2

the ½ in. shelves, which are now pinned in the required positions; that is, about 1 ft. up from the bottom of the bookcase.

The Standard.—Prepare the standard from the same kind of wood. Plane and square up two pieces, each

5 ft. 7 in.×2×1 in. and make with a plough plane two grooves $\frac{5}{16}$ in. wide ×⅛ in. down the centre face of each piece. Glue these together groove-to-groove, cramp up and leave the usual time to dry. The grooves now glued together form the hole through the standard for wiring.

Measure 2 ft. 1¾ in. from the base of the standard and turn in a lathe or otherwise shape this part down to 1⅝ in. diameter, to form the circular spindle on which the bookcase revolves.

Measure up from the turned end 1¾ in. and cut a tenon, size 1¼×1 in. Now cut out the lower base, 12 × 12 × 1½ in., and cut a mortice through the centre of it to fit the tenon.

Fit the standard into the base and slope back the ends of the mortice ready for wedging. Next, taper the standard by planing it down to 1⅝ in. at the top, cut it off to the required length and fix a standard electric key-switch lamp-holder and then remove or push it.

Purchase or make the lampshade and fit it on by planting round, near the top of the standard, a piece of wood about ¾×½ in. for it to rest on.

Cutting Washers.—Now cut out of copper or brass sheet (24 B.W.G.) two large washers as follows: With a pair of metal snips cut out two square pieces, size 3×3 in., find the centres by diagonal lines, and strike circles, one on each piece, of exactly the same diameter as that of the wooden spindle. Punch out these circles with a small cold chisel or saw out the waste with a fret-saw.

Then carefully flatten the squares with a hammer and file the circular holes so that the spindle fits easily in them. Then trim off the outsides of the washers to 2½ in. diameter and clean them up. These washers can be carefully cleaned up by placing a sheet of fine emery paper on the table and fastening it down with drawing-pins. Then rub the washers round and round until they are quite flat and smooth. Polish them with metal polish or smear on a trace of mutton fat or tallow. This is to prevent squeaking when the bookcase is revolved. Note that copper is kinder in this respect than steel or zinc.

Knock four 1½ in. domes of silence on the underside of the stand, or very small castors may be fixed about ¾ in. in from the edges.

The advantage of domes of silence is that they serve the same purpose as castors and cannot get out of order.

Clean up all parts with glass-paper. All being ready for gluing up, lay the standard on the table with the lower end of the standard projecting about 2 ft. 2 in. from the end of the table.

Cramp or hold down the standard, put the first washer on the circular end and push on the bookcase; then follow on with the second washer.

Then use plenty of hot glue all round the tenon and glue on the stand, taking care that it is square with the standard.

Now gently push and glue in the wedges, but do not hammer them in. Place two pieces of ½ in. stuff on the floor so that you can stand the work on them and verify whether the standard is vertical.

When you have corrected any fault, leave the standard for five minutes, replace it on the bench and tap in the wedges. Give one tap on each wedge to avoid disturbing the 90 deg. angles. Put the complete fitment aside for a day to allow the glue to dry, saw off the wedges, clean up and polish, and wire and refix the lampholder.

LINEN CUPBOARD

A CUPBOARD for storing linen is best arranged with shelves, in order to prevent turning over a lot of articles to get a particular one, and so that every item will be visible. The arrangement shown in Figs. 1 and 2 fulfils this condition with the addition of a bottom drawer for articles of a general nature.

The outer frame is practically a box built up of 1 in. planed deal, 13 in. wide. The shelves and divisions are of the same material, except the top shelf, which is of ¾ in. stuff. The sides extend from the floor to the top, the top being of 1¼ in. stuff projecting over the sides for ½ in. and the front for 1½ in., the latter to cover the top edge of the door.

The sides are housed into grooves in the top board, the grooves extending from the back of the board to 1½ in. from the front. The grooves are ⅜ in. deep and 1 in. wide and the side boards fit up into them, thus making a presentable front appearance; the edges of the top board are rounded or square to choice. A square edge conforms more with modern ideas than a round. This top board is extended so as to cover the top of the door and to project ½ in. over the sides so that when the door is closed it overlaps both sides (ends) and front by ½ in.

Dimensions.—The bottom of the cupboard is arranged to stand on corners of the side pieces as shown in Fig. 2, and the bottom board is housed into the side boards in a channel extending to

½ in. from the front the bottom board being cut back that amount so that the front edge comes flush with the front edge of the side, but does not show the end of the groove on the front. The shelves, made of 1 in. wood (except the top one, which is ¾ in.), are also fitted in grooves ⅜ in. deep, again not extending to the front by ½ in., a piece ½×⅜ in.

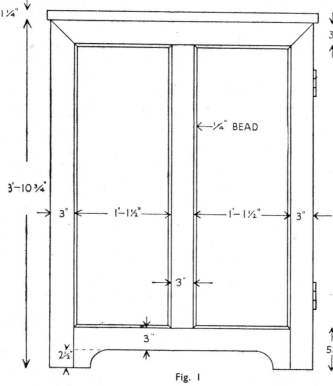

Fig. 1

ends of the sides are curved as shown at A in Fig. 2, which allows a space for sweeping dust and dirt away from underneath.

The bottom drawer is 10 in. deep, so that the first shelf comes at 10 in. from the bottom board (not the floor level). The space above this is divided into three parts by two shelves as shown, and they are 2 ft. 10 in. long and 12½ in. wide. They will then extend back from flush with the front edges of the side pieces to within ½ in. of the extreme back. This leaves room for a backing of either plywood or ½ in. stuff, to be nailed in at the back edges of the shelves, and (in the case of the ½ in. backing) will lie flush with the back. If thin plywood is used it will not come level with the back, but a bead can be planted round the inside to hold the panel up to the line of the shelf-backs and retain it in position

from falling or being pushed back.

The Bottom Drawer.—The bottom drawer is shown in Figs. 3 and 4. The front board is of 1 in. stuff, 2 ft. 10 in. long and 10 in. wide. The sides are let into the ends as in Fig. 3, and glued and nailed, the front thus showing no joint. The bottom is of 3/16 in. plywood, grooved into the sides and front at ¼ in. from the lower edges. The back is let into grooves made in the inside faces near the rear ends of the sides and is of

being cut off the corners of the shelves to let their front edges come flush with the front edges of the sides. The overall width of the cupboard is 3 ft. The height from the floor to the top is 4 ft. Allowing for the thickness of the top board above the groove, the side timber will be 3 ft. 11⅛ in. in length. The bottom board should come 3 in. from the bottom edge of the side members so that the whole of the cupboard does not rest on the floor. The lower

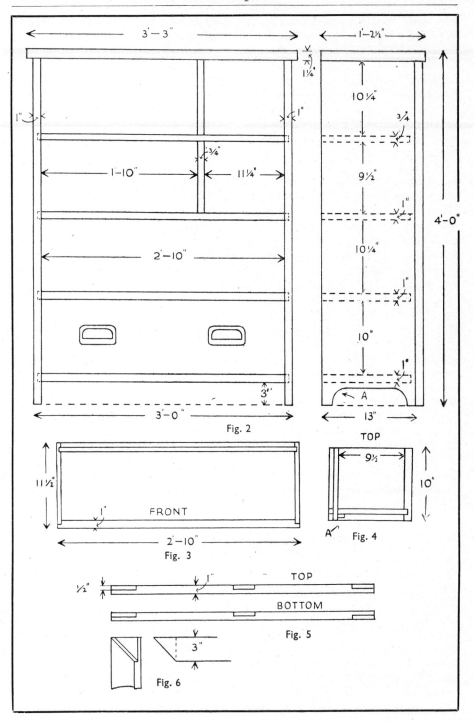

Fig. 2

Fig. 3

Fig. 4

Fig. 5

Fig. 6

½ in. stuff in a ½ in. groove, Fig. 4. It projects beneath the bottom for a distance of ⅛ in. and is nailed through into it; a strip A is glued along the underside in the ¼ in. space and this is then bradded through the bottom from the underside and through the back into the strip A which is ¼ in. deep and ½ in. wide. The arrangement is shown in Fig. 4.

The door is illustrated at Figs. 1, 5 and 6. It is 3 ft. wide and 3 ft. 10¾ in. high. It fits flat against the front edges of the sides, underneath the top board which projects forward beyond it (as previously described), and it extends down below and in front of the bottom board of the cupboard.

The framing of the door is made of 1 in. stuff, 3 in. wide. The top corners are halved and mitred as shown in Figs. 5 and 6 and screwed together from the back. The panels are of ¼ in. stuff, or two pieces of plywood can be used, one at the back of the other. The panels are of importance in holding the door-frame square, and they should fit exactly into the frame and be held centrally by ¼ in. beading glued and bradded into the frame back and front of the panel.

The door can be hung on either side by butt hinges let into the faces of the side and the back of the door. A hook catch at the side will secure it.

The front of the drawer can be fitted with two pressed brass, recessed drawer-pulls. Since the front of the drawer comes flush with the front of the side and shelf framing, the door will close up against it and there will be no room for projecting drawer-handles, but if the drawer is made ¼ in. less in depth (back to front) then light hinged brass drawer-pulls can be used and room will be provided between them and the back of the door.

There is also a small amount of space represented by the depth of the beading at the back of the door which gives about ⅛ in. of the room at the back where the drawer-handles come.

The finish can be to taste. It is a good idea to stain the panels a dark shade before building them into the door and to stain the beading, which is used to hold them, a contrasting colour. The rest of the cupboard can be finished with pale shellac varnish, or the whole can be enamelled ivory white or any shade to choice. The panel and beads and top board may be in a different shade of enamel. The inside can be left as when planed and sandpapered, or the fronts of the shelves and the drawer may be stained, varnished or enamelled.

CABINET BEDSTEAD

AN occasional bedstead is valuable in a house where bedroom space is limited. The one described and illustrated in this article takes up little room when closed and has the neat appearance of a cabinet. It is made of yellow deal, either varnished or painted, and is shown in section in Fig. 1.

The sides of the cabinet are 16 in. wide—made up of boards ¾ in. thick (with the top and bottom of the same material) and the front and back are 2 ft. 9 in. wide, as indicated in Fig. 2.

The first thing to construct is the back. This consists of ½ in. matching—built up to the required width and nailed to two cross battens A and B, Figs. 1 and 2.

The top edge of one batten A is 12 in. from the board forming the bottom and helps to support the head board of the

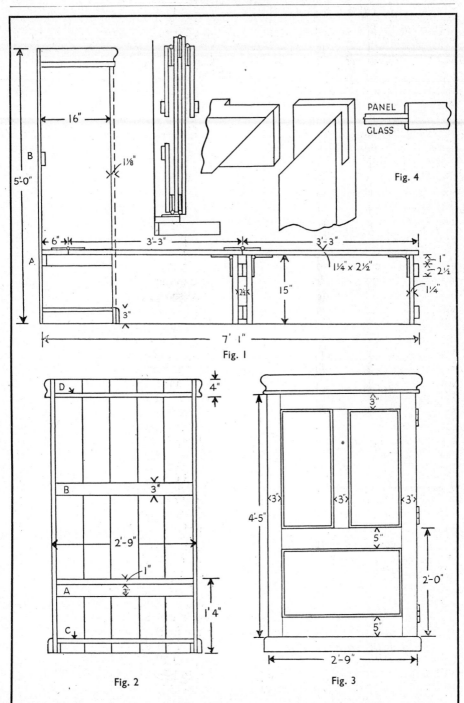

PANEL
GLASS

Fig. 4

Fig. 1

Fig. 2

Fig. 3

folding bed, its top edge being 13 in. from the bottom board.

The other batten B is midway between this and the underside of the top board.

Now make the top and bottom boards, C and D, which are 2 ft. 7½ in.× 16 in., followed by the sides, each 5 ft. in length and of the same width as the top and bottom boards. These members should be constructed of boards ¾ in. thick and built up to the desired width with two 9 in. wide boards, the long edges of which are fastened together by means of tongued and grooved glued joints. The surplus wood can then be sawn and planed to give the desired width.

Fixed to the sides and front at the top is a moulding with mitred corners of standard section and 4 in. deep to form an ornamental cornice.

Two short pieces of 2×1½ in. deal are screwed to the sides, while the lower part of the matching forming the back is nailed to the back edge of a board forming the bottom.

To enable the plinth moulding to stand beyond the face of the door, a 2 ft. 9 in. length of 3×1⅛ in. stuff is fastened to the front edge of the bottom member and the ends of the side battens, by means of screws.

A skirting or plinth 3 in. × ¾ in. with a bevelled or rounded top edge is nailed to the sides and front. The ends should be mitred and fixed with lost-headed nails which are punched down just below the surface.

This will complete the cabinet except for the door and the bedstead.

The Door.—The door stiles and top rail are made of 1⅛×3 in. deal and are shown in Fig. 3. The top edge of the second rail is 2 ft. from the bottom inside floor level, 5 in. wide and of the same 1 in. stock. The bottom rail is also 5 in. wide. The joints in the door frame may be ordinary mortices and tenons, the rails being morticed into the stiles. A method equally strong and easier to make is illustrated in Fig. 4.

Panels are fixed in by beads to avoid the trouble of rebating. The top panel may be divided by a 3 in. munting as shown, halved into the top and middle rails, or it may be one panel with a glass mirror having a backing of three-ply. The bottom panel should be of ¼ in. board, with the grain running vertically. Three-ply can be used here if desired, but it should be thicker than the three-ply panel at the back of the glass. Fig. 4 shows a section of the panelling. The beading should be ¼ in. thick and rounded at the edge, the rounding coming flush with the face of the door framing. At the back the beading may be square-edged and flush with the frame.

Some makers may like to have both the upper and the lower panels of a superior wood, and a good figured panelling such as ash or oak will add to the appearance. In such cases a mirror could be fitted to the back so as to come into use when the door is open. It will then back up to the wood panel and be fixed by round-nosed beading. In all cases the beading should be glued and fixed with panel pins. An attractive finish is made by using gilt beading for the front fixing of the panels. This is a matter of taste.

The framing of the door should be a little full in length and width and should be planed down to fit exactly on the face of the cabinet. It is hung on three 2 in. wide brass butt-hinges 4 in. in length, let half into the cabinet side edge and half into the back of the door. The top and bottom butt-hinges should be 3 in. from the top and bottom of the door and the third hinge should be centrally between them. A latch fastening should be fitted at the closing edge with a plate fastening in the cabinet side board. The door may be hung from whichever side is the more suitable.

The Folding Bed.—The folding bed is formed of two sections each 3 ft. 3 in. long and 2 ft. 6 in. wide overall. The top rails are $1\frac{1}{4} \times 2\frac{1}{2}$ in. and are connected to the legs. These legs are of the same sized stuff and hinged to the under sides of the top rails by strap hinges as indicated. The middle pair should be sunk flush. They are shown above the level for clarity. The legs are joined across by battens of the same cross section, the battens being screwed to the legs at 2 in. from the bottom and 2 in. from the top. They keep the side rails rigid and yet have no cross bars coming at the same height at the top of the rail, so that a sagging bed does not meet a cross rail.

The section nearest the cabinet is hinged to a 6 in. cross piece nailed on to the back batten previously mentioned, and, at its ends, on cross battens screwed to the cabinet sides. The middle hinges joining the two sections may be recessed into the rails.

Long strap hinges with the butt uppermost are used for fastening this section. The second section is hinged to the first by similar hinges so that it folds down over the first section and both are then folded up to lie at the back of the cabinet, the three legs folding down as shown in the side view of the bed section in Fig. 1.

Two legs are used at the centre so that the weight of the sleeper shall not be taken by the attachment of the strap hinge which joins the two sections of the bedside rails.

To prevent the two central legs spreading and letting the bed down, a hook and eye is fixed on each side. This is released when folding the bed. To prevent the end legs leaning in and letting the end of the bed down, a larger hook and eye is used. These

hooks and eyes (four will be wanted) can be made of a piece of $\frac{3}{16}$ in. iron rod bent round at one end and screwed through the eye to the inside edge of the bed rails to act as a hinge and hooking into a screw eye in the side of the leg at the other end.

The top should be covered with a double thickness of the stoutest bed canvas, nailed to the bed rails at the side and ends. The edges of the sacking should be folded over and tacked to the rail ends with gimp pins. Then a strip, $\frac{1}{4}$ in. wide, of upholstery leather should be laid on top and fastened through the four layers with clout nails at intervals of not less than $1\frac{1}{4}$ in. The closer the better.

The bed framing and legs should be made of best yellow deal entirely free from shakes or knots. The whole of the inside of the bed cabinet and all the woodwork of the bed should be sized and varnished with oil varnish of a dark shade. This will prevent the ingress of wood-eating insects and allow easy cleaning by wiping with a cloth.

The outer finish of the whole cabinet can be to the choice of the constructor. It can be stained to represent walnut or oak and varnished, or it can be painted. If painted in two shades, it will look well. It may be enamelled. In any case, if painting is decided on for a finish, the inside (not the bed itself) should be enamelled white, after painting with lead undercoating and rubbing down with glass-paper.

Use cast brass for the fittings, not cheap, pressed brass, plate hinges now in common use, and wrought iron strap hinges 2 in. wide and 10 in. long. When open they should be let into the top of the bed rails flush, and it is well to paint them with lead paint before fixing them. This will prevent rust.

PORTABLE WASHSTAND

THE portable washstand illustrated in Fig. 1 consists of a substantial cabinet of plywood with a hinged lid and a deep enamelled basin, while the interior is sufficiently large to accommodate a waste water receptacle and a water jug, as well as a separate compartment for holding toilet requisites.

As indicated in Fig. 1, the overall

front by a top and a bottom rail.

The door is of the panelled frame type to match the sides. The lid is a piece of $\frac{1}{2}$ in. thick plywood fitted with battens round the edges on the underside, the joint and laminations of the plywood being covered with a thin edge moulding. The basin is supported by a piece of $\frac{3}{8}$ in. plywood; the shelf underneath

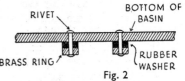

Fig. 2

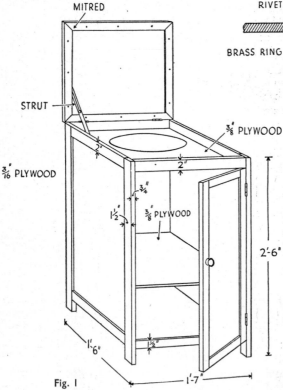

Fig. 1

and floor are made of the same material.

The Frames.—Make a start by constructing the two side and back frames. The material for the uprights as well as the bottom rails and the frame members of the door, is a cheap hardwood of $1\frac{1}{2} \times \frac{3}{4}$ in. section, though good yellow deal could be used if free from knots and shakes. The top rails are $\frac{1}{2}$ in. wider than the rest, as shown.

All frame members are, except the front top and bottom rails, grooved $\frac{3}{16}$ in. (full) and $\frac{1}{4}$ in. deep to accommodate the edges of the plywood panels. The grooves should be formed after the parts have been marked out and cut to length, and the sheets of plywood must be glued into their respective grooves and kept cramped until the glue has set. Screwed and glued butt joints

dimensions of the cabinet are 2 ft. 7 in. high (including the lid), 1 ft. 7 in. wide and 1 ft. 6 in. deep.

The carcase consists of two side frames and a back frame panelled with $\frac{3}{16}$ in. plywood, held together at the can be used at the corners or glued dowel-joints if preferred.

The three frames can then be screwed together and the top and bottom rails added.

Before cutting the piece of plywood that supports the basin, measure the actual basin so that a hole of a suitable diameter can be cut to fit it. Use a pad saw for cutting the hole, and smooth the edges with medium grade glass-paper.

The dimensions of the shelf are the same as those of the basin support, and both members rest on $1 \times \frac{1}{2}$ in. strips, glued and pinned to the inner faces of the sides and back. The parts should be sawn and trimmed quite square, and they should be recessed at the corners to clear the frame. The floor is $\frac{1}{2}$ in. longer and wider than the shelf as it is fixed by short screws to the underside, of the bottom rails.

In making the lid, the ends of the battens underneath should be neatly mitred at the corners and they should be fixed to the plywood by screws driven in from the underside into the top.

The edge moulding is $1\frac{1}{2}$ in. wide and $\frac{1}{4}$ in. thick and the corners are neatly mitred at the joint. Two $2 \times \frac{3}{4}$ in. butts should be used for hinging the lid, and a suitable metal strut of the jointed type must be fixed to keep the lid open.

The door can be on either side and a small handle and ball catch are needed.

Fitting a Drain Plug.—It is preferable to empty the basin by simply withdrawing a plug and allowing the contents to run into a receptacle underneath, so a suitable hole will have to be made at the bottom of the basin to accommodate the plug. Rubber plugs, $\frac{3}{4}$ in. in diameter, can be obtained for a few pence at most hardware shops. The best way to make the hole is to scribe a $\frac{3}{4}$ in. diameter circle in the middle of the bottom of the basin and then drill a series of small holes as close together as possible round the guide-line. The unwanted piece can then be removed with the aid of a small cold chisel, and the rough edge made smooth with a fine half-round file. A socket for housing the stopper can consist of a piece of $\frac{3}{16}$ in. brass, drilled and filed to form a ring which should be securely riveted to the underside of the basin. A washer cut from a piece of sheet rubber should be inserted between the brass ring and the basin to keep the latter watertight when in use. This is illustrated in Fig. 2.

A proper flanged socket with a screwed lock-nut can be used if desired, in which case all that is necessary is to insert the fitting into the hole, place the washer in position and screw up the lock-nut from underneath.

If the cabinet is intended for use in a bathroom, it can be finished in enamel to match the bath; but if required for a bedroom the fitment can be finished to correspond with the rest of the furniture.

BOX SEAT FOR BEDROOM

THE purpose of the box seat shown in the sketch, Fig. 1, on p. 161, is twofold, for it also gives additional storing space—very useful for those with limited cupboard accommodation.

The construction is simple, as this piece of furniture consists simply of a long substantial box and lid, the exterior of which is covered with art cretonne. Sea grass, flock or other suitable material is used for forming the padded seat.

The overall dimensions are 5 ft. 7¼ in. long × 2 ft. wide and approximately 1 ft. 9 in. high, as shown in Figs. 2, 3 and 4, which illustrate the front and back members, ends and the underside of the lid respectively.

Necessary Timber.—Planed yellow deal is used for the frames, while planed plain-edged deal boards 6 in. wide and ⅝ in. thick are employed for covering the four frames forming the body. The framework of the lid is made with 3 × 1 in. planed batten, which is to be clad with 6 × ⅝ in. boards. The floor is ½ in. matching.

Each frame is fastened to the other by means of countersunk-headed screws (No. 8) in the manner shown in Fig. 5.

Construct the front and back frames first. These are identical in size. The two horizontal rails A and B in Fig. 2 are 5 ft. 3 in. long, the end uprights C and D 1 ft. 6 in. in length and the intermediate one E, 1 ft. 2 in. The ends should be sawn to length and squared and the planing should be done with great care. This applies to members of all frames.

All members of a frame are fixed together by means of 3 in. wire nails, one nail at each joint.

Note that the bottom rail B is not flush with the lower ends of the vertical pieces C and D, but is 1 in. above them, as shown.

Cladding the Frame.—Square up the frame and tack a piece of waste wood across the corners to keep it square, and then prepare the boards. In sawing the boards to length, cut them 5 ft. 9¼ in. long to allow for a ⅝ in. overlap and 1 in. for waste at each end, the latter being sawn off after the boards have been fixed.

The boards are fixed to the frame by means of 1½ in. oval brads, and it is an advantage to glue the long edges as the assembling proceeds.

Having fixed the boards, remove the waste at the ends first by making scribing lines. When marking these, do not overlook the ⅝ in. overlap which hides the ends of the boards of the side members.

Now construct the end members, Fig. 3. They are made on exactly the same lines as the long sections except that the ends of the covering boards are sawn flush with the end uprights.

The front, back and ends can now be screwed together as indicated in Fig. 5. Two screws at each corner will give ample strength. Bore screw-holes in the first uprights to be joined to clear the screws, countersink the tops of the holes and drive the screws well down.

The Floor.—The next operation consists of sawing the matching to length to form the floor. Cut the boards to length, taking care to see that the ends are square. Before fixing them to the upper edges of the bottom rails, verify the squareness of the assembled parts. To do this, place a piece of batten diagonally across two corners and carefully mark on the batten the outer extremities in the manner indicated in the diagram Fig. 6. If square, the distance between the corners C D should be the same as A B. If the faces of the corner pieces are not planed correctly the structure will be out of true, so the constructor should take care to make a good job of the planing at the outset.

Nail the pieces of batten across the upper corners to keep it square and then fix the flooring down with 1 in. oval brads.

If it is desired to line the interior to cover up the unsightly framework, a cheap quality of thin plywood can be used, in which case it will be necessary

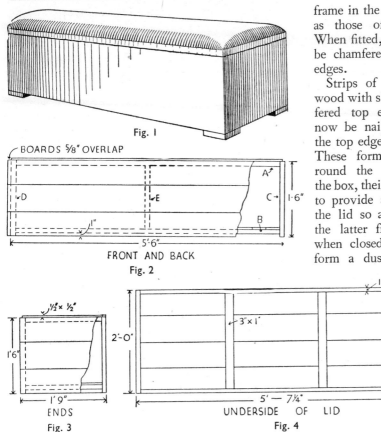

Fig. I

BOARDS ⅝" OVERLAP

FRONT AND BACK
Fig. 2

ENDS
Fig. 3

UNDERSIDE OF LID
Fig. 4

frame in the same manner as those of the body. When fitted, these should be chamfered round the edges.

Strips of ½ in. square wood with slightly chamfered top edges should now be nailed down to the top edges of the box. These form a shoulder round the top edge of the box, their object being to provide a seating for the lid so as to prevent the latter from shifting when closed and also to form a dustproof joint.

to fix strips of wood between the uprights and on top of the floor to obtain a fixing.

Round gimp pins ¾ in. long can be used for fixing the plywood.

Details of the Lid.—The construction of the lid is illustrated in Fig. 4. The lid is inverted to show the details distinctly. The members forming the frame are of 3×1 in. stuff, fixed narrow edge up, while the two cross-pieces of the same material are fixed with their wide faces flat and flush with the top edges of the frame. These parts should be fastened together with screws and not nailed; a couple of 2 in. No. 8 screws should be used at each joint.

The top boards are nailed to the

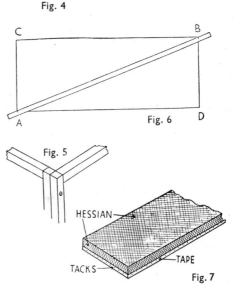

Fig. 5

Fig. 6

Fig. 7

F

Now make four feet measuring 3 in. square and $\frac{1}{2}$ in. thick and screw one to the bottom at each corner, or, if preferred, fit four screw-on castors. If wood is used, the feet should be stained.

The lid should now be fixed to the body by four stout hinges, 3 in. long and 1 in. wide. The leaves of the hinges should fit into shallow recesses cut in the back members of the lid as well as the top of the box.

Remove the hinges for the time being as the next process consists of padding the top and sides of the lid.

Upholstering.—Procure some stout hessian or canvas, a supply of strong linen tape $\frac{1}{2}$ in. wide and some galvanized tacks. Cut the hessian large enough to cover the top, including the front, back and sides. Stretch the material and fasten it down all round near the lower edge of the lid, using the tape to prevent the heads of the tacks from slipping through the hessian, as illustrated in the diagram Fig. 7. Then cut a similar piece about 6 in. wider and longer than the first one and fasten it down at the front and back as before

so that it forms a sack open at both ends. Fill the space tightly with the stuffing material, starting in the middle and working towards one end, manipulating some of the padding into the sides as the work proceeds. Start again at the middle and repeat the process, working towards the other end, and then fill the end and fix the covering down with tape and tacks. Fill the opposite end and fasten as before.

The cretonne is then cut to size, stretched over the seat and fastened with gimp braiding and gimp pins.

The sides and ends of the box are not padded and therefore may simply be covered with the cretonne cut to size, sewed at the back and fastened with gimp braid at the top and lower edges.

Before fixing the lid, touch up the top edges of the box either with paint or stain. Then fix the hinges.

To keep the lid in position when open, fix leather straps of suitable length and 1 in. in width to the inner faces of the sides of the lid and box, one at each end. Holes should be punched near the ends of the straps and fixture made with round-headed screws and metal washers.

CHILD'S COT

THE construction of a child's cot of the type shown in the dimensioned drawings, Figs. 1 and 2, is simple. The cot is designed with a view to using a ready-made wire mattress mounted to a wooden framework and costing less than ten shillings.

The usual dimensions of such a mattress are 4 ft. long × 2 ft. wide, but if a wire mattress is unnecessary, the bottom of the cot can be arranged with slats across it to support a mattress of a different kind.

Sides and Ends.—Figs. 1 and 2 show a front elevation and an end view

of the cot. The sides and ends are composed of strips of $\frac{3}{8}$ in. wood, $1\frac{1}{2}$ in. wide, let into horizontal rails. The ends of these strips or slats are housed in grooves formed in the under faces of the top rails and the top faces of the lower ones the spaces in the grooves not occupied by the slats being filled in with pieces of $\frac{3}{8}$ in. square hardwood. This method avoids the process of cutting mortices with a chisel.

Plated metal drop-side fittings may be obtained for about four shillings per set, but the expense of these could be saved by using pieces of electrical conduit for the guides and hardwood buttons for keeping the side or front in position when in use.

The legs as well as the rails should be of a reliable hardwood, but if the cot is to be finished with enamel the slats can be made of good deal.

Dowel-joints are used for fixing the rails to the legs, and a start can be made by preparing the latter. These are 1½ in. square and 3 ft. 2 in. long, but 1⅜ in. wood may be used if desired. If the surface is not already planed when purchased, the rough wood should be

locate the positions for the dowel-pins at the ends, and bore them ¾ in. deep. Next form the groove either with a plough or a combination plane. Care must be taken to see that the groove is in the exact centre of the narrow face. Start ploughing the groove from the farther end and work back to the end nearest you, until the full depth of the groove is cut.

Now mark the positions of the slats on the grooved faces of the rails. To save labour, cramp the four long rails together and mark them all at the same

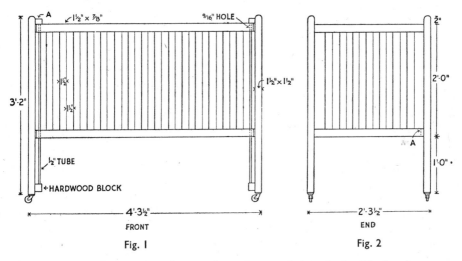

FRONT

Fig. 1

END

Fig. 2

planed to size and cut to length, namely 3 ft. 2 in., and then marked and bored for the dowel-pins which form the joints. This is shown in Fig. 3.

If difficulty is experienced in obtaining prepared wood 1½ in. wide and ⅜ in. thick for the slats, they can be cut from ½ in. thick (⅜ in. finished) prepared boards 7 in. wide. The strips should be sawn a little wider and longer than the finished sizes, the narrow faces smoothed with a plane and the ends cut square.

The Rails.—Work on the rails can then begin. Mark, saw to length, and

time, and then deal with the short ones in the same manner.

As a number of short pieces of equal length of ⅜ in. square wood will be required for filling in the spaces in the grooves, a gauge should be improvised for cutting them to length. The gauge can be in the shape of a bench-hook having a slot in the top piece and a stop on the flat board as indicated at A in Fig. 4. The saw is inserted into the slot, which guides the blade, while the end of the wood to be cut is butted up against the stop.

Having cut the requisite number of

square pieces, glue and pin them into the slots, using liquid glue and 1 in. panel pins for the purpose. Sink the heads of the pins about $\frac{1}{16}$ in. or less below the surface by striking them on the top with a hammer and a fine nail punch made from a wire nail filed to a taper. One face-edge of each rail will now have a number of mortices although they have not been made in the orthodox manner.

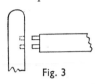

Fig. 3

Skim the grooved faces of each piece with a plane.

Then construct the two end frames by gluing the ends of the slats into the mortices.

Then glue the wooden pins into the legs and complete the joints by brushing glue on to the ends of the rails. Square the frames, fix them in cramps and allow the glue to harden.

Construct the back frame in the same way and prepare the front long rail. There are no grooves in this one. Then join the members to the end frames with glue.

The ends of the front rail are not fixed to the legs but the rail is set back flush with the back faces of the front pair. The ends are dowelled into the two side frames, as shown at A in Fig. 2. This arrangement ties the front legs

together without having to rely on the guides and the drop-front.

The drop-front consists of two horizontal rails and vertical slats which are glued into grooves in the same way as the side frames and back.

Front Guides.—A hole is bored with a $\frac{9}{16}$ in. diameter bit near each end of the rails as shown in Fig. 1, to allow the vertical guide rods to pass through. It is essential that these holes be absolutely vertical, otherwise the wood will bind on the guides when they ought to slide easily.

The guides are made of close-joint enamelled steel electric-light conduit, $\frac{1}{2}$ in. in diameter. The rods are threaded

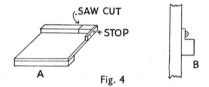

Fig. 4

through the holes in the rails and kept in position on the legs by fixing small blocks of wood drilled to fit the tube and screwed to the legs as illustrated at A in Fig. 1. The illustration at B in Fig. 4 shows a button for keeping the front in position when in use. Two such buttons will be required and these are fastened to the inner side faces of the front legs by means of screws which should not be driven in too tightly.

ILLUMINATED SHAVING MIRROR

THE illuminated shaving mirror, fitted with tubular electric lamps, shown in the figure is of good proportions and throws light correctly. It is made of three solid pieces of wood, hinged together, on which three mirrors are fixed.

Two strip electric lights are fixed on

the movable side mirrors so that the light may be thrown at any desired angle.

The shelf above the mirrors reflects light downwards. Below the mirrors there is a shelf for hairbrushes and shaving tackle. The mirror may be fixed to a wall or stood upon a table, in which case the bottom shelf should be larger and heavier—say 2 ft.× 7 in.× 1 in. Use only dry timber of the best quality. Austrian wainscot oak, mahogany or American walnut would be suitable.

Measurements.—Saw, plane and square up one centre panel for the back, size 1 ft. 6 in.× 9 × ½ in; two side panels each 1 ft. 1½ in. bare × 4 × ½ in.; one top shelf 1 ft. 6 in.× 4½ × ½ in.; one shelf under the mirror 1 ft. 6 in.× 4 × ½ in.; one lower shelf for brushes, etc., 1 ft. 4½ in.× 4 × ½ in.; and two brackets each 4¼ × 4 × ½ in.

Take the three back panels and hinge them together in the following way: on the centre panel measure down from the top 1 ft. 1½ in. and square a pencil line across.

Mark out on the edges of all three panels the positions of the hinges, as shown. The hinges should be 1½ in. narrow brass butts.

Set the gauge to half the thickness of the hinges and mark lines on the face and back of each piece. Carefully chisel out these grooves so that half of the hinge is set into each piece of wood.

When screwing the hinges on, see that the butts are on the face-sides as shown, and the centres of the pins are level with the edges of the wood.

Fixing the Lights.—Before actually hinging the three panels together it is best to get the strip lights and lampholders and carefully mark grooves in the positions shown on the side panels.

Slightly hollow them out with a gouge, so that the strip lights and lampholders rest in them. These lights can be wired to the wood later on.

Now, on the underside of the middle shelf and on the face of the lowest shelf, square lines across (½ in. apart).

These lines are to become the grooves

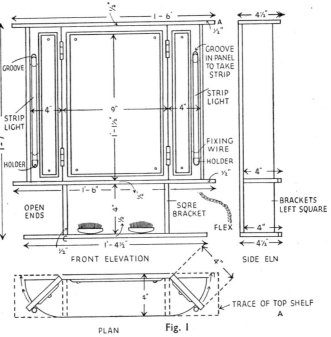

FRONT ELEVATION   SIDE ELN

PLAN   Fig. 1

(⅛ in. deep) in which the two square brackets will be fixed by housing joints.

Then gauge ⅜ in. from the face-edges of each piece, as the grooves are stopped ⅜ in. short of the face-edges.

Chisel out these grooves carefully and fit in the brackets. The outer sides of these brackets are flush with the edges of the centre 9 in. panel.

Next, sketch out with pencil and compass the quarter-circles on the ends of both shelves, saw these out with a small bow-saw and finish with a spoke-shave and glass-paper, Nos. 1½ and 1.

The whole of the work should now be cleaned up with glass-paper and care should be taken to test, with a steel rule, the surfaces of the three back panels to see that they are perfectly flat beds for the mirrors.

Sizes of Mirrors.—The plate glass mirrors should be of the following sizes: One 1 ft. $\frac{1}{2}$ in.×8 in. and two each 1 ft. $\frac{1}{2}$ in.×3 in. with $\frac{1}{8}$ in. holes ready bored for fixing.

The mirrors may be bevelled, but square finished edges will be best, as they do not reflect confusing lines of light.

Bore with a twist-drill all the necessary $\frac{3}{16}$ in. holes for fixing the brackets and shelves, and countersink them.

Then hinge the three panels. True up the top edges and screw down the top shelf; move the side panels backwards and forwards to see that they do not touch the underside of the shelf.

To obviate this, plane a little more off the wings than you do off the centre panel, and, when screwing down the top shelf, get the pull on the backs of the screws so that the shelf is a trifle less than 90 deg. with the back.

Now screw the brackets to the two lower shelves, countersinking the heads of the screws in the case of the upper shelf, and fill up the holes with stopping of the required colour. Then screw this shelf on from the back and up from the lower edge of the centre panel. Staining and polishing must be done now. If the wood is walnut, wax polish it. If it is light oak, use transparent polish of this colour. For dark oak, mix vandyke brown powder with .880 liquid ammonia to make a paste, then thin out with cold water to the required colour.

After staining it will be necessary to rub the work with a piece of coarse canvas to take the grain down. Then wax polish.

Put the brass back plates on the back for fixing to the wall.

Light Reflectors.—Purchase two small strips of tinfoil, just enough to cover the strip light grooves, and brush a little thin glue into the grooves, then lightly place on the tinfoil and pat it down with a clean handkerchief. The tinfoil reflects the light, looks well, and protects the wood from heat.

The mirrors should next be fixed with chromium-plated round-headed screws, which can be purchased with the mirrors.

Fixing is a delicate operation and it is necessary to have a perfect screwdriver. A bradawl of the same diameter as the screw-head will do, so long as it is square across the edge, which can be slightly blunted and squared on an oilstone.

Try the screwing on a piece of oak first. It may save breaking a mirror.

Place the glass in position and mark the holes with a long-pointed pencil.

Take off the glass and bore holes in the wood. Replace the mirror and carefully screw it on, guarding the glass with a thumb and finger.

Now wire the lampholders with flex and fit the strip lamps into the holders.

Get some fine silver wire and, just outside the grooves, bore tiny holes about $\frac{1}{32}$ in. diameter right through the panels. Put in the strip light and thread the silver wire through the holes so that the wire projects about 1 in. beyond the back of the panels. Twist the ends round and round carefully until it pulls up hand-tight only on the strip.

BEDSIDE CABINET

THE bedside cabinet shown in Fig. 1 is for a bed less than 2 ft. from the ground. The height can, of course, be altered to suit any bed.

The illustration shows a bed cabinet, the flap of which goes over, when opened, the left-hand side of the bed.

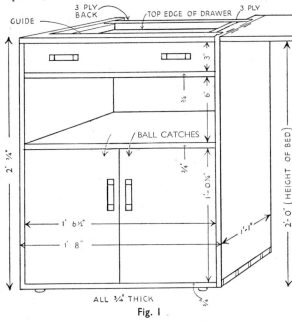

GUIDE — 3 PLY BACK — TOP EDGE OF DRAWER — 3 PLY

BALL CATCHES

1' 6½"

1' 8"

ALL ¾" THICK

Fig. 1

detail A in Fig. 2), by gauging lines ¾ in. from the four ends. Then set out the sockets and saw down carefully. Place the ends in the vice and put the bottom piece on the ends of the sides and mark through the cuts of the sockets with a small tenon saw. Complete the marking on the sides and saw down; then chisel out the dovetail and fit them together roughly.

Take apart and, with a pencil, square lines across for the shelves in the positions shown.

These shelves should be dovetail-grooved in the following way. Set a gauge to ¼ in. and gauge lines all round the ends of the shelves, also gauge lines on the back edges of the sides to give the depth of the grooves. Cut down with a chisel the gauge-lines on the shelves to $\frac{1}{16}$ in. deep and slope down from the edge to $\frac{1}{16}$ in. deep so as to form the dovetails. See detail C in Fig. 2.

As these dovetails and grooves are set back ½ in. from the front edges of the cabinet, saw out from the front edges of the shelves ½ × ¼ in.

Now chisel out the grooves ¼ in. deep, but stopping them ½ in. from the front edge. Fit these shelves in and then take them apart again.

Notch out the ends of face-edges of the top front rail ½ × ½ in. and drop this

The hinges may be reversed to serve the right-hand side.

Suitable woods to use are mahogany, Austrian wainscot oak or walnut. Procure dry, first-quality wood.

Square and plane the following pieces of wood:

Two pieces for the sides, each 2 ft. ¾ in. × 1 ft. 1 in. × ¾ in.; one piece for the bottom, 1 ft. 8 in. × 1 ft. 1 in. × ¾ in.; two shelves, each 1 ft. 7 in. × 1 ft. ½ in. × ¾ in.; two top rails, each 1 ft. 7½ in. × 1½ × ¾ in.

Dovetail Joints.—Dovetail the bottom and sides together, as shown (see into the sides. Drop the back rail in but do not notch it.

Note the back rail comes against the plywood back. Take the work apart again, and on the inner faces of the two sides plough grooves $\frac{1}{4} \times \frac{1}{4}$ in. and $\frac{1}{4}$ in. from the back edges. Put together and fit in a plywood back $\frac{1}{4}$ in. thick.

Now square up the drawer front to 1 ft. $6\frac{1}{2}$ in. $\times 3 \times \frac{3}{4}$ in. and fit it in.

wood back and cramp the carcase. Allow twelve hours to dry, then plane off the sides of the drawer and fit it in.

Next square up two panels each 1 ft. $\frac{3}{4}$ in. $\times 9\frac{1}{4} \times \frac{3}{4}$ in. for the doors and fit them in, making the heart sides the face sides (front).

Then fix a pair of $1\frac{1}{2}$ in. brass butt-hinges on the doors ($1\frac{1}{2}$ in. brass butts) sinking the whole thickness of the hinges into the hinging edges of the doors.

Now square up a piece of wood, size

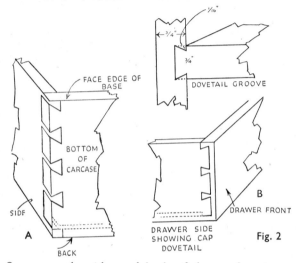

FACE EDGE OF BASE

DOVETAIL GROOVE

BOTTOM OF CARCASE

SIDE

A

BACK

DRAWER SIDE SHOWING CAP DOVETAIL

B

DRAWER FRONT

Fig. 2

D

Square up the sides and back of the drawer to the required size, $\frac{1}{2}$ in. thick only.

Lap-dovetail the drawer together as shown at detail B, groove the sides and front and slide in from the back a plywood bottom $\frac{1}{4}$ in. thick.

Glue up the drawer, test for squareness and allow twelve hours to dry.

Clean up the whole carcase and finish with Nos. $1\frac{1}{2}$ and 1 glass-paper.

Assembling Details.—Put it together in the following sequence, using hot, thin, clean glue. (1) Glue in the bottom; (2) the top rails; (3) the top shelf; (4) the bottom shelf.

The shelves will have to be pushed or knocked in from the back edges of the sides. Next, slide down the ply-

1 ft. 2 in. $\times$ 1 ft. $\times \frac{3}{4}$ in., for the handles. On the edges of the wood set out the profiles as shown in detail D in Fig. 2. Square lines across and saw with a 6 in. tenon saw down the lines to $\frac{1}{2}$ in. bare. Shape the four handles and finish off while they are in one piece. Then divide them.

Screw the handles on drawers and doors from inside and countersink the screw-heads' surface so that they can be filled with stopping of the required colour.

Put two $\frac{3}{8}$ in. ball catches on each door as shown in Fig. 1. To do this drill $\frac{3}{8}$ in. diameter holes $\frac{3}{4}$ in. deep at about 1 in. from the edges of the doors, then knock in the ball catches level with the surface. Fix on the underneath of the carcase four domes of silence ($1\frac{1}{2}$ in.

in diameter) or castors. Domes of silence are better as they do not get out of order.

Screw a strip of wood between the top and bottom of the cupboard $1\frac{1}{2} \times \frac{3}{4}$ in. Set this back $\frac{3}{4}$ in. from the front edges so that it forms a stop for the doors.

Countersink and fill up the top holes.

The arrangement of shelves inside the cabinet is left to the discretion of the constructor. Probably it will be best simply to fix them on battens about $\frac{5}{8} \times \frac{3}{8}$ in. and to screw the battens on.

The shelves can then be easily altered if required.

Hinges.—The hinged lid or flap should now be squared up to 1 ft. 8 in. × 1 ft. 1 in. × $\frac{3}{4}$ in. Make the heart-side the face (top) side. It will be best to have one long piano hinge stretching

from rail to rail as strain may be put on the lid when open.

The hinges should come well over ($\frac{3}{4}$ in.) to the inner edges of the sides and should be screwed down with long screws into the end grain.

The wood in this case should be equally taken out of the sides and lid, so that the hinges are flush when the cabinet is open.

Note the lid might be increased in length if necessary. It would then overhang on one side when closed.

Before hinging the lid, staining and polishing should be done.

If the wood is American walnut, wax polish it. If mahogany, stain with a hot solution of bichromate of potash, rub down with canvas and wax polish. If oak, use a light oak polish.

Methods of darkening are given in Modern Methods of Wood Finishing.

CHILD'S PLAY PEN

THE play pen, constructional details of which appear in Fig. 1, may be easily moved from place to place.

It is sufficiently strong and balanced

The frame would be best made out of American whitewood (not deal) and the railings out of birch or beech, so that they will withstand strain on them.

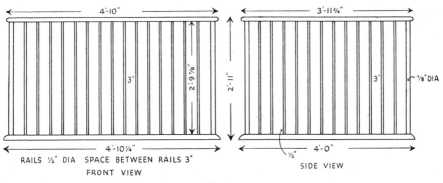

RAILS ½" DIA   SPACE BETWEEN RAILS 3"
FRONT VIEW

SIDE VIEW

Fig. 1

for a child to pull itself by the rails. Every part is rounded over and a wood should be chosen that does not splinter.

F*

Plane and square up the following pieces of whitewood: two pieces for the long top rails, each 4 ft. 10 in. by

$1\frac{5}{8} \times \frac{1}{2}$ in.; two pieces for the top end rails, each 3 ft. $11\frac{3}{4}$ in. $\times 1\frac{5}{8} \times \frac{1}{2}$ in.; two pieces for the long members of the base frame, each 4 ft. $10\frac{1}{4}$ in. $\times 1\frac{7}{8} \times \frac{5}{8}$ in.; two pieces for the ends of the base frame, each 4 ft. $\times 1\frac{7}{8}$ in. $\times \frac{5}{8}$ in.

These two pieces of framework are fixed together with open mortice and tenon joints, as shown in Fig. 2.

The Bar Holders.—Mark the face-sides and face-edges on all pieces. The face-sides are the top wide faces of the frame and face-edges are the inside edges.

all round as these rails go through the base.

Now make the top frame in the same way, except that you gauge $1\frac{5}{8}$ in. from the ends and only gauge the centre-lines on the under side of it, as the rails only go in $\frac{3}{8}$ in.

Make and fix this top frame in the same way as the base. Put the base frame together again, stand the top frame vertically on its edge and mark off the corresponding $3 \times \frac{1}{2}$ in. lines across it.

Now mark the corner upright rails by

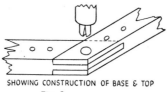

SHOWING CONSTRUCTION OF BASE & TOP

Fig. 2

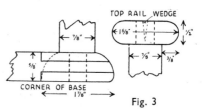

TOP RAIL WEDGE

CORNER OF BASE

Fig. 3

Make the base frame first, as follows. Measure $1\frac{7}{8}$ in. from the ends of the two long pieces and, with chisel or marking knife, square deep lines all round.

Measure the same distance from the ends of the short pieces and square pencil lines all round.

Set the gauge to one-third and then two-thirds of the thickness of the wood and gauge round all the edges from the $1\frac{7}{8}$ in. lines and across the end edges as well.

Saw down the tenons and open mortices, taking care that the saw-cuts are taken out of the waste side of the lines.

When sawing the long and the short pieces, look on the right and left of the saw, keeping the gauge-lines in.

Having cut out the mortices and tenons, fit them together to verify that all is correct. Next, take the frame apart and gauge centre-lines on both sides of all the pieces, then set out 3 in. spaces and $\frac{1}{2}$ in. rails all along each piece. Square across pencil-lines and take them

squaring four 3 ft. $\times 1$ in. $\times 1$ in. lengths of wood and square all round the shoulder-lines, which are 2 ft. $9\frac{7}{8}$ in. apart. Saw out the little tenons at the ends $\frac{1}{2}$ in. in diameter. These may be rounded, as shown, or left square.

Then plane the lengths to octagonal shape and continue to take off the ridges until they are round. Finish with middle 2, fine 2, and 1 glass-paper.

Making the Bars.—Now make all the $\frac{1}{2}$ in. diameter rails in the same way and cut off exactly to the required lengths, and see that they really are $\frac{1}{2}$ in. in diameter.

When making these, take an odd piece of wood and bore a $\frac{1}{2}$ in. diameter hole in it, so that each rail can be tried to ensure a tight fit.

Ready-made hardwood dowel-rods could be used if desired.

Bore all the holes with the same bit, right through the base frame and $\frac{3}{8}$ in. into the underside of the top frame.

Then glue up each frame, cramp, and leave for twelve hours to dry.

If there are no cramps to hand, place

the frame on the floor and knock in some 2½ in. wire nails outside the frame. Little wedges of wood can then be driven in between the nails and frame to push the shoulders up tight.

Test for squareness and put in 1½ in. panel pins in the exact centres of the corner rail-holes. When dry, bore (or mortice square) these ⅞ in. holes and fit in the four upright rails.

Remove these rails and round over the edges of the frames as shown with a small iron smoothing plane, but be careful not to strain the frame and break the joints. Parts of the inside edges will have to be chiselled up into the corners unless a bullnose plane is used.

Glass-paper every part smooth, taking care there are no splinters.

Take the corner rails and saw little wedge-shaped pieces out, like the wedge in a hammer (see Figs. 2 and 3.)

Make some hardwood wedges in readiness and glue up. Use hot glue and work in a hot room, otherwise the glue will chill before all the rails are put in place.

Working quickly, and starting at the right-hand corner of the base-frame, dip each rail rapidly into the glue pot, which should be kept hot on the stove, and put them in the holes.

It is best to have someone following up and tapping them home with a hammer and keeping them as upright as possible.

Leave these for a moment and with a small stiff brush (round sash tool) put glue in all the holes. Here again a helper is required. Put this frame on the table and turning the base-frame upside down, tap the rails into the holes. Use a piece of flat wood, about 6×2×1 in., held under the hammer, to avoid denting the wood.

Put the pen on the floor and tap in the little corner wedges. Wash off all glue with hot water and allow to dry.

Finally glass-paper again to a smooth finish and leave the wood natural colour.

BATHROOM FITTINGS

As a bathroom is subject to moisture, it is important to make woodwork as waterproof as possible. To do this, there is no better way than a couple of coats of priming paint and a finish of good enamel, the colours of which should harmonize with the decorative scheme. To avoid the effects of dirt and dust, the larger fittings, such as the soiled linen hold-all and stool, should have more or less plain surfaces, that is to say, exterior panelling should be avoided.

The Linen Hold-all.—As will be seen in Fig. 1, this is a corner fitment with a curved front. Where a corner is not available, a rectangular hold-all could be made on similar lines.

For the hold-all shown, a supply of 1×1 in. yellow deal will be required for the upright parts of the framework, a length of batten 1½ in. wide and 1 in. thick for the horizontal rails, and two pieces of board 2 ft. in length×5½ in. wide and ¾ in. thick for the curved members, sufficient ³⁄₁₆ in. alder plywood for covering the front, sides and bottom, and a piece of ⅜ in. plywood for the lid.

Fig. 2 shows a plan of the framework, while Fig. 3 illustrates one side of a frame. The side rails represented at A and B are joined to the uprights D, E, F by means of dowels, while the ends of the curved piece C are let into recesses ½ in. wide cut sufficiently deep in E and

F to allow the top of C to be flush with the tops of the uprights and the rails. Short blocks of wood are screwed to the side faces of E and F immediately below the ends of the curved member C to reinforce the joint. Screws are then driven into holes bored near the ends of

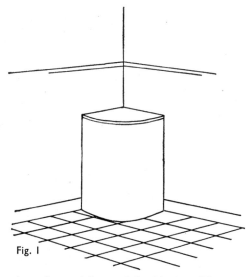

Fig. I

C into the uprights and the blocks. The same method of construction applies to the bottom of the framework.

As the making of the curved pieces may appear difficult, a few words on the subject will not be out of place. The best way to construct these parts is first to make a paper template or pattern for each piece, paste it on the board, cut round the outline with a pad saw and trim the edges with a spokeshave. In making the templates, all that is necessary is to procure a piece of paper about 16 in. square, draw two lines 15 in. long at right-angles to each other and strike an arc of 15 in. radius joining the two points. In the absence of a large compass, use a thin strip of wood with a small notch at one end to accommodate a pencil point and an ordinary pin driven through exactly 15 in. from this point. Then, with the pin point stuck

in the corner formed by the right-angle, draw the arc by holding the pencil vertically in the notch and moving it from one point to the other. Fig. 4 shows the operation.

Having assembled the frame, the plywood is cut to size. The front of the

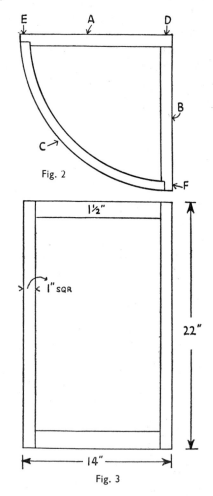

Fig. 2

Fig. 3

piece forming the bottom must, of course, be shaped to suit, and then pinned down to the upper edges of the lower portion of the frame, thus leaving a gap of 1½ in. between the underside and the floor. Next fit the curved front. This piece can easily be bent to the

Fig. 4

The Stool.—The illustration shown at Fig. 5 represents a bathroom stool built on similar lines to the hold-all; that is to say, it consists of an internal framework, clad with plywood, and a hinged lid. This type of stool has an advantage over the four-legged type as it provides temporary accommodation for soiled towels and proves useful for holding a stock of soap and other bathroom accessories.

Reference to the drawing shows that the overall dimensions are 18 in. long,

contour of the front frame members if it is cut so that the grain of the front and back of the ply runs vertically. The sides of this piece of plywood should overlap the outer edges of the vertical posts by $\frac{3}{16}$ in. to cover the edges of the side covering pieces, which are the next items to be fitted. The sides and front pieces are fixed by means of glue and thin panel pins $\frac{5}{8}$ in. long. As the heads of these are so small, there is no object in punching them below the surface as paint will entirely cover them.

The lid is the final item. A pattern should be cut out and pasted to the $\frac{3}{8}$ in. plywood and the piece cut to shape with a pad saw. The edges are then trimmed with a spokeshave, the pattern is removed and the lid hinged either to the right or left of the top framework.

Before applying any finishing medium, glass-paper the exterior smooth. The interior and exterior should be enamelled.

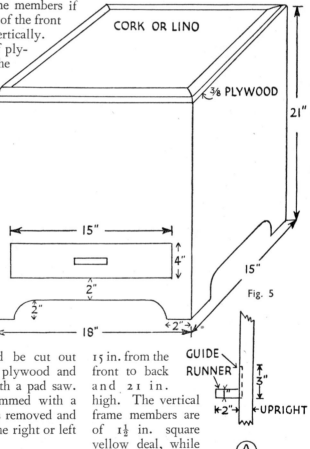

CORK OR LINO

$\frac{3}{8}$ PLYWOOD

21"

15"

4"

2"

15"

2"

2"

18"

Fig. 5

GUIDE

RUNNER

3"

2"

UPRIGHT

Ⓐ

15 in. from the front to back and 21 in. high. The vertical frame members are of $1\frac{1}{2}$ in. square yellow deal, while the rails are of 2×1 in. stuff. For easy construction, dowel-pins are used for joining the

rails to the uprights and the same type of joint is used in the rails that keep and hold the frames apart.

A couple of drawer-runners are fixed between the front and back bottom rails. The runners and guides are formed by screwing a piece of deal $\frac{1}{2}$ in. thick and 3 in. wide, at right-angles to a piece of

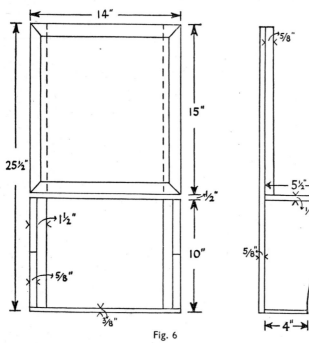

Fig. 6

2×1 in. batten runners with their guides being fixed by means of screws driven in through the fronts of the rails and into the ends of the runners. The method of forming the runners is detailed at A in Fig. 5.

The drawer is of simple construction and comprises a plain deal front, back and sides, all of which are $\frac{1}{2}$ in. thick. These parts are fastened together by screws and a $\frac{3}{16}$ in. plywood bottom is fixed. The sides and back are made $\frac{3}{16}$ in. shallower than the front to enable the latter entirely to cover the long laminated edge of the drawer bottom.

The bottom of the compartment above

the drawer consists of a piece of $\frac{1}{4}$ in. plywood supported by $\frac{1}{2}$ in. square fillets glued and pinned to the plywood casing.

The lid, which forms the seat, consists of a piece of plywood $\frac{3}{8}$ in. thick around the top and flush with the edges to which is fixed a $\frac{3}{4}$ in. quarter round beading. This is to enclose the space, which is filled with a piece of compressed cork $\frac{3}{4}$ in. in thickness, costing about half-a-crown. A piece of thick cork lino may be substituted for the compressed cork, in which case a $\frac{1}{4}$ in. bead will be needed. Glue is used for fixing the seating material.

In preparing the plywood with which the framework is covered, do not forget to cut a drawer aperture in the front piece. Glue and thin panel pins are used for fixing the plywood.

Shaving Mirror.—The shaving mirror, Fig. 6, is another useful bathroom accessory of simple design and consists of two essential items—namely, the framed mirror and the shelf unit to which the mirror is fixed. (See page 274).

Start by making the mirror frame. This measures 15 in. long and 14 in. wide overall, as will be seen by referring to Fig. 6, and consists of plain oak moulding 1 in. wide and costing about $2\frac{1}{2}$d. per foot run; it is so cheap that there is little to be gained in purchasing the plain wood and forming the rebates yourself, even if you possess a rebate plane. The ends of the pieces are mitred. Having prepared these mitres, the frame may be assembled with glue and a lost-headed nail at each corner, the head of which is sunk below the surface when the glue is dry and the hole filled with plastic wood.

The shelf unit of yellow deal consists of two sides, each 10 in. long, $5\frac{1}{2}$ in. wide at the top, 4 in. at the bottom, $\frac{5}{8}$ in. thick, and shaped as shown.

picture-frame sprigs and then a piece of stout brown paper glued on to cover the aperture and prevent the entry of dust.

To give the front and side edges of the top shelf a finish, suitable lengths of a half-round bead with mitred corners are pinned on, the side pieces being extended to the back edge of the frame support. The beading is not shown in the drawing.

The shelf unit is now ready for

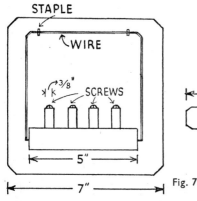

Fig. 7

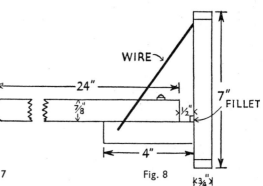

Fig. 8

To ensure accuracy and save time, the two pieces, when cut to size and squared up, can be tacked together and the curved edges cut with a pad saw and finished with a spokeshave.

The two shelves are of the same length, but the upper one is $5\frac{1}{2}$ in. wide and the lower 4 in. The former is fixed by lost-headed nails, while the latter is fastened to the underside by means of 1 in. brass countersunk-headed screws.

The frame supports at the back are $1\frac{1}{2}$ in. wide and $\frac{5}{8}$ in. thick and $25\frac{1}{2}$ in. long. They are fixed to the back edges of the sides by 1 in. brass screws. The frame is fixed by the same means.

Before fixing the mirror in the frame, however, it is advisable to give the latter two coats of paint and a final coat of enamel. When dry, the mirror can be placed in position and a backing of $\frac{3}{16}$ in. plywood fixed by driving in

enamelling. When dry, the mirror can be attached and fixed to a wall by means of brass mirror plates sold for the purpose.

Collapsible Towel Rails.—At Fig. 7 is seen a collapsible towel airer, preferable to the ordinary type fitted close against the wall, as the arms upon which the towels rest are hung projecting fan-wise, which allows the free circulation of air. (See page 274).

To construct the fitment (see Fig. 8) a piece of hardwood 7 in. square and $\frac{3}{4}$ in. thick for the base, a piece of similar wood 5 in. long, 4 in. wide and 1 in. thick for the arm support, four strips of hardwood—oak preferred—each 2 ft. long, $\frac{7}{8}$ in. wide and $\frac{3}{8}$ in. thickness for the arms, will be required.

Also, four japanned No. 6 round-headed screws, $1\frac{3}{4}$ in. long, for supporting the arms, and a piece of thick galvanised iron wire, a few tinned iron wire staples for fastening the wire and four brass washers to clear the shanks of the fixing screws.

Make the base and arm support first and trim off the sharp corners with a chisel to give the parts a finish.

Drill a hole near each top corner of the base for accommodating the screws which hold the fitment to the wall, and bore a hole of the same diameter as that of the wire, 1 in. deep in the centre and 1 in. from the front, in each side of the arm support.

Then drill a perfectly upright hole $\frac{1}{2}$ in. from one end of each arm, of sufficient size to clear the shank of the round-headed screw. Remove the sharp edges and corners of the strips and screw them to the support, not forgetting to place a washer under the head of each screw. These screws should not be driven in tightly but sufficiently to allow the arms to swing freely, though not loosely.

Bend the wire to shape with pliers and fasten it about 1 in. below the top of the base, using the staples for the purpose, thus forming a hinge. To complete the job, insert the ends of the wire into the holes in the sides of the arm support and fix a thin fillet of wood to form a ledge just above the back of the support when in a horizontal position.

When not required, a gentle pull on the arm support will disengage it from the ledge and allow the arms to hang down vertically. The fitting should be enamelled to match the rest of the articles described.

KITCHEN CABINET TABLE

THE cabinet table shown in Fig. 1 will be found useful in a modern kitchen where room for storage is generally at a premium.

As will be seen from the illustration, the space between the legs accommodates two roomy drawers immediately under the top rails, a smaller drawer to the left, and, under it a small cupboard. This could be utilised for storing bread in a suitable enamelled metal bin, while a larger cupboard with double doors occupies the remaining space on the right.

The Construction of the framework and drawers is carried out in yellow deal and plywood is used for facing the top, cladding the ends and back, partition, floor and the cupboard doors. Panelling has been avoided for two reasons. First, because surfaces devoid of ledges are more hygienic, as they do not harbour dust, and secondly, the construction is simplified, inasmuch as

no grooves or rebates are required to accommodate the panels, the plywood being simply glued and pinned to the framework. Moreover, such a surface can be given a high-gloss enamel finish which can be washed.

The amount and sizes of material can easily be ascertained from the fully dimensioned drawings of the framework shown at A, B and C in Fig. 2, which illustrate a front elevation, side view and a plan respectively, the latter being given with the top removed to show the framework more easily.

A start can be made by sawing and planing the four legs to size, after which each front face of a leg should be numbered, marking the front left-hand leg No. 1, the corresponding right-hand one No. 2, the back left and right Nos. 3 and 4 respectively. The legs are then marked out for the mortices which house the tenoned ends of the rails.

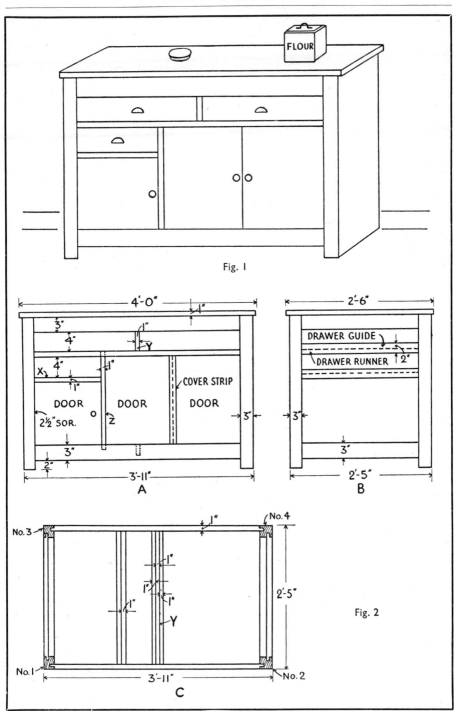

Fig. 1

Fig. 2

Joining the Rails.—At A in Fig. 3 is shown the mortice and tenon joint used in joining the top rails to the legs, that illustrated at B represents the joint for the bottom rails, and the detail at C shows the method of joining the long drawer rails. Mortices will also be

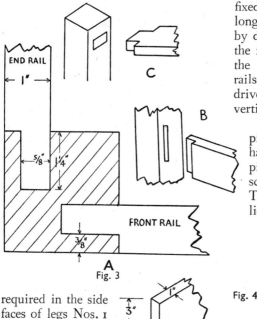

END RAIL

1″

⅝″   1¼″

FRONT RAIL

⅜″

A
Fig. 3

C

B

required in the side faces of legs Nos. 1 and 3 to take the tenoned ends of the short drawer rails as indicated at X in Fig. 2, A.

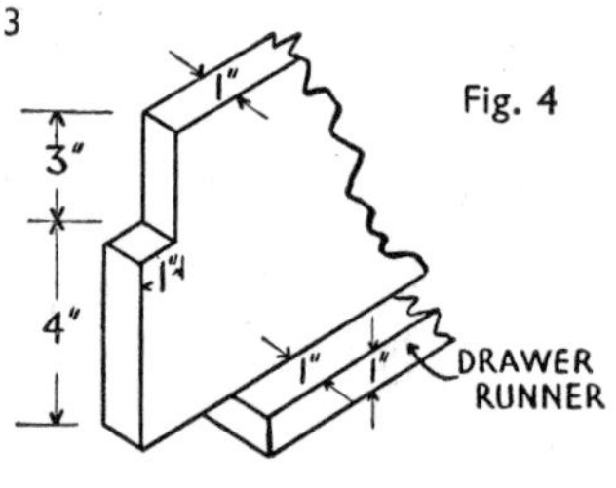

Fig. 4

DRAWER RUNNER

1″   3″   1¼″   4″   1″

The mid-rail or cross-piece represented at Y in Fig. 2, A and C, separating the two top drawers is 8 in. wide and the ends are cut away as shown in Fig. 4 to allow the front edge to be flush with the face of the top rail. A piece of 3×1 in. planed stuff is fixed by screws to the lower narrow face of the cross-piece in order to form runners for the drawers as shown.

The partition z (A, Fig. 2) consists of a frame, the two uprights and horizontal members of which are 2½ in. wide and 1 in. thick. The ends are

halved to form halved joints and fastened together with screws. The upper and lower ends are cut as indicated in Fig. 5 to allow the face edges to lie flush with the front faces of the long drawer rails and the front and back rails. The top of the frame is fixed by driving screws through the long drawer rails, the lower portion by driving screws through the faces of the front and back bottom rails, while the interior end of the short drawer rails are fastened by means of screws driven in through the sides of the vertical pieces of the frame.

The intermediate horizontal cross-piece forms the guide for the right-hand end of the small drawer. A piece of 2×1 in. planed stuff is screwed to the guide to form a runner. The top of the latter must of course lie flush with the short drawer rail.

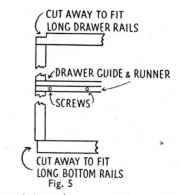

CUT AWAY TO FIT
LONG DRAWER RAILS

DRAWER GUIDE & RUNNER

SCREWS

CUT AWAY TO FIT
LONG BOTTOM RAILS
Fig. 5

The remaining drawer guides and runners at the leg end of the drawers are constructed by letting pieces of 2×1 in. planed batten into the legs and forming the runners with 1 in. square stuff screwed to the sides as already mentioned.

The framework is finished when a cross-piece, 2½ in. wide and 1 in. thick, has been fixed between the long rails at the bottom to support the floor of the cupboard.

It should be noted that all mortice

and tenon joints should be glued.

The top consists of $\frac{3}{4}$ in. thick boards faced with $\frac{3}{16}$ in. thick alder plywood. The width is made up by gluing several boards a couple of inches longer than the finished length. Allow the glue to dry and then saw to size and finish the edges with a plane.

Using Panel Pins.—The piece is then screwed down to the top of the framework with $1\frac{1}{2}$ in. No. 8 counter-sunk-headed screws, the tops of the holes being countersunk to allow the screw heads to lie flush or just below the surface. The next operation consists of cutting the plywood facing to size and gluing it down to the top, and further securing it by means of $\frac{3}{4}$ in. panel pins, driven in so that their heads are flush. They should not be punched down below the surface or their object will be defeated by the thinness of the plywood. This point should also be observed when using panel pins for fixing the ends and back.

If ordinary Scotch glue is used for fixing the plywood to the top it is essential that it be applied very hot and its consistency not too thick, also that heavy weights should be applied to the surface and allowed to remain there for at least a day.

The piece of plywood forming the floor of the cupboards is supported by the rails and should be cut so that the narrow ends butt against the plywood sides and the back edges against the plywood back. The front edge covers only $\frac{1}{2}$ in. of the front bottom rail, the remaining $\frac{1}{2}$ in. towards the front forming a rebate against which the lower edges of the door butt.

The Cupboard Doors of plywood $\frac{1}{2}$ in. thick, should be square and an easy fit, otherwise, when finished with enamel, they may not close properly, if at all.

A thin strip of wood $\frac{1}{2}$ in. wide should be glued and pinned $\frac{1}{2}$ in. away

from the front edge, to the underside of the long drawer rail to act as a door stop, and a similar strip should be fastened in the same manner to the vertical opening-edge of the right-hand door. This latter piece should project $\frac{3}{8}$ in. beyond the edge to cover the adjacent door-edge to prevent the entry of dust. A door stop should be fitted to the underside of the short drawer rail.

The doors should be hung with $1\frac{1}{2}$ in. long $\times \frac{1}{2}$ in. brass butts and suitable fastenings fitted to keep the doors shut.

The Drawers.—The length of these is 2 ft. but could be made shorter if desired. Plywood $\frac{1}{4}$ in. thick is used for the bottom, $\frac{7}{8}$ in. thick deal for the fronts and backs and $\frac{3}{4}$ in. stuff for the sides. The ends of the fronts should be cut away at the back to house the ends of the sides, and the inside faces of the four frame members grooved $\frac{1}{4}$ in. deep and $\frac{1}{4}$ in. wide to take the plywood bottoms. The grooves should not be made nearer the bottom edges than $\frac{1}{2}$ in. as this distance allows sufficient room for gluing a number of triangular blocks to the sides and the bottom of the plywood. These give additional support where strength is needed.

The fixing of the ends and back sheets of plywood is a matter of simple gluing and pinning and should present no difficulty provided the pieces have been cut and trimmed with accuracy.

Before attempting to apply enamel, the doors should be removed and the drawers taken out, and the whole thoroughly rubbed down with fine glass-paper. Any knots appearing on the surface should be treated with knotting, and all screw holes and cracks filled with plastic wood which must be levelled off flush with the surrounding surface.

A priming coat of good lead paint may then be given, rubbed down with glass-paper when dry, dusted, and another coat of flat paint applied, which, when hard, must also be lightly rubbed down. This is followed in due course by the final coat of enamel, which must be applied in a dustless room whose temperature should not be below 60 deg. F.

STORAGE CABINET FOR FRUIT

THE storage of fruit is simplified by using a cabinet built on the lines illustrated in Fig. 1. It is constructed of good yellow deal, but a cheap hardwood such as Oregon pine could be used for the framework.

The cabinet is 2 ft. wide, 3 ft. high

corners, and for joining the top and bottom rails at the front and back.

To give extra strength, the back is provided with a cross-brace as shown at B in Fig. 3. The pieces forming the brace are halved at the centre so that they lie flush.

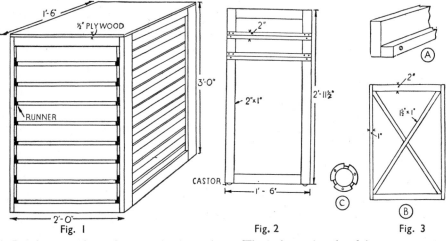

Fig. 1   Fig. 2   Fig. 3

and 1 ft. 6 in. from front to back, and consists of two side frames held together by rails and a top consisting of plywood $\frac{1}{2}$ in. thick.

Eight trays are provided which slide in and out like drawers, and the cabinet is fitted with small castors.

Simple Construction.—Details of the side frames are shown in Fig. 2. They consist of two uprights and a top and bottom rail, 2×1 in. planed wood. The tray runners are fixed between the uprights by screws. Each runner consists of a length of 2×$\frac{1}{2}$ in. batten, having a strip of $\frac{3}{4}$×$\frac{1}{2}$ in. wood screwed to it to form a ledge as shown at A in Fig. 3.

Glued dowel-joints are used at the

The sides and ends of the trays consist of planed wood 2 in. wide and $\frac{3}{4}$ in. thick, and ordinary screwed butt-joints are used for fixing the parts together. The bottoms of the trays consists of slats or strips of wood 1 in. wide ×$\frac{1}{2}$ in. thick. These run from the front to the back and are fixed to the underside of the frames by screws spaced 1 in. apart. On no account should a solid bottom be used instead of slats as the latter allows free circulation of air, an essential factor in the storage of fruit.

Use screws for fixing the plywood top. Small ball-shaped castors as shown at C in Fig. 3 could be used in lieu of ordinary wheel castors.

VEGETABLE SAFE

THE safe shown in Fig. 1 is easy to construct and is made of red or white deal.

About 90 ft. of $2\frac{1}{2} \times 1$ in. battens will be required. Plane and square these up

Before doing this, it is better to stain them to the required colour. A medium brown stain will be best as this does not show up the dirt. Mix some vandyke brown powder and .880 liquid ammonia

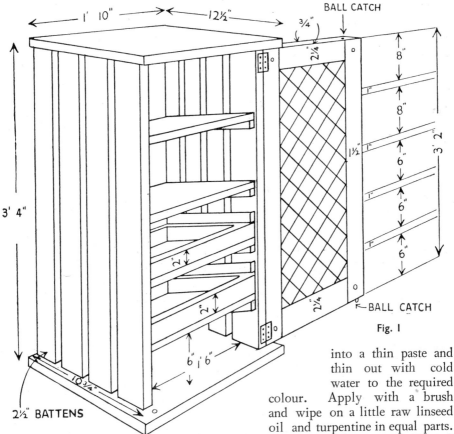

Fig. 1

into a thin paste and thin out with cold water to the required colour. Apply with a brush and wipe on a little raw linseed oil and turpentine in equal parts. The oil prevents the stain coming off when the safe is washed.

and cut the top and bottom also out of deal or American whitewood, size 1 ft. 10 in. $\times$ $12\frac{1}{2} \times 1$ in. Square these, then cut the battens up into eight 3 ft. 2 in. lengths and square their ends.

These eight battens and the top and bottom can at once be assembled by screwing and countersinking from the top and bottom.

Use of Battens.—Find the position for the screws, bore and countersink below the surface and screw the eight battens at top and bottom together.

Screw four battens across the back to keep the structure rigid and for the trays to shut against, about $2\frac{1}{2} \times 1$ in.

These can be screwed from the sides as they are in the clear.

The positions of these battens are immediately behind the shelves and trays.

Nail on a sheet of perforated zinc or small-mesh wire netting from the back of the safe. This completes the back.

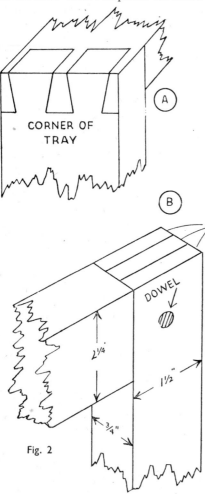

Fig. 2

Now square up twelve battens to the required length and screw them on the sides, so that the shelves may rest upon them. These battens are set back $\frac{1}{4}$ in. from the front edge.

In the case of the lower two trays,

two battens will have to be screwed to each side, one above and the other underneath the trays, to form runners for the trays, as shown in Fig. 1. The shelves can be made of $2\frac{1}{2}$ in. battens and screwed in from the sides.

Now make the two trays. Plane up sufficient wood 2 in. wide × $\frac{1}{2}$ in. thick, and from it cut four pieces each 1 ft. 6 in. × 2 × $\frac{5}{8}$ in. thick, four pieces each 1 ft. 6 in. × $9\frac{1}{2}$ × $\frac{5}{8}$ in. Dovetail them together as shown in detail at A in Fig. 2. Set the marking gauge to $\frac{5}{8}$ in. and gauge lines round both ends of the eight pieces. Mark out the sockets of the dovetails on the four front and back pieces and saw them down with a dovetail saw, keeping the saw cuts inside the lines.

Put the short pieces in the vice, one piece at a time, and, placing the long piece in position and holding it firmly, put the saw into the cuts made and draw it towards you, thus scratching the lines on the end of the short piece. Complete marking out the pins, which are left up, on the short pieces. Saw down outside the pins and chisel out the wood between them, working alternately from the front and back.

Chisel out the sockets and fit and glue up these two frames. Then glue, pin or screw on some little $\frac{3}{8} \times \frac{3}{8}$ in. strips inside, and bevel with the edge so that you can drop in the $\frac{5}{16}$ in. thick plywood bottoms.

This method of fitting the bottoms is better than grooving them in, as they can be taken out and washed when necessary.

Trays and Door.—Plane up the outsides of the trays and fit them so that they run easily. Screw on the four battens that form the runners.

The door shuts over the front edges of the sides, so that it allows the trays to be pulled out.

The size of the door is therefore 3 ft. 2 in.×1 ft. 8 in.×$\frac{3}{4}$ in.

Square up two pieces 3 ft. 2 in.×$1\frac{1}{2}$ ×$\frac{3}{4}$ in. and two others 1 ft. 8 in.×2 ×$\frac{3}{4}$ in. to form the stiles and rails.

Gauge the lines for, and square with a chisel, the shoulders of the tenons on the short pieces as shown at B in Fig. 2 and draw the mortice lines on the long pieces with a pencil. Saw down the tenons and mortices, cut out the waste and fit the frame together. Try for size and plane off surplus wood until it is only a shade too large.

This is easily done before gluing, as each piece may be planed off on the bench. Now glue the framework together and allow twelve hours to dry. Then, with a fine-set sharp plane, take off from the edges a few fine shavings so that the door opens easily and is flush with the sides.

To make a good job of this frame, put a $\frac{3}{8}$ in. diameter beech dowel through each tenon, as shown.

Put on the hinges, sinking them in the edges of the safe and frame of the door; that is, half the thickness of the hinge in each case. Put them on the frame of the door first.

Purchase a piece of perforated zinc, size 2 ft. $11\frac{1}{2}$ in.×1 ft. 6 in., and paint it in sympathy with the colour scheme of the kitchen. Zinc takes paint or enamel well, but the colouring medium must not be took thick.

When it is painted, allow it to dry and fix it on the inside of the door.

Now purchase two $\frac{3}{8}$ in. ball catches, drill holes and tap them well down in the positions shown in Fig. 1 on top and bottom of the door.

Next, square up the wood for the handle, c in Fig. 2, size $4\frac{1}{8} \times 1 \times \frac{7}{8}$ in. A piece of hardwood is best for this. Square and saw at the two lines across the front and gauge and saw out the two ends, gauging $\frac{3}{16}$ in. from the back. Then round over the front with a chisel as shown. Bore two holes and screw and glue it on to the door.

Hinge the door, gouge out small hollows on top and bottom to take the ball catches and finish the rest of the staining.

A $\frac{3}{8}$ in. stop chamfer can be put round the inner edges of the door if desired.

A SIMPLE ICE SAFE

AN ice safe is the next best thing to a refrigerator, and the illustration at Fig. 1 and the accompanying working drawings (Fig. 2) show an efficient type which can be made at little expense.

The safe consists of a framework of 2×2 in. timber supporting panels on each side, the inner space being filled with ground cork, glass-wool, sawdust or other non-conductors of heat.

The safe measures approximately 2 ft. wide, 1 ft. 6 in. from front to back and 3 ft. high, and rests upon a low base.

It may be more convenient to have an ice safe of greater height, but science proves that cooler air is found near the floor.

The Lining.—The inner panels of the safe consist of ¼ in. asbestos-cement sheeting, while the outer covering is of plywood ⅜ in. in thickness.

First, saw the four uprights of the framework indicated in Fig. 2. The

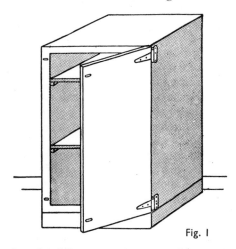

Fig. 1

length of these is 2 ft. 8 in. Plane all faces square and put them aside for the time being.

Next, construct the top and bottom frames. Two pieces each measuring 1 ft. 6 in. and 2 ft. long, will be required for each frame. The ends should be halved together so that the members lie flush.

Screw these parts together with 2 in. No. 8 brass countersunk-headed screws, to each joint in the position shown in Fig. 3.

Drill a clearing hole in the centre of each joint to pass a 4 in. No. 10 brass screw and drive the screws into the centres of the ends of the uprights.

Square up the frame with a try square

and brace the outside corners by fixing temporary battens across them. Before proceeding further, the height of the two shelves must be settled as cross-pieces consisting of 1½ in. wide × ¾ in. planed batten must be fixed at these positions as supports.

Cold air descends, so the ice chamber should be at the top. Measure a distance of 8 in. from the underside of the top frame and mark a line across each inner face of the uprights. The lines indicate the positions of the top edges of the shelf battens. House the ends of the battens into recesses 2 in. long and ¾ in. deep, which must now be sawn and chiselled out of the uprights. Fix the battens with 1½ in. No. 6 brass screws, countersinking the holes so that the heads lie flush.

Similar battens can be fixed at equal heights at any desired distance below the top ones. Cut and fit these battens in the same way. This completes the framework.

Cutting Asbestos.—Now cut and fix the asbestos-cement sheets to form the lining of the framework. If the sheets are new, they may be a little soft and can be cut with an old tenon saw. Hard sheets can be cut by scoring deep grooves with the top edge of a triangular file. When sawing or grooving, see that the material is placed on a flat surface and is well supported.

Fit and fix the bottom piece first. The size of this is 2 ft. × 1 ft. 6 in. Cut this piece square and cut out the corners, 2 in. square, to clear the uprights, and then cut a piece of exactly the same size for the top. Fix these in position with 1 in. galvanized lath nails. Drive the nails into the centre of the wood. The nails will drive easily if the sheets are soft; but, if hard, drill small holes to take the nails. This will prevent breakages of the asbestos.

Now prepare some ½×½ in. wood

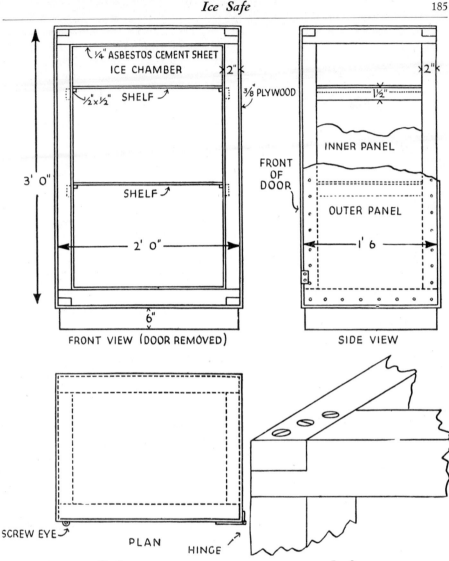

FRONT VIEW (DOOR REMOVED)

SIDE VIEW

SCREW EYE↗   PLAN   HINGE↗

Fig. 2

Fig. 3

with saw and plane and fasten a fixing fillet on the top and bottom lining pieces previously fixed. The faces of these pieces should be flush with those of the interior of the framework.

Then cut the back panel and fix it to the top and bottom fillets and continue by fixing the two sides, using galvanized lath nails as before.

Now attend to the outside. Mark out,

saw and plane the edges of a piece of ⅜ in. thick plywood for the back. This piece measures exactly 1 ft. 6 in. wide and 3 ft. high (long). Proceed in the same way with the sides. These should be of the same length as the back and ⅜ in. wider than the outside edges of the framework. The ⅜ in. overlap covers the edge of the back, the front edge of the plywood being made flush with the front face of the frame-work.

Now cut the top panel 2 ft. ¾ in. wide, which allows ⅜ in. at each end to cover the top edges of the sides. The back to front dimension of this piece is 1 ft. 6⅜ in. The front edge of this is flush with the front face of the frame and ⅜ in. overlap hides the top edge of the back panel.

A similar piece must be cut to cover the bottom. In all these pieces drill holes ½ in. from the edges, spaced at a distance of about 4 in. apart. The holes should be large enough to clear the shanks of 1 in. No. 6 screws.

See that the outer panels are right for size before proceeding with the insertion of heat-insulating packing. To do this, lay the safe on its side or end, as the case may be, and fill each section. Then fix the covering panel with brass screws.

Now cut four strips of ½ × ½ in. section wood for the shelf supports and fix them to line up with the inner supports in the sides of the frames and make two framed shelves to fit, and cover them with very fine mesh gal-vanized wire netting. This material allows the cold air created by ice in the top chamber to pass through and reach the bottom.

Plywood Door.—The door is built on the same lines as the body of the safe, that is, the front consists of a thick panel of plywood fastened to a frame of 2 in. square deal and lined at the back with an asbestos sheet.

Make the frame first, to fit exactly the interior of the safe and then fix the outer panel of plywood.

This panel covers the entire front, while the edges of the back panel should be flush with the frame. The space between the front and back should be, of course, filled with the insulating material. Black japanned hinges known as cross garnets, 6 in. long, should be screwed to the outside of the door and side of the safe.

To keep the door closed, a couple of brass screw-eyes should be fitted to the body frame upright. The rings of the screw-eyes pass through holes near the clearing edge of the door and the door is secured by means of hardwood wedges, which can be anchored to the side with pieces of cord.

A tray of thick sheet zinc for holding the ice must now be made. The ice should rest upon a grid and not on the bottom of the tray.

There yet remains to construct the base or the plinth. This may consist of a simple platform of ¾ in. planed boards 2 ft. wide and 1 ft. 6 in. from front to back.

The whole fitment should now be rubbed down with glass-paper and care-fully finished with white enamel.

A ROLLER TOWEL RAIL

THE essential of this kind of towel rail is to have a simple method of taking out the roller.

The illustrations, Figs. 1, 2 and 3, show how such a rail may be made easily and cheaply.

Plane and square up a piece of syca-more or American whitewood to size 1 ft. 9 in. × 4 × ¾ in. and two pieces for the brackets, each size 3½ × 2¼ × ¾ in.

Find the centres of these pieces as shown in detail sketch, Fig. 2, and bore two holes ¾ in. in diameter, one hole in each piece.

Housing Brackets.—On the right-hand bracket only, saw down with a tenon saw and take out the slot into which the roller drops. Saw off the bevels from each of the two brackets and file or plane the edges smooth. Then bore holes for screws in the back piece, countersink and clean the three pieces with fine Nos. 2, $1\frac{1}{2}$ glass-paper. Next tightly screw on the two brackets from the back. Note the screws should go hand-tight through the back piece to ensure that the two brackets

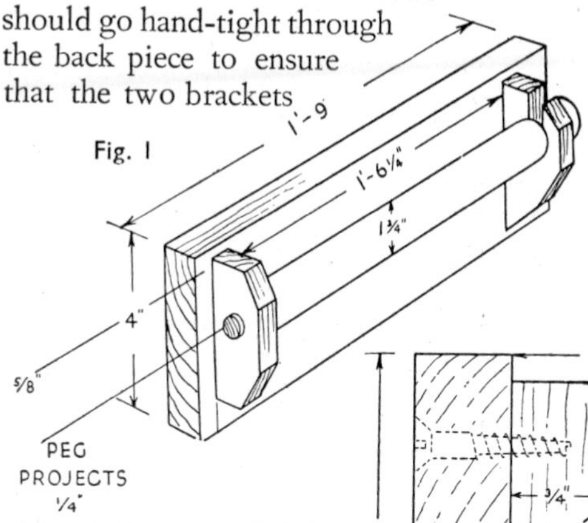

Fig. I

1-9

1-6½

1¾"

4"

5/8"

PEG
PROJECTS
¼"

will pull up tightly.

House the brackets into the back piece $\frac{1}{4}$ in. deep. In this case the brackets should be $2\frac{1}{2}$ in. wide to allow $\frac{1}{4}$ in. for letting in. Hold each bracket in turn to the back piece in its exact position and mark round with a sharp pencil. With try square, marking knife or sharp pencil, square across lines on the inside edges of the pencil lines and gauge the lines on the ends of the slots. To chisel these out, clamp the back piece down on the bench, then, holding a 1 in. firmer chisel upright with the face side out, mallet down the long lines, and with a $\frac{1}{2}$ in. chisel, cut down, by hand pressure only, the end of the slots.

Now turn the $\frac{1}{2}$ in. chisel, bevel side down, and cut out the slots $\frac{1}{4}$ in. deep.

Finally glue and screw the brackets in.

The next thing is the roller. A piece of sycamore or birch will be best as the pivot end and the button will not

break off if made in a hard wood.

Square up one piece of wood to size 1 ft. 9 in. $\times 1\frac{3}{4} \times 1\frac{3}{4}$ in. Now, as the collar on the right and the pivot on the left have to be cut while the wood is in its square form, proceed as follows.

Measure from the right-hand end of the wood $\frac{5}{8}$ in., then $1\frac{1}{2}$ in. from the same end, and square lines all round with a marking knife. Now, measure from the left-hand end $1\frac{1}{4}$ in. for the pivot; then gauge to $\frac{1}{2}$ in. bare from the edges of both ends, and carefully saw down all the squared lines to $\frac{1}{2}$ in. bare and chisel a groove out all

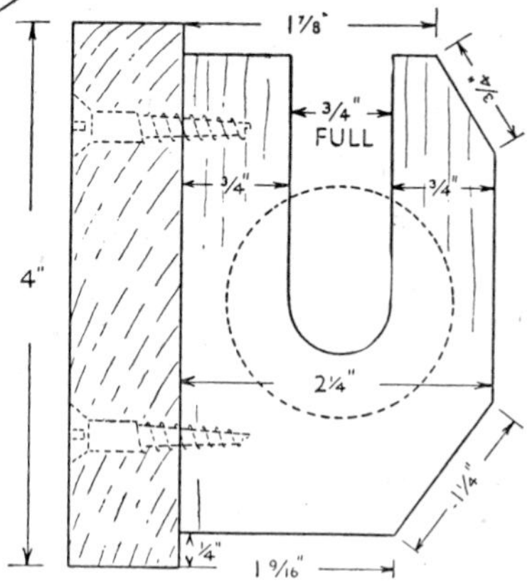

4"

1⅛"

¾"
FULL

¾"

2¼"

¾"

1½"

¼"

1 9/16"

END VIEW

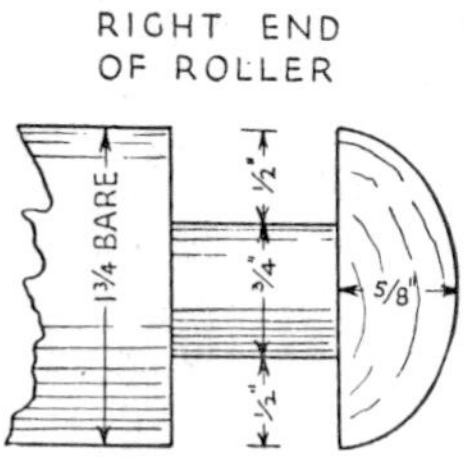

RIGHT END
OF ROLLER

1¾ BARE

½"

¾"

½"

5/8"

Fig. 2

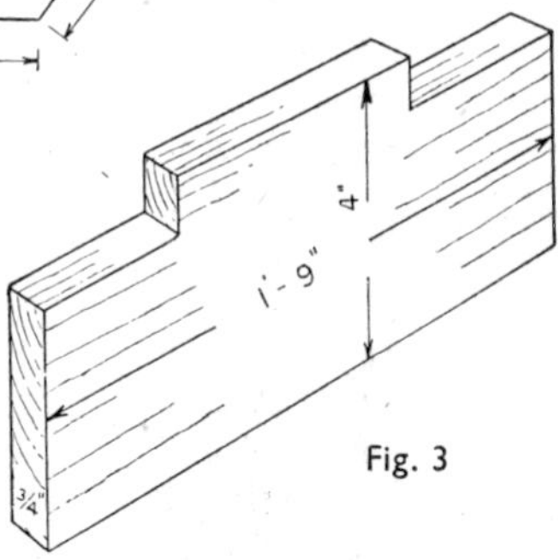

1-9

4"

¾"

Fig. 3

round. This can be sawn out both ways on the pivot end. Round the collar and pivot with a chisel, file and glass-paper.

Forming the Roller.—Then set out an octagon in the right end, carry the lines down the length of the wood and carefully plane off. Plane off the ridges and the roller now has sixteen faces. Plane these ridges off and keep on taking them off until the roller is round. Remember to take off finer shavings as the work proceeds. Now round off the button as shown in the detail, Fig. 2, then carefully smooth the roller with Nos. 2, $1\frac{1}{2}$ and 1 glass-paper.

The $\frac{3}{4}$ in. hole in the left-hand bracket must now be enlarged with a coarse half round file so that there is play for the roller to be put in at that end and dropped into the other.

It may also be necessary to ease off the wood down the sides of the slot.

The sketch appearing at Fig. 3 shows an alternative shape for the back.

The corners of the brackets should be sawn out square $\frac{1}{4} \times \frac{1}{2}$ in. so that they are in sympathy with the back. The button in this case should not be rounded over.

To give a final finish to the work, go over it with some white wax or light oak polish and polish with a soft duster. Do not polish the roller.

WRINGER STAND

THE stand shown in Fig. 1 may be painted in any colour to brighten the scullery. The top is best left plain, as the wringer is clamped or screwed to it.

Plane and square up four legs each 3 ft. × 2 in. × 2 in. These should be of best deal. Treat in the same way two top rails 1 ft. $3\frac{1}{2}$ in. × 4 × 1 in., two short rails, $6\frac{1}{2}$ × 4 × 1 in., and one long stretcher 1 ft. 7 in. × $2\frac{1}{2}$ × 1 in. and one piece for the top 1 ft. 6 in. × 6 × 1 in.

Lay two of the legs on the floor and, with a piece of chalk, mark the centre line A as shown. Then set out, full size, the drawing of the end of the stand including the top and bottom rails.

This drawing should be exactly to measurements.

Using the Drawing.—Place the two legs on the drawing, get someone to hold them, and place on top the two rails. By this means you can mark off the bevelled shoulders of the rails, both top and bottom, and also square horizontal lines across the top and bottom ends of the legs. Set the bevel (movable square) to the required angle and square round the legs in pencil the positions

of the mortices. Then gauge the sides of the mortices, which are $\frac{3}{8}$ in. wide.

Now draw lines across with the bevel set to the same angle, at each end of the top and bottom rails. Saw them off to the required lengths, measure 1 in. in from each end and strike a line across, with bevel and try square, down the edges, and carry the bevelled lines across the back of each rail.

As the rails are set in $\frac{1}{4}$ in. you need only make half-tenons, $\frac{3}{8}$ in. wide.

Remember to set back the mortices at the tops of the legs $\frac{3}{4}$ in. This makes the top tenons $3\frac{1}{4}$ in. long.

Cut out the mortices and tenons, fit them in one by one and assemble this end, from which you can get the positions and angles of the tenons on the other end. Mark this out and assemble it.

The two ends are now complete except for morticing in the stretcher and the long rails. Find the centres of the rails on each of the lower rails and mark out the mortices as shown. Measure $1\frac{1}{4}$ in. from each end of the stretcher and square lines across and round each end. Notch out each end

½ in. This leaves the size of the tenon 1½ × 1 in.

Cut the mortices through, saw out the tenons and fit the stretcher in. Bevel back the ends of the mortices ¼ in. Do this from the face sides.

Now square round the shoulders of the tenons on the two long rails and cut the tenons and take out the mortices on the inner sides of the four legs and fit these in.

The First Gluing. —Take apart the two end frames, clean them with glass-paper and glue them up.

These are not easily cramped, so, after they have been glued, put the frame on a table or bench and knock in some 2½ in. wire nails outside the legs and opposite all the mortices. Then drive in some small wedges between the legs and nails. This will pull the shoulders up. While still in this position, bore some ⅜ in. holes through the legs and tenons and drive in some ⅜ in. beech dowels. Saw the dowels off and wash off the glue. Then clean up.

When dry put one end frame on the floor, then glue in the stretcher and the two long rails. Glue and knock on the other end frame and cramp this up.

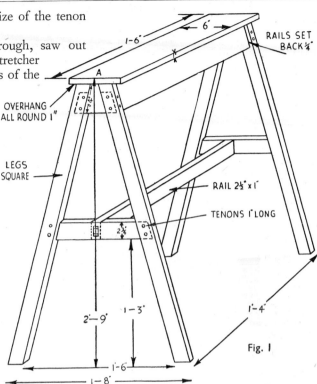

OVERHANG ALL ROUND 1"

LEGS 2" SQUARE

RAILS SET BACK ¼"

RAIL 2½" x 1"

TENONS 1" LONG

2'-9" 1'-3" 1'-4"

1'-6"

1'-8"

Fig. 1

Bore and knock in the dowels and wedge up the stretcher rail. Test for squareness.

If a clamp is not to hand, put some 1½ in. wire nails in where the dowels go, to hold the work together. Then take out each rail one by one and substitute a dowel for it.

Saw off the top and bottom of the legs to the required angle and see that the whole stand is firm.

Allow twelve hours to dry. Then screw and nail on the top, clean the work up with glass-paper and paint to the required shade.

BROOM RACK

NOTHING ruins a broom more quickly than allowing it to rest, when not in use, business end down on the floor. The life of a broom will therefore be greatly lengthened by making the broom shelf depicted in Fig. 1.

The one shown, details of which

Fig. I

appear in Fig. 2, consists of a length of board 5 in. wide and $\frac{5}{8}$ in. thick fixed to a back board of the same width and thickness and measures 3 ft. 6 in. long for accommodating three brooms of normal size.

To make the fitment, procure a piece of 4 in. prepared board 11 in. wide $\times$ $\frac{3}{4}$ in. thick ($\frac{5}{8}$ in. finished), mark a line down the centre of the wide face and rip the wood down with a saw. Plane the narrow faces and run the plane along the edges to remove the arris, as the sharp edges are termed. Saw off the corners and trim them with a sharp chisel to give the holder a neat appearance.

Cutting Slots.—Now set out the position of the slots. Along the wide face of one of the pieces scribe a line

$2\frac{1}{2}$ in. from the front edge, and along this mark the centre of the slots. With a try square and pencil, mark the lines $\frac{5}{8}$ in. on each side of the centre lines to meet the first scribed line, and then trace curves at the back.

Place the board, front edge uppermost, in the bench vice and with a pad saw carefully saw out the slots and remove the roughness with medium glass-paper.

Now draw a centre line along the back of the back board and drill five screw holes, one $1\frac{1}{2}$ in. from each end and the remainder at equal distances apart. In addition, bore two screw holes as indicated at A for taking the fixing screws.

Assemble the two members together with screws driven in from the back, and further strengthen the holder by

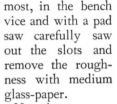
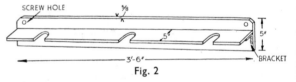

Fig. 2

fitting three 2 in. iron brackets to the underside of the shelf and the back board. Fix one of the brackets in the centre and the other two about $1\frac{1}{2}$ in. from the ends. Plain iron brackets can be obtained at most cheap stores for about a penny each.

Stain and varnish or paint, according to taste.

AN IMPROVED BOOT AND SHOE RACK

THE ordinary open boot and shoe rack allows dust to accumulate on its contents. The one shown in Fig. 1 is totally enclosed.

The overall measurements are 2 ft. 6 in. high, 2 ft. wide and 12½ in.

fitted with four pairs of rails for supporting the footwear, and consists of enamelled steel tubes such as are used for electric lighting purposes. This material costs about a penny per foot and is much to be preferred to wooden rods.

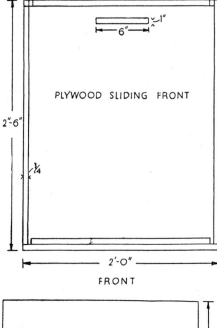

FRONT

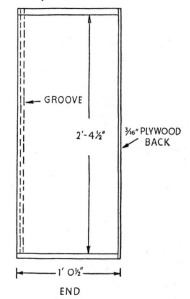

END

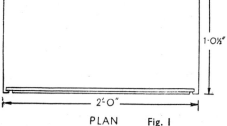

PLAN   Fig. I

from the back to the front. In order to save space, the front slides vertically in grooves in the side members instead of the customary hinged door.

Good yellow deal is used for the base, sides and top, and plywood for the front and back. The interior is

Building the Sides.—First prepare the two sides. They are 2 ft. 4½ in. long × 12½ in. wide. These can be built up to give the width by using two boards 6¼ in. wide fastened together by means of 1½ × ¾ in. battens screwed at the top and bottom. Before fixing the boards together, plough a groove ¼ in. deep × ¼ in. wide in the inner face of each front piece. The groove should be formed ¼ in. back from the front edge, as indicated in Fig. 2.

Next, prepare the base and top, using planed battens for fastening the boards together as at the sides. The battens should be fixed ¾ in. from either end and not flush.

Assemble the sides, base and top together with 2 in. No. 8 screws and then prepare the back. The latter is a sheet of $\frac{3}{16}$ in. birch plywood and is 2 ft. 6 in. long × 2 ft. wide. It must be cut perfectly square. Fix the plywood to the back with $\frac{1}{2}$ in. oval brads, taking

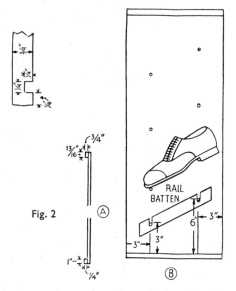

Fig. 2

care to keep the edges flush with the outer edges of the carcase.

Now prepare the front sliding panel which consists of a piece of plywood 1 ft. 10$\frac{7}{8}$ in. wide × 2 ft. 5$\frac{1}{4}$ in. in length and $\frac{3}{16}$ in. thick. Saw and plane this square and fix a strip of wood $\frac{13}{16}$ in. wide × $\frac{3}{4}$ in. thick flush with the top

edge as indicated at A in Fig. 2. Prepare and fix a similar strip $\frac{1}{4}$ in. thick and 1 in. wide at the bottom and trim off $\frac{1}{2}$ in. at each end to enable the panel to enter the grooves.

Make a horizontal handle 6 in. long and 1 in. square and fix it to the front of the panel by means of $\frac{3}{4}$ in. No. 6 screws driven in from the back.

Filing the Rods.—The next thing to do is to prepare the side bearers for the rods. These are shaped as indicated at B in Fig. 3, and are screwed at an angle to the sides. Cut the rods to length by using a triangular file. File across the seam first and continue filing round the tube until the file mark meets at the seam, then sever the piece by placing it, seam outwards, across your knee and breaking it in the same manner as one would break a piece of wood.

Trim the ends smooth with a file and place the rods in position. The fitment is now complete and can be finished as desired. Before applying any finishing medium, smooth the exterior with glass-paper, rubbing it in the direction of the grain. If art enamel is to be used, stop any knots with knotting and fill the screw holes with plastic wood. Give the surface two undercoats of flat paint of the colour desired, rubbing each coat down with fine glass-paper after it has dried, then apply the enamel with a soft brush.

COAL BOX WITH METAL CONTAINER

THE dimensioned drawings shown in Figs. 1, 2 and 3 illustrate a coal box in wood with a removable, metal container. The top forms a padded seat. The container is designed with a false grid bottom, allowing the larger lumps of coal to rest upon it, while slack falls through, and may be

shovelled up through the door in one end. The seat, door and grid container may be omitted, and the construction simplified accordingly.

The wood case may be made either in solid oak, preferably of the less expensive and more easily worked varieties (e.g., Japanese or Australian)

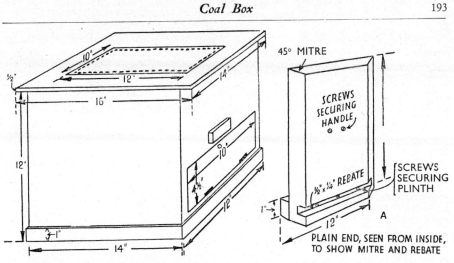

COAL CABINET WITH SHOVEL DOOR
OUTER WOOD CASE IN ½" STUFF

45° MITRE

SCREWS
SECURING
HANDLE

½" x ¼" REBATE

SCREWS
SECURING
PLINTH

A

PLAIN END, SEEN FROM INSIDE,
TO SHOW MITRE AND REBATE

Fig. I

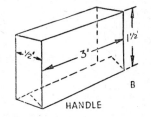

HANDLE

or other hardwood, or in laminated wood faced with oak (or other) ply, in either case of ½ in. thickness. If solid oak is employed, it may be necessary, if difficulty is found in procuring boards of sufficient width, to butt-joint and glue, side by side, boards of about half the specified widths, so as to obtain the sizes. On the other hand, if laminated wood is used, the edges of the top, the plinth and the handles will require facing with ply, neatly mitred.

The Joints.—Reliance is placed generally upon simple mitred joints which, if accurately cut and surfaced, glued and held in cramps until set hard, will give ample strength; the bottom, however, is cut ⅜ in. larger each way than the internal dimensions of the case and is fitted and glued into a ½×¼ in. deep rebate cut on the inner sides of the two sides and two ends, ¼ in. above their lower edges as shown at A in Fig. I.

But first the plinth is glued and screwed on (from the inside of the rebate) with three ¾ in. screws, countersunk.

The top is hinged to one of the sides

and may be fitted, inside, with a brass quadrant stay and stop to hold it open, if desired. The padded seat is stuffed with horsehair or flock and upholstered with leather or leather-cloth of any desired shade, and is held in place with a fillet of the same material, run round the edge and tacked to the wood with brass-headed or leather-covered nails at intervals of, say, 1 in.

The handles, B in Fig. I, are rectangular blocks of wood, 3×1½×½ in., with a finger groove gouged in the bottom edge, glued and held on to the ends of the cabinet with two ¾ in. screws driven from the inside. It will save some fiddling mitre work with ply, if these are cut out of solid timber.

The shovel door is hinged at the bottom to fall outwards, and is fitted in the middle of its top edge, with a

G

ball-spring catch, to hold it in the closed position, and with an external button with which to open it.

The Coal Container.—The metal container is made of flat galvanized sheet iron of twenty or twenty-two gauge (black plate is not recommended, since even if painted, the moisture almost always present in coal, eats it into holes comparatively rapidly). The ends are tapped $\frac{1}{2}$ in. over the sides and rivetted.

The top rim is reinforced with No. 8 W.G. galvanized wire bent to a rect-angle, over which the edges of the sheet forming the sides and ends are tapped. The top and bottom of the shovel-hole are similarly reinforced, as shown in Fig. 2 by two lengths of the same wire.

This may also be used for the cross bars forming the grid; but this size is barely substantial enough, and it would be preferable to use eight lengths of No. 7 W.G. or even $\frac{3}{16}$ in. galvanized wire here.

The carcase may be marked and cut out of one sheet as shown in Fig. 3, allowing $\frac{1}{2}$ in. for all laps, and the two sides and one solid end then bent up at right-angles and the tops beaten over and secured with, say, six rivets down each side (it is not necessary to rivet the top laps over the wire stiffener). The aperture end will obviously be separated in the process of cutting, and should have its edges lapped and rivetted to the sides of the container in a similar manner to the solid end, but with the substitution of two stiffen-ing cross wires for four of the rivets.

Before bending up, however, there are two things to do: form the aperture for the shovel-hole, and mark the centres for the holes to fit the various wires and rivets. The metal is not entirely removed from the aperture, A, Fig. 3, but cut at what will be the bottom and the two sides of the hole, and the

flap so created is bent inward at an angle of approximately 120 deg. The centres for the wires—eight for the grid and two stiffeners—also for the rivets, including those holding the handles, should be carefully set out in accordance with the dimensions, but the holes should not actually be drilled until the carcase has been bent up into its final shape, and all is ready for riveting. Work on the rivets first and leave the wires to the last.

Wiring the Bottom.—The drilling should be carried out with drills of exactly the diameters of the wire and rivets to be employed. The wires themselves should be cut to a length equalling the full outside width of the container, or even a shade more, and when driven into position the ends are secured by liberally sweating them with solder. The bottom of the flap is next lapped from above downwards and round the last grid-wire seen on the right of the illustrations in Fig. 2; lastly the $\frac{1}{2}$ in. strip left at the bottom of the shovel-hole is similarly tapped around its stiffening wire.

There now remains to make and fit the collapsible handles. The two oval loops are bent up from the No. 8 W.G. wire, and each will require a sleeve cut out and made from the galvanized sheet, to be drilled, as shown, with two holes for rivetting on the inside of each end of the container, near the top, in the centre.

If the sizes given are carefully fol-lowed, the container should prove an easy fit in the wood cabinet, $\frac{1}{4}$ in. clearance having been allowed in every direction.

Nevertheless, it is advisable that the container should be made, complete, *before* the wood for the cabinet is cut, and the one measured against the other, to avoid any possibility of a misfit.

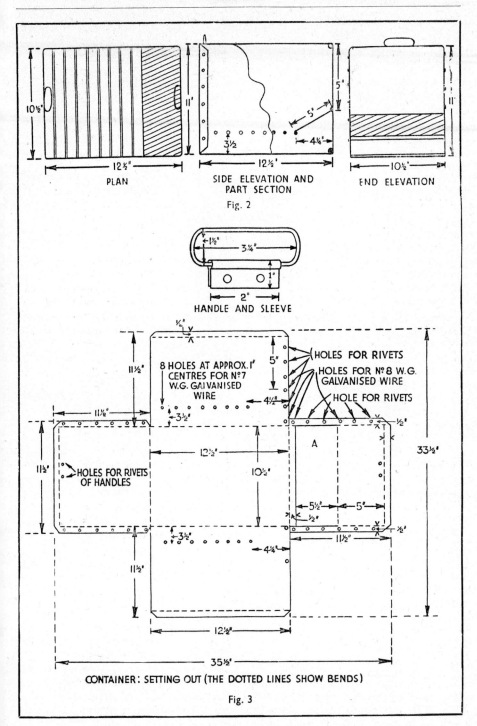

PLAN

SIDE ELEVATION AND
PART SECTION

END ELEVATION

Fig. 2

HANDLE AND SLEEVE

HOLES FOR RIVETS

HOLES FOR Nº 8 W.G.
GALVANISED WIRE

HOLE FOR RIVETS

8 HOLES AT APPROX. 1"
CENTRES FOR Nº 7
W.G. GALVANISED
WIRE

HOLES FOR RIVETS
OF HANDLES

A

CONTAINER: SETTING OUT (THE DOTTED LINES SHOW BENDS)

Fig. 3

WOODEN COAL BUNKER

A WOODEN coal bunker to hold a ton or half-ton of coal can be constructed according to the details given in the accompanying drawings. It is made of deal scantlings for the frame and ¾ in. weather boards for the outer covering. Fig. 1 shows the bunker complete and Fig. 2 the framing.

The structure is 5×3×4 ft. high at the front and 5 ft. deep at the back to

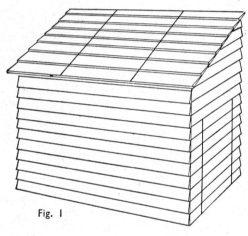

Fig. 1

allow sufficient slope in the roof to carry off water. The framing consists of posts 2½ in. square of rough, good quality, sawn timber. They are connected by side and end rails, and the top members are at an angle to form a support for the roof. The bottom rails are at ground level and the posts project 2 in. below the lower edges of these rails in order to allow them to be bedded in a cement floor, which is the only suitable base for an outside coal bunker.

The side and front middle rails are 2 ft. 6 in. and the back 3 ft. 6 in. from the ground and are of 1×2 in. stuff let in flush with the outside faces of the posts, the joint being shown in Fig. 3.

They are fixed with galvanized nails or may be secured with galvanized screws. The three front posts can be laid alongside each other and marked and the recesses for the top, middle and bottom rails cut across with a saw and the remainder removed with a chisel. The same can be done with the three back posts. The end rail is similarly cut to lie flush with the middle rail.

The Back and Front.—The end middle rail and bottom rail, at the end most convenient for the situation the bunker has to occupy, are connected by uprights A and B halved in at the top and bottom. These are central with the width of the end and 14 in. apart. They form an aperture for the removal of the coal when the supply is getting low. The two intermediate sloping members form an opening in the top of the bunker for shooting coal in from sacks and also for the removal of coal until it is reduced to a level which enables it to be shovelled and heaped to the far end of the bunker and conveniently withdrawn from the end opening. The end opposite the small door could have its top horizontal rail fitted just below the top of the front post, as shown, and a big door fitted to fill that space. This arrangement would allow one to get into the interior for the purpose of shovelling the coal to the opposite end when the supply gets low, as the physical effort necessary to reach the end from the small door would be heavy. This is, however, a refinement which may be incorporated and will be dealt with later.

The framing having been constructed, it should be moved to the place made ready for it. This will be a flat surface

6×4 ft. prepared and levelled and with 2 in. of concrete laid down. Holes should be sunk for the six posts and these should be inserted as the framing is lifted into position. The whole levelled and the holes filled with cement. An inch layer of sand and cement should be laid over the surface and well into the holes around the posts.

If the bunker has to back up against a wall or fence the back weather board should be laid along the back and nailed with zinc or galvanized nails before the framework is cemented in position.

If the bunker be backed up to a brick wall, neither the back boarding nor the middle post and the rails will be required; the end posts being simply nailed to the wall with flat-head staples driven in at the side, but a rail to support the back of the roof will have to be fixed along the wall at the height of the back end posts. The top of all the posts must be sawn off to suit the angle of the roof, and the top edges of the front and back rails will also have to be bevelled to the same angle.

Fixing Weather-boards. — The weather-boarding should be laid across the front and the end to be entirely closed, beginning at the bottom with the thick edge downwards. The boards should be 5 in. wide and overlap an inch so that twelve weather-boards will therefore be required for the front. The end opposite the aperture will be similarly treated until the boards reach the top of the front post, after which the boards will have to be cut to an angle at the ends as they continue to the height of the back post until they line up with the top edge of the end top rail. Similarly in the aperture end they will be laid from the bottom up each side of the short posts, but not reaching to their

inside edge. They should be 1 in. from the inside edge to allow a space for the door to close up against the post (the door being made of similar weather-boarding), but above the door-head they should be continued all along and tapered off at the ends to match the fall of the roof and extend right up level with the top of the roof end rail.

In the same way the boarding will be fixed on the top. It should start at the

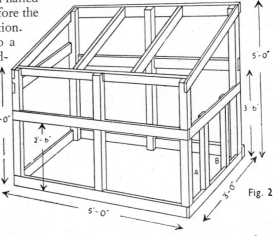

Fig. 2

bottom with the thick edge of the weather-board overlapping 2 in. to clear the rain from the front, and should extend beyond each end

Fig. 3

of the bunker for 2 in. for a similar purpose. This top boarding should be fixed on each side of the aperture and the inner ends flush with the two centre top cross-pieces.

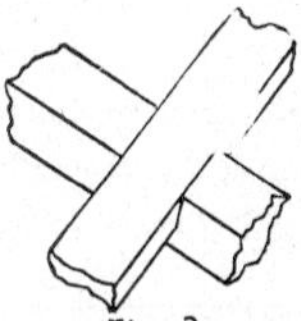

The back of the hatch rests on the top back rail. It consists of weather-boards, as shown in Fig. 1, on two battens of 3×1 in. stuff. The ends of the battens at the back should be cut away so that the top weather-board rests upon the face of the top back rail (or the rail on the wall in the case of a lean-to bunker) and the bottom ends treated in the same manner to enable the front top board to rest on the front top rail of the bunker, while a fillet nailed to the sides of the sloping pieces keeps the cover in position. The cover does not need any hinges. It is simply lifted to one side when the bunker is being replenished and replaced afterwards.

The end door is made with plain $\frac{3}{4} \times 5$ in. weather-boards nailed on two battens. The width of the door is equal to the width between the inside ends of the covering boards and rests against the uncovered parts of the two posts which form the opening.

The battens fit between the rails and a pair of cross garnets are screwed through the top board into the battens and to the weather-board above it. Suitable wooden buttons fixed just above the lower edge of the weather-boards will keep the cover closed when not in use.

Two or three applications of creosote should be given to the exterior as well as the interior of the bunker to give it a finish and preserve the wood.

MAKING AND FITTING CLOTHES POSTS

THE clothes post illustrated in Fig. 1 is removable and is also provided with a loose box for accommodating the clothes line.

Obtain a 9 ft. length of good yellow deal, remove the roughness with a plane and bore two $\frac{3}{4}$ in. holes with the aid of a twist-bit, 4 in. from the top, through adjacent sides as shown, and cut two pieces of dowel rod, 8 in. long, round the ends to remove the sharp edge and drive them into the holes.

A Pulley Hoist.—If a pulley is preferred to pegs, there are several ways of fitting one. An easy method is to procure a galvanized pulley sheaf as used for wireless aerials, and attach it by galvanized wire to a strong screw-eye in the post, as illustrated at A in Fig. 2. Another way is to get a bracket pulley and fix it to the post with wood screws. This is indicated at B.

The method represented at C is perhaps the best, but the top end of the post requires to be morticed right through to house the pulley. The mortice should be as wide as the thickness of the pulley plus $\frac{1}{4}$ in. to enable a washer $\frac{1}{8}$ in. thick to be inserted between the wood and the pulley at each side of the latter. A $3\frac{1}{2} \times \frac{1}{4}$ in. bolt serves as a spindle. It is fixed by a suitable nut.

The top of the post should be provided with a cap shaped from a piece of wood 1 in. thick, and to give the cap a finished appearance, the top edges should be chamfered. The cap also keeps moisture from entering the end grain of the wood. A piece of sheet zinc will do equally well. Use galvanized iron nails for fixing the metal, as uncoated nails will rust.

At a distance of 1 ft. from the bottom end, pieces of planed batten 1 in. thick $\times 1\frac{1}{2}$ in. will be needed for a collar, the top edges of which should be bevelled as shown and fixed by galvanized nails.

An iron cleat, costing a few pence, will be required for anchoring the line. This should be fixed by screws at about 3 ft. 6 in. above the ground level.

The box measures 7 in. wide, 7 in. back to front, and is provided with a sloping hinged lid. The thickness of

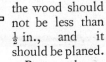

the wood should not be less than ½ in., and it should be planed.

Brass butt hinges should be used for fixing the lid, and a couple of holes drilled in line near the top at the back, to accommodate the ends of two nails driven slantwise into the post.

The socket into which the post fits may be either

COLLAR

Fig. 1

the top of the socket a little above the ground. Make a suitable wooden cap or stopper to keep out the soil when not in use.

To make a cement socket, excavate the soil to a depth of 12 in. and about 12 in. square, and, in the centre of this, suspend a length of 3×3 in. wood to act as a core and then fill the hole with cement mortar. The wood core should be carefully planed, slightly tapered from top to bottom and coated with grease to enable it to be withdrawn when the cement has set. A strong cement mortar can be made by mixing one bucketful of portland cement with three bucketsful of clean sand, thoroughly incorporating them together in the dry state and then mixing with

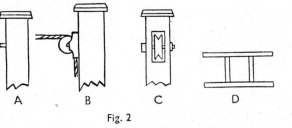

Fig. 2

of wood or cement. The latter is better, as wood—especially soft wood—rots very quickly below the ground. A wooden socket should be made of timber at least 1 in. thick and the two opposite sides should extend 6 in. beyond the others as indicated at D in Fig. 2.

The Post Socket.—Give the wooden socket two or three coats of creosote before burying in the ground. Fill the hole with broken brick, stones, and ram it well down, taking care to keep

water. Any cement mortar left over can be used for making a cover by constructing a mould and then filling with cement. If this method of socket construction is adopted it will be necessary to taper the lower end of the post.

In order to preserve the post, give it either two or three coats of lead paint or creosote.

When a woven rope is employed for a clothes line it should always be removed after use and not allowed to remain out in wet weather.

A PORTABLE BOOT SCRAPER

FIG. 1 shows a portable boot scraper, useful for placing outside the garden workshop or back door. It consists of two side pieces of 3×2 in. deal, 11 in. long, which supports five strips of iron

Fig. 1

13 in. in length, 1 in. wide and $\frac{1}{8}$ in. thick. Two cheap household brushes with stiff bristles, costing about sixpence each, are screwed to pieces of wood 7 in. long × 3 in. wide and 1 in. thick and these are fixed to the side members.

To keep the boot scraper from slipping about, an objectionable feature in a great many of the portable type, a hole is provided at each corner through which a metal skewer is pushed into the ground.

Two pieces of iron are screwed to the underside of the end members to keep them apart.

Making the Base.—After having sawn and planed the two end base members, cut the ends to the shape shown in the constructional drawings in Figs. 2 and 3, and then make five slots $\frac{3}{16}$ in. wide right across the inner face of each. These are made a trifle wider than the thickness of the iron strips to enable them to be withdrawn.

Cut recesses in the undersides to take the two iron distance pieces. These are

1 in. wide and $\frac{1}{8}$ in. deep to enable the faces to lie flush when fixed with screws.

Now saw and plane two pieces of $\frac{3}{4}$ in. square wood 9 in. long as shown at A in Figs. 2 and 3, and fix them to the inner faces of the end members, keeping their top edges 1 in. below the top edge of the slotted pieces.

These square pieces support the scraping irons and prevent them from slipping to the bottom. Bore a hole of $\frac{3}{16}$ in. diameter at each corner as indicated.

Next, prepare the upper pieces of the ends c, and on each inner face fix a brush by screws driven in from the outer face, as shown.

The Metal Parts.—Now for the metal work. Procure sufficient iron of the width and thickness specified to produce five pieces 13 in. long and two pieces 16 in. in length. Use a hack saw for cutting and file the ends square.

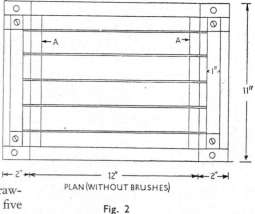

PLAN (WITHOUT BRUSHES)

Fig. 2

Slightly round the bottom corners of the shorter ones for easy insertion into the slots.

Drill two holes near each end of the longer pieces to clear No. 8 brass countersunk-headed screws, in the centre and spaced 1 in. apart and 1 in. from the end. Countersink the tops of the holes

Give the whole scraper a couple of coats of lead paint. Clean the metal strips and paint them with aluminium

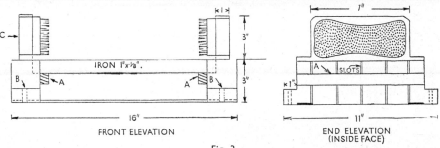

IRON 1"x⅛".

3"

3"

16"

FRONT ELEVATION

1"

A SLOTS

1"

11"

END ELEVATION
(INSIDE FACE)

Fig. 3

to allow the heads of the screws to lie flush, and then fix them in the recesses provided in the end members.

paint. When dry, insert the strips into the grooves and secure the scraper to the ground by means of the four skewers.

A NEEDLEWORK BOX

An interesting example of light cabinet-making is the needlework box illustrated in Fig. 1.

The box measures $7\frac{3}{4} \times 6\frac{1}{2} \times 5\frac{1}{4}$ in. deep and accommodates a shallow, partitioned tray at the top, a space below for scissors, crochet-hooks and the like, and a drawer for reels of cotton, silk, and thread, fitted with upright wooden pegs for the reels.

Mahogany is used for the construction and if neatly made and finished carefully with french polish applied with a very soft brush would make an acceptable gift.

As the thickness of the wood does not exceed $\frac{1}{4}$ in. it can be conveniently sawn with a fretsaw.

The top of the lid, the bottom of the compartment and the base of the box are cut from wood $\frac{1}{8}$ in. thick, while the rest of the body is of material $\frac{3}{16}$ in. in thickness.

To construct the box, follow the dimensions shown in Fig. 2, and a start can be made by marking out and

G*

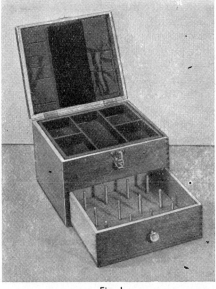

Fig. 1

cutting the exterior parts. Make sure that all items are square.

Although the corner joints may be formed by simply butting the members and gluing them together, a much stronger joint is that known as a corner lock joint. This type of joint is made by cutting away small portions at equidistant intervals along the edge of one member to be joined and forming a

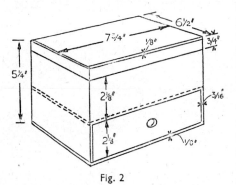

Fig. 2

series of projections in the joining edge of the other. The projections engage in the gaps and when accurately made and glued form an exceptionally strong joint. Such a joint is seen at A in Fig. 3.

Assembling the Parts.—When the parts are ready for assembling, fix the ends to the front and back using tube glue. If the members are butted together, use thin panel pins or pins minus their heads to strengthen the joint. The pins are unnecessary with a corner locked joint.

While the glue is still wet, fix on the bottom. Tube glue and $\frac{1}{2}$ in. panel pins may be used for this, unless thin brass countersunk-headed screws are preferred, but, if the latter are used, care must be taken not to split the wood as they are likely to do in a position so near the edge.

Make sure that this part of the work is square and then bind string tightly round to keep the parts cramped together. To prevent damage to the corners, pieces of thick cardboard should be interposed between the string and the wood.

Then assemble the lid, fixing the parts together with tube glue, and bind

string round it in the same manner as that of the body. If these parts are assembled in the evening, the glue will be hard by morning.

The bottom of the compartment can now be fitted. To do this, glue and pin supporting fillets of $\frac{1}{4}$ in. square section stripwood on the inside faces of the body as indicated by the dotted lines in Fig. 2 and glue the bottom member to them.

Fig. 3, B shows details of the tray while the illustration at C in the same figure indicates the method of notching the partition strips where they cross each other at right-angles. The ends of the strip should be housed in shallow grooves cut in the inside faces of the tray. If it is found inconvenient to cut square grooves, they can be V-shaped,

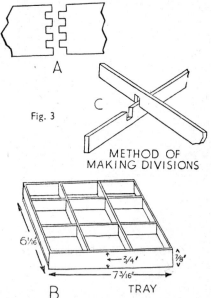

A

C

Fig. 3

METHOD OF MAKING DIVISIONS

B   TRAY

in which case the ends of the strips will have to be shaped accordingly to fit. These should be a tight fit and all parts fixed together with glue. The tray rests on a couple of $\frac{1}{4} \times \frac{1}{8}$ in. fillets glued to the front and back faces of the interior.

Making the Drawer.—At A in Fig. 4

is seen details of the drawer. Make up the frame consisting of the front, back and sides and fasten on to the bottom. A piece of wood $\frac{1}{4}$ in. thick cut to fit the frame is bored to take three rows of four pegs upon which the reels are placed. The pegs are pieces of $\frac{3}{16}$ in. diameter dowel rod each $1\frac{3}{4}$ in. long and are glued into the holes in the base. The bottom of the projecting pieces should lie flush with the underside of the base, which, when the assembly is completed, it should be fixed to the bottom of the drawer-frame by two short countersunk-headed screws driven in from the underside of the box.

There is no need to finish the interior with a high gloss. All that is necessary is to give the surfaces a few spots of linseed oil applied with a soft linen rag. This, if rubbed well, will impart a pleasing dull polish, but too much oil must be avoided.

The exterior should be well rubbed down with fine glass-paper and given several coats of french polish applied with a camel hair mop, allowing each layer to harden before applying the next.

To complete the work, the lid should be hinged to the body with small brass butt hinges, a small mahogany knob fixed to the front of the drawer and a suitable fastener as that illustrated at B in Fig. 4 secured by small round-headed brass screws driven into the front of the lid and the box.

If it is desired to form a cushion under the top of

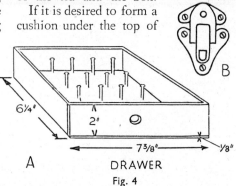

A   DRAWER

Fig. 4

the lid for accommodating needles and pins, it can be accomplished by gluing a piece of silk over a foundation of tightly-pressed cotton wool.

To prevent the bottom of the box from scratching polished surfaces, it is an advantage to glue a piece of neatly-cut baize on the underside.

TROUSER PRESS AND TIE PRESS

THE trouser press and the tie press shown in Fig. 1 are simple and efficient. In each case they consist merely of two pieces of wood hinged together.

This really is the best method, as there are no parts to screw down. The trousers are folded carefully and put in the press, with the turn-ups projecting from the far end, the lid dropped down and secured by the catch C first then D and E, Fig. 1.

Time taken is a few seconds only, the tie press takes even less.

The trouser press may be made of deal, oak, mahogany or walnut, and the one shown in the illustration A in Fig. 1 is 3 ft. × 1 ft. 4 in. Each board finished $\frac{5}{8}$ in. thick. It is not advisable to make the press smaller.

Beginning Work.—To make the trouser press, plane and square up two pieces of wood each 3 ft. × 1 ft. 4 in. × $\frac{5}{8}$ in. To prevent these wide boards from warping, it is important to determine which side of the board is to be face side. This is done by looking at the ends of the boards and placing the heart side up, which is shown by the annual rings.

Now on the back board, screw on three strong brass catches, these can be purchased or fretsawn with a metal fretsaw in the following way: get a piece of brass or other metal about $\frac{1}{10}$ in. thick, clamp the metal so that it projects $1\frac{1}{2}$ in. beyond the bench, mark out to cover the edges of the brass hinges which project from the back edges of the wood, as shown in the details at c in Fig. 1.

Through each piece of metal, bore six holes as shown in the illustration with a $\frac{3}{16}$ in. metal twist-drill; counter-sink the holes and fit in the screws.

Place the metal strips in position

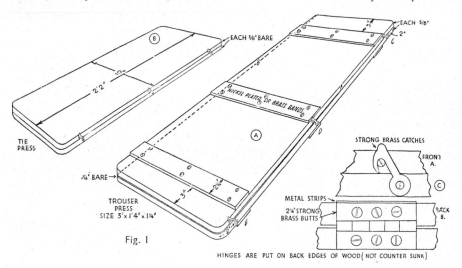

Fig. 1

HINGES ARE PUT ON BACK EDGES OF WOOD (NOT COUNTER SUNK)

the catches on the metal with a scriber (a stout steel knitting needle will do), bore the holes for the screws first and then fret out the metal catches. Round over all edges with small files (those sold at most chain stores at sixpence a card are quite good).

Now screw on three strong $2\frac{1}{4}$ in. brass butts (hinges). These are screwed flat on to back edges of the trouser press with the inside of the hinge facing outwards. When screwing the second piece, leave $\frac{1}{16}$ in. bare space between the two boards.

Metal Work.—Buy sufficient metal —i.e., about 8 ft. 3 in. $\times 2\frac{1}{4} \times \frac{1}{16}$ in. (No. 16 Birmingham wire gauge)—and cut this up into six pieces each 1 ft. $4\frac{1}{8}$ in. long $\times 2\frac{1}{4}$ in. wide. The extra $\frac{1}{8}$ in. is

exactly over each hinge. To do this, place the metal flush with the front edge of the press so that the extra $\frac{1}{8}$ in. covers the edge of the brass butt-hinges, then screw on the six metal strips—i.e., three on the back and three on the front of the press. These metal strips are an additional safeguard against the wood warping.

With a small file, file round the back edges, carrying these latter edges well over to the edges of the brass butts. Round off the sharp edges of the press and round off the corners with a chisel, file and glass-paper (Nos. $1\frac{1}{2}$ and 1). Shut down the press so as to find the exact position of the small round-headed screws that are screwed into the top piece and screw them in.

Finally, clean up the wood with 1½×1 in. glass-paper, working with the grain.

A useful hint to prevent the trouser press from scratching the polished surface of a table is to screw two battens underneath the extreme ends, size 1 ft. 4 in.×1½×⅜ in. and cover these with velvet or baize.

A Tie Press.—The tie press, B in Fig. 1, is easier to make as there are no metal strips.

Square up two pieces of wood to size, each piece 2 ft. 2 in.×9×⅜ in. bare. Screw on four hinges, size 1 in., in the same way as the trouser press, true up the edges of wood and put on the fasteners (clips) and clean up with glass-

paper, etc., as before mentioned. This press will hold a number of ties.

The pull on hinges gives the necessary pressure. Being screwed on the back edges (see trouser press) prevents the wood from splitting.

To give the presses a nice appearance, polish them on the outside only with beeswax and turpentine. Wax polishes may be obtained to suit the colour of the wood you use. If dark oak colour is required, mix vandyke brown powder and .880 liquid ammonia (50-50) into a paste, and thin out with water to the required colour. Leave it to dry, rub with canvas and then wax-polish, putting on and rubbing off the polish with a soft cloth.

A FOLDING
TABLE TENNIS TOP

THE modern home seldom contains a room sufficiently large to accommodate a table tennis table of standard size, measuring 9 ft. long × 5 ft. wide, but a smaller one may be used with equal success.

The dimensions of the table-top here described and illustrated are 7 ft. long × 3 ft. 9 in. wide, but these measurements can be suited to the space available.

As will be seen by Figs. 1 and 2, the table-top consists of two sections of equal size and of the same construction, hinged at the centre to facilitate portability.

The top itself is of ⅜ in. plywood.

This is fixed to a frame of 2×1 in. planed yellow deal battens.

Thinner plywood could be used, but the more solid the base the better the

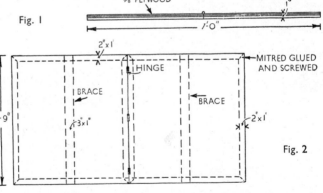

Fig. 1

Fig. 2

bounce, and it is for this reason that extra cross braces are fixed underneath the plywood top.

Good birch plywood, which will give an excellent surface, can be obtained for about sixpence per square foot cut to size, so that this item will cost approximately fourteen shillings.

Fixing the Top.—There are several methods of fixing the top to the side and end battens. If a rebating plane is available, a good job can be made by forming a rebate in the top inner edges and sinking the plywood into these. These rebates should be 1 in. wide and ⅜ in. deep as shown in Fig. 3. Another method is to fix the plywood to the battens so that the edges of the plywood are flush with the sides. In both cases

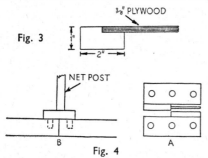

Fig. 3

Fig. 4

the corner joints can be simply mitred together and fixed with glue and No. 6 2½ in. screws. This is the method adopted in Figs. 1 and 2.

The cross bearers of the rebated frame are ⅝ in. thick and 3½ in. wide. The ends of these should be cut to fit exactly between the side members, and both pieces should be fixed by means of 4 in. No. 6 screws driven through the side members into the ends. The bottom faces of these members must lie flush with the lower faces of the sides.

Cross bearers 1 in. thick are used in the plain frame and can be fixed by screws.

It is wise to smooth the top face of the plywood with fine glass-paper and then apply the colouring medium, which should be green, and to paint the battens before assembly. A good oil stain should be used for the plywood as water stain may raise the grain. Glossy paint must be

avoided as it casts confusing reflections.

Precautions.—If the rebate construction has been used, care should be taken to prevent paint getting into the rebates as this would prevent the glue by which the plywood is fixed into the rebates from adhering properly. The same applies to the top of the battens where the flush side method is adopted.

When the paint is dry, apply cold glue to the rebates, or the top faces of the frame, as the case may be, and also to the cross braces and the underside of the panels where they join. Then drive in 1 in. oval brads at intervals of about 3 in. near the edges of the plywood to secure the battens further.

Punch the heads of the brads so that they lie just on the surface and fill the holes with plastic wood. When dry, smooth level and touch up with stain. Do not drive nails in that portion of the plywood above the cross pieces as it is essential that the surface be perfectly smooth.

Loose butt-hinges as illustrated at A in Fig. 4 should be used for fastening the two sections. Such hinges allow the section to be entirely disconnected when not in use.

The Hinges.—The leaves of the hinges should be recessed into the end battens to enable the ends to butt together without any gap. The centre pins of the hinges will project a small fraction of an inch above the surface at the joint, but as this is the same position as the lower edge of the net their presence will not matter.

To prevent the pins of the hinges slipping out of their sockets the bases of the net posts are provided with dowel pins on the underside, which engage in corresponding holes drilled in the battens as indicated at B in Fig. 4. The posts themselves consist of pieces of ⅝ in. dowel rod, the lower ends of which fit in holes in the bases, as shown.

RACQUET PRESS

THE press shown in the detailed drawing Fig. 1, is made of seasoned English beech. Birch or American black walnut would do equally well.

Two frames will be required. First plane and square up two pieces of wood exactly to $11\frac{1}{4} \times 1\frac{1}{16} \times \frac{1}{2}$ in., and two pieces to $8\frac{1}{16} \times 1\frac{1}{16} \times \frac{1}{2}$ in. It is important to keep to these sizes so that the frame of the racquet is cramped in the press nearly all round. See illustration.

Now measure $1\frac{1}{16}$ in. from each end of all the four pieces of wood and square lines across and all round. Then divide the $\frac{1}{2}$ in. thickness of the wood into three parts and gauge the two lines round the edges and ends of each piece. The joint shown is a bridle joint, sometimes called an open tenon. The centre of the wood is cut away on the short pieces, forming an open mortice. The two outside pieces are cut away on the two $11\frac{1}{4}$ in. strips, forming the tenons.

Gauging the Tenons.—When sawing down the tenons on the long pieces, put the wood in the vice upright and, when sawing the left-hand line, look on the right-hand side of the saw; when sawing the right-hand line, look on the left of the saw, and leave the gauge lines in. Never saw on a line, as the thickness of the saw-cut puts out the measurement.

Saw off the outsides of the tenons and chisel out the mortices on the short

pieces. Fit and glue up the frame work, allow it to dry for twelve hours and then true up the surfaces with a smoothing plane.

Purchase a set of wing nuts and bolts Three of these will be ordinary ones but the fourth one will be hinged.

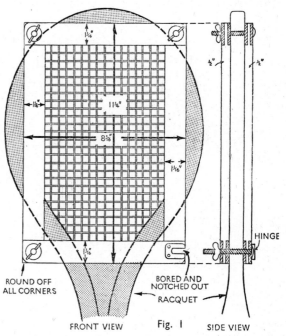

ROUND OFF ALL CORNERS

BORED AND NOTCHED OUT

RACQUET

FRONT VIEW Fig. I SIDE VIEW

HINGE

Examine the lower right corner in the illustration, Fig. 1. Then drill a hole in a spare piece of wood and fit in the bolt. The hole will probably have to be $\frac{5}{16}$ in. diameter. This is a necessary precaution and may save the press being spoilt.

With a twist-drill, bore a hole in each corner of the press and, in the case of the lower right hole only, saw from the edge into the sides of this hole, forming a slot as shown.

Put the three other bolts in and screw up tightly. Clean off the edges so that front and back frames are the same size.

Take the frames apart and, with a sharp ½ in. chisel, pare off the corners to round them. Smooth off with a file and 1½ and 1 glass-paper. Clean up the framework and take off all sharp corners.

Assembling.—Then screw the frames together again to find the exact position for the hinged nut and bolt in the lower right-hand corner. Screw this hinge on, completing the press so far as construction is concerned.

To ensure the press keeping its shape, soak it thoroughly in a mixture composed of three parts of linseed oil to one of turpentine.

Do this until the wood has absorbed all the oil it can take. Between applications, it is advisable to rub the oil in with a cloth every time it appears on the surface of the wood.

Leave the racquet press in a warm room for a few days and then polish it with dry beeswax worked · into the grain. Warm a piece of beeswax by the fire and rub it with a piece of canvas. Then rub the canvas on the wood.

A PORTABLE TOOL CASE

THERE are many jobs outside the workshop and the portable tool case shown in Fig. 1 will be useful for carrying tools on such occasions.

The construction is simple, strong and convenient.

The body is divided into four sections, the largest one for accommodating tools such as planes and the smaller ones for holding little tools, nails and screws. The lid is provided with divisions, the upper one for housing a small hand saw, the lower division to the right for chisels and the space to the left for boring bits.

The arrangement of the body and lid compartments and details of construction can be clearly seen by referring to Fig. 2 at A and B respectively.

The whole of the body is made of best quality yellow deal ½ in. thick except the top of the lid, which is ⅜ in. in thickness. As deal boards are seldom wider than 11 in., the lid and the bottom will have to be built up to obtain the desired width, viz., 16 in. Two pieces of 9 in. prepared stuff should be used for these items and the

surplus sawn off and the edges trimmed with a plane.

A glued butt-joint could be used for joining the timbers longways, but better results will be obtained if the edges to be joined are grooved and fitted with a loose tongue, which is afterwards glued up.

In any case, the following prepared wood, including sufficient for waste, will be required for the body.

One board 3 ft. 6 in. long × 8 in. wide and ⅜ in. thick for the top of the lid and a board of the same length and width, but ½ in. thick for the bottom. A 6 ft. 6 in. length ½ in. stuff, 8 in. wide, for the sides and ends.

In addition, a piece 3 ft. long, 6 in. wide × ½ in. in thickness will be required for the partitions in the body, while 3 ft. of 1¼ × ½ in. planed batten will be ample for the divisions in the lid.

A piece of thick leather strap, 9½ in. long × ⅞ in. wide, will make a suitable handle. Eighteen 1 in. No. 6 brass countersunk-headed screws will be necessary for fixing the top of the lid to the lid frame members, and the same

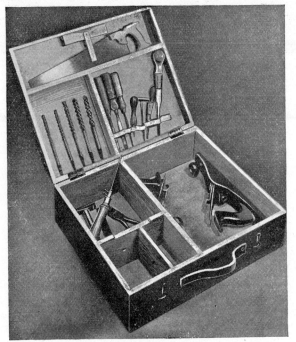

Fig. 1

surplus being sawn and trimmed up with a plane after gluing.

If the tongued and grooved method of forming the joint is used, plough a $\frac{1}{8}$ in. wide groove in the edges to be joined in the lid members as well as those of the bottom. The grooves should be ploughed $\frac{3}{8}$ in. deep, and this will require a feather or strip $\frac{3}{4}$ in. wide for the joint. In forming the joint it is essential that the edges be true and only a faint line should be observed.

Glue the edges and feathers of the pieces to be joined, cramp them up and let them remain in the cramps until the glue is dry.

When ready, the pieces can be removed from the cramps, the surplus wood sawn off the sides and ends and trimmed up squarely with a plane.

Prepare the sides of the body, taking care to see that the ends are square. As

number of similar screws $1\frac{1}{4}$ in. long for fixing the bottom. Also sixteen $1\frac{1}{2}$ in. No. 6 screws for fixing the side ends.

For hinging the lid, a pair of $2 \times \frac{1}{2}$ in. brass butts and a dozen $\frac{3}{4}$ in. No. 6 brass screws for fixing them should be obtained together with a pair of 2 in. brass hooks and eyes to keep the lid closed.

Simplified Construction.—To simplify construction the joints are screwed butt-joints. The front and back of the body should overlap the ends of the sides and not vice versa, as the front should always present as neat an appearance as possible, unbroken by avoidable joints, as is the case of constructing drawers.

Start by making the top of the lid and the bottom of the box. The timber for these should be sawn $\frac{1}{2}$ in. longer at the ends than the finished size, the

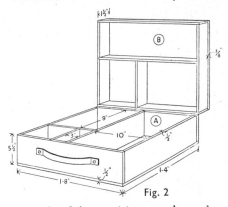

Fig. 2

the ends of the partitions are housed or recessed into the sides and the ends of the body, the latter should now be grooved to accommodate them. To do this, mark the lines across the wood at the correct position and saw at the guide lines, taking care to keep the teeth of the saw within the waste part to ensure a good fit. If the saw cuts into the material on the other side of the lines the resulting joint will be sloppy when it ought to be tight.

The best way to remove the waste material after having sawn to depth is to place the member in the vice and use a sharp chisel first from one edge to the centre and then from the opposite side to the centre and then neatly level the bottom of the channel.

The operation is then repeated with the ends and sides of the lid.

Assuming that the glued joints in the top and bottom boards are quite firm, the parts may be assembled. A number of screw holes should first be drilled in those parts to receive the plain portion underneath the heads of the screws. These holes are necessary as they ensure tight joints.

Screwing and Joining.—As the screwing operation may prove awkward at the outset, it is a good plan to fix the first member to be joined between the jaws of the bench vice and place its fellow member over the supported piece, seeing to it that the edges are flush and then driving in the screws. The same method can be applied in joining the next member and, when this is finished, remove the work from the vice and complete it on the bench.

The frame is now ready to receive the top of the lid or the bottom according to which frame has been assembled first. Both the lid and the bottom are fixed in the same way by simply driving the screws into the edges of the frames. Before driving the screws, make sure that the edges of the board are flush with the sides and ends of the frame.

Now fix the partition pieces into their respective grooves. Use plenty of glue and wipe off the surplus with a rag.

The next job is to fix the hinges. Recesses should be cut in the lower edge of the lid and the upper one of the body. The recesses are cut to a depth equal to the thickness of a leaf of the hinge, so that the surfaces lie flush with those of the wood. See that the hinges are placed squarely before driving in the screws because any other position will strain the joints when opened.

The leather handle is now fastened to the front by means of screws; a small washer being inserted between the leather and the underside of the screwhead. The hooks and eyes are then screwed to the body and lid.

To keep the chisels in position, small loops of thin leather are used, the blades being protected by fitting a length of $\frac{1}{4}$ in. stripwood to form a groove in the back member of the lid. The hand saw and tenon saw are held by means of similar loops and turn buttons which fit over the handles.

To protect the bare wood and give it finish, the exterior should be glass-papered and then stained and varnished.

STORE CUPBOARD FOR TOOLS

THE store cupboard shown in Fig. 1 is easy and inexpensive to make. Purchase 100 ft. of $2\frac{1}{4} \times 1\frac{1}{8}$ in. pine or deal battens. These are usually sup-

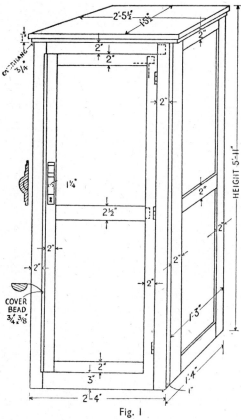

Fig. 1

plied in 10 ft. or 12 ft. lengths. Also, two 12 ft. lengths of $3 \times 1\frac{1}{8}$ in.

This will make the whole of the outside framework of the store cupboard.

Plane and square up the front framework, i.e., two pieces each 5 ft. 10 in. $\times 2 \times 1$ in., one piece 2 ft. 2 in. $\times 2 \times 1$ in. and one piece 2 ft. 2 in. $\times 3$ ft. $\times 1$ in. These four pieces have to be morticed and tenoned together. The mortices

are $1\frac{1}{8}$ in. deep. Take the two long pieces, and with a pencil, square lines across, and all round on one end of each piece. Measure from the extreme end $\frac{1}{2}$ in. and 2 in., then square lines all round. This will give the size of the exact length of mortice which works out to $1\frac{1}{2}$ in. long. These pieces are to become the top of the cupboard.

On the same long pieces, but measuring from the other ends, mark off $\frac{1}{2}$ in. and 3 in. and square lines all round. The length of these mortices is $2\frac{1}{2}$ in. and the width of the tenons is one-third of 1 in. Now cut the mortices and tenons and glue up this front piece of framework only.

Then work on the side pieces of the framework in the same way, but note they are only 1 ft. 3 in. (out to out) wide and they have a 2 in. rail across the centre, as indicated in the drawing in Fig. 1.

Frame up the back, size 5 ft. 10 in.$\times$2 ft. 2 in. and put in a 2 in. rail across the centre, the same as the sides.

Plywood Panels.—Now purchase sufficient plywood to panel the sides, back and front. The plywood should be $\frac{3}{16}$ in. thick. For the back, birch will do; but for the front and sides it will be better to have baywood (swamp mahogany), Columbian pine or ash. As the three pieces of framework are now set up, it is easy to arrive at the sizes of the plywood panels. When measuring for these, allow $\frac{3}{16}$ in. extra all round as they are grooved into the frames $\frac{3}{16}$ in. deep. Cut out and square the panels. Take all three sets of framework apart and plough a $\frac{3}{16} \times \frac{3}{16}$ in. groove on all face edges. These, of course, are the inside edges.

The grooves should be ploughed and run out from mortice to mortice and the ends of the grooves finished with a chisel.

Fit in the panels and glue up the three sets. Four sets of framing, including the front, are now complete. Screw them together by boring $\frac{3}{16}$ in. holes $\frac{1}{4}$ in. deep in the front frame only, and then bore through the frame with a $\frac{1}{4}$ in. twist-drill so as to countersink the screw-heads $\frac{1}{4}$ in. below the surface.

Screw this front frame on to the sides and then screw the back framework in the clear—i.e., from the sides. Plug up the screw holes with $\frac{3}{8}$ in. dowels.

Square up, fit and nail in the bottom of the cupboard from the sides and back rails as it fits in the clear. Punch in the nails below the surface.

The Cupboard Top.—Cut out the top of the cupboard, size 2 ft. $5\frac{1}{2}$ in. $\times$ 1 ft. $5\frac{1}{2}$ in. $\times$ 1 in., and rebate all round as shown. The $\frac{3}{4}$ in. overhang at the back enables the top of the cupboard to touch the wall. This keeps it steady and prevents dust getting behind.

Screw or nail on the top of the cupboard. Next, purchase sufficient white or red deal for the six shelves, Fig. 2. This should be 14 in. wide $\times \frac{1}{2}$ in. thick. Buy also some battens $1\frac{1}{4} \times \frac{1}{2}$ in. Screw these in their appropriate places inside the cupboard to support the shelves.

Square up the shelves and fit them in. The corners must be notched out so that they fit up against the panels.

Now cut out and square up the framework for the door. Mortice, tenon and groove it in the same way as the side framework, fit in the panels and glue up. Allow it to dry, then fit it into the front of the cupboard.

Plane and square up four battens, each 1 ft. $9\frac{1}{2}$ in. $\times 1\frac{1}{4} \times \frac{3}{8}$ in. These are then screwed on to the framework inside the door to provide tool racks.

The ends of these battens should be bevelled off $\frac{3}{8} \times \frac{1}{4}$ in. to give a neat appearance.

Plane and square up one lowest batten, size 1 ft. $9\frac{1}{2}$ in. $\times 2 \times \frac{3}{8}$ in., bevel it and screw on. This batten will take a tenon and dovetail saw. Plane and square up one piece 1 ft. 8 in. $\times 1 \times 1$ in. for the rack for files, as shown in detail at B in Fig. 3. This piece should be hollowed out from end to end ($\frac{3}{4} \times \frac{3}{4}$ in.) with a gouge. Fix it by pinning from the bottom of the hollow on to the edge of the rail. Note, this strip of wood is fixed in the clear and rests against the plywood panel.

Screw two very small dresser hooks on to the middle rail to take the 2 ft. rule. Block off the hand saw by gluing in a small block. (See top batten in Fig. 3.) This will prevent the saw knocking against other tools.

Finishing Touches.—Block off the other battens at their centres, glue and screw them through the battens into the plywood. This will need care, for the plywood is only $\frac{3}{16}$ in. thick. Now screw on 2 in. brass hinges. The whole of the hinge thickness may be taken out of the door. Cut the keyhole and screw on the lock to the inside framework of the door. Do not let the lock in. The bolt will then shoot forward behind the framework. Make a half-round cover bead $\frac{3}{4} \times \frac{3}{8}$ in. and pin it on, as shown in the illustration Fig. 1.

Next make the wooden handle out of a piece of American walnut or other hardwood. Square up a piece of wood $3 \times 1\frac{1}{4} \times 1\frac{1}{8}$ in. and shape it as shown at A in Fig. 3. Clean it up and screw it on with small brass round-headed screws.

Then clean up the whole of the cupboard, including the door, with fine

Nos. 2, 1½ and 1 glass-paper. Hinge the door.

The six shelves make ample provision for the tools used by a woodworker. Generally speaking, the heavier tools such as a jack and trying plane are placed are of baywood, Columbian pine or ash, the following finish will be effective.

Mix some grey dye with boiling water according to the maker's directions. Apply it to the framework only with a brush. Allow it to dry, lightly

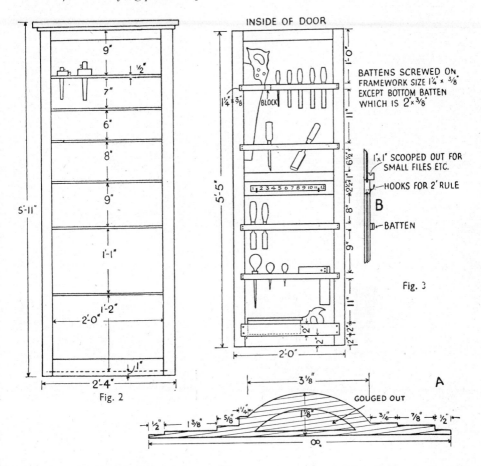

Fig. 2

Fig. 3

at the bottom of the cupboard, working upwards, shelf by shelf, with tools of lesser weight.

Holes can be bored in the top shelf for marking and mortice gauges as indicated in Fig. 2. It may be advisable to put in a few vertical divisons for such things as bottles of stain and polish.

If the storecupboard framework is made of red or white deal and the panels glass-paper with the finest grade and rub with canvas.

Wax polish the whole of the cupboard, panels and framework with light oak polish or a good transparent floor polish.

Put the polish on and rub off with a soft cloth. The cupboard will have a silver-grey framework standing out from the lighter tones of the panels.

CIRCULAR SAW BENCH

A SMALL circular saw is an important labour-saving device for the amateur woodworker. With such a machine, ripping, cross-cutting, rebating, grooving and a number of other important

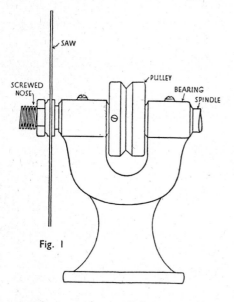

Fig. 1

when being sawn. The table is hinged at the back to the bench-top so that the height of the table can be adjusted to expose less depth of saw—as required, for example, in grooving.

The saw spindle and bearings consist of a small polishing head having a $\frac{5}{8}$ in. diameter shaft screwed at each end as shown in Fig. 1. This device can be obtained at most tool shops for about five or six shillings, while a 6 in. saw disc costs about four shillings.

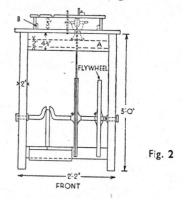

Fig. 2

operations can be carried out in a fraction of the time taken by hand-operated tools, with less physical exertion and with greater accuracy.

A circular saw disc, 6 in. in diameter and capable of cutting any of the usual timbers up to 1 in. thick, is illustrated in the drawing appearing at Figs. 1 to 6 and here described.

Machine Details. — The machine consists of a bench carrying the saw, a spindle to which it is attached, and the treadle, driving-wheel, flywheel and crankshaft by which the saw is driven. Upon the top of this bench is a box-like structure forming an upper table which partially encloses the saw, and carries a fence or guide for guiding the wood

The crankshaft shown in the drawings was purchased for eighteen pence from a second-hand machine dealer, as was the 20 in. grooved driving-wheel. The flywheel, a wheel taken from an old mangle, was obtained from a dealer in old iron.

Pivot bearings are used for suspending the crankshaft, and these are simply $\frac{5}{8}$ in. Whitworth bolts with pointed ends that fit into corresponding tapered holes drilled in the ends of the crankshaft. The bolts are $3\frac{1}{2}$ in. long and a nut near the end of each keeps them in position and allows for adjustment.

The treadle consists of two pieces of board kept together by means of battens on the underside, and motion is imparted to the crank by a connecting rod consisting of a piece of flat iron bent at each end to form hooks. The upper hook is attached to the crankshaft and the lower one to a piece of $\frac{1}{2}$ in. iron rod fixed to the underside of the treadle by pieces of thin brass strip bent to the shape of saddles and held in place by screws.

The treadle is hinged to the lower edge of the back bottom nails as shown in Fig. 3.

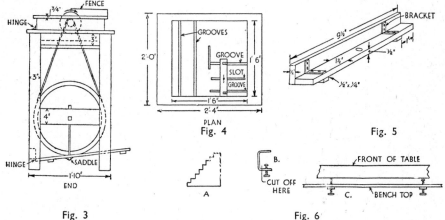

Fig. 3

Fig. 4 / PLAN

Fig. 5

Fig. 6

The Bench.—To make the saw-bench the following material is required. Four pieces of 3×2 in. yellow deal, each a little over 3 ft. long for the legs, two pieces 1 ft. 10 in. long and one 2 ft. long of the same section material for the top side-rails and the bottom back-rail respectively. Three 2 ft. 2 in. lengths of $4\frac{1}{2}$×1 in. are wanted for the top-front, back rails at the top, and the mid-rail shown at A in Fig. 2, and two pieces 4 in. wide ×2 in. thick for the cross-rails which house the bearing bolts, together with sufficient mahogany, oak or other hardwood for the table. This material might be obtained from an old dining-room table. To this must be added sufficient yellow deal for making the bench top and the treadle and a 20 in. length of hardwood for the fence, Fig. 5.

If prepared wood is used, the width and thickness will be slightly smaller than those specified.

Make the bench first by sawing the legs to length and perparing the mortices into which the tenoned ends of the rails fit. The outside faces of all rails should be flush with the outside faces of the legs. Glue the parts together and use wood screws to strengthen the joints. Then cut the mid-rail so that it is a tight fit between the two top side-rails. This member carries the saw spindle and bearings. Do not fix this for the time being. Drill the holes in the lower side rails for the pivot bolts. These holes should be bored accurately and squarely as the crank shaft must be dead in line for true running.

Make the bench top by joining the boards together with 2×1 in. battens screwed to the underside. The battens should be fixed so as to clear a hole about 9 in. square cut in the centre of the bench-top. Do not fix this member at the moment.

The Treadle. — Now make the treadle. This is 2 ft. long and 11 in. wide and is constructed from two boards $5\frac{1}{2}$ in. wide and $\frac{3}{4}$ in. thick with 2×1 in. cross battens underneath. Screws should be used for fixing these parts together in preference to nails. Make a square hole with the aid of a pad saw in the centre and 9 in. from the back edge to allow the connecting rod to pass through, and fix a 4 in. length of $\frac{1}{2}$ in. diameter iron rod across the centre of the hole. This rod is kept in position by two pieces of brass as indicated in Fig. 3, or, as an alternative, the ends of the rods could be flattened by heating them to redness and hammering them to shape. The flat faces are then drilled to take suitable screws and the rod fixed by means of a screw at each end.

Next construct the top table. This is of hardwood $\frac{3}{4}$ in. thick.

The sides and ends are 3 in. wide and the joints are glued and screwed butt-joints. The top should be planed quite flat and smooth and two long grooves $\frac{1}{2}$ in. wide $\times \frac{1}{4}$ in. deep cut on the left-hand side of the centre as shown in the plan in Fig. 4. On the right-hand side, two grooves extending from the side edge to the centre must also be made, as well as a slot of the same length as the two grooves. The slot should be $\frac{3}{8}$ in. wide to enable a $\frac{1}{4}$ in. diameter fastening bolt to pass through to hold the fence in position. The bottom projections of the fence, Fig. 5, fit the grooves and keep the fence parallel to the saw. The long channels are for accommodating a cross-cutting device and a jig for cutting mitres. Screws are used for fixing the table top to the sides.

Fig. 5 shows details of the fence. This component consists of two pieces of hardwood each $9\frac{1}{2} \times 1\frac{1}{2} \times \frac{1}{2}$ in. thick. The parts are fixed together by means of screws driven in through the vertical member into the edge of the horizontal one and strengthened by small iron brackets, as shown. The small projecting pieces of wood underneath are $\frac{1}{2}$ in. wide $\times \frac{1}{4}$ in. thick and are also

fixed by screws with their heads countersunk.

Now fix the bench-top by means of stout screws driven into the top edges of the top-rails and fasten the table to the bench by hinges at the back as indicated in Fig. 3.

Mounting the Shaft. — Assuming that the mechanical components, including a rawhide or leather belt (the former is recommended) are to hand, place the wheels on the crankshaft and suspend the assembly between the pivot bolts. Give the bearings a drop of oil and make sure that the shaft runs freely without play. This can be ensured by adjusting the bolts. Then place the spindle component, without the saw, in position on the cross member A.

The top of the belt on the small pulley should be as close to the underside of the table-top as possible as the nearer it is the more the saw will project above the top, a desirable feature.

Then mark the position of the ends of the cross-piece on the inside faces of the top side rails and fix the cross-piece by means of stout screws driven in through the rails into the ends of the cross-piece.

It is essential that the faces of the saw disc be parallel with the long edges of the bench top. Lightly nail a strip of wood, whose long edges are parallel, across the aperture to act as a guide. The saw assembly can then be moved along till the teeth at the front and back of the disc just touch the edge of the straight-edge. Having satisfied yourself on this point, fix the saw assembly permanently in position, using screws to suit the holes in the base.

Place the belt over the pulley and driving-wheel and fasten it together with a suitable belt fastener. Rotate the driving-wheel to verify the alignment of the belt. Shift the driving-wheel along the shaft in whatever direction required and tighten the fixing bolt.

Couple up the connecting rod, not forgetting to apply oil to each end and also to the spindle bearings. Then drive the saw at a high speed in the direction indicated by the arrow in Fig. 3—that is, towards the operator—and then bring the table very gently down to the saw so that the latter cuts the slot for the saw.

In order to prevent the near end of the table from moving sideways, two blocks of wood should be screwed down to the bench-top so that they lie against the sides of the table as shown at B in Fig. 2.

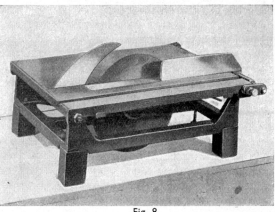

Fig. 8

Adjusting Saw Depth.—The constructor has the choice of two simple methods of providing a means of adjust-

Fig. 7

ing the height of the table to enable a smaller depth of saw to be exposed above the surface.

One way is to prepare a block of wood with a series of steps or ledges on one face, as indicated at A in Fig. 6. This component is placed under the lower front edge of the table so that the edge rests on a step to suit the work in hand.

Another method, and the better, is to provide a screw adjustment whereby absolute accuracy is ensured.

This can be done by lowering the front top rail of the bench for a distance of about 4 in. during the construction of the bench and utilising a couple of cheap screw cramps as indicated in Fig. 6 at B. The legs of each cramp are cut off at the positions indicated and holes are drilled in the remaining piece to enable them to be screwed to the bench-top in position immediately below the lower front edge of the table, as shown at C in Fig. 6. To prevent wear at where the tops of the screws make contact with the edge of the table, sink a piece of brass or other suitable metal into the wood at these points.

Here are a few hints for operating the saw. Always run the saw at as high a speed as possible.

Ripping.—In ripping, set the fence accurately; see that it does not project beyond the centre of the saw and that it is parallel. Do not force the work under the influence of the saw too quickly, but allow the saw to do its job, by feeding the wood gently and evenly as the cutting proceeds. Forcing results in a hot saw and this means a distorted saw.

Circular saws, like hand saws, do not remain sharp for ever. When replacing the saw on the spindle, make sure that it is correctly centred or uneven wear of the teeth will result.

It sometimes happens, when ripping a piece of wood, that the edges of the severed part of the wood at the back of the saw close and tend to project the wood towards the operator.

On large machines this would be a serious matter if means were not provided to prevent it. This is done by fixing a reeving knife to the table top at the back of the saw. A similar device could easily be adapted to a small machine in the shape of a screw filed wedge-shaped.

Those readers who are fortunate enough to have a small electric motor and require a saw for cutting larger and thicker wood cannot do better than construct a circular saw on the lines of the one shown in Figs. 7 and 8. The machine illustrated is factory-built, and will take a saw 10 in. in diameter. It is provided with plummer-block bearings and striking gear for shifting the belt. Note the reeving knife at the back of the table as mentioned in a previous paragraph.

Such a machine could easily be constructed of wood.

AN AQUARIUM

THERE are several ways of making an aquarium but the one illustrated in the accompanying drawings and explained in the following paragraphs is extremely simple.

The following points should be observed. First, it is essential that the glass used in the aquarium should be sufficiently thick to withstand the weight of the water, for it must be remembered that a gallon of fresh water weighs 10 lb. and occupies a space of 277 cu. in., so the total weight of water occupied by the aquarium under review, which measures 1 ft. 9 in. × 1 ft. × 1 ft., will be nearly 110 lb. On this basis nothing thinner than 32 oz. glass should be used. The same applies to the uprights and these should not be less than of 1 in. square section material. Secondly, the joints must be watertight; not even an occasional drip can be tolerated.

Waterproof Cements.—The constructor has the choice of several waterproof cements including one made of a mixture of red-lead and white-lead bound with a little gold size.

This will give a watertight joint provided the edges and sides of the glass where the cement joint is formed are first given a coat of gold size. Another reliable cement is composed of litharge —a lead compound—plaster-of-paris, silver sand and powdered resin in the proportions of 4 : 4 : 4 : 1. The ingredients are simply mixed together with a small quantity of raw linseed oil to form a plastic mass of about the same consistency as putty. All this material can be obtained at most oil and colour stores.

Teak is undoubtedly the best wood to use as it is durable when subjected to both wet and dry. If teak cannot be obtained, oak is the next best.

The aquarium, a front and end view of which is shown in Fig. 3, consists of a solid base 2 ft. 2 in. × 1 ft. 5 in. × 1 in. thick upon which the four uprights are fixed the upper ends of which are held together by a frame, Fig. 1. Two faces of the uprights which are 1⅛ in. section are grooved to a depth of ⅜ in. and ¼ in. wide to take the side edges of the glass. The bottom edges of the glass are housed in the grooves formed by screwing ½ in. square wood on the face and near the edges of the base as shown in Fig. 2, or if a plough plane is available the grooves could be ploughed in the base itself. The former

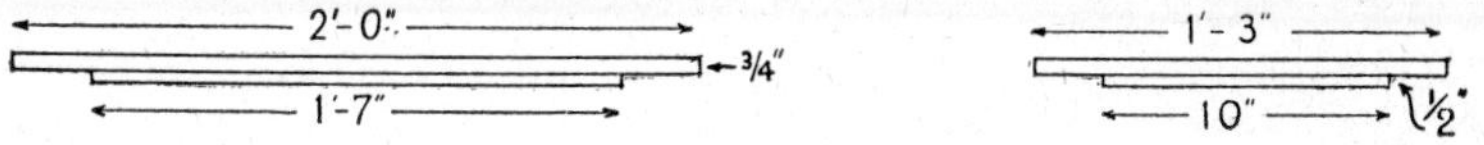

underside, and the face made perfectly level with a smoothing plane.

Now mark out on the face of the base the position of the uprights and the strips for forming the groove, the latter being ¼ in. wide. Drill suitable holes

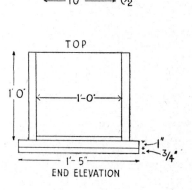

Fig. 1

Fig. 3

FRONT ELEVATION · END ELEVATION

DOWEL

¼ THICK

Fig. 4

PLAN

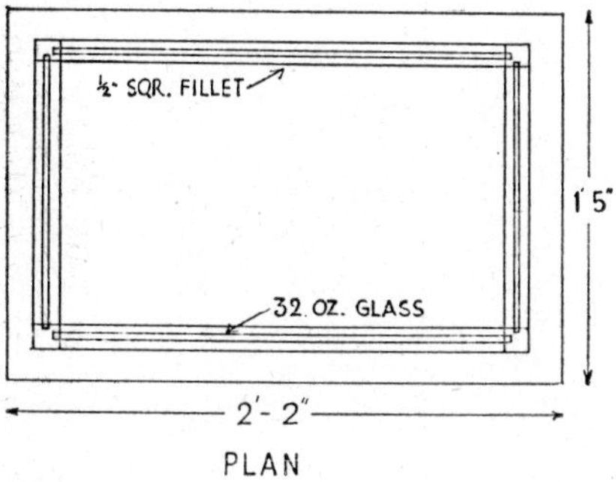

Fig. 2

method is simpler than, and just as satisfactory as, the latter.

As it is difficult to obtain a single piece of wood of sufficient width for the base, it can be made up of two lengths of equivalent width by grooving the adjacent edges to be joined and inserting a loose tongue. In joining these parts it is advisable to use marine glue which is unaffected by damp.

The underside can then be reinforced by means of a couple of 2×¾ in. battens secured by screws screwed in from the

for taking the fixing screws of the corner posts, drill clearing holes in the strips and fasten them down temporarily with brass screws, spaced not more than 3 in. apart, in order to see that everything fits.

The Top Frame.—The top, Fig. 1, consists of a plain frame of 2×¾ in. stuff the ends of which are mitred and fitted with a false tenon by slotting the ends and gluing and dowelling a slip of wood into the slots as indicated in Fig. 4. The sharp corners of the frame should be removed with a chisel and the arris, or sharp edges, smoothed by a plane. Suitable lengths of ¼ in. square section wood are then screwed to the underside to support the outside faces of the glass, but it is better to leave this until the glass has been fitted.

At this stage the framework can be

dismembered, including the strips forming the base grooves, and preparations made for cementing in the glass.

Mix the cement as mentioned in a previous paragraph and apply a thin layer to the underside of the grooving strips and fasten these down to the base by the screws. Then apply a layer to the enclosed space and bed on the bottom piece of glass, pressing it gently here and there so that it beds evenly. Apply more cement to the inner edges and bevel the joint in the same way as a glazier bevels off putty in fixing a window pane. Fill the grooves in the base as well as those in the uprights. Press the short edges of the glass into their respective grooves in the uprights, apply cement to the bottoms of each

any leak, empty out the water, allow the container to dry and apply cement at the faulty spot.

The whole of the woodwork interior and exterior should be given two coats of good paint and finished with enamel.

A Supporting Table.—An aquarium of this description requires a substantial table or stand. This can be made of good quality yellow deal if it is to be enamelled afterwards, as there is no advantage gained by constructing it of superior wood.

Such a table is illustrated in Fig. 5 and is of the simplest design. The legs are of 2 in. square stuff free from knots and other imperfections, while the top rails are 3 in. wide × 1 in. thick morticed into the legs and secured with glue.

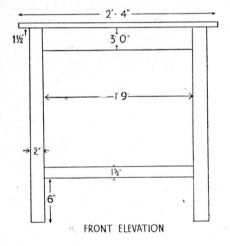
FRONT ELEVATION

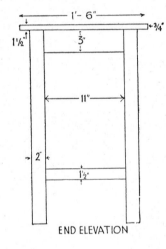
END ELEVATION

Fig. 5

upright and fix the whole in position by driving in brass screws from the underside of the base. Trim off surplus cement and allow the cement to harden. When hard, fix the $\frac{1}{4}$ in. square fillets to the underside of the top frame, making sure that the fillets butt against the glass.

Fill the aquarium with water and watch for leaks. Locate the position of

The bottom rails are also morticed into the legs and are $1\frac{1}{2}$ in. × 1 in.

The top measures 2 ft. 4 in. × 1 ft. 6 in. wide and is constructed by gluing two $\frac{3}{4}$ in. thick tongued and grooved boards together and fastening them to the frame by means of buttons screwed to the underside which engage into slots made near the top edges in the inside faces of the top rails.

SIMPLY MADE BIRD CAGES

THE bird-cage illustrated in Fig. 1 is of simple design and of a type that looks well on a small table. It is of sufficient size to house a pair of budgerigars or love birds.

As will be seen in Fig. 1, the cage consists of a framework, the front, sides and top of which are wired, while the back and base are of solid wood. A shallow tray with a zinc inside-facing is fitted at the bottom to allow easy cleaning, and two wire doors at the front and a wooden one at the back allow convenient access. The framework without any wires is seen in Fig. 2.

Tools and Materials.—The necessary tools include a hand saw, tenon saw, plane, screwdriver, side-cutting pliers, to which must be added a small metalworker's hand-drill, or archimedian drill as used by fretworkers, for boring holes to accommodate the wires, also soldering iron with solder and flux.

The table below gives a list of the wooden parts required with their measurements in inches:

In addition to the wooden parts, a supply of proper tinned bird-cage wire and punched bar for supporting the wires will be needed. This wire is

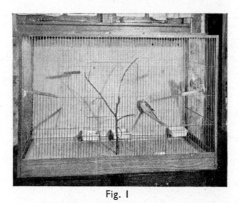

Fig. I

manufactured specially for the purpose and is practically rustless owing to the tinned surface.

Punched bar consists of a thin strip of tinned metal having a series of holes $\frac{1}{2}$ in. apart punched in the centre of the width to accommodate the wires. The stock length is

No. 4.	Uprights—A, B, C, D ..					$24 \times \frac{1}{2} \times \frac{1}{2}$
,, 3.	Horizontal pieces—E, F, G	..	..	..	..	$35 \times \frac{1}{2} \times \frac{1}{2}$
,, 2.	,, ,, H, I	..	..	..		$17 \times \frac{1}{2} \times \frac{1}{2}$
,, 2.	,, ,, J, K	..	..	..		$17 \times 3 \times \frac{1}{2}$
,, 1.	,, ,, L ..	..	..	..		$35 \times 1 \times \frac{1}{2}$
,, 1.	,, ,, front of tray	..	..	..		$35 \times 2 \times \frac{1}{2}$
,, 1.	Plywood panel for back	..	..	..		$36 \times 24 \times \frac{3}{16}$
,, 1.	,, ,, ,, base	..	..	..		$36 \times 18 \times \frac{1}{4}$
,, 1.	,, ,, ,, bottom of drawer	..	..			$35 \times 17\frac{1}{2} \times \frac{3}{16}$
,, 1.	Half-round moulding ..	..	..	..		$108 \times \frac{1}{2}$
,, 1.	Back of tray ..	..	..	..		$35 \times 2 \times \frac{1}{2}$
,, 2.	Sides of tray ..	..	..	..		$17\frac{1}{2} \times 1 \times \frac{3}{8}$

The whole of the framework, including the front of the tray, should be of hardwood, as this enables simple screwed butt-joints to be employed.

4 ft. Both items can be purchased cheaply at most bird dealers.

Eight or nine punched bars will suffice. Two doz. 1 in. No. 5 and

4 doz. $\frac{5}{8}$ in. No. 2 countersunk-headed screws will be needed for joining the parts together, and for fixing the plywood base and back.

Start the constructional work by marking and cutting the four uprights A, B, C, D, Fig. 2, to length, taking care to see that the ends are square.

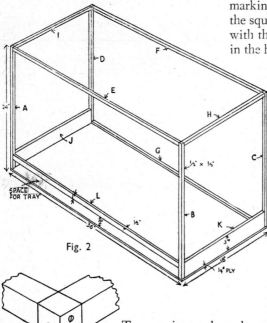

Fig. 2

Fig. 3

To save time and ensure accuracy you will find it an advantage to cramp these parts together and then mark out and saw them, rather than mark and cut singly. Next prepare the horizontal members E, F, G, in a similar manner following with I, H, J and K, then L, and finally the drawer front M.

The next items consist of marking out and boring the screw-holes near the ends of the uprights for making the joints. In doing this be sure to bore the holes a trifle larger than the gauge or thickness of the screw, as this procedure allows the parts to be joined to butt together tightly. Countersink the tops of the holes to allow the screws to lie flush with the faces. Fig. 3 shows a corner joint and position of the screws, which you will observe are staggered, or not in line, so that one screw will not foul the one at right angles to it.

Now prepare the back plywood by marking it out cutting it just outside the squared lines, finishing off the edges with the aid of a sharp plane. The door in the back panel is marked out squarely and cut with a fretsaw. A small hole of sufficient size to take the saw blade should be made at one of the corners. If the sawing is done carefully, the piece cut out can be used for the door. Scribe lines $\frac{1}{4}$ in. from the edges on the back face for the centres of the fixing screws. Eight holes are required in the length, spaced at equidistant intervals, and five near the edge in the width.

The base is the next item to receive attention. Mark out, saw and plane the edges to the dimensions given, namely 3 ft. ×1 ft. 6 in. wide, making sure that the member is square, otherwise the framework will be out of true when assembled.

Mark and drill the holes for the fixing screws as before except that only four are required at each end of the width, and none in the front.

At this stage the parts should be assembled together to see that all fit correctly. There are several ways of doing this, but you will find the most convenient method will be to start by building up the back frame from C, D, F, G, and screwing on the plywood back, the edges of which should be flush with the outer edges of the frame. Next screw the members A, B, E and L forming the front frame; and when this frame is completed add the cross pieces

H, I, J and K. Now fit the completed back to the cross members and finally turn the carcase upside down and fix the base. A $\frac{3}{4}$ in. No. 5 countersunk-headed screw should be driven through the plywood into the centre of each upright. At this stage there is no need to insert all the small fixing screws.

Panel pins $\frac{1}{2}$ in. long could be used instead of screws for fixing the plywood to the framework, but the little extra cost of screws and the added time and labour of drilling the holes and driving them in is well repaid in that the plywood will not twist and draw them out, as it might do if pins were used.

Mounting the Wires.—The next procedure is to dismantle the parts, except the back, in order to drill the holes for the wires. Accuracy and patience are needed in doing this, otherwise those wires which ought to be vertical may slope and horizontal wires be at anything but right-angles.

Before actually dismantling the parts it is a good plan to pencil and mark the parts alphabetically on the face side, in a similar manner as that shown in Fig. 2. This will save time and avoid confusion when ready for reassembly.

Starting with the front top horizontal member E, the holes are drilled right through from the top, while the corresponding holes in L are drilled $\frac{1}{4}$ in. deep; the ends of the wires rest on the bottoms of the holes. The holes in the back horizontal piece F are bored right through from the back and the ends of the wires are housed in holes $\frac{1}{4}$ in. deep in the back of E. The top cross-pieces H and I are bored right through from the top to coincide with the holes $\frac{1}{4}$ in. deep in the tops of J and K respectively.

It has already been stated that the holes in the punched bar are of $\frac{1}{2}$ in. pitch, which means that their centres are $\frac{1}{2}$ in. apart, so a strip of this material

can be used as a gauge for drilling the holes in the various members. Fix the strip down to the piece to be drilled, using a few small screws spaced about 6 in. apart and fix it down in the manner indicated in Fig. 4. A $\frac{1}{16}$ in. diameter drill should be used for boring. Such a drill will just clear the holes in the guide strip and make a hole of sufficient size in the wood to ensure a good fit for the wires.

Before attempting to drill the stopped holes ($\frac{1}{4}$ in. deep) in E, J, K and L, you

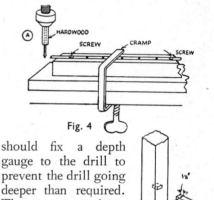

Fig. 4

should fix a depth gauge to the drill to prevent the drill going deeper than required. The gauge can be a piece of hardwood fitted tightly over the drill as illustrated at A in Fig. 4. In setting the gauge do not forget to allow for the thickness of the guide strip, which is just under $\frac{1}{16}$ in.

Fig. 5

Having completed the drilling operations, the position for the small recesses for taking the ends of the punched bar should be marked on the uprights A, B, C, D, and the cross-pieces H, I. Three horizontal bars will be required in the front and sides and two at the top. The bars should be spaced at equal distances apart, while the recesses should be $\frac{3}{16} \times \frac{1}{16} \times \frac{1}{8}$ in. deep. The latter can be cut with a sharp bradawl. Fig. 5 shows a recess.

The parts can now be reassembled

and the bars and wires fitted. Proceed with assembling in the manner already explained and then spring the bars into their respective positions. Having cut the wires to length, start at the front by pushing them through the top member and the holes in the bars and finally into the lower member, using the pliers to ease them through. Treat the sides in a similar manner and finally the top. Take care not to bend the wires.

Soldering.—Fix a strip of half-round moulding to the top members and a narrow strip at the back of the top back member F. Then, after making sure that the bars are parallel, proceed by soldering the wires at the bars. In order to keep the bars in their correct position during soldering, a couple of pieces of wood notched at intervals to take the bars, A in Fig. 6, can be inserted between the top and bottom members or the top and back member as the case may be.

The soldering process is simple and should not take much time if the iron is sufficiently hot. Flux round each joint in turn until all have been treated, and use a matchstick for applying it. Then follow up with a hot well-tinned soldering iron.

The wire doors in the front cover apertures made between the thick bar

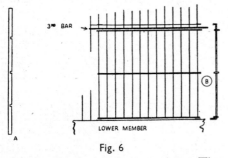

Fig. 6

and the lower wooden member. The openings are 6 in. long and as high as the distance between the bars namely $5\frac{1}{4}$ in. approximately. The position

they occupy is 2 in. from either end. This means that the fifth vertical wire (from the wooden uprights) to the fifteenth inclusive will have to be removed. This is done by cutting the wires as close as possible to the bars,

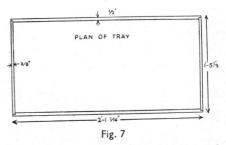

Fig. 7

using the cutting pliers for the purpose, and then filing smooth any rough projections.

A diagram of a door appears at B in Fig. 6. The construction is simple. The end wires must be left sufficiently long to enable loops to be formed and bent at right angles for fastening it to the cage. Solder is employed to join the wires to the punched bars.

No difficulty should be experienced in making the movable tray, Fig. 7, the sides of which are housed and screwed, not nailed into the front and back. The plywood bottom should be cut $\frac{1}{16}$ in. undersize, that is 2 ft. $10\frac{15}{16}$ in. to allow a little play between the sides of the drawer and those of the cage, while the front and back members must also be reduced in length by the same amount to correspond. Cut the parts accurately to size, make the frame, and attach the bottom, using $\frac{1}{2}$ in. No. 4 brass screws, seeing that the heads lie just below the surface. Cut a piece of zinc to fit and lie loosely on the bottom.

Fit the wooden door at the back and hang it with small $\frac{1}{2}$ in. thin brass hinges and small screws.

Make a couple of turn-buttons and screw them to the lower member of the cage to keep the drawer from opening.

A couple of shallow earthenware trays will suffice for food and water, and twigs for perching can be arranged in the interior by unscrewing the plywood back.

A suitable nest-box is illustrated diagrammatically at Fig. 8. It is a

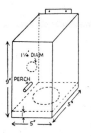

simple box of rectangular shape, 9 in. high, 5 in. wide and 5 in. deep. The bottom is of 1 in. deal, the centre of which is gouged out to a saucer shape. The front, top and back are of plywood, while the sides are of ¼ in. deal. A

Fig. 8

1¼ in. diameter hole is drilled about 6 in. from the bottom edge and in the centre, as shown. A small perch of ¼ in. dowel is fixed about 2 in. below the hole. One side is hinged to allow access to the interior.

A smaller hanging cage, suitable for a canary, is illustrated in the diagram shown at Fig. 9. The constructional work is on similar lines to that already explained. All four sides, as well as the top, are wired. The main dimensions are shown, and hardwood should be used in its construction.

A couple of perches made from ¼ in. diameter dowel are fitted, the ends being provided with saw-kerfs or slots which fit over the wires.

In hanging the cage from a ceiling,

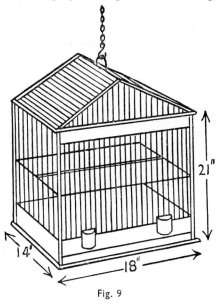

Fig. 9

care must be taken to find a joist into which the suspension hook should be screwed. The hook should not be fixed into a lath as laths are not sufficiently strong to withstand the weight.

A GARDEN ROOM

THE problem of the extra room, which often crops up in these days of small houses and small incomes, can be solved by constructing a garden room. No longer would it be necessary to turn a friend out after a pleasant evening, because a garden room can easily be converted into a temporary bedroom on such occasions.

The building need not be costly and elaborate, but it should be well constructed, weatherproof and designed to harmonize with the surroundings. The working drawings illustrated in Figs. 1 and 2 conform to these requirements.

The Dimensions.—The size of the erection shown is 9 ft. wide × 14 ft. long and 7 ft. high at the eaves and 8 ft. 6 in. at the ridge. These dimensions may be varied to suit particular circumstances, but it is false economy to make the building too small. It consists of a framework clad with V-jointed

H

matched boards of ⅝ in. finished thickness, while the floor is constructed of tongued and grooved boards which, if properly fitted, are draughtproof.

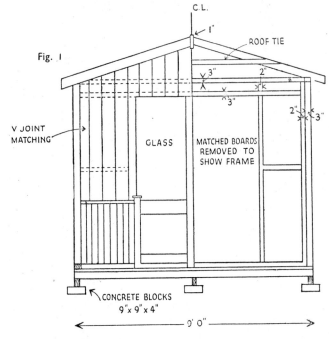

Fig. 1

C.L.

1"

ROOF TIE

3"   2"

3"

2"   3"

V JOINT MATCHING

GLASS

MATCHED BOARDS REMOVED TO SHOW FRAME

CONCRETE BLOCKS
9"x 9"x 4"

9' 0"

As an alternative, asbestos-cement sheets could be used for cladding the walls.

The roof projects 6 in. beyond the back wall and 4 ft. 6 in. beyond the front one. The latter covers a small veranda 4 ft. wide which has rails at the sides and along part of the front. This veranda adds slightly to the cost, but it has the advantage of allowing one to sit out of doors sheltered from the sun's rays during the summer months. The rails at the sides could be substituted by square mesh trellis upon which rambler roses could be trained.

Another good feature is the double doors which open outwards on to the veranda.

As the structure should have as much light as possible, a double casement window is provided in each side, while another window could be included in the back if required. A rectangular bay, extending from the eave of the roof to the floor, on one side of the structure, 4 ft. long ×2 ft. wide and having windows at the front and two sides could be incorporated with little additional trouble and expense. This extra space would accommodate a small table, or the space below the windows could be cased in to form a cupboard.

All these details should, of course, be decided and put down on paper in a working drawing before starting practical work.

Preparing the Site. —A dry site should be chosen for the garden room. If such a position is not available, the ground should be drained and made up with broken bricks, stones and other similar material and well rammed down, as it is essential that the foundation be firm. If this requirement is not observed the structure will, in a short time, be out of plumb.

The site should be pegged out by driving in pegs at the corners corresponding with the dimensions of the floor. To ensure dryness, the floor joists should be raised well above the ground. An easy and satisfactory method is to make a number of small concrete blocks for the plates to which the floor joists are fixed to rest on. Fifteen such blocks measuring approximately 9 in. square and 4 in. thick will be required and placed at equidistant intervals to form three rows of five each along the length of the floor.

Make the blocks in the following manner: Make a frame 47× 28 in. wide (internal measurements) and 4 in. deep, and fix a bottom consisting of boards ½ in. thick to form a tray. Divide the interior into fifteen 9 in. divisions, using ½ in. thick wood for the purpose.

Mix sufficient portland cement and clean washed sand in the proportion of one part cement and three sand to fill the tray. The mortar should not be too sloppy and it is essential that the top of the mixture should be smoothed level with the top of the tray. Allow a couple of days for the cement to harden, remove the sides of the frame and withdraw the blocks.

The blocks can now be placed in their respective positions on the site and the surfaces levelled either by adding or removing soil underneath them as the case may be. Use both straight-edge and spirit level.

This procedure is preferable to using bricks, which are apt to sink in the ground owing to insufficient bearing area.

Constructional work can now be put in hand.

Place three 14 ft. lengths of 4×2 in. scantling narrow edge up on the blocks.

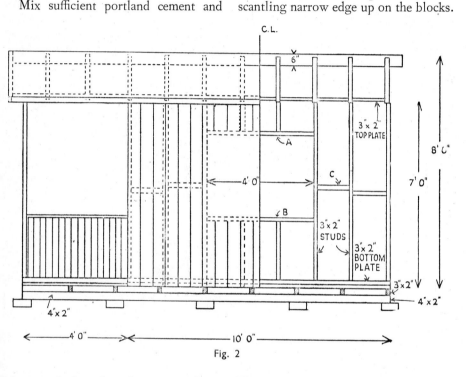

Fig. 2

These form the plates to which the joists are fixed and can be held temporarily in position by pegs driven on either side of them into the ground. Then fix the joists, which run across the width. One at each end will be required, together with seven intermediate ones spaced at equal distances apart. The joists are of 3×2 in. stuff and are fixed narrow edge up to the plates by means of 3 in. wire nails driven in from the sides.

Now fix the floorboards. These will

have been ordered in 14 ft. lengths. Nail the boards down with 2 in. floor brads, taking care to keep the tongued and grooved edges well cramped together.

It may be mentioned that the three joist supports, the joists themselves and the undersides of the floorboards should

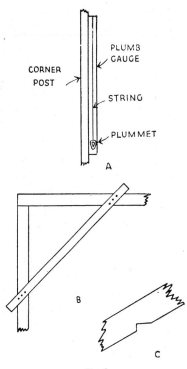

Fig. 3

have a liberal supply of creosote applied before fitting. Creosote is cheap and an excellent preservative.

Frames for Sides.—At this stage it is advisable to make the side frames. The flat floor will enable you to do this part of the work with ease.

Fig. 2 shows the general arrangement of a side frame. The studs or uprights are simply nailed to the top and bottom plates. Wire nails 5 in. in length should be used for this, but before driving in the nails the top plates should be drilled

to receive them, otherwise they are liable to split the wood, especially at the ends.

The two end uprights at the front, the lower and side faces of the top plates, and rafters and the corresponding faces of the lower plates, where the latter project beyond the front wall, should be smoothed with a plane, as these parts are not hidden from view. Note that the two horizontal members A and B are required to take the window frames. Short horizontal pieces C of the same material should be fixed between the studs to give stability and for supporting the matching. These are not in line and so allow nails to be driven in straight.

Next, make the frame for the back, the construction of which is carried out on similar lines to that of the sides. If a window is required as suggested, two horizontal pieces must be fixed in the desired position for the window frames.

The members of the front frame are shown in Fig. 1. The construction of these is quite simple and straightforward.

The frames are fixed to the floor by means of $7 \times \frac{1}{2}$ in. diameter bolts and nuts, 3 in. each side and 2 in. the front and back respectively.

The holes for these, both in the plates and floor, should be bored a trifle larger than the diameter of the bolts to allow for slight adjustment. The edges of the bottom plates should be flush with the edges of the floor.

As erecting frames 14 ft. in length is awkward for one person a helper should be asked to hold a side frame and the back frame together while the nuts of the holding-down bolts are being tightened. The end posts of these two members are then bored, suitable bolts passed through the holes and the nuts tightened to secure these frame members together. The remaining side frame is then treated in a like manner and finally the front bolted in position.

At this juncture it is advisable to test for verticality by means of a plumb-gauge as illustrated at A in Fig. 3, and having made necessary adjustments, the framework should be braced temporarily by nailing a batten diagonally across the top faces of the top plates as illustrated at B in Fig. 3.

A pair of tall household steps will now be required to enable you to reach the ridge-board which is the next item to fix. This member is 14 ft. × 6 in. × 1 in. and fits into the recesses at the apex of the front and back frames.

The roof rafters of 3 × 2 in. stuff should all be cut to the same length. The ends should be sawn to an angle to correspond with that of the roof, and notched to form a bearing on the top plates of the side frames. This detail is shown at C in Fig. 3.

The rafters are then nailed to the ridge-board and to the top plates. Care must be taken in fixing these to see that they are all in line and the top faces level with each other, as neglect may result in a wavy roof.

Each pair of rafters should be tied together with 2 × 1 in. battens to prevent the weight of the roof from forcing and spreading out the tops of the side walls. They also provide a means of support for the lining material, to be fixed after the completion of the exterior part of the structure.

Cladding the Frame.—The next process consists of cladding the framework with matching. This is quite simple, but the following points should be noted.

The boards are fixed vertically and cut 4 in. longer than the distance between the upper edge of the top plate and the lower edges of the bottom plate of the side and back walls. This allows a 4 in. overlap to cover the side and back joists.

If the outside is to be painted, which is preferable to creosoting, the joints should receive a coat of priming paint before erection, as it is obviously impossible to get to the joints after the boards have been fixed. Squeeze the joints up as tightly as possible. If it is found necessary to use a hammer, a piece of matching with the groove removed and the tongue remaining, should be used for striking upon, as the bare hammer-head will damage the groove, making it difficult to fit the corresponding tongue of the adjacent board.

It is also wise to test the verticality of the boards from time to time as the cladding proceeds. Any small adjustment necessary, due to inequalities in the wood, can be remedied by a little give and take at the joints.

Now for the roof. The remarks made about the walls apply to this except that the painting can be omitted and the boards are fixed horizontally.

Covering the roof with a suitable waterproof material now requires consideration. There are several excellent products advertised for the purpose. Such materials have excellent wearing and weather-resisting properties, are inexpensive, and usually obtainable in rolls of 12 yd. length and 36 in. width at ironmongers and oil and colour stores. Slates made of the same material may also be obtained in red, green and blue colours. They are light and easily fitted.

Start fixing the roofing material at the eaves and work upwards to the ridge. A 4 in. overlap should be allowed at the ends to enable it to cover the edges and be nailed underneath. The same applies to the lower edges along the length of the first piece to be fixed and a 4 in. overlap should be provided at the horizontal joints. Planed 1½ in. battens spaced at not more than 2 ft. apart should be nailed between the ridge and the eaves.

This completes the main part of the erection.

Attention should be given to the doors and windows. The former are simple doors, the stiles and top rails of which are 3½ in. wide, while the lock rails and bottom ones are 6 in. in width. The rebates for holding the glass in the top position as well as those for supporting the panels in the lower part can be cut with a rebating plane or the recesses can be formed by nailing strips of wood to form false rebates. The latter method is simple and satisfactory and saves planing recesses. The same procedure will serve for the window sashes.

Mortice and tenon joints should be used for the doors and sashes, and all should be hung on strong iron butt-hinges. A good rim lock fitted on the inner face of the opening stile of the right-hand door should be fixed, with a box catch plate screwed to the corresponding face of the other. Bolts must also be fitted to the top and bottom on the inside face of the opening stile of the left-hand door.

The apertures in the walls for the reception of the sashes are lined with yellow deal 3 in. wide at the sides and top, with a sill of 5×2 in. material and bevelled towards the front on the top face.

Do not forget to make the weather groove near the front edge on the underside of the sill. This prevents water from creeping between the joint and the interior.

The rails at the sides and front of the structure are of 2× 1½ in. wood and the uprights may be of either square section or slats, as shown. The ends of the vertical pieces at the sides are morticed into the bottom plates of the framework and the underside of the rails while those at the front are let into the lengths of planed 3×2 in. stuff nailed down to the floor and the top rails.

Assuming that work on the exterior is complete, including fixing the barge boards which cover the rafters at the roof edges, the next item is to line the interior. The builder has the choice of several kinds of material for this. Thin matched boards ⅜ in. finished thickness may be used if the appearance of the groove at the joint is not objected to. Compressed wall boards $\frac{3}{16}$ in. thick are excellent for lining when it is desired to decorate with wallpaper. Plywood also makes a good lining and looks well if panelled. It is best to cover the ceiling first and then the walls.

The whole of the exterior except the floor and top of the roof should receive at least three coats of good lead paint. Before applying the paint, go over all knots with knotting and then apply the priming coat. This should then be rubbed down with glass-paper when dry and followed by an undercoat of flat paint which, when dry, is also rubbed down and the final coat applied.

It is a mistake to finish a building of this description with a sombre paint. Cheerfulness should be the predominating note, and it is suggested that a medium stone colour be used for the body of the building and the window frames and sashes be painted light green.

A SUMMER HOUSE

READERS who contemplate building a summer house cannot do better than make one on the lines shown in the accompanying illustrations and here described.

Such a structure, with folding doors at the front, as seen open in Fig. 1 and closed in Fig. 2, is more suitable for the English summer than the more formal type with a permanently open front which can only be used comfortably on warm and sunny days.

The erection has a 3 in. concrete floor and measures 9 ft. in length, 6 ft. wide, 6 ft. 3 in. to the top of the upper plate and approximately 8 ft. 3 in. to the ridge.

As will be seen by referring to Fig. 3, the ends of the roof are hipped, a method of construction which enhances the appearance of the structure.

An ordinary plain eaved roof is

Fig. 2

slightly less expensive but the small additional outlay and labour involved in constructing the one shown will be justified by its appearance.

If desired, a wooden floor could be substituted for concrete, but the latter has the advantage of being easily cleaned and does not deteriorate.

The illustration at Fig. 3 is a view of one end, where a large double casement window is incorporated, while Fig. 4 shows the opposite end with a door.

Substantial Build. — The summer house is substantially built and consists of a framework with $3\frac{3}{4}$ in. square section corner posts; the outside being covered with 6 in. tongued and grooved weather-boards $\frac{3}{4}$ in. thick, fixed flush

Fig. 1

Fig. 3

must be made for the bolts that are used for securing the bottom plates. Eight of these will be required, each measuring $6 \times \frac{1}{2}$ in. diameter, so arranged that they come in the centre of the plates and about a foot from each corner.

The ends of the bottom plates are halved and morticed to take the tenoned ends of the uprights, while the front plate is also morticed at the centre to house the tenon at the end of the intermediate post.

The top plates are of the same width as the lower ones and 3 in. thick, the studs or vertical members being of 3×2 in. stuff. In fixing these, the back narrow faces must be kept flush with the inside edges of the plates as the remaining $\frac{3}{4}$ in. towards the front allows the weather-boards to lie flush with the corner posts and outside edges of the plates.

In marking the positions of the studs, five of which will be needed, for the back framework, first scribe a line across with the posts. The back and ends of the framework in the interior are lined with asbestos sheets $\frac{3}{16}$ in. thick, and the roof members covered with $\frac{1}{2}$ in. tongued and grooved matching, finished with varnish.

Constructional details of the framework are pictured in Figs. 5, 6, 7 and 8, which show a front elevation, door-end view, window-end view and roof-plan respectively.

The bottom plates are of wood $3\frac{3}{4} \times 3$ in. laid with the widest face uppermost, and as the front bottom member is subjected to wear, it is made of oak, but yellow deal is used for the others as well as the remainder of the framework.

With regard to the site, much will depend upon the general layout of the garden, but where circumstances permit it is advisable to choose high ground having a south aspect.

In preparing the concrete, provision

Fig. 4

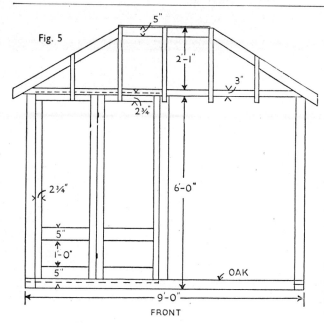

Fig. 5

5"

2-1"

3"

2¾"

2¼"

6'-0"

5"
1'-0"
5"

OAK

9'-0"

FRONT

The Roof. — The construction of the hipped roof is really not difficult. The best way of going about it is first to mark out the centres for the rafters on the top plates. These are of 3×2 in. wood spaced 1 ft. 6 in. apart, as shown in the plan of the roof members, Fig. 8. Then cut the ridge-board which is 1 in. thick and 5 in. wide and a trifle longer at each end than the finished size, 3 ft. 4 in. This may now be held temporarily in position by nailing two pieces of wood across the front

the top face in the centre of the bottom plate and mark off the other positions from this, as indicated in the diagram, Fig. 9. The plates are notched $\frac{1}{2}$ in. deep, 2 in. wide and 3 in. long to take the ends of the uprights as shown in Fig. 10 and are secured with 6 in. wire nails.

The door posts at the door end are of 3×2 in. wood, the ends of which are morticed into the top and bottom plates.

Two long horizontal members, A and B in Fig. 7, are incorporated at the opposite end frame. The lower one supports the sill and the upper one the top part of the window-frame. The sides and top of the window-frame consist of wood $3\frac{3}{4}$ in. wide and 1 in. thick, the outside edges of which will be flush with the weather-boards when fixed. In fitting the window-frame and sill it is imperative that the angles be perfectly square or else trouble will be experienced when fitting the sashes.

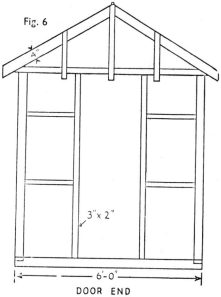

Fig. 6

4"

3" × 2"

6'-0"

DOOR END

and back top plates and fixing a couple of uprights to support each end of the ridge. The top of the ridge should be 2 ft. 1 in. above the level of the top plates.

The next procedure is to cut and fix

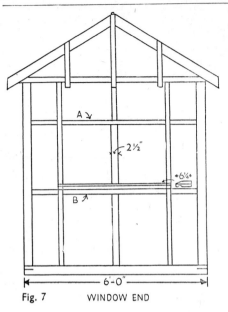

Fig. 7   WINDOW END

plates. the latter are bevelled off a trifle. The lower ends of the rafters which overlap the plates 3 in. are then trimmed off to length.

Having finished fixing the roof members, the temporary ridge support may be removed and the weather-boards at the ends and back of the structure cut and nailed. Before actual work on this can be started, fillets consisting of 2 × 1 in. battens will have to be cut and nailed to the side faces of the posts to form fixings for the weather-boards.

These are fastened of course $\frac{3}{4}$ in. from the face edge to allow the boards to lie flush. No difficulty should be experienced in dealing with the boards as it is simply a question of accurately marking, sawing to length and fixing them with 2 in. cut nails.

the common rafters —marked A, B, C, D, E and F in the plan—starting with the centre one B, and fixing its fellow member E and then the other four in rotation. The top ends of the rafters are fixed to the sides and 1 in. below the top of the ridge.

This operation is followed by cutting and fixing the hip-boards, which are 1 in. thick and 4 in. wide, after which the end centre rafters, and finally the jack rafters, as the short rafters are called, can be measured and the upper ends cut to suit the angles.

In order to allow sufficient bearing surface under the lower edge of the hip-boards at the corners of the wall

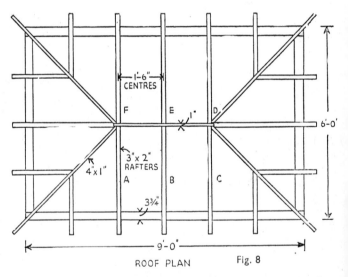

ROOF PLAN   **Fig. 8**

The double doors at the front are hinged at the middle and supported by hinges fixed to the inside faces of the front end posts; an arrangement which allows them to be folded back against the ends inside the building when not in use. The top and bottom of these doors butt against the inside faces of the top and bottom plates respectively and a wooden fillet $3\frac{3}{4}$ in. wide $\times \frac{5}{8}$ in. thick is nailed down the centre of the inside face of the centre post to enable the faces of the opening stiles to lie flush. The arrangement of this is clearly indicated at A in Fig. 11.

Double Doors.—Each leaf of the double doors is 6 ft. high and a trifle over 2 ft. wide and the side door is of the same dimensions. The doors have

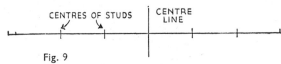

Fig. 9

stiles $2\frac{3}{4}$ in. wide, $1\frac{5}{8}$ in. thick and top rails of the same width. The middle and bottom rails are 5 in. wide; the space between them being filled in with $\frac{3}{4}$ in. weather boards on the outside, let in flush, and $\frac{3}{8}$ in. plain boards on the inside, also let in flush. These boards are fixed to $\frac{1}{2}$ in. square supporting fillets nailed to the inside faces of the stiles and rails.

The upper portion of the window is divided into six sections separated by one vertical and two horizontal sash bars. The labour in fitting the sash bars is time well spent as it means the replacement of only a small piece of glass if one is broken.

The sill at the bottom of the side casement windows projects $2\frac{1}{2}$ in. beyond the surface of the weather boards and the window sashes are $1\frac{1}{4}$ in. thick with stiles $1\frac{1}{2}$ in. wide, $1\frac{1}{2}$ in. top rails and 2 in. bottom rails.

A cover strip of $\frac{3}{8}$ in. stuff is nailed round the outside of each sash and projects $\frac{3}{8}$ in. beyond the opening stile and the top and bottom rails, thus forming a rebate as shown at B in Fig. 11.

This strip keeps out moisture and prevents draughts.

In addition to the cover strips, a planed batten $1\frac{1}{2}$ in. wide, 1 in. thick at the back and tapering down to $\frac{3}{4}$ in. in the front is fixed immediately above the window. Its length is the same as that of the window sill, and, like the sill is weather-grooved on the underside, near the front.

The ends of the roof rafters are covered all round with facia boards 6 in. wide $\times \frac{3}{4}$ in. thick, and soffit boards 5 in. wide enclose the exposed undersides of the rafters.

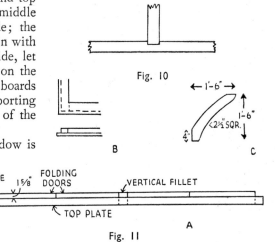

Fig. 10

Fig. 11

The whole of the roof is covered with $\frac{1}{2}$ in. tongued and grooved matching and then covered with red asbestos tiles and circular ridge and hip tiles of the same material.

A 4 in. gutter of semi-circular section is fitted to the facia boards and kept in position with brackets and a down pipe is connected to the gutter, which discharges into a circular corrugated galvanized iron tank at the back of the structure.

To give the front an attractive

appearance, four shaped brackets as detailed c in Fig. 11 should be fixed at the top corners of the front posts. These may generally be procured at a saw-mill equipped with a band saw, but if any difficulty is experienced in this direction, pieces of 3×3 in. straight wood, fixed diagonally, can be substituted.

The interior surface of the walls consists of asbestos sheeting which is fixed to the uprights, and the joints covered with strips of thin wood, while the interior of the roof consists of matchboards with neat covering strips at the joints.

Suitable bolts should be fitted to the folding doors and a good quality rim lock fixed to the side door.

Three or four coats of good lead paint after the preliminary operation of stopping the knots and punching down the nail heads, will finish the structure.

A LEAN-TO GREENHOUSE

THE lean-to greenhouse illustrated in Fig. 1 affords ample room for plants and also provides a covered entrance to the side door of the house.

Fig. 1

It is provided with a door at each end—a feature which allows the house door to be entered from either the front or back garden, as the case may be.

Ample ventilation is provided by means of a small window over each door, one of which can clearly be seen in Fig. 3, which is an end view.

The structure measures 11 ft. ×7 ft., while the height at the eave is 6 ft. 6 in. and 8 ft. 9 in. at the ridge, and rests on a concrete foundation 3 in. thick.

The first thing to do is to prepare the site for the concrete foundation. This may necessitate either excavating the soil or making it up to bring the top of the concrete to a convenient height below the house doorstep. If the latter has to be resorted to, the soil must not be allowed to come above the damp-course or a damp wall will result.

Marking the Site.—In any case, the site must be marked out by driving in four pegs, one at each corner, at the correct distance apart. Having done this, a stout front board and two side ones should be fixed to enclose the floor-space. These boards, which must not be less than 7 in. wide, are supported by a number of pegs placed between the marking pegs, as shown in Fig. 5, and it is essential that the top edges be level with the top of the concrete as tested with the spirit level.

The next operation consists of partly filling the enclosure with small pieces of broken brick, stones, slag or cinders to a depth of 4 in. and consolidating it by ramming. The site is now ready to receive the concrete.

A good concrete mixture consists of one part portland cement, two parts clean three parts sand can be proceeded with.

Mix the ingredients, remove all dust from the concrete surface, sprinkle it with water if dry and fill the enclosure with the mixture until it is perfectly

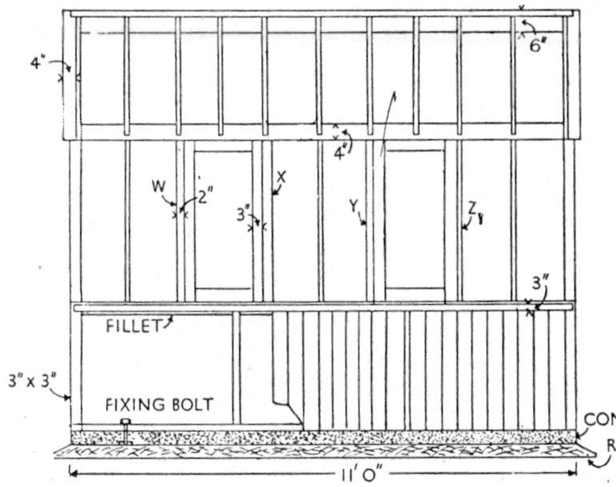

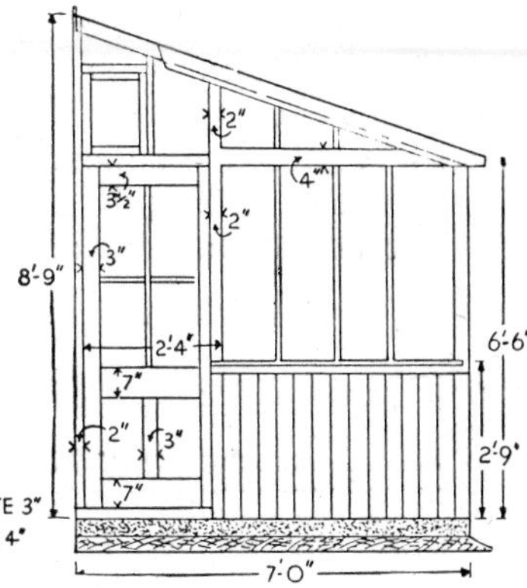

FRONT VIEW
Fig. 2

END VIEW
Fig. 3

sharp sand and four parts washed shingle about 1 in. diameter, all of which can be obtained at a builder's merchant's.

Measure the ingredients with the aid of a bucket and mix them thoroughly in the dry state on a large mixing board with a shovel, by first mixing the sand and cement until it assumes a reddish-grey colour. Then add the aggregate, as the more solid stuff is termed, and continue mixing; it cannot be mixed too much. Then add a little clean water from a water-can fitted with a rose and mix, adding more water as the mixing proceeds until the whole becomes a plastic mass, not too wet. Moisten the bed of rubble, shovel the concrete into the enclosure and bang it down level with the back of the shovel to a thickness of 2 in.

Allow this to harden and protect it from strong sun and drying winds by covering it with wet sacks. The longer it takes to dry the better the concrete will be. When hard, the finishing layer consisting of one part cement and

level with the top edges of the supporting boards. To ensure that the level is correct and the surface smooth, use a straight-edge made of a long board and with the aid of a helper hold it edgewise with the lower end resting on the frame boards and draw it from the back to the front, giving it a sawing sideways motion, as indicated by the arrows in Fig. 5.

Holding down Bolts.—When filling the enclosure with concrete, three bolts 6 in. in length and $\frac{1}{2}$ in. in diameter should be let in at a distance of 2 in. from the front edge and spaced approximately 1 ft. from each end and one in the centre. Two similar bolts are also fixed at the same distances in the side or end edges. These are for holding the bottom sills or plates in position. The top of each bolt should project 3 in. above the level of the concrete except the two back ones in the end plates. These should only project 2 in. so that the top of the nuts lie flush with the top of the plates. This is necessary because any projection at these points would prevent the door from closing. A thin iron plate about 1½ in. square should be drilled and filed to fit the shoulder of the bolt to prevent it turning when tightening the nut.

Having completed the concrete foundation, proceed with the constructional work.

Start by cutting the bottom plates or sills to size and drilling the bolt holes. The corners of these plates butt as

plane is not available it should be chiselled out with a narrow chisel.

The next item consists of fixing the top plate, and, to save the making of complicated joints, this is fixed with bolts and nuts as illustrated in detail at c in Fig. 6.

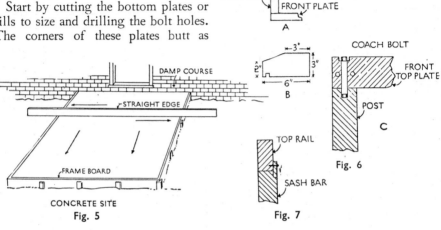

CONCRETE SITE
Fig. 5

Fig. 6

Fig. 7

shown in the detail at A in Fig. 6, and are held firmly in position by the holding bolts. If any reinforcement is needed at the joints, a right-angled bracket could be screwed to the inside faces, but this will be unnecessary if the nuts are screwed well down.

It is advisable to make the frame of the front of the structure first. The two corner posts are fixed to the bottom plates by driving in a couple of 6 in. wire nails from the underside into the bottom of the posts. This method is simple, saves the making of joints. The same method applies to the two intermediate posts, 6 in. nails having been driven in from the bottom and from the top of the window sill.

Fig. 6 B shows a section of the window sill. Note that a groove is made near the front edge of the underside to prevent the entry of water. The groove should not be omitted and if a plough

At this stage it is advisable to fix the ridge-board. This is 6 in. wide, and its lower edge is fixed 8 ft. 5 in. above the level of the floor. The board must be perfectly level and the ends must correspond with the floor edges. This position can readily be found with the aid of a plumb-bob and line. The ridge-board is fixed by means of long wall-nails having a flat shank and a head at right-angles to the shank; the lower edge of the board rests upon the nails and the heads keep it back to the wall. In using these nails, drive them into a mortar joint of the brickwork, but, if the mortar is too soft, it is wise to cement the nails in with neat portland cement.

Erecting the Frame.—Having fixed the ridge-board satisfactorily, it will be as well to get the front frame erected. Before doing this, however, it is a good plan to square up the frame and fix temporarily a batten diagonally across each corner, to keep it square.

You will need a helper to assist in erecting the front frame on the fixing bolts and to hold it in position while you fix a strut between the ridge-board and the top of the frame. This temporary strut will be helpful when testing vertically, as it is absolutely essential that the front should be plumb upright.

The next procedure is to build up the sides. It matters little which side is started first, as they are both built in the same way.

The best way is first to nail the back post and door post to the bottom plate and fix the latter down by means of the nuts and bolts. Then fix the 4 in. horizontal cross-rail, the outer end of which is secured to the front top rail by means of 5 in. coach bolts as shown at c in Fig. 6.

Nail the sloping top rail to the ridge board and horizontal cross-rail. See that the ends are cut to correspond with the angle of the roof, and fix the window sill, door-head and the framing for the small ventilating window.

Repeat the operations on the other side of the structure and fit the vertical pieces which form the window frames, marked w, x, y and z in Fig. 2.

This is followed by cutting and fixing the sash bars to the roof. These are 2 in. wide × 2½ in. deep, the fronts of which should project 3 in. beyond the front top rail. Fix the sash bars to the front and sides by cutting them 1¼ in. longer than the distance between the top of the sill and the underside of the top plates. The ends are then cut as shown in Fig. 7 and screwed from the back to the members. This method is entirely satisfactory and eliminates the complication of mortices. The other parts of the rebates for supporting the glass are formed by nailing 1 × ¾ in.

strips in line with the rebates in the sash bars.

The tongued and grooved matching should be at least ⅝ in. finished thickness and is nailed to fillets about 1 in. square, nailed to the underfaces of the window sills, and the bottom plates as shown in the front view, Fig. 2.

The stiles and rails of the doors are 1½ in. thick yellow deal, the foot and lock rails being 7 in. wide, while the width of the top rail is 3½ in. and the stiles also 3½ in. The joints are mortice and tenons and the lower panels are of matching nailed to the fillets.

The ventilating windows as well as the casements in the front are also morticed and tenoned. The former are hinged at the top, casement fasteners being fitted to the lower rails to keep them open at any desired position within the limits of the fasteners.

Before fitting any glass, the whole of the framework should be prepared for a priming coat of paint. All knots should be treated with knotting to prevent them spoiling the finished work.

The priming paint should consist of red and white lead mixed with linseed oil and can be obtained ready mixed. Before applying the paint, make sure that the woodwork is absolutely dry, otherwise blisters and other imperfections will appear in the finished work.

Use 21 oz. horticultural glass for the roof and allow at least a 1½ in. overlap between adjacent pieces.

Ordinary glass is used for the front and side leading to the back garden and this can be cut to measure, allowing ⅛ in. less in both width and length than the corresponding measurements of the rebate.

The side facing the front garden is glazed with translucent glass to ensure privacy.

Having completed the glazing, two

coats of good lead oil paint should be given. A stone colour is more suitable than a green as the latter soon becomes shabby.

A cast iron or zinc gutter with a down pipe should be fitted with brackets to the top horizontal plate, and the surface water led either to a large water butt at one end or to a catch pit at some convenient spot in the garden. The gutter should be painted inside and out.

A FRONT DOOR PORCH

THE porch shown in Fig. 1 is modern in design and the square, step back treatment is consistent even to the

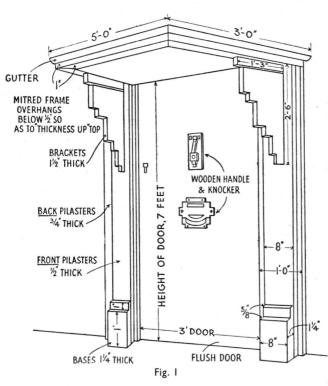

GUTTER

MITRED FRAME
OVERHANGS
BELOW ½ SO
AS TO THICKNESS UP TOP

BRACKETS
1½ THICK

BACK PILASTERS
¾" THICK

FRONT PILASTERS
½" THICK

WOODEN HANDLE
& KNOCKER

HEIGHT OF DOOR, 7 FEET

5'-0"   3'-0"

1'-3"

2'-6"

8"

1'-0"

⅝"

1'4"   3' DOOR   8"

BASES 1¼ THICK   FLUSH DOOR

Fig. 1

knocker and letter-box. The 7×3 ft. door may be altered to suit individual requirements.

It is not necessary to make the surround and canopy of heavy timber. The canopy has only to keep rain off.

The wooden structure can easily be fastened to stone or brick, as long as there is a flat surface to screw it to.

First cut out two back pilasters in oak or pine, size 12 in. wide and ¾ in. thick and as long as necessary to clear the door top and the door framing. The canopy is nailed on to the pilasters from above.

Bore ⅜ in. holes, ¼ in. deep only, on the back pilasters, three at the top and three at the bottom. Set these holes in 1 in. from the edges and ends and then bore holes at convenient distances down the sides, about 1 ft. apart.

These back pilasters have to take the entire weight of the structure.

Now bore through the bottoms of all the ⅜×¼ in. holes with a $\frac{5}{16}$ in. twist-drill.

Wall Fittings.— Mark out on the wall the exact position of these pilasters taking care that the lines are vertical. Place the back pilasters in position, get someone to hold them, and, with the $\frac{5}{16}$ in. twist-drill, give a few turns to mark the exact positions of the holes on the brickwork.

Take away the pilasters and, with the same drill, bore into the brick 1½ in.

deep. These holes can also be made with a rawlplug tool.

Carefully plug the holes in the brick with whitewood pegs, fitting them in very tightly. Saw off the pegs level with the face of the wall, screw on the back pilaster but do not plug up the large holes in the pilaster itself.

Now square up two front pilasters 8 in. wide × ½ in. thick and the same length as the back ones, and make the two brackets.

Square and plane up two pieces of wood, each 2 ft. 4 in. × 1 ft. 1 in. × 1½ in. bare. Set out the shapes as shown in Fig. 2 on both sides of each bracket. Put them, one at a time, in the vice, and with a tenon saw cut the lines that go across the grain. The other lines should be cut with a hand or panel saw.

Clean up the edges with a chisel and Nos. 2 and 1½ glass-paper. Then nail on the two pieces 1 ft. 3 in. × 2½ × 2 in. that form the top fillets. See that the nails will not be in the way of the screws in the canopy when screwed down on the fillets.

Find the position of the brackets on the top centre of the front pilasters and bore, countersink and screw them on from the back.

Then cut out and square up the two bases, size 1 ft. 1 in. × 8 in. × 1¼ in. Square lines across and saw out the square mouldings, as shown. Clean these up and screw them on from the back. See that they bed down on the pilaster faces.

The two front pilasters, brackets and bases are now complete. Screw them firmly in the same way as the back pilasters were screwed to the wall.

The Canopy.—Sound yellow deal, 1 in. thick, will do perfectly well for the canopy. If the rest of the work is in oak, the edges of the canopy may be faced with oak.

Cut out, plane and square up a piece of deal, size 4 ft. 8 in. × 1 in. (bare) × 2 ft. 8 in.

Mitre round the edges a framework 2 in. wide × 1 in. thick all round, just like a picture frame, and nail it on. This may be of oak, if it is on an oak

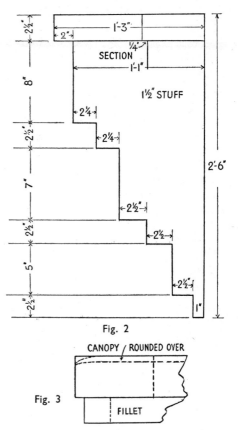

Fig. 2

Fig. 3

porch. Fix a mitred fillet ⅝ in. underneath so as to thickness up the top. Plane the top face of the canopy slightly round so that the rain will run off into the small gutter which is fixed on the edge.

The gutter is not essential, as the canopy is large enough to prevent the rain drippings falling on anyone standing underneath.

Clean up the top and place it in position to find the positions of the screws by which means it is screwed on to the tops of the back pilasters and brackets.

Bore the holes for screws $\frac{5}{16}$ in. in diameter and partly screw the canopy on to see that everything is right. Make any necessary adjustment, take it down and make the top waterproof.

Purchase some Burgundy pitch, which is sold at about ninepence per box. Two boxes will be enough to cover the top. Melt the pitch in an old saucepan on the gas stove. Use a low gas as the pitch is inflammable. Stir the mixture till the pitch has melted and then, with an old brush, apply it to the face side, the rounded side and $\frac{1}{2}$ in. down the edges, and allow it to dry.

Purchase a sheet of thin zinc or copper. Bore $\frac{1}{4}$ in. holes all round the sheet about $\frac{1}{2}$ in. in from the edges and countersink the holes.

Screw on the canopy before fixing the zinc or copper. When this is done, screw on the metal. All screw-heads that show on the work should now be plugged up with oak dowels.

Plane up several $12 \times \frac{3}{8} \times \frac{3}{8}$ in. (full) pieces of wood. Then, holding the wood in one hand against the bench stop, round it with a smoothing plane.

Glue and knock in the oak dowels and clean up the whole porch with Nos. 2 and $1\frac{1}{2}$ glass-paper.

Finishing the Porch.—If the porch, door, knocker and letter-box are all in seasoned wainscot oak, it would be best if the oak were left untouched to weather to a silver grey.

For a slightly darker shade, mix raw linseed oil and turpentine in equal parts and apply with a brush. Allow to dry.

A darker shade still may be obtained by brushing with strong soda in hot water and oil and turpentine.

Another way is to brush it with .880 liquid ammonia, then oil and turpentine, to give a shade darker again. It can be stained to a rich brown colour by mixing sixpennyworth of bichromate of potash with one pint of boiling water. Apply and finish as before.

Try all these finishes on odd pieces of wood until you get the required shade.

If the porch is made of pine or deal it will be best to paint it. Stop the knots, apply two coats of undercoating and finish with a coat of high-class paint of a colour to tone with the front of the house.

For instance, any of the following schemes would look well:

Scheme A.—Door crimson, blue, orange, green or maroon with the brackets, knocker, letter-box and edges of the canopy black. In this case the window-frames should also be black.

Scheme B.—Paint the whole canopy in any of the above colours as a contrast to the existing door.

Scheme C.—Paint the whole canopy cream, not white, except the brackets, bases and edges of the canopy. These will form a contrast if painted black.

When decorating with black and cream, use seven-eighths the area of cream to one-eighth the area of black.

KNOCKERS, LETTER-BOXES AND FINGER-PLATES

KNOCKER and letter-box should, if possible, be made of the same wood as the door. As the door weathers, so do the fittings, thus unifying the door and its furniture.

The Knocker.—The following description shows how to make and fix an oak knocker and a letter-box, details of which appear in Figs. 1 and 2.

Saw out and square up one piece of

oak, size $9\frac{1}{4} \times 3 \times \frac{1}{2}$ in.; another piece, $8\frac{1}{2} \times 1\frac{7}{8} \times 1\frac{1}{2}$ in.; and two small pieces, $\frac{7}{8} \times \frac{11}{16} \times 1\frac{1}{4}$ in.

Mark out two half mortices in the $9\frac{1}{4} \times 3 \times \frac{1}{2}$ in. piece of wood in the positions shown in Fig. 1, and mark out corresponding tenons on the two small

the $8\frac{1}{2} \times 1\frac{7}{8} \times 1\frac{1}{2}$ in. piece and mark out on both edges the lines and shape, shown in the side view.

Put the block in the vice and, with a 6 in. dovetail saw, cut down all the lines to the required depth and pare out with a chisel to the profile shown.

Now draw out on the front and back the lines shown in the front view. Saw down and cut these out in the same way, taking care to fit the knocker quite loosely in between the two little posts.

Then centre the two little posts on their inner sides and bore, with a $\frac{5}{16}$ in. twist-drill, two holes $\frac{1}{2}$ in. deep only. These holes must not go right through the wood.

Find the same centre on the striker and bore right through.

Cut off a piece of copper rod $1\frac{3}{4}$ in. long $\times \frac{5}{16}$ in. diameter. Put together and fit in.

Round off the end of the knocker (see side view) and scoop out the wood between the two little posts, as shown by the dotted line in the side view. This enables the knocker to be lifted right up.

Turn over the $9\frac{1}{4}$ in. back plate and slope the ends of the mortices and cut out two small wedges to fit.

Now rebate ($\frac{1}{4} \times \frac{1}{4}$ in.) the edges of the back plate and clean up the whole knocker with Nos. $1\frac{1}{2}$ and 1 glass-paper, taking off all the sharp edges.

Assemble the two posts, pivot and knocker as these have to go in together.

With hot, clear glue, glue in the posts, turn the knocker over and glue

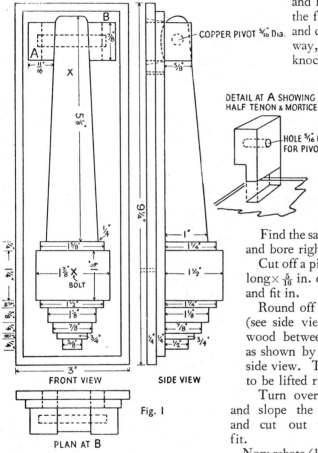

DETAIL AT **A** SHOWING
HALF TENON & MORTICE

COPPER PIVOT ⁵⁄₁₆ Dia.

HOLE ⁵⁄₁₆ Dia.
FOR PIVOT

FRONT VIEW   SIDE VIEW

Fig. I

PLAN AT **B**

pieces. Saw out the half tenons carefully and cut the mortices through the $9\frac{1}{4}$ in. piece. These mortices should be cut half-way through from the front and half-way from the back.

Knock these two little posts into the back plate. The tenons project $\frac{1}{4}$ in. which will be sawn off later. Then take and tap in the two wedges. Do this by hitting once, alternately on each post.

Leave twelve hours to dry, then saw off the wedges and tenons and clean off the back.

Fixing to the Door.—To fix the knocker on the door, bore two $\frac{5}{16}$ in. holes through the back plate in the positions marked x in the illustration. Hold the back plate in position on the door, with the knocker lifted up, and mark the positions of the bolts on it. Bore these two holes through the door $\frac{5}{16}$ in. diameter and bolt on the knocker

$8\frac{1}{2} \times 4 \times 2\frac{3}{4}$ in. and mark it " face side " and " face edge."

Gauge a line along the face $1\frac{1}{2}$ in. from the face edge and another $\frac{1}{4}$ in. from the face edge. From the back, gauge a line $\frac{3}{8}$ in. all round and carefully saw out the block from the front so as to leave the handle in relief on the $\frac{3}{8}$ in. letter plate. Be careful to leave all your lines well in, as a certain amount of wood is required when planing down the back plate. Do this next.

Then clamp the plate to the bench and, having marked out the shape of the handle, bow saw it out and clean

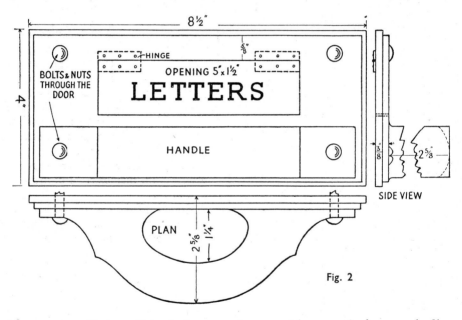

Fig. 2

by two nuts and bolts sufficiently long to go through so that the nuts can be screwed up from inside.

If a very loud knock is required, a dome of silence should be hammered on the back of the knocker before fixing.

The Letter-box.—The oak letter-box and handle shown in Fig. 2 are cut from a solid block of oak.

First square a block of oak to size,

it up with a spokeshave and files. Then drill or bow saw out the centre hole in the handle, size $2\frac{5}{8} \times 1\frac{1}{4}$ in. and clean it up to shape as shown in the plan.

Now round over the front edges with a spokeshave and let the round part run out flat and square at the ends. Round over the centre hole with a gouge, letting it die out on to the back plate.

Mark out the letter-slot and carefully drill or saw this out, then clean up exactly to lines.

Bore the holes for the nuts and bolts, $\frac{5}{16}$ in. in diameter, and rebate the front edge of the plate $\frac{1}{8} \times \frac{3}{16}$ in.

Cut a piece of $\frac{3}{8}$ in. oak to the exact size of the letter-slot. This must be slack so that, when hinged, it will fall into position.

Turn the plate over and screw on two $1\frac{1}{4}$ in. stamped brass hinges with the insides of the hinges outwards. These hinges must be slack and well oiled.

A $\frac{1}{8}$ in. bevel all round the opening will improve its appearance.

Little pieces must be cut from the door to take up the hinges which project from the back of the plate.

Clean up the plate and handle, and bolt it on in the same way as the knocker.

The light oak knocker and letter box can be left unstained or may be coloured to agree, or contrast, with the door.

Finger - plates.—When making a door-plate the first consideration will be the wood. American black walnut, Australian walnut, mahogany, teak, dark oak and ebony go with most colour schemes and do not show finger marks.

To make door-plates from any of these, obtain wood about $\frac{3}{16}$ in. or $\frac{1}{4}$ in. thick. Square and plane it to size, $3\frac{1}{2}$ in. wide and about $\frac{1}{8}$ in. thick. It would stand out too much from the door if thicker. Then, with a metal smoothing plane, run a $\frac{1}{16} \times \frac{1}{8}$ in. bevel all round. The plates may be of any length desired.

Bore a hole $\frac{1}{4}$ in. from each corner with a $\frac{1}{8}$ in. twist-drill and countersink so that the brass screw-heads are level with the face. This gives a smooth surface for dusting and polishing. Put in other necessary screw-holes down the sides and then polish the plates with beeswax and turpentine. Any well-known wax polish will do.

Another scheme would be to make the door plates out of holly or sycamore and dye them to the desired colour. Purchase dye of the required colour and make it in liquid form as directed. Stir well and put the dye on with a brush, allow to dry, then smooth with Nos. 1 and 0 glass-paper and polish with light wax polish.

The upper plate should be 1 ft. 10 in. to 2 ft. above the keyhole, and the lower plate about 10 in. under it. They should be placed as near as possible to the edge of the door without interfering with the closing.

TABLE LIGHTING AND DECORATION

AN effective way of furnishing a dining table is to have an oiled silver cloth. These cloths need no washing as they have only to be wiped with a wet cloth. At each end may be placed an oak candlestick with a black or silver candle as in Fig. 1 and, in the middle of the table, the two-tiered oak centre-piece for fruit, Fig. 2. To com-plete the scheme, oak mats could be placed under the plates to save marking the table.

The following article shows how to make these furnishings.

Candlesticks. — To construct the bases of the oak candlesticks, square up a piece of Austrian wainscot oak to $9\frac{1}{8} \times 4\frac{1}{2} \times 1\frac{1}{2}$ in. for the two bases, each

$4\frac{1}{2} \times 4\frac{1}{2}$ in. The $\frac{1}{16}$ in. on each is to allow for the tenon saw-cut when halving them. The two candlesticks are morticed into this $9\frac{5}{8}$ in. piece and the work is carried as far as possible before dividing it.

Now square up two pieces of oak for the candlesticks, size $12\frac{3}{4} \times 1\frac{3}{8} \times 1\frac{3}{8}$ in.

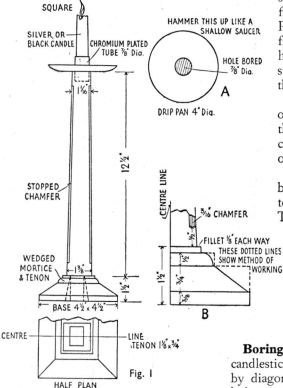

SQUARE

SILVER, OR BLACK CANDLE

CHROMIUM PLATED TUBE ⅞" Dia.

HAMMER THIS UP LIKE A SHALLOW SAUCER

HOLE BORED ⅞" Dia.

DRIP PAN 4" Dia.

A

1 1/16

12½

STOPPED CHAMFER

CENTRE LINE

³/₁₆ CHAMFER

FILLET ⅛ EACH WAY

THESE DOTTED LINES SHOW METHOD OF WORKING

WEDGED MORTICE & TENON

1⅜

½

½

¾

³/₈

1½

BASE 4½" x 4½"

B

CENTRE

LINE TENON 1⅛ x ¾

Fig. I

HALF PLAN

Measure up from the base of each piece a distance of $1\frac{3}{4}$ in. and square a line round with a chisel or marking knife. The tenon projects through the base $\frac{1}{4}$ in. and is sawn off later on. Then gauge lines for the tenons which are $1\frac{1}{8} \times \frac{3}{4}$ in.

Take the base and square a fine pencil line across the middle, and, with a marking knife, square across two lines $\frac{1}{16}$ in. right and left of it. This leaves two squares each

$4\frac{1}{2} \times 4\frac{1}{2}$ in. Centre these by drawing diagonals with a pencil and mark out the $1\frac{1}{8} \times \frac{3}{4}$ in. tenons, taking care that the long sides of the mortice are with the grain.

Cut these mortices out by drilling two holes through each base with a $\frac{1}{2}$ in. centre-bit. Pare carefully down the sides and ends of the mortice, finishing to the lines exactly. Pare down half of the mortice from the face and the other half from the back. Slope the sides of the mortices $\frac{1}{4}$ in. for the wedges.

Now saw down the tenons on the candlesticks, keeping the gauge lines in, and saw carefully across the shoulders of the tenons.

Fit the candlesticks into the base and test with a try square to see that they are vertical. To do this, place, right and left of the projecting tenon, two small pieces of wood $\frac{1}{4}$ in. thick so that the candlestick will stand upright. This is important and cannot be done so exactly if the testing is left until the final gluing.

Boring and Tapering.—Take the candlesticks out and centre the top ends by diagonal lines. Then bore a $\frac{7}{8}$ in. hole 1 in. deep with a sharp centre-bit. This is very difficult and the brace must be held upright or the hole will come through the sides when the candlesticks are tapered to $1\frac{1}{16}$ in. Do this tapering next by marking off with a pencil the $1\frac{1}{16}$ in. diameter at the top. Then, with a metal smoothing plane, plane off to the lines.

Now fit two pieces of chromium-plated or stainless steel tubing, each $2 \times \frac{7}{8}$ in. in diameter, into the holes. Get the tubing before boring so as to fit the holes to it. Different makes vary slightly in diameter.

For the drip pans, take a piece of aluminium sheet, $8\frac{1}{4} \times 4\frac{1}{4}$ in., and strike two circles upon it, each 4 in. in diameter. Mark the centres by a tap with a sharp nail. Cut out the circular pieces with a pair of metal snips. Then, starting from the centre and with a pencil compass, strike as many concentric circles upon it as possible, $\frac{1}{4}$ in. apart. This is a guide when hammering it up to a concave shape as indicated at A in Fig. 1. To do this, round the head of a hammer slightly over and smooth it with fine emery paper. Then, starting from the centre, hammer with sharp taps between the $\frac{1}{4}$ in. lines, gradually working to the outside circles. It is important to hammer a series of marks all round between each $\frac{1}{4}$ in. circle and keep them just touching each other. Turn the drip pan over from time to time, and with an ordinary hammer tap outwards gently to level the edges. Then file and finish them half-round and smooth with emery paper.

Bore out the $\frac{7}{8}$ in. centre hole and smooth the edges of this also. On the two candlesticks, with a sharp 2 in. chisel, cut the $\frac{3}{16}$ in. stopped chamfers—i.e., bevel off the edges.

The Bases.—These are still in one piece $9\frac{1}{8}$ in. long. Mould them as far as possible while they are together, as follows: From the edge, gauge a line all round on the face side, $1\frac{3}{8}$ in. in from the edge. From the face side, and on the edges, gauge a line $\frac{1}{8}$ in. down. Saw down the centre dividing line to the depth of 1 in. only. Rebate this out and gauge and rebate out the second step as shown by the dotted lines detailed at B in Fig. 1.

Then round off the oval moulding with a $\frac{3}{8}$ in. chisel or gouge and plane off the long bevel. The top $\frac{1}{8}$ in. fillet and ovolo can now be worked through

the centre of the block. When this has been done, divide the block by sawing it in half. Then complete the moulding of each block and clean up

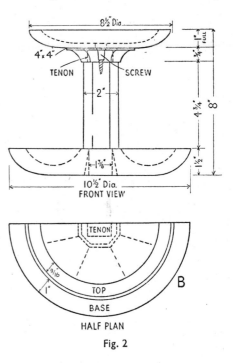

Fig. 2

the candlestick with Nos. $1\frac{1}{2}$ and 1 glass-paper.

Now cut two little wedges of oak or walnut to wedge up the tenons.

Dip the tenons into hot glue, then put them in the mortices, dip the wedges in the glue, push and tap them in, tapping once on each wedge alternately.

Put the candlesticks on the $\frac{1}{4}$ in. thick pieces and test for squareness. An extra tap on either wedge will bring the candlestick over more to the side you tap on. Now remove all the glue with clean hot water and allow to dry. Then glass-paper down, working in the direction of the grain with Nos. 1 and 0. This completes the candlesticks.

Oak Fruit Stand.—To make the oak centre-piece for fruit, square up a piece of oak for the base, size $10\frac{1}{2} \times 10\frac{1}{2} \times 1\frac{1}{2}$ in.; a piece for the top tier, size $8\frac{1}{2} \times 8\frac{1}{2} \times 1$ in. full; a piece for the centre stem, size $6\frac{3}{4} \times 2 \times 2$ in. and a small piece $4 \times 4 \times \frac{3}{4}$ in. which is directly under the top tier of the bowl.

Constructional woodwork should always be done before the wood is shaped. So mark out the tenons on each end of the centre stem by a gauge and chisel, to the sizes shown in Fig. 2, viz., $1\frac{3}{8}$ in. square. To do this, square a line all round with a chisel $1\frac{3}{4}$ in. from the base of the stem, and square a line $\frac{3}{4}$ in. from the top all round also.

Set an octagon out in pencil on the

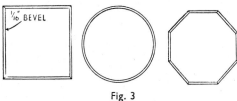

Fig. 3

top and bottom ends of the stem and carry the pencil lines down the sides as a guide to planing off later on. Saw out the tenons.

Find the centre of the base by means of diagonal lines, set out the mortice $1\frac{3}{8}$ in. square, drill out the waste and afterwards pare to the lines with a chisel.

Cut out the mortice in the same way through the $4 \times 4 \times \frac{3}{4}$ in. piece of wood. Then slope the ends of mortices $\frac{1}{4}$ in. at each end to receive the wedges, and make the wedges. Do the same to the base mortice.

Fit the table centre together, but do not put in the wedges. Plane the stem to an octagon as shown. Then strike all the circles as shown on the top bowl and the base.

Now gouge out the wood to the

dotted lines shown with a $\frac{7}{8}$ in. wood carving gouge, holding the gouge handle with the back of the hands up. With elbows extended, weight of the body on the left arm, gradually carve out the hollows. A mallet may be used if necessary. It will be best to carve out the top bowl first.

When carving out the base, do not forget to leave the little $\frac{1}{8}$ in. fillet at the base of the stem.

As the stem is octagonal, you will find that octagonal radial lines will result; see dotted lines in the half-plan B in Fig. 2. Leave the gouge cuts in. They complete a hand-wrought appearance.

If you wish, these hollows can be turned out on a lathe.

Hollow out with the same gouge the octagonal piece, $4 \times 4 \times \frac{3}{4}$ in.—and glue the three pieces together. Wedge up as before, taking care that the stem is upright. Leave for twelve hours to dry, then saw off the projecting wedges and clean up.

Fix the top bowl by boring in its centre a $\frac{3}{8}$ in. hole, $\frac{1}{8}$ in. deep only. In the centre of this hole bore another hole through, $\frac{5}{16}$ in. in diameter. Glue and screw on the top. As the screw is countersunk $\frac{1}{8}$ in., plug up with a piece of oak.

It may be necessary to hammer in some $\frac{3}{8}$ in. veneer pins to secure the outside octagonal edges of the 4×4 in. piece. Punch the pins in and fill up.

Clean up the centre-piece with Nos. $1\frac{1}{2}$ and 1 glass-paper, and take off the sharp edges so that it is comfortable to handle.

Table Mats.—To make the oak table mats as shown in illustration 3, plane up half a dozen pieces of seasoned Austrian wainscot oak to size, $8 \times 8 \times \frac{5}{16}$ in.

The mats may be made square,

octagonal, or round. It is best to make them out of the solid wood so that they can be scrubbed from time to time.

If they are made of oak-faced plywood, hot plates will eventually take off the thin film of oak.

Mark out the wood the shape you require. With a dovetail saw, cut them out and clean up the edges, face and back.

If light oak has been used, the best polish is a branded one of light oak colour. These polishes do not show marks from hot plates. They are easily and quickly applied and burnished with a soft cloth.

If the dining-room table is of dark or brown oak, a beige oiled-silk cloth would be best. The furnishings would then look better if fumigated as follows. Put the articles in an air-tight box, half fill a tea-saucer with .880 ammonia, place it in the box and quickly shut the lid. If there are any cracks or openings in the box, paste them up with paper. Leave for twelve hours, then rub the articles with canvas and burnish them with a chain burnisher. This gives the wood a beautiful brown colour with a patina that cannot be obtained in any other way.

Another method, after fumigating, is to polish them with a dark brown wax polish put on and rubbed off with a light soft cloth.

It is not advisable to stain oak. Any colour can be obtained by chemical process.

BUILT-IN FURNITURE

TAKE the mantelshelf of a room as the highest line, and suppose that bookcases and cupboards are to be built in on each side of it as in Fig. 1. Make them the same height as an existing sideboard.

The cupboards and bookcases shown are for a room 12 ft. wide. The recesses left and right are 2 ft. 10 in.×3 ft. 6 in. wide respectively and they are 10 in. in depth. The chimney breast is 5 ft. 8 in. wide. The mantel face is $\frac{3}{4}$ in. oak, thus making the total depth of the recess 10$\frac{3}{4}$ in.

These measurements may be modified to suit any room.

Preparing the Recess.—Remove the skirting on the right and left of the mantel. First place a straight-edge on the floor against the face of the mantel so that it reaches the left-hand wall and mark a vertical line on the wall and skirting. Then mark the right-hand wall.

With a tenon saw, cut off the skirting each side to the lines drawn.

Take off the unwanted skirting with a screwdriver or cold chisel. Screw in the bookcases, as nailed work legally cannot be taken away unless the house is your own property.

Cut and square four pieces of deal for the four upright sides of the bookcases, size 3 ft. 7$\frac{1}{2}$ in.×8×$\frac{3}{4}$ in., and glue, on the face edges, pieces of $\frac{3}{4}$ in. oak × 2$\frac{3}{4}$ in. wide.

Rub the glue well out and allow twelve hours to dry. Then fit them in and plane off flush with the mantel.

Then cut two top pieces out of oak— namely, one piece 2 ft. 10 × 10$\frac{3}{4}$ × $\frac{3}{4}$ in. and the other 3 ft. 6 in. × 10$\frac{3}{4}$ × $\frac{3}{4}$ in. and two bottom pieces of deal the same sizes but faced up with 2 × $\frac{3}{4}$ in. oak.

Fit all the pieces in the recesses, mark them for easy identification and square lines across the insides of the upright pieces for the grooves of the shelves, which can now be cut out.

The Shelves.—These may be of $\frac{3}{4}$ in. deal faced up with oak as before described.

The sizes are as follows: Two pieces 2 ft. 9 in. $\times$ 10$\frac{3}{4}$ $\times$ $\frac{3}{4}$ in., two pieces 3 ft. 5 in. $\times$ 10$\frac{3}{4}$ $\times$ $\frac{3}{4}$ in. for the shelves,

these holes with a $\frac{1}{4}$ in. drill. The holes will later have to be plugged up with $\frac{5}{16}$ in. oak dowels. The carcases may now be placed in the recesses, to be taken out later.

No backs are required, unless the walls are damp, in which case it will be best to back with plywood $\frac{1}{8}$ in. thick.

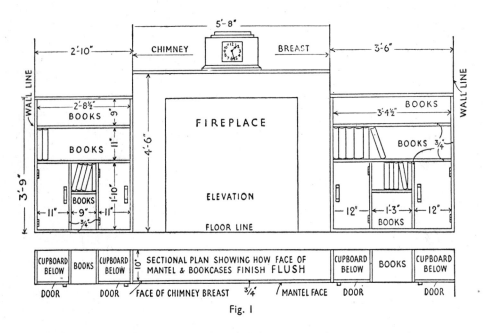

Fig. 1

and four pieces 1 ft. 10$\frac{1}{2}$ in. $\times$ 10$\frac{3}{4}$ $\times$ $\frac{3}{4}$ in. for the upright divisions of the cupboards; one piece 9$\frac{1}{2}$ $\times$ 10$\frac{3}{4}$ $\times$ $\frac{3}{4}$ in. and one piece 1 ft. 3$\frac{1}{2}$ in. $\times$ 10$\frac{3}{4}$ $\times$ $\frac{3}{4}$ in. for the small shelves between the cupboards.

House in the long shelves $\frac{1}{4}$ in. deep only, as shown at A in Fig. 2.

Fit the carcases roughly together and try them in the recesses. Take them apart, mark and cut the grooves for the upright cupboard divisions and small shelves.

Now bore holes, countersink them and screw up the carcases.

When screwing on the tops, bore holes $\frac{1}{4}$ in. deep with a $\frac{5}{16}$ in. twist-drill; then bore through the bottoms of

This can be painted on both sides to keep out damp.

Cupboard Doors. — The doors shown are of the flush type. They are small and can be built of clean pine or deal by gluing together, in the case of the 11 in. door, three pieces of dry pine, each piece being 1 ft. 10$\frac{1}{4}$ in. $\times$ 4 $\times$ $\frac{1}{2}$ in. For the 12 in. door, wider pieces will be needed.

Rub the joints well and leave them for several days to dry. It is best to leave them in a warm room, standing on their ends. Reverse them from time to time, to counteract tendency to warp.

When dry, plane, square-up and fit. Face them with $\frac{5}{16}$ in. thick oak plywood. Cut the plywood a trifle larger than the soft wood panels (doors). Then fix the latter to an old table by knocking in veneer pins against the outer edges, but below the thickness of the deal. Working quickly in a warm room, cover the surface of the deal, then the underside of the oak ply with hot thin glue, and with a circular motion and hard pressure rub out the glue. Wipe the face of the oak with hot water to prevent it kicking up, and drive in a few $\frac{3}{8}$ in. veneer pins to keep it down.

Put a heavy weight on it and allow twelve hours to dry.

Then plane up the edges with a small metal plane, planing away from the oak ply by working obliquely.

Now glass-paper the edges smooth,

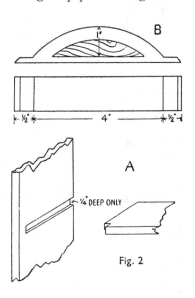

Fig. 2

fit in the doors and smooth the carcases with Nos. $1\frac{1}{2}$ and 1 glass-paper.

Hinges and Fastenings.—Put the hinges on the doors (2 in. brass butts) after having cut recesses to a depth of the total thickness of the hinges in the edges of the doors.

On the tops and bottoms of the doors,

at a distance of about 1 in. from the long edges, put on some $\frac{3}{8}$ in. ball catches—one on top and the other on the bottom of each door.

Now make the wooden handles, B in Fig. 2. First square up a piece of wood, 1 ft. $8\frac{3}{16}$ in. × 1 × 1 in. As each handle

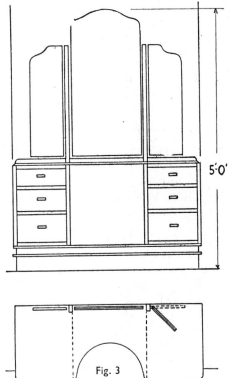

Fig. 3

is 5 in. long, square lines across at 5 in., allowing $\frac{1}{16}$ in. for each of the three saw cuts. Measure $\frac{1}{2}$ in. from left-hand end of the wood, then 4 in., then $\frac{1}{2}$ in. and $\frac{1}{2}$ in., and so on until all four handles are marked out. Do not saw through into four pieces, but saw down to $\frac{3}{4}$ in. deep at all these lines that you have squared across, and groove out the flat parts first.

Then, with a 1 in. chisel, round off the handles and file and glass-paper them smooth. Put the piece of wood in the vice and gouge out the finger holds as shown.

Finally, saw the piece of wood up into the four complete handles and clean up the end grain.

Screw on the handles as shown in illustration 1. Screw them on from

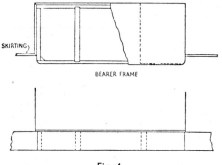

SKIRTING

BEARER FRAME

Fig. 4

inside the doors and plug up the countersunk portion.

Then plug up the tops of the book-cases with $\frac{5}{16}$ in. oak dowels, saw off the waste and clean up the top surfaces.

Completing the Case.—Only four screws are necessary for fixing each bookcase. Bore one $\frac{5}{16}$ in. hole in the centre of each side between the long shelves only.

Place the bookcase in position, hold it in place, and with a bradawl and hammer mark the positions of the holes on the walls.

Take out the bookcase and, with a $\frac{5}{16}$ in. twist-drill, bore 1 in. deep into the walls. Make some whitewood pegs to fit the holes exactly; hammer them in and saw off the waste.

Then, placing a bookcase on its side, screw on the door hinges. When mark-ing the position of the hinges on the sides, see that the centres of the pins are on the edges of the sides.

Now make eight little door stops (which prevent doors being pushed in too far), size about $1\frac{1}{2} \times \frac{3}{4} \times \frac{5}{16}$ in. and glue and pin them on securely.

Staining or polishing should now be done. The best plan is to polish the built-in furniture to match other furni-ture in the room.

If the furniture is Jacobean oak, the colour may be obtained by mixing vandyke brown powder with .880 liquid ammonia. Mix it to a paste and then thin out with cold water to the required colour. Try it out on an odd piece of wood. Then, when the stain is dry, rub the bookcase with coarse canvas and polish with wax polish.

Bedroom Furniture. — Another example of built-in furniture is shown in Fig. 3 which illustrates a dressing table with mirrors.

Space being restricted, it may not be possible to tilt the centre glass so it has been increased in height and remains fixed. The two side mirrors swing inwards, as indicated.

A form of unit construction has been used, consisting of a base or platform built into the recess, two drawer units, and a shaped top carried right across the recess. The recess allows a person to sit close to the mirror with their feet on the platform below. The dimensions may be altered to suit any recess.

The framework of bearers, Fig. 4, to rest on the floor must fit in the recess between, and at the same height as, the existing skirting boards. Deal may be used for all members except the front one. This must be of the same wood as the remainder. On the top boards the same method is followed, ordinary wood at the back and better wood for finishing at the front, all tongued and grooved. These boards must be long enough to cover right up to the wall and will thus fit on top of the skirting boards as well as the bearers.

The bearer frame may be joined in any manner most convenient, such as

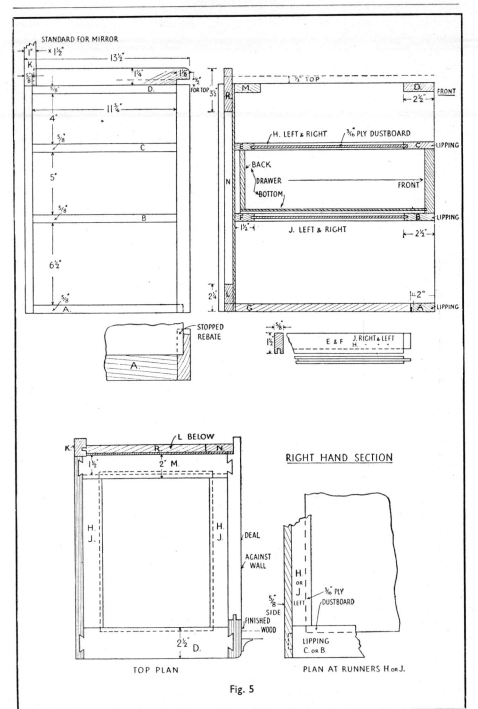

Fig. 5

mortice and tenon at the back but as no screws or nails are to show on the front, angle pieces are shown, and the front ends and the front piece itself secured by these. A pair of inner bearers may be cut to fit between the front and back ones, or the ends may be notched in. The frame is cut and fitted into

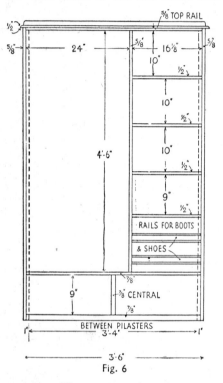

Fig. 6

position. The top is made and trimmed to size last of all in case the walls are not square.

Both side units are constructed in the same way except that, at the back, the standard for the centre mirror is fixed in the right-hand corner in one case and in the left-hand corner in the other.

Two Kinds of Wood.—It is not necessary to use the better wood for the whole of the two sides which will be against the walls. These are of ordinary finished timber faced or edged with better stuff for polishing. The

other pair of sides flanking the open space under the top centre being exposed to view, must be of the better wood. This is indicated in Fig. 5. Oak, mahogany or walnut are three suitable woods for the polished parts.

Each case unit consists of one inner side $\frac{5}{8}$ in. thick and the other $1\frac{1}{8}$ in. thick, against the wall. The bottom, G, of deal $\frac{5}{8}$ in. thick, is edged with $2 \times \frac{5}{8}$ in. lipping of the better wood, grooved, tongued and fitted into a stopped rebate cut in each side.

Runners $\frac{5}{8}$ in. thick $\times 1\frac{1}{2}$ in. are made into a frame consisting of the back runner E, side runners H, left and right, of deal with a finished lipping C, $2\frac{1}{2} \times \frac{5}{8}$ in.

E and C have tenoned ends to fit in the sides of the case, while the back and front ends of H runners are fitted into E and C.

Dustboards.—The inner edges of all four pieces are grooved to take a sheet of $\frac{3}{16}$ in. plywood to make a division or dustboard between the top and middle drawer. A second frame consists of runners F, J left and right and lipping B with a ply dustboard as before.

A standard $1 \times 1\frac{1}{2}$ in. is fixed at the back inner corner right down to the bottom. It has a stopped groove on its 1 in. wide face to suit a tongue on the back edge of the $\frac{5}{8}$ in. side of the case. It also has a tenon for the back bar which is fitted later to prevent anything from being pushed down the back.

When the sides and parts have been cut and fitted, the dustboards placed in their frames, each case may be assembled, and the plywood back and top rails dovetailed into the sides.

The shape of the top is indicated in Fig. 3 and is cut and finished after the grooved and tongued wood has been secured into a rectangle to fit the recess.

Mirror backings of $\frac{1}{2}$ in. plywood

for each glass are marked out to shape. All three mirrors have a $\frac{3}{8}$ in. bevelled edge all round.

A Wardrobe.—A suggestion for the arrangement of a built-in wardrobe is in Fig. 6. This is built to stand on a platform fixed in the recess in the same way as the dressing-table. On the left it has a section high enough to take overcoats, as well as suits. This is fitted with a metal slide for hangers. On the right-hand side are four compartments for folded articles, and, below these, a section with rails for boots and shoes. The whole of this part is enclosed by doors and, below it, and at the same face level, are two large drawers, 9 in. deep.

The case consists of four posts 1 in. square. To these are fitted the sides and bottom. The back is of $\frac{1}{4}$ in. thick plywood and rails dovetailed into the top edges of the sides and posts to keep the whole firm.

The right-hand side should be grooved or trenched at the specified spacing for housing the edges of the shelves. The grooves do not extend right up to the back face of the door. Similar trenching is required for the division between the compartments and the one between the left and right drawer, also for the horizontal division over them. Stopped ends are employed, and the same manner of using lipping or edge-pieces of better wood for exposed and finished parts.

The doors may be framed, panelled or flush pieces of grained wood fitted with a lock for the left-hand door.

BENDING WOOD

IT is sometimes necessary to give wood a curved surface instead of a flat one.

This actual curving, called a bull nose, is frequently found in the bottom riser of a staircase where the bottom stair tread comes beyond the post supporting the handrail. It is also found in mouldings that are run round curves, for picture rails and chair rails.

The curved riser of a staircase is often cut by machinery. It saves the time of the workman, if it does not save labour.

Thick Boards.—A 6 in. wide board $1\frac{1}{4}$ in. or $1\frac{1}{2}$ in. thick and the necessary length is planed up true. At one end a line is scribed about $1\frac{1}{2}$ in. from and parallel to the end. The length of the curve required is marked out and another line parallel to the first is scribed. These two lines are guides for the saw-cut made so that $\frac{1}{8}$ in. of

wood is left. The waste is removed with saw, chisel and plane. The saw is mentioned again because it will aid chiselling if a series of cuts is made parallel with the first cut and about an inch apart. If the part to be bent is

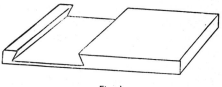

Fig. I

rather long it may be possible to employ the hand saw to cut the length down after chiselling away part of the waste. Fig. 1 shows a length of wood prepared for bending.

A quicker method would be to cut the wood down from the edge with the saw, holding the wood in the bench vice. Then cut a separate strip and screw it on the end.

A curved end is built up to the desired bend with shoulders to take the undercut part shown, and wedges are driven in to make these parts engage and hold.

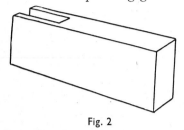

Fig. 2

Lengths of wood to be curved are sometimes steamed. This requires steam boxes and templates and is not worth the time and expense to the amateur.

Another way to get a board to take on a required curve is to make a saw cut down the middle as shown in Fig. 2.

Moulding.—All that has been said before refers to bending wood that shows only the face of the wood. The cut-away parts are hidden, but when bending moulding, the whole of it is

seen and so a part cannot be cut away.

For this purpose another method is adopted. If the curve is an exterior or convex curve, the back is treated, but if the curve is an interior or concave one, then the face of the moulding has to be cut. Fig. 3 shows how this is done when the back of the moulding is cut to make an outward curve. Saw cuts are made at intervals to suit the curve. The sharper the bend, the more saw cuts will be required. It is also advisable to make some of the cuts deeper than the others. This will allow

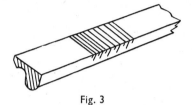

Fig. 3

the extreme back to close in more.

Plywood is at times very useful for curved cabinet work and may be bent over two or three supports to make the required curve.

CUTTING DOWN A WARDROBE

IT is not unusual to find when moving furniture from one room to another that a piece is too big to go through the doorway. This article deals with one specific example—a wardrobe.

The wardrobe, Fig. 1, was one of those models measuring some 6 ft. 9 in. high consisting of an upper part or cupboard with a large drawer underneath. Unfortunately the cupboard and base containing the drawer were made in one piece and not detachable as are a great many wardrobes of similar design. Originally this piece of furniture was hauled into the room through the window after removing the sash.

After careful measurement, it was found that the wardrobe could be manœuvred into the other room if the base were removed. The question was how to do this without disfiguring a good piece of furniture.

Choosing the Cut.—An examination of the constructional details of the wardrobe revealed that the two panels at the sides of the door were attached to the top of the drawer-top or board by means of glued blocks as indicated by the dotted lines in Fig. 2, while the sides as well as the back (of the tongued and grooved boards) extended from the top down to the

Fig. I

after the removal of the glue blocks. Careful use of hammer and chisel removed the blocks.

The top edge of the beading was used as a guide for marking guide-lines for sawing, and removed later by prising it up with a chisel and withdrawing the panel pins.

Then came the task of severing the top from the bottom. This was done by placing the wardrobe on one side and packing it up with flat pieces of wood to keep it a few inches above the floor. The two sides were sawn through very carefully and then the back, pieces of wood packing being placed in suitable positions to prevent the sawed slot from closing in on the saw and binding it.

Having accomplished the most difficult part of the job, that of sawing the wood perfectly square, the wardrobe was carried through the doorway, to the new position.

Refixing the Top.—The next thing was to reinstate the top portion on the bottom. A narrow ornamental bead B surrounded the front and sides, the top of which was level with the top of the drawer board.

It was decided to saw through the sides and back and to remove the glued blocks, which secured the front panels.

First the door was removed. This necessitated the removal of two metal pegs used for hinging purposes, fixed to top and bottom edges of the door by screws. Then a length of $1\frac{1}{2} \times \frac{3}{4}$ in. batten was fastened temporarily across the front to keep it square

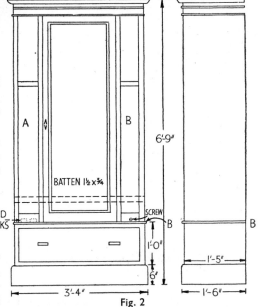

Fig. 2

I

base. This was done with lengths of $1\frac{1}{2} \times 1$ in. planed batten. Having placed the top part of the wardrobe in the exact position on the base, the battens were screwed, wide faces downwards, to the top board of the lower part, in the manner shown in Fig. 3, and screws driven in

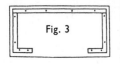

Fig. 3

through the sides and back into the narrow faces of the battens, while a screw driven through each front panel into the short battens behind them fixed these parts securely.

The beading was then refixed about $\frac{1}{8}$ in. higher than its original position to hide the joint made by the saw. The final operation consisted of fixing the door once more in position.

SIMPLE DOOR MAKING

THE doors dealt with in this article are simple and their construction is quite within the powers of the amateur.

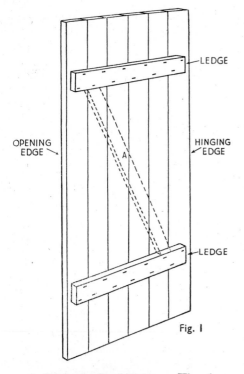

OPENING EDGE

HINGING EDGE

LEDGE

LEDGE

A

Fig. I

A Plain Ledged Door.—The door shown in Fig. 1 would be suitable for a poultry house or a shed of light construction. It consists of a few tongued and grooved matched boards held together by nails driven into battens at the back. For strength and appearance, V-jointed matching is to be preferred.

A suitable size for such a door must be left to the constructor's decision. It should not be narrower than 2 ft. or less than 5 ft. in height, nor of thinner material than $\frac{1}{2}$ in. finished thickness.

In constructing a door of this description, choose boards that are a multiple of the width and, in estimating the number of boards, do not forget that the tongue of one long edge forming the edge of the door and the groove of the board forming the other have to be removed. In addition, an inch should be allowed at each end for trimming off after the boards have been fastened in position. The battens should be 3 in. wide and $\frac{3}{4}$ in. thick.

The Construction. — To construct the door, skim the battens with a sharp plane if using rough sawn wood. Chamfer the face edges and cut the ledges to size. These should be 1 in. less than the overall width of the door, thus allowing $\frac{1}{2}$ in. on each side for the door-stop against which the door rests when closed. If the matched boards are in lengths, cut them to a length of 5 ft. 2 in. Remove the tongue of the first board by planing it in the direction of the grain, or remove most of the tongue with a sharp chisel used also in the direction of the grain, and then remove inequalities with a plane. The latter method is quicker, but care must

Fig. 2

be taken not to chisel too deeply and thus spoil the edge of the board.

Next, carefully mark the position of the ledges on the first board with the aid of a try square and fix the board to the ledges, using the lines as a guide. Reverse the work so that the face side is uppermost, place the boards in position and mark guide lines for the nails as the nail-heads should be in neat lines.

Use $1\frac{1}{2}$ in. wire nails. The ends of these will project a $\frac{1}{4}$ in. above the faces of the ledges. When all the nails have been driven, reverse the door again—that is, ledge side up—and clinch the ends of the nails. To do this, first support the heads on a piece of iron or other hard substance so that, in clinching, the nails are not driven back. Then strike the ends of the nails at an angle so that they lay parallel to the ledges and flush with the surface.

The final operation consists of squaring lines across the top and bottom of the boards representing the true length and sawing off the waste.

A Cupboard or Cabinet Door in Plywood. — The illustration in Fig. 2 represents a door of simple construction, suitable for a cupboard or cabinet. It consists of a squared piece of thick plywood, the unsightly edges of which are covered with narrow strips of deal. Such a door can be made more ornate by the addition of a thin, flat moulding fixed to the face and flush with the edges to represent rails and stiles, as the cross-members and vertical pieces of a framed panelled door are called.

Another door of similar construction is seen in Fig 3. Here a moulding is fastened at a short distance from the edges on to the plywood face, which gives a pleasing effect.

A panelled door of light construction where a thin sheet or panel of wood is fixed in grooves between the frame members is shown at Fig. 4. Doors of this description are suitable for a great number of purposes including cabinets and cupboards.

There are several ways of making a panelled door of this type. One method is to purchase hardwood with a groove already planed in its edge to take the panel as shown at *a* in Fig. 6. Another way is to obtain plain wood and plough the groove yourself.

A third method eliminates the use of a proper groove and, in its place, a rebate is formed on one of the inner edges of the frame members against which the panel lies, a small bead being fixed within the rebate to keep the panel in position.

Still another and the most simple way is to make a false rebate by fixing a strip of wood to form the recess on the inner edge of the finished frame and fixing the panel by a similar strip.

Glass may be substituted for plywood in the rebated frames; such doors being useful for china cabinets, etc.

In constructing comparatively small doors of this type from grooved wood, a stub or short tenon at the end of each rail to fit into the groove of the stile will give a satisfactory joint provided the parts are properly glued together. This joint is depicted at A in Fig. 5.

For larger doors, it is advisable to use dowel-joints or, better still, mortice and tenon joints.

In making dowelled-joints, the ends of the members which butt together must be square, and it is essential that the holes to receive the pins are bored accurately. If done carelessly the finished door will, in all probability, be out of square and twisted.

Fig. 3

A glance at B in Fig. 5 will enable you to see at once how the dowelled-joint is applied when rebated material is employed.

Mortice and Tenon Joints.—To construct a panelled door with mortice and tenon joints proceed in the following manner:

Saw the rails and stiles to length

Fig. 4

plus 1 in. at each end for waste, and plane each member to the desired thickness and width, keeping the long edges perfectly square from time to time and test by a try square as the work proceeds. The rails are tenoned into the stiles as illustrated by the dotted lines in the illustration at C in Fig. 5. If the door is to be small, make all members of the same width but, if the door is comparatively large, it is usual to make the bottom rail a trifle wider.

Frame Members.—The next process is to mark the frame members. To ensure accuracy it is advisable to make a full-size sectional drawing of the parts representing the height and width of the door. This is shown in Figs. 6 and 7.

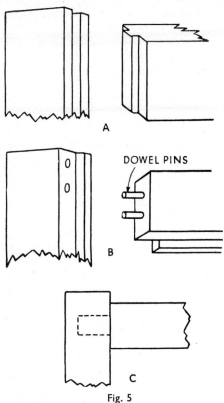

Fig. 5

It is a good plan always to make similar drawings before constructing any kind of framework.

As an example, it is assumed that a door 3 ft. high and 1 ft. 8 in. wide is required and that the stiles and rails are 2 in. wide × $\frac{3}{4}$ in. thick. The depth of the groove is $\frac{1}{4}$ in. and its width $\frac{1}{4}$ in. Place a stile on the drawing as indicated in Fig. 8, and mark on the face edge the points A, B, C, D, and F.

Clamp or otherwise fix the two stiles together, square lines at the marked positions across both face edges at both ends. Separate the parts and

extend the lines A B and E F across the working face and the back edge of both members. Extend C and D representing the depth of the groove partially across in the manner shown in Fig. 9 which illustrates one end only.

The Mortices.—The next procedure is to mark out the mortices. Reference to the illustration will show that the mortice is cut between B and D, the space between A and D being that required for the haunch or small part of the tenon. The distance between A and D is equal to about one-third of the length of the tenon so that in the case under review the length of the mortice B D will be $1\frac{3}{4}$ in. — one-third of $1\frac{3}{4}$ in. = $1\frac{1}{6}$ in. say $1\frac{1}{8}$ in.

Lay the stiles aside for the time being and proceed by marking out the rails in a similar manner. Place a rail on the drawing representing the width, not forgetting the extra inch at each end for waste, and mark on the face edge the position E F and G H as indicated in Fig. 10.

From these marked points square lines all round, fasten the rails together and mark across the edges of the unmarked

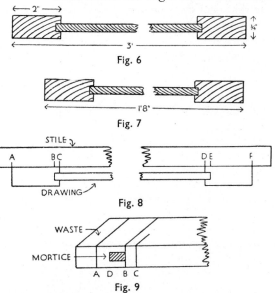

Fig. 6

Fig. 7

Fig. 8

Fig. 9

one and then take them apart and complete the making.

The Tenons.—The next operation requires the use of a mortice gauge. As it is usual to make the thickness of the tenon approximately one third that of the material, the thickness of the tenon in this case will be $\frac{3}{4}$ in. — one-third of $\frac{3}{4}$ in. = $\frac{1}{4}$ in. Take a $\frac{1}{4}$ in. chisel and set the mortice gauge to it and adjust the fence of the gauge so that the lines will be in the middle of

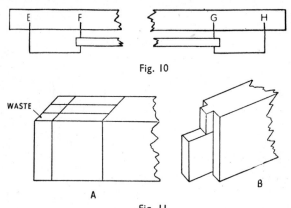

Fig. 10

Fig. 11

the thickness of the work. Mark lines on the ends of the rails and then the stiles, working from their working faces. The marked out tenon is shown at A in Fig. 11.

The tenon is formed by first cutting the full tenon and then marking the haunch or a small projection at the top and removing the waste. The completed tenon is shown at B.

An easy way to make the mortices is to bore a number of holes close together, half-way through the thickness of the wood and completing them from the other side. A twist-bit of slightly smaller size than the width of the mortice should be used and the remaining waste removed with a very sharp chisel. The parts are then ready for grooving.

The plywood panel should be then cut square to size and the parts assembled

temporarily to ensure that everything fits well.

After dismembering the door, the parts should be glued together. The assembly should then be cramped and left for at least twenty-four hours, to enable the glue to harden.

The final operations consist of removing the ends of the tenons where they project beyond the stiles and the waste part at the ends of the stiles themselves, all of which should be removed carefully with a tenon saw. A skim over the framework with a finely-set plane completes the job.

A Plywood Door.—A useful plain door may be made of plywood for a large cupboard or even a room. It consists of two sheets $4\frac{1}{2}$ mm. ($\frac{1}{4}$ in.) plywood securely glued to a substantial frame. Doors measuring as large as 6 ft. 6 in. high and 2 ft. 6 in. wide can be made successfully provided the frame is strong.

In constructing the frame of a door of the above dimensions, the stiles should not be less than 4 in. wide, and 1 in. thick, while the top one may be the same width, but the middle and bottom rails should be at least 6 in. in width, and two intermediate ones 3 in.

The joints may be either dowelled together or morticed and tenoned and fastened with glue. Another alternative is for the top and bottom rails to be tenoned into the stiles and the middle and intermediate rails dowelled.

Care must be taken to ensure that the frame is square and not in winding, which can only be attained by accurate workmanship and careful cramping after gluing.

In fixing the plywood, which should be $\frac{1}{16}$ in. each way larger than the finished size of the door, place the frame flat on the floor and use plenty of hot glue, reinforced with panel pins to keep it in place. Then turn the frame over and repeat the operation on the other side. Place some weights over those parts that have been glued and allow it to harden.

When dry, trim up the edges of the plywood so that they are quite flush with the outer edges of the frame, and glue a ⅛ in. thick cover strip on the long edges to hide the edges of the ply. Cover strips are unnecessary at the top and bottom as they are hidden.

A Greenhouse Door.—A greenhouse door constructed on simple lines is shown in Fig. 12. It consists of a frame, the stiles and rails of which are 1½ in. thick. The width of the stiles is 3 in. and that of the top, middle and bottom rails are 3, 4½ and 4½ in. respectively

The upper half is divided vertically by a piece of 2×1½ in. sash bar, the other rebates for supporting the glass being false ones obtained by nailing lengths of ½ in. square wood to the inner edges of the frame—in line, of course, with the rebate in the sash bar.

The lower portion of the door is filled in with V-tongued and grooved matching which lies flush with the faces of the stiles and rails. This section also has false rebates to which the matching is fixed, while a brace running diagonally across this portion prevents the door from sagging on its closing side and provides an additional face for supporting the matched panel.

Through tenon and mortice joints of the wedged type should be employed for the fastening of the stiles and rails and they should be glued together and pinned through with dowel pins.

Instead of the orthodox method of letting the ends of the sash bar into the

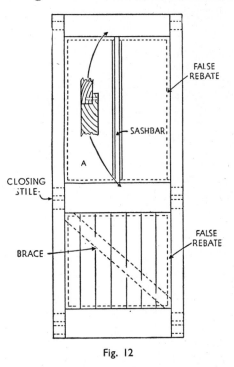

Fig. 12

top and middle rails, the piece is made an inch longer at each end than the distance between the rails and the face of the bar cut away to a depth of 1½ in. This leaves a piece 1 in. long × 1/12 in. thick at the back which is screwed to the back faces of the rails. See Fig. 9A.

TABLE FOR SEWING MACHINE

A CABINET table for a sewing machine must be sufficiently high, with a knee-hole wide enough, a drawer for odds and ends, a cabinet on the left-hand side—with the door handle high enough to prevent bending to open it—and fitted with convenient shelves inside. Also enough table space on the left for the work to lie on, a cover sufficiently high for a high arm lock-stitch machine and large enough to provide room for the worker to leave scraps of material, etc., under the cover.

The cabinet table shown in Fig. 1 is modern in design, constructed of oak left natural colour, with ebony handles and the ends of the dovetail pins are also ebonised. The cover for the sewing machine forms part of the design of the cabinet as a whole, even the wooden handle is in keeping with the drawer and cabinet handles.

Prime Austrian wainscot oak should be used when making this cabinet table and machine cover, but alternatively walnut or mahogany could be employed.

Construction.—Proceed by first planing and squaring up the following pieces of oak. Two pieces for the upright ends, each 2 ft. $5\frac{5}{8}$ in. × 1 ft. 6 in. × $\frac{5}{8}$ in.; one piece for the table top 3 ft. × 1 ft. 6 in. × $\frac{5}{8}$ in.; one piece for the upright end of the cupboard 2 ft. $5\frac{1}{4}$ in. × 1 ft. 6 in. × $\frac{5}{8}$ in., and one piece for the bottom of the cupboard, 1 ft. $\frac{5}{8}$ in. × 1 ft. 6 in. × $\frac{5}{8}$ in.

Then indentify the pieces by marking them "top and bottom" on each piece "face side," "left end," "right end," "upright side of cupboard," etc.

Gauge lines all round the top at each end $\frac{5}{8}$ in. from the edge. Gauge two similar lines on the "left end" and one line only on the top of the "right end."

Set out the dovetails on the gauged ends and mark them with a $\frac{1}{4}$ in. chisel, I, II, III, IV. Saw down the sockets first and mark out on the side pieces a replica of the saw cuts by pulling the saw through the socket-cuts, complete the marking, saw down, chisel out and fit these pieces together.

Take this apart, and on the top end of the "upright right side" of the cupboard, gauge a deep line $\frac{1}{4}$ in. all round from the edge. Slope the wood down $\frac{1}{16}$ in. from the edge so as to form a shoulder for the dovetail grooves. Stop the dovetail $\frac{1}{2}$ in. back from the face edge by sawing out a piece of wood $\frac{1}{2} \times \frac{1}{4}$ in.

Now on the underside of the top, measure 1 ft. and 1 ft. $\frac{5}{8}$ in. from the left-hand end and square lines across with a pencil. Measure $\frac{1}{16}$ in. inside both of these lines and square across with a chisel or marking knife. Gauge $\frac{1}{2}$ in. from the face edge so as to stop the groove and gauge $\frac{1}{4}$ in. down on the back edge for the depth of the groove. Then saw, chisel out and fit in.

Assemble all this again by first knocking on the top, then the dovetail-grooved partition, and finally the bottom of the cupboard.

See the "right end upright" is vertical. Then square up the shelf under the drawer to 1 ft. $11\frac{1}{2}$ in. × 1 ft. 6 in. × $\frac{5}{8}$ in. To avoid mistakes, mark out the dovetail-grooves for this shelf inside the kneehole while the work is still assembled. Then take apart and make the dovetail-grooves (stopped $\frac{1}{2}$ in. from the front). Carefully note that the shelf has to be grooved $\frac{1}{4} \times \frac{1}{4}$ in. and the ends also, to a length of 4 in. to take a three-ply back. Do this, and set back the grooves $\frac{1}{4}$ in. Next plough $\frac{1}{4} \times \frac{1}{4}$ in. grooves down the upright ends of the cupboard, set these grooves $\frac{1}{4}$ in. from the back to allow for the three-ply back, which now cut out and fit in.

Clean up the whole carcase with a fine-set metal smoothing plane and glass-paper with Nos. $1\frac{1}{2}$ and 1. Then with hot, thin glue, glue up the carcase, taking care to leave the top until the last, i.e., after the backs have been slid into the grooves. Then glue and knock down the top securely. Cramp up, test for squareness in all directions and allow twelve hours to dry. Note that the rebate edged round the top must not be done yet. Now square up the drawer front. This is $\frac{5}{8}$ in. thick and the sides and back $\frac{1}{2}$ in. thick. Dovetail these together and groove the sides and front $\frac{1}{4} \times \frac{1}{4}$ in. and slide in a three-ply bottom. Glue up and allow to dry. Then fit it in the cabinet and clean off, taking care to see that the face of the drawer is flush.

The Door.—Cut out and square up the cabinet door, size 2 ft. $4\frac{3}{8}$ in.$\times 11\frac{3}{8}$ $\times \frac{3}{4}$ in. Fit this in and put hinges on the door ($1\frac{1}{2}$ in. brass butts).

If this door is made of thoroughly dry Austrian wainscot (quartered) oak there will be no need to laminate the work. But if the oak is not thoroughly satisfactory, it will be best to glue (and cram) together two $\frac{5}{16}$ in. (thick) pieces of oak with the grain running two different ways—i.e., the vertical grain outside the door.

Next put two $\frac{3}{8}$ in. ball-catches on the top and bottom of the door, about $\frac{3}{4}$ in. in from the edge.

Turn the cabinet over and put eight domes of silence on the bottom ($\frac{1}{2}$ in. diameter.)

For those who wish to make the oak cover for the sewing machine the following directions should be carried out.

First, square up two pieces of oak for the front and back, each 1 ft. 6 in.$\times 12$ $\times \frac{1}{2}$ in. bare; two pieces for the sides, each 1×1 ft.$\times \frac{1}{2}$ in. bare; and one piece for the top, size 1 ft. 6 in.$\times 1$ ft.$\times \frac{5}{8}$ in.

Dovetail the four sides together as shown, fit and test for squareness and glue up. Leave this to dry, clean up

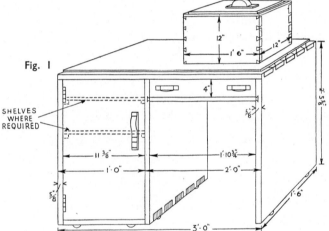

Fig. 1

SHELVES WHERE REQUIRED

and then refer to how to make the handle which is described below.

When the handle is finished, glue and screw it on the top of the cover from underneath. Countersink the screwheads well below the surface and stop the holes with beeswax and small pieces of resin and whiting, melted together.

Then glue and pin on the top of the cover, punch the heads of the pins, stop up the holes and clean off with Nos. $1\frac{1}{2}$ and 1 glass-paper.

The Handles for both the cabinet table and the cover, Fig. 2, may be constructed of either ebony or oak.

Saw out and square up a piece of wood for the two drawer handles, size $10 \times 1 \times \frac{7}{8}$ in. Mark the profiles (shape) of them on both edges of the wood, saw down and saw out the little steps first—most carefully—with a 6 in. tenon saw. This leaves the centre block in relief. Then place the handles, still in one piece, on their sides in the vice and gouge out the finger-grips as shown in section at A. Finally, round over the top to shape and clean up with files and glass-paper and sever the two handles.

Saw and square up a piece of wood for the cupboard and machine cover handles size $11\frac{1}{2} \times 1\frac{1}{4} \times 1\frac{1}{4}$ in. Mark shapes and

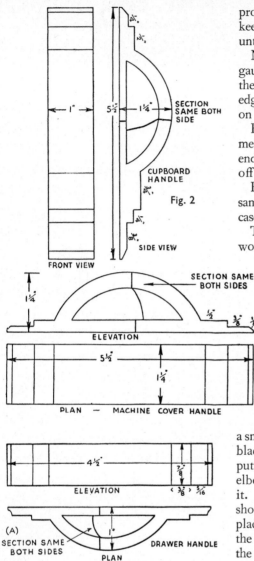

SECTION SAME BOTH SIDE

CUPBOARD HANDLE

Fig. 2

SIDE VIEW

FRONT VIEW

SECTION SAME BOTH SIDES

ELEVATION

PLAN — MACHINE COVER HANDLE

ELEVATION

(A)
SECTION SAME BOTH SIDES

DRAWER HANDLE

PLAN

proceed in the same way as above, and keep the handles in one piece of wood until finished, then divide them.

Now resume work on the carcase and gauge a line all round the face side of the top for the rebate $\frac{5}{8}$ in. in from the edges, and a line $\frac{1}{8}$ in. down all round on the edges.

Rebate this down with a finely set sharp metal shoulder plane. Plane across the ends first. This, of course, will take $\frac{1}{8}$ in. off the dovetails. Next, hang the door.

Rebate the top of the cover in the same way. The size of the rebate in this case will be $\frac{1}{2}$ (bare) $\times \frac{1}{8}$ in.

Then, finally, finish up the whole work with Nos. $1\frac{1}{2}$, 1 and 0 glass-paper and screw on the handles and plug up as before described.

Regarding the shelves in the cupboard, these should be of $\frac{1}{2}$ in. oak, placed where required on small battens, so that they may be altered from time to time.

If the whole work, including the handles are of oak, just polish with light oak polish. If the handles are of ebony, carefully paint in the sockets of the dovetails only, using a small pencil brush and a little dull (flat) black enamel. To do this successfully, put the left arm on the top of the fitment, elbow out and the weight of the body on it. The right hand with the brush in it should be held vertically and now placed over the left wrist, then with the brush still held vertically, paint in the desired shapes.

NURSERY FIRE GUARD

A FIREGUARD should have a heavy base to prevent the child from pulling it over, and as an additional safeguard should be hooked to the wall.

The solid oak fireguard shown in Fig. 1 is suitable for protecting a small child, but the height and length may be increased to suit individual requirements.

It is best to make the fireguard big enough so that it can be placed outside the existing fender.

Where there is no fender it is advisable to pin on metal strips as shown, although if the wood is treated and made fireproof, as described at the conclusion of this article, there is no real necessity for doing so.

It is best to make the frame of the fireguard in oak and the rails of birch.

framework. This component is the same size as the base, but only $\frac{5}{8}$ in. thick.

Fit this together and see that the two frames are exactly the same size, then glue them up and leave them for twelve hours to dry.

Now saw and plane up the four corner

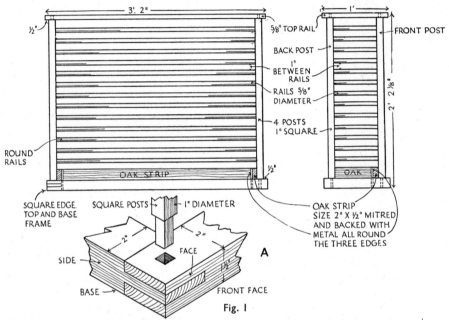

Fig. I

Construction.—Start with the base by squaring up one piece of oak 3 ft. 2 in.$\times 2\times 1\frac{1}{2}$ in. for the front, and two pieces each 1 ft.$\times 2\times 1\frac{1}{2}$ in. for the two sides.

Now set out the bridle joints "open mortice and tenon," on each corner, as shown in detail at A. To do this, divide the thickness of the wood into three parts and gauge lines round the four ends that go together.

Then measure 2 in. from all these four ends and square round pencil lines.

Saw down on the insides of the lines of the front piece and outside the lines on the two side pieces, chisel out the waste and fit together.

Do the same with the top three-piece

posts, and note that they are square in section.

The size of each post is 2 ft. 2$\frac{1}{2}$ in.$\times 1\times 1$ in. Measure a distance of 1$\frac{3}{4}$ in. from the left-hand end of each piece and square a line all round with a chisel, then measure 2 ft. from this line and square another line all round these lines to indicate the shoulders of the tenons. Saw these shoulders down $\frac{1}{8}$ in. and pare off, thus leaving the "stub" tenons $\frac{3}{4}\times\frac{3}{4}$ in.

Now, taking care to centre by diagonals the true centre for the mortices both on the top frame and base frame, set them all out to $\frac{3}{4}\times\frac{3}{4}$ in.

Then, with a $\frac{5}{8}$ in. centre-bit, drill holes through, working from both sides in each case to prevent splitting the wood.

Next, square the round holes by paring the wood from each side with a very sharp chisel, fit in the posts and note that the tenons project a little.

Identify each post with the framework it belongs to by marking AA, BB, CC, DD, and so on.

With the aid of a pencil, set out on the four posts the centres for the round rails in the following way: Work from the base and first measure 2 in. from the shoulders and square all round for the oak strip. Next space out the centres for the rails and square lines round. Now gauge a faint line down the centres of the two inner sides of the front posts and on one inner side of the back posts. Where the lines cross are the centres for drilling. Purchase enough $\frac{5}{8}$ in. diameter birch dowelling to make all the rails and saw them up carefully to 2 ft. $11\frac{1}{2}$ in. in length for the long rails and $9\frac{1}{2}$ in. long for the side ones.

On a spare piece of wood drill a hole $\frac{5}{8}$ in. diameter and fit one of the rails (dowels) to try it out.

Drill all the holes on the two inside faces of the front posts and the one inside of each back post, to $\frac{1}{4}$ in. (full)

deep. This little extra depth is to give room for the glue which is forced to the bottom of each hole.

Before proceeding to glue up, clean up all the work with Nos. $1\frac{1}{2}$ and 1 glass-paper, not forgetting to round off all the sharp edges, both of the posts and the top and bottom frames.

Gluing Up.—Proceed by gluing up the two sets of end rails, test for squareness and see that the posts measure 11 in. from "out to out" and prove it by applying each end to the mortices in the frames. Wash off any surplus glue and leave at least twelve hours to dry.

Then glue in the front rails, the top frame and the base and wash off all glue with hot water. Stand the guard up and test for squareness. Leave the work for twelve hours to dry and saw off the projecting tenons.

Cut out three strips of oak, $2 \times \frac{1}{2}$ in. and fit them "in the clear" above the base as shown. Take them out and pin some metal strips inside—then pin in from the ends.

To Render the Wood Fireproof.—first wash it in a solution of hot salt and water, then apply oil and turps. Stain to the colour required.

WASTE-PAPER BOX

THE solid oak waste-paper box shown in Fig. 1 is best made of Austrian wainscot oak out of $\frac{1}{2}$ in. sawn stuff for the sides, $\frac{3}{4}$ in. stuff for the bottom and $2\frac{1}{2}$ in. stuff for the solid top.

Proceed by sawing, planing and squaring up the following material.

Four pieces for the sides, each $8\frac{3}{8} \times 12\frac{1}{2} \times \frac{3}{8}$ in. (note the grain runs the short way); one piece for the bottom, $9\frac{5}{8} \times 9\frac{5}{8} \times \frac{5}{8}$ in.; one piece for the top, $9\frac{3}{8} \times 9\frac{3}{8} \times 2\frac{1}{2}$ in.

The best way to square up the four sides is to plane up a piece of oak 2 ft. 10 in. long $\times 12\frac{1}{2}$ in. wide $\times \frac{3}{8}$ in. Shoot (square) the right-hand end. With the face-edge nearest to you, measure off from the right $8\frac{3}{8}$ in., then square a line across with a chisel or sharp marking knife. Now looking on the right of the saw and keeping the cut line in, make a tenon saw cut $\frac{1}{8}$ in. deep.

This will enable you to see exactly how wide the saw cut is.

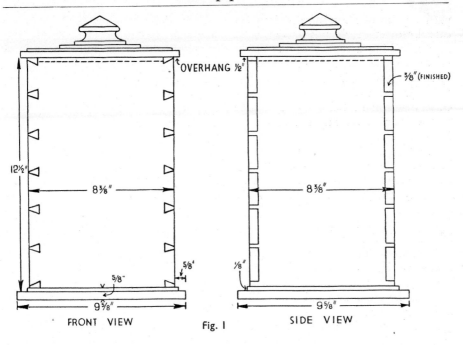

OVERHANG ½"

3/8" (FINISHED)

12½"

8⅜"

8⅜"

5/8'

5/8"

⅛"

9⅝"

9⅝"

FRONT VIEW

Fig. I

SIDE VIEW

Then measuring 8⅜ in. again from the left-hand edge of the cut just made, square across again and proceed until you have four pieces marked and partly sawn.

Saw through the cuts, shoot the ends of each piece, set the marking gauge to ⅜ in. and gauge round both ends of all four pieces.

Set out the dove-tails as shown in the elevation, Fig. 1. Saw them down, keeping the cuts on the waste side of the lines.

Indentify all pieces by marking 1—1, 2—2 and so on. Then with the "side view" piece, Fig. 1, fixed in the vice with one of its long edges just above the bench-top level, place the side piece in position and, with the aid of a friend,

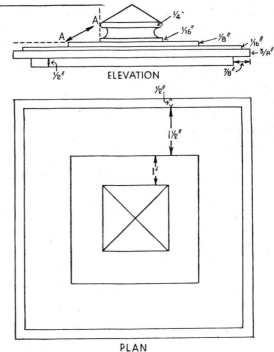

2¼"

A

A

¼"

1/16"

⅛"

1/16"

3/8"

½"

⅞"

ELEVATION

½"

1½"

1"

PLAN

Fig. 2

put the point of the tenon saw into the cuts already made, draw it towards you, thus scratching a replica of the dovetail on the side. Complete the marking by squaring pencil lines down the sides, then saw down outside these lines and chisel out all the wood between the pins on the side pieces and the sockets on the front and back.

Fit the four sides carefully and assemble. These four sides may now be glued, cramped and left for twelve hours to dry. When gluing, test carefully for squareness.

Now gauge a line $\frac{1}{2}$ in. in from the edge all round on the face-side of the piece of wood forming the bottom, and then gauge $\frac{1}{8}$ in. down from the face on the edges and rebate down as shown.

Screw the bottom on and countersink the screw-heads.

The loose top, details of which appear in Fig. 2, could be made out of two pieces of wood, but it will be best to make it from a solid block.

Note that the "face side" is the bottom of the lid. Set the marking gauge to $\frac{7}{8}$ in. and scribe a line all round on the face side "underside." Then from the face side gauge a line $\frac{1}{2}$ in. down on the edges, all round. This will form the rebate later on, but do not saw it out yet.

The next thing is to get rid of the bulk of the wood, so as to leave the centre block standing up square.

Proceed by gauging $1\frac{3}{8}$ in. from the face side and round the edges. The gauge should be set full "$\frac{1}{16}$ in." to allow for shouldering down afterwards.

Now gauge a line 3 in. in from edges, and with a tenon saw very carefully saw out the four waste blocks of wood, keeping all your gauge lines "well in."

It is best to finish this surface and edges now, indicated at A in Fig. 2, with a fine set and sharp shoulder plane.

The Handle.—While you still have a flat surface to grip in the vice, mark and gauge the profile of the handle on the front and back "i.e., with the grain sides."

With a gouge, hollow through across the grain, taking care to leave the little $\frac{1}{16}$ in. fillet as shown.

Then with a sharp $\frac{3}{4}$ in. chisel having a long bevel, pare through the two sides of the pyramid, by working three parts of the way from the front, then quarter of the way from the back. This is to prevent breaking the end grain. Shape the front and the back in the same way and round off the edges.

Next gauge and shoulder down the other two fillets and finally saw out and finish the rebate underneath and fit it.

Clean up carefully all these mouldings with Nos. $1\frac{1}{2}$ and 1 glass-paper and then finish with wax.

HOW TO CONSTRUCT AN IRONING BOARD AND SLEEVE BOARD

EVERY kitchen should be equipped with an ironing board and sleeve board. They are labour saving and much more easy to work with than the kitchen-table top.

The Ironing Board in Fig. 1 must project beyond the table when pressing trousers, etc., and naturally must be supported at the other end by placing it on the rail of a chair, a convenient ledge or another small table, but for most ordinary ironing it can be placed upon the table.

To make the ironing board, square up a piece of American whitewood, size 3 ft. 6 in. or 4 ft. long, 15 in. wide and 1 in. thick. Draw a centre line down it, parallel to the grain, and mark off the taper at one end 9¾ in. wide, as shown.

Saw off the surplus wood and smooth the edges, using a jack plane for the purpose.

Saw and square up two battens, one 15 × 2¾ × 1 in. and the other 9¾ × 2¾ × 1 in. Bore a number of holes in the wide faces of these to clear 1¾ in. No. 8 brass countersunk-headed screws, and countersink the tops of the holes.

Before fixing the battens to the board, make sure that the heart side of the latter is uppermost to prevent warping. To ascertain the heart side, glance at the end grain and observe which way the curves of the annular rings which surround the heart of the tree run. The

face side of the board is the one opposite the concave curves of the rings, as indicated at A in Fig. 1.

Fix the top board to the battens by driving in screws from the underside.

Slightly round the four sharp corners and the top edges with a rasp, plane and glass-paper.

Cover it with a piece of old blanket or similar material in the following way. Put the blanket on the table and place the board on it, upside down. Then, with a pair of scissors, cut out the material about 1 in. larger all round. Turn the board over and place the

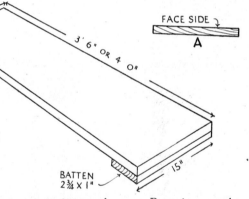

BATTEN 2¾″ × 1″

Fig. 1

BATTEN 2¾ × 1″

covering on the top. Press in a number of drawing-pins to keep the material in position, making sure that it is quite smooth. Turn the edges of the material over the edges of the board and secure them by driving in galvanised tacks, spaced about 3 in. apart. Remove the drawing-pins and in a similar way cover the blanket with an old sheet. Finish the board by tacking linen tape all round the edges.

A Self-contained Folding Ironing Board, Fig. 2, can be made with the

aid of the dimensioned drawings illustrated in Fig. 3. All woodwork may be
of good quality yellow deal.

The top board measures 3 ft. 8 in.

Fig. 2

long, 8 in. wide and $\frac{3}{4}$ in. thick. One
end is sawn to form a point, while the
other is fitted with a shallow tray, the
bottom of which is faced with asbestos
upon which to stand an iron.

The legs are made from planed batten

$1\frac{3}{4}$ in. wide $\times \frac{5}{8}$ in. thick and each pair
of legs is wider at the bottom than at
the top, being held in position by wood
cross-braces $\frac{7}{8}$ in. wide $\times 1\frac{1}{4}$ in. thick.
The pair of legs marked A in Fig. 3 is
held in position to the top board by
means of a piece of $\frac{1}{2} \times \frac{3}{16}$ in. iron bent
to shape, as shown, while the top of
the legs B rest against a stop consisting
of a piece of batten $1\frac{1}{4}$ in. wide $\times \frac{3}{4}$ in.
thick, screwed to the underside of the
top member.

The top should be covered with
flannel or an old blanket and finished in
the manner already described for the
plain ironing board.

The Sleeve Board, Fig. 4, has the
advantage of standing firmly on the
table. It may be cramped to the edge of
the table if desired. The top is raised
$5\frac{1}{2}$ in. above the base, thus enabling
those parts of the garment not actually
being ironed to keep out of the way of
the worker.

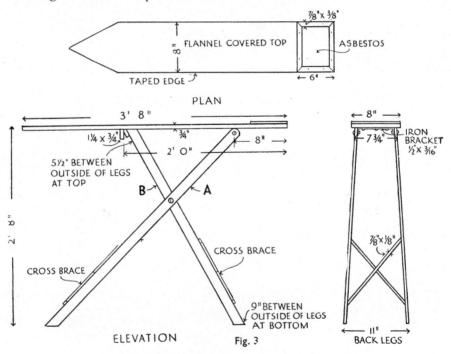

Fig. 3

To make the sleeve board, a dimensioned drawing of which appears in Fig. 5, saw and plane and square up a piece of good quality deal, 2 ft. 3 in. long, 7 in. wide × $\frac{3}{4}$ in. thick for the top and another piece 2 ft. long × 7 × $\frac{3}{4}$ in. for the base. Also two pieces 6 × 7 × $\frac{3}{4}$ in. and 7 × $3\frac{1}{2}$ × $\frac{3}{4}$ in. for the upright supports, A and B respectively.

Start work on the base. With a pencil and try square scribe across the face a line 1 in. from the left-hand edge and another line $\frac{3}{4}$ in. from the first one. These lines give the width of the groove. Set the marking gauge to $\frac{1}{4}$ in. and from the face side (top) scribe a line on each edge to indicate the depth of the groove. Cut down to depth inside the waste between the guide lines and

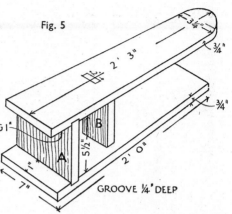

Fig. 5

Fig. 4

finish the slot with a sharp chisel. Next mark and prepare the mortice to take the lower end of B. The hole should be made 2 in. long and $\frac{3}{4}$ in. wide. Remove as much waste as possible

with a twist-bit and finish the mortice with a chisel. Slightly round the corners at the right-hand end. This completes the base.

Now take the top member and mark out the positions of the groove and mortice in the same manner as described above.

Cut the groove and the mortice and then mark the taper on the top face. Saw and plane down to the marked lines, not forgetting to round the narrow end as shown.

Mark out and cut the tenons on both ends of the support B. Assemble the parts to verify that they are a good fit. If satisfactory, glue the parts together and reinforce the back support A with $1\frac{1}{4}$ in. No. 8 countersunk-headed screws. Cover the top as already described.

PORTABLE CAKE STAND

Details of this useful piece of drawing-room furniture are to be found on page 119

SHAVING MIRROR

An easily constructed and efficient bathroom accessory with a shelf and recess attached to hold brushes, shaving tackle, etc. Working diagram and construction on page 174

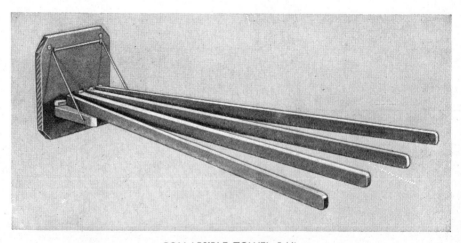

COLLAPSIBLE TOWEL RAIL

An ingenious space-saving device described on page 175. The spars fold back when not in use.

BUILDING CONSTRUCTIONS AND PROCESSES

PRACTICAL NOTES ON BUILDING A HOUSE

As comparatively few people are in a position to pay cash down for a house, the all-important problem of ways and means must be solved. This is not a very difficult matter. Funds can be raised by borrowing the majority of the necessary capital from a building society and repaying the principal plus interest by monthly or other instalments.

In a great many cases the society would probably advance an amount up to 75 per cent. to 80 per cent. of the valuation of the house. Thus, a responsible person who wished to build a house—say, costing £1,000—would, in the majority of cases, be able to obtain a loan of £750 to £800, the balance of £200 to £250 representing the purchaser's deposit.

Most societies allow a purchaser to repay the loan over any period up to fifteen years or even twenty years, and this does not prevent him from selling the house in the interim if he so desires; moreover, the new purchaser may take over the mortgage by arrangement with the society.

Loans from Local Councils. — Another satisfactory method of raising money to build a small house, is to approach the local Council or the County Council who have powers to make advances under the Small Dwellings Acquisition Act. This excellent piece of legislation was introduced and passed in Parliament some years ago with the object of assisting those individuals to purchase their houses by easy instalments at a low rate of interest, which at the present time is 3½ per cent. Under this scheme, advances up to 80 per cent. of the value of the property as estimated by the Council's surveyor can generally be obtained by approved persons provided the property is within the area controlled by the Council advancing the money. The total cost of such a house must not exceed £800. Repayment is made by monthly instalments, as in the case of most building societies. One of the conditions under which advances are made under the Act, is that the would-be purchaser must himself reside in the house within a period of six months of making the purchase for three years, after which time he is allowed to sell it if he so wishes. This condition, however, is not always enforced.

The purchaser can reduce his mortgage in sums of £10 or multiples of £10 at the expiration of every six months dating from the time of purchase. The amount paid off can be alloted to reducing either the amount of the monthly instalments or the period of the loan.

Insurance Companies. — A good many insurance companies advance money on favourable terms for house purchase; a popular scheme being a loan in conjunction with an endowment life assurance. This plan is sometimes a blessing in disguise as it has the great advantage that should a purchaser die at any time before the mortgage is repaid, the property immediately becomes mortgage-free, even if only one instalment has been paid, by virtue of the insurance policy, which of course remains in the possession of the society. Before a loan of this description is granted, the applicant is required to undergo a medical examination.

Choosing the Site.—In choosing a site on which a house is to be built, make a point of securing, if possible, one with a top surface of loam and a gravel sub-soil. Such a soil is ideal since the top layer is excellent for vegetation and gravel forms a firm and dry foundation, from which moisture can freely drain away.

Although not always possible, a clay soil should be avoided as it both shrinks and expands and is liable to produce settlements in the building, causing cracks which may or may not be serious.

Another very important point sometimes overlooked is to find out whether there are any restrictions as to the cost of other dwelling houses that might ultimately be erected on the chosen site. Unless some such restriction is imposed, it is quite within the rights of other purchasers (in some districts) to erect a residence of obsolete tram cars, or make it into a dump for disused cars.

Road Charges. — Enquiry should also be made as to the probable cost of road charges if the road has not already been made up and taken over by the authorities. This may be a costly affair, especially if the house occupies a corner site.

Choosing a Builder.—Perhaps the most difficult task of all is selecting a builder to carry out the proposed work. It does not necessarily follow that the larger the firm the better the work. Builders in a small way of business often give better value than some firms employing dozens of tradesmen. In any case it is wise to get estimates and specifications from several house constructors of good repute who will, in most cases, also submit designs based on the purchaser's requirements. Estimates and specifications can then be compared, but the contract should not be signed until the specifications and estimates have been scrutinised by some capable person having an expert knowledge of building construction, unless of course you are competent to judge for yourself.

As a guide a typical specification of a small well-built two-floored house, together with a few notes of interest on the subject, will be found in the following paragraphs.

Specification of Proposed House at————————————
For————————————
Preliminary Items—   ——
Maintenance.—The contractor shall keep the work in repair for a period of six months after the date of the certificate of completion, and any damage, defects or imperfections of any description that may arise during that period, owing to carelessness, defective workmanship or materials shall be made good at the contractor's expense.

Protection of Work. — The contractor from the time of the order being placed in possession of the works, will be held responsible for all damage that may occur by or in consequence of the carrying out of the works to any person or thing whatsoever and will be required to make good, compensate as the case may demand.

Acts.—The work to be carried out in conformity with the Local Acts and By-laws and to the satisfaction of all interested local authorities.

Notices.—Give notices to the local

authorities, gas, water and electricity supply companies. Obtain all consents, licenses and pay all fees and charges in connection therewith.

Plant. — Provide all scaffolding, planking, strutting, plant, tools, and all other things necessary for the complete execution of the works. Remove all surplus plant and materials as and when necessary.

Water.—Provide an adequate supply of water for the purpose of the work. (Town supply.)

Materials and Workmanship. — The materials, workmanship and articles shall be of the best quality and execution.

Protect Work.—Protect work in progress from injury due to sun, frost or drying winds until properly set. Also sub-contractor's work. No mortar or concrete to be used when the temperature is below 39 deg. F.

Clear Away.—Clear away all old materials, dirt rubbish, and superfluous matter and materials as they accumulate, from the whole plot.

Leave Clean.—Twice scrub floors and clean all paving, steps and stairs. Clean windows inside and out and leave the whole of the premises clean and perfect at completion.

Excavator.—Excavate to the foundations of house down to virgin soil. To be inspected and approved by the local building authorities.

Clear all vegetable matter from the whole area of the site and cover same with hardcore ready to receive concrete.

NOTES.—The builder is not allowed to proceed with laying the concrete foundation until the trenches have been examined and approved by the local building authorities. Another inspection and approval is needed after the concrete foundation has been completed and a further examination after the damp-course has been laid.

Concretor. — Concrete to foundations 9 in. of reinforced concrete consisting of clean shingle, approved brand of cement properly mixed and turned, three times dry and twice wet. Mixed to the proportions of three of shingle and one of cement, with one of sand. A suitable number of steel bars with overlapping joints to be incorporated.

Concrete the whole of the site 3 in. thick with concrete mixed in the same manner and in the same proportion.

NOTES.—The quality and proper mixing of concrete is of the utmost importance. Improper mixing greatly reduces the strength of concrete however good the ingredients used in its composition may be.

Steel bars reinforce the concrete and therefore make a stronger job than plain concrete.

Concreting over the whole site within the area of the foundation prevents damp rising which would be unhealthy. It also protects the woodwork of the ground floor from rot.

Drainer.—Excavate trenches and lay on concrete 4 in. first quality glazed earthenware pipes, to be run to intercepting chamber and connected to sewer by corporation.

All collar joints to be properly made in neat cement and trowelled off round and to be watertight.

Manholes to be at all junctions and excavated for, bricked up and trowelled off round channels in a workmanlike manner.

Render float and set to inside of brickwork.

Fix necessary fresh air inlets.

Grease down cast-iron manhole covers 24 × 16 in.

Fix all gullies with double gratings where required.

On completion the whole to be tested and approved by the local council and certificate of habitation issued.

NOTES.—Manholes are needed at every junction, and the covers are greased down to prevent the escape of foul air.

The concrete bed under the drain pipes prevent them from being damaged should there be a slight subsidence of soil.

The trenches must not be filled in with soil until the whole system has been tested and approved by the authorities.

Bricklayer.—Bricks to be hard facing bricks of approved quality and to be laid in cement mortar of an approved brand of cement, clean sand free from all salt and dirty nature, to be mixed to the proportions of three of sand and one of cement, mixed in small quantities and to be used straight away and not re-used after once setting.

All exterior walls to have 2 in. cavities and tied with proper galvanised wall ties at approximately every three feet apart, and ever six courses.

Cavities to be kept clear of all mortar droppings.

No brickwork to be carried on in frosty weather.

All sleeper walls to be honeycombed.

Air bricks to be fixed under ground floor and under roof plate at equal distances round the whole of the building. Above the ground floor, walls to be carried up in 4 in. hollow blocks covered with 1 in. rough boarding and tile hung. Tiles nailed on every one, with proper lap.

Chimney pots to be short terra-cotta, neatly bedded on in cement.

Chimney stacks to be carried up in brickwork with double damp-course below and above joint of roof. Sett-offs of chimney stacks to receive tiles, properly bedded on and made water-tight.

Lead flashings neatly cut in and properly dressed.

Flues to be parged in cement.

All face work to be pointed in neat cement.

Window heads to receive thick bitumen aprons.

Fireplaces to be approved by owner p.c. sum £7 10s.

NOTES.—The quality of cement mortar specified is quite good and the conditions regarding mixing in small quantities and to be used straight away is in order because mortar loses its effectiveness after it has become dry.

Cavity walls seem to be the order of the day and provided they are carefully constructed generally form a dry and warm building.

The ties are made of galvanised iron and are designed so that a portion hangs down in the centre in order to allow any moisture to drip down between the cavity to the bottom of the wall.

An accumulation of mortar droppings in the cavity between the walls would defeat the object of the cavity and in all probability cause dampness—hence the paragraph relating to mortar droppings.

Lead flashings refer to a method of rendering joints, such as those between the chimney stacks and roofs, watertight.

Parging is the term given to the flue linings.

The reference to the fireplaces means that the owner can choose his own fittings up to a prime cost (p.c.) of £7 10s. Should a more expensive fireplace be required the owner would have to pay the difference.

Damp-course.—A damp-course of double slate to be laid in cement under all plates, including main walls and honeycombed sleeper walls.

Internal partition walls to be built in 4 in. and 3 in. partition blocks laid in cement mortar same quality and proportions as already stated.

Steps of front porch to be carried out in 8×8 in. quarry tiles.

NOTES.—The damp-course is of the greatest importance, for unless the work and the materials are up to the highest standard the bugbear of dampness will surely arise. A double slated damp-course is accepted by most architects as being the best, although there are some who prefer a high-grade bituminous damp-course interleaved with lead.

Sleeper walls are the low walls which support the joists and flooring on the ground floor. They are honeycombed in order to ensure a good circulation of air, via the air bricks. This is one of the least precautions against what might be termed the house owner's greatest enemy—dry rot.

The blocks used for partition walls refer to hollow blocks specially designed for the purpose and make better walls than those constructed of coke-breeze.

Carpenter and Joiner.—All timber to be of yellow deal of dry, clean and good quality.

Roof to be supported by 4×2 in. common rafters, 9×2 in. hip rafters, 4×3 in. plates, 4×3 in. purlins, 7×1 in. ridge. All to be spiked and properly nailed together to form the roof.

The whole roof to be covered with ½ in. boarding and one-ply felt ruberoid, properly lapped, battened and counter battened with ¾×1 in. battens ready to receive tiles.

Valleys to be double felted to form secret gutter.

Facia board 7×1 in. prepared.

Match boarding to soffit of eaves.

¾ in. elm boarding to gables.

Top ceiling joists to be of 4×2 in. strutted at equal distances.

First floor joists to be of 8×2 in.

Herringbone strutting to be equally spaced between the joists.

All ceilings to be ½ in. insulite composition boarding properly nailed to joists and finished with an approved plaster.

The ceilings of hall and dining-room to have 3×2 in. false joists securely nailed to the underside of the composition boarding instead of being plastered, and spaced about 12 in. apart.

3 in. plain cornice to all rooms.

2×1 in. picture rails.

4×1 in. rounded skirtings.

Door linings to be of 1 in. clean deal properly fixed to brickwork with 3×1 in. double half-round architraves with 6×1¼ in. plinth blocks, ½ ovolo moulded stops.

Doors to be plain, 6 ft. 6 in. ×2 ft. 6 in. hung on 4 in. cast-iron butts. Mortice locks and bakelite furniture.

Flooring of first and ground floor to be of Columbian pine tongued and grooved and secret nailed.

All joists round hearths and chimney breasts to be properly trimmed.

Front door to be made in Japanese oak according to pattern and to be hung on 4 in. brass butts to solid oak frame with oak sill, weathered and throated.

All sashes and frames to be 1¾ in. sashes, 3×4 in. frames. Solid rebated and ovolo moulded. 3×6 in. weathered sunk and throated sills.

Every other sash to open.

Wood lintels over all heads to be covered with expanded metal ready for plastering. Lintels to be 1 in. deep for every foot span.

W.C. seats to be in bakelite, double flap in bathroom, single flap ground-floor lavatory.

Double draining boards on each side of sink in kitchen to be made of teak hardwood, grooved and properly bedded on to sink. Cupboards to be formed underneath. Cupboard catches on doors.

A suitable larder to be constructed on one side of draining board and a cupboard on the other side with four tiers of shelves in each. Marble in larder and wood in cupboard.

Sash and frame to larder to be 2 ft. × 18 in. overall, to open inwards and provided with a fly screen.

Cupboard doors and larder door 2 ft. 6 in. × 6 ft. × 1½ in. to match remainder.

Dresser with two glass doors to measure 4 ft. × 3 ft. to be made with three rows of shelving with necessary brass cup hooks, to hang on wall.

Doors glazed with 21 oz. glass.

Stairs to be in deal, 1¾ in. treads and risers. 1½ in. wall and 2 in. outer strings, 4 in. newel posts round or acorn-shaped newel tops with oak panelled balustrade.

Mopstick handrail. Soffit of stairs to be panelled with oak moulding slip.

Garage doors to be of 2 in. clean deal, ledged and braced and hung on 2 ft. 6 in. cup cast-iron hinges.

The walls of the hall to be treated with plastic paint.

NOTES.—Common rafters are those which are fixed between the roof ridge or top board and the top plate of the wall. Hip rafters are the lengths of timber which form the angle between the sides of the roof, while purlins are horizontal members that support and strengthen the roof.

The facis board carries the gutter and the soffit is attached to the undersides of the rafters where they project beyond the wall.

Plumber and Ironmonger.—All furniture to be bakelite, either round handles or lever locks of good quality, with keys, striking plates, etc., 3 in. bronze bolts for casement doors, two at each.

One Berlin black letter-box to be let into brickwork.

Berlin black Yale pattern lock, knocker and handle and Berlin black Gothic latch for front door.

Two foot bolts and two chains bolts for garage doors with yale pattern latch.

Two holes to be cut in cement outside for keeping garage doors open.

30 in. iron cup hinges to be fixed to garage doors and gates of required size and strength.

All keys to doors to be handed to owner on completion.

Supply and fix one 35 gal. copper cylinder in linen cupboard.

One 60 gal. cistern of galvanised iron 14 gauge with ball valve and lid to be fitted in roof.

Supply and fix two low pedestal W.C.'s as selected.

Chromium plated wastes of latest pattern to all basins, bath and sink.

Supply 24 × 18 × 10 in. white glazed sink, chromium plated taps, waste and chain to be built in between the walls in bathroom.

Wash-hand basin to be fixed in bathroom with suitable brackets.

Run all cold water services in heavy lead pipes with properly wiped joints.

Pipes to be hidden where possible.

Hot water pipes to be run in ½ in. copper tube, 1 in. flow and return to boiler and cylinder ½ in. services.

Cisterns to be tested before being taken over by owner.

Boiler to be of a suitable domestic type.

Tap to be put in garage to be bibcock of brass.

Half-round 4½ in. gutter on brackets to be screwed to fascia.

2½ in. stack pipes, 4 in. L.C.C. iron soil pipes.

All shoes, stop ends outlets, cistern heads as required. Chromium plated hat and coat hooks in all cupboards.

Stop-cock to be fixed in service pipe on entry into house and draw off tap fixed directly over to empty main.

All pipes in roof to be protected against frost.

NOTES.—Bakelite, a manufactured product which can be moulded into various shapes, is rapidly taking the place of metal for lock furniture, electric light switch plates, etc. Such fittings are inexpensive, can be obtained in numerous colours and designs and have the advantage of not having to be cleaned.

Chromium-plated metal has the advantage of retaining its lustre and colour.

The Half-Built House showing Built-in Garage—Front View

Deep sinks are the order of the day. Such sinks can only be fully appreciated by those individuals who have experienced working at a shallow one.

Copper Piping for the hot-water system is a modern innovation. Among the many benefits to be derived from their installation is that

The same—Back View

they are not so unsightly and are not so likely to furr up as heavy gauge iron barrel.

There are many types of domestic boilers, using many varieties of fuel. An excellent kind is one that is self-regulating—that is, as the water heats up it automatically closes a damper and reduces the draught and therefore the amount of heat and incidentally fuel.

A water tap in the garage is one of those conveniences very often over-

looked and should never be omitted.

A draw-off tap to empty the water mains is also another item which should not be forgotten.

Plasterer.—The whole of internal walls to be rendered in cement and set in sirapite. Make good after all trades.

The plastering in kitchen and bathroom, etc., to be specially prepared to receive paint.

Glazed Tiler.—Tile sink and draining boards with 6×6 in. ivory tiles and black edging and birdbeaks.

Floor of cooker and boiler recesses to be rendered in cement.

Bathroom and ground floor cloakroom to be tiled in 4 ft. high with 6×6 in. ivory white tiles, black edging and birdbeaks.

Roof Tiler.—Tile roof with antique-finish best quality British-made tiles, bonnet hips and half round ridge.

Notes.—Roofing tiles form one of the most important items of house construction. Beware of cheap foreign tiles of the semi-glazed variety. They are likely to split and flake at the no distant future. Insist on British tiles—always. They can be depended upon.

Electrician.—One lighting point to include plain pendants without shades and lamps to be installed in all rooms and one power point of 15 amp. capacity in dining-room, lounge, hall, bathroom and each bedroom.

All work to be carried out in strict accordance with the rules and regulations of the Institution of Electrical Engineers and the supply authorities.

All wires to be of best quality 600 megohm grade vulcanised india-rubber and of British make and protected by Simplex close-joint enamelled steel conduit properly bonded and effectively earthed.

All power plugs to be three-pin combination switch-plugs, surface type.

Each power plug to be protected by separate double pole fuses enclosed in a Home Office type fuse board and a similar board of 5 amp. capacity per way to be supplied and fixed to suit the arrangements of the lighting wiring.

One iron-clad double-pole combined main switch-fuse of a capacity to suit the power circuit and a main switch-fuse for lighting circuit fixed near the entry of the supply company's mains.

Notes.—It is of the utmost importance that the electrical installation be carried out in a safe and efficient manner, and executed by competent electricians. This part of the house construction is generally done by sub-contractors, so make sure that the sub-contractor is one of good repute.

Painter and Decorator.—Ground-floor joists to be creosoted immediately after completion. All woodwork to be prepared and stained with Darkaline of an approved shade and varnished throughout the whole of the house. Gutters to be painted inside and out with bitumastic black. Hot-water pipes where showing to be painted in accordance with the decorations of the room in which they appear. Exterior woodwork sashes and frames, eaves, gutter boards and soffits to receive three coats of best quality lead oil paint. All paintwork to be stopped and primed and finished in an approved colour. Kitchen W.C. and bathroom walls to be painted and finished in Silexore.

Walls in all rooms to be distempered or papered with paper 2s. per piece.

Clear 21 oz. glass to all windows except W.C. and bathroom, or any other where obscured glass is required.

Obscured glass to be small ripple or cathedral.

Form ash and brick rubble drive with smooth surface from garage to entrance gates.

Supply and fix stock pattern oak gates, hung on cup hinges of required strength to 6×6 in. oak posts properly cemented in and made tight.

Supply and fix one small 3 ft. gate with post, etc., for tradesmen's entrance with path similar to garage drive.

POINTS ABOUT HOUSE PURCHASE

GOOD water and plenty of it; that is still the first point to look for in a new house in the country. With that, naturally, goes efficient drainage. Unless these are satisfactory, or can be made so, the house is not suitable.

If the company's water is laid on, well and good. But find out whether it is hard. Hard water means furred kettles and hot-water pipes. It may be worth while to install a water-softening plant.

Should a well be the source of supply, there is a greater need for investigation. In no circumstances proceed until a sample has been examined by an analyst. Boring to tap a fresh source of water is costly.

Testing the Drains.—The drains must be tested. The nose is some guide, but the smoke-test is more certain. The professional surveyor uses a smoke-cartridge, made for the purpose, flushing it down the W.C. The handyman can carry out for himself the directions given with it. Septic tanks and cesspools can be a source of trouble. The former call for expert advice; as to the latter, if the cesspool is of the type that requires periodical pumping out it is needful to ascertain whether the rates cover this service. It is, in any case, wise to inquire about the amount.

See that the flushing cisterns, the main cistern (if any) and the plumbing are complete and in working order. It is a great advantage if every delivery pipe from the main cistern has its stop-cock fitted for use. If these pipes and, above all, the supply main are run on the north or east walls of the house (and they often are), they should be lagged with canvas or felt against frost.

Sounding the Walls.—As to the structure itself, the most important considerations, particularly in an old house, are the soundness of the roof and the dryness of the walls. Fortunately, damp usually betrays itself. In the rooms immediately beneath the roof, look carefully at the ceilings and upper walls, especially about the angles of the chimney breasts and in corners, for discoloration and mould. Such signs give ground for further investigation. They may be due merely to a tile or slate or two having become damaged or missing. On the other hand, the general soundness of the roof must be suspected. You should go up into the attic or loft and examine at close quarters the slating or tiling and the woodwork that support them. Strictly speaking, it will be to the good if you find the slates or tiles are not visible by reason of an inner lining of boarding or (in modern houses) felt; these make for warmth. If the day is at all windy, notice if it is draughty up there; that means a cold house. If dealing with thatch, see that it is whole and preferably bound down with galvanized wire netting.

Checking for Damp. — Scrutinize floorings and skirtings for soundness. Gaps between the two mean draughts and dust. On the ground floor, look out for damp. Normally, modern houses have a damp course built into the brickwork of the walls about a foot above ground-level, with air-bricks below it to ventilate the floor timber. Not all old houses are so safeguarded, and even if they are, garden soil may have been piled up above the level of this course, defeating its purpose. A soundly built house, too, has double walling with a cavity between so that rain will not penetrate to the inner wall. Damp walls may be due to defective or choked guttering and down-pipes, causing rain water to spill over and drench them; but this, of course, can be verified.

Dampness is a source of dry-rot. If the house smells musty without apparent reason, have two or three floorboards lifted in different places on the ground floor. Dry-rot, once firmly established, is very difficult to get rid of, for it is capable of spanning many feet in search of fresh areas of woodwork. Dry rot may also be responsible for a shaky roof or unsound stairs.

Vermin.—It is hardly necessary to warn you against buying or renting a house that is infested by rats, mice or black beetles; look for their traces.

Cracks in walls and ceilings may be superficial and capable of easy repair, or due to structural defects such as a faulty foundation. Consult an expert in case of doubt. If the ceiling plaster is cracked and has the appearance of sagging, prod it gingerly with a stick. Should it give noticeably, it is pretty sure to come down sooner or later.

Details to be checked include the sound fitting of windows. See that the glass is whole and, in the case of sashes, whether they slide easily or need new sash-cords. See that the latches and locks of doors work and that each has its properly-fitting key. Look for evidence of smoky chimneys—usually smoke stains betray a bad chimney.

To conclude, however attractive a house may appear, if it is really old, have it vetted by an architect-surveyor.

IMPROVING A SMALL HOUSE

THE following paragraphs contain descriptions of alterations carried out in a small pre-war terrace house, in order to modernise it. The article has been written for readers who may have similar homes and wish to make improvements. The alterations were made at such odd times as were at the disposal of the owner, covering a period of several years and show what can be done by a man of ordinary intelligence who can use tools.

Fig. 1 represents a rough plan of the ground floor before the alterations and additions were put in hand. The ground floor apartments consist of a small hall with the usual staircase, a sitting-room, kitchen, scullery, and an outside lavatory and coal cellar. The upper floor contains three bedrooms as indicated in Fig. 2.

Installing Electricity. — The first thing tackled was the installing of electric light and power, taking down all the gas fittings and sealing off the ends of the pipes, special care being taken to see that all such joints at the gas plugs were absolutely gas tight, thick red lead paint being painted on the gas threads for this purpose. Then followed the actual installing of the electric light, which was carried out in the close-joint conduit with continuity fittings, such as elbows, tee-pieces and junction boxes so that it could be efficiently earthed; a very important item rightly insisted upon by the supply authorities.

While this was being done the supply company laid the necessary service cable. A position for the meters, under the stairs, was mutually agreed upon and as the distance from this point to the front boundary hedge measures 30 ft., a charge was made of £3 15s., which works out at 2s. 6d. per foot run, the usual charge in most districts.

As there was no means of gaining access to the space between the roof and the first-floor ceilings to allow tubes to be fixed on the top of the joints, a trap door had to be made for this purpose and the joists cut and trimmed to take it, otherwise it would have meant running unsightly tubes on the faces of the ceilings below.

As some of the walls between the

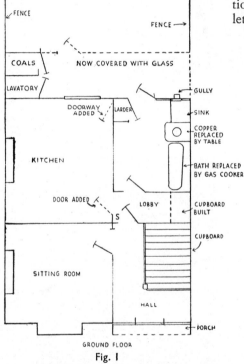

GROUND FLOOR
Fig. I

rooms on the upper floor were lath and plaster partitions, no difficulty was experienced in concealing the tubes where they ran down to the switches. A hole was bored in the wall-plates at the top which allowed the tubes to be inserted in the hollow space within. In one wall only did a channel have to be cut to bury the tube. Tubing and wiring the ground floor presented no

difficulty as the floor boards under which they were run were quite easy to take up. Most of the walls on the ground floor were brick. As it meant much cutting away to bury the switch tubes, and the decorations of some of the rooms were in good order, it was decided to group the switches and place them in the lobby. Incidently this method of grouping saved a considerable amount of conduit and wire and should therefore be noted. The position of the switches is indicated by a letter S; in Fig. 1.

The hall light, a lamp which could

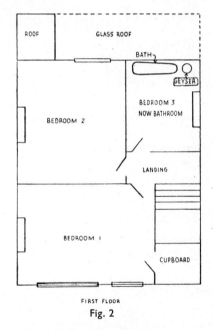

FIRST FLOOR
Fig. 2

be turned down at the pull of a cord, was operated from the lobby and the first floor landing, while the two large bedrooms were fitted with plugs for bed-lights. A power plug was installed in every room.

Kitchen to Living-room. — The next item was the conversion of the kitchen into a living-room. This apartment contained an old-fashioned kitchen

Fig. 3

brick copper and a bath as shown in Fig. 1 which took up valuable space. The brickwork of the copper developed an unsightly crack and the copper itself showed signs of decay, while the bath, an old painted affair, badly needed a few fresh coats.

A few hours work with hammer and cold chisel demolished the copper and the flue was effectively blocked with a few of the old bricks and portland

stove. A low open grate was fitted in its place and a suitable oak surround constructed, as shown in Fig. 3. Through an oversight of the builder, no door had been provided between the kitchen and the small adjacent lobby. To isolate the latter, which was useless from a practical point of view, a door was made and fitted as indicated in Fig. 1, and the lobby was made serviceable by constructing a cupboard from floor to ceiling.

The larder door opened into the scullery and this meant that food had to be brought through the scullery into the living-room. A doorway was cut in the wall and a door fitted at the back of the larder so that access could be obtained from the sitting-room. The door on the scullery side was retained, (See Fig. 4.) After these improvements had been carried out, a picture rail was added, the walls and ceiling re-decorated and the woodwork repainted.

The Scullery.—contained a projecting

Fig. 4

cement and sand mortar. The plaster was made good with Keene's cement. The bath was retained for a time until a new porcelain one had been installed in the small unused bedroom which was converted into a bathroom. In place of the old copper, a modern gas copper was obtained, which, when not in use, was housed under a flap table attached to the wall, and the space formally occupied by the bath was partly filled by an up-to-date gas cooker.

The New Bathroom.—In the bedroom which was made into a bathroom, the bath was placed under the window and the waste pipe carried down an outside wall to discharge in a gulley below. Cold water was obtained from a pipe connected to the main supplying the sink immediately below.

To overcome the difficulty of obtaining hot water for the bath, a semi-rotary pump was installed in the scullery. This scheme eliminated the weary process of carting bucketsful of water up the staircase. The pump gave satisfactory service for some years when it was replaced by a gas geyser.

Improvement in the hall was effected by enclosing the space under the stairs. This space was made into a cupboard for overcoats, hats and other outside wearing apparel.

An electric bell was fitted at the side of the front door to ring in the lobby. This replaced a mechanical bell which required constant winding up.

With regard to the original sitting-room, except for the addition of a picture rail, re-painting and re-decorating and fitting bookshelves, nothing else was done to it. Little was done to the bedrooms except the usual re-decoration.

The Back of the House.—The last job so far as the house was concerned was to concrete the area between the lavatory and coal cellar and the right-hand fence, and then cover it in with a glass roof, part glass front with a garden door, and matchboarded side.

This proved equivalent to an extra room for it contained a large table upon which electric ironing and other various odd jobs, including carpentry, could be carried out in a good light.

The size of the glass lean-to was 12 ft. 6 in. long ×6 ft. 6 in. wide. The surface soil was removed to a depth of 12 in. to enable the finished surface of the concrete to come just below the level of the air-bricks. The excavated site was then carefully levelled and filled with small brick rubble to a depth of 5 in., rammed down tightly and levelled to form a solid base. On the top of this was added concrete made up of one part portland cement, two parts sand and four parts aggregate, consisting of small washed stones. To give a durable smooth surface, an inch top layer of cement mortar consisting of one part cement and three parts sand was applied. When the floor had been allowed to harden a course of bricks placed longways, technically termed stretchers, was laid along the front edge, except a gap to be occupied by the doorway, and along one side. The bricks were then given a coat of cement on both sides and along the top and upon this was placed a damp-course consisting of specially prepared bitumen felt sold for the purpose. The damp-course prevented moisture rising to the sill or bottom plates of the structure and preserved the wood from rot.

The height to the eave was 6 ft. 8 in. from the floor level and the height at the back 10 ft. 10 in. The slope of the roof thus formed corresponded with the roof covering the lavatory and coal cellar and allowed the rain water to get away quickly to the gutter where it discharged through a down pipe into a nearby surface-water gulley.

Before the work of enclosing the site was put in hand, a guard was fitted to the house roof above to prevent snow from falling and damaging the glass below. The snow-guard consisted of stout, square mesh, galvanised pea-guards carefully straightened and supported by iron brackets bent to shape and fixed with galvanised screws to the facia board to which the gutter is attached. An illustration, Fig. 5, is given for those readers who might require a similar device at some future time. Before erection, the brackets were given two coats of aluminium paint.

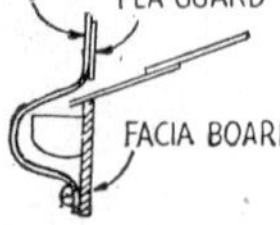

Fig. 5

The end posts and door posts consisted of 3×3 in. prepared yellow deal, the top and bottom plates of 3×2 in. and the window sill of 5×2½ in. stuff sloped off at the front and provided with a weather groove under the front edge to prevent entry of water. The front was provided with a casement window, while the roof was fitted with a ventilator.

The intervening space between the bottom plate and the window-sill consisted of ¾ in. tongued and grooved V-matching and similar material formed one side. The sash bars were spaced to suit the width of best quality horticultural glass of stock size. A purlin, or long horizontal support, consisting of 3×3 in. material was placed in the centre immediately under the roof sash bars to take the weight and prevent the roof from sagging. After erection the structure was primed with red lead paint, glazed and then given a further two undercoats and a final coat of lead oil paint.

A small lean-to shed, with the floor well above the ground, was built against the coal cellar wall. In this were housed garden tools, carpenter's tools, paint pots, and other handyman's items.

EQUIPPING A SMALL MODERN HOUSE

LET us suppose we are dealing with a house of, say, two reception rooms, kitchen, three bedrooms and bathroom, and that there is need for economy. True economy in the long run, assuming that the house has been purchased or taken on a long lease, may involve more outlay than is at first thought reasonable. It is better to pay the price for durable goods, even if everything cannot be bought at once, than to have to make early replacements.

Floor Coverings.—Start with the floors. Consider the possibility of putting down parquet in the living rooms. This is obtainable in thin layers of a variety of hardwoods, all ready for fixing, at a price comparable with that of a good carpet with the felt underlay that a good carpet deserves.

It lasts, it requires a minimum of labour in cleaning and it looks well, with or without rugs upon it. And rugs of the right shape and design can be handmade in the home nowadays. Fig. 1 shows a typical example of such a rug. Their tendency to slip can be overcome by mounting them on non-slip backing.

An alternative to parquet is an oak floor such as that illustrated in Fig. 2. Linoleum, preferably of the thick, spongy variety, is specially suitable for bedrooms and is almost a necessity for the bathroom. Even those who prefer a fully carpeted bedroom will find it expedient to lay a surround of linoleum. It is more lasting, and more easily cleaned than stained floor-boards, though, if the flooring is sound staining can be satisfactory.

Fig. I

Linoleum should be fixed with paste to concrete flooring only. When laying it over boarding, especially if new, tack it down, over a paper-felt underlay, with brads designed for the purpose.

Fig. 2

This will eliminate the possibility of bottling up damp and starting dry-rot. If the joint between the floor and skirting is not already rounded, it can be

K

rounded by bradding on lengths of wood beading of quarter-circle section, running the linoleum up over it and forming a neat finish with a small beading, also obtainable in lengths from the woodwork shop.

The existing kitchen floor may be of wood, cement or tiles. The first is not easy to keep clean, the last two are cold to the feet. There is nothing to equal rubber flooring here. It may be had in many colours, plain, variegated or patterned like tiling.

Stair carpet shows unequal wear and should be taken up and relaid in a different way periodically. Rubber stair carpet is now obtainable and may be bought in a continuous length or in separate pieces to cover the tread and nosing of each step.

Wall Treatments.—Treatment of the walls depends to a certain degree on the age of the house. If the house is new, the walls are certain to be not quite dry and, in drying out, may stain the wall-covering.

The wisest course with new walls is to start with plain distemper, preferably one of the oil-bound water paints. Dark tones should be avoided, particularly if the room is none too light. Many consider there is nothing so satisfactory as a buff tint, which is not only cheerful but forms an excellent background for pictures. If there is a preference for different tints in different rooms, keep them delicate and do not use violent contrasts, which have the effect of

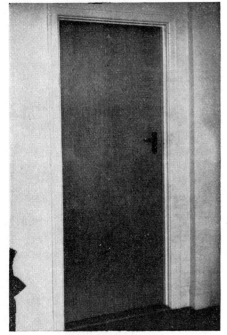

Fig. 3

apparently decreasing the size, not only of the rooms but of the whole house.

Wallpapers can be substituted after a year or two if desired. Conversely, if paper already exists, but its pattern is not liked, distemper may be applied on it after a coat of sealer, and possibly renewed once, after which it will be a case for stripping. If you choose a patterned design, remember that the smaller the room the smaller should be the scale of the pattern. There is a

vogue for coloured ceilings nowadays. The hint about keeping the tints on the light side particularly applies here.

For dining-rooms and sitting-rooms, if means permit, wood panelling may be considered. It is obtainable in thin layers of solid wood or as plywood with or without beading for the joints. For the kitchen and bathroom walls, white tiles are ideal; but an effective substitute is found in white gloss-enamel made for walls. If it is of cellulose lacquer, which is practically everlasting, the wall must be perfectly dry and a sealing coat be first applied.

Cellulose lacquer is, indeed, an excellent finish for all woodwork that has to be painted. However, the less paintwork to keep clean, the better the housewife will be pleased. Hence, the popularity of flush, laminated wood doors as represented in Fig. 3, with chromium, oxidized or hardwood fittings. Window-sills, if not in hardwood, should be of tiles. Paintwork, however good, is bound to get dirty and scratched.

The Windows.—You may have to deal with both sash and casement windows. Since blinds are out of fashion—if they must be used, a spring-roller design is worth paying for—draw-curtains will probably be required, and these give scope for individual taste in material, design and arrangement. Deep sash windows often lend themselves to floor-length hangings and formal pelmets; shallow casements look attractive with window-length curtains and a simple frilled valence.

It is worth while going to the expense of installing metal runways and roller-hooks for curtain fastenings; they save tears, time and temper. The curtain fabric itself should be of some fadeless washable material, stout and preferably lined. For rooms that happen to be overlooked, subsidiary curtains of a light net, in one of the many admirable patterns, hung with curtain rings from light rods fixed just above head-level, will form an efficient screen without excluding too much light. Alternatively they may be hung from spring coiled wire, but this rusts easily and hangs up when the curtains are pulled.

Lighting Points.—Lighting may be arranged in numerous ways. It is desirable to have ample light in working quarters. There should be a point over the kitchen sink as well as over the

Fig. 4

kitchen table. A shaving light in the bathroom is a boon. Indirect lighting has done away with the heavy shadows. Often lighting is concealed within the cornice rail, and even if this is not practicable, tubular lamps, with or without concealing reflectors, may still be employed. It is, however, an advantage to have a wall plug to serve a portable lamp for close work.

In passages and stairways it is advisable to have two-switch control systems. In bedrooms, the principle may be applied to the door and bed switches. Nowadays, houses are sometimes provided with wireless points in several rooms. It is important to ascertain that the wiring of the circuits carries a fuse to avert fire-danger.

The possibilities of gas lighting are not so great, but by-pass burners in conjunction with gas switches (plungers operating pneumatically through very fine brass tubing that may be run any distance) make gas nearly as convenient as electricity.

The modern house is usually equipped with gas-points for fires, and an inset fire such as the one depicted in Fig. 4 is favoured by many. There are, however, kinds that can be removed in favour of a fire of coals, the flexible gas tubing should be fitted with the kind of terminal that plugs in and automatically cuts off the gas when withdrawn. A gas poker with a similar fitment will make the starting of the coal fire very easy. A gas iron, Fig. 5, also offers possibilities where electricity is not available.

There is an increasing tendency to plan the dining-room and kitchen with the fireplaces back to back, and to fit an oven and hot-water boiler between so

Fig. 5

that the heat from either fire will serve them. An interesting innovation combines with the duplex firing facilities doors and shelves so disposed that they form an enclosed hot-plate-cum-hatch-way between the two rooms. A hatch is one of the most labour-saving devices in domestic equipment. The best substitute is a trolley dinner-wagon.

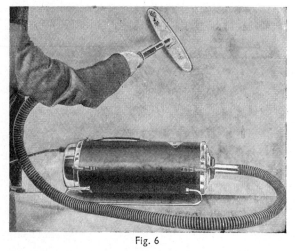

Fig. 6

See that the wheels are large and tyred with rubber, so that it may be moved about with ease.

Hot Water.—If a separate boiler is installed for supplying hot water to kitchen sink and bathroom, let it be large enough to supply one or two bedroom radiators and a hot cupboard as well. The additional cost of boiler and fuel will be trifling, and that of piping and radiators will be paid for in a year or two by saving on other forms of heating. Alternatively, there are sitting-room fireplaces that serve a small radiator in the room directly above at no extra fuel cost whatever.

Solid fuel independent boilers of the slow combustion kind are little trouble to run once the knack has been acquired, but even that may be saved by the use of a gas-fired hot-water storage system, which is equally efficient but rather more costly in operation. Whether such things as the totally enclosed slow-combustion cooking-range and refrigerator are to be regarded as luxuries or necessities depends largely on the number of persons normally living in the house; if it is fewer than four, it would take some years of economy to pay off the rather heavy outlay. A vacuum cleaner, Fig. 6, is a necessity.

The things to consider when spending extra money are easy chairs and beds. Whether the beds should be divans, which are space-saving and allow the bedrooms to be used also as sittingrooms, is a question for personal choice. Bedroom chairs may as well be of the semi-easy type.

Washstands are disappearing in favour of fitted wash-basins, as represented in Fig. 7. These are neatly placed in corners or recesses and completely enclosed with doors. See that every basin waste is fitted with a trap.

Built-in basins bring up the question of built-in furniture. Divans may be built into recesses; make a permanent platform of timber, 8 in. or a foot above

Fig. 7

the floor, to take a box-spring mattress and the thing is done. Recesses are obvious places for hanging cupboards, doing away with wardrobes.

ERECTING A PARTITION

MANY houses have a bedroom measuring about 20×14 ft., running from the front of the house to the back, with a window at each end and a fireplace in the centre of one of the long walls, as

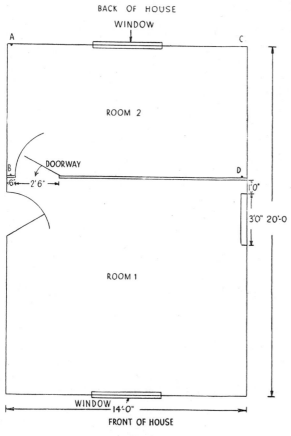

BACK OF HOUSE

WINDOW

A   C

ROOM 2

B   DOORWAY   D

6"   2'6"   1'0"

3'0" 20'-0

ROOM 1

WINDOW 14'-0"

FRONT OF HOUSE

Fig. I

indicated in Fig. 1. Such a room is ideal for converting into two small ones, and the cost of making the alteration can be reduced to a minimum by doing it yourself.

It is possible to divide such a room into two rooms of equal size, by covering in the fireplace, but this would spoil the appearance of both rooms. It is better to make one room larger than the other and so retain the fireplace in one of them.

It is a matter of taste whether the smaller room shall be at the back of the house or at the front. In either case the partition should not be erected closer to the fireplace than a distance of 1 ft.

The best time for carrying out the work is just before redecorating, as this will enable both sides of the partition to be finished in accordance with the decorative scheme of the rooms. On the other hand, the partition could be painted to match surrounding woodwork.

Important Points.—Before starting work, it is good to consider one or two details. If the floor in the room is covered with linoleum in good condition, there will be no need to take it up. The partition can be built upon it and cut afterwards at the skirting. A carpet should, of course, be taken up.

If possible, arrange the doorway so that it comes near the end opposite the fireplace and not in the centre of the partition. A doorway in the centre of a small room is not conducive to economy of space.

Another point which should be

decided is the material for cladding the framework of the partition. Tongued and grooved V-jointed matching makes for stability and could be used if the new wall is to be painted. But if the partition is to be papered, the matching should have a perfectly flat surface, which can be obtained by using an

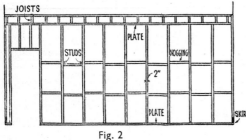

Fig. 2

overlay of plywood $\frac{1}{8}$ in. thick.

Another method is to cover the framework with one of the many excellent kinds of building boards. Alterations may be necessary to the lighting. If the house is wired for electricity the work should be done before the framework is covered in as it enables tubes carrying the lighting wires down to a switch to be concealed; the ends of the wires being simply threaded through a hole

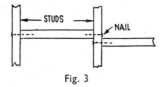

Fig. 3

in the wall-covering during erection, and connected to the switch when complete.

It is customary to hang the door in the doorway so that it opens towards the bed and closes on to a nib of projection not less than 6 in. wide. If this principle can be followed so much the better.

The framework consists of a top and bottom plate to which a number of

vertical studs or posts are secured by nails. The section of the wood (deal) should not be less than 3×2 in. and this is arranged narrow face outwards as illustrated in Fig. 2.

Materials Required. — Assuming the height of the room to be 8 ft. 6 in., the length of the struts will be 8 ft. 2 in. Four such pieces will be required for the ends and the door posts while eight intermediate ones will also be needed. These intermediate studs should be spaced at an equal distance apart. Two nogging pieces as illustrated in Fig. 3 should be fixed between each stud to make the structure rigid. Each of these will measure a little over 1 ft. 9 in. in length.

The head of the door will require a further 2 ft. 6 in. length and the short studs above it, two pieces each 1 ft. 8 in. in length.

The top plate is in one piece and extends across the room from one wall to the other. It should, however, measure an inch less than the distance between the walls, to enable it to be manipulated into position without damage to the plaster.

In determining the length of the long and short bottom plates, do not forget that about an inch must be deducted to allow for the skirting board at the ends.

Before marking the position for the top plate, ascertain which way the ceiling joists run in order to obtain a fixing. In a room of this size, it is usual to place the joists across the shortest span, but this is not always the case as the joists may run longitudinally and be supported near the centre by a girder.

Top Plate and Joists.—If the joists are found to run lengthwise, mark out on the ceiling the position of the top plate by first measuring the distance from wall A to B in Fig. 1 and then cutting a piece of batten of that length.

Then mark the position D from the wall at C with the aid of the batten, and also make two intermediate marks measured from each side of the window. Draw a line across the ceiling passing through these marks. If the joists run across the room, and a joist does not happen to come in the desired position, it will be necessary to fix the top plate a few inches towards the back window, so that it can be fixed to the bottom of the joist. A guide line can then be made.

Having cut the plate to length, bore a number of screw holes to clear 4 in. No. 8 screws and fix the plate in position. The latter operation will need a helper to hold the plate firmly against the ceiling while you drive in the screws.

The next operation, that of marking the position for the bottom plates, calls for a string and plumb-bob. Partially drive a nail in one side and near the end of the top plate and from the nail suspend a plumb-bob so that the bottom of the latter just clears the floor. Allow the bob to come to rest and mark the position; then repeat the process at the other end and draw a line joining these two points. Cut the plates to length, bore screw holes and fix the pieces down to the floor, using 3 in. No. 8 screws.

Now mark on all plates the position of the end uprights, door-posts and studs, and cut these parts to length. Each end post will need to be recessed near the ends and on the face in contact with the wall to clear the skirting.

Now fix the whole of the parts together by using 3 in. nails driven in slant wise. Then add the nogging pieces, door head and the short studs above it.

At this stage alterations to the electric light should be carried out.

Wall Fabrics.—When these have been done, the covering material can be added to the framework. Tongued and grooved matching is nailed on vertically with 1 in. cut nails, the heads of which are punched just below the surface after completion. This operation is unnecessary if the boards are to be overlayed with plywood.

The Doorway.—Fit a lining to the doorway. The thickness of the wood for this is 1 in. and equal in width to the thickness of the door-post (3 in.) plus twice the thickness of the covering material, so that the edges of the lining lie flush with the back and front surfaces.

It is a good plan to house the top ends of the members into recesses cut $\frac{3}{8}$ in. at the ends of the head piece. The door lining is then fixed.

An architrave consisting of either an ornamental or a plain moulding is then fixed round the edges of the door lining on both sides to cover the joints. The width of this moulding should correspond, if possible, with that of the other doors.

Two short and two long pieces of wooden skirting-board about 1 in. thick and of a width to correspond with the existing skirting will be needed for finishing the partition. These should be fixed with 2 in. cut nails driven into the bottom plate and the studs.

If you have facilities for making a suitable door, and can carry out a piece of accurate joinery, make your own door. The alternative is to buy one. In these days doors are inexpensive and can be obtained in a number of good designs. A purchased door may have to be cut down and planed, but this is a simple matter.

The door should be hinged with substantial 3 in. cast-iron butts, and a length of door stopping $1\frac{1}{2}$ in. wide $\times \frac{1}{2}$ in. thick nailed to the inside faces of the door lining.

FITTING A DOMESTIC STOVE

THE old-fashioned kitchener is generally being replaced nowadays by the small, economical self-contained domestic stove, finished with porcelain enamel as the example illustrated in Fig. 1.

Such a stove, whether it be of the open or closed type, shows a saving of

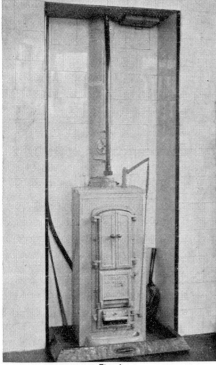

Fig. 1

anything up to two-thirds of the cost of running compared with an ordinary range. A modern domestic stove can be fitted by any practical man.

Readers who are not familiar with the principles on which a domestic hot water system works should study Fig. 2, which shows the usual arrangement of pipes in a small house.

It is hardly necessary to point out that the diameter of the new pieces of pipe must be of the same diameter as the existing ones, and that steam barrel must be used and not the thinner stuff used for conveying gas.

When buying the material, do not forget a loose-handled drain cock for the bottom of the return pipe to drain off the water when occasions arise.

As it is unlikely that you possess tools for cutting the screw-threads on the ends of the pipes, your local hot water fitter or ironmonger from whom you purchase the materials will do this for you for a small additional charge.

The parts should be connected up to the stove to verify that all is correct, after which the pipes should be disconnected and the stove removed to enable walls and floor to be finished.

Installation.—The stove can then be fixed permanently in position and the pipes connected up as before, but this time the joints must be perfectly watertight. To effect this, paint the screwthreads with thick red and white lead paint and wind a few twisted strands of hemp moistened with paint in the channels between the threads, and screw the pipes and fittings up tightly, using a large pair of pipe grips for the purpose.

Now fix the sheet-iron cover-plate and seal the edges with portland cement. Cut the flue pipe to suit, with the aid of a file, allowing a couple of inches to project above the iron to prevent soot falling into the pipe.

Finally, attach the flue pipe sealing ring, generally supplied with the stove, to prevent cold air entering at the joint between the pipe and the sheet iron.

The system can now be tested. Fill the apparatus with water either by operating the stop-cock or by removing the wooden plug in the storage tank outlet, and watch for leaks. If all is well, fill the stove with fuel, get the water hot and look again for leaks. If necessary, tighten up the joints.

To give the pipes a finished appearance, paint them with metallic paint such as aluminium, bronze or other colour to suit the surrounding decorations.

Hot-water Principles.—The cold water storage tank which feeds the hot water system is generally placed in the loft or between the roof and ceilings of

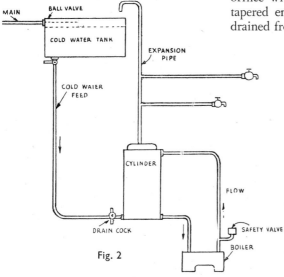

Fig. 2

the top-floor rooms. This tank is supplied with cold water direct from the main through a ball-operated valve which automatically regulates the height of the water in the tank. From the tank, the cold water flows by gravity via the feed pipe, indicated by the arrow, into the bottom of the hot water cylinder of copper, or a small closed galvanized iron tank. The water then traverses the return pipe and into the boiler where its temperature is raised by the fire. As hot water is lighter than cold, it rises in the flow pipe into the top of the cylinder

where it mixes with the cooler water below. Hot water is drawn off from the taps connected to the expansion pipe as shown, one end of which is connected to the top of the cylinder while the other is open-ended and terminates over the storage tank and acts as a safety valve should the water boil in the cylinder.

Drain the System.—The first thing to do when substituting a domestic stove and boiler for a range is to turn off the water supply at the cold water feed cock situated near the storage tank; or, if such a cock is not fitted, to plug the orifice with a piece of wood having a tapered end. The water must then be drained from the system by opening the draw-off cock usually provided for this purpose and turning on the hot water taps.

The range can be taken apart by removing all portable parts such as the oven door and fire bars, and then undoing the nuts, bolts and screws that hold it together. Many of the fastenings will, no doubt, be rusty and difficult to remove, and as there is nothing to be gained by removing each portion intact, the use of a hammer and cold chisel will save a lot of time. Thin cast-iron from which the parts are made is easy to break by this method.

As soon as practicable, remove the boiler by cutting the floor and return pipes at some convenient place just above the boiler and then disconnect the pipes at the first joints which may be a socket as illustrated in Fig. 3. The cutting can be done with a hack saw—or, better still, with a wheel pipe-cutter, the proper tool for the job. This tool might be hired from the local hot water fitter for a few pence.

The aperture is now clear of encumbrances except for the two down pipes which have to be extended and connected to the new stove.

Walling the Recess.—At this stage consider the method to be adopted for finishing the recess. The walls may be

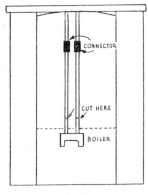

Fig. 3

finished in portland cement and sand, or they may be rendered in portland cement mortar and finished with Keene's cement plaster and painted, or they may, if preferred, be fitted with glazed tiles. Tiles are undoubtedly best, but are also expensive. The floor may be either cement or covered with quarry tiles.

Having come to a decision about this, measure the roof of the aperture for the cover-plate. The latter consists of a piece of sheet iron about $\frac{1}{8}$ in. thick and is held in position by channels cut in the brickwork and supported underneath by two lengths of $1 \times \frac{1}{4}$ in. irons fixed, one at the front and the other at the back, between the side walls.

Cut the channels about $\frac{1}{2}$ in. deep in the sides and back of the brickwork.

Mark the iron with a pointed tool such as a fine bradawl and carefully cut the metal to size by means of a cold

chisel and hammer. Having cut the slots for accommodating the water pipes, fix the cover plate temporarily in position so that the position of the holes for the flue pipe can be marked thereon.

To do this, place the stove in the exact position it is eventually to occupy, and with a plumb-bob and string, plumb the centre of the flue-socket of the stove in the manner indicated in Fig. 4 and mark the corresponding centre point on the cover-plate. Remove the iron and, with a pair of compasses, scribe a circle of the same diameter as that of the flue pipe, then cut the hole with a cold chisel and hammer and finish by using a half-round file.

Estimating Pipe Lengths.—Next, ascertain the lengths of pipe and fittings required for extending the existing flow and return pipes and connecting them up to the boiler.

The amount of pipe and number of

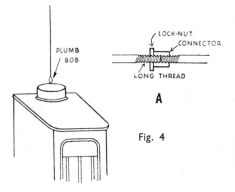

Fig. 4

fittings such as bends will be determined by the type of stove being installed. Some stoves have the water-pipe sockets at the back, others at the side, while in several makes one socket is placed at the top. In any case, the upper ends of the new pipes must be fitted with running threads as illustrated at A in Fig. 4 to enable them to be connected up to the old ones.

PANELLING A ROOM IN PLYWOOD

PANELLING walls in wood is undoubtedly not only the most charming way of dealing with walls but also preserves them and saves the expense and labour of constantly re-painting, papering or distempering.

The sketch, Fig. 1, shows a room panelled in oak-faced plywood.

A Scale Drawing.—Details of the panelling are shown in Fig. 2. Before beginning work on a room, draw the stiles and rails so as to bring the size of the panels as near to 2 ft. 1 in.× 1 ft. 4 in. as possible.

Take off the old skirting and plane and bevel some lengths of oak skirting, size $7\frac{1}{2}\times\frac{7}{8}$ in.

Begin by fixing this to the longest wall—in the clear (against the end walls). Screw this on this way: on the face of the skirting, bore holes $\frac{3}{8}$ in. diameter and $\frac{1}{4}$ in. deep only (this is for

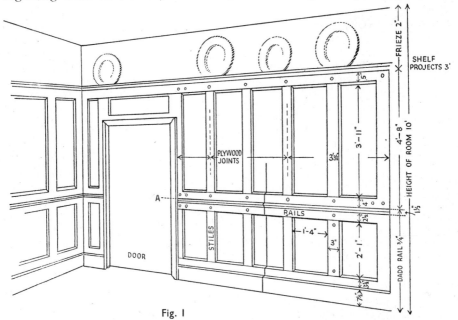

Fig. 1

dado lines $1\frac{1}{2}$ in. apart all round the room at a height of 3 ft. 4 in. from the top line A. Make a scale drawing of the setting out of the panels and skirting below the dado lines as it is better to make this part of the panelling first (and, if desired, leave it panelled to the dado rails only).

Consider carefully each plain stretch of wall and on the scale drawing, set out

countersinking and plugging with oak pegs). Then at the bottoms of these bore through with a $\frac{5}{16}$ in. twist-drill.

Now wedge the piece of skirting in place and with the $\frac{5}{16}$ in. drill bore just through so as to mark the positions of the holes on the wall. Take away the skirting and with the same $\frac{5}{16}$ in. twist-drill bore holes in the wall 1 in. deep.

Make some soft wood plugs, round

them carefully to a tight fit, hammer them in and saw off level with the wall.

Put the skirting again in place and screw up.

Make some 13 in. lengths of oak dowels $\frac{5}{16}$ in. diameter, glue and hammer them in, carefully saw them off and file level. These pegs hide the screws.

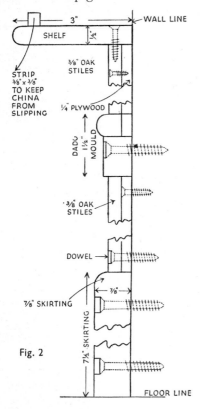

Fig. 2

Finish this skirting all round the room first, then plane up sufficient strips of oak—some 3½ in. wide and some 2½ in. wide—all these pieces are ⅜ in. thick only.

Now plane and mould the necessary lengths of dado moulding and fix this all round the room as before described and plug up the screw-heads. Next, mark the position of the rails (horizontal) and stiles (vertical) on the wall.

Fixing the Plywood.—Everything

is ready now for fixing the oak-faced ¼ in. plywood. This is fitted close up under the dado moulding and on to the skirting.

Cut the plywood up (the grain must be the long way of the panels) so that the joins come behind the stiles as shown, and all screws that fix the plywood to the wall must be countersunk flush with the face of it, in positions behind the rails and stiles. Then screw up the plywood.

Saw off the two end stiles, size 2 ft. 7 in. × 3 × ⅜ in. fix them tightly in the clear. Then bore them as described and screw them right through into the wall as shown, and plug up.

Now screw on the top and bottom rails in the same way and finally the 2 ft. 1 in. × 3 × ⅜ in. stiles.

This completes one length of panelling below the dado moulding.

Work round the room in the same way, and then proceed with the panelling above the dado. First carefully measure down from the ceiling 2 ft., draw the line all round for the frieze then draw another line ½ in. above the first line (the ½ in. is taken out of the frieze which is actually 1 ft. 11½ in.).

Now fix and screw the two end stiles as before, then the top and bottom rails. Fix the plywood on the walls and finally the shorter stiles.

Cut out the required lengths of shelf 3 × ½ in. thick, then tack on a strip of wood ⅜ × ⅜ in., about ½ in. from the front of the shelf, clean up the shelf and pin the strip on with 1 in. panel pins. Before fixing this, hammer in the pins so that their points almost come through the underside of the shelf.

The panelling shown is for a room, size 15 ft. × 10 ft. 2 in. × 10 ft. high. The measurements may be increased or modified in the case of a larger or smaller room.

The general practice is to take one-third of the total height for the dado rail, and measuring down from the ceiling, take a little less than one-third of the wall space left, this determines the width of the frieze. Regarding the panels: do not make them much larger (to save work) or they will be out of proportion to the size of a room as shown in the illustration.

Large panels make a small room look smaller still.

It is not advisable to use birch plywood; this wood does not take stain well.

Woods and Finishes.—As an alternative to oak-faced plywood, Columbian pine might prove cheaper. It has a beautiful grain and looks well if only wax polished. French polish or linseed oil turn it yellow.

For finishing the oak-faced plywood two methods are suggested.

1. Leave it a natural colour.
2. Polish with turpentine and wax only.

Should a darker effect be required, stain it with vandyke brown powder and .880 liquid ammonia (mixed 50-50) and thinned out with water to the required colour. Then polish with beeswax and turpentine.

CONVERTING A WINDOW INTO A DOORWAY

WHEN it is desired to convert an existing window into a doorway, it saves time to have the new doorframe and door made ready to fix as soon as the opening has been cut and finished.

The general construction of a sliding type of window is shown in the sectional drawings in Fig. 1, elevation Fig. 2, and end sectional elevation Fig. 3. The first thing to do is to remove the moulding A from all round the window, then the piece B and the shelf.

To Remove the Sashes, take out the beading c from all round and pull the sash forward; cut or unnail the end of the cord and let the weight drop. Follow on by taking out the centre strip of beading, D. This will allow the other sash to be pulled out and cut free as with the first one.

The remaining woodwork to be removed consists of a hollow box frame containing the weights. This is made up of the parts marked E, F, G, fixed to the lining board H. In some the bare frame, E, F, G, may now be prised loose and cleared away with assistance from the other side.

Removing Brickwork. — Before knocking away any brickwork, mark

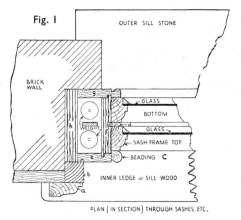

Fig. I

OUTER SILL STONE

BRICK WALL

GLASS

BOTTOM

GLASS

SASH FRAME TOP

BEADING c

INNER LEDGE or SILL WOOD

PLAN (IN SECTION) THROUGH SASHES ETC.,

out the size of the proposed opening on the plaster inside the room and then cut through the plaster to the brick surface, using a hammer and sharp cold chisel. This will lessen the spread of cracks when the adjoining bricks are being knocked out. Remove all plaster from the area of the opening.

Some of the brickwork beyond the area of the opening must be removed round the ends of the sill before it can be taken out. The edges of the cutting will be in steps as indicated in Fig. 4, as only the nearest full-length or half-brick is removed. These notches are made good afterwards with pieces of

If there is any timber spanning the opening across the top of the window under the brick arch, it should be left in place and the door-frame and door arranged accordingly. But if it is only a plain opening, a lintel must be fitted. Cut the brickwork back for a distance equal to half a brick and insert a length of stout timber so that the end of the

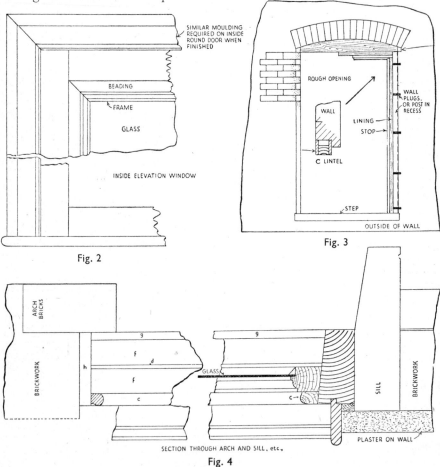

Fig. 2

Fig. 3

Fig. 4

brick which have been removed from the opening, and cemented in with a mortar consisting of three parts of clean sand and one part of portland cement mixed with water.

wood rests in the space on each side of the opening.

The timberwork required will depend upon the shape of the wall in plan. Some openings have a step back, or increase in size on the inside and this space can be used to take a door-post.

When the opening is the same width all through, fix wooden plugs into the side joints between the bricks and nail a lining board to these on each side with a piece of the same width to span the top. In both types, a strip of planed batten for a stop is fixed all round at a distance to suit the thickness of the door, whether the door is required to open outwards or inwards.

To complete the framework, an architrave moulding is fixed on the inside of the opening, while the joints between the door-posts and brickwork are filled with neat portland cement.

If it is not intended to make or buy a new door, a second-hand one can often be obtained at a reasonable price from a local dealer.

FITTING A TRAP-DOOR FOR A CEILING

MANY modern houses are not provided with an entrance to the loft or roof-space. If the householder wishes to make use of this space, the provision of a trap-door entrance can be effected cheaply and efficiently. The following points should be considered before beginning work:

The making and fitting of a trap-door necessitates the cutting away of certain ceiling joists, and it is essential to choose a position where the removal of part of the joist or joists will not decrease the ultimate strength of the ceiling to any appreciable extent. Another point is that however well a trap-door may be fitted it does not help the appearance of a room. For this reason the bathroom or passage ceiling might be used. If the choice rests between the two, select the latter as the ceiling of a passage is well supported by the walls on either side.

Before the joists can be cut it will be necessary to remove part of the lath and plaster ceiling and, as this is a messy job, the floor should be protected with dust sheets. Its covering can be taken up and removed for the time being.

The first thing to do is to pencil guide-lines on the ceiling indicating the size of the opening, bearing in mind that the aperture should be large enough to enable trunks, pieces of furniture and odd lumber to pass through. It may be that the joists are arranged as shown in Fig. 1, in which case it would be possible to obtain an aperture 2 ft. 6 in. wide and nearly 3 ft. in length by sawing through and removing the piece of the centre joist indicated by A in the illustration.

Finding the Joists.—Before actually marking the position, however, it is necessary to locate the centre joist and the inner faces of the two outer ones, B and C. This can be done by tapping the centre of the ceiling with a light hammer. The ceiling will sound hollow except at the position of the joist. When the centre joist has been located, insert the blade of a bradawl to find the edge and from this point measure a distance of about 16 in. Insert the bradawl again to find the inner face of B and repeat the operation for locating C. Measure equal distances from each wall to give the width and draw guide lines parallel to the wall. Along these lines make a series of bradawl holes about $\frac{1}{2}$ in. apart, as shown in Fig. 2. Then insert the blade of a pad saw near the inner face of one of the outer joists and cut through the laths and plaster, using the edge of the joist as a guide for the blade. Do the same at the other joist and with an old wood chisel sever the plaster between the holes made by the bradawl. If this is done carefully the surrounding plaster will not be damaged, so eliminating extensive making-good. The unwanted laths and plaster can then be removed. A dustpan held near the ceiling will catch loose material.

Now cut the centre joist. Squared guide lines should be marked at the correct position prior to the cutting, as this joist must not be sawn irregularly.

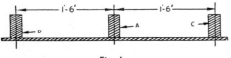

Fig. I

Lining the Opening.—The aperture is now ready to receive the lining, Fig. 3, that surrounds the space and supports the trap-door. This is really a shallow box minus a bottom, and can be made from planed deal 4 in. wide and ¾ in. thick. Screw the sides and ends together and brace the ends by fastening pieces of thin batten diagonally across those members to keep it square. Then screw the lining to the joists after boring the necessary clearing holes in the box to take the screws. The bottom edge of the lining must be flush with the underside of the laths.

As it is essential that the frame be quite square, it may be necessary to place thin slips of wood between the joists and the outer faces of the frame. Strips of wood 1½ in. wide and about ½ in. thick are then bradded to the wide faces of the lining to form a ledge upon which the trap-door rests. The top edge of the strips should be 1 in. below the top edge of the lining.

Making the Trap.—The length and width of the trap-door can now be ascertained from the fixed lining. The finished size should be ⅛ in. smaller in length and width than the lining to allow for play.

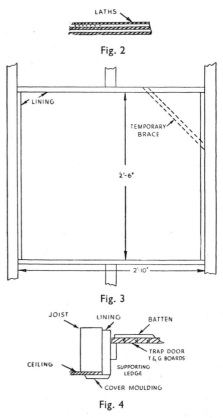

Fig. 2

Fig. 3

Fig. 4

The trap-door can be made from planed tongued and grooved boards fixed together by means of a couple of battens at the back. The thickness of the boards should not be less than ½ in. while the battens should be at least 3 in. wide and ¾ in. in thickness. Use screws for fixing rather than nails.

There remains to cut and fix the cover moulding to hide the joint between the ceiling and the bottom of the lining. This can be either a plain or ornamental moulding, according to taste. Plain moulding with bevelled edges looks well and conforms to modern decoration. In both cases the ends must be accurately mitred. Fig. 4 shows details of the arrangement. This completes the constructional work.

As the trap-door should be as inconspicuous as possible, it should be painted to match the ceiling, after having treated all knots with knotting and given it a couple of suitable undercoats.

CONVERTING THE LOFT INTO A SERVICEABLE ROOM

IN many houses there is a loft under the roof, empty except for a water tank in one corner. This space may be turned into a useful room for many purposes—a study, radio den or workshop. Heavy work is, of course, out of the question. It must be remembered that the joists are only intended to carry the ceiling of the rooms below, and if boards are put down above, much walking about and general use might cause the ceiling to crack or fall.

Floor Support.—The safest method is to add extra joists alongside the existing ones to span the space between the walls and to rest on the same wall plates. These new joists should not be fixed in any way to the old ones and must be at least 1 in. greater in depth than the others, so that, when the floor boards are fixed to them, the floor will be supported clear of the existing joists and no unreasonable weight will come on them.

Advantage should be taken of any existing uprights or struts of the roof members to fix a light partition across to make the end walls. The same series of uprights can perhaps be used for the foundation, or line, of the side walls, thus enclosing a space in the centre of the span for the proposed room.

The construction of the roof members and the distance spanned will be different in various houses, so each case must be dealt with on its merits.

Use Existing Features.—Make as much use as possible of existing constructional features, so when there are no vertical posts at intervals along the length these must be added and it may be possible to fix the top ends to the side of the slanting rafters that run from the roof ridge to the wall plates, while the bottom ends rest on the new joists. When the roof members do not come over or near enough to allow the posts to be fixed to the new joists below, a sill piece or plate should be fixed across at right-angles to the run of joists as in Fig. 3 and the posts attached to this, so that any weight or strain is distributed over all the joists.

If the horizontal members spanning the rafters are too high, suitable timbers can soon be fixed across at a height to give support to the ceiling boards and also allow adequate head room. This arrangement forms a normal rectangular room, but as extra head room is sometimes wanted, it may be better in some cases to have the ceiling boards fixed to the bottom edge of the existing collar beam right down the centre and to include part of the slope in the ceiling as indicated in Fig. 2. The side walls are then carried on a suitable framework set up to cut off the lower parts of the slope, which are useless if included in the room, unless a built-in cupboard can be arranged.

The Entrance Hatch.—When planning the floor the hatchway must be taken into consideration as the entrance,

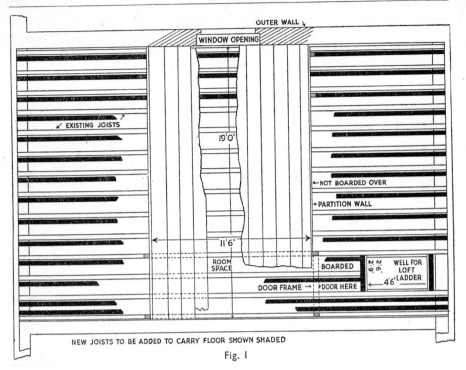

OUTER WALL

WINDOW OPENING

EXISTING JOISTS

19'0"

NOT BOARDED OVER

PARTITION WALL

11'6"

ROOM SPACE

BOARDED

WELL FOR LOFT LADDER

2'6"

4'6"

DOOR FRAME → DOOR HERE

NEW JOISTS TO BE ADDED TO CARRY FLOOR SHOWN SHADED

Fig. I

and this should not come inside the room. It is best to have a floored passage or landing as indicated in the plan, Fig. 1, with the door of the room a little distance away so that one does not step out of the room into the hatchway. The latter is also better railed round with a hinged bar across the opening.

The size of opening should be such that the entrance and exit is safe and comfortable, without the usual scramble. There is also the question of getting material such as wall boards up into the room. The stock sizes of ceiling and wall boards are either 3 ft. or 4 ft. wide, and it must be remembered that the smaller the boards the more joints there will be, and also more battens to be fixed behind to carry the edges and provide something to which to nail them along all joints, even though two edges can be fixed on the width of one

run of batten, as shown in Fig. 4.

Having gained some idea of the size of the room, the overall length should be compared with the widths of standard sheets to see how many will be required, and it is as well to give some thought here to the finish and decoration of the room. A panel arrangement of walls and ceiling is effective, or they can be painted, distempered, or papered. As planed battens are used to cover the joints between the sheets in a panelled room, and too many joints will spoil the effect, large sheets will be required to run the width standing on the floor and the length extending up the wall and across the ceiling in 3 or 4 ft. bays. The wall sheets are fixed first and the ceiling last, the meeting joint all round being covered with a wooden beading. Alternatively the ceiling and the top part of the walls can be papered with white lining paper to make a surround above the picture rail and whitewashed as in other rooms.

Wall Boards.—For cladding walls and ceiling, the most inexpensive material is Building Board. This is a manufactured board in sheets of two main kinds, fibre board and plaster board.

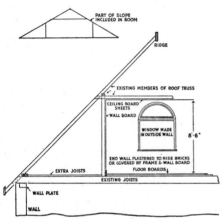

Fig. 2

Fibre board consists of a mixture of wood pulp and is compressed into solid sheets of stock sizes ranging from 3 to 4 ft. wide ×6 to 16 ft. long, and in thickness from $\frac{3}{16}$ to $\frac{1}{4}$ in.

Plaster boards under various trade names incorporate plaster compressed between sheets of fibre and pulp. They have the advantage of being fire- and vermin-proof and they insulate against heat, cold and noise. They take any kind of finish and are obtained in stock sizes and thicknesses up to $\frac{3}{8}$ in.

The best way to estimate quantities is to measure the size of the room and make a rough plan as in Fig. 5. On this can be marked the widths of the sheets in 4 or 3 ft. spaces along the walls. Also mark the lines across for the ceiling which will give the sizes of the pieces and also the lines of the battens for the panelling. The number of sheets of each size can be found

from this. Dividing the total area of wall and ceiling surface by the area of one sheet does not indicate how they must be cut.

The odd 6 in. in the wall height can be made up by fixing a skirting board along the wall and standing the bottom edge of the sheet on this, see Fig. 4. The door and window opening have not been deducted as the sheets are cut to fit round.

If help cannot be obtained when fixing the ceiling, some form of prop, as shown at A in Fig. 3, will be useful to hold the sheet in position while it is nailed. The nails should be galvanised and have large flat heads. These are obtainable from the firm supplying the sheets.

A fine tenon saw is the best cutting tool as it does not tear the edges. Plaster boards are hard on the cutting edge of the saw so do not use your best.

Fixing Wall Boards.—The sheet to be cut should be placed on the floor with lengths of batten underneath to support it in two or three places; one

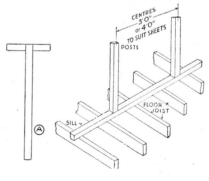

Fig. 3

length being just under and alongside the cutting mark to support that part while being cut.

Commence nailing at the middle and work outwards towards the corners, spacing the nails about 12 to 16 in. apart in the middle of the sheet and about ⅜ in. in from the edges and spaced here about 6 to 8 in. apart.

With fibre board, it is usual to leave a gap of about ⅛ in. between the edges of the sheets to allow for natural expansion, but with plaster boards the joints are butted together. Cross supports or battens are fixed behind to provide firm nailing surfaces for all four edges, the batten being wide enough to serve for two edges; 2×2 in. timber would be suitable.

Against a brick wall the batten framework can be made of timber ⅞ in. thick × 2 in. wide nailed to wall plugs. Packing pieces may be required to ensure a vertical wall.

Filling the Joints. —Flush joints are obtained by filling the cracks with composition cement used in a plastic state, working it well into the joints and finishing flush with a paperhanger's scraper. Rolls of fabric strip 2 in. wide are also supplied for sticking over the joints. As it is fixed from top to bottom, draw the scraper downwards with enough pressure to free it from wrinkles and bring the plastic filling through into the fabric strip, scraping off the surplus.

All nail holes should be filled in with plaster and the places brushed over with shellac. Sizing is not usually necessary with fibre boards. Plaster boards must be sized or primed with a mixture of size, varnish and paint of the desired colour. For distempered surfaces or wallpapers on plaster boards it will be found more satisfactory to use varnish size first.

It is well worth the extra trouble to have a window made in the end wall. For artificial light, electricity is most convenient. The cable can run to convenient points outside the room for both wall and ceiling and only the leads for switches and points brought through, so that no wiring shows in the room. A light should be provided over the hatchway, and for greater convenience the light should be arranged

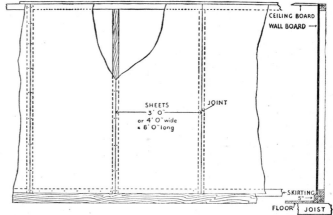

Fig. 4

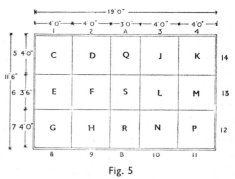

Fig. 5

for switching on and off from the top and bottom of the steps.

Water Cisterns often make a lot of noise when filling and can be silenced by means of a length of tube fixed to the valve and extending to the bottom of the tank.

LAYING A NEW FLOOR

HAVING stripped the floor of all old woodwork, go over the whole of the exposed walls, including the sleeper walls, with a blow-lamp as this is the only means of destroying possible spores of dry rot. At the same time look at the air bricks, the perforated bricks or iron grids placed in the outer walls, just below the floor level. These air bricks may be blocked up. Fresh air is necessary if floors are to be kept in good condition.

Now measure up for the new material. The wall plates upon which the joists are fixed are generally of 4×2 in. deal laid in a mortar composed of cement and sand, with a layer of special damp-course bitumen felt between the sleeper walls and the cement.

This prevents damp from creeping up the brickwork and reaching the timber. Fig. 1 shows the general arrangement of the floor.

Materials.—If the floor measures say 14 ft. by 13 ft. giving an area of approximately 182 sq. ft., order two squares (100 sq. ft. = 1 sq. super) because it is usual on such jobs to add 10 per cent. for waste in sawing and the reduction in width of the boards due to the machining of tongues and grooves. The boards should be of the same thickness as that of the original ones, which are generally ⅞ or ¾ in. finished, the difference of ⅛ in. being the waste due to planing.

The wall plates (4×2 in.) should be purchased in single lengths a trifle over the finished size, and this applies also to the joists which are generally of the same section. Several pieces of skirting will also be found necessary.

If it is necessary to make a joint in the joist, the ends to be formed should be scarfed, and fixed in such a position that the joint is supported by the wall plate, as illustrated in Fig. 2.

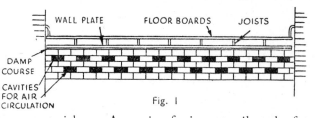

Fig. 1

A supply of 4 in. cut nails and a few pounds of 2 in. floor brads will be wanted for fixing the joists to the plates and the floor-boards to the joists respectively. In addition, a quantity of portland cement and clean sand will be needed for bedding the plates. Finally, half a gallon of creosote should be obtained for treating the whole of the joists, plates and the undersides of the floor-boards and back of the skirting before they are fixed.

Creosote is an excellent preservative and should never be omitted.

Wall Plates and Damp Course.— Fix the wall plates by stretching and fixing a couple of lines between the walls to indicate the height of the top faces of the plates.

Mix a quantity of cement mortar in the proportion of one of cement and three of sand. Then add water from time to time and mix again so that the whole forms a plastic mass.

Place the bitumen felt in position on the sleeper wall and put a layer of mortar on top, using a bricklayer's trowel for the purpose. Now place the plate in position and tap it down with the handle of a trowel until the top face coincides with the lines. Proceed in this way until all the plates have been bedded in.

The plates should be cut a trifle under size, say about 1 in. less at each end, as the ends must not be allowed to touch any brickwork.

The mortar must now be allowed to set hard. Then the fixing of the joists can be done. Mark the position of these on the top of the plates and fix the joists with 4 in. nails driven in from the sides —one at each side.

Laying the Boards.—Fix the floor

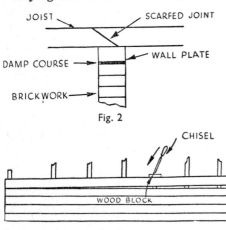

Fig. 2

Fig. 3

boards in the following way: start at one end or a side of the room, as the case may be, and fix the first board, tongue towards the wall, but not touching it. Follow on with the next board, inserting the tongue into the groove of the first, and nail this down at the back edges only and proceed in a like manner until all the floor boards are in position. The remainder of the nails can then be driven in the front edges to complete. Take care to drive the nails in the centre of the joists and in line. Do not allow the hammer to bruise the work. If difficulty is experienced in fitting the tongues into the grooves, persuade them

with a hammer; but insert an odd piece of tongued board to take the blows to prevent damage to the edges.

It is essential that boards should fit tightly at the outset as they will shrink in time and leave unsightly edges.

Fig. 4

No difficulty should be experienced in fixing the boards, but it sometimes happens that one is not quite straight, causing trouble in getting the tongue to fit in the groove at the opposite end. To overcome this defect, insert the tongue into the groove at one end and nail the board down at this point. Then prise the board into position by using a chisel driven into the joists as indicated in Fig. 3, as fixing proceeds. A wooden block must first be inserted between the blade of the chisel and the edge of the board to prevent damage to the latter.

Do not let the last board touch the wall. Go over the whole floor and punch the nail-heads down below the surface.

Skirting.—Now fix the skirting-board. Plug the walls at intervals of about 2 ft. by scraping out the mortar of the vertical joints between the brick-work to a depth of about 3 in., cut a number of wedge-shaped plugs and drive them between the prepared joints, as indicated in Fig. 4. Mark the top edge of the skirting indicating the position of the fixings and fix the board with 2 in. cut nails, using the marks as a guide. Punch the nail-heads completely below the surface.

This completes the woodwork. If the skirting is to be painted or enamelled glass-paper the surface with a medium grade paper and follow with a finer grade, remove the dust and treat the knots with patent knotting. Then give the wood a priming coat of paint consisting of red lead, turpentine and a little linseed oil. When dry, rub the surface with fine glass-paper and give it an undercoat of flat paint of the same tint as that of the rest of the paintwork. Allow it to dry and surface this coat with glass-paper as before, remove the dust and apply the finishing coat.

If the floorboards are to be entirely covered with lino or carpet there will be no need to fill in the nail holes, but if the surround is to be stained and varnished, fill in the holes with plastic wood and, when dry, rub the surface level with glass-paper before applying the finishing medium.

HOW TO DEAL WITH DEFECTIVE CEILINGS

ISOLATED cracks in ceilings, generally due to settlements in the joists, can be made good when the room is being redecorated, and small patches may be cut out and re-plastered provided the surrounding ceiling is firm.

Treatment of Cracks.—Essential tools are a small pointed trowel, scraping knife as used in paper-hanging, any convenient brush for damping, and a small home-made float as shown in Fig. 1. If a smoothing trowel is available, the metal blade will produce a smoother surface than the wooden one. Another square of wood with a handle grip underneath is useful for holding a supply of plaster while working. Keene's cement is the usual material for repairs. This substance, obtainable in small quantities, should be stored in an air-tight tin in a dry place.

Small cracks do not require cutting out. Scrape away loose fragments and wet with clean water, brushing well into the crack. Then work new cement into place, strike off the surplus and smooth off with the float.

Large cracks need cutting out. First mark parallel lines on each side of the crack and about ⅜ in. away, following the course of the crack as in Fig. 2.

Use a length of wood placed along one of the pencil lines as a guide. Begin by scraping along it with the point of the scraper, or by using a sharp chisel or knife. Scraping the lines fairly deep prevents the crack from spreading outwards, gives a neat edge and only a narrow slit on the surface if the tool is

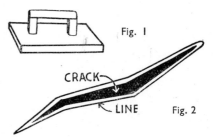

Fig. 1

CRACK LINE Fig. 2

held to cut under the surface and remove plaster from the back without enlarging the width. A few taps may be necessary to sink the blade through the plaster.

Clear away all loose pieces sticking between the laths. Wet the crack thoroughly and allow the water to reach all the inner surfaces. This is repeated at intervals during the work and should not be neglected, or the existing plaster will draw all the moisture from the new before it has time to set hard.

A clean biscuit-tin lid, a sheet of metal or a flat board for mixing are better than a small bowl as it is easier to scrape all the powder from the outside to the middle where the water is poured.

Work the mixture well into a smooth and fairly wet state.

A quantity is taken on the board and pressed, a little at a time, into the open slot, using the point of the trowel to work it well to the back. After a certain amount has been placed in this manner the work is again wetted and another layer added, until the slot is filled. Finish off smooth by the alternate use of a wet brush and a float.

Larger patches are treated in a similar manner by building up round the edge of the cleaned space and working to the centre, getting the plaster well behind the laths all the time.

Ceiling Falls.—When the fall is a large one, test the surrounding ceiling by pressing gently against it with the open hands. Any movement up or down will indicate how much plaster has left its support. Sometimes a large area will sag without falling, and will remain in this uncertain state until an extra shock sends it crashing down. A ceiling in this condition is a menace and should be dealt with at once. The best and cheapest way, especially if the house is near main road or rail traffic, will be to clear the room, cover the floor and strip off all the plaster and laths ready for fixing ceiling board. Take care round lighting fixtures. Withdraw all nails and make good the wall plaster up beyond the old ceiling level and clear all rubbish away before starting repair work.

Covering With Builder's Boards. —Measure the ceiling for width and length and make a rough sketch on the lines of Fig. 3.

The choice of material rests between fibre board and plaster board. The first is a mixture of wood pulp and fibre compressed into sheets 3 or 4 ft. wide ×6 to 16 ft. long, $\frac{3}{16}$ (4 ply) or $\frac{1}{4}$ in. (5 ply) in thickness. The second incorporates plaster compressed between sheets of wood pulp. Standard sheets are as for fibre boards, but the thickness is $\frac{3}{8}$ in. Both kinds are easy to saw and may be nailed or screwed in position. It is advisable not to use asbestos sheets as this material is hard to saw by hand, and unless very carefully handled and drilled breaks and cracks.

On the rough plan, mark off widths of 3 ft., either across the room or from end to end. A 6 ft. length is about the largest for easy handling, so find where the ends of such sheets will come in relation to the joists. One joist can carry the meeting edges of two sheets. It may be more economical to use sheets 4 ft. wide, but with a plain ceiling to be papered before whitewashing, any odd cutting and fitting will not matter.

A panel effect entails extra care in selecting the size of sheets and the run of the battens.

Fig. 3 is a plan of a typical ceiling area to be covered. After measuring, it was found that the best sheet would be 4×6 ft. The actual list was as follows, although a certain amount of sizing and fitting was necessary afterwards to allow for walls being out of the square in places.

3 ft. 9 in.×5 ft. 9 in. long ..	4 pieces
3 ft. 9 in.×6 ft. long ..	2 ,,
4×4 ft. 7 in. long	1 piece
4×5 ft. 9 in. long	1 ,,
4×6 ft. long	1 ,,

Battens to hide the joints may be $\frac{1}{4}$ in. thick and 1×2 in. wide. They should not be out of proportion to the size of panels. Suggested sizes are: 1×$\frac{1}{4}$ in., 1$\frac{1}{4}$×$\frac{1}{4}$ in., 1$\frac{3}{8}$×$\frac{3}{8}$ in., 1$\frac{1}{2}$×$\frac{1}{2}$ in., 1$\frac{1}{2}$×$\frac{3}{8}$ in., 1$\frac{3}{4}$×$\frac{3}{8}$ in., 2×$\frac{1}{2}$ in.

At the crossing of the battens they may be halved or if well fitted and secured the ends may butt against the piece at right-angles. It will depend upon the size of the room which way the longest runs are placed to avoid more cutting.

The sheets are best placed on the floor for cutting, with a length of batten underneath in line with the cutting mark so that this edge is well supported. One or two pieces of the same thickness underneath will keep the sheet level. A fine-toothed saw will leave the cleanest edge, but plaster board dulls the teeth.

Galvanised $1\frac{1}{4}$ in. oval brads or French nails spaced about 12 to 16 in. apart in the middle of the board and about $\frac{3}{8}$ in. in from the edges and 6 to 8 in. apart will secure the boards to the joists. Fibre boards are fixed with a gap of about $\frac{1}{4}$ in. between adjacent edges as illustrated in Fig. 4 to allow for expansion, but plaster boards may be butted together.

Commence covering the ceiling from one corner, nail at the middle of the board and work outwards towards the corners.

Joints between plaster boards may be filled with plastic cement. Over this is placed a strip of fabric about 2 in. wide. This is pressed down firmly and evenly by drawing the scraping blade downwards with enough pressure to bring the cement through the mesh.

Fibre boards may be finished with any kind of wall paint, distemper or enamel. All nail heads are covered with plaster-of-paris and brushed over with shellac.

Varnish size is required on plaster boards before distempering.

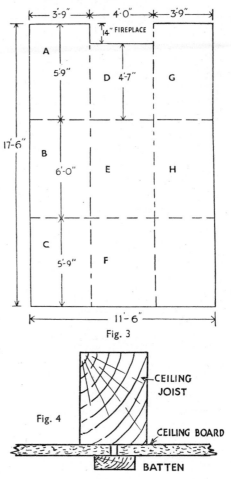

Fig. 3

Fig. 4

CEILING JOIST

CEILING BOARD

BATTEN

MAKING A SERVING HATCH BETWEEN THE DINING ROOM AND KITCHEN

WHERE the dining-room adjoins the kitchen, meals may be prepared and served more easily and quickly if a serving hatch is made in the dividing wall, illustrated in Figs. 1 and 2. These show the hatch viewed from the kitchen and dining-room respectively.

The partition wall, being on the ground floor and perhaps near a fireplace on the kitchen side, is likely to be of brickwork at least $4\frac{1}{2}$ in. thick. Some partitions may be of coke breeze blocks about 4 in. thick. The cutting of the opening and the making and fitting of the timber framework shown in Fig. 3 will be practically the same for either.

Wall Construction.—Walls dividing the upper floor rooms may be of lighter construction, such as lath and

Fig. I

plaster on a timber framework, with or without bracing members. This construction is therefore to be expected in a large house converted into flats.

The room diagram shown in Fig. 4 shows the convenience of making the hatch, and is characteristic of many cases. A cooker and hot-water boiler are installed near the table, sink and the hatch through which meals are to be passed. An opening measuring about 2 ft. 3 in. high and a couple of feet wide will be wide enough to take a large tray.

The kitchen side of the hatch is fitted with a cupboard, the top of which forms a table. This cupboard could be substituted by a drop-flap table, which, when not in use, is let down and the supporting brackets folded back behind.

Flap Tables.—A drop-flap table in

hardwood similar to that suggested for the kitchen could be fixed directly under the hatch, or a low sideboard could be placed there, the top to come just below the sill of the hatch. In the latter case, moulding to match the sideboard should be used round the opening.

If a drop-flap table is used, the top should be about 3 ft. from the floor, and as the sill to which the shelf part of the hatch is fitted is 2 in. thick it will be necessary to mark the wall 2 ft. 9 in. up from the floor for the bottom of the sill.

The lintel over the top of the opening is 3 in. thick, and the top edge of this, 2 ft. 7 in. above the 2 ft. 9 in. mark, or 5 ft. 4 in. from the floor.

The opening in the brickwork should be a trifle over 2 ft. 5 in. wide and 2 ft. 7 in. high, with recesses cut back at each end 2¼ in. deep into the wall to house the ends of the lintel and sill, as indicated in Fig. 3.

The frame members, Fig. 3, should

Fig. 2

be prepared ready for fixing. The overall size of this is 2 ft. 5 in. wide × 2 ft. 2 in. high, made of yellow deal 5¼ in. wide, which is the approximate thickness of the wall, plus the plaster on each side.

The ends of the horizontal members of this frame should be trenched or grooved to house the grooved ends of the vertical pieces. The grooves should be $\frac{1}{2}$ in. deep and $\frac{1}{4}$ in. wide and the tongues on the side members of the same size.

When the brickwork has been cut away, the lintel should be fixed first to take the weight of the walling.

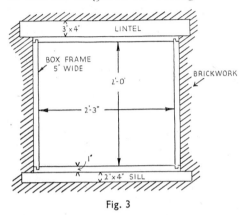

Fig. 3

Cutting the Opening. — Measure and mark out the full size of the aperture and remove the bricks with a hammer and sharp cold chisel.

Cut the lintel, which need not be planed, to length, and fit the ends into the recesses in the brickwork. Do the same with the rough sill.

Now fix the box lining. This is fastened to the lintel and sill with $2\frac{1}{2}$ in. No. 10 wood screws, countersunk below the surface.

As it is unlikely that the box will fit exactly between lintel and sill, thin strips of wood should be inserted between these members to make a tight fit. To keep the box lining square, it is advisable temporarily to brace the corners with thin diagonal battens.

If the edges of the fitment project beyond the surrounding plaster, the amount of projection should be marked, the box removed and planed down to the marks.

Damage to Brickwork.—Any gaps between the sides and brickwork should now be filled in with portland cement mortar in the proportion of three of sand to one of cement. Fill the space so that it is within $\frac{3}{4}$ in. of the face of the plaster. Damp the bricks before applying the mortar. Now nail a couple of thin strips of wood along the outside faces of the lintel and sill to form a key for the new plaster and then mix sufficient Keene's cement for facing purposes. Before applying the plaster, moisten the surrounding plaster, mortar and woodwork.

The Door. — There are several methods of fitting the door. One is to hinge it from the kitchen side so that the door is flush with the edges of the box lining. Another way is to have a sliding door moving in vertical runners, as in Fig. 1.

The hinged door may consist of a single piece of plywood $\frac{3}{4}$ in. thick. Strips of deal 1 in. wide and $\frac{3}{8}$ in.

Fig. 4

thick should be fixed all round the inner faces of the box lining, $\frac{3}{4}$ in. away from the edge on the kitchen side.

Brass butt-hinges may be used and a suitable button screwed to the opposite edge of the box frame to keep the door shut. A hardwood handle, or a small metal knob should be fixed near the closing edge of the door.

The corners of the finishing moulding on the dining-room side should be mitred and the edge of the shelf faced with a piece of 1 × 1 in. hardwood with rounded edges. The ends of this piece extend about a couple of inches beyond the outer edges of the moulding.

ENCLOSING THE BATH

THE usual cast-iron, silicate enamelled bath with the curled edge is not very attractive in appearance. The bathroom can be considerably improved by enclosing the bath as shown in Fig. 1, where a panelled surround and a neat top edge make it a more pleasing part of the bathroom furniture.

Since the bath is usually placed beside a wall, the panelling need only be on the side and the two ends, and can be attached to the wall at the back. As baths vary in size, not only in length but also in width and depth, specimen measurements only can be given on the drawings.

Figs. 1 and 2 show the completed job. The side is in two panels and the ends have a panel each. The top fits under the overlapped edge of the bath so that the rounded edge of the bath is above the surrounding rectangular frame. The drawing is to scale and is suitable for baths of the following measurements: 5 ft. 9 in. long, 2 ft. 4 in. wide at the widest part and 2 ft. wide at the tap and waste end, standing 21 in. from the floor to the underside of the turn-over edge.

The top board, shown in the plan view in Fig. 3 fits up around the bath and under the lip of the turn over top edges. It would best be made in two pieces of timber of $1\frac{1}{4}$ in. yellow deal nailed together with a batten at each end so as to make up a width of 2 ft. 7 in. and a length of 6 ft. which would allow $1\frac{1}{2}$ in. each side wider than the widest part of the bath and the same at each end. The dotted lines show the inside edge of the top board where they come near the bath sides.

Marking the Top Board.—The shape to be cut can be marked roughly by smearing the top edge of the bath with a black colouring medium and laying the top board on it.

If the bath is against a wall, the board should be placed close to it. When the board is lifted, the centre of the top curve will be marked on it, and, if roughly cut out with a pad saw 1 in. inside of this marking, we shall have two boards which will fit up around the bath. Let the battens be screwed to the boards and as near as they can be to the two ends of the bath below the turn-over top edge. These battens can be replaced when we come to fit it all up.

The Top Board in two halves, having been prepared and cut to shape, length and width, is placed around the bath and wedged up from the floor with four corner posts, $2\frac{1}{4}$ in. square; each post coming at such a position that its two outer faces (side and end of the bath) come within 1 in. (full) of the edge of the top board. These posts should be wedged in between the floor and the underside of the top board as tightly as possible. They should be fastened by screws driven in diagonally, from each side, into the floor at the bottom and up into the top board at the top. They must be tested with a plumb before finally screwing up. The corner posts at the back should be nailed to the wall (if the bath fits against the wall) and cut in at the bottom if there is a skirting board.

The top is now in position, Fig. 4, and the posts fixed. Incidentally these should have been painted with red lead before fixing and the top of the board should be nicely planed. At the joint between the two boards (indicated by the dotted lines in Fig. 3) the boards

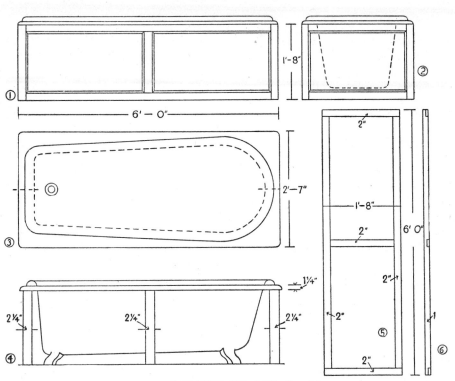

ENCLOSING THE BATH—Figs. 1-6

should have been clamped together with glue between them and the battens, previously described, nailed up from below. These battens should reach from the wall or back framing to within 1 in. (full) of the front edge of the board. Since the grain here is across the narrow dimensions of the timber of the top board, the value of the batten will be appreciated. A number of thick screws should be used, taking care that they do not come within $\frac{3}{16}$ in. of the top of the board.

Sides and Ends.—All is now ready to fit the side panel and the two end panels. These are made of framing of 1 × 2 in. timber which may be left rough at the back but planed on the front and sides. The framing is shown in Fig. 5. The front consists of two panels and the two ends a single one; the corners can be made by simply halving the two rails, top and bottom into the upright members. This is shown in the edge view in Fig. 6. The central member is 2 in. as are the ends, and the complete front panelling is of a length to just overlap the upright posts by 1 in. at each end. The end panels are made in the same way.

The width of these panels is made $\frac{1}{8}$ in. wider than the depth between the underside of the top board and the floor. The actual panels are let into the frames and butt against a beading at the back. They are made of $\frac{3}{16}$ in. plywood or $\frac{1}{4}$ in. sound yellow deal. The latter is more suitable. It need be planed only on the front surface and should fit the framing tight and bed against the $\frac{3}{8}$ in. beading $\frac{1}{4}$ in. wide, planted in at the back and be fixed by a round nose beading planted at the front. This panelling should be done before fitting the whole side and ends into place around the bath.

Then side and ends are fitted into place and nailed in with sunk-headed brads. The brads at the top should come an inch away from the corner on both sides so that, when all is fixed, the top edge of the top board and the corners at each end of the front can be rounded so that no sharp edges are anywhere able to hurt people.

The finish can be as desired. The most appropriate is perhaps a good painting with lead paint and rubbing down, then a coat of dead white also well rubbed down and finally a coat of the finest white enamel.

Panels can of course be of any other shade to match the decoration of the bathroom, but the top board and the framing will, whatever the room decoration, look best in white enamel. This will match the overturn of the bath edge which rises quite naturally from the flat top of the surround.

FIXING FLOOR AND WALL TILES

Preparation is necessary before covering a floor area with tiles, the amount depending upon the construction of the floor. If this is the usual boards on joists, the boards must be removed and the joist ends in the door way leading to the adjoining room trimmed and perhaps supported according to the direction in which they run. The space below will require making up to nearly the original floor level with concrete spread over the existing bed already in position over the floor area. The new concrete must be of such thickness that a layer of cement and the thickness of the tiles will bring the surface flush with the floor level in the adjoining room.

Thickness of Tiles.—In some houses the scullery has a concrete floor either a step down from the kitchen or one up from that floor. In the first case, the extra thickness of tile and the layer of cement in which they are bedded will not matter, but where the concrete floor is above that of the next room some thought must be given to the extra thickness of the proposed work. The labour of breaking up and removing the existing concrete cannot be undertaken,

so the best way is to roughen the surface to form a key for the cement, lay the tiles, and then—having found out how much thicker the new floor is—add a suitable thickness of board to the top surface of the step which, in most cases, will be of wood, so that it is all level, and then remove the door from its hinges and saw and plane off enough from the bottom to clear the new thickness of step, as indicated in Fig. 1, A and B.

The first step should be to measure the floor and make an outline sketch with the dimensions, and note how these dimensions run out in odd inches—for example, 10 ft. 9 in., 5 ft. 3 in. For a length of floor an odd 3 in., 6 or 9 in. over the feet measurements it would be as well to obtain tiles 6 in. square and some half tiles—i.e., 3 × 6 in.—as these can be put down in rows, as indicated in Fig. 2A without a lot of extra cutting to odd sizes.

When obtained, the tiles should be placed in water and left to soak until required for use.

Preparing Floor.—Apart from making the existing concrete surface rough to give the new work a grip, it is essential that it shall be level when finished, and if the area is of fair size it may not be easy to float large sections of the space with cement and keep it level. In any case, the tiles can only be put down in sections while the operator occupies part of the floor to kneel on.

A start should be made on the far side where no one will have to step in order to get to the sink or back door. For all cement mixing should be done outside on a board, and water will be required during the work.

The surface of the concrete can be roughened by means of a cold chisel and hammer. Sweep up all dust and chips and make one length of floor space wet, sufficient to take, say, four rows of tiles. Mix up enough cement to float over this space only, and to ensure a level foundation place a long strip of wood by the wall and another some distance out. If an inch thickness of cement is needed, then the wood should be 1 in. thick. Test these strips as they lay by means of a spirit level and, where necessary, insert a little packing under them to correct the level. A straight-edge board is required just long enough to span the two strips, Fig. 2B.

Spread the cement over the floor between the two wooden strips and level off as near as possible with a trowel. The straight-edge float is placed against the wall at the far end, held down on the wood strips and given a backwards and forwards motion. At the same time, advance it to move the surplus cement forward to fill the hollows, leaving a level surface behind.

Unless the tiles are arranged in regular fashion, they will look unsightly. Where a row is started with a whole tile, the next row must start with a half tile,

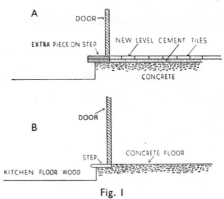

Fig. 1

as shown in Fig. 2A. Thus the joints in one row do not come in line with those in the next.

Before the tiles can be placed, the

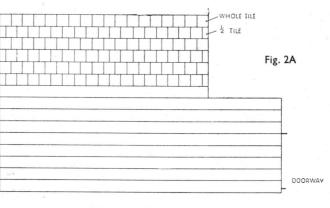

FLOOR TILES

wood strips are removed and the hollow spaces left carefully filled in with cement to the surrounding level.

The damp tiles are then placed in position one by one and each given a tap with the handle of the trowel to bed them firmly. Having completed one section, the next strip is prepared with the levelling strips in the same manner, care being taken to see that the edge of the new section is blended, and level, with the previous work.

Wall Tiles.—If a brick wall is to be covered, first rake out all the joints in

Fig. 2B

the brickwork and give the wall a coating of cement made of one part of sand to one part of cement. After smoothing this, brush it lightly with a stiff brush to form a key for the cement used to fix the tiles. Neat cement is required for this. Half tiles should be used to start alternate rows, as for the floor work.

Towards the top, the plain effect may be broken by using tile strips as shown in Fig. 3 in some contrasting colour to match the paintwork.

The straight-edge is also used from time to time to check the surface to see that there is no bulge in any part.

The surface of new tiles is often unsightly, having a white stain which cannot be removed by scrubbing. The usual treatment is to rub over well with linseed oil several times at intervals of a few days and to follow this with a good rubbing with a special kind of dark red

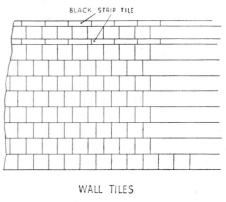

WALL TILES

Fig. 3

floor polish for tiles. This polish will soon clear the whiteness and should be used with the same frequency as ordinary floor polish.

HOW TO FIT A MODERN WASH BASIN

THE illustration appearing in Fig. 1 depicts a modern hand basin with chromium-plated taps, white porcelained brackets, chain and plug and an outlet cleaning trap, the cost of which would be about 45s., while the cost of the piping and pipe fittings will depend on the length of the runs which, from the economic as well as the practical point of view, should be kept as short as possible.

A grade of iron pipe known as steam barrel must be used for conveying the hot water, a thick lead pipe for the cold supply and a lead pipe for the waste.

Running the Pipes.—The diagram shown in Fig. 2 shows a method of connecting up the pipes. It will be seen that the new hot-water pipe is connected to the expansion pipe just above the hot-water cylinder; the pipe feeding the cold-water tap is joined to the cold-water supply main. The waste pipe is run under the floor-boards and discharges into the nearest hopper. This pipe should have a slight fall and be carried along or across the joists without sag, so that no water is allowed to remain in the pipe.

If the room to be fitted adjoins the

bathroom, the various connections can be made to pipes in that room.

Fix the brackets to the wall. The height of the top edge of the basin when fixed should not exceed about 3 ft., and care must be taken that the brackets are level both horizontally and vertically.

Plugging a Wall.—If the wall is of brick, plug it with long wooden fixings, taking care when making the plug holes not to hammer too vigorously or you may damage the wall, especially if it is one brick thick. The secret of success in plugging a wall is to use a small sharp cold chisel and to give the latter a number of light blows rather than a smaller number of heavy ones. Cut and remove the plaster where the hole is to be as this will prevent the plaster being damaged outside that area.

If the wall is of lath and plaster, it may be necessary to fix a couple of horizontal battens across at the back and secure them at the ends by stout screws driven into the vertical studs, as indicated in Fig. 3.

It will now be necessary to take up a

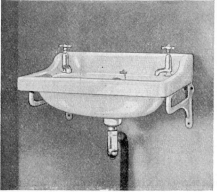

Fig. I

few floor-boards to conceal the pipes and to measure up the run to ascertain the lengths of the pipes and fittings required. Do not under estimate the amount of pipe required, but add on at least a foot to each length.

L

When ordering the material you should also hire a pipe vice and a stock and die of a diameter to suit the external diameter of the steam barrel. A hack saw and pipe grips will also be needed.

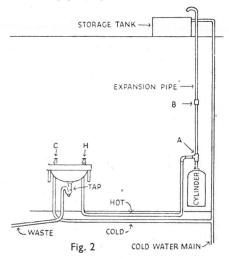

Fig. 2

Start the pipework by installing the hot-water service. The first thing to do is to cut off the hot-water supply either by turning off the cock generally to be found near the cold-water cistern in the loft space under the roof or by plugging the outlet orifice with a wooden plug. Then drain the pipes by turning on the hot-water taps. There is no need to cut off the cold water at this stage, but no fire must be lit under the boiler.

Joining Pipes.—With a hack saw or pipe cutter, sever the expansion pipe at a distance of about 9 in. above the top of the cylinder as a tee-piece is to be inserted here for joining the new pipe. Remove the longer piece of pipe by unscrewing it at the nearest joint, and then unscrew the shorter piece. Cut a thread on the severed end of the 9 in. length and screw on a tee-piece, as at A in Fig. 2.

To make the joints in the screwed barrel water-tight, apply a mixture of white and red lead, linseed oil and turpentine to the screwed threads. This compound should be of the consistency of thick cream and painted on with a brush. It is also necessary to wind on a few strands of hemp previously treated with the paint, round the bottom

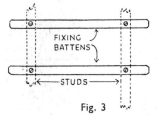

FIXING BATTENS

←——STUDS——→

Fig. 3

of the threads to ensure a permanent water-tight joint when screwed up.

At the upper end of the tee, screw in a short connecting piece or nipple and then reinsert the upper end of the longer pipe into its fitting, B in Fig. 2, to ascertain how much metal must be removed at the opposite end. Mark the pipe, remove it and saw off the waste. Cut a thread equal in length to that of a connector, plus the thickness of a lock nut, run these fittings on the thread, lock nut first, connector last, and screw the pipe in position at the top, not forgetting to apply the paint and hemp. Screw the connector over the nipple and then tighten the lock nut, again using paint and hemp at the bottom of the threads. Details of the connection are shown in Fig. 4. Fit the rest of the water pipe and then connect the end to the tap.

Now install the cold water and the waste pipes. Get a plumber to make the connection unless you know how to make wiped joints in lead pipes, a process demanding great skill. This operation will, of course, necessitate shutting off the cold-water supply at the main and draining the pipes by opening the taps.

Waste Discharge.—If the hopper into which the waste pipe is to discharge is some distance away, do not run the pipe outside the wall of the house as

frost is likely to block the pipe. Run it underneath the floor-boards as far as possible and keep the length of pipe

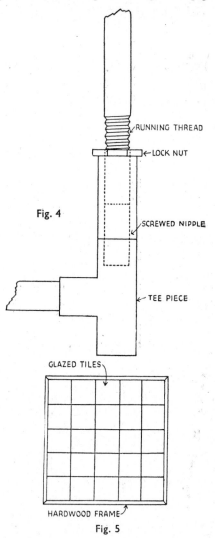

RUNNING THREAD

←LOCK NUT

Fig. 4

SCREWED NIPPLE

←TEE PIECE

GLAZED TILES

HARDWOOD FRAME

Fig. 5

outside as short as you can. When the connections have been made, the water may be turned on and the basin put into service.

If desirable, the space below the basin could be enclosed to form a cupboard for toilet requisites.

The wall at the back of the basin is

likely to get splashed with water, so it is desirable to make a splash-back. This could consist of a wooden mitred frame housing a number of white or coloured tiles, each measuring 6 in. square. The frame should be about 2 ft. high and a trifle wider than the width of the basin fitment. The tiles can be glued to $\frac{1}{4}$ in. thick plywood backing, the joints filled in with thin plaster-of-paris and then inserted and fixed into the rebate of the frame. The frame shown in Fig. 5 is neatly fixed to the wall by means of brass back plates.

FITTING A CUPBOARD UNDER THE STAIRS

MANY small houses are designed with an open recess underneath the staircase. In such cases the appearance of the hall will be enhanced by enclosing the space, thus providing a cupboard for accommodating coats, hats and articles such as the vacuum cleaner.

Fig. 1 shows a typical example. Although measurements will vary in different cases, the general layout will remain the same.

The tools required are a hand saw, small plane, hammer, screwdriver, rule, and a rawlplug tool for plugging the wall.

The upright A, forming the door post, is of 2 in. square deal as is the short one B at the opposite end. The post measures 6 ft. 9 in. and the bottom is cut away to clear the skirting, as shown, while the top is cut to suit the angle between the wall and ceiling of the space. The same applies to the top of the shorter post.

Although these posts are hidden from sight, it is a matter of minutes to skim the wood with a plane and so give the job a finish.

General Details. — The wall to which the door part is to be fixed will often be of brick. To obtain a firm fixing it will be necessary to plug the wall. If this is the case, find a mortar joint in preference to boring bricks.

Make the top fixing not less than a foot from ceiling, a corresponding one at the same distance from the other end and another midway between the two. Use No. 8 countersunk-headed iron screws 4 in. in length.

The small upright B may be screwed direct to the edge of the wide wooden upright of the staircase indicated at C.

Matchboarding $\frac{1}{2}$ in. thick (finished) is used for enclosing the space. Therefore, the top batten should be fixed $\frac{1}{2}$ in. back from the face of the string, as the outside sloping part of the staircase is called, to enable the faces of the boards to lie flush with that member.

The undersides of the stairs will in all probability be covered with laths and plaster to form the ceiling so it will be necessary to find a solid fixing. This can be done by inserting a blade of a bradawl into the ceiling to find the positions of cross members.

The position of the fixings on the ceiling, half a dozen will do, should be marked and the top batten D cut to length and placed up to the marks. The batten can then be marked for the screw holes. Screws, 2 in. in length and of No. 6 gauge, will suffice for fixing the batten.

If the floor is of wood the lower batten E is simply screwed directly down on it; but in the case of a tiled floor, plugs must be inserted for fixing. ·

The rawlplug tool is as suitable for making holes in tiles as it is in brickwork. A number of gentle taps on the

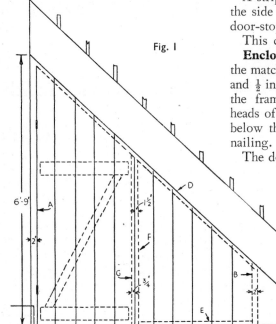

Fig. I

top of the tool are better than a few heavy ones, and if these instructions are carried out there is little risk of breaking the tiles.

There remains the task of fixing the upright forming the short door post F. This piece is of $1\frac{1}{2}$ in. square stuff, skimmed with a plane, sawn at the top and to suit the slope and fixed by driving in nails on the skew.

It is important that the post be quite parallel to its fellow member A in order to obtain a good fit for the door.

A strip of $1 \times \frac{3}{4}$ in. wood is nailed to the side face of the upright to act as a door-stop, as indicated at G.

This completes the framework.

Enclosing.—The next item is to fix the match-boards. These are 5 in. wide and $\frac{1}{2}$ in. in thickness, and fastened to the frame by $1\frac{1}{2}$ in. oval brads, the heads of which should be punched just below the surface after completing the nailing.

The door is of the same material and is held together by two ledges 4 in. wide $\times \frac{3}{4}$ in. thick. To prevent the door from sagging, two braces, or diagonal pieces of $2 \times \frac{3}{4}$ in. stuff, are fixed between the ledges, as shown.

A pair of 2 in. iron butt-hinges should be used for hanging the door and a small metal latch fitted to the opposite side.

Knots appearing on the surface of the cupboard should be treated with knotting preparatory to applying a primary coat of lead paint after which the nail holes may be stopped with putty.

Two coats of undercoating should be applied of a colour to suit the finishing coat. The final coat should, of course, match the paintwork of the staircase.

MAKING A WOODEN GATE FOR THE TOP OF THE STAIRCASE

A WOODEN gate at the top of the stairs should always be fitted where small children have their nursery above the ground floor. The one shown in Fig. I can be made in a few hours.

The drawing, Fig. I, shows that the gate is 2 ft. 6 in. high and the width 2 ft. 6 in. These measurements could be modified to meet any requirements.

Double gates could be used where the span is of exceptional width, one of which could be kept closed by means of a bolt fixed at the bottom of a closing stile.

When arranging gates of this description, it is an advantage to fit loose butt-hinges so that the gates can be removed when necessary.

Before making the gate it is a good plan to prepare and fix the post on the wall side which should line up exactly with the newel or main post on the opposite side.

In the majority of modern houses the faces of the newel posts are quite plain, which makes it easy to fix a plain stop for the gate to close against, but, in older houses, the post may be of a more ornate design in which case it will probably be necessary to cut out a stop to conform with the contours of the post.

The Wall Post.—This consists of a piece of 2 in. square planed yellow deal 2 ft. 9 in. long, the top being bevelled off to give it a neat finish. The back face of the bottom end of the post is cut away to a depth just to clear the skirting, to which it is attached by means of screws. A screw is also used for fixing the post to the wall. As the latter will probably be of brickwork, the wall will have to be plugged to ensure a good fixing. A suitable position for the fixing screw is 9 in. from the top of the post, and a clearing hole should be bored in the wood at this point to clear a 4 in. No. 8 iron screw of the countersunk headed type.

Make sure that the post is perfectly upright and in line with the newel. Verticality can be tested by means of a plumb-bob and string.

There is nothing of an intricate nature in the construction of the gate. The stiles or vertical pieces as well as the rails or horizontal members can all be made from yellow deal, but hardwood is better. These are 2 in. wide × 1 in. thick, while the bars are $\frac{5}{8}$ in. diameter

hardwood dowel rods which may be purchased cheaply at most dealers.

Simple mortice and tenon joints are used for fixing the rails and stiles together. These parts should be cut an inch or so longer than the finished sizes, accurately marked out, joints formed and the surplus wood removed. They can then be fitted temporarily together to ensure that all fits well, after which the members can be taken apart and the position marked on the rails for the dowel holes. As the bars are all of the same length and the holes in each rail are at the same distance apart the three

Fig. 1

rails can be cramped together and marked.

The holes in the top and mid rails are bored right through but the bottom ones are drilled only $\frac{1}{2}$ in. deep with a $\frac{5}{8}$ in. twist-bit. It is essential that the holes be perfectly clean and upright.

Inserting the Bars.—As the dowel rods may be a trifle too thick to ensure their easy insertion into the holes, each rod should be smoothed with medium glass-paper and then finished with glass-paper of fine grade.

Cut the rods about an inch longer than the finished size. Place the bottom rail horizontally between the jaws of a bench vice, give the ends and sides where they enter the hole an application of thin glue, insert the rods and tap them home with a mallet. Make pencil marks in the end rods indicating the position of the bottom edge of the mid rail, place the mid rail over the ends of the rods and tap it down to within 2 in. of the marked lines. Apply a little glue to each rod and tap the rail down so that it coincides with the marks, making sure that the rail is parallel to the lower one.

The outer rods should be marked near the tops in the same way as before and the top rail added after the glue has been applied to the rods.

The stiles can now be glued to the rails and the gate fixed in cramps until dry. The projecting ends of the rods can then be sawn off flush with the top of the upper rail.

To complete the gate, fix a strip of deal 1½ in. wide × ¾ in. thick to the top of the upper rail to hide the ends of the rods. The top edges should be slightly rounded and the piece can be glued to the rail, while a couple of thin screws 1 in. long will strengthen the joint.

Fasten the gate-stop to the newel by screws, hinge the gate to the wall post and fix a suitable bolt or latch for keeping the gate shut.

The final item is to finish the gate with stain, varnish, or paint to match the staircase.

PRACTICAL NOTES ON GEYSERS

THERE are two kinds of geyser in which the gas is burned, the white flame, and the Bunsen flame types. The former uses gas direct as in an old-fashioned gas burner. It does not mix air with the gas before it issues from the burner. The other type uses a Bunsen flame like the household gas cooker. This mixes air with gas and gives a blue flame. The heating properties of this type are greater for a given gas consumption but the geyser is sometimes less safe than the white flame type.

Fume Dangers.—No geyser is safe unless there is efficient and continuous circulation of pure air through the geyser itself: from the inlet for air to the burners, to the exit after the hot gases have risen in the geyser flue and escape, by reason of their heat, into the atmosphere. The Bunsen or atmospheric burner denudes the atmosphere of oxygen. Hence a double danger of insufficient oxygen and air contaminated by combustion fumes.

The bathroom should have a vent below the geyser.

This should preferably be not more than 4 in. above the level of the floor of the room. This ventilator will act in two ways. If carbon monoxide is given off by the geyser, it will fall, being heavier than the atmosphere, and instead of filling up from below and eventually reaching the head of the occupant of the bath, it will flow out of the vent at floor level.

The section of a house given here, Fig. 1, shows several alternative arrangements of geysers and flues. The floor outlet is at A. The outlet for the gas flue is important. It cannot be allowed in the bathroom and must be conducted into the open air or some other space sufficiently ventilated.

Often the geyser is provided with a sheet metal flue pipe which runs through the outside wall and extends upwards for a few feet as at B. It is important that the outlet of this pipe should be so arranged that down draught cannot get into the flue and blow back on to the burners. Where the geyser is on the ground floor, the flue pipe should be taken through the wall to an outside vertical pipe, which should not be placed too near the wall, since air eddies often come down a wall. The outlet should be well above the point at which the flue emerges from the wall and should be about a foot or 18 in. from the face of the wall, if on the first floor. It should on no account come up under the eaves of the house or under outwardly projecting guttering. If the top end of the pipe comes anywhere near the gutter or eaves, it should be carried out and up past them.

The Vent Pipe.—It should have a mushroom cowl at the top to stop down draughts and to prevent birds building nests in the pipe. The cowl should be of such a shape that air currents striking it act as extractors and draw hot air out of the geyser.

At c the pipe is extended right up through the roof and at D it terminates in the false roof or attic space. The latter arrangement avoids all danger of down draughts and of obstruction by birds, but it should only be adopted if there is ample air space and ventilation in the roof. At E the flue is shown carried into the existing chimney. This is a very good method, and in the case of the bathroom it can generally be arranged by carrying the flue through the ceiling and then into the chimney breast in the party wall or stack.

When the geyser is on the ground floor it is generally away from chimney flues and the arrangement at B will be found most suitable. It is convenient and safe to have a baffle fitted on the flue above the geyser. This absolutely prevents down draught. It is generally a light mica swinging vane which closes when the air direction is altered but opens again immediately the draught is with-

drawn and lets rising fumes out again. Its normal position is open.

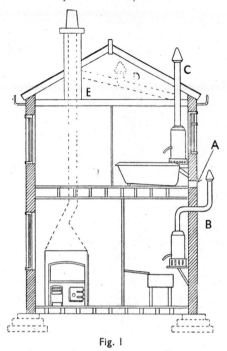

Fig. 1

When fixing a geyser, it is important to see that the gas and water supply pipes are of adequate size. A pipe smaller than that intended by the designer will not give heating satisfaction. For gas as now supplied, the following sizes of gas and water pipes (inside diameter) for geysers of varying capacities are recommended.

Gallons per minute	Gas pipe	Water pipe
$1\frac{1}{2}$	$\frac{1}{2}$ in.	$\frac{1}{2}$ in.
2	$\frac{3}{8}$,,	$\frac{1}{2}$,,
3	$\frac{3}{4}$,,	$\frac{3}{4}$,,
4	1 ,,	1 ,,

Water Pressure.—This is for cistern water supply when the cistern is above the first floor. In the cases of bungalows, where the cistern is nearer the geyser, the water pipes should be 25 per cent. bigger in bore. The bottom of the cistern should be at least 10 ft.

above the top of the geyser to get the best results; but, where such height is not available, the same effect can be obtained by increasing the bore of the water pipe from cistern to geyser. For geysers with automatic valves controlling the gas, the water pressures should not be less than 5 lb.—that is, the pressure obtainable with the cistern 10 ft. above the geyser. But geysers can be had with light-pressure valves when this cannot be obtained. In such case the pipe bore must still be greater.

It is often an advantage to have a separate meter for the geyser and often the gas meter in a house is too small if a geyser is subsequently fitted. Geysers consume more gas than any other domestic gas appliance.

As a guide to the size of meter, it may be stated that a geyser heating 2 gals. of water per minute should have a ten light gas meter. For 3 gals. it should be twenty lights, and for 4 gals. fifty lights.

In a good geyser, 25 to 30 ft. of gas (depending upon the calorific value) will heat 30 gals. of water to 40 deg. F. above that of the cold water supply, or from 60 to 100 deg. F.

Here are some figures as to temperatures, sizes of baths, times required and size of geyser required, to give a fully efficient service. To give a hot bath averaging 98 deg. F. with a 5 ft. cast-iron bath in 20 mins. a 2 gal. geyser is required. For a 5 ft. 6 in. bath for the same time and temperature a 3 gal. geyser, and with a larger bath a 4 gal. geyser. If a hotter bath is required—say about 105 deg. F.—for a small bath (5 ft.), a 3 gal. geyser will be required and so on in proportion.

Taking the average price of gas and the average size of bath (5 ft. 6 in.), a hot bath costs about twopence.

MODERNISING THE KITCHEN

To bring an old-fashioned kitchen up to date, new appliances should take the place of obsolete ones. The old range should be replaced by a modern stove burning coke, I in Fig. 1. These stoves take up less space than the range and are much more economical.

They are made with a vitreous enamel surface and do away with the black-leading and polishing which constituted a tedious labour with the older kinds. Enamel surfaces and chromium plating are kept clean by wiping and will stay clean without labour.

Kitchens differ so much in shape and in size that not one example will serve for all; but Fig. 1 shows a lay-out for a kitchen of a shape often found. The sink A should be near the window, as shown in Fig. 2 to get good light and efficient ventilation.

A sink in a dark corner means undiscovered dirt and grease. The modern sink is of glazed earthenware and should be of fair size and have a clear space below it, while a draining board B should be made removable for scouring.

Soft Water Economy.—Near the sink should be a water softener, C. This is connected to the cold water tap by a rubber hose and an instantaneous coupling. The spout of the water softener should project over the sink. Cooking utensils and kettles are thus freed from fur deposit so that less fuel is used to boil the water, the saving being as much as 50 per cent. Soft water also requires much less soap for all washing purposes.

The old copper should be removed and

replaced by a portable gas-fired boiler D which can be stored in a corner when not in use. A useful type is shown in Fig. 3. Where electricity is laid on, an electric washer and ironer E which combines a washing machine to take the place of the boiler, and a rubber roller wringer and roller ironer in one unit, will take the places of the copper, mangle and wringer and occupy little space in a corner. It enormously reduces the time of the weekly wash and is one of the most efficient of labour-saving appliances.

Modern Dressers.—The old-fashioned open type of kitchen dresser should be discarded and one of the new kitchen cabinets F put in its place. The inside shelves are enamelled, the pull-out table G is covered with a white enamelled metal sheet sliding, when not in use, between the bottom cupboards and the top glass or wood doors which enclose the shelves. It is shown (dotted) open.

The gas or electric cooker H should be placed as near as possible to the cabinet, in good light and away from draughts which interfere with heat efficiency and may be dangerous in the case of a gas cooker.

Wallpapers should be avoided. The walls should be sized and painted, and the colour should be pale so as to get as much light as possible in corners farthest from the window. The ceiling should be white, preferably painted. Doors and windows should be enamelled. It costs more than ordinary paint, but lasts much longer and can be wiped clean with a damp cloth.

The floor should be kept clear so

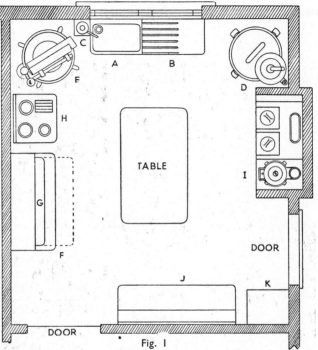

Fig. I

that it can be easily swept with a broom in every corner. Thick plain linoleum is the best covering

Electricity.—Lighting of the kitchen must be good. The best light is a reflected light from a central bulb with an opal globe of large diameter below it, so arranged that the light is thrown all over the ceiling and for a foot along the walls each side. With such lighting there will be no shadows.

Wall plugs, in a house supplied with electricity, should be fitted in the kitchen for such things as irons or an electric toaster, and separate plugs, with earthing plugs attached, should be provided for the electric washer and ironer which should have a separate circuit directly wired via a special fuse-box from the main switch and terminal board.

Shelves are a necessity for spare crockery and household utensils, but they should be enclosed in shallow cupboards with doors. Plate racks should be fitted so that plates are instantly

lined with tiles with a moulding surround of the same material. These should be white or light coloured to tone with the walls.

Clean Cookery.—If the cooker is in a corner, it should be of a size which will allow a brush to be used on the walls and floor all round it to allow

Fig. 2

available without taking them from piles. The usual closed type of dresser (J) is suitable but should be narrow.

Where possible, the corners of walls and skirtings should be rounded and the latter should not have dust retaining mouldings. The lower part of the wall, to a height at least 4 ft., should be of a darker colour than the rest and should be marked off by a band of contrasting colour as a finish. The kitchen door should have finger plates. This is more important in a kitchen than in the living rooms.

Where the sink is in the kitchen, the wall surrounding the sink should be

grease to be easily removed. It should be surrounded by enamelled iron plates fastened to the wall and extending from the top of the skirting to at least 18 in. above the top grid of the stove. This should be done even if the cooker has an overhead plate rack with an enamelled back.

Ample ventilation should be provided. A hinged fanlight should be fitted above the outside door and if the cooker must be arranged alongside the chimney-breast, a hood with a fume pipe at least 6 in. in diameter should be taken from the hood into the chimney to carry off the cooking fumes. A great preventative of cooking odours reaching the rest of the house is to fit a pneumatic or hydraulic door-spring to the inside door so that it will always close behind anyone leaving the kitchen.

A handsome piece of kitchen furniture is a two tiered dumb waiter on rubber tyred castor wheels as illustrated in

against the wall in an unoccupied corner.

Brushes and cleaning apparatus should be kept out of sight, and a rack in a shallow cupboard (K) about 5 ft. high and 8 in. deep should be provided so that soft and hard brooms can be hung head upwards to prevent bending of the bristles. Such a cupboard could

Fig. 3

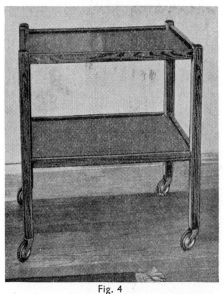

Fig. 4

Fig. 4. It makes for speed and neatness in serving and removing meals. It should have a place reserved for it

hold underneath, boot and stove cleaning tackle and the housemaid's box. It might also accommodate coal scuttles.

SINKING A WELL FOR A DOORMAT IN A WOODEN FLOOR

A DOOR mat that slips under your feet can easily be made fast by sinking a shallow well in the floor to enable the top of the mat to lie flush.

First measure the length and width of the mat, adding $\frac{1}{4}$ in. to both dimensions as the mat should not be a tight fit in the recess.

Marking the Recess.—As an aid to

marking the position of the recess on the floor-boards, it is quite a good plan to set out the size on a piece of paper and then to cut the latter out squarely with a pair of scissors. The pattern may then be placed on the floor-boards and a thin nail partially driven in at each corner. All that is necessary is to place a straight-edge against the nails, and using this as a guide, to pencil-mark the boards. This method saves time and ensures accuracy.

Outside the marked lines on the floor indicating the oversize length and width of the mat, make other lines $1\frac{1}{2}$ in. away from them. The area enclosed within these lines represents the size that the aperture has to be cut in order to accommodate the mat and a wooden surround.

Now lift a floor-board that crosses the area of the well. Little difficulty will be found in lifting a plain edged board; but before lifting a tongued and grooved board, the tongues will have to be removed on both edges. To lift a plain edge board, first punch down the nails with the aid of a nail-set, insert a cold chisel between the joint, place a small block of wood under the chisel to act as a fulcrum and force down the tool in the manner indicated in Fig. 1.

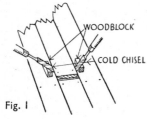

WOODBLOCK

COLD CHISEL

Fig. 1

To remove a tongue from a tongued and grooved board, bore a small hole between the joint, just large enough to take the end of a pad saw blade, and cut through the tongue with that tool.

With a small hand saw, saw through the floor-boards at the outer marked line, taking care to cut the edges of the boards squarely to enable the surround to butt evenly against them. In order to obtain the length or the width it may be necessary to cut into the floor-

board lengthwise, as shown at A in Fig. 2, in which case a pad saw should be used.

Treatment of Joists.—Cutting away the top of the joists requires a wood chisel and mallet in addition to a saw.

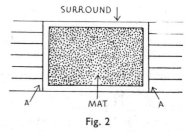

SURROUND

MAT

A   A

Fig. 2

It may be that only a single joist will have to be cut, or perhaps two or even three, depending upon the position of the joists and the size of the aperture.

If the joist comes in the middle of the opening and if two opposite edges of the aperture coincide with the inner faces of two outer joists, as represented in Fig. 3, the height of the joist A should be reduced by an amount equal to the difference of thickness between the floor-boards and the mat plus the thickness of the new piece of sunk flooring. Assuming the thickness of the mat to be 1 in. and the new boards $\frac{3}{4}$ in., the depth of wood to be removed will be 1 in.

Cut across the top of the joist where it is to be recessed and then make a series of similar saw cuts at intervals of about 1 in. This allows the waste to be removed in sections and is much better than attempting to chisel it in the solid. Fig. 4 shows how this is accomplished.

A length of planed batten $1\frac{1}{2}$ in.

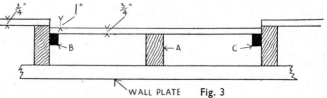

$\frac{3}{4}$"   1" $\frac{3}{4}$"

B   A   C

WALL PLATE   Fig. 3

wide × 1 in. thick is then nailed to the sides of the joists, as indicated at B and C in Fig. 3, to support the ends of the sunk floor.

Another arrangement of joists is indicated in Fig. 5 where the ends of the boards do not come sufficiently near the sides of the joists to obtain support. To overcome this difficulty, recess the joist as before and cut the well boards 3 in. longer than the length or the width, as the case may be, of the opening. A length of planed wood 1½ in. wide and ¼ in. thick is then fixed by screws on top and flush with the ends of the boards, the new floor manipulated into position and the ends fixed by driving in a few 2 in. No. 8 countersunk-headed screws, as shown.

To finish the job, a neat surround or frame consisting of planed batten 1½ in.

wide × 1 in. should be nailed down, wide face up to the sunken floor. The ends of the batten should be neatly

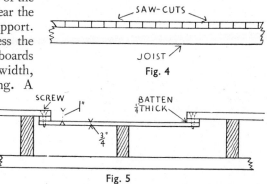

Fig. 4

Fig. 5

mitred, and if the original floor-boards have been cut squarely the edges should butt against the surround without unsightly gaps.

PRESERVATIVES OF WOOD

NOWADAYS, painters treat outside woodwork in the following way:

Go over the work with under coating so that the wood can absorb it and leave a reasonably smooth surface. Glass-paper this with middle 2 and fine 2 and then apply a coat of paint of the required colour. Two coats are sometimes necessary if a glossy surface is required, which is easier to keep clean. A coat of varnish should afterwards be applied.

The woodwork outside a half-timbered house of Tudor type needs special treatment to achieve mellow colour and charm.

Paint it with creosote and leave it at that, or stain it with vandyke brown powder and .880 spirits of ammonia (mixed 50-50) and then apply two or three coats of raw linseed oil.

Gate posts or any woodwork that is to go below the ground should be coated

with Burgundy pitch. Melt some Burgundy pitch in an old saucepan and quickly apply it to the wood, as illustrated in Fig. 1. Take care, for it is inflammable. This will prevent the wood rotting and is better than ordinary tar.

If the fencing is of oak, it is better to leave it untouched. It will last a life-time and weather to a silver grey. There are some fifteenth century oak lych-gates still in existence that were not preserved in any way.

Death Watch Beetle.—Inside wood-work and furniture require special attention to prevent attack by the death watch beetle.

The best way to eradicate these pests is to saturate the wood with paraffin and petrol. If there are many worm holes, this will be a long job, for the liquid should be squirted into each hole with a small glass syringe, as indicated in Fig. 2. Then go over the whole piece with turpentine and beeswax (mixed 50-50) and polish with an old rag.

Do not buy antique furniture that has

Fig. I

signs of worm, for it will rapidly infect other pieces in the house.

Wet Rot may be retarded by the application of paint and varnish, but the cure is to ascertain the cause of the wet and remedy it.

Latter-day furniture and fittings were made of hardwoods such as oak, American walnut, satin walnut, mahogany, ash, birch and elm, but now many new woods are used, of which examples are sycamore, Indian laurel, padouk, cherry, pearwood, French walnut and macassar ebony.

Polishes.—Furniture must be treated according to wood and colour with french polishing or one of the following polishes. For dark woods, such as dark oak, mahogany, walnut, macassar ebony, use a dark oak polish made up as follows:

Melt together over the gas stove, sixpennyworth of real beeswax, $\frac{1}{2}$ pint of turpentine and a piece of resin the size of a marble. Add to this as much vandyke brown powder as would cover a sixpence (in the case of mahogany, a pinch of rouge) and allow this to get

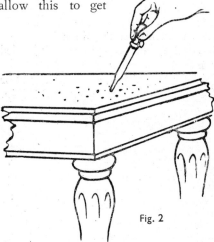

Fig. 2

cold before using. Apply and polish with a soft rag. For light wood such as sycamore, pearwood, ash, birch, elm and Indian laurel, use a light oak polish or make it as before with beeswax, resin and turpentine, but omitting the vandyke brown.

MIXING AND PREPARING PAINTS

PAINTS prepared and mixed at home from dry or wet pigments can be made in any desired colour and waste is avoided by making the exact quantity needed. Disadvantages are the trouble which has to be taken and the risk of wrong quantities spoiling the quality.

Care will obviate such risks.

Materials and appliances must be kept ready for the job. A number of cans are required, some quart bottles, a square of thick glass, several metal rods, sticks of non-resinous wood, an old table knife, and two or three earthenware vessels, as indicated in Fig. 1.

The use of dry or wet pigment is dictated by the colour used and the quantity required. For a large quantity of paint of normal colour, pigment in paste form should be purchased, as it is cheaper. A little dry pigment can be kept in stock in case a very small quantity is required, but for colours such as ultramarine, chrome yellow and vermilion, dry pigment only should be used and this in very small quantities. These colours are very expensive and are very powerful stainers, so that only very small amounts are required.

Dry Mixing.—Dry pigment should be placed upon the glass square and a little pure linseed oil added. Then grind the pigment into the oil with the knife, using a circular motion and considerable pressure as illustrated in Fig. 2. The pigment should be ground, adding oil as required, until a sticky but smooth paste is formed. The procedure then becomes the same as for paste pigments.

Mix the paste with raw linseed oil and turpentine, the proportion of linseed oil being about three times that of the turpentine, and copal oak varnish. If glossy paint is required, more varnish must be used. The method used in mixing is to stir the paste well into the different oils, adding each gradually and stirring with a metal rod.

The mixing should be done in a clean can, and each oil should be mixed until no hint of streakiness remains. The process is shown in Fig. 3.

The paint is finished off with patent

Fig. 1

dryers and turpentine added to thin to the desired consistency. If the paint is not to be used at once, it should be sealed down in the can with a piece of

Fig. 2

wax paper under the lid. This will prevent the formation of scum.

Mixing to Colour.—Mixing paints to various colours requires care and a knowledge of the colours being worked. For instance, white paint, either lead-white or zinc, has a yellowish tinge.

Therefore, to all white paints, a very small quantity of prussian or cobalt blue should be added, stirring in slowly and cautiously. This will make the paint an intense white.

An aid to mixing colours is a chart giving the different orders of colours and how they are formed, which can

Fig. 3

usually be obtained from a text book on art or physics.

When mixing paint for a two-coat job, the colour should be divided into two parts. Turpentine, with a little carbonate of lead, should be added to the part used as a first coat. The other portion should be varnished and linseed oil dryers included for a second coat.

When mixing colours, make enough for the job, as it is very difficult, unless a formula is kept, to make the exact colour again. If a big job is being done, and the quantity of paint required uncertain, it is best to have on hand two clear glass jars with wide mouths, one large and the other small. These jars are both graduated with inch marks as illustrated in Fig. 4, enamelled or etched with hydrofluoric acid. The basic paint (usually white) is measured off in the large jar, and a rough measure

jotted down. The added colours are measured in the smaller jar, and notes made of each addition. It will then be possible to repeat the colour exactly.

Popular Colours.—The following are quantities for useful colours:

Lead-white: 7 lb. white lead, $\frac{1}{2}$ lb. dryers, 1 quart raw linseed oil, 1 pint turpentine, 1 pint copal oak varnish. Mix the white lead and dryers first.

Zinc-white: six parts zinc-oxide ground in oil, four parts raw boiled oil, two parts turpentine, $\frac{1}{2}$ oz. liquid dryers to each 1 lb. mixture. For use at the seaside, add small part carbonate of lead (poisonous).

Green: add brunswick green to zinc-white. Mix a small portion first on glass, testing tint and noting proportions as directed. Pea green: fifty parts white, one part green. To remedy blue tone, use a little chrome yellow ground in oil. Four parts copal oak varnish one and a half parts turpentine, 1 oz. patent dryers to every 2 lb.

Fig. 4

Stone: mix white-lead paste with two parts copal oak varnish, three parts raw linseed oil, one part turpentine. Stain with equal parts yellow ochre and burnt umber in oil. Use ½ oz. dryers to every 1 lb.

Heliotrope: two parts zinc-white, three parts red, four parts ultramarine blue.

Flat paint can be made by adding to white-lead paste 1 oz. dryers for every 1 lb., one part raw linseed oil and five parts turpentine. It is better to purchase metallic paints such as silver, gold and aluminium. Mix each colour thoroughly before the next is added. Use metal rods for mixing and wooden rods for stirring the paints during use. Never mix in a dirty can.

PRACTICAL HINTS ON PAINTING AND VARNISHING

A SURFACE to be painted should be free from all foreign matter. If it has been painted before, it should be stripped and cleaned.

Soda water is best for cleaning new or previously-painted surfaces. Prepare several buckets of soda water before beginning work on a big job. The prepared solution can be warmed up as required. White rags should also be ready for applying the soda water and for wiping off and drying.

Preparing Walls.—Even a new plaster wall should be washed off with soda before distempering. If old paint or distemper is not stripped off, it is essential to wash it with a strong solution. The soda water should be washed off before painting is commenced.

Furniture, carpets and floors should be covered with newspaper, for paint splashes in spite of every care. Rags should be kept ready to wipe fingers and brush.

Two single gadgets will be found of great help; one prevents the hands becoming soiled through the handle of the brush being covered with paint and the other stops the paint spilling down the can. For the brush, cut a piece of linoleum about 6 in. long, tapering in width from 3 to 1 in. Wrap it round the brush handle, starting with the 1 in. end to form a cup below the bristles to take all surplus paint, and held on with a piece of twisted wire, as in Fig. 1.

To prevent paint spilling down the can, cut a piece of tinplate in the form

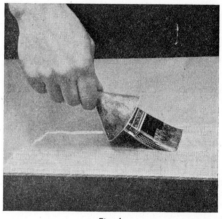

Fig. 1

of an oblong, with a square section cut out near one end. The other end of the tinplate is bent over the rim of the can so that the piece with the hole in it projects into the can. The paint brush is then wiped on the edge of this hole, as seen in Fig. 2, after being dipped in the paint, instead of on the side of the can.

Keep an old and worn distemper brush by you to brush down walls.

When painting moulded work, as shown in Fig. 3, have a variety of brushes of different sizes to fit the mouldings, and brush corners thoroughly before leaving to dry. Be careful to brush off excess paint which otherwise may form into beads and ridges.

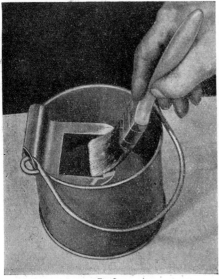

Fig.2

Blow-lamp and Scraper.—When a surface has been cleaned of paint by burning with a blow-lamp, rub it down with pumice-stone and turpentine. Never keep the blow-lamp on one spot longer than necessary to melt the paint, as there is a great danger of burning the wood. Always keep the scraper clean and dip it in paraffin frequently while working, as shown in Fig. 4. Keep the scraper pressed nearly flat against the surface, as a wide angle may lead to dents or notches.

When repainting articles from which old paint has not been stripped, give two undercoatings.

Knots in new wood, or in old wood that has been stripped, should be treated. Shellac knotting should be used over and around the knots as shown in Fig. 5. Two coats for new wood, one for old.

Shellac varnish, to which a little spirit has been added, gives good results if knotting preparation is not available.

Work is often spoiled because each coat of paint is not allowed to harden before a fresh one is applied. Blistering and flaking off result if this precaution is not taken. At least twenty-four hours should be allowed for a coat of ordinary oil-bound paint to dry.

Varnishing.—Amber varnish is the best for general use. It can be prepared in the following way. Take a hard glass flask and put in $2\frac{1}{8}$ oz. of pulverised amber chips. Heat over a burner. When melted, add $\frac{1}{4}$ pint of artists' linseed oil, which has previously been heated to the same temperature in another vessel. Pour slowly on to the melted amber, stirring all the time with a clean hardwood stick. Let the mixture simmer until stringy and then pour in slowly $\frac{1}{4}$ pint of turpentine, also heated. Stir all the time. The colouring may alter through variation of heat or stirring.

If varnish fails to dry on a polished surface, clean off all traces of it with

Fig. 3

acid or spirit, and rub the surface with pumice powder, or powdered bathbrick and water. Wash thoroughly, brush, and varnish again.

Dark patches which appear on varnished doors should be treated with weak oxalic acid, applied to the patches only, and washed afterwards with diluted vinegar.

Paint and varnish brushes should be kept clean when not in use. Clean them with soft soap, warm water and paraffin after use, and leave to soak in petrol or paraffin. To remove excess petrol or paraffin when using again, brush a clean flat board as shown in Fig. 6 until no mark is left.

Varnishing in cold weather is often difficult because the material becomes stiff. A small quantity of heated linseed oil poured in before use is a good preventative. It is also advisable slightly to heat the varnish.

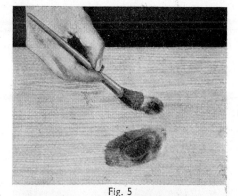

Fig. 5

Fig. 4

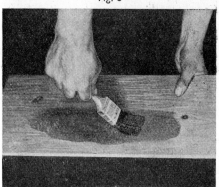

Fig. 6

More dryers should be incorporated in paint during winter than in summer.

To remove the smell of paint, place in the room two bucketsful of water, each containing 2 oz. of vitriolic acid. In country districts, a bucket of hay standing near new work is good for removing the smell.

ENAMELLING FURNITURE AT HOME

THE use of enamel for some furniture is recommended as this paint provides a finish which is durable and easily cleaned.

Preparing the Surface.—Great care should be taken in the preparation of the surface. The article, if enamelled before, should be cleaned of old paint with a dissolving solution. It is then necessary to rub well with pumice-stone and water, and coarse glass-paper and finish off with a finer grade.

If the article is new, grease, dirt and stains must be removed with warm soda water applied on a leather or soft cloth. One part soda to three of water should be used and the surface washed thoroughly. The article must be dried.

Fig. 1

Stop knots with patent knotting and then give the article a rub down with No. o glass-paper. Where dirt is ingrained, rub lightly with coarse glass-paper and then with fine. Wrap the glass-paper round a block of wood or cork and apply it in the direction of the grain, as shown in Fig. 1.

Both new, unfinished surfaces, and those from which old paint has been removed must then be brushed with a soft, wide brush, as in Fig. 2, to take away all dust left from the glass-papering.

Undercoats.—Although it is best to buy branded enamels, which are skillfully made to exact proportions, the primary coating can be prepared at home. This consists of zinc-white ground in turpentine, with a quantity of pale oak varnish added. Four parts white, one part turpentine and one part varnish is a good mixture, although on old furniture it is better to use more varnish.

The primary coat is applied with a soft, wide brush as quickly as possible and left to dry thoroughly. It is then rubbed down with fine glass-paper until very smooth. Use the finest obtainable, as the surface should not be noticeably scratched at all. Then brush the surface again and apply the enamel.

A camel-hair brush of 1 in. width should be used and it must be clean. A new brush is not a necessity. A brush which has been broken in on other work and thoroughly cleaned will give the best results. New brushes must be cleaned in water and dried before use.

Only one coat of enamel should be needed over the primary coat. The brush should be worked downwards and then across at right-angles to eliminate brush marks as much as possible. Speed is essential, as enamel begins to set quickly and, after a few minutes, will show brush marks badly. Always work one way and, if possible, use only two or three strokes to cover the surface.

Fig. 2

When enamelling articles which are beaded, or in corner or recess, care must be taken to prevent the formation of beads of enamel. For these parts, use a brush which will fit well in; do not use too much enamel and do not dab. When wiping an enamel brush on the side of the tin after dipping, wipe the tip of the bristles with a sideways motion, and not on the flat of the brush as in painting.

A Good Filler.—It is sometimes necessary to use a filler when re-enamelling old work. The filler is used to raise indentations, to fill the cracks and to give a smooth surface for the final coat. Good commercial fillers are obtainable or a home-made filler can be prepared as follows. Take equal parts of paste of white-lead, finely powdered whiting, and mix to a stiff cream with japanner's gold size. Strain through fine canvas. The filler can be put on with a putty knife or a stiff brush.

To obtain a clean surface, lightly dip a putty knife in turpentine and press gently against the filler just before it sets.

After using the filler, rub down with glass-paper and give another coat of flat white for enamel backing.

Articles should never be enamelled in either a cold or a hot room. An even reading of about 70 deg. F. is the best. Never dry enamelled articles in a current of hot air or with heat. This tends to harden the surface, leaving the underneath liquid and will produce cracks.

White enamel can be made as follows: For each gallon of enamel required, take 4 lb. zinc oxide. The oxide should be ground into a mixture of very pale copal varnish (three parts), dammer varnish two parts, and french oil varnish one part, adding a little dry blue as required. The furniture may also be given a matt finish by dulling the enamel with pumice powder applied with a soft cloth after the final coat has dried. The powder can be applied in parts only to produce a varied effect.

STENCILLED DECORATION

A STENCIL is a thin piece of metal or prepared paper in which a design has been cut to allow repeated reproduction of the design by brushing coloured pigments through and on to the article to be decorated.

The variety of design is endless and may be adapted to cupboard doors, waste-paper baskets, lampshades, linen baskets, screens, book ends and covers, cushion covers, bedspreads, and many other articles.

Uses for Stencilling.—Wall decorations include dadoes, borders, panel surrounds, frieze work for the nursery and play-room in animals, birds and familiar characters. On a background of plain or shaded tint, flower groups in the corners and part way along the skirting are effective; suitable and

varying designs may show iris, foxglove, delphinium and other flowers. Stencilled wall decorations carried out on large sheets of rush matting secured to the walls by means of stained wood battens are a ready way of dealing with the conversion of a lean-to greenhouse or small conservatory into a rest room, or covering the whitewashed walls of a club room for Scouts or Guides.

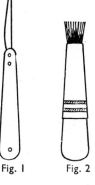

Fig. 1   Fig. 2

An old book of wallpaper samples or lino patterns will often provide ideas for stencils. Original designs may be drawn to suitable size with compasses and rule. French curves are handy for many outlines impossible to produce with compasses, and squared paper is another great help with the proportions of a design and enables work to be done without a tee-square. Complicated designs are built up of one or more simple elements repeated or varied, but the simpler ones are most effective: avoid too much detail.

Stencilled designs may be applied to any material that is capable of taking colour or pigment, such as plaster, linen, wood, leather, canvas, paper, hessian, twill and cotton.

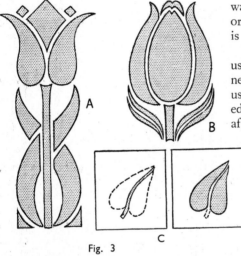

Fig. 3

The Outfit.—The tools are few and cheap. The small knife used for cutting stencils must be of good steel that will retain a sharp edge and point. The ready-made article of the shape shown in Fig. 1 costs from 1s. to 2s. 6d., but an ordinary penknife may be used provided it has a comfortable handle and a blade of suitable shape. An old one could be ground to shape. The objection to a penknife is that it is liable to shut in slipping, so the blade should be locked in the open position by placing

a piece of metal tube over the handle and flattening it to shape with enough projecting forward to prevent the blade shutting.

Small holes are punched with hollow tools made from assorted sizes of steel tubes ground at the ends to make cutting edges.

Any hard surface will do for cutting upon, but wood grain is liable to lead the cutting blade astray. For all-round results, there is nothing better than a piece of plate glass or frosted glass, as this surface gives a better grip. Punching is done on hardwood with a piece of card between wood and stencil plate.

Colours are used in the wet state, so waterproof card or paper is best. Waxed or oiled manila paper for the purpose is obtainable from artists' shop.

Drawing and other papers may be used, and cardboard of various thicknesses; but unless waterproofed before use, the colour will soak into the cut edges and cause smudged work, and after frequent use the stencil will break apart.

Waterproofing may be carried out by treating the cut stencil with coats of varnish or french polish mixture, but these require ample time to dry hard before use. Painter's knotting can also be used and dries quickly. Boiled linseed oil with a little turpentine gives a transparent stencil but requires a long time to dry.

Waterproofed plates allow the necessary cleaning to prevent colour filling small cuts and marring the result. All plates should be cleaned after use.

The usual type of stencil brush shown in Fig. 2 has short hairs, usually hog's hair, in a tuft varying from $\frac{1}{4}$ to $1\frac{1}{2}$ in. in diameter. Such can be purchased from threepence each, or a clean paint brush may be cut to suit.

Suitable Colours.—The pigments may include stains and dies, pigments

Fig. 4

mixed with oils and varnishes, and those mixed with water and gum.

Artists' oil colours dry slowly and water colours are only suitable where moisture will not affect them. Poster colours in a large variety of colours are waterproof, but waterproof-coloured inks are inclined to spread under the stencil if applied with a brush. The method with these is to use a spray diffuser and, provided the jet is so made that the spray will not fan out over a large space, little material is wasted, although masks to cover portions will be required.

An excellent colouring medium is prepared by mixing powder pigments with the white of an egg, an equal quantity of water and a few drops of vinegar. It takes some time to dry, but sets hard and is insoluble.

Stencils must be cut in such a way that they will not fall apart after cutting. For example, if a circle is marked out by double lines and these are cut all round, the centre will fall out and give a stencil for a large round dot. Centre-pieces

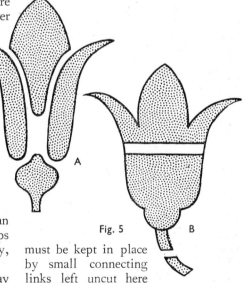

Fig. 5

must be kept in place by small connecting links left uncut here and there (Fig. 3, A and B). When placing the links in a design, always

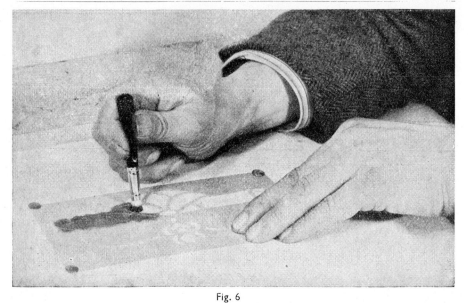

Fig. 6

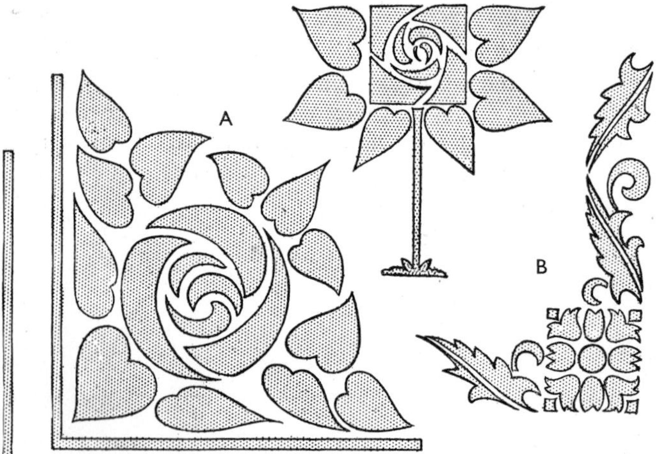

cutting some stencil details, such as a leaf. In Fig. 3c, the body of the leaf is marked out, leaving the centre rib blank or the same colour as the surrounding background. By marking the plate with a simple border and again cutting out only the dark parts, in this case the background, and stencilling these, the body of the leaf is left blank for filling in with another tint.

Fig. 7

arrange them so that they help towards the foundation of the design and indicate the desired shape as at A in Fig. 5. The effect of incorrectly placed links is indicated at B, where the result is not so definite.

Reversing Designs.—In the illustrations the dark portions are the parts to be cut out. There are two ways of

When cutting a stencil, the knife should be held as indicated in Fig. 4.

Fig. 6 shows how to apply the pigment. The brush is not drawn across the stencil, as in ordinary painting, but used in vertical dabs.

A modern type of a panel corner is depicted at A in Fig. 7, a suggestion for a wall border is represented at B.

HOW TO USE CELLULOSE LACQUER

CELLULOSE lacquer is easy to apply, dries in an hour or so, is durable, produces a hard and mirror-like surface which can be safely washed with ordinary soap.

It can be applied over old paint, provided such paint is in good condition but it should not be used to cover new oil paint as lacquer solvent attacks linseed oil.

Precautions to Observe. — The liquid constituent is extremely volatile and gives off a highly inflammable vapour. For this reason it should never be used near a naked light. Another important point is that the lacquer must be thinned only with a special thinner supplied by the makers of the lacquer. If brush-work is in view, make sure to get "brushing" lacquer, not the other kind.

The lacquer must not be applied with a cheap brush as it usually sheds bristles, and any attempt to remove them ruins the surface. Get a good brush with soft bristles set in vulcanised rubber.

Before using the lacquer, stir the liquid thoroughly, as indicated in Fig. 1, in the same way as for oil paint. Straining is unnecessary; no skin is formed and thinners are not required at the outset, the lacquer being sold ready for use.

Rubbing Down the Wood.—If the lacquer is to be applied to new wood the latter should be prepared by rubbing down the surface in the direction of the grain, Fig. 2, with fine glass-paper, dusted, and then brushed over with a suitable filler to seal the pores of the wood. If a smooth surface is wanted, this process should not be omitted,

Fig. 1

especially if the wood is soft. Open pores in wood allow the lacquer to soak in and result in a patchy surface.

The filler can be purchased or prepared at home by making a strong solution of gelatine in water. It can be applied with the lacquer brush if it is cleaned and dried afterwards.

Allow the filler to dry, then give the surface a further glass-papering and remove the dust.

Make sure that the wood is dry before applying the lacquer. Dampness is fatal. It is also important that the work should be carried out in a dry, cool place, as humidity in the air may cause condensation to form on the work and so spoil it. A hot atmosphere is as bad as it makes the lacquer set too quickly.

The lacquer should be laid on as rapidly and evenly as possible. The part being lacquered should be covered by a single stroke of the brush, and the sections should be joined before the lacquer has had time to become tacky.

Do not attempt to remove brush marks as the work progresses. These will flow out before it sets. As the work proceeds, it may be necessary to clean the brush in the special thinning solution in order to allow the lacquer to work freely. It may also be found necessary to thin the lacquer. Give the lacquer an occasional stir. Fig. 3 shows the process of applying the lacquer.

A Second Coat.—Before applying another coat, make sure that the first one is hard and then proceed as before. Do not let the brush remain on the surface longer than is necessary because the new coat tends to dissolve the undercoat, a feature which not only renders the lacquer difficult to apply, but will produce a bad finish.

It is a waste of time to apply cellulose lacquer to an old painted surface that is chipped and blistered. It is far better to remove it entirely by blow-lamp and scraper or one of the numerous chemical paint removers. On the other hand, if

Fig. 2

the paint is only dull and discoloured, a coat of cellulose lacquer will give it new life. Before applying the lacquer, dull the surface with fine glass-paper and wash it down with a damp chamois leather to remove the dust and allow

the work to dry. The surface is then ready to receive its new coat, which is done as already explained.

If the old paint has been varnished, the coat can be removed by softening the

Fig. 3

varnish with strong liquid ammonia and then scraping.

On Metal.—Cellulose lacquer can be used with equal success for finishing metal objects, but the surfaces to be treated must be devoid of rust, dirt and grease, the removal of which is effected with fine emery cloth.

If the articles have been previously painted, first remove the oil paint and make a fresh start. The result will be more satisfactory.

Transparent Lacquer. — Cellulose lacquer is also supplied in the form of a transparent wash in various colours. This can be used to deepen or to alter the tone of metal vases, trays, etc., but it is particularly successful when used as a decoration on glass.

The cheapest tumbler may be transformed into a richly tinted goblet, while plain glass vases may be enriched with an endless variety of warmly transluscent patterns.

The same care must be taken over its application.

Cellulose lacquer can also be sprayed on the surfaces, thus obviating the use of a brush. Fig. 4 shows a useful portable apparatus for applying the lacquer by this process. The sprayer can also be used with oil paint.

The outfit consists of a foot pump, compressed air container fitted with a pressure gauge, and a spraying pistol to which is attached a glass container for holding the lacquer. The latter can be of a kind specially prepared for spraying or brushing lacquer thinned; two-thirds lacquer to one-third thinner.

Briefly, the action of the sprayer is as follows: Compressed air at a pressure of about 20 lb. per sq. in. issues from the air jet of the trigger valve controlled pistol over a similar jet connected by a metal tube immersed in the finished medium. The velocity at which the compressed air issues from

the pistol jet and passes over the container jet draws the liquid up the tube and through the jet and drives it forward in the form of very fine spray.

Such an outfit is useful for painting quickly small work, such as cycle

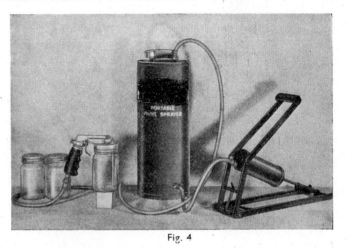

Fig. 4

frames, motor-car mudguards, doors, furniture and the numerous odd jobs that have to be done in the home, garden and workshop.

ENAMELLING A BATH

ORDINARY enamel should not be used for a bath. It is not sufficiently elastic to withstand the effects of expansion and contraction due to hot and cold water, nor the effects of bath salts. Special bath enamel is now obtainable at most oil and colour stores; this, if properly applied, gives a durable and porcelain-like finish.

The number of tools and the variety of materials will depend upon the condition of the old enamel. If this has only lost its gloss and shows no sign of cracking and peeling off, all that is

necessary is to give the bath a couple of undercoats and one or two coats of enamel. On the other hand, if the bath has got into such a condition as to expose bare metal and rust, the best course is to remove the old paint entirely and start at the beginning rather than attempt patching.

A good brush with which to apply the medium is essential and this brush should be flat and not less than 2 in. wide. Do not begrudge the 2s. or so you may be asked to pay for a good brush. Brushes of inferior quality shed their bristles while work is in progress. Before using the brush, make sure it is free from dust. In addition to the enamel, a suitable undercoating must be provided.

The best undercoating to use is that

Fig. 1

recommended and prepared by the manufacturers to suit their enamel.

Renewing Paint.—If the condition of the bath is such that it does not warrant the removal of the old paint,

Fig. 2

the first thing to do is to prepare the surface for the first coat by ridding it of all traces of grease and soap. This can be done effectively by rubbing the surface with powdered whiting applied

with a damp flannel, and then rinsing the bath with warm water.

Next lightly rub the surface with fine sandpaper to remove gloss, as it is essential that the surface be matt, that is, dull, before applying coats. After sandpapering, remove all traces of grit with hot water and allow the bath to dry.

Make sure that the taps do not leak. An occasional drip of water on the work will spoil it. If new washers cannot be fitted at the time, either make

Fig. 3

the taps watertight by stopping them with corks as indicated in Fig. 1, or hang a tin under each tap to catch the drips as shown in Fig. 2. The first method is the better because tins get in the way when applying the enamel.

Thoroughly mix the contents of the undercoating tin before use by stirring it up with a stick of clean wood, making sure that no sediment is left at the bottom. In order to eliminate lumps, it is advisable to put the medium through a strainer, as illustrated in Fig. 3.

Undercoats.—Now give the interior of the bath a coat of thin undercoating, brushing it on evenly and taking care not to apply too much at a time as a thick coat causes cracking, and is fatal to durability. Allow the paint to dry and harden thoroughly. This may take twenty-four hours, after which the paint should be lightly rubbed down with fine sandpaper. Remove all dust and apply another undercoat. Allow it to harden and apply fine sandpaper as before.

The enamelling process requires great care. It is essential that the enamel should be applied without interruption and as rapidly as possible. It sets very quickly.

If the temperature of the bathroom is below 60 deg. F. and there is no handy method of raising it, such as by use of an electric stove, it is advisable to defer the enamelling to a warmer day.

The enamel must be thoroughly mixed before attempting to apply it. If it is found too thick for easy working do not add thinners such as turpentine, but pour the contents of the container into a convenient receptacle and place it in a bowl of hot water in the manner shown in Fig. 4. This will reduce the consistency of the enamel and allow it to flow easily.

Fig. 5 shows a diagram of the sequence of operations in applying enamel to a bath fixed close to a wall. Start in the middle of the long edge 1 and work downward toward each end 2 and 3. Continue round 2 and 3 and the bottom, 4, and finally the front side and the top edge 5, making sure that the entire surface has been covered. If a small gap between the joints is apparent, remedy the defect at once by just touching the place two or three times with the tip of a brush lightly charged with enamel.

Do not attempt to lay it on as in painting, as this would leave a mark when dry. Remember that one of the secrets of success in enamelling is to join up each section before they set.

Having completed the enamelling, the surface must be allowed to set and harden, a process which will take two or three days or even more. Keep the bathroom free from dust but allow plenty of ventilation.

Before using the bath, fill it with cold water and allow it to remain there for a day. When filling the bath, make a practice of turning on the cold water tap first until the bath is partially filled and then adding the hot water. If this

Fig. 4

is done and the precaution taken to swill the bath with water after use to get rid of soapy deposits, the enamelled surface should, with ordinary care and normal use, last several years.

Repainting.—A bath that is so bad as to necessitate removal of the old paint before it can be refinished, should be treated in the following way. Apply to the inside some special chemical paint-softener obtainable at most oil and colour stores, or a home-made preparation consisting of lime, caustic potash and water, mixed to the consistency of a paste. Apply this with a fibre brush, or a piece of rag wrapped and tied to the end of a stout stick. Allow the softener to remain on the surface for a considerable time before scraping it and the old paint off. Use an old knife for scraping purposes. Care is needed when handling these preparations as they are likely to cause damage to other articles if allowed to come in contact with them. Protect the hands with rubber gloves.

Having scraped off every particle of old paint and removed the judge, clean rusty areas by scraping and the use of

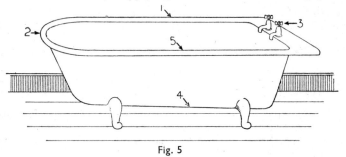

Fig. 5

emery cloth. Then remove all traces of the alkali with vinegar and water and swill the bath out with copious supplies of water. When dry, give the bare metal two coats of aluminium paint, allowing the first coat to dry before applying the second. After sandpapering the final coat of aluminium paint, give the surface two coats of undercoating and finish with the enamel as previously described.

If it is desired to give the bath two coats of enamel, the gloss of the first must be removed. This can be done effectively with fine pumice-powder, carefully applied with a damp flannel.

COLOUR SCHEMES AND DECORATION

GENERALLY speaking, there are three accepted ways of ensuring colour harmony, which are simple to carry out, viz. :

Dominant Harmony, when different tones of the same colour are used, as light, medium and dark blue; light, medium and dark red or any two or three tones of any one colour. Note the dark tones should be about one-eighth area only to the remaining seven-eighths of the other tone, or tones.

Complementary Harmony, i.e., combinations of two or three complementary colours, viz.: two colours—blue and orange, violet and primrose, crimson lake and green, black and grey, etc. Three colours—green, violet and grey; mauve, pink and grey; primrose, violet and blue; orange, violet and blue; crimson lake, violet and blue, etc.

Colour Contrast, i.e., yellow, red and blue. These three primary colours were used by Italian Renaissance artists as symbolising "life" in the following category: morning-yellow, evening-red, night-blue.

The latter colours are especially suitable for a child's room, as children love bright colours, but they need

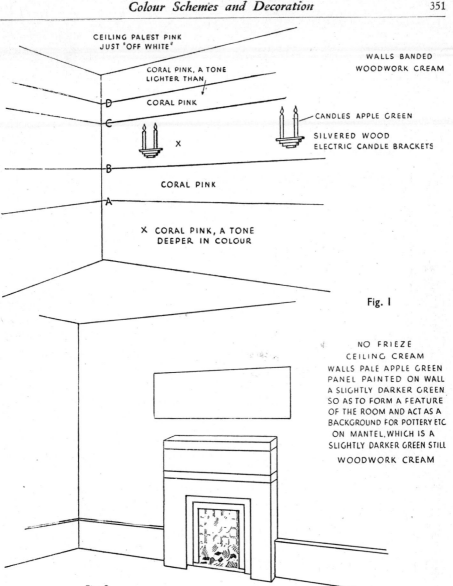

CEILING PALEST PINK
JUST "OFF WHITE"

WALLS BANDED
WOODWORK CREAM

CORAL PINK, A TONE
LIGHTER THAN,

CORAL PINK

D

C

CANDLES APPLE GREEN

SILVERED WOOD
ELECTRIC CANDLE BRACKETS

X

B

CORAL PINK

A

X CORAL PINK, A TONE
DEEPER IN COLOUR

Fig. I

NO FRIEZE
CEILING CREAM
WALLS PALE APPLE GREEN
PANEL PAINTED ON WALL
A SLIGHTLY DARKER GREEN
SO AS TO FORM A FEATURE
OF THE ROOM AND ACT AS A
BACKGROUND FOR POTTERY ETC
ON MANTEL, WHICH IS A
SLIGHTLY DARKER GREEN STILL

WOODWORK CREAM

Fig. 2

handling carefully to avoid placing the yellow next to the red. The arrangement should be yellow against blue and blue against red.

All the colours mentioned can, of course, be toned to the lightest and most delicate variations of shade.

With regard to colour tones, all the light colours, as primrose, cream, buff, stone, coral pink, very pale blues and greens, etc., are receding colours.

Dark reds, blues, browns, greens, greys and black are advancing colours. The darker they are the more they advance.

Receding Colours make a small

room look larger, as they reflect light, while advancing colours make a large room look smaller, or their effect on a small room is to make it appear still smaller as they absorb light.

Apart from considering the size of the room, its situation has to be taken into account.

For a room facing north, it will be best to gain a "sunshine" effect by colouring the walls primrose, cream or coral pink, etc., while rooms facing south should be decorated in the quieter colours such as pale green, pale blue or pale grey.

It should be observed that light tones of the same colour, or light shades of complementary colours are much more effective than violent contrasts.

The illustration in Fig. 1 shows diagrammatically a modern style in colour decoration called banding. These horizontal bands help to make a small room look larger, and used in conjunction with the receding colours mentioned carry the illusion much further.

Great care must be taken not to make these bands aggressive so it will be best to keep them a tone lighter than the wall in order to create a shadow effect. The placing of the bands is most important. Starting from the floor level, take one third of the total height of the wall and draw the line marked A. Then taking half the total height of the wall above, draw line B.

Now measure down from the ceiling a little more than half of the wall space left and draw line C. Then divide the space between C and the ceiling into seven parts and measure down from the ceiling four parts and draw line D.

The colour scheme suggested is in tones of coral, but it could be carried out with equal success in any colour provided a pale shade is employed.

Colour scheme, Fig. 2, is also modern. The walls are perfectly plain and there is no frieze. This is an advantage in a room with a low ceiling, as it adds height to a room, whereas a frieze has the effect of lowering a ceiling.

This scheme in tones of green, as indicated would be very refreshing and restful for a sunny room.

The mantel panel should only be a tone darker than the wall and the mantel a tone of green, still darker. The horizontal bands on it "come back" to the same colour tone as the panel, which, by the way, is painted on the walls.

It is interesting to note that the cream ceiling "comes back" on the skirting and gives unity in decoration.

Scheme three, Fig. 3, shows an ordinary room with a frieze, dado and skirting. The moulding of the frieze may be painted in the same deep ivory as the skirting and the dado line or moulding, of the same colour.

The colour gradations in this room are interesting. Starting from the ivory white ceiling, the ivory gradually deepens in tone. The dove-grey walls should be of the same tone as the light ivory frieze.

This scheme could be equally well done by leaving out the dado as shown but in this case the dove-grey walls would be carried down to the skirting.

Colour scheme No. 4, Fig. 4, shows a panelled-out effect, without actually panelling the room. The divisions are strips of paper carefully pasted on, or if there is a really good wall surface they can be painted direct on the wall.

The panelling-out needs some thought; the smaller wall surface should be taken first. Then—as far as possible—set out the panels in a right proportion as shown.

Pale primrose (or lemon) walls with cobalt blue divisions would make a very happy room with a sunshine effect, that would be an ideal treatment for a north room.

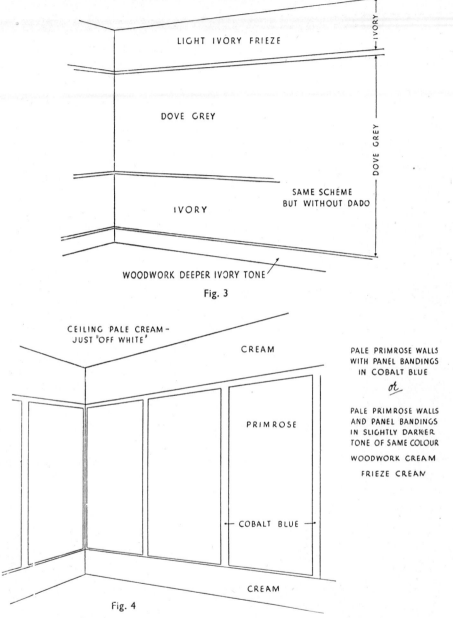

CEILING IVORY WHITE

LIGHT IVORY FRIEZE

IVORY

DOVE GREY

DOVE GREY

IVORY

SAME SCHEME
BUT WITHOUT DADO

WOODWORK DEEPER IVORY TONE

Fig. 3

CEILING PALE CREAM –
JUST "OFF WHITE"

CREAM

PRIMROSE

COBALT BLUE

CREAM

PALE PRIMROSE WALLS
WITH PANEL BANDINGS
IN COBALT BLUE

or

PALE PRIMROSE WALLS
AND PANEL BANDINGS
IN SLIGHTLY DARKER
TONE OF SAME COLOUR

WOODWORK CREAM

FRIEZE CREAM

Fig. 4

Alternative treatments are as follows: For a room facing south, either grey, light blue, light green, mauve, lilac or turquoise could be used with advantage.

When planning a colour scheme for any one room, the furniture and the colours of the cushions, etc., should be taken into consideration.

M

STAINING AND VARNISHING FLOORS

BEFORE applying the stain and varnish the condition of the floor-boards must be examined and repaired if necessary.

The long edges of the boards of an old floor very often will be found to project above the remainder of the board due to curling. If this is so, the boards should be carefully levelled with the aid of a sharp smoothing plane.

If possible use the plane in the direction of the grain and in any case do not set the plane iron too deep. Before using the tool it will be necessary to punch down the heads of the floor-brads below the surface. This should be done carefully, as any brads left unpunched will cause havoc with the cutting-edge of the plane iron.

In some instances it will be found that gaps occur between adjacent boards in which case the recesses should be filled by gluing in narrow strips of wood, sawn and planed to fit them. The strips should be made so that they project a trifle above the surface of the boards, the surplus wood being planed down level after sufficient time has been given for the glue to dry.

Knots projecting above the surface of the wood should be levelled carefully with a sharp chisel.

Having prepared the floor in the manner described the parts to be stained and varnished should be smoothed first with a medium grade glass-paper.

Remove all dust as any grit and dirt allowed to remain will spoil the work.

Staining.—Do not be tempted to use a spirit varnish stain—which is a preparation of stain, methylated spirit and varnish, as this material when dry does not stand up to hard wear and it has the further disadvantage of showing a pronounced white mark when even slightly scratched. It also chips very easily. So use a good quality oil stain and apply it with a soft flat brush or use a clean soft cloth, moistened with stain.

Water stain is not recommended for use in rooms where the appearance of the surround is of great importance, as soft wood absorbs it so rapidly that it is likely to make the colour darker than that required.

It is a good plan to have the colour of the surround slightly darker than the predominating colour of the carpet or the lino square. This arrangement will give a much better effect than having the wood of a lighter colour than the floor covering.

Having applied the stain, allow it to dry thoroughly before attempting to put on the varnish.

Use a soft brush for varnishing but do not proceed with it if the temperature of the room is much below 60 deg. F. If necessary use an electric stove or an oil stove to raise the temperature. This will allow the varnish to flow on smoothly without any tendency to drag.

In applying the varnish see that the surface being treated is covered by one application of the brush, and be sure not to leave any part uncovered.

Allow at least a week for the varnish to harden before treading on it or putting furniture on the surface.

It may be mentioned that it is useless to attempt to apply stain and varnish to a floor that is in a very bad state of preservation. In this case the difficulty can be overcome by facing the surround with thin plywood, about $\frac{3}{16}$ in. thick.

This material is inexpensive and is simply fastened down to the floor-boards by $\frac{3}{4}$ in. panel pins. If this method is resorted to, make sure that the ends of the pieces butt together closely so as not to leave unsightly gaps, and do not forget to place the best side of the plywood uppermost.

Plywood can be stained and varnished.

Those who prefer a very dark surround of a semi-matt finish can obtain it by applying japan-black thinned with a little turpentine.

Before applying the japan, however, it is wise to give the floor-boards a coat of size to prevent excessive absorbtion.

The surrounds of unimportant rooms can be stained with a solution of permanganate of potash and water. This mixture although purple in colour gives a brown tint, the shade depending upon the strength of the solution.

RENOVATING OLD FURNITURE

R ENOVATING and restoring old furniture is interesting work, but great care must be taken not to destroy the character and craftsmanship of the old

designer of this period, worked in Honduras mahogany. These two facts are of great help in determining the style and maker of an old piece of furniture.

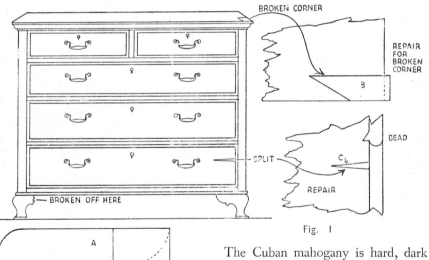

Fig. 1

work. For instance Chippendale invariably worked in Cuban (Spanish) mahogany, and his furniture was made and carved out of the solid wood. Sheraton, another famous furniture

The Cuban mahogany is hard, dark in colour and shows flecks of chalk in the grain. Honduras mahogany is much lighter in colour and the grain runs in streaks in opposite directions.

This article describes how to restore and renovate a Chippendale chest of drawers, and this description may also be followed in restoring solid mahogany furniture of later periods.

First of all, take off the drawer

handles, locks, etc., and identify them by numbers so they can be easily replaced.

Next, take out all the drawers and thoroughly wash every part with hot soda water. This will remove all the old polish if it is genuine Chippendale and has not been repolished with french polish; in the latter case, it must be washed again with American potash. When doing this, do not get the potash on your hands as it may take off the skin.

Repairing Faults.—Having taken off the old polish, all defects, fakes, splits, etc., will be disclosed, and so it will be necessary to look at every part and repair them where necessary.

Generally speaking, the drawer bottoms usually require repair. To effect this, take them out and rejoin them.

Again, the dovetails in the drawers may have broken loose; in this case, soak off all the old glue in hot water and glue them up again with hot thin glue.

The more common faults, however, are found in the carcase. If there are any cracks in the back they must be "shivered up." This is done by gluing in thin strips of the same kind of wood.

The drawing A in Fig. 1 shows how to mend a broken leg by turning the chest upside down and examining the fixing of the leg. These legs generally break off where shown. Chisel the broken surface carefully and test for squareness.

Saw out a small piece of Cuban mahogany to the required size, glue and cramp this on firmly with wooden hand-screws, allow twelve hours for the work to dry and then bow saw and carve it to shape.

Now supposing a corner is broken off as shown at B, proceed by carefully sawing out the broken corner in dovetail form, as shown. Pare down the edges perfectly square and bevel off the end of a narrow piece of Cuban mahogany. Fit this in, then glue it, tap it in gently and allow twelve hours to dry. The projecting piece should be sawn off to the dotted line, afterwards.

Next, turn over the chest and carve the moulding and clean off.

Splits in the front or sides of the drawers are best "shivered up" with wedge-like pieces, as seen at C. Glue these in and clean up.

Now wash the chest in American turpentine to kill any wood-worms. Look for worm holes and ruthlessly cut out the infected parts, making good with Cuban mahogany as described before.

When the work is complete, carefully paper up every part with Nos. $1\frac{1}{2}$, 1, 0 and "flour" glass-paper. Take care to paper with the grain.

Staining and Polishing. — Then make a saturated solution of bichromate of potash mixed with hot water in the proportions of 3 oz. bichromate of potash to 1 pt. of hot water.

Stain the whole chest with this, allow to dry, then with canvas rub off the yellow powder that will have formed on the surface.

Next, mix genuine beeswax polish— i.e., "wet wax"—as follows: 4 oz. beeswax to $\frac{1}{2}$ pt. of American turpentine and a piece of resin the size of a marble. Melt these together in an old tin on the gas stove, with the gas jet turned low.

Allow the mixture to cool, then work it well in the wood with a brush, rags, etc. Give it a good polishing with coarse canvas and then with a silk cloth.

Locks and Handles.—Thoroughly oil the locks and screw them on to the drawers.

The handles should then be put into very strong boiling soda water, thoroughly polished, washed in soap and water and rinsed in warm water.

It would spoil the appearance of the chest to put the handles on in this polished state, so purchase twopenny worth of hypo-sulphate of soda and twopenny worth of perchloride of iron and mix with ½ pt. of hot water.

Immerse the handles, boil them for a few minutes, take out, rinse in cold water and screw them on.

To make the drawers run easily, smear the sides of them—the runners and guides—with polish

FIXING A MIRROR AND GLASS SHELF IN A BATHROOM

THIS article deals with how to fix a mirror with a separate glass shelf, on which brushes and shaving tackle may be placed.

The size of the mirror shown is 1 ft. 8 in. × 1 ft., but the dimensions may, of course, be varied and the mirror placed horizontally if required.

The glass shelf is placed 4 in. below the mirror and the supporting wood brackets are placed directly underneath the side bevels of the mirror above.

Having decided upon the size and purchased the mirror, the first thing to do will be to make the clips. Mirror glass of good quality is about ¼ in. thick. The mirror shown is bevelled, but it may also be purchased with a smooth round edge.

Carefully measure the thickness of the mirror and cut out a strip of hardwood about 6 × 2 in. and of the same thickness as that of the mirror, and bevel or round the edge of it so as to be an exact replica of the mirror edge. This piece of wood is used to bend over the copper clips which are to be silvered later on.

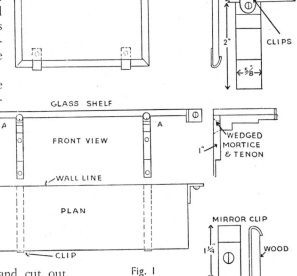

MIRROR SIZE 1·8″ X 1′

WALL LINE

DETAILS A A

GLASS

CLIPS

2″

⅝″

GLASS SHELF

FRONT VIEW

A   A

WALL LINE

PLAN

CLIP

WEDGED MORTICE & TENON

1″

MIRROR CLIP

1¼″   WOOD

½″

Fig. 1

The Clips.—Make these in the following way: Take a piece of sheet copper, size 8×8 in. (19 B.W.G.) and clean and polish it. Then file a true face edge and gauge a line along the face side and $\frac{1}{2}$ in. from the edge. Square lines across 2 in. apart, as each of the four clips is 2 in. "in the flat."

Find the positions of the holes, bore and countersink them carefully, using a $\frac{1}{4}$ in. twist drill. Now flatten the copper by tapping outwards with a smooth-faced hammer. File the edges round and clean up the front and back.

If the copper is hard, anneal it by heating it up to redness and plunging it into cold water. Then clean and polish it again. Cut off the $\frac{1}{2}$ in. strip and round the other edge, then cut off the four 2 in. pieces and round the ends.

Now take the little piece of wood and bend over the copper, as shown in the illustration. This can be done with the fingers first and, finally, by tapping the copper over the wood.

Fixing the Mirror. — Hold the mirror on the wall in its position (with the help of a friend), test to see that it is straight, then with a pencil draw a faint line round the edges, on the wall.

Take the mirror down, determine the positions for the clips, hold them in place and mark with pencil as before.

As the backs of the clips are let flush into the wall, take a $\frac{1}{2}$ in. chisel and cut round inside the lines first, then work back to the lines and cut out the plaster carefully to the thickness of the copper. Now, with a $\frac{3}{8}$ in. twist-bit, bore the four plug holes 1 in. deep and plug each with whitewood. Then screw on the four clips. Paste a piece of paper over the screw and clip so that the mirror —which slides in from the sides—will not get scratched.

The Shelf Brackets.—Before fixing the glass shelf, it is best to make the two mahogany brackets first. To construct these, square up two pieces of hardwood each 6×2×$\frac{5}{8}$ in., for the tops of the brackets, and two pieces each 6×1×$\frac{5}{8}$ in. for the uprights which are fixed to the wall. Mortice and tenon these together in pairs as shown, take them apart and cut to shape.

Then bore and countersink $\frac{1}{4}$ in. holes on the upright pieces. Next put the top pieces in a vice, mark, bore and screw on the two oval clips, which prevent the shelf from slipping forward.

These brackets may be screwed instead of morticed. Glue up the two brackets, allow them to dry and clean up and glass-paper with Nos. 1$\frac{1}{2}$ and 1.

Carefully cut out two pieces of suede leather (that taken from an old pair of gloves will do), the sizes of which should be 6×$\frac{5}{8}$ in. Glue them to the tops of the brackets and trim.

Next, find the exact positions of the brackets which should be in alignment with the bevels on the mirror above.

Mark through the holes with a pencil to get the exact hole centres. Bore 1 in. deep holes in the wall, using a $\frac{3}{8}$ in. twist-bit and plug up with a tightly fitting round whitewood plug. Saw off the plugs level with the surface wall.

Put the brackets in position again and with a bradawl bore holes in the plugs, putting screws half-way in only.

Purchase some liquid silver paint (not aluminium) and paint the brackets, including the top suede edge allow to dry and screw the brackets on to the wall. Touch the screw-heads with the paint and also the clips.

Fixing the Shelf.—Carefully rest the glass shelf (size 1 ft. 8 in.×6×$\frac{1}{4}$ in.) in position on the brackets and proceed to make the right-angled clips that keep the glass shelf from slipping sideways.

Cut off two pieces of copper 2×$\frac{3}{4}$ in. round the edges, bore $\frac{1}{4}$ in. holes at one end of each and bend them to slightly more than right-angles, as this will give a hand-tight fit when the glass shelf is pushed in between them.

With the glass shelf held firmly in position, push the clips well up against the glass to get the position of the holes,

take the glass down and bore and plug the walls as before.

Screw on the clips, silver them, place the shelf in position and turn upwards the two oval clips on the front edge. These also should be silvered.

GLAZED ROOF VERANDAH

IT is sometimes convenient to have a covered space outside the house against the kitchen or scullery where, for example, a mangle or washing machine can be placed, giving more room inside the house. The coal cellar door or any outside bunker for coke or wood may come under this cover for convenience in wet weather.

Outside a living or other reception room a similar addition makes a nice light airy lounge when the weather is unsettled.

This usually consists of a glazed roof supported on posts along the front and sides, and on a wall plate at suitable height at the back. The ends and front may have glass down to about the usual window-sill level and below this the spaces between posts are filled in with weather-boards or brickwork.

The timber work of the front head and gutter board should be arranged at a height that will throw the least shadow across the house windows and when viewed from inside the house, the run of woodwork should not cross the

general line of vision. To admit as much light as possible, all timbers should have their narrowest faces inwards and outwards. For example, if the wood is 3 × 2 in. in section, the 2 in. wide face is on the outside and inside, leaving the 3 in. face to make up

Fig. I

the thickness from inside and outside.

The Floor is of concrete, either cement or tile faced, and it is suggested that the ends of the posts are bedded in the concrete.

A floor space of about 6 ft. from the house wall to the front and 12 ft. long inside is given as an example in Fig. 2. The roof has a rise of 3 ft. at the back.

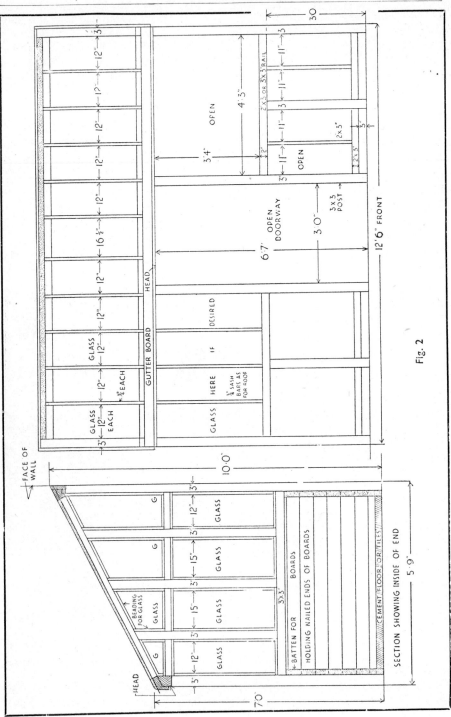

Fig. 2

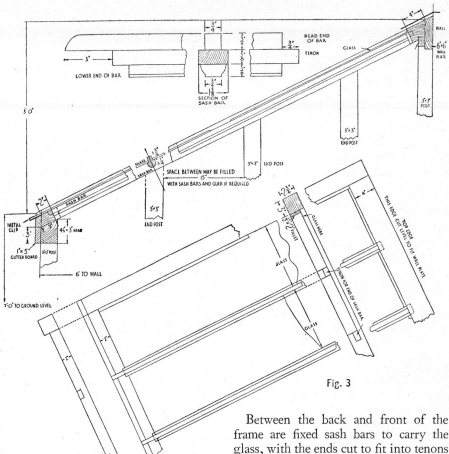

Fig. 3

As a guide when arranging the length, it should be noted that the glass is usually 12 in. wide and the sash bars supporting the edges have a rib ¾ in. thick down the centre, spacing the edges of the glass this distance apart, so the complete length should be some number of glass widths plus the ¾ in. ribs in between and the two widths of frame member making up the ends.

From the details in Fig. 3 it will be seen that the roof consists of a framework built up of 3 × 2¾ in. timber at the ends, 4 × 2¾ in. for the back top edge, and 3 × 2 in. along the front. These members are joined by mortice and tenon joints.

Between the back and front of the frame are fixed sash bars to carry the glass, with the ends cut to fit into tenons and slots. The centre rib is carried over the top faces of the frame to the front, as shown. To support the glass at the top end a fillet is fixed inside the frame to correspond with the same depth as the shoulder on the sashbars, and between each bar.

Twenty-one oz. glass, 12 in. wide is suitable. Start at the bottom so that the end overlaps about 1½ in. The next piece and each one to the top overlaps on the sheet below by about 1½ in. each time, in the same manner as slates.

The wall plate is secured to substantial wall plugs. Iron hooks—preferably galvanised—may also be used. Posts are used at the ends.

At the front, posts too are employed to support the head, the top face of which is cut to fit against the wall plate, and the front edge of the frame is cut to correspond to the vertical face of the post. The gutter board also helps to keep the frame in position.

Fig. 2 shows the outside front view of such a construction, closed with glass above and weather-boarding below. A fillet would be required all round inside the posts and sill to nail the edge and ends of the boards to, also a horizontal piece along the ground between posts for the bottom fixing. The top face of the sill bar should be planed so that it slopes towards the front so that water running down the glass will not stay in a pool at the bottom. Fillets are also required all round the other timbers to take the glass which is put in from the outside and finished round with putty.

The Doorway can, of course, be in one of the ends if more convenient (as in Fig. 1) and also fitted with a suitable door with glazed upper panels.

The top edge of the frame is covered by a strip of zinc set into the nearest joint line in the brick wall and bent over to cover the frame to allow moisture to drip on to the glass.

New woodwork should be given a preliminary coat of red lead paint.

A light zinc gutter should be fixed to the gutter board and a 2 in. down pipe of the same material fitted at one end of the gutter to take away surface water.

NOTES ON CENTRAL HEATING

CENTRAL heating boilers are self-contained units and are not connected to the kitchen range hot water circulating boiler which supplies the taps of lavatories, baths and kitchen sink.

Fig. 1 shows a suitable form of kitchen boiler for this type of installation. The boiler may be used also for the direct heating of the kitchen since it may have a grate which may be opened when a kitchen fire for airing, toasting or kettle boiling is required.

The fire is in direct contact with the water space which is surrounded by a non-conducting jacket so as to conserve heat. Where it is not desired to use coke, coalite, anthracite or other fuel a boiler can be had of similar type but heated by gas, in which case there is no fuel to be stored, no ashes to be removed and little attention required. Gas companies are now quoting special low rates for gas used for central heating.

Circulating pipes of steel tube are connected from the boiler to the different rooms where radiators of varying heating surface are placed for warming the atmosphere.

The Circulation is on the usual thermo principle; the hot water rising from the top of the boiler up to an expansion tank sometimes fixed in the roof or an airing cupboard, provided it is installed above the level of the radiators, then to the radiators themselves and back to the bottom of the boiler. Fig. 2 shows a plan of two floors of a moderately sized house with the position of the central boiler and the radiators marked.

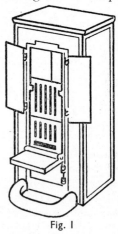

Fig. I

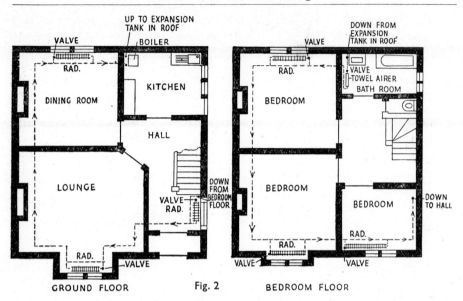

Fig. 2

GROUND FLOOR   BEDROOM FLOOR

It is an advantage to arrange the boiler in that part of the kitchen (or even an outside scullery or outhouse) where a direct down take pipe can be run up

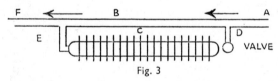

Fig. 3

the corner of the walls to the attic or roof. Where, as in the plan, Fig. 2, the bathroom is above the kitchen—a very general arrangement—the pipe can be taken inconspicuously in a felt-lined wooden casing. It need not stand out from the corner more than 4 in. in each direction. The pipes can then be laid along and at the back of a false skirting or under the floor-boards as in the plan. The main difficulty to be avoided is to so arrange the lay-out that a pipe does not have to curve downwards and rise again (as for instance to pass a doorway) if it can be avoided, since such falls and rises interfere with the easy circulation of the water and may

possibly cause air traps which would interfere with the flow. Sometimes pipes have to be laid below the flooring to avoid this and where such is necessary the lay-out should be arranged so that such pipes can lie in the direction of the joists, as cutting the joists to take the pipes weakens the floors, while boring the joist is equally impracticable once the house is built.

The System.—Because it is desirable that each radiator in the installation shall be capable of being turned on or off at will or adjusted for flow and therefore for heat, it is necessary that these should be coupled to the hot water main in a "shunt" arrangement as shown diagrammatically in Fig. 3. The hot water flows along in the direction of the arrow from A and passes along B, past the radiator and along in the direction towards F. A branch out at D leads to a cock or valve by means of which as much hot water as desired can pass through the radiator and back into the main line at E. When the cock is closed the circulation continues

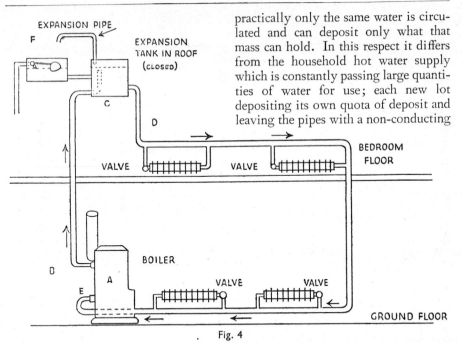

EXPANSION PIPE

F

EXPANSION TANK IN ROOF (CLOSED)

C

D

BEDROOM FLOOR

VALVE   VALVE

BOILER

D

A

E

VALVE   VALVE

GROUND FLOOR

Fig. 4

practically only the same water is circulated and can deposit only what that mass can hold. In this respect it differs from the household hot water supply which is constantly passing large quantities of water for use; each new lot depositing its own quota of deposit and leaving the pipes with a non-conducting

uninterrupted along to F and the radiator is shut off or, if the valve is partly closed, it is partially cut off. In this way the amount of heat can be regulated or no heat taken to the radiator.

Fig. 4 shows in diagrammatic form the coupling up of the system. A is the boiler, hot water leaving it at B, passing up to the expansion tank C in the loft or attic, from where it falls by gravity down the pipe D and around the bedroom floor and ground floor, back to the bottom of the boiler at E. A ball valve in a cistern F keeps the level of the water in the expansion tank C constant and makes up for any small loss of water through evaporation. Otherwise the system is self-contained as far as the supply of water is concerned, virtually the original mass of water flowing round continually under thermo syphonic automatic circulation.

This feature ensures that the pipes of the system do not get choked by lime or other deposits from the water, since

coating. This undesirable effect is avoided by using virtually the same water over and over again, and the incrustation in the pipes is infinitesimal. The heat conducting properties of the radiator is unaffected while the circulation pipes continue to have full sized bores—not obstructed by deposit which would seriously throttle the circulation and would greatly reduce the heating efficiency of the system.

The boilers are usually fitted with a safety valve in a suitable part of the system so that any obstruction which might cause a dangerous rise of pressure is avoided.

An arrangement can be included by means of which in weather where the temperature is high enough to enable the radiators to be cut off, the system can be still used to heat the water in a supply tank. This hot water is obtained by means of an "indirect cylinder."

Made of copper or galvanised steel it contains an inner heater connected (as are the radiators) to the heating up flow line. The heated water flows through the heater and raises the temperature of the water in the cylinder, where it is stored till drawn off by the taps (bath, lavatory, kitchen, etc.).

Such a system should not cost more than about twopence per day per room with the added advantage, when the indirect cylinder heating as described is installed, of having constant hot water for lavatories, baths and sinks.

LAYING AN OAK FLOOR

THE oak floors in a great number of old farm houses are usually of board 10 ft. to 13 ft. in length × 8 in. to 11 in. wide and $1\frac{3}{8}$ in. thick. These boards were often pegged to the joists, but before this was done they were laid loose for some time to take up the shrinkage. Many of these boards were tongued and grooved and had iron tongues let $\frac{1}{2}$ in. into each board.

Oak floors to-day are usually laid in strips (slats) on a sub-floor, either old or new. These slats are fixed crosswise on the old or new floor; that is, the grains of the two floors cross each other at right angles as illustrated in Fig. 1.

Types of Wood.—Before starting to lay an oak floor, however, it is advisable to consider the general sizes of the woods on the market which are sold for the purpose by specialist firms.

Generally speaking, Japanese oak slats can be bought in the following sizes. Six feet in length—average about 8 ft. 4 in. in width and $\frac{1}{4}$ in. thick; also 3 in. × $\frac{1}{4}$ in., etc.

Austrian wainscot (quartered) oak is better than Japanese oak or American. The latter wood especially is not so reliable owing to its tendency to warp. Slats of Austrian oak generally run about from 4 in. to 5 in. wide × $\frac{3}{8}$ in. or $\frac{7}{16}$ in. thick, and from 6 ft. in length and upwards.

All these slats are provided with machined tongues and grooves along their lengths, while each length has a groove, running across one end and a tongue at the other, as indicated in Fig. 2. In addition the slats are dry, well seasoned and flat in their lengths and widths, which is a great advantage.

Method.—Assuming that you wish to lay an oak floor with 3 in. wide oak slats in a room floored with ordinary deal boards, proceed in the following manner.

First punch down the heads of the nails well below the surface, with the aid of a heavy hammer and a substantial nail punch. Go over the work systematically, taking particular care not to leave any nail heads unpunched, as otherwise damage will be done to the cutting edge of the plane which is used in the next operation.

The old floor will now have to be traversed with a coarsely-set smoothing plane. The object of traversing, which is done by working the plane in a more or less semi-circular motion and principally in the direction of the grain of the wood, is to level the floor and not to smooth it.

As the work proceeds, test the surface of the floor in all directions, using a straight-edge for the purpose. This levelling process is one of the most important parts of the business of laying an oak-slatted floor, as it is absolutely essential that the old floor be quite flat and true each way.

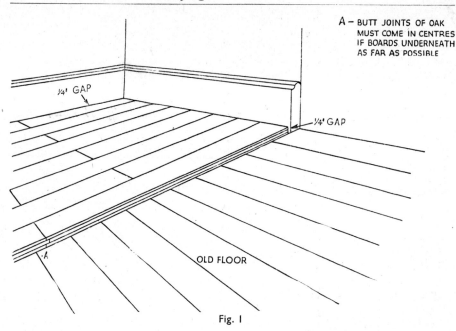

A – BUTT JOINTS OF OAK
MUST COME IN CENTRES
IF BOARDS UNDERNEATH
AS FAR AS POSSIBLE

¼' GAP

¼' GAP

OLD FLOOR

·A

Fig. I

Having satisfied yourself that the levelling process is correct clear away all shavings, dirt and dust.

Now procure a thin special pliable bitumen felt, or, failing this, thick tarred brown paper and lay this material, starting at the far end of the room (away from the door), smoothing it down and outwards with the hands.

A few dabs of hot glue, brushed on here and there on the old floor will help to keep it flat while the first slats of oak are put down.

Laying the Slats.—Choose a wall that is continuous, that is, one with no recesses, projections, etc., and of course one where the old floorboards are at right-angles to it. Measure a distance of $3\frac{1}{4}$ in. away from the bottom of the skirting, at each end. Mark these parts accurately on the floor and partially drive in a 2 in. wire nail at both positions. Between the nails stretch a length of thin string and fasten the ends to the nail. The string forms a guide line, Fig. 3, with which the outer top edge—that is, the edge farthest away from the skirting—of the first length of slats laid must coincide.

Take the first long strip and fasten it down to the floor by driving in a couple of panel pins—one near each end and near the back. Make sure that the grooved edge of the slat is toward the skirting and the front top edge coincides with the string line.

It will be seen that a space of $\frac{1}{4}$ in. is left between the back edge of the slat and the skirting. This gap is purposely provided to allow for expansion which sometimes takes place in a newly laid oak floor. The same amount of gap must be left between the ends of the boards and the skirting.

Verify that the front of the edge of the slat is correct with the line, and hammer in panel pins as before, spaced at intervals of about 1 ft.

Then take the second slat that goes to make the total length, saw off the end so that there is a space of $\frac{1}{4}$ in. at the skirting end, insert the tongue into the groove and drive in panel pins at the back.

It is absolutely essential that this first complete length of oak be truly laid as otherwise difficulty will be experienced in fitting the rest.

Now secret-nail the front edge of the

Fig. 2

slats by driving in panel pins at the top back edge of the tongue. The pins should be spaced about 8 in. apart and driven in at an angle of 45 deg., as shown in Fig. 4. Do not put in less pins than that stated as the fastenings prevent subsequent squeaking. Punch the heads well below the surface by the use of a thin nail punch or a wire nail filed and tapered towards its end.

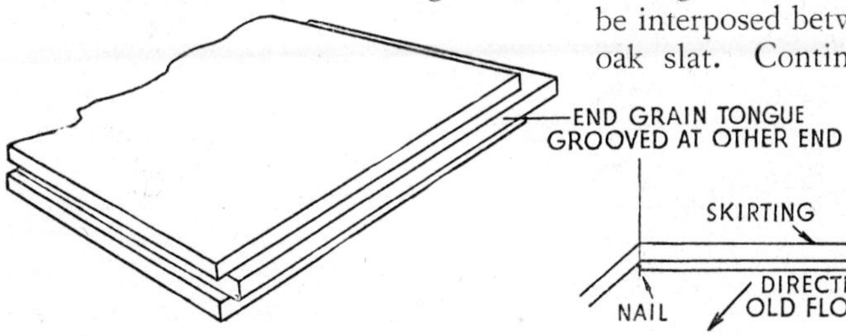

slats. This also keeps them in position when skew nailing the tongues. Another method is to drive the blade of an old narrow chisel into the floor and prize the slat up against the other while nailing. A small block of wood should be interposed between the blade and the oak slat. Continue the work in this

END GRAIN TONGUE
GROOVED AT OTHER END

SKIRTING   GUIDE LINE

NAIL   DIRECTION OF
OLD FLOOR BOARDS   NAIL

Fig. 3

fashion, cutting the boards with a sharp hand saw as necessary to trim round projections, fireplace, bay window, etc., not forgetting to leave a $\frac{1}{4}$ in. gap at the ends for expansion.

Having completed laying the slats, go over the work with a finely set sharp smoothing plane and then clean off with glass-paper Nos. 0 and 1.

Obtain a suitable quantity of $\frac{1}{2}$ in.

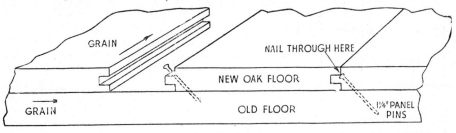

GRAIN

NAIL THROUGH HERE

NEW OAK FLOOR

GRAIN   OLD FLOOR   1¼" PANEL PINS

Fig. 4

Proceed with the second row of slats by first inserting the tongues into the grooves, making sure that the joints butt tightly. If necessary, tap the boards, but in doing so use a smooth piece of wood about 12 × 3 × 1 in., and hold this against the edge of the oak to prevent the hammer breaking the tongues.

To keep the slats tightly in position, drive a few nails into the old floor so that they press on the near edge of the

quarter round oak moulding and pin this to the skirting to cover the gaps.

Finally, remove all dust and fill up any cracks between the slats with melted beeswax, applying it with the grain as in glass-papering. Stain to the desired shade and allow the stain at least twelve hours to dry. Then give the floor a vigorous polishing with either a home-made polish of beeswax and turpentine or a high-class proprietory preparation of wax polish.

MODERNISING A FIREPLACE

IT is a very simple thing to encase these fireplaces with wood, which may be taken out when moving to another house. The work can be done very cheaply, for it is possible to make the wood mantel out of old packing cases (machinery cases) which, if treated properly, would look quite as well as red deal, pine or American whitewood.

The latter two woods are, however, cheap and save labour, for if packing case wood is used it must be glass-papered to obtain a proper surface. If a really fine, smooth surface is required it is best to use the pine or whitewood.

If the furniture is of Jacobean design it will be best to make the mantel out of packing cases. If the furniture is modern the fireplace should be made of pine or whitewood.

The following article deals with how to modernise an old iron mantelpiece, size 4 ft. 4½ in.×4 ft. 1 in. out to out, with packing case wood. The measurements here given may have to be altered to fit your special requirements.

Construction.—First saw out the following pieces of wood: one piece size 4 ft.×9×¾ in. for the frieze, two pieces each 4 ft.×9×¾ in. for the two sides.

Now take out all the nails and, if necessary, wash the wood in soap and water. Allow time to dry, then plane diagonally to ⅝ in. thick. This is best done with a smoothing plane, using short circular strokes in a diagonal direction. Do not worry about the resulting rough surface so long as it is reasonably level.

Next, fit the two side pieces under your iron mantelshelf, hand-tight. You will see in diagram A, Fig. 2, that the iron shelf is hollow. With these pieces still in position, place the frieze on them—well up under the iron shelf and pin it on to the side pieces with long veneer pins.

Then take this structure down (you will need a friend to help you) and place it upside down on a table. From the back, screw on the two side pieces—five screws in each case.

Replace the structure so as to obtain the width of the side returns; see side view in Fig. 1. These will be the same length as the sides and about 3 in. wide. Cut them to length and scribe them on to the skirting moulding. This is best done by using a cardboard template.

Now saw and chisel these pieces out (see D, Fig. 1) and fit from time to time.

Take down the structure and pin on the two returns from the front with 1½ in. panel pins, 6 in. apart.

Cut out and square up a piece of wood, size 3 ft.×8×½ in., for the bases and their returns (on the outer edges only). Set the gauge to 1 in. and gauge a line along the face (top) edge. Then on the face edge gauge a line ¼ in. from the face side. Rebate this out, or it may be done with a chisel.

As the bases are butt-joined, cut two pieces the exact length of the 3 in. side width, pin them on and then pin on the two front pieces.

See that the bases project beyond the sides (pilasters), EE Fig. 1, for although they are not "returned," here they prevent the movable copper panels FF from slipping out.

The work should now be turned over and the bases firmly screwed from inside.

Now run out some moulding, details of which are shown at C in Fig. 2. About 5 ft. 6 in. will be required. Work this moulding in the same way as described for the base moulding.

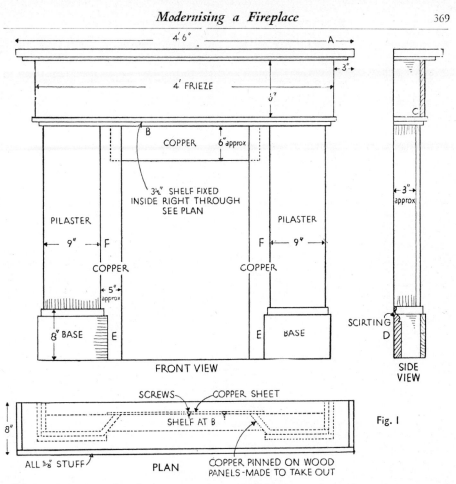

Fig. 1

Then cut a piece for the 3½ in. wide shelf and pin this in position so that the front edge comes level and below the face of the frieze. This means the shelf will have to be notched out at both ends 9 × ¾ in.

Now pin on the end pieces of moulding and then the front piece so as to cover the end grain of the return pieces.

As this part of the structure is now complete, give it a good wash down with warm water then allow it to dry and then give it a good glass-papering with middle 2 and fine 2.

Next cut a piece of wood the exact size of the old iron mantelshelf. Run out, as before described, sufficient moulding to go round, as shown in the diagram A. Pin this on all round, keeping the moulding level with the face side of the shelf so that it will drop well down (hand tight) and cover the unsightly iron moulded edge. Wash the shelf and paper it as described above.

The Metal Panel.—Purchase a sheet of copper, brass or chromium metal, size 1 ft. 3 in. × 6 in., and bore a series of holes ⅛ in. in diameter along the top edge about ⅜ in. in from the edge.

If a hammered effect is required put it on a piece of hardwood, and with a small round-headed hammer, tap it down from the centre in parallel strokes outwards to the ends; then, still from the centre, tap it out vertically to top and bottom edges. From time to time turn the metal over and flatten it with a mallet, still working outwards.

Lacquering.—Clean the copper with metal polish and to save labour, lacquer it in the following manner:

Purchase a small bottle of colourless lacquer and a camel-hair brush of large size. Put the copper sheet on the gas stove with the jet burning low.

Test the heat of the copper by touch-

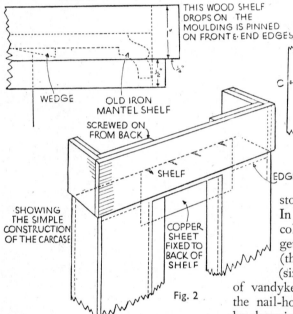

DETAIL A

THIS WOOD SHELF DROPS ON THE MOULDING IS PINNED ON FRONT & END EDGES

WEDGE   OLD IRON MANTEL SHELF

SCREWED ON FROM BACK

SHOWING THE SIMPLE CONSTRUCTION OF THE CARCASE

SHELF

EDGE OF SHELF

COPPER SHEET FIXED TO BACK OF SHELF

Fig. 2

probably be about 5 in. wide. They fit up under the 3½ in. shelf and behind the inside projections of the base. Fit these in first, then prepare the copper sheets as before described and screw the metal on with small copper round-head screws.

The angle of these copper panels will be 45 deg. approximately, but as they rest against the dropped copper sheet it will be easy to find the exact angle required and then the inside edges of the pilasters can be bevelled off to fit.

Fit the mantel in, drop on the shelf and fit in the copper side panels.

Staining and Polishing. — When everything is satisfactory, determine the colour you require it and make up some stopping to fill the nail holes. In this case, dark brown is the colour suggested, so melt together a small piece of beeswax (the size of a walnut) and resin (size of a marble). Add a pinch of vandyke brown powder. Punch in the nail-holes and apply the stopping by dropping it in the holes.

Now give the whole work a good glass-papering, taking care to work with the grain and pressing on the forward stroke.

Mix some vandyke brown powder with some .880 spirits of ammonia and mix to a paste. Thin with cold water to the required colour. Stain the work, using the brush with the grain, allow to dry, then vigorously rub the mantel with coarse canvas (hessian).

Finally, polish it with one of the well-known wax polishes.

ing it, and when a trifle warmer than comfortable to the hand, put on the lacquer quickly with round even strokes, taking great care not to go over any part twice. It is advisable to experiment on a small piece of copper first, and remember that the metal must be perfectly clean.

Now screw on the copper to the back edge of the 3½ in. shelf, so that it hangs down and hides the top tiles.

The Side Panels.—Next cut out and bevel the edges of the two side panels, as shown in the plan Fig. 1. These will

FITTING A PUMP TO A BATH

A PUMP for raising hot water from a copper in a scullery to a bath situated in a room on the floor above, and where there is no hot water supply, is a great convenience.

The installing of such a pump is neither costly nor difficult.

The pump used for the job is a device known as the double acting semi-

Fig. 1

rotary pump, actuated by a to and fro movement of a handle about a foot in length. Such a pump costing about 25s. is illustrated in Fig. 1, while the internal mechanism is pictured in Fig. 2.

It is essential to fix the pump near the source of supply, in this case a gas-heated copper, and not at the bath end. Iron pipes can be employed but the use of a thick lead pipe will save labour in the screwing for attaching elbows. Lead

pipe also has the advantage of being easily bent.

Lifting Floor-boards.—It will be necessary to lift one or two floor-boards and perhaps to slot several joists in the room above. To remove the floor-boards first punch the nails down as far as possible and insert a cold chisel on each side of the board and prize it up. To prevent bruising the boards more than necessary, insert a block of wood between the chisel and the board.

Cut a hole in the ceiling sufficiently large to allow the pipe to pass through easily. To do this, push the blade of a bradawl between two laths at the position required, enlarge the hole with a screwdriver and cut the laths with a pad saw. If this is done carefully, little damage will be done to the plaster surrounding the hole.

Fig. 2

In measuring up to ascertain the length of the pipe do not forget to allow about a foot extra for bending over the edge of the bath and make provision for a short piece below the inlet of the pump.

If you cannot solder lead to brass, get a plumber to fit the brass fittings that connect the pipes to the pump.

As lead piping is not easy to handle owing to its weight, get an assistant to lend a hand whilst getting the pipe through the hole in the ceiling and fastening it to the wall. In bending the pipe the radius of the curve should be as large as possible and care must be taken not to flatten the pipe. Use galvanised iron saddles for supporting the pipe and use round-headed screws for fastening them.

Mounting the Pump.—The pump should be mounted upon a block of wood about $1\frac{1}{4}$ in. thick and 9 in. wide and about 12 in. in length. Chamfer the front edges, bore suitable holes for the screws which hold it to the wall, and, after fixing the block, mount the pump. Screw the connecting caps down tightly to the inlet and outlet flanges of the pump and connect the pump to the tap on the copper by means of a short piece of canvas hose.

The joint between the hose and lead pipe can be made more or less permanent either by a suitable clip or by binding it with copper wire. The connection at the tap, however, must be of an adjustable type so that the hose can be removed when not in use.

Now fill the copper with water, turn on the tap and operate the pump to see that it works well and that the system does not leak. If all is correct, light the gas under the copper and try it again when the water is hot as a leakage may appear at the screwed joints owing to expansion. For this reason, it is advisable not to pump boiling water; a temperature of 160 deg. F. should not be exceeded.

As the interior of the pump and the lead pipe may be greasy and dirty, a handful of common washing soda can be added to the first lot of hot water. This should be followed by another supply of hot water, after which the system will be ready for use.

In order to give the system a workmanlike finish, the pipes can be painted with aluminium paint and the mounting block treated with ordinary lead paint of a colour to match the surrounding decoration. Any damage around the hole where the pipe goes through the ceiling can be hidden by cutting a small cover of thin plywood, screwing it to the ceiling and painting it to match the latter.

In the event of iron pipes being used it will be necessary to apply red-lead paint to the screw-threads and to wind a few strands of hemp between them at each joint. This prevents leakage.

MODERNISING DOORS

FLUSH doors have many advantages over the usual framed, moulded and panelled door. They are easy to dust, keep clean and repaint, and we all know the difficulties experienced when repainting a panelled door where the mouldings have shrunk with the panels away from the stiles.

This shrinkage problem has also to be considered when making a flush door. It is most important to have all the wood of good quality and well seasoned. Even then the grain should be opened by roughly planing each piece and leaving the wood for some time in a hot kitchen, turning the pieces from time to time to prevent any possible warping.

The best woods to use for the door frame and stock (core) are Canadian yellow pine, good quality deal, or Gaboon mahogany. This latter wood is light in weight, very easy to plane and does not warp or twist. Apart from these good qualities, it is not very

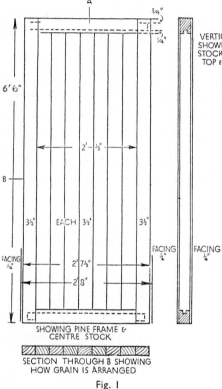

VERTICAL SECTION AT **A** SHOWING HOW CENTRE STOCK IS GROOVED INTO TOP & BOTTOM ONLY

SHOWING PINE FRAME & CENTRE STOCK

SECTION THROUGH B SHOWING HOW GRAIN IS ARRANGED

Fig. I

expensive. Plywood is used for facing the door.

The door shown in Fig. 1 is 6 ft. 6 in. × 2 ft. 8 in. × 1⅜ in. Purchase sufficient lengths of wood 4 × 1 in. to do the whole door. Then roughly plane it and leave to dry as before described.

When dry, begin work on the outer frame.

Construction.—Take four pieces of wood — namely, two pieces each

6 ft. 8 in. × 4 × 1 in. for the stiles and two pieces each 2 ft. 4½ in. × 4 × 1 in. for the rails.

Plane the face side of each piece, test and mark it. Then plane the face edge of each piece and also test and mark it.

Set the marking gauge to 3½ in. wide, mark the pieces and plane off to the gauge lines.

Gauge ⅞ in. thickness and plane off to the gauge lines.

On the long pieces, square across pencil lines all round 1 in. from each end, then measure inwards from these lines 3½ in. and again square all round. This gives the positions of the rails.

It should be observed that the 1 in. extra on the ends is for knocking up and to prevent the mortices from breaking through the ends. These "horns" are sawn off after the door is glued up.

Set out the mortices on the stiles between the 3½ in. lines, gauge them to ⅜ in. wide and cut them out 2⅛ in. deep.

Square the shoulder lines all round 2 ft. ½ in. apart on the short pieces, with a chisel. This leaves 2 in. for each tenon, which is ⅜ in. thick. Gauge and saw these out. Then plane a groove down the face edges of these two short pieces ⅜ in. wide × ¼ in. deep, details of which appear at A in Fig. 2.

Fit this frame together and "face it up" true on each side.

Now cut the seven pieces for the centre core, each 6 ft. 1 in. × 4 × 1 in. and glue them together in pairs (two pieces at a time). Leave these for twelve hours to dry, then reduce each pair to 7¼ in. wide.

Glue the three pairs together and more than make up the final width by gluing on the last 4 in. piece. Leave to dry.

Then saw off the ends to the required

length and run out a $\frac{3}{8} \times \frac{1}{4}$ in. tongue on each end.

Fit on the top and bottom rails and see that the tongues run easily in the grooves.

When doing this, check off and plane the joined core to the exact width required—that is, the width from shoulder to shoulder of the tenons—as there are no grooves in the stiles.

Now glue up one stile and the two rails, slide in the core and glue on the other stile. Cramp up tightly with several sash or tee-cramps.

Leave as long as possible to dry. Afterwards remove the cramps, clean up and put the door on the floor of a warm room for some weeks, turning it over each day.

When the door

If the door is to be painted, good quality alder or birch will suffice. Other plywoods available are oak, mahogany, walnut, Oregon pine, Columbian pine, etc. Oregon pine and Columbian pine show very beautiful grain markings.

Now plane and square a piece of wood of the same kind as the ply facing, 6 ft. 7 in. $\times 2\frac{1}{2} \times 1\frac{3}{8}$ in.

Put this in the vice and gauge two lines $\frac{3}{8}$ in. apart—down the centres of the two long edges. This is the width of the tongue. Now gauge a line all round $\frac{1}{4}$ in. and another all round $\frac{3}{4}$ in. from the edges.

The $\frac{1}{4}$ in. line gives the depth of the rebates on each side. The $\frac{3}{4}$ in.

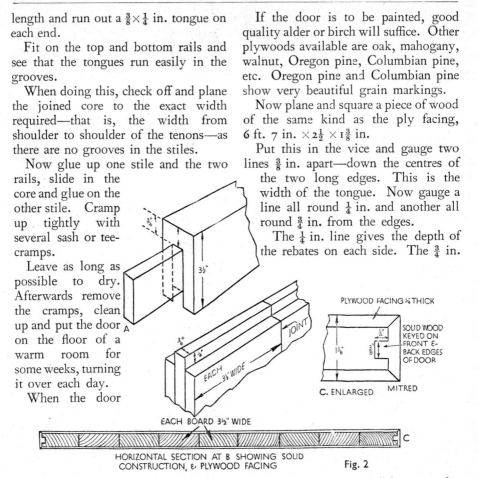

C. ENLARGED   MITRED

HORIZONTAL SECTION AT B SHOWING SOLID CONSTRUCTION, & PLYWOOD FACING   Fig. 2

has "settled down," tooth it across the grain by working a toothing plane towards the centre. Failing this, hold together a couple of firmer chisels and with the corners of the blades scratch (score) across the grain as many lines as you can. Hold the handles of the chisels towards you at an angle of 45 deg. This will give a rough surface which will hold the glue.

Then plough a groove down the outside edges of both stiles, $\frac{3}{8}$ in. wide $\times \frac{1}{4}$ in. (full) deep.

Facing.—The plywood for facing should be 6 mm.; that is, about $\frac{1}{4}$ in. thick—not less.

line is where you saw off the strips after you have rebated the four outer edges, so as to leave the tongue standing up as shown in detail at B in Fig. 2.

Fit these strips into the two grooves on the door stiles, but do not mitre the ends yet.

With plenty of clean hot glue stick them on and cramp up. Clean off the glue with a hot wet rag, not too wet. Leave the work for twelve hours to dry.

With a metal shoulder plane, plane a 45 deg. bevel on the $\frac{1}{4}$ in. projecting edges. This is a skilled tool operation, so go carefully about it.

Now square the edges of the plywood

faces to the exact size required and note this ply is 6 ft. 6 in. long (or whatever the door height is) as the top and bottom of the door is not faced, but is stained and polished or painted to match the ply facing.

Gauge a line ¼ in. from the two long edges and on the back of the ply facing. Then with a fine set trying plane or a jack plane, bevel off to 45 deg. the two edges on each piece and fit them in.

Gluing.—The gluing up will need some preparation. Here are a few points:

1. Do the work in a hot kitchen.
2. Have ready (and keep hot on the stove) two large glue pots full of clean, thin (tacky) glue.
3. Put the door on the kitchen table (or small table) so that the door projects over the edges of it.
4. Have a clean cloth ready—in a saucepan of hot water, and plenty of hand-screws or G cramps.
5. Have a couple of helpers at hand.

Everybody must work quickly in the following way: Slop (pour) the glue quickly on the door and brush it over with a large brush. Put on the plywood facing and push it up and down between the mitred edges, so as to rub out the glue. Damp the face of the plywood with the hot, slightly wet rag. See that the plywood is flush with the edges and then put a big weight on the centre, such as another table upside down. Put plenty of hand screws round the edges and leave to dry. Wipe off all the surplus glue with the hot, wet rag.

Then turn the door over, placing it on an old blanket or large cloth to prevent scratching the ply-face already done, and proceed with the other side.

Thoroughly clean up the edges first, then the face and back with Nos. 1 and o and flour glass-paper and polish.

To convert an old panelled door into a modern flush one, proceed in the following manner:

First study the existing architrave (surround moulding). This generally runs away down by a series of mouldings to the face of the door.

Note, flushing the door will make it about ⅛ in. thicker on each face, and so when rehanging it may be necessary to put a small fillet on the architrave to "thickness up" to the new door face. Or, of course, a new flat (not moulded) architrave may be substituted.

Take the old door off, remove the hinges, lock, handles, etc.

With a blow-lamp, burn off all the old paint, etc., from the rails and stiles only. If a blow-lamp is not available, the old paint may be taken off with strong American potash or other chemical paint-remover.

When dry, plane over the rails and stiles and tooth (roughen) them as before described. See that the surface on each side is perfectly flat.

The sunk panels may be "thicknessed up" to the level of the stiles by pinning on strips of deal planed to suit. This need not be done if you do not object to the slightly hollow sound that is heard when the door is tapped.

Now groove and key on the end strips as before described. The thickness in this case will vary according to how much the old door has shrunk.

Pin a strip on the top edge—if necessary, and on the lower edge also where the floor is worn away.

Allow time for the glue to dry. Then glue the plywood facings on the front and back as already explained, clean up and polish as required.

A WELL LAID OUT SMALL GARDEN

THINGS TO DO IN THE GARDEN

SUGGESTIONS FOR LAYING OUT THE GARDEN

THE aspect and size of the plot will determine features that can be included with success. There are few plots, even in towns, that cannot be turned into beautiful gardens if thought is given to the requirements of the plants it is desired to grow. Many gardens have shady spots, and although most flowers require sun, there are certain kinds that prefer partial or complete shade. If the garden is small, it may be impossible to include all desired features. Have variety by all means, but do not attempt too much. A simple design should be tried rather than a complicated one. The former will be easier to carry out, easier to keep in order and generally more attractive.

A short garden of fair width may be laid out to look much longer by suitable proportioning of beds and curvature of their outline.

The plainness of the fence-line may be broken at intervals by climbers and rambler roses of various kinds. Flowering shrubs break up groups of herbaceous plants and can be used with effect to fill odd corners. When the garage intrudes on the view, erect a trellis-work against it and train suitable plants on it.

The Pathway.—Gardens must have pathways, but these should not be too wide and out of proportion with the space. Avoid long, straight stretches. Try to think of the path as something more than just a way leading to the bottom of the garden. Let it lead from one interesting feature to the next. Stepping stones may be sunk in the grass to provide a dry walk after rain.

Drawing of Garden Plan. — A variety of suggested layouts is given herewith, and if a personal plan is drawn on similar lines, it will be of great assistance. We would suggest that a large scale drawing be made to show in detail how the garden will look when finished. Keep this drawing for reference and make a tracing to work from. This working plan should have as many dimensions as possible for the widths of paths and borders. Run the dimensions from one fixed place such as the outside wall of the house, or the edge of the concrete surround. To reproduce on the ground the curved outlines of flower beds, mark off on the plan distances of, say, 3 ft. or 5 ft. along the fence-line for as far as the beds extend. At each interval thus marked, measure outwards to the edge of the bed curve and write in the distance. Distances of less than a foot over an established dimension should be to the nearest 3 ins. For example, a width between 3 ft. and 4 ft. would be near enough for garden purposes if made

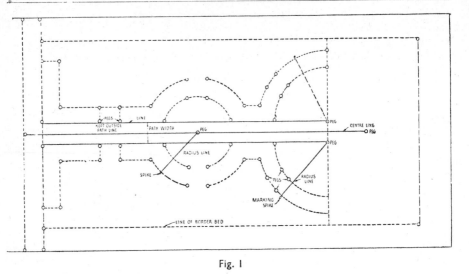

Fig. I

3 ft. 3 in., 3 ft. 6 in., or 3 ft. 9 in., do not bother with the odd 4, 5, 7 or 8 in., either when making the plan or pegging out the ground.

Those who cannot successfully draw a garden plan should proceed on the following lines.

Laying out the Garden.—Clear the ground of all builders' rubbish and large weeds and dump it clear of the site. Cut a supply of wooden pegs about 16 or 18 in. long, out of rough timber about 2 in. square. Include a few longer ones of larger section for marking main points. Two stout garden lines for setting out and, if possible, a long tape measure, 50 to 66 ft. as used by builders, a mallet or hammer for driving in pegs, an 8 ft. length of 3 × 1 in. timber marked off in feet and half feet as shown in Fig. 2B will complete the equipment required. If a builder's tape cannot be obtained, the work can be laid out by means of the lines pegged out to give true direction and the measurements marked with the measuring rod which, for greater convenience, could be 10 feet long. Two rods, one long and the other shorter,

for offset measurements might be desirable.

A plan like Fig. 4 is easy to lay out. Starting from the house line, the width of the path can be pegged out, then the width of the flower bed from the fence on each side of the garden and at the bottom. Measure across the garden at one end and drive in a big peg half-way. Repeat this at the other end and secure a length of line tightly between the pegs. This will establish the centre line for the path and circle. Set off the width of the central path and drive in pegs to mark the edges of the pathway. Run the garden line along the pegs and check up the widths. Put in pegs to indicate the shape and corners of the flower beds. Establish the centre of the circle on the centre line and drive in a stout peg, a round one if possible. Make sure it will stand a fair strain, as this peg is to take a marking line for the circle. Make a secure loop in one end of a length of line and tie a peg or metal spike to the other at a distance equal to half the diameter of the circle. Now walk round the centre peg, keeping the line taut, and drive in a circle of pegs for the outline of the path. Lengthen the line and peg out the curved flower bed in the same manner. The curved beds at the end are done in the same way except that the centres for the quarter-circles are off the main centre line at a distance apart equal to the path width as indicated on Fig. 1.

Flower Beds.—Curved flower beds

An increase of 3 to 6 in. will give a fair curve, so try a peg at 3 ft. 6 in. At the next peg along the fence-line, move out to 3 ft. 9 in. or 4 ft. The curve then sweeps in towards the fence, so as you proceed from peg to peg decrease the distance by about 3 in. at a time. If a sharper curve is required, try the effect of 6 or 9 in. Walk away and judge the effect from various points

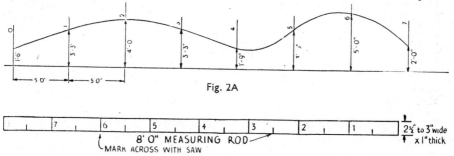

Fig. 2A

Fig. 2B

as in Fig. 2A are set out by marking off along the fence-line and inserting pegs at intervals of, say, 5 ft. for a long garden or 3 ft. for shorter plots. Now, with the measuring rod held at right-angles to the fence, start at the first peg and establish the width at the start, say at 3 ft. from the fence. Then move to the next peg, lay the marking rod on the ground and, if not working to a dimensioned plan, judge how far out you would like the bed at this point.

and vary the positions of the pegs accordingly.

Where possible, the pegs should be left in even after the flower beds have been dug, until the grass portions have been dug and levelled.

Garden Designs.—For a narrow garden, a show of bloom from early to late in the year can be obtained when the borders are shaped to curved outlines extending the full length as shown in Fig. 3. Planting is done in groups to

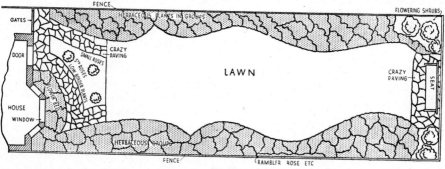

Fig. 3

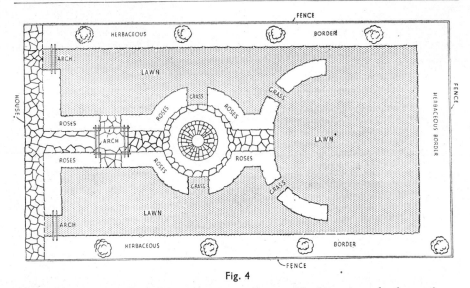

Fig. 4

give contrasting and blending colours, each group merging into the next. To make the most of the space, plant tall flowers at the back, then those of medium height, with the short varieties in front. This will give a bank of bloom from back to front, and if the heights are varied along the beds as well the effect will be undulating waves of colour. A long path has not been included except near the house, and this leads to the edge of the lawn, round a bed to include about three standard or shower roses with dwarf border plants or polyantha roses. At the bottom of the garden a seat is arranged on crazy paving flanked by flowering shrubs or trees such as cherry, lilac or laburnum. As a protection from sun or wind a screen behind the seat could be included, or if the seat is placed to one side and both get plenty of sun, select that which gives the main sunlight from the back, thus avoiding glare direct on the face.

Fig. 4 is a much more formal design with a central path for a little more than half-way flanked by straight and curved flower beds for roses and bedding plants, leaving the side borders for herbaceous plants with flowering shrubs at intervals. This divides the lawn into three portions. Arches span the entrances to the left and right lawns and cross the main path twice. The centre of the circular path might be finished in old red brick with a stone or lead figure in the centre.

A larger plot of irregular shape could be treated as shown in Fig. 5. Here the frontage to the roadway is between 45 and 50 ft., with a straight depth on the left of 170 ft. and a back fence line of about 98 ft.

A central entrance gate and path leads past grass plots on each side, through a rose screen and flower beds to the path in front of the house. The front ground-floor rooms are thus screened from the road, but have a pleasant outlook, while on the other side the aspect from the roadway is good. Following the curved path across the lawn, there are herbaceous borders of curved outline along the fences. The lawn on the right goes past the side of the garage and ends in flowering shrubs and border plants along the drive to the garage. The walls of the latter are

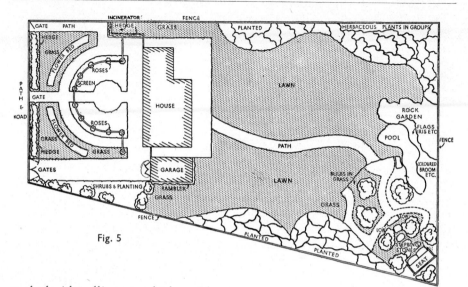

Fig. 5

masked with trellis, over which ramblers are trained. The path proper ends near the pool which has been shaped to natural outlines and backed by a rock garden in grey stone.

The rock garden slopes off to the flower bed and forward to odd rocks in the grass. The other end of the pool extends into the grass under trees where a woodland effect has been aimed at, the paths being mere indications of footways with stepping stones leading through low flowering shrubs to a seat in the corner. Bulbs are planted in the grass.

Fig. 6 illustrates a suggestion for dealing with the end of a plot which tapers off as many do on the curve of a road.

In this case, the ground is very uneven and tilted sideways in places, the general slope being upwards towards the back. By means of pegs and string lines, the general level is found and the places marked for correction of level. Lines are set out across from fence to fence to mark the edge of the seat step, the centre of the pool and the two steps down to the lawn, and the surplus soil

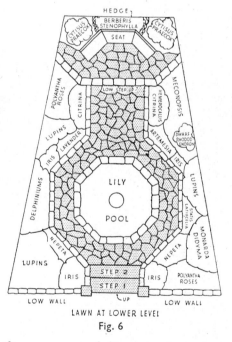

LAWN AT LOWER LEVEL
Fig. 6

from one part of the garden is used to build up the others to the desired levels, including the soil from the foundations of the path and that excavated from the pool.

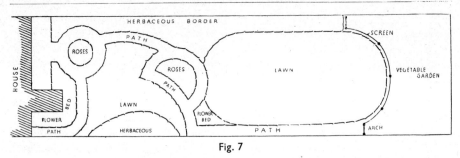

Fig. 7

The bordering of the pool may be raised above the level of the crazy paving and the low wall edge to the flower beds can be at a different height, just enough to retain the soil. The stone steps are best set on a foundation of bricks faced with cement, but the low wall along the lawn is built dry with a certain amount of backward slope at the top. Spaces are left here and there for the planting of wall plants to hang down the face of the wall and from over the top. A few suitable plants for the borders are also indicated on the plan.

In Fig. 7 use is made of both curves and straight lines with a long herbaceous border on the left almost to the end of the larger lawn which extends right across the garden to the path leading through an arch which, in turn, shuts off the vegetable garden.

MAKING A ROCK GARDEN

FIRST decide what the rock garden is to represent and then aim to make it a natural miniature. One may represent a mountain valley, a boulder-strewn bank or a slope showing an outcrop of rock and stones. There may be a boldly fashioned cliff with a pool at the foot, into which a small cascade falls. Various features will suggest themselves as the work proceeds.

Remember that it is not quantity of stone that gives the best effect. Use as little as possible of the right kind, a few large rocks being more effective than a cartload of oddments. The complete rock garden should be built and arranged for the benefit of the plants to be cultivated using suitable composts for different kinds and making conditions as nearly natural as possible.

Choice of Site.—In a small garden, one may not have much choice as to position, but the essential requirement is to keep the site away from the shade and drip of trees. Where the site is on good loam, previously cultivated for a number of years, the natural drainage should be enough provided the mounds are based on a foundation or core of turfy loam mixed with stone chips of the kind that will retain moisture to help the plant roots. Broken bricks of the soft dark red and yellow kind can also be used, as they contain a large percentage of sand and, when they weather away, will improve the soil.

On new ground and on soil of a clay nature, a proper drainage foundation, as shown at Fig. 1, should be made. Clear a space large enough to accommodate the proposed banks and remove the soil for a depth of at least 15 in., making a shallow pit of the whole site. Choose one end—that nearest a flower bed if possible—and make the bottom of the excavation slope that way, as indicated. If the soil is ordinary loam, that taken out can be broken up and heaped for future use, but if it is clay it will be valuable on the rose beds.

The pit is now filled with broken bricks, clinkers, broken slates and

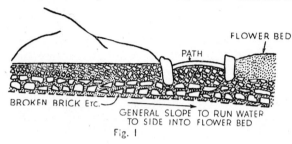

FLOWER BED

PATH

BROKEN BRICK ETC.

GENERAL SLOPE TO RUN WATER TO SIDE INTO FLOWER BED

Fig. I

flower-pots, placing the larger material at the bottom. The top need not be levelled off, but may remain raised in the positions where mounds are to be made later, but not allowed to come too near the surface.

It may be possible to obtain enough soil from other parts of the garden, or a load can be obtained locally. If the

may be used for the core provided it is not clay and large lumps are broken up.

Height and General Shape. — Unless the site is of fair size, it will be impossible to build high as the soil will only wash down with the rains. If only a few feet in average width, it is best not to build to a greater height than 3 or 4 ft.; but when several yards wide the slopes can be carried up to 5 or even 6 ft. in places.

Always arrange an irregular outline, no straight lines or regular curves. Here and there place a bold piece of rock and elsewhere have receding bays. Keep the largest rocks at the lower parts—but do not carry the stone all the way round the margin to outline it. Leave gaps where cushion growths may spread forward on the ground level. Let gaps taper down to ground level in gentle slopes and not end in unsupported banks of soil as these will wash away. This arrangement is indicated in Fig. 2.

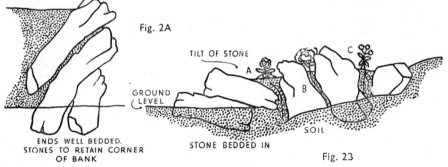

Fig. 2A

TILT OF STONE

A

C

B

GROUND LEVEL

SOIL

ENDS WELL BEDDED. STONES TO RETAIN CORNER OF BANK

STONE BEDDED IN

Fig. 23

latter, the soil should be fibrous loam for the main core over the bricks, the finer stuff with stone chips being used to finish the upper layer to a depth of from 2 to 3 ft. It is as well to build somewhat higher than required as the soil will sink and a great reduction in height spoils the effect.

The rougher soil from the excavation

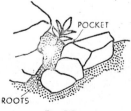

POCKET

ROOTS

Fig. 2C

Kinds of Rock to Use.—One material to avoid is the pale yellow glazed and similar milk-white stone so frequently seen at the side of garden paths. The most suitable and effective

pletely filled with soil mixed with sandstone chips and grit so that the plant roots may be well established, as in Fig. 2B, rocks B and C, and in Fig. 2C. Any that require special compost, with

Fig. 3

stone is dark grey. Limestone, tufa, and harder sandstone are also used.

Soil Pockets.—When placing the rocks, see that they are well bedded with a backward tilt so that rain will run back into the soil for the benefit of the plants, as in Fig. 2A and in Fig. 2B. The spaces between rocks must be com-

peat and leaf mould, can be provided for in this way without digging up much of the other part.

A larger rock garden as shown in Fig. 3 may be roughly divided by a pathway curving through and around, with flat stones as steps and landings placed between the banks.

SIMPLE STONEWORK

THE simplicity of stonework for constructing garden features is often overlooked because the finished results are so effective that the average man thinks there must be more skill attached to it than is really so.

Much may be done with cement and a heap of small pieces of crazy paving

by making the material up into units as shown in Fig. 1A, for low border walls, small corner pillars, and steps. The height is not intended to be much over 12 or 15 in. or they will be too heavy to move, and for any purpose, will depend upon the thickness of the material obtainable. Wall units are

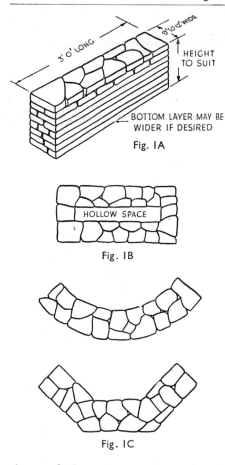

Fig. IA

BOTTOM LAYER MAY BE WIDER IF DESIRED

3' O" LONG

9" TO 12" WIDE

HEIGHT TO SUIT

HOLLOW SPACE

Fig. IB

Fig. IC

about 3 ft. long ×9 to 12 in. wide. In some positions the wall may be made hollow from top to bottom but, with closed ends as at 1B, and, when in place, this may be filled with soil ready for growing plants along the top. The smaller pieces of crazy paving should be used and the inner and outer walls will be about 4 or 5 in. wide with a space of about 5 or 6 in. in between.

Cap Stones and Pillars.—The cap stones are flush with the end if the wall is to butt against a pillar but at the other end the last piece is left off as indicated at Fig. 2, being fixed in position on the next unit so that it overlaps and

N

forms a tie between the two and, except for the complete vertical joint at the end of the wall itself, the whole looks more continuous when finished.

Here and there and at the ends, pillar units may be introduced to break up the run of walling. Some of these may be hollow towards the top to contain suitable plants but if it is desired to plant something larger such as a shrub or a small fir tree, then the whole depth should be made to contain soil for the larger roots.

Walls with curved outline, right-angled corner pieces and corner sections slanting are indicated in Fig. 1C. All of these are built on the same lines.

It is suggested that a board foundation be made similar to a mixing board for cement. Nail a rough wooden fillet on to this to form the outline of the outside of the wall in plan. Also have a straight-edge board for testing the length and face as the work proceeds. All stone should be well soaked with water before use.

Fill the space inside the base fillet with cement and strike off level. On this, place the first layer of pieces in the same manner as when laying crazy paving. Use the straight-edge or a line stretched between pegs as a guide to keep the edges about level, arranging the pieces as indicated. On this put another layer of cement, taking care whenever possible, to keep the new edge joints clear of the joints in the first row so that no two joints are in a straight line. This will key the layers together similar to the bond in brick work. Scrape off surplus cement from the face of the joints.

The cap pieces are wider than the width of the wall, and in this and all layers the odd corners are filled in flush with cement.

Pillars may be on the same lines and

are built two or three layers higher than the wall before the caps are added. In plan the sides may be equal to the width of the wall, but if required to stand out from the face of the wall the square dimension should be increased by about 2 in. For example, for a wall 9 in. thick the pillars would be 13 in. square and would be most effective as end pillars at the side of steps as in Fig. 2. For those at intervals in the general walling only the front face need stand out beyond the wall face.

Steps.—Steps are built as in Fig. 2. The top unit consists of three layers of 1 in. thick pieces cemented into half-circle and the bottom step is also three layers thick, but to a greater radius. Garden steps should have easy

metal spike, also pushed through a hole in the bar.

Bird Bath (Fig. 3).—The column is built of rough-faced stones or lumps of rock-garden stone too small for their real purpose. Stone trays can be purchased, or a slab may be cut with the proper type of chisel. An alternative is to make the trays from a slab of crazy paving with smaller pieces cemented along the edges and made watertight with cement inside. The height may also be less if desired.

Cover for the Manhole (Fig. 4).— One of the most unsightly things about the garden is the iron cover of the drain manhole. A removable cover to go over this is shown in Fig. 4. This consists of a tray made up of pieces of

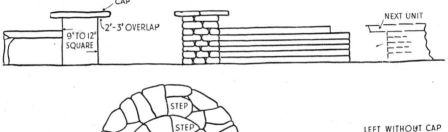

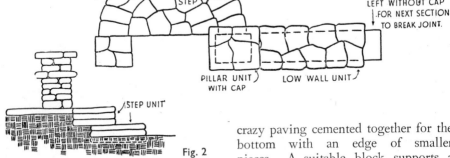

Fig. 2

rises and ample treads or spaces for the feet.

Circles may be marked out by means of a length of 3×2 in. wood with a hole in one end, through which a length of gas pipe is inserted and driven into the ground for the centre. The marking point at the necessary distance can be a

crazy paving cemented together for the bottom with an edge of smaller pieces. A suitable block supports a smaller tray and both are planted with rock-garden plants to hang over the edges.

Dry Walling (Fig. 5).—When the garden is being laid out there is often opportunity to make a dry wall against a natural bank—that is, a wall built without cement, with gaps or pockets of

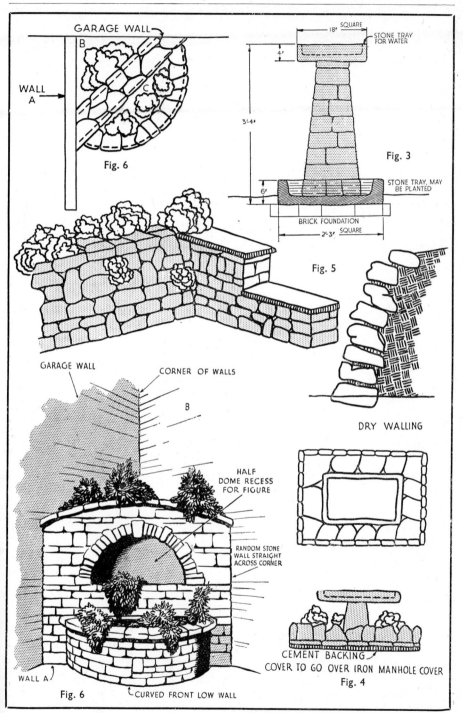

GARAGE WALL

B

WALL A

C

Fig. 6

18" SQUARE

STONE TRAY FOR WATER

4'

3'-4"

Fig. 3

6'

STONE TRAY, MAY BE PLANTED

BRICK FOUNDATION

2'-3' SQUARE

Fig. 5

GARAGE WALL

CORNER OF WALLS

B

DRY WALLING

HALF DOME RECESS FOR FIGURE

RANDOM STONE WALL STRAIGHT ACROSS CORNER

CEMENT BACKING

COVER TO GO OVER IRON MANHOLE COVER

Fig. 4

WALL A

Fig. 6

CURVED FRONT LOW WALL

soil extending into the wall to the soil at the back to which roots may have access. Such a wall is not difficult to build and is beautiful in spring and summer if filled with flowering and foliage plants.

Fairly large stones are required to give stability and the whole wall leans backwards against the bank. The larger pieces are placed at the bottom, most of them being arranged more or less parallel with the face of the soil bank, but some should be placed at right-angles so that the greater part is embedded in the soil to strengthen the wall.

Each layer is placed slightly farther back so that the plants will get a fair share of rain. Use stones of varying size and, when the plants have become established, the appearance will be perfectly natural.

The best time of the year for this work is about September and the planting should be done as the wall is built to ensure that the roots are properly spread in a good layer of soil right through the wall. They will then have time to become established and push their roots into the soil behind the wall before the next season's hot weather sets in. Small plants are better than large ones as they settle down more quickly.

In Fig. 6 we give a suggestion for filling an odd corner where two walls meet. A random stone wall is built across the corner to a suitable height and finished with a curved top. The corner faces of the existing walls should be covered with waterproof cement and the bottom of the corner pocket filled with old bricks with a layer of soil so that plants can be grown in the pocket to hang over the wall. Suitable pieces of stone are set out as an arch built on a rough timber centre. The recess formed under the arch is circular in plan and section and could be of cement, moulded as described elsewhere. The lower part is a low wall filled with soil and planted. The recess could contain a figure; the lower pocket could be made watertight for growing water-lilies.

BRICKWORK IN THE GARDEN

THERE are many uses to which bricks may be put in the garden, such as steps, dwarf walls, posts, bases for sundials, bird baths and figures, pathways and panels in stone paths. The ordinary pale house bricks should be avoided as their colour is not pleasant and their smooth surface and rigid outlines are too hard to blend with garden surroundings.

Select rough-faced varieties of dark red, yellow, brown, plum and other colours. Two or more colours may be used in groups, lines, bands and simple patterns, placing the bricks sometimes on edge for one part of the work and flat for the other parts. Rough-faced tiles on edge are used for edging and panels in between, also in selected courses in brick walls and for a finish towards the top of pillars.

Simple Paths. — For pathways, simple arrangements look well, such as the example illustrated in Fig. 1. Here the main path has bricks on edge in groups of three each way, with dark bricks also on edge but a little higher for the borders.

The same type of border will do for the arrangement in Fig. 2, where the path bricks are laid flat, but in diagonal rows. Widths are adjusted to suit the requirements in both types.

Pillars for the pergola are one brick

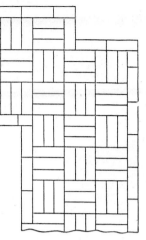

Fig. I

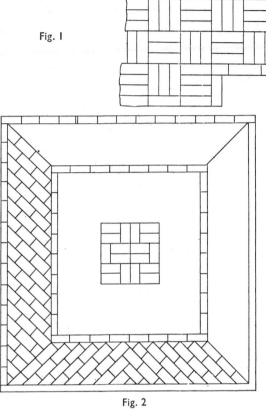

Fig. 2

for a sundial, circular in plan. The bricks are laid on edge for the upper layer of each step, these being placed on a foundation of bricks laid flat. For a more perfect fit round the circle the bricks are rubbed down to taper towards the centre and fitted into place with narrow mortar joints. For the inner circle, tiles on edge make a contrast, or kidney stones set closely together in cement between an edge of bricks relieve the brickwork. These stones, on the same lines as in an old-fashioned cottage path, may be used in panels or as the complete centre section of a path. Such an arrangement is seen in Fig. 5A.

Two artistic arrangements of brick paths are shown round a square pool in Fig. 2 and 5B. The centre pillar supports a bird bath, fountain or figure and is carried out in bricks and tiles, with a set-back panel effect for the centre.

The sharp corners need not be carried down all the way, but between the last one or two upper and lower courses the corners may be rubbed off flat or rounded.

or 9 in. square, and if built with coloured bricks placed at random as regards tint, blend well with the surroundings. Fig. 3 shows a walk of stone flags with a brick panel in each bay and an edging of dark bricks.

Low walls for the front garden may be set out on the lines of Fig. 4A, and the spaces between left open or filled with odd pieces of broken or clinker bricks. As an alternative the whole wall may be of clinker brick burnt into odd-shaped lumps of two or three bricks in a piece, as indicated at B in Fig. 4.

A Sundial.—The illustration at C in Fig. 4 shows brick steps and the base

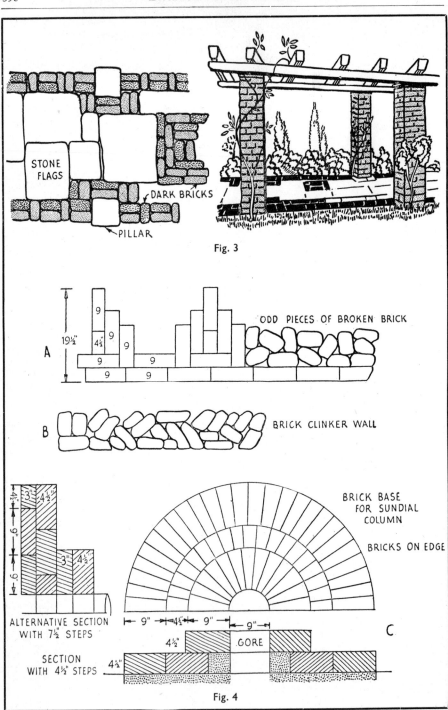

STONE FLAGS

DARK BRICKS

PILLAR

Fig. 3

A — 19½" — 9 4½" 9 9 9 9 9 9 ODD PIECES OF BROKEN BRICK

B — BRICK CLINKER WALL

4½" 3" 4½"
9"
9" 3" 4½"

ALTERNATIVE SECTION WITH 7½ STEPS

SECTION WITH 4½" STEPS 4½"

BRICK BASE FOR SUNDIAL COLUMN

BRICKS ON EDGE

9" — 4½" — 9" — 9"

4½" GORE

C

Fig. 4

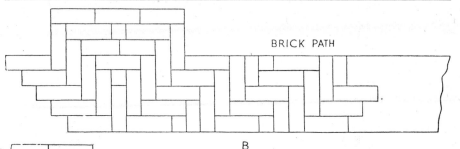

BRICK PATH

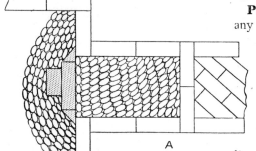

A

Fig. 5

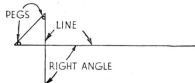

B

PEGS

LINE

RIGHT ANGLE

A

A

B

B

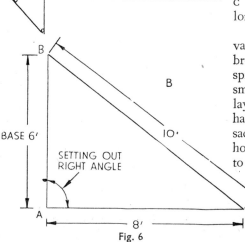

BASE 6′

B

10′

SETTING OUT
RIGHT ANGLE

A

8′

C

Fig. 6

Preliminary Work.—The site for any work such as a pathway, pergola walk or steps must be prepared by removing the soil to a depth of from 3 in. to 1 ft., according to the nature of the soil. To keep the excavation within size, lines are pegged out to mark the width and directions. To ensure that corners will be at right-angles, cross lines are first set out as indicated in Fig. 6A. By this method the pegs are out of the way and only the line indicates the edge to which the work is built. The corners can be checked by means of a square prepared in the workshop, or a very handy rule to remember is that if a base distance of 6 ft. is set out as in Fig. 6B from A, a line 8 ft. long from A will be at right-angles to the base provided the points C to B are 10 ft. apart If this is too long, the lengths may be reduced.

The soil in the bottom of the excavated area must be rammed well and broken bricks, tiles, clinkers and stones spread, rolled in and levelled off with smaller clinkers or cinders. Over this a layer of cement is placed and left to set hard. Cover the work at night with old sacks as a protection against frost. In hot weather, the sacks should be wetted to prevent the cement drying too quickly. This is an important precaution in dealing with all work in cement or concrete which if allowed to dry too quickly is liable to crumble.

PRACTICAL RUSTIC WORK

RUSTIC work is used in the garden for arches, pergolas and screens and is constructed, as a rule, of larch poles of suitable sizes.

The form of construction shown in Fig. 1A may be adapted to suit varying requirements; for example, as shown, it consists of twin uprights with cross members over the top to span the path, and a baseboard linking the two butts where buried in the ground. For an ordinary arch, one unit of two uprights on each side of the path, with two cross members and two to four shorter pieces on top of these again at right angles will complete the job.

A pergola can be built on the same lines using uprights of not less than 3 in. in diameter. Space the pairs of twin uprights about 6 ft. apart and link them across with poles that project at the sides as indicated, and lengthways by means of five spaced poles. Top side rails are generally added and another may be fixed lower down, with or without struts as desired. In Fig. 1B, three units are used as a screen to mask where one path joins another at right angles. The two outer units are repeated on the opposite side to form arches and these two are spanned across to form a wider arch over the other path.

A screen could be made on the same lines as the closed-in side of Fig. 1B, with perhaps, increased spacing between units.

With unbarked larch, the poles for uprights should be skinned for a distance well above ground level and soaked in wood preservative. Galvanised coach-screws should be used for fixing the cross members, then should it be necessary to remove a

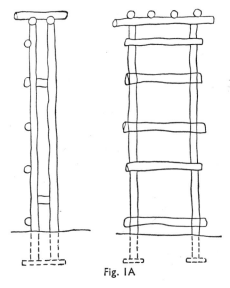

Fig. 1A

member at any time, the screws will come out easily.

Galvanised iron nails and screws should always be used in place of the ordinary kind.

The woodwork is not usually painted as it weathers in time to a silver grey that goes well with the foliage of climbing plants.

Bird Shelter and Feeding Tray.— Another rustic item for the garden is illustrated in Fig. 2. This structure consists of three poles of larch, each with a square wooden base-plate at the bottom. The top ends are notched to fit under a fairly thick piece of timber, sawn from the end of a log. The feeding tray is of rough sawn timber with outer edges and ends left rough, and only roughly cleaned up where the edges of the boards join together.

The shelter has two pieces notched together as indicated to form four divisions and the four sides have

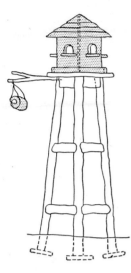

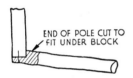

END OF POLE CUT TO FIT UNDER BLOCK

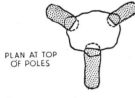

PLAN AT TOP OF POLES

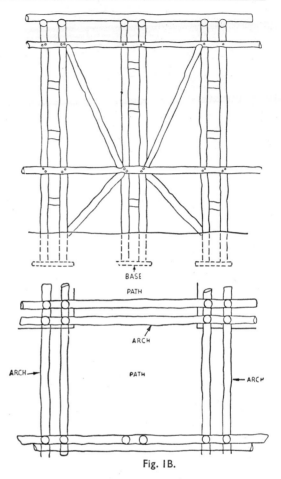

BASE

PATH

ARCH

ARCH→

PATH

←ARCH

Fig. 1B.

PLAN AT TRAY

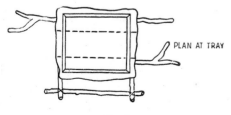

Fig. 2

openings, one into each compartment. Light forked branches nailed underneath the tray form perches. The legs can be used for climbing plants.

Garden Shelter.—A shelter is a useful addition to a garden provided it is in keeping with the surroundings. The one illustrated in Fig. 3 is 5×8 ft. on the outside. The supports for the roof are six poles on the top of which is fixed a timber frame made out of 4×4 in. stuff, halved at the corners as indicated in the lower plan on Fig. 3. A simple roof truss of two rafters braced across should be erected on this at each side of the centre where the

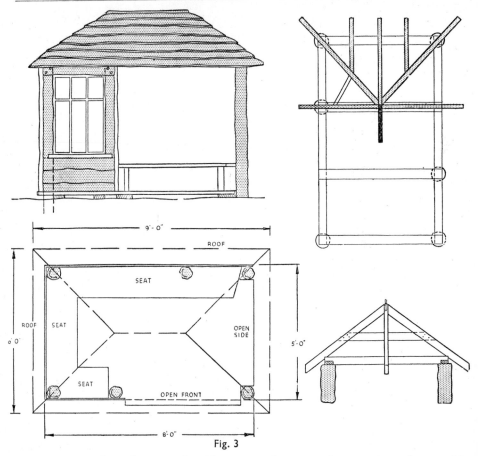

Fig. 3

ridge starts to slope down at the sides. From the ridge board, a rafter extends to each corner and another from the ridge to mid-way along each side. If necessary, bracing pieces can be fixed between these members for additional strength. All rafters are notched to fix over the wall-plate or framework on top of the poles. The roof is completed by shingle boards lapped or a plain boarding covered with heather thatching would add to the rustic appearance. Rubber composition in strips, or tile-shaped in green or red, may also be obtained for fixing to plain boarding.

The poles are well-bedded in the ground, after having been treated with wood preservative or tar, or they could be set in cement.

The floor shown is raised on old sleepers or similar timber and the floor boards cut away round the base are of the poles. A plain boarded seat on brackets is indicated. One end and part of the front is open, the back and other side being closed in with weather boards or rough shingles as on the roof. Part of the front may include a window as shown. A ready-made frame can often be obtained cheaply where buildings are being pulled down, and the surrounding boarding cut to suit. The whole of the woodwork is treated with wood preservative or paint.

A PORTABLE GARDEN TOOL SHED

A PORTABLE shed of light construction for the storage of garden tools and accessories is shown in Fig. 1. The structure measures 5 ft. wide and 6 ft. from front to back, while the roof is 7 ft. 6 in. above floor level at the front and 1 ft. lower at the back.

The walls and roof are constructed of $\frac{5}{8}$ in. matching attached to a framework consisting of $1\frac{1}{2}$ in. square scantlings, fixed by screws to a floor of $\frac{3}{4}$ in. tongued and grooved boards supported on 2×2 in. joists. Each wall, the roof and the floor are separate units so that the structure can be easily dismantled and re-erected upon another site, with the minimum of trouble.

Timber Needs.—Materials are approximately as follows: two squares of $\frac{5}{8}$ in. matching for the walls and roof, half square $\frac{3}{4}$ in. T. and G. flooring for the floor, 150 ft. run $1\frac{1}{2}$ in. scantling for the frames and roof rafters, and 20 ft. 2×2 in. for the floor joists, besides several pieces of wood for constructing the ventilator over the door and other minor purposes. In addition a supply of $1\frac{1}{4}$ in. cut nails will be needed for fastening the matching to the frames, together with some 4 in. wire nails for fixing the frame members, a few No. 8 iron screws for fixing the sections together, two lengths of roofing felt, 1 yd. wide, and some $1\frac{1}{2}$ in. galvanised iron clout nails for fixing it. Also a pair of 12 in. cross-garnets for hanging the door, a substantial rim lock for the door, a piece of glass for glazing the ventilator and a casement stay for keeping the ventilator open.

From the dimensioned drawings Figs. 2 to 6 inclusive, ascertain the exact lengths of wood required, then it can be delivered in lengths which avoid waste.

The Floor.—Make a start with the floor, being sure to choose a level part of the garden. Cut the four joists to length as indicated in Fig. 5, remove the tongue of the first floor-board

Fig. I

shown at A with chisel or plane, and nail it down to the joists, keeping the long trimmed edge flush with the ends of the joists. Lightly fix another board to the joists at the opposite end as indicated at B, as an aid to keeping the floor square whilst the remaining boards are being nailed in position.

Insert the tongue of the second board to be fixed into the groove of the first, seeing to it that there is no gap between the joins, nail it down and continue in this way until the whole of the joists are covered.

Trim the ends of the boards and saw off the projecting part of the last board, as its long edge must be flush with the ends of the joists.

Now construct a pair of side frames to the dimensions given in Fig. 2, using wire nails for joining the parts together. When made, test the lengths for correctness by placing them in position on the floor. The frames should measure 3 in. less than the length of the floor. Carry on the work by making the front and back frames as illustrated in Figs. 3 and 4.

Matching the Walls.—The walls are now ready to receive the matching. Saw the boards 3 in. longer than the height of the frames to allow them to overlap by this amount at the bottom edges of the lower plates and thus cover the floor-boards and joists. Start by nailing the boards to the front section. The outer edges of the boards should project ⅝ in. beyond the outer uprights, while the inner edges of the boards should be flush with the inner edges of the door posts. Do not fill the space above the head of the doorway shown between A and B in Fig. 3, as this aperture accommodates the ventilator.

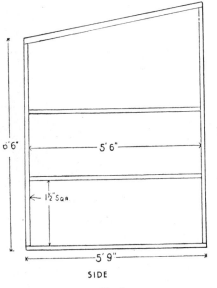

SIDE

Fig. 2

Next fix the boards to the back section, not forgetting to allow ⅝ in. overlap at each end as at the front. Then cut the matching for the sides, allowing a couple of inches extra to the finished sizes. These boards are nailed so that the top edges project 2 in. above the sloping members. The surplus wood can be sawn off flush with the top after all the boards have been fixed. This method of obtaining the angle at the tops of the boards is much to be preferred to marking and sawing individual boards.

Now fasten all four sections together by means of 3 in. wood screws. One screw should be driven in 6 in. from the top and another at the same distance from the bottom at each corner, keeping the outer faces of the lower plates flush with the edges of the floor. Screw the plates down to the floor with No. 8 2½ in. screws. Eight such screws will be required, two for each plate.

The Roof.—The roof should be treated in a similar manner. The outer rafters are 5 ft. 6 in. long and spaced at a trifle over 6 ft. from each other, as indicated in Fig. 6, while the inner ones are only 4 ft. 9 in. in length as they fit between the top plates of the side section.

Before placing the roof in position, fix the roofing felt. Start laying it from the back edge and work towards the front, allowing 2 in. at the ends and sides for turning under the edges of the wood.

Fix the roof to the walls by driving screws through the front and back rafters into the front and back sections, and secure the intermediate rafters by driving screws through the sides and into the ends of the rafters.

The little tool shed is now complete except for door and ventilator. The door is made of matching nailed to three 3 × ¾ in. deal cross-battens at the back, while it is hinged to the left-hand door post by means of two 12 in. cross-garnets. The rim lock should be fitted to the inside of the door, after cutting suitable holes with a pad saw for allowing the handle spindle and the key to pass through.

A strip of wood 1½ in. wide and of the same thickness as the matching should be fixed to cover the head of the door,

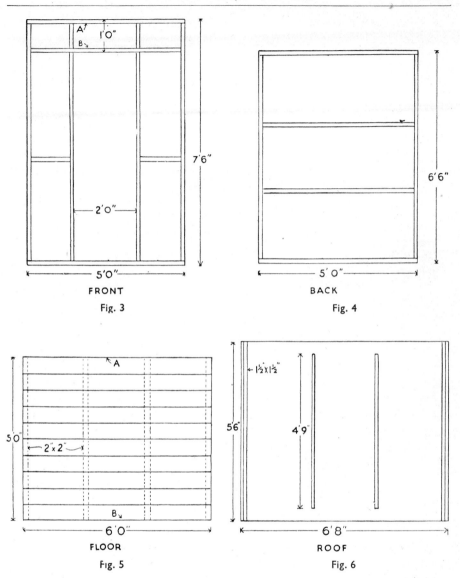

FRONT
Fig. 3

BACK
Fig. 4

FLOOR
Fig. 5

ROOF
Fig. 6

B in Fig. 3, and the member A above it, and a ventilator 2 ft. long ×9 in. wide made to fill the space. This can be constructed of planed batten 1½ in. wide × ⅞ in. thick with halved joints secured by screws at the corners. False rebates for supporting the glass can be of ⅜ in. square wood. Before fixing the glass, give the frame a priming coat of paint, and when dry fix the glass into the recess with putty. Hang the ventilator from the top by using 2 in. butts and fix a suitable casement stay.

Give the whole structure two coats of creosote or other wood preservative, both inside and outside.

A SKYLIGHT FOR A WORKSHOP

A SKYLIGHT is often a welcome addition to the inadequate lighting of a garden workshop or shed. Instructions to make and fit a suitable light to a shed measuring about 12 ft. long and 8 ft. wide having an ordinary eaved roof are given here. For larger structures, the dimensions of the skylight should be proportionately increased, but the simple construction can remain practically the same.

Fig. 1 shows a section of one side of the roof. Here it will be seen that the sloping boards are nailed to two horizontal rafters—one A at the top near the ridge and the other B on the inside of the top plate of the wall.

Selecting the Position.—The most useful place to fix a skylight is midway between the ends and between the two rafters of the front section of the roof, and in order to

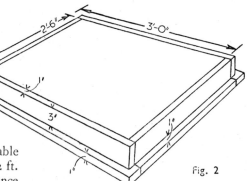

Fig. I

obtain plenty of light it is advisable to make the skylight not less than 2 ft. 6 in. wide and as long as the distance between the two rafters.

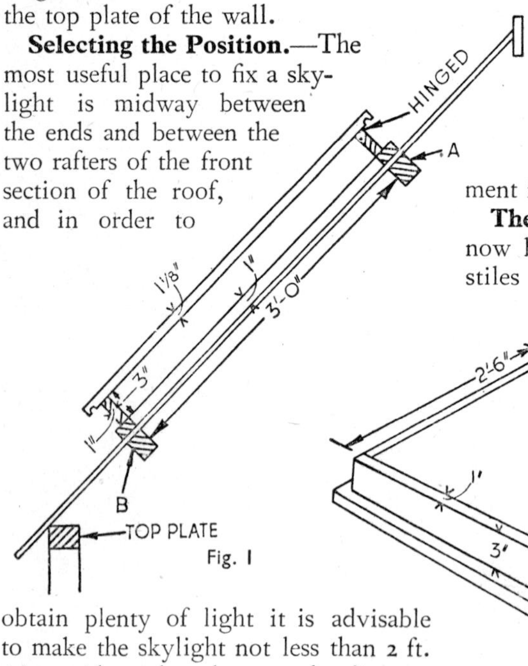

To lessen the labour of sawing, make the width a multiple of the width of a board and separate the boards at the joints. If this is done the only cutting will be across the boards at the top and bottom rafters respectively.

Having decided upon the width of the aperture, remove the roofing felt by cutting it with a sharp knife guided by a straight-edge. Then cut the boards across at the inner edges of the rafters with a pad saw, until the cut is sufficiently long to take the blade of a hand saw with which the cutting is completed. The boards can then be removed at the joints.

Make a plain flat frame similar to a picture frame without the rebate, of 2×1 in. planed batten of the same internal dimensions as that of the aperture and make another frame shaped like a box of 3×1 in., batten and screw the two frames together. The completed fitment is shown in Fig. 2.

The Sash.—The skylight sash can now be made. Make the top rail and stiles 2½ in. wide and 1⅛ in. thick, and

Fig. 2

the bottom rail the same width but ½ in. thinner. In the centre of the top face of the upper rail, cut a channel 1⅛ in. wide and ½ in. deep to house the end of the centre bar which divides the sash along its length. This bar should be 1⅛ in. wide, 1½ in. in depth, and as long as the sash.

The underside of the bar is cut away at the top end to allow it to lie flush with the upper rail, while the lower end is recessed on the underside so that the top projects ½ in. above.

Mortice and tenon the ends of the stiles and rails, glue them up and strengthen the joints with dowel pins driven into holes bored through the frame and tenons. Then fix the centre bar by means of countersunk-headed screws. Fix strips of ½ in. square planed wood around the inside of the sash frame and centre bar, except the lower rail. These should be fixed at a distance of ½ in. from the top edge by means of 1¼ in. oval brads.

To prevent moisture creeping under the edge and entering the skylight, a round groove about ¼ in. wide × 3/16 in. deep should be cut on the underside of the sash, at a distance of about ⅜ in. from the outer edges.

Both the box frame and the sash should now be treated with knotting and then given a coat of lead priming paint, after which the sash may be glazed with 22 oz. glass.

Glazing.—Have the glass panels cut ⅛ in. less in width than the distance between the rebates and allow 1 in. overlap in the length, as the bottom edge of the glass should extend beyond the inner edge of the lower rail.

Before placing the glass in position, apply a thin film of putty to the bottom of the rebates to form a bed. Then place the glass into the recess and press the sheet gently all round to exclude surplus putty. Drive in a few headless brads to keep the glass in position. Apply more putty to seal the joints and level off neatly with a knife.

The box frame can now be screwed down over the aperture in the roof. Brass butts and screws should be used for hinging the skylight sash to the box frame in preference to iron ones as the latter soon rust.

All cracks should be filled with putty to ensure watertightness and the whole finished with two undercoats and a finishing coat of lead paint.

When dry, strips of roofing felt can be nailed to the sides of the box frame and roof to make all watertight.

To complete the work a suitable japanned iron-hinged strut having a series of holes should be fixed near to the front of the inner face of the sash, with a peg to correspond on the frame to keep the skylight open when desired.

GARDEN ORNAMENTS IN CEMENT

PORTLAND cement is a cheap substitute for stone in the construction of garden ornaments. Reproductions of human figures, animals, birds, etc., will give scope for the artistic skill of the maker and quickness in moulding the cement before it sets.

For some ornaments, such as a bowl for a fountain or plants, vases and ornamental boxes, mechanical moulds can be made which will produce the desired article.

Moulding a Bowl.—In making a bowl, a large mould would be difficult to construct and hardly worth making for one article. The best method is to use sweeps or templates as shown in Fig. 1 (page 401). The work may be carried out on a suitable mixing-board or on level ground. In the latter case, see that the surface is flat and hard.

Apparatus required includes a length of gas pipe as a centre pin. This is shown driven into a hole bored in a large block of wood which is in turn fixed to the centre of the baseboard, care being taken to see that it is vertical and firm. Round this is built a core consisting of a mound of clay mixed with old bricks to give it a body. The upper layer of clay should be worked into the shape and size of the inside diameter and depth of the bowl reproduced the reverse way up in the solid. A template is required for this. The template is a wooden board with the inner edge shaped to the profile of the inside of the bowl. The top end is provided with a metal strap and eye to slide over the vertical gas pipe. In the last stages of shaping the core surface, this template is fixed in the position indicated, and moved round in short sweeps to scrape the surface of the clay into correct curves. Fill up hollow places with moist clay pressed firm, and bring the sweep or template round again to give the correct curves. Remove the template and leave the core to dry.

A second template is required, shaped to the curve of the outside diameter and depth of the finished bowl and the space between its outline and the surface of the core will be the thickness of cement for the walls of the bowl.

The cement is applied to the surface of the core and spread nearly to the right thickness, then the sweep is brought round with a backward and forward motion, a little at a time, pushing the surplus cement before it. The surplus should be carefully removed and used to fill hollow places, always slightly advancing the sweep until the whole circuit of the job has been completed.

Finishing the Cast.—In this way the cement will have become smooth and of the required shape. It must be stiff and is best left for twelve hours or more to set before being lifted clear of the baseboard. Should it refuse to come away from the core, turn the whole job over, soak the back of the core with water and dig the clay and core out with a trowel. Most of it will come away readily. The finished job can be cleaned and is ready for fixing to its pillar. The hole where the gas pipe has passed through will be essential for drainage if the bowl is to contain plants, and if for a fountain it will serve to lead the jet pipe through or for a drain plug.

The suggested proportions of materials for the cement mixture for casting ornaments and slabs are as follows:

Three parts sand to one part of portland cement, well mixed, both before and after adding water, and worked to a fairly stiff consistency. Use the mixture directly after being made, and only mix sufficient for the work in hand.

Cement may be coloured by adding suitable powders during mixing. They should be sprinkled over the cement while it is being mixed and not thrown all in one spot. A few lumps of soda added to the water used will dry off the cement quickly and should be used only for moulded or cast work and not for modelled pieces.

Imitation Tree Stumps.—A tree stump with roots and the end of a side branch as shown in Fig. 2, moulded in cement coloured with a mixture of green and brown, can be used to fill an odd corner of the garden and, hollowed to contain soil, will hold a suitable rock plant. A log moulded on similar lines placed or cemented at the foot of the roots will form a soil pocket for planting. An ornament of this kind could be used to hide a manhole cover. Fig. 3 on page 387 shows a stone bird bath and a similar one might be cast in sand and cement.

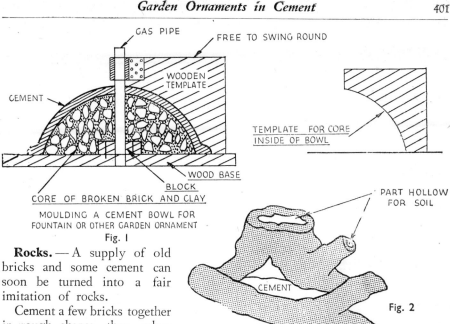

GAS PIPE

FREE TO SWING ROUND

WOODEN TEMPLATE

CEMENT

TEMPLATE FOR CORE INSIDE OF BOWL

WOOD BASE

BLOCK

CORE OF BROKEN BRICK AND CLAY

MOULDING A CEMENT BOWL FOR FOUNTAIN OR OTHER GARDEN ORNAMENT

Fig. I

PART HOLLOW FOR SOIL

CEMENT

Fig. 2

TREE STUMP & LOG MODELLED IN CEMENT FOR ODD CORNER FILLING. PLANTED WITH ROCK PLANTS TO HANG DOWN OVER STUMP & FILL THE WELL BEHIND THE LOG WITH A CUSHION GROWTH FLOWING OVER THE LOG

Rocks. — A supply of old bricks and some cement can soon be turned into a fair imitation of rocks.

Cement a few bricks together in rough shapes, then, when ready, cover each group with cement and sprinkle with plenty of sand. The surface should also be marked like natural rock. A dark green or grey tint can be given to the cement.

Crazy Paving.—Cement pieces for crazy paving $1\frac{1}{2}$ in. thick are made by preparing a mixture of 34 lb. of cement and $1\frac{1}{8}$ cu. ft. of sand and spreading it on a level space of ground bordered by $1\frac{1}{2}$ in. thick wood battens to form a space of 1 yd. square. Strike the surface level with a straight-edge and after being left for two or three hours cut into pieces of crazy shape with a trowel. See that the blade goes right through. Cover with sacks for protection from the sun and wind and keep these damp during hardening. The pieces are then lifted on a spade and stacked until the required quantity has been made.

To save time and trouble in sorting pieces to fit for path work, wood battens should be placed the width apart of the proposed path. Mix the cement, spread and cut as before, but instead of stacking move the pieces a row at a time in the right order to that end of the path which is to be constructed first, leaving a starting space so that it will only be necessary to turn round to find the next piece to fit.

Blocks can be used for pergola posts or walling for pools and sunk gardens. Large ones are for paved paths, courts or for surrounding the house. They are cut to whole squares and half squares in order that the joints may be broken when laid. The usual thickness is 2 in. and the size of square can be varied in any one path so as to avoid regularity. For the same reason do not choose the size used for street paving stones.

For pergola posts the width of small blocks should be equal to half the length, but for wall blocks a few longer or shorter ones here and there help to keep the joints nicely placed.

SIMPLE GARDEN FURNITURE

THE following simple pieces of garden furniture could be made of Indian teak and left natural colour.

Teak can be bought cheaply at ship-breaking yards. The natural oil in the wood enables it to stand up to constant wetting and drying better than any other.

Alternatively the garden furniture could be constructed of pine or deal.

To make the garden seat illustrated in Fig. 1, plane and square up two back posts each 3 ft. 2 in. × 2 × 2 in. and two front posts each 2 ft. 7 in. × 2 × 2 in., four long rails each 3 ft. 7 in. × 2½ × 1 in., one long top back rail 3 ft. 7 in. × 3 × 1 in., four side rails each 1 ft. 4 in. × 2½ × 1 in., and four pieces 3 ft. 7 in. × 3 × 1 in. for the top of the seat.

Making the Seat.—Mortice and tenon the front and back framework first. Square lines across with a chisel 1 in. from each end of each piece and take the lines all round. Now gauge the lines around the edges for the tenons which are one-third the thickness of the wood.

Place all these rails together to see that the shoulders of the tenons are in a straight line.

Set out the mortices on the front and back posts in the positions shown by squaring pencil lines all round.

As these mortices are set in the centre of the thickness of the 2 in. posts, gauge lines from the sides of the posts to leave the mortices ⅓ in. in width.

Cut the mortices out to 1⅛ in. deep, saw down and cut off the tenons.

Put these two frames together and mark and cut out the mortices for the short rails.

Knock the parts together and see that every joint fits well. Take it apart and shape the ends of the posts.

Then prepare some dowels. Square up some strips of hardwood 1 ft. × ⅜ × ⅜ in. and round them by holding the strip on the bench and planing with a smoothing plane. Then file and glass-paper them to ⅜ in. diameter.

All is now ready for gluing up. Glue and cramp up the back first. While the cramps are still on, drill holes, insert the dowels and saw off the waste.

These cramps may be taken off at once and the front and end pieces of the framework glued, cramped and dowelled in the same way.

While this gluing up is being done, test for squareness in each direction.

Wipe off surplus glue with hot water and allow twelve hours to dry.

Smooth with Nos. 2 and 1½ glass-paper, then finish off the tops of the posts and round over all sharp edges.

Next cut and square up the four 3 in. wide battens which form the seat.

These battens are flush with the faces of the end rails, and the front batten is flush with the front framing.

It will therefore be necessary to saw out from the front two corners of this piece 2 × 1¾ in.

Clean and glass-paper all these battens and round off sharp edges. As the battens are screwed to the frame, bore two holes at each end ¼ in. deep, with a ⅜ in. twist-bit and then bore through the bottoms of the holes with a 5/16 in. twist-drill, so as to countersink the screws, which can now be plugged up with ⅜ in. dowels.

Give the whole seat a finish with glass-paper and see that every sharp edge is smoothed off.

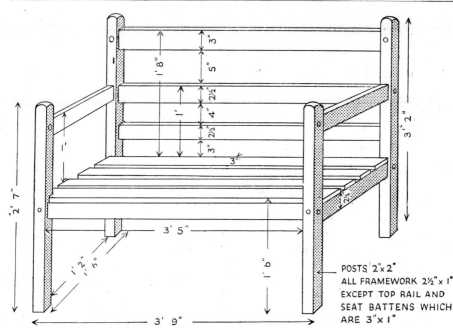

Fig. I

POSTS 2"x 2"
ALL FRAMEWORK 2½"x 1"
EXCEPT TOP RAIL AND
SEAT BATTENS WHICH
ARE 3"x 1"

STOOL 1' 6" x 1' x 1

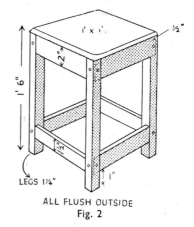

ALL FLUSH OUTSIDE
Fig. 2

If the wood is to be left natural colour, rub it with coarse canvas and dry beeswax. Rub the block of beeswax vigorously with the canvas and then rub the wood with the canvas. This gives a charming polish.

To make teak a rich brown, mix equal parts of turpentine and raw linseed oil, apply it with a brush or rag, and leave it for a few days to dry. Then rub up with canvas as before.

Garden Stool.—The little stool shown in Fig. 2 is a combination piece. It may be used for a seat at the table or it can be used beside the garden seat as a table.

Plane and square up the following pieces of wood: four legs each 1 ft. 5 in.×1¼×1¼ in., four top rails each 11×2×1 in., four bottom rails each 11×1½×1 in., one piece for the top of the stool, 12×12×1 in.

Square round the legs pencil lines for the mortices, as shown. The top mortices are set in ½ in. from the top ends of the legs and are 1½ in. long.

As the rails are flush with the top and legs, it will be necessary to set out the mortice gauge pins to one-third and two-thirds of an inch and gauging from the face side and face edge, carry the lines along between the pencil lines which run across and round the legs. The mortices are on the inner sides of the legs.

Next, take the eight rails and from each end of each piece measure inwards 1 in. and square deeply round the lines with a chisel.

Take the four top rails and gauge back $\frac{1}{2}$ in. from the top edge, or face edge.

Saw out the tenons and chisel or drill out the mortices. As the tenons are 1 in. long, they will clash together when you knock up the work, so pare off the end of each tenon to a mitre of 45 deg., inwards.

Fit each joint separately and mark both mortice and tenon with a corresponding number. Roman numerals are best, as they can be marked with a $\frac{1}{4}$ in. chisel as I, II, III, IV, V, VI and so on. This is better than using a pencil, as such marks are rubbed out when glass-papering.

Now clean up all pieces of wood with Nos. 2 and $1\frac{1}{2}$ glass-paper. Get the dowels ready and glue, cramp, dowel and clean off as described in making the garden seat.

Fix on the top by boring $\frac{3}{8}$ in. holes in suitable position $\frac{1}{4}$ in. deep only, and through the bottoms of the holes bore through with a $\frac{5}{16}$ in. drill. Then screw down the top and plug up the holes with $\frac{3}{8}$ in. dowels.

Plane off the edges and round the corners of the cushion top so that it is comfortable for sitting.

Glass-paper the whole stool and take off all the sharp edges. Then polish as described before.

The rails of this stool are placed low so that the feet may be rested and kept off wet grass.

Warp-proof Table.—The table shown in Fig. 3 has battens round and underneath the top to keep the latter from warping, and the set back of $\frac{3}{8}$ in. gives the effect of moulded edges. Battens on the base keep it off the wet ground and prevent decay.

Plane and square up the follow-ing pieces of wood: one piece 1 ft. 6 in.×1 ft. 6 in.×1 in. for the top (this may have to be joined), one piece 12×12×1 in. for the base, one piece 2 ft. 2$\frac{1}{2}$ in.×11×1 in. for cross supports, two pieces 2 ft. 2$\frac{1}{2}$ in.×5×1 in. for the other two cross supports.

Sufficient battens are necessary, 1×$\frac{3}{4}$ in., to go round the top and base. The heart side of the wood forms the face sides both of the top and the base. Turn them over and centre the under-sides by drawing diagonal lines from corner to corner.

Mark off in pencil $\frac{1}{2}$ in. right and left of the diagonals and parallel to them, two lines for the grooves 11×1 in., in which the uprights are housed $\frac{1}{4}$ in. deep.

Now cut out these grooves $\frac{1}{4}$ in. deep only and square these lines round and across the top and under the base to find the positions for the screws. Keep inside the lines of the grooves when chiselling.

Fix the uprights together as shown at A in Fig. 3. Draw two pencil lines 1 in. apart down the centre of the 11 in. wide piece, bore and countersink $\frac{3}{8}$ in. holes at convenient distances on the centre line and tightly screw on the left-hand piece as shown in the illustration. Between these screws, mark off the positions for the $\frac{3}{8}$ in. hardwood dowels. Bore about $\frac{7}{8}$ in. deep in both the 11 in. and 5 in. pieces and bevel off the edges of the dowels. Then glue and knock in the dowels, test for square-ness and, before the glue is dry, force the uprights into the top and bottom grooves without glue, and leave to dry.

Take off the top and base and screw on the 1×$\frac{3}{4}$ in. battens. These should be screwed on across the grain first, and their full length should be 1 ft. 5$\frac{3}{4}$ in. for the top and 11$\frac{3}{4}$ in. for the base.

The other four battens are screwed on in the clear.

All iron wood screws should be

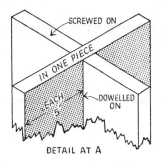

SCREWED ON

IN ONE PIECE

EACH 5"

DOWELLED ON

DETAIL AT A

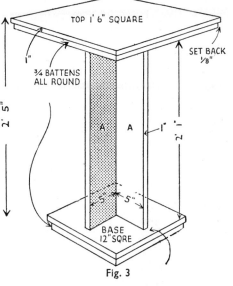

TOP 1' 6" SQUARE

SET BACK ⅛"

¾ BATTENS ALL ROUND

2' 5"

A A

1'

2'

5" 5"

BASE 12" SQRE

Fig. 3

oxidized to prevent rust if they are used for outside work.

Put the screws in the lid of an unsoldered tin. Put the tin on the gas stove and heat the screws until nearly red hot, then plunge them into olive oil.

Clean up and glass-paper the whole table. Glue and screw the upright into the top and base.

Test for squareness and plug up the holes in the top and base as described before.

Clean up and polish as before.

The base of this table also allows the feet to be kept off wet grass.

Those who make this garden furniture in deal or pine should look on the furniture as being a part of the garden and paint or dye it to harmonise with the surroundings.

AN ORNAMENTAL FOUNTAIN

A GARDEN POOL, especially if provided with an ornamental fountain, is always a pleasing feature in any garden. There are several ways of providing the water supply. One method is to run a metal pipe through the centre of an ornamental centre piece consisting of loose pieces of crazy-paving or rock built round the pipe, and connect it to a garden hose as indicated in the diagrammatical sketch Fig. 1. This method has several disadvantages. First, it is illegal to use water supplied from the mains for garden purposes unless a special charge is paid, and in some districts the water supply authorities insist upon having a water meter installed. Another disadvantage is that in a good many cases the water is at such a low temperature and so hard that it is unsuitable for certain kinds of fish and aquatic plants. Also, a fountain supplied in this fashion requires an outlet for waste water.

Another method to supply water for the fountain is to use a large rain-water tank and feed the fountain from this. It is essential to have the tank several feet above the level of the jet, as shown in Fig. 2.

An Electric Pump.—Where electricity is available, a very much better scheme is to install a small electric motor-driven pump on similar lines to that shown in Fig. 3.

Among the many advantages of such an arrangement may be mentioned the

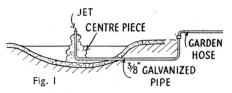

Fig. 1

following: There is no waste of water, as the water is supplied from the pool and the same water used over and over again. The temperature of the water is not affected and the circulation and aeration are beneficial to aquatic plant —and fish—life. The current consumption of the motor is low, it takes but little more electricity than an electric lamp bulb of about 100 watts. No overhead costs are incurred when the fountain is not working.

The pump, Fig. 4, is of the centrifugal type directly coupled to a small electric motor, thus making it a self-contained unit. Such a unit is best housed in a chamber, the sides of which should be

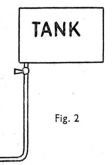

Fig. 2

of concrete of not less than 4 in. thick or of cement-faced brickwork, while the bottom may consist of a layer of small stones and coke to allow efficient drainage. The top is covered with a concrete slab fitted with a suitable handle in the centre so that it can be easily lifted off. The pump unit should be bolted down to a concrete foundation, as shown.

A suction pipe, preferably of galva-

nised barrel, is fitted to the centre hole of the pump and the delivery or discharge pipe is connected to the side one.

In fitting these pipes, sharp bends should be avoided as much as possible as acute angles offer resistance to the water and therefore reduces the efficiency of the installation. The end of the suction pipe should not be allowed to rest upon the bottom of the pond, but should be bent upwards so that the top is just below the centre of the depth of the water. The end should have an efficient strainer.

The pump end of the delivery pipe should be fitted with a stop-cock, as shown. The connections between the delivery and suction pipes and the pump are best made with thick rubber hose held in position by suitable clips, sold for the purpose.

Lack of space prevents a detailed description of how to make the pond, but the concrete should be not less than 4 in. thick. A good mixture to use is one made up in the proportion of one part Portland cement, two parts of clean sharp sand and two parts broken stones or old brick rubble of about ¾ in. diameter, and if a smooth surface is desired it can be obtained by applying a final layer of cement mortar, consisting of cement and sand in equal proportions. The same quality of concrete may be used for the pump chamber.

Wiring.—There are several methods of installing the electrical wires from the house supply to the pump chamber.

One way is to run ordinary vulcanised india-rubber insulated cable in lengths of galvanised iron conduit attached to a convenient fence to run in a shallow trench in the ground where necessary. If this method is resorted to it is important to make the whole system water-tight. This can be done by binding the connecting screw-threads with hemp treated with paint and then screwing up the junction tightly.

A better way is to use proper underground cable of the armoured type and

plug, fed from the fuse side of the switch.

Self-contained electric pump units can be obtained at most of the large stores.

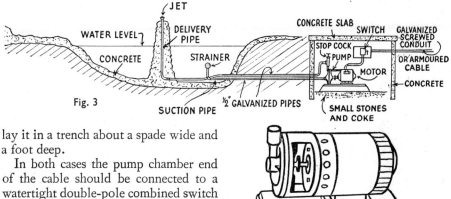

Fig. 3

lay it in a trench about a spade wide and a foot deep.

In both cases the pump chamber end of the cable should be connected to a watertight double-pole combined switch fuse; and a similar switch, which need not be of the watertight type, inside the house.

The controlling switch in the pump chamber should not be mounted directly upon the wall, but on either a slate or varnished hardwood baseboard. The motor can be connected to a watertight

Fig. 4

The one shown in Fig. 4 runs at a speed of approximately 3,000 revolutions per minute. The pump is of gunmetal and the shafts are rustless. Such a pump unit costs about £5.

GARDEN WATER SUPPLY

THE difficulty of keeping a long garden watered during the summer can easily be overcome by installing a metal water pipe arranged with outlet taps at convenient distances apart in the garden as indicated in Fig. 1. This allows a short length of hose to be connected to any of the taps and the watering proceeded with in comparative comfort.

In arranging a pipe system of this description ¾ in. galvanised water barrel should be employed as the coating of zinc protects the pipe from rust. This costs about 50s. per 100 ft.

The Taps.—For convenience the outlet taps should not be spaced further apart than every 35 ft. and where the

total run of piping exceeds 100 ft. a larger sized pipe should be employed. The taps should be of a type having a screwed nose to take the threaded connecting flange of the hose as seen in Fig. 2. Such taps, known technically as bib-cocks, can be purchased for about 5s. each at most ironmongers.

It is neither advisable nor desirable to bury the pipe. It can be fixed along a fence or a wall at an average height of about 6 in. above ground level. If a fence is not available the piping could be supported on short wooden posts of about 2×2 in. section, spaced at a distance of about 6 ft. apart.

The posts should be creosoted thoroughly before inserting them into the ground and the pipe securely held in position with galvanised saddles either screwed into the top or one side of the post. Galvanised screws only should be employed for securing the

in the scullery or the garage, it is as well to discard the tap and fix a screwed nosed one in its place so that a short piece of hose can be conveniently connected to the garden pipe.

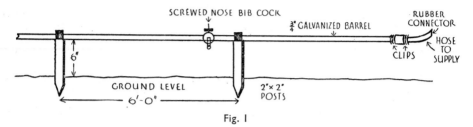

Fig. I

saddles. This method of pipe fixing also applies when the pipe is to be installed along the fence.

If the pipe is to be run on the side

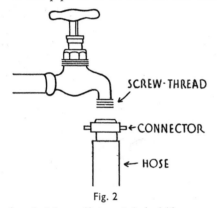

Fig. 2

of a brick wall special holdfasts are obtainable which are simply cemented into small holes made in the mortar between the joints of the brickwork.

In arranging the pipes the end nearest the main water supply should be slightly above the level of the opposite end and not vice-versa.

As the garden pipe will possibly be fed from an ordinary tap situated either

This permits the fitting of a screwed union which is much more satisfactory than the ordinary cup-shaped tap connector, as the latter type is liable to leak at the rubber joint or slip off the tap if not adequately fixed to it. The other end of the hose is connected to the garden water pipe with a rubber connector, fixed by screwed clips.

In fitting the pipe sections together the junctions formed by the connecting sockets and tee-pieces should be made perfectly watertight. This can be done by twisting together a number of strands of hemp moistened with a mixture of red lead and linseed oil or thick oil paint, and winding the prepared material into the grooves between the threads of the male part of the junction. Before wrapping the prepared caulking round the threads brush a little paint on the threads themselves.

If it is proposed to instal a garden water pipe system, it must not be forgotten that the water supply authorities make a special charge for water used for gardening purposes and they should be consulted before the work is put in hand.

A BRIDGE OVER A POND

A SMALL bridge over a garden pond, provided the latter is of not less than about 8 ft. in diameter, considerably enhances the appearance of the pool.

The one described and illustrated in Fig. 1, in this article slopes upward from the banks of the pond towards the centre, and is to be preferred to the ordinary level type.

Construction.—Procure four pieces of yellow deal, each 9 ft. 6 in. long, 4 in. wide and 2 in. thick and four pieces 1 ft. 6 in. long and two pieces 1 ft. 2 in. all of the same width and thickness.

Remove the roughness from the wood one at each end to take the ends of the frames. These should be about 12 in. deep, 18 in. wide and 9 in. long and of a shape shown in Fig. 3. It will be seen that the outer end of a pier projects 2 in. above the level of the wide face. The ends of the frames butt up against this projection and take the strain off the bolts at the opposite ends and prevent the frames from flattening out.

The Piers.—Excavate the soil near the edge at both sides of the pond and fill the excavation with concrete made in the proportion of one part Portland cement, one part clean, sharp sand and

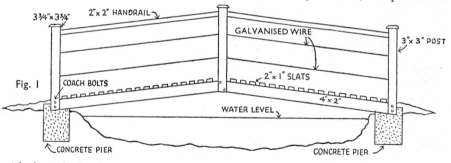

Fig. 1

with the aid of a sharp jack plane, mark and saw the wood to length and construct two frames to the dimensions shown in Fig. 2. The parts can be fastened together with 6 in. wire nails. The ends of the side members that meet at the centre of the span should be sawn at an angle and the faces of the end cross pieces planed so that when placed together butt together tightly. When complete, bore a couple of holes in each of these end pieces to clear ½ in. bolts.

At this stage it is necessary to fix the frames over the pond, but before this can be done a couple of concrete piers or platforms should be made— three parts aggregate, consisting of clean broken brick, small stones, etc. The projection at the top as well as the sloping top face can be formed by means of a wooden frame, which should be greased to prevent it from sticking.

Allow sufficient time for the concrete piers to become thoroughly set and hard and then place the bridge frames in position, bolting them together at the centre with 5 in. galvanised iron bolts. Before inserting the bolts give them a good coat of grease.

Now saw up a sufficient number of cross slats to form the pathway over the bridge. These can consist of 2×1 in. planed batten, spaced 1 in. apart.

At this stage it should be decided whether the bridge is to be painted or creosoted, because to get the best

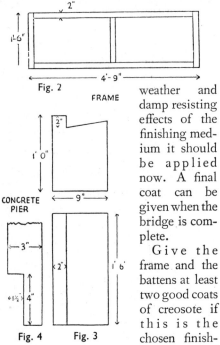

Fig. 2
FRAME
CONCRETE
PIER
Fig. 4   Fig. 3

weather and damp resisting effects of the finishing medium it should be applied now. A final coat can be given when the bridge is complete.

Give the frame and the battens at least two good coats of creosote if this is the chosen finishing medium, or a priming coat of lead oil paint followed by an undercoat.

Having prepared and painted or otherwise finished the slats, nail them down to the frames using $2\frac{1}{2}$ in. galvanised wire nails for the purpose.

The Handrails and Posts.—These should not be too high, neither should they be too heavy-looking. A height of 2 ft. above the track will look well. The end and centre posts are best prepared of 3×3 in. stuff and the tops should be covered with hardwood caps bevelled along the top edges to allow moisture to run away easily.

The top handrail can be of 2 in. square material with rounded top edges, and the ends morticed into the posts.

Two thickish stranded galvanised iron wires will look quite well if threaded through holes bored in the posts stretched tightly and anchored at the end posts. Vertical wooden slats are not recommended for a small bridge as it gives a heavy appearance.

The bottom ends of the posts can be shouldered as shown in Fig. 1, so that they can be fitted to the sides of the frames by means of $\frac{1}{4}$ in. coach screws.

MINIATURE ROCKERY FOR A CONSERVATORY

A ROCKERY with a small pool in front for goldfish adds greatly to the attractiveness of a conservatory. The one described here and illustrated in Fig. 1 is considerably lighter than a rockery built up "in the solid."

For its construction the following are the chief requirements: A baseboard upon which to construct the rockery, a quantity of portland cement and sand for forming the structure, a suitable length of closely woven wire netting for the foundation upon which the

cement mortar is applied, a few feet of $\frac{1}{2}$ in. square wood to support the wire netting during the constructional processes, some pieces of clinker and sundries such as nails, screws, etc.

The Base.—This should measure about 2 ft. 6 in. back to front, 2 in. wide and 1 in. thick, built up of boards which need not be planed on the faces, but the edges trimmed up with a plane.

The boards can be held together by four 2×1 in. thick battens fixed by screws driven in from underneath. The fixing battens are not shown in the constructional drawings Figs. 2, 3 and 4.

Having completed the baseboard, cut two side pieces shaped as shown at A in Fig. 2. These can be portions of an old box, since the wood need not be of good quality nor need it be planed. They should be ½ in. thick.

Next make a wooden frame like a tray without a bottom and fix it securely to the baseboard, keeping the faces flush with the edges. This frame forms a trough for holding water when the rockery is complete. The sides of the trough should be about 3½ in. high and ½ in. thick, and can be fastened together with 1½ in. wire nails. Fix a piece of batten 1½ in. wide × ½ in. thick, narrow face between the side pieces at the top at the back, and fasten a similar piece at the top about 4½ in. in front of the back piece. These cross members are shown at B in Figs. 3 and 4. The space between them will form a long pocket between the sides for plants.

Covering the Structure. —Cover most of the structure with the wire netting, by tacking it down with 1 in. panel pins and bending the heads over the wire to form staples. In doing this the ½ in. square wood referred to in the list of requirements is useful for supporting the wire at intervals between the sides. The netting should not be put on flat but should be bent and crumpled here and there to represent the jagged edges of rocks and also to form pockets for plants. The netting between the back and front battens should be bent down for a distance of about 4 in. to form the rectangular recess. The sides as well as the interior and the top of the trough should be studded with a number of tacks driven in so that the heads remain about ⅛ in. above the sur-

face. These form a key for the cement mortar. It is advisable to do this at the top of the side pieces and cross-battens and round the edges of the base.

Mixing the Mortar.—To make the mortar, mix together in the dry state equal quantities of clean washed sharp sand and portland cement. Turn it over several times in order to make sure that the ingredients are thoroughly incorporated. The mixing is best done on a large, clean tin tray or if you like to

Fig. I

go to the trouble of knocking one together—a mixing board of planed wood with raised edges.

Collect the dry formed mortar in a heap, make a crater in the centre and pour some clean water into it. With a plasterers' trowel gradually fill in the crater with mortar from the sides, mixing the mass as the operation proceeds and adding water from time to time. The consistency should be that of thick clotted cream.

Before applying the mortar to the foundation, thoroughly moisten the whole of the surface with water applied with a brush. Then apply the mortar by taking some up on the back of the trowel and throwing it into position.

This is better than spreading it on as the force produced by throwing it keys the mortar to the netting.

The cement for the trough should be applied in the normal way with the trowel, but left rough to form a key for the next layer. The depth of this preliminary

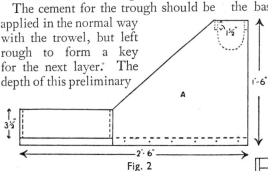

Fig. 2

coat should be $\frac{1}{4}$ in. and it should be allowed to harden before putting on the next.

A Fountain.—It may be noted at this point that a small fountain may be added in the centre of the trough as shown in Fig. 1, by building a centre piece of cement round a central core of wood. A hole should be bored at the correct position in the wooden base before applying the mortar and a core made of hardwood tapering slightly upwards from the base and long enough to project a couple of inches above the water level. Before fixing the core it should be glass-papered perfectly smooth and well greased to prevent it from sticking to the sides of the hole. The core can be driven out with a few taps of a hammer when the structure is complete.

An overflow pipe must not be forgotten. This may consist of a piece of brass or copper tubing $\frac{3}{8}$ in. in diameter, the top of which must coincide with the water level. The best position for the tube is about 1 in. from one of the back corners of the trough. To ensure a watertight joint it is advisable to solder on a metal flange in the manner shown in Fig. 5, and to roughen it and

the exterior of the tube with a coarse file to form a key for the cement.

A hole must, of course, be bored in the baseboard to clear the pipe. The latter can be held in position during the cementing by small wooden wedges driven from the underside of the baseboard into the space between the hole and the pipe. The flange should be bedded in cement and should not rest directly on the wooden base.

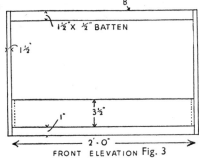

FRONT ELEVATION Fig. 3

When the first covering has set hard, the second layer can be applied. Moisten the prepared surface with water and put on the coating to a depth of about $\frac{3}{8}$ in.

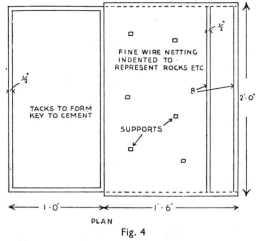

PLAN

Fig. 4

As this work proceeds, pieces of clinker and similar material can be added to form soil pockets, etc. Moisten these before cementing them in. They can either be entirely covered with cement or they can be left as they are according to taste.

When the second coat is dry, a final layer of cement and water should be applied. The thickness of this layer should be about $\frac{3}{16}$ in.

If a fountain has been made as suggested, the wooden core can be knocked out and a brass or copper tube of about $\frac{1}{4}$ in. diameter inserted and fixed into the hole. The lower end can be fixed by boring a hole in the centre of a cork and driving the cork into the hole in the bottom of the baseboard, while the top is better fixed with cement so that water cannot leak down the side of the pipe and find its way to the baseboard. A suitable jet can be soldered to the top of the tube.

A Stand for the Rockery.—It is advisable to make the top of the stand 6 in. wider at the sides and front than the length and width of the baseboard of the rockery as this additional space allows small drooping plants in flower pots to be placed along the edge, thus adding greatly to the appearance of the rockery.

Procure sufficient planed yellow deal boards, $\frac{3}{4}$ in. thick to form the top and join them together by means of battens screwed on from underneath. The front, back and side top rails can be made of $\frac{3}{4}$ in. stuff $3\frac{1}{2}$ in. wide, while the bottom rails are best made from battens $\frac{3}{4} \times 2$ in. The long rails are sawn $1\frac{1}{2}$ in. longer than the distance between the outer side faces of the legs while the short rails are cut flush with the front and back faces of the legs so that when secured by screws to the legs the ends of the long rails cover the end grain of the short ones. The legs are 2 ft. 4 in. long $\times 2\frac{1}{2}$ in. square section deal.

In assembling the parts the top is merely screwed down to the narrow faces of the top rails which are screwed to legs. The lower rails are kept 6 in. above the bottoms of the legs.

The whole of the stand should have three good coats of lead paint. Apply spirit knotting to all knots and then brush on a coat of white and red lead paint. When dry, rub down with fine glass-paper, stop up the screw holes with putty and then apply an undercoat of green flat paint. Allow it to dry thoroughly, treat the surface with glass-paper as before, remove the dust and give the table a coat of good quality gloss paint, preferably green.

When the stand is dry the rockery can be placed upon it, after having bored holes in the top to clear the fountain tube and the waste pipe.

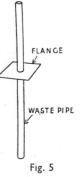

FLANGE

WASTE PIPE

Fig. 5

Water Supply for the Fountain.— A large square biscuit tin will act as a cistern. Solder in the bottom a short length of short brass or copper pipe of the same diameter as that used for the fountain. Give the exterior and the interior of the container a couple of coats of paint. Then make a shelf of sufficient size to accommodate the tin and support it on two iron brackets fixed on a wall, about 2 ft. above the level of the table. Connect the supply astern to the fountain by means of a piece of rubber tubing. A small tap should be inserted at some convenient place in the rubber tube, or a small spring clothes peg could be clipped over the pipe when not in use.

A similar tin should be used under the overflow pipe to take the waste.

HEATING AND LIGHTING POINTS SHOULD BE EASILY ACCESSIBLE

ELECTRICAL REPAIRS AND CONSTRUCTION

MAINTAINING AN ELECTRICAL INSTALLATION IN GOOD REPAIR

A<small>N</small> electric installation demands as much attention as the gas and water systems. Make a periodical examination of the various components, and effect necessary repairs at once.

Fortunately, most breakdowns in the domestic electric light and power systems are due to minor defects which are easily remedied.

Defects in the main wiring seldom arise unless the installation is old or was badly installed at the outset. But it is good to have the wiring tested every six months by an electrician who, for a small fee, will report on its condition. Examination of the components other than the actual wiring, which is not dealt with in this article, should be carried out systematically.

Carry a pencil and paper and jot down items such as defective switches, flexes, and any accessories that need attention. Start from the main switch, then the distribution fuse-board from which the various circuits radiate, and test the switches, fittings, plugs, lamps, wherever they are installed.

Always Switch Off.—It will be an advantage in some cases to have the main switch, which entirely disconnects the installation from the supply, at the on position, but no work should be carried out with live installations.

The Fuses.—Start by examining the fuse-board, first making it dead by opening the main switch.

This fitment, Fig. 1, has on it a number of porcelain fuse-carriers

arranged in pairs (a pair to each sub-circuit) and separated by a fillet, generally of asbestos or ebonite. Each

Fig. 1

fuse-carrier supports a thin wire between its terminals which blows or melts should a current in excess of the normal flow through it.

When replacing a blown fuse, it is essential that the wire should be of the correct thickness. Cards of wire can be obtained cheaply at most electrical shops. One should be hung beside the fuse-board so that it is ready when wanted. Care must be taken when replacing a fuse not to screw up the terminals too tightly over the ends of the wire, as they may cut it, although the breakage may not be visible. To ascertain whether the fuse is intact, insert a knife or bradawl under the wire and lift slightly to put a little tension on it, as indicated in Fig. 2.

In one kind of fuse-board, known as the channel type, the fuse-carriers are held in position by means of bent metal clips that grip the metal ends of the carriers as shown in Fig. 3. If your fuse-board is of this type, make sure

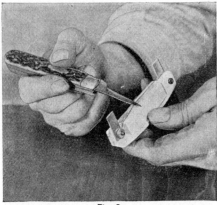

Fig. 2

that the clips make tight contact with the carriers and that they are free from corrosion or you may be troubled with flickering lights. The clips may be adjusted with pliers, while slight corrosion can be removed by judicious scraping with a penknife.

If corrosion has rendered the metal so fragile that they cannot be adjusted or scraped without breakage, it is wise to discard the fuse-board and replace it with a modern one.

Replacing the Fuse-board.—The fitting of a new fuse-board is simple. Disconnect and remove the old one. First remove the fuse-carriers and the glazed cover, and disconnect the top row circuit wires by unscrewing the terminal screws, starting at the left-hand end.

Label each wire 1, 2, 3 and so on, as each individual wire is withdrawn,

in order that they may be connected to the new fuse-board in the same sequence. Then disconnect the bottom row of wires and label these in the same manner, finally withdrawing the thick cables from the bus-bar terminals. The circuit wires are now ready to be connected to the new fuse-board.

Remove the cover and fuse-carriers from the new fuse-board and drill suitable holes in the latter for fixing. Then connect each wire to its respective terminal and fix the board with screws. A fuse-board should never be fixed by nails. Replace the cover, fit suitable fuse wire to the carriers and reinstate them in their sockets. Turn on main switch to test installation.

Many faults arise from defective ceiling pendants. These fittings usually consist of a ceiling rose to which the circuits are attached and from which

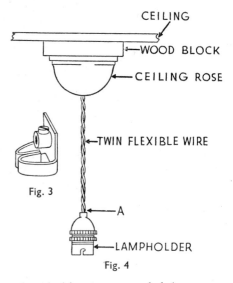

Fig. 3

Fig. 4

a lampholder is suspended by means of a twin flexible wire, Fig. 4.

Faulty Ceiling Lights.—If the lamp in such a fitting fails to light when switched on, and assuming that the fuses are intact and other lights on the same circuit light in the normal way, examine the lamp to ascertain whether the filament is intact. As the filament of a pearl or frosted lamp cannot easily be seen, test the lamp in another fitting. It is wise to treat a clear lamp in the same way as a broken filament cannot always be discerned. If the lamp is in order, examine the lampholder.

The bayonets or projections that make contact with the small metal pieces at the top of the lamp-cap may be out of alignment. This may be due to a broken porcelain interior which holds the bayonet-sockets, or the locking-ring which keeps the interior, top and bottom of the holder together has worked loose, causing the bayonets to be in line with the lamp leads instead of at right-angles to them.

A broken interior cannot be repaired. If the lampholder only needs adjusting, remove the locking-ring and reinstate the porcelain interior in its correct position.

Other defects associated with lampholders are weak springs inside the bayonets, causing imperfect contact, and stuck bayonets. The former cannot be remedied, while the latter can generally be eased back into position with pliers. A drop of thin lubricating oil will be helpful.

In modern lampholders made of bakelite a separate porcelain interior is omitted, as the bayonets are moulded in the bakelite, but the principle upon which they act is the same.

Faulty Flex.—The next part to examine is the twin-flex connecting wire. The most likely place to find

any fault is near to the wire's entry into the top of the lampholder, as indicated at A in Fig. 4. If the wire is defective at this point, and the other part is in good condition, the lampholder should be removed, the faulty end cut off, the wires bared and refitted to the lampholder. On the other hand should the flex be hard and brittle it will be safer to rewire the pendant.

Obtain some double-vulcanised india-rubber-covered flex in preference to the

Fig. 5

single vulcanised kind. It is thicker and may cost a penny per yard more but will last four times as long as the other.

When making the connections at the ceiling-rose, make sure that all strands of the flex are securely fixed under the terminals, and take care to anchor the wires correctly so that the terminals do not take the weight of the pendant. In the event of the ceiling-rose being out of order or cracked, replace it with the type shown in Fig. 5, which is easily fixed and has an excellent device for gripping the flex.

The flex by which most portable electrical devices is connected to plugs and sockets is a weak part of the installation and is subjected to a great deal of wear. All connecting leads should be kept in first-class order, and

O

as soon as the rubber covering shows signs of perishing, they should be renewed.

Flex should not be allowed to remain alive, even if a switch is inserted at the

Fig. 6

further end of the wire as, for example, a key-switch on a standard lamp. Disconnect the lead from the circuit by removing it from the plug socket, or by opening the switch where the connection is by means of a combination switch-plug. Do not use ordinary flex wires and staples when extending or adding extra points. Insurance companies object to this makeshift.

Good switches are remarkably efficient and trouble-free on the whole. Bad

contact between the knife blades and the metal terminal-pieces upon which the blades make and break the circuit, giving rise to flickering lights, is a common defect, easily remedied with a screwdriver by bending the contact pieces as shown in Fig. 6. Other faults which sometimes arise include a broken spring or a broken link connecting the switch knob to the knife blades. If these defects occur it is better to replace the switch rather than attempt to repair it.

Switch Blocks upon which surface switches are mounted sometimes become loose on the wall. It will be necessary to disconnect and remove the switch to get at the fixing screws. If the wall plugs are loose, refix them with neat portland cement; allow it to set and then refix the block and switch.

Switch Plates which cover sunk switches should be examined, and if any are found loose they should be tightened by screwing up the fixing rings.

To keep heavy duty switches—such as those used for electric radiators—in good condition, always make a point of breaking the circuit by first opening the controlling switches on the radiator itself as this gradually reduces the load and prevents excessive arcing at the contacts of the master switch.

ADDING BRACKET POINTS IN A LOUNGE

THIS article will help those who wish to carry out an extension of their electric light system and who have little knowledge of electricity.

To explain the process, it is assumed that it is desired to add four bracket points in a lounge in which one centre light, consisting of the conventional bowl fitting suspended from the ceiling,

is the only one installed, and to replace the bowl fitting with a fixture fitting close to the ceiling.

The job should, if possible, be undertaken just before the room is to be redecorated as the work involves cutting plaster to bury the tubes which carry the wires down to the brackets and possibly the tube housing the switch wires.

No work should be carried out before switching off at the main.

Earthing.—When carrying out alterations or additions where metal-sheathed wires or metal conduit are used, keep the sheathing or tubes continuous and efficiently earthed. This will prevent the tubes or sheathing from becoming alive in the event of a fault or leakage.

There are many electric light brackets of different designs to be obtained at reasonable prices and it is a good plan to obtain these, ready wired with flex, as indicated in Fig. 1, before the main wiring begins. By so doing, suitable heights and spacing for the brackets can be actually tested.

Consumption of Current.—Electricity supply undertakings often transmit current at a pressure of 240 volts. By dividing the number of watts by the

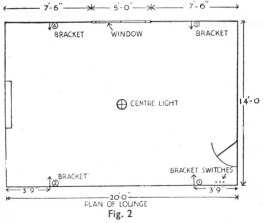

Fig. 2

voltage, the total amount of current consumed is obtained. Thus, in this instance the current will be $\frac{340}{240}$ or approximately $1\frac{1}{2}$ amperes.

This extra current might overload the fuse to which the circuit wires of the room are connected, so the best plan would be to run an entirely new circuit back to the fuse-board and connect the new wires to a pair of separate cut-outs, as illustrated in the diagram Fig. 3.

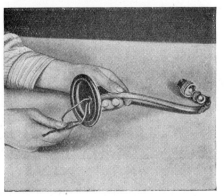

Fig. 1

Brackets are usually fixed about 6 ft. above the floor, and the spacing may be carried out on similar lines to that illustrated in the plan of the lounge, Fig. 2.

In this instance a pair of brackets is fixed to the inner wall and another pair on the opposite one as indicated by 1, 2, 3 and 4 respectively. These, with the centre light, give a total of five lamps and, assuming that a 100-watt lamp is to be fixed in the ceiling fitting and 60-watt lamps in the brackets, the total consumption will be 340 watts.

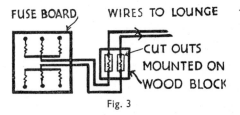

Fig. 3

The old wires running down to the existing switch could be disconnected, drawn up the tube and the ends sealed off in a suitable metal box. This method eliminates interference with wires in other rooms that may be connected to the lounge circuit. It also obviates the necessity of cutting an extra chase or channel as the original switch tube can be used for accommodating the new wires.

In disconnecting the switch it will often be found that one or more wires are twisted together and connected to one terminal, while a single wire is joined to the opposite one. Mark the insulation or covering of the single wire by making a nick in it with a penknife as this wire must be sealed off separately

Three ⅝ in. pin grip, inspection type, T-pieces with inspection lids.

Seven ⅝ in. pin grip elbows, inspection type.

Two ⅝ in. pin grip couplings.

Three three-way circular joint-boxes, inspection type.

One three-way wooden switch box.

Three one-way sunk switches with fixing rings.

One three-way switch plate.

Fig. 4

from the others after they have been drawn up the tube and housed in a joint-box. The twist should be taken out of the others with pliers so that the wires may be withdrawn from the tube.

The Wanted List.—For the wiring work, the following materials, all of which can be obtained at the local electricians, will be necessary:

Suitable lengths of ⅝ in. diameter close joint conduit.

Some 1/.044 red coloured and some black 600-megohm vulcanised india-rubber-covered electric lighting wire.

One reel electrician's adhesive tape.

One ⅝ in. earth clip.

Several porcelain cable connectors.

These components are illustrated in Fig. 4.

The first thing to do is to switch the current off at the main. Then disconnect and remove the old switch by the door and take down the centre bowl fitting. Get out the run for the new tubes by lifting the floor-boards in the room or rooms above. In preparing the run for the length of tubing indicated at A in Fig. 5, choose a floor-board as near as possible to the door frame B near the wall to enable the board to be taken up if possible in one piece. Then cut traps at the positions marked c to allow the short pieces of tube which branch out from the main run to be inserted under the floor and coupled together.

If a trap is not already provided above the centre light, it will be necessary to cut one.

The boards forming the traps should be sawn across with a pad saw and the cut should be a sloping one as indicated in Fig. 6. If, in removing the floor-board A, a tube branching out to one running down to the switch in the lounge is exposed, it will be an easy matter to undo the fitting, especially if a trap is made just above the tube where it drops down to the switch.

Drawing Out Wires.—In most cases, an elbow will be found at the top of the switch tube as shown in Fig. 7, so it will be necessary first to undo the screw A that secures the joint and then ease up the elbow in the direction of the arrow to expose the wires. It may then be possible to draw up the wires one by one by inserting the end of a small screwdriver to lever up the first wire. The elbow can then be removed as well as the short length of tube B connecting it to the main run.

The next operation is that of fitting a joint-box and sealing off the wires. Cut a piece of tube an inch long, file the ends quite smooth, remove the enamel to enable the box to make good metallic contact with the tube and couple up the box, not forgetting to tighten up the screws. Fig. 8 shows the arrangement.

Sealing Off.—Now seal off the single wire previously marked. Cut off the surplus, remove the insulation for a distance of $\frac{1}{2}$ in. to expose the naked

wire, insert the end into the metal portion of the china connector and screw up the fixing screws. Repeat the process with the remaining wires, all of which should be connected together in one connector. Having satisfied yourself that the ends of the wire do not project beyond the connector, bind each connector with adhesive tape as bare metal touching the metal box would cause a fault. The wires are then neatly tucked

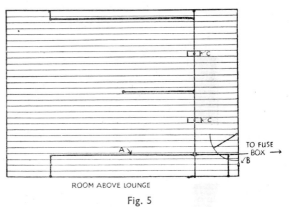

ROOM ABOVE LOUNGE

Fig. 5

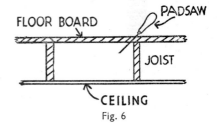

Fig. 6

into the box and the cover put on. Fig. 9 shows the wires housed in the joint-box.

The wires at the centre light are treated in the same way. All black wires are connected together by one connector and the single red one by itself.

In cases where it is found impracticable to draw up the old wires and thus prevent the tube from being utilised for the new ones, the best thing to do is to cut away the wall, fix a joint-box at the switch outlet and there seal off the wires. The box should be sunk sufficiently deep to enable it to be covered with plaster.

This will involve the cutting of a chase or channel in which to sink a new switch tube.

Wall Channels.—Next, chase the walls from the ceiling down to the bracket positions.

Mark guide lines, spaced $\frac{3}{4}$ in. apart, from these positions up to the ceiling, and then ascertain whether the top of each chase-to-be is clear of obstruction such as a ceiling joist. This can be done by inserting the blade of a fine screwdriver into the ceiling a small fraction of an inch away from the wall. If the blade goes through the ceiling

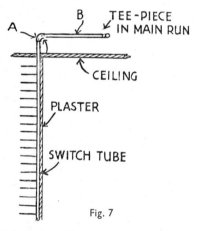

Fig. 7

with little effort, it may be taken that the path is clear, but, if it strikes something more solid than a ceiling-lath, a joist is in the way. Try again at a distance of a few inches to the right or left until the correct position is found and then alter the guide lines to suit.

Cut the plaster sufficiently deep enough for fresh plaster entirely to cover the tube when making good the walls. Use a wide chisel such as that illustrated in Fig. 10, and cut carefully to avoid knocking out more plaster than is necessary.

Then, if the original switch tube can be utilised, cut out the old switch-box or fixing and cut a cavity for the new one.

The next step is to slot the joists

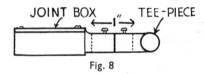

Fig. 8

where necessary so that the tubes lie just below the top surfaces. Then cut the tube to suitable lengths and fix the elbows and T pieces, taking care that no sharp edges remain at the ends of the tube and that the enamel is removed at the joints to ensure good metallic contact.

Wiring Up.—Fig. 11 is a diagram of how to run the wires. Starting at the fuse-board end, a red wire A should be taken down to the switch outlet. This wire feeds all the switches. Leave about a foot of wire at each outlet for connecting.

Then run another red wire B from bracket No. 1 to No. 2 and another c back to the switch. These two bracket points are controlled together by one switch as are the pair on the opposite wall. Mark the covering of the wire at the end of c at the switch outlet by cutting three nicks to enable it to be distinguished from the others when connecting up the switches. Run similar wires to the bracket points on the opposite wall, that is, one red D from the switch outlet to No. 3 and another E from No. 3 to No. 4. Mark the switch end of D with two nicks.

One more red wire F runs from the switch outlet to the centre light. One nick should be made in the switch end of this wire.

A black wire z (all black wires are shown dotted) is now run from the fuse-board end to the bracket 1, another from 1 to 2, another from 1 to the centre light, yet another from the centre light to 3 and finally one from 3 to 4.

The wires are simply drawn through the tubes by removing the caps from the fittings.

The next job is to fix the switch-box,

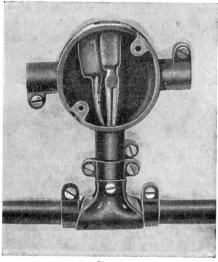

Fig. 9

after having drilled the top to accommodate the end of the down tube. Cement the box with neat portland cement and do not let the edges of the box project beyond the face of the plaster.

It is also advisable to fix the wooden fixing blocks at the bracket outlets. These can be cemented in the same way as the switch-box. The faces of the blocks should be ⅛ in. below the level of the surrounding plaster, so that when it is made good nothing projects except the wires.

Before proceeding with any other electrical work in the room, the plaster should be made good with Keene's cement and the room redecorated. The switches can then be fixed and connected. Remove about ¼ in. of the insulation from the ends of the wires, and take off the outside brading and tape of the covering for a distance of about one inch. Be careful to note the marked ones. If necessary, mark numbers on scraps of paper and slip them over the wires. Do not cut the wires too short. Rather allow an extra three or four inches on each wire more than is necessary.

Connect the unmarked wire to the right-hand terminal of the top switch and loop another piece to the corresponding terminal of the middle one and another short length from this one to the bottom switch.

Now deal with the marked wires. Connect the one with the single nick to the left-hand terminal of the top switch. This switch controls the centre light and should be at the top. Then connect the wire having two nicks to the centre switch and finally the remaining wire to the bottom one. The former controls the right-hand pair of brackets and the latter the opposite one.

Tuck the wires neatly into the box and fix the cover plate with the fixing

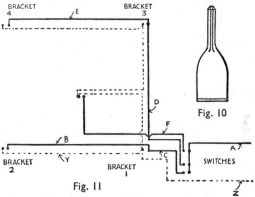

Fig. 10

Fig. 11

rings, taking good care not to scratch the plate.

Connecting.—The next job consists of fixing and connecting the flex of the brackets and centre light to the circuit wires. The brackets are usually fixed to the walls by screws driven into the fixing blocks behind the plaster and the latter to the ceiling. All wires are connected by means of china connectors —two at each outlet.

One connector is joined to a red circuit wire and one wire of the flex, while the other connector joints one or more black wires to the other wire of the flex. The connections are then taped up and tucked out of sight either below the brackets or in some other position dictated by the design of the fixtures.

Then fix and connect the cut-outs near to the fuse-board. The cut-outs should be mounted upon a hardwood block and connected as indicated in Fig. 3.

The enamel should be removed at a convenient position near the end of the tubing and an earth clip fixed at this point. Connection is then made from the clip to a main cold water pipe by means of a length of seven strand 22 gauge copper wire.

OVERHAULING DOMESTIC APPLIANCES

It is always good to look upon each part or unit of an electrical article as a separate circuit, and, in diagnosing a

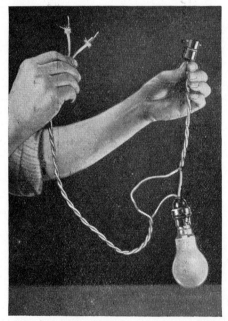

Fig. 1

fault, to test each of these circuits in turn for continuity.

Test, for example, the flex, then, if

it is a heating appliance, the heating element and so on. In this way all the parts will come under inspection, and the fault will be found by a process of elimination.

It is obvious, then, that it is necessary to have some form of continuity tester.

A Simple Tester.—The easiest to construct is one that works from the lighting supply Fig. 1. This takes the form of a long piece of twin flex, with one wire cut somewhere in the middle to receive a lampholder. On one end of the flex is a plug, for fitting into the light or into a wall plug, and the two wires at the other end are bared for about an inch up. These bared ends may be soldered to stiffen them, or small plugs, such as are used for aerial plugs on a wireless set, fitted to them. The lowest wattage lamp available is used (a 5-watt if possible). This can be an ordinary filament lamp, or, better still, a neon lamp.

If the tester is plugged into the supply and the two bared ends touched together, the lamp will light; and if these lamps are placed across a circuit, through which there should be continuity and the lamp lights, this is an indication that the circuit is in good order. Care must be taken, however, only to use this tester when standing on a dry floor. When the repair is done in a room with a stone floor, stand upon a piece of dry wood.

In practically all electrical appliances the most common source of trouble is the flexible lead.

The first proceeding, therefore, in tracing a fault in a vacuum cleaner is to look at the connections in the plug on the end of the lead, and at the ends of the flex. A slight pull on the flex will generally reveal a break near the end, and the flex can be cut off above the break and the plug put on again.

If no fault is discovered, the lead itself must next be tested.

Dust-bag Cleaners.—In a vacuum cleaner of the dust-bag type, where the whole cleaner is moved in the action of cleaning, the lead is generally divided into two parts—the external part for plugging into the supply (or, in other

Fig. 3

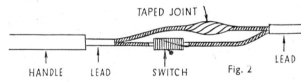

TAPED JOINT

HANDLE   LEAD   SWITCH   Fig. 2   LEAD

words, at the switch), and the part which runs down from this point in the hollow of the handle. One wire of the external lead connects direct to one wire of the lead in the handle, the other two wires being connected together through the switch (see Fig. 2). The latter section usually ends in a socket fixed in the base of the handle which receives a plug attached to a lead from the motor as in Fig. 3. Sometimes the internal section of the lead runs straight through the bottom of the handle and plugs into an attachment on the motor casing itself (see Fig. 4).

First of all, test the lead as a whole. To do this, disconnect it from the motor

—i.e., unplug it from the base of the handle or from the motor casing—and see that the switch is turned on. Now touch the pins of the plug with the bared ends of the continuity tester, as shown in Fig. 5. If the lamp lights, there is a short circuit. If it does not light, joint the two ends

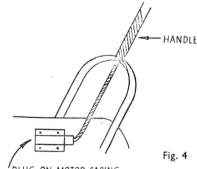

HANDLE

PLUG ON MOTOR CASING

Fig. 4

of the lead at the bottom of the handle with a piece of wire (fuse wire is the most convenient) and touch the prongs of the plug with the tester, as before.

If the lamp lights the lead is in order, but if it does not there is a break in the circuit, either in the lead or in the switch.

Locating the Fault.—The next step, if the lead is at fault, is to find where the break is, and to do this it is necessary

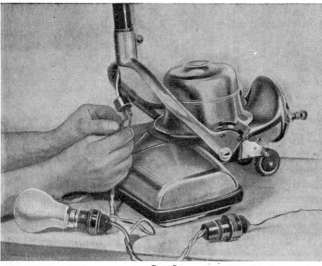

Fig. 5

to disconnect the external part from the part inside the handle and from the switch.

In the majority of cleaners it will be found that a section of the handle at the top is removable, being only held in position by a bolt. When this is taken off, it is easy to get at the switch, which can be withdrawn after its fixing screws are removed.

Some of the wire from inside the handle will be drawn up with the switch and it will be seen that the connections are as illustrated in Fig. 2. The wire that is not connected to the switch will probably have a taped joint beside or underneath the switch. If this is so undo the join and disconnect the other wires.

Join the two ends of the external lead and test for continuity as before.

If no continuity is indicated, replace the flex from this point.

Should there be no join—i.e., the external and internal—leads are in one piece, except for the insertion of the switch, test between the plug or socket, as the case may be, and the plug at the end of the external portion. Test each wire of the lead with the switch turned off, if it has not previously been removed.

If no continuity is obtained there must be a break in the wire that is not connected to the switch. In this case, cut the wire beside the switch and test as previously explained as though there had been a join.

When replacing the flex, insulate the join with adhesive insulating tape. A joint of this description is all the better for being soldered, though this is not essential. Similarly, the connections to the switch should, for preference, be made by making little circles at the end of the wire and tinning these over with the soldering iron.

Now for the lower half of the lead.

This may be tested for continuity in the same way as the whole lead was tested—i.e., by joining the wires at the base of the handle. Replace if necessary by drawing the wire out from the bottom.

If the lead terminates in a fixture at the base of the handle, this may be removed in the same way as the top of the handle, by withdrawing the bolt. If it plugs into the motor casing, do not forget to leave a little slack to allow for the movement of the handle.

The next step is to test the switch. This may be done by touching the terminals with the tester wires with the switch turned on.

If there is no continuity, it will most likely be found that the fixed contacts are not quite pressing against the movable ones and this may be adjusted by a screwdriver. Should a great deal of trouble be experienced in obtaining continuity through the switch, the best course is to buy a new one from the makers.

Tracing Motor Troubles.—Having eliminated the flex and the switch, the next thing for attention is the motor.

The most common source of trouble here is the brushes, which may be removed by unscrewing the two little black knobs on each side of the motor, as seen in Fig. 6.

Make sure that the brushes are pressing firmly against the commutator (the metal split ring which can be seen through the brush holders). It may be that the brushes are worn too low or are sticking in their holders. When worn, replace them, and when they are sticking rub their sides on a small piece of emery cloth. Should this still not produce a satisfactory result, the tension on them may be increased by stretching the springs slightly.

If necessary, the next step is to uncover the motor. The removable part of the casing is usually held in position by means of a circle of bolts, and when these are removed the casing can be taken off.

Next undo the nut or other fastening from the centre of the fan, and the armature (the revolving part of the motor) can be withdrawn.

Look at the connections to the brush-holders and if these are in order, join the two external motor connections with a piece of wire and test for continuity across the two brush-holders. If there is no continuity there is a break in the winding and the motor will have to be returned to the makers for re-winding.

If no faults are found, dust out the inside of the motor, clean the commutator with a piece of very fine sandpaper—not emery—and reassemble, making sure that all parts turn easily and that the fan is not catching on anything.

Should the motor still not run satisfactorily, or should it sometimes fail to start without the fan being first given a

Fig. 6

twist or should it get unduly hot, then the probability is that the trouble lies in the winding of the armature, and in this case again the motor will have to be returned for re-winding.

Another fault that is commonly found in vacuum cleaners, even when the motor is running well, is a lack of suction.

This may be caused by several things. The entrance to the bag may be choked with dust, in which case the cure is a good clean. There may be a puncture or a small tear in the bag. It is possible to patch a bag with an ordinary cycle tyre patch and rubber solution, but a more satisfactory repair can be achieved by the use of a piece of fine canvas and a solution, or specially prepared material sold for the purpose.

will allow) merely by undoing two clips on the outside of the case (see Fig. 7).

Test and examine the connections from the casting to the motor and then proceed as before with various tests of the motor itself.

In this type of cleaner, lack of suction may be caused by a leak in the hose. This may be patched by making a band of canvas and securing it by

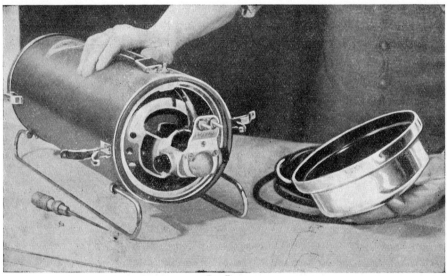

Fig. 7

Another method is to use a marine glue and canvas which makes an exceedingly strong mend.

Hose Cleaners.—The repair and tracing of faults in a hose type of vacuum cleaner, where the motor is housed in a long metal container as in Fig. 7, is very similar to that of the detachable dust-bag type.

Test the flex as before, beginning by an examination of the plugs (in this case at both ends of the flex which is in one piece only).

The motor unit can, as a rule, be withdrawn (as far as the internal connections from the cleaner casing

means of one of the solutions mentioned. Another method is to force a band of rubber, made out of a piece of cycle inner tube, over the puncture and bind it tightly round with insulating tape or cord.

The tracing of faults on practically all small motor driven appliances is very much the same, so if the procedure described here is carried out, electrical fans, hairdryers, and several other things that are used in the home, can be serviced.

The Washing Machine.—The same principle may be applied to the servicing of an electric washing machine. Instead of the fan that was removed to withdraw the motor in the vacuum cleaner, there will be a belt pulley.

The brushes will be under cover, owing to proximity to water, and it is essential to keep an electric motor dry. This cover usually takes the form of a band of steel, the two ends of which are bolted together. The switch will be larger than one on a vacuum cleaner and for this reason will probably be found easier to adjust.

Make sure that all covers and plugs are screwed tight, to exclude as much moisture as possible.

The actual gearing of the machine, which connects the motor to the rotating and the wringer rollers, is unlikely to require much attention, and, when it does, as a rule, the trouble does not require very much tracing and is usually cured merely by the renewal of the part.

Electric Fires.—Another very common electrical appliance that frequently requires attention, is the electric fire.

This may take one of several forms. There is the bowl fire, which is generally of about 500 watts and has one cylindrical element.

Another type is the flat bar-element type, which consists of one, two or three 1,000-watt spirals, wound on a rectangular porcelain former. In the case of a two or three-bar type, a switch is usually incorporated for the purpose of switching off one bar. The diagram for the connections of this type of fire is shown in Fig. 8.

In order to trace a fault in an electric fire, first test the flex for continuity, from the connections on the element, or switch as the case may be, and then test the element in the same way.

Should the element be at fault, the break can usually be seen, and if it is near the end, the spiral can be stretched a little and reconnected to the terminal.

This repair may last a considerable time, but it is possible that the spiral may burn out again almost immediately. This is because the wire used in heating spirals forms a coating of oxidization very quickly when it gets hot for the first time, and this oxidization forms a sort of case hardening, which, when broken, never re-forms satisfactorily. It also forms an insulation between the turns of the spiral.

During the repair of a spiral, this coating of oxidization is nearly always damaged, and the consequence is, that the element seldom has the same lasting power as when new.

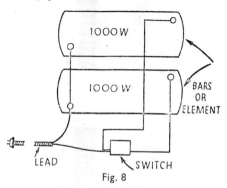

Fig. 8

When reconnecting a spiral to the terminal, double the wire back for about an inch and then make a loop of the doubled wire. Also make sure that the turns of the spiral where it has been stretched or handled are not touching one another as the insulation that the oxidization provides has probably been damaged.

A fault that is often overlooked and which frequently causes the element to burn out is loose connections on the terminals of the spiral. Always make sure that these are as tight as possible.

Occasionally, in the case of a multibar fire, an obscure fault is caused by the mica insulation between the switch and the casing breaking down. The mica is sometimes replaceable, but more often it is necessary to replace the whole switch.

It will be noticed that no particular make of apparatus is specifically dealt with, owing to the fact that there are slight variations in construction in practically all different makes. However, if the principles outlined in this article are applied, with the addition of a certain amount of ingenuity, no great difficulty should be experienced with the servicing of apparatus of any make.

ELECTROPLATING FOR THE AMATEUR

S UCCESSFUL application of the commercial principles of electroplating on a small scale can be accomplished by the amateur at small cost and without cumbersome apparatus. There are numerous small articles that can be plated easily, such as spoons, cigarette lighters, ash trays, propelling pencils.

Details of the Process.—The principles of electrolysis—and, therefore, of electroplating—are, briefly, these. If a

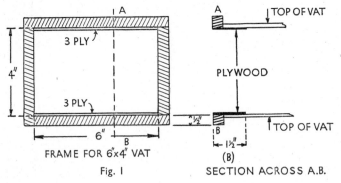

FRAME FOR 6"x4" VAT

Fig. I

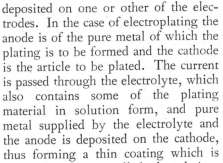

SECTION ACROSS A.B.

(B)

current is passed through certain liquids, these liquids are decomposed. The process is called electrolysis, and the liquid is called an electrolyte. The current is passed through the liquid by means of metal plates which are immersed in it, and these plates are called electrodes; the one by which the current enters being called the anode, and the one by which it leaves the cathode. Some of the constituents of the liquid are liberated by the current and are deposited on one or other of the electrodes. In the case of electroplating the anode is of the pure metal of which the plating is to be formed and the cathode is the article to be plated. The current is passed through the electrolyte, which also contains some of the plating material in solution form, and pure metal supplied by the electrolyte and the anode is deposited on the cathode, thus forming a thin coating which is called the plating.

As previously stated, the apparatus for our plant is not large. It consists of a small tank or vat, a 6-volt car battery, a sliding resistance graduating from 0-6 ohms, and an ammeter calibrated from 0-10 amps.

The vat should be of glass so that the electrodes can be seen without removing them. Porcelain will do, however, if a glass vat cannot be obtained. It should not be less than 6 in. long, 4 in. wide and 6 in. deep.

Next, make a frame to fit over the top of the vat to carry connecting rods, which will in turn support the electrodes.

Making the Vat.—First of all, make an ordinary frame of $\frac{1}{2}$ in. to $\frac{3}{4}$ in. square wood, the internal measurements of which are the same as the internal measurements of the vat. Now get two strips of plywood, of the same length as the internal length of the long side of the vat and about 1½ in. wide and screw them to the insides of the corresponding sides of the frame. The whole thing should fit firmly on top of the vat. The frame at this stage is shown in Fig. 1.

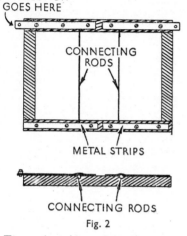

CONNECTION GOES HERE

CONNECTING RODS

METAL STRIPS

CONNECTING RODS

Fig. 2

Fig. 2 shows how the connecting rods are fitted to the frame. The rods themselves are of the same length as the extreme width of the frame, and are about ¼ in. thick. They can be of steel, copper or brass, but when finally ready for use they must be thoroughly cleaned with emery cloth to ensure good contact. The frame is grooved out where the rods will fit to a depth of about half or slightly more of the thickness of the rod. A strip of thin metal, about 1/16 in. thick, which may be of brass though any metal will do, is first thoroughly cleaned on the underside and then placed on top of the rod and screwed firmly down on either side of it. One of the strips holding each rod should protrude about ½ in. over the end of the frame and this projection can be drilled and a terminal bolted in, or the wire which will be connected to it can simply be

secured with crocodile clips. The two strips on the same side of the frame should be fixed so that their ends do not touch. A gap of about ½ in. will suffice.

The electrodes are suspended in the electrolyte from the connecting rods by means of hooks, which can be made out of steel, and should be about 2 in. in overall length.

Where possible, the anode should be drilled and the hook passed through; but where this is not possible and where the articles to be plated (which forms the cathode) are not adaptable for suspension on a hook, 5-amp. fuse wire can be used to tie round the electrode and then round the hook. In this case the position of the wire should be altered from time to time during the process, in order to ensure an even plating.

The electrolyte should fill the vat up to the level of the top of the article to be plated.

Fig. 3 shows the vat complete with electrodes.

Battery Connections.—The connections to the car battery can be secured by

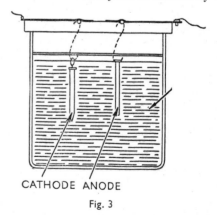

CATHODE   ANODE

Fig. 3

means of spring battery clips, which are very large crocodile clips and are specially made for car batteries, or by ordinary terminals such as are fitted to cars. The positive lead from the battery is taken, through the ammeter and resistance, to the anode and the negative to the cathode, see Fig. 4.

The lower the current used for plating and the longer the process takes, the more satisfactory is the coating. If the process is carried out speedily, the plating is liable to peel off. The best current will be found to be of about $1\frac{1}{2}$ to 2 amps.

If a car battery is not obtainable, two or three very large 2-volt accumulators may be connected in series. If some difficulty is experienced in obtaining very large cells, banks of two or three

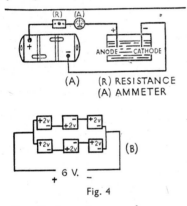

(A)   (R) RESISTANCE
(A) AMMETER

(B)

Fig. 4

small cells in series may be connected together in parallel, this arrangement being called series parallel (see B in Fig. 4).

The article to be plated must be thoroughly cleaned and polished. This can be done by means of caustic soda, or by rubbing with fine graphite paste, and then washing off in petrol or benzine to remove grease.

Plating with Silver.—Silver-plating is still, perhaps, the finest plating available, especially for domestic articles, although nickel and chromium have largely replaced it. The electrolyte for silver-plating consists of silver cyanide, potassium cyanide and water. About $\frac{1}{2}$ oz. of silver cyanide to $\frac{3}{4}$ oz. of

potassium cyanide, both dissolved in about a quart of water. If this is not sufficient to cover the article, more can be added in the same proportions. Accuracy is not of great importance in these measurements and they are only approximate. For small work approximations are quite satisfactory. The anode is of pure silver, which can be obtained in leaf form. Another pure silver article can be used as anode, without appreciably deteriorating it.

Gold and Nickel. — Gold-plating may be carried out in a similar manner. Gold is also obtainable in leaf form. In this case the electrolyte consists of a solution in water of potassium cyanide and gold chloride, using about ten times as much of the former as the latter.

Nickel is suitable for articles that are likely to get a large amount of wear. It can be highly polished and it is not so liable to tarnish. Its price is something under two shillings per pound, and can be obtained from any chemical stores. For these reasons it is probably the best plating material for the amateur.

Great care must be taken to get the article absolutely clean and smooth; this is of especial importance in the case of nickel-plating. The electrolyte in this case consists of a solution in water of nickel sulphate and ammonium sulphate with rather more of the latter, and a little citric acid. The anode is of pure nickel.

Copper, Brass and Zinc.—Copper-plating can be done by cleaning the articles as before and immersing them in an electrolyte consisting of a solution in water of copper sulphate, with just a little sulphuric acid. Another solution for this purpose consists of a solution of cyanide of copper and cyanide of potassium. With both solutions, the anode is of copper.

Brass may be used as a plating material, the anode being brass and the electrolyte a solution in water of cyanide of potassium, zinc cyanide and copper cyanide with a rather larger quantity of potassium cyanide.

Zinc plating (galvanising, as it is often called) is carried out with an anode of zinc and an electrolyte of a solution in water of zinc sulphate and sodium sulphate.

The amateur cannot do satisfactory chromium plating, chiefly because a large plant is necessary to obtain a large current. The solution used as an electrolyte is, however, of chromic acid and a small amount of chromium sulphate. The anode, in this case, is lead and the chromic acid has to be replenished from time to time.

The best metals for the amateur to use for plating are silver, nickel, copper and brass, and with these he should be able to obtain a satisfactory coating.

SIMPLE BATTERY CHARGERS

IN designing a battery charger, the first thing to be considered is the number of cells it will be required to charge. The simple chargers described below are designed to suit a man with six or a dozen accumulators and perhaps a car battery to keep charged.

If your lighting system is a direct current supply, the making of a charger presents very few difficulties and we will deal with a D.C. charger first.

Necessary Parts.—First of all we shall want a baseboard on which to mount our components. This should be of fairly thick plywood, say $\frac{3}{8}$ in., and about 12 in. wide × 18 in. long. In each corner screw a piece of wood about $\frac{3}{4}$ in. to 1 in. thick × 1 in. square to serve as distance pieces so that when the board is fixed to the wall there is a space at the back for the wires.

Next, we require an ammeter, an ordinary moving iron type will do, calibrated from 1 to 5 amps. This should be screwed to the board at the top and in the centre. Below the ammeter, fix three batten holders, preferably of bakelite, drilling holes behind their positions to allow the wires to come through from the back. Under these, fix a double-pole switch (this is always wise on a D.C. plant of this description because of the high

voltage) again drilling holes for the wires to come through. Lastly, drill two fairly large holes (about $\frac{1}{2}$ in.) underneath all and about 6 in. apart.

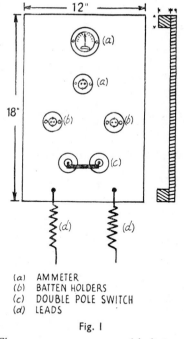

(a)	AMMETER
(b)	BATTEN HOLDERS
(c)	DOUBLE POLE SWITCH
(d)	LEADS

Fig. I

The components assembled in the suggested manner are shown in the diagram Fig. 1 and the wiring in Fig. 2.

Make the two leads for connecting to

the cells of single No. 18 gauge vulcanised rubber lighting wire, and about twice as long as the distance they will have to reach. Bring them through the two holes at the bottom of the board (all the wiring being done at the back) and then wind them on to a broomhandle or some other round article of similar thickness, slip the spiral off again, and you will have a springy coil. This will greatly facilitate handling the lead and it will wear much better than an ordinary straight piece of wire.

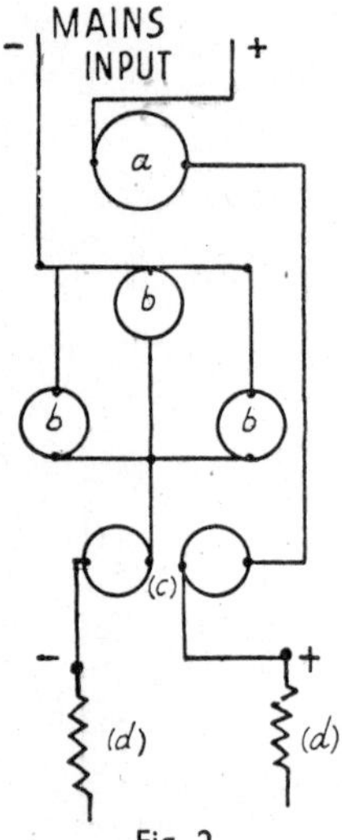

MAINS INPUT

Fig. 2

The purpose of the batten holders is to accommodate resistance l a m p s, which can be the ordinary common lighting lamps or carbon f i l a m e n t lamps. The latter are to be preferred, as they are more easily obtainable in high wattages and are less likely to damage with handling.

It will be noticed in Fig. 2 that the lampholders are connected in parallel. The method of increasing the amperage through a group of cells, therefore, is to increase the number of lamps in the lampholders or, of course, to put in lamps having a higher wattage.

Estimating Wattage.—On 240-volt mains, three 100-watt lamps will give an amperage of 1 to 1.5 amps. to about twenty cells connected in series. It will probably be found that it is not necessary to use so large a wattage as this at first, as the back E.M.F. (pressure) from the cells is obviously less when the cells are in a discharged condition than when they are charged. The amount of current

passing drops as the cells become charged, and has to be increased as explained. It is best, therefore, to have one very large lamp (say 200 watts) and two smaller ones.

For charging car batteries, it is a good idea to plug into one of the lampholders a 500-watt or 750-watt bowl fire. This on 240 volts will give about 3 to 4 amps on a 12- or 6-volt car battery.

A second circuit can be added to the charger by taking a wire from the mains side of the first ammeter (see Fig. 2), to one side of the ammeter of the new circuit and a wire from the mains side of one of the three lampholders to one side of one of the lampholders of the new batch. If preferred, instead of bringing the leads through from the back and using them direct they can be brought to terminals on the front of the board (the terminals taking the place of the two $\frac{1}{2}$ in. holes).

Inserting Fuses. — There is one important detail that should be remembered when finally installing a charger of this type. If the point from which the power is obtained is not separately fused, it is as well to insert a pair of 5-amp. fuses. These can be mounted upon a hardwood block and fixed alongside the charger, or can be incorporated in the board itself. There is plenty of room for a fuse-holder on each side of the ammeter. To connect, take each of the mains input leads to a fuse and then the other side of one fuse to the ammeter and from the other fuse to a lampholder.

For an A.C. (alternating current) charger, there are three things that must first be obtained, a rectifier, a transformer and a variable resistance (two of these will be required for a two-circuit charger). The rectifier for preference, should be a Westinghouse metal rectifier, capable of supplying 5 amps. at 25 volts for one circuit or 10 amps. for two circuits. The transformer must have an input voltage equivalent to that of your mains supply, and an output voltage slightly higher than is required from the rectifier, say, 30 volts, and must have an output of 300 volt-amps. for a two circuit charger. The variable resistances should be of

Fix the blocks of wood on the back as before to allow wiring room at the back. Mount the transformer at the top, the rectifier below, and the ammeters, resistances and switches at the sides as illustrated in Fig. 3. It is advisable to make two circuits from the start on A.C. as it is not so easy to add circuits, and it will be noticed that

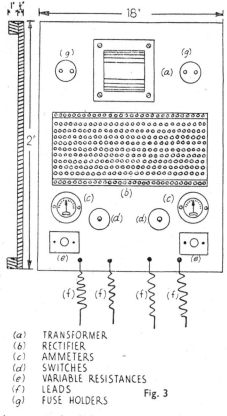

(a)	TRANSFORMER
(b)	RECTIFIER
(c)	AMMETERS
(d)	SWITCHES
(e)	VARIABLE RESISTANCES
(f)	LEADS
(g)	FUSE HOLDERS

Fig. 3

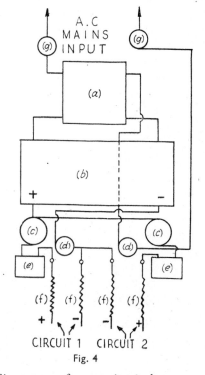

Fig. 4

the vertical sliding type, graduating from 0 to 50 ohms. and, of course, capable of carrying a current of at least 5 amps. Other components that are required are two tumbler switches, two 5 amp. fuse-holders and two ammeters (calibrated 0-5 amps.). These should be mounted on a baseboard similar to that of the D.C. charger, but about 18 in. wide × 2 ft. long.

the diagrams are for two-circuit chargers.

Shielding the Rectifier.—The rectifier can be shielded by means of perforated zinc such as is used on the construction of meat safes, etc., but care must be taken to allow plenty of space between the shield and the cooling fins of the rectifier. The zinc can be bent to shape to fit over the rectifier, and the top and bottom edges bent back about ½ in. deep to form a flange for screwing to the baseboard. The fuses can be mounted on each side of the transformer and should be loaded with 5-amp. fuse wire. The wiring is shown in Fig. 4.

This charger will be satisfactory for charging six 2-volt cells in series on each circuit and, of course, more than one bank of six can be put on one circuit by connecting each bank of cells in parallel with the next bank. There is no necessity always to have six cells per bank, but if connected in series parallel as this method is called, a like number of cells must be maintained in each of the banks connected together. Thus you can have two sets of three or two sets of four, and so on. It must be remembered that the ammeter reading in this case must be divided by the number of banks connected together in order to obtain the reading per bank.

ALTERING BATTERY-OPERATED BELLS TO MAIN

THE trials and troubles of battery-operated domestic electric bells can be eliminated by using the electric light supply, provided the current is alternating.

No extensive alterations in the existing bell wiring are necessary. A few

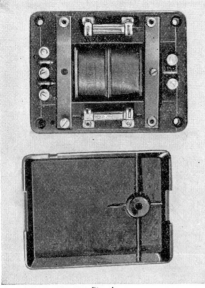

Fig. I

feet of twin-insulated bell wire and staples for fixing, a short length of twin lead-covered electric light cable, a lighting switch, a bell transformer, a few screws and a piece of insulation tape complete the list of materials. The tools required are a light hammer, screwdriver, soldering iron, solder and flux, and perhaps a tool for plugging the wall.

The Transformer.—A good type of bell transformer is shown in Fig. 1, and can be had at most electrical stores for about six shillings. It measures 4×3 in., and the parts are housed in a bakelite case.

The transformer reduces the high voltage of the supply to one suitable for operating the bell and indicator, which may require three, five or eight volts.

The transformer is a simple piece of apparatus and consists of a number of thin iron stampings upon which are mounted two separate coils of insulated wire, known respectively as the primary and secondary coils. The primary coil comprises a large number of turns of thin insulated wire and is connected to the supply, while the secondary has a few turns of comparatively thick wire, and is connected to the bell system. The pulsations of the alternating current flowing in the primary coil set up magnetic impulses in the core, as the metal stampings are called, and induces a corresponding current in the secondary. The ratio of the voltage in the secondary and primary will be approximately that of the numbers of turns in their respective windings.

In order to keep the length of connecting cable as short as possible, the transformer should be fixed near to the source of supply. The best place will be at the side of the distributing fuse board to which it can be connected. A switch should also be inserted in this circuit so that the transformer can be cut out in the event of a fault developing in the bell installation.

A good place to mount the switch is at the side of the transformer, and to do this the transformer and switch should be mounted on a small wooden board having fillets at the back to provide a space between the board and the wall. As the connecting wires will pass through the wooden base the latter must be drilled with suitable holes. Such a board with the transformer and switch mounted upon it is illustrated in Fig. 2. Should the wall be of brick, it will be necessary to plug it to obtain a good fixing.

Fixing Wires.—Having disconnected and removed the batteries, the battery wires should be extended from this point to the transformer. In fixing the twin bell wire, leave about a foot at each end for connecting purposes, and when using staples for keeping the wire in position see that they are not driven in too far, otherwise one may cut through the insulation and set up a short circuit. The use of insulated staples with a piece of fibre over the metal loop will obviate this risk.

One pair of bared ends of the extended bell wires are connected to the battery wires by twisting each pair together and applying a little solder to each joint to ensure perfect contact and then

binding each joint separately with a short length of insulation tape, slack wire being twisted round a pencil or similar article to form neat coils. The other ends of the wire are connected to the secondary terminals of the transformer. Three such terminals are generally provided to give voltages of three, five and eight volts respectively. It is advisable first to connect the wires

Fig. 2

to the terminals giving three volts, and, if this pressure is not sufficient to operate the bells normally, a higher voltage can be tried.

Lead-covered Cable.—The next operation is to fix the lead-covered lighting cable and to connect it to the fuse-board. Before doing any work on the fuse-board, turn off the current by opening the main switch. On no account must the board be touched when alive.

Having fixed the lead-covered wire and allowed about a foot or so at each end for connecting, remove the lead sheathing for this distance by lightly nicking it at the top and underside and then bending it. This will sever the lead. The unwanted piece can be removed by holding the main sheathing with one hand and drawing the

LEAD COVERED LIGHTING WIRE

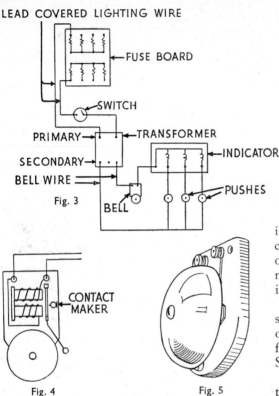

FUSE BOARD

SWITCH

PRIMARY → ← TRANSFORMER

SECONDARY → ← INDICATOR

BELL WIRE

Fig. 3

BELL

PUSHES

CONTACT MAKER

Fig. 4   Fig. 5

terminal of the upper fuse-clip and the other to the bottom terminal of the lower fuse-clip of a pair of fuses. The other end of the lead-covered wire is treated in the same manner and connected to the top or primary terminals of the transformer. This completes alterations to the wiring, a diagram of which appears in Fig. 3.

There remains the task of altering the bell. This involves nothing more than cutting the contact maker out of the circuit, leaving the magnet coils connected as indicated in Fig. 4.

If the bell is corroded, it should be substituted by a new one of a type specially made for use with a transformer. Such a bell is shown in Fig. 5.

When the work is complete the current can be turned on at the main switch and the bells tested. If too weak, make the adjustment on the secondary terminals of the transformer.

short piece off with the other. Remove about ½ in. of the insulation from the wires and connect one wire to the top

A BATTERY-OPERATED BED LIGHT

THE battery-operated bed light here described and illustrated is a device which should appeal to readers who have no electric light installed in their homes.

Fig. 1 shows an illustration of the completed article which consists of a piece of hardwood, although plywood or a faultless piece of deal could also be used, upon which is mounted a metal container for housing the battery, a miniature holder and flashlamp bulb, a switch for operating the light,

while two metal clips fixed to the back keeps the fitting in position on the bed rail.

Referring to Figs. 2, 3 and 4 which give constructional details, it will be seen that the base-board measures 6 in. long, $3\frac{3}{4}$ in. wide $\times \frac{3}{8}$ in. thick and the metal container 3 in. in width, $3\frac{1}{4}$ in. long and $1\frac{3}{8}$ in. deep, which is of sufficient size to house a two-cell cycle lamp refill dry battery of standard size, costing 8d. The lampholder is of the miniature screw-in type, and the lamp, whose voltage is 2.5 volts, is of the same kind as that used in an electric torch. These two items together cost about 7d.

Although the bed light is intended primarily for intermittent lighting—that is to say, for switching on for a minute or two at a time—the battery is capable of running the lamp for several hours continuously and the light will be powerful enough for the user to read by it provided the lamp is not too far away.

Start construction by making the base. To give a neat appearance the top corners should be rounded or cut off square,

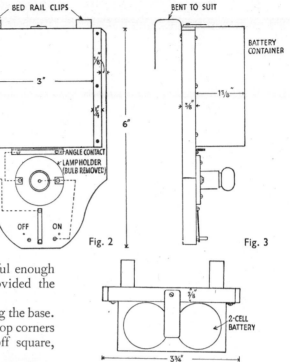

Fig. 2

Fig. 3

Fig. 4

Fig. 1

while the bottom will look well if shaped as shown in Fig. 2. As the wood is comparatively thin a fretsaw may be used for cutting the shape, or if this tool is not available a pad saw can be employed for roughing out and then the work smoothed with a spokeshave and glass-paper.

A piece of tinplate from a tobacco tin—or, better still, a piece of thin sheet brass, as that metal does not rust—should now be cut to a length of about 8 in. and marked out as shown in Fig. 5. This measurement leaves a surplus at each end which facilitates bending, and the metal can be removed afterwards.

Bending Tinplate.—The best way to bend the metal is to begin with the ends. Sandwich the metal between two squared pieces of wood so that the line of bending coincides with the top edges of the wood. Place the whole in a vice and force the projecting length down with the fingers, finally tapping it with a hammer until it is square. Then fashion the opposite end. The remainder of the bending can be done by forcing the metal down over the edge of a square block of wood. Drill three small holes in each fixing flange to take the screws for fastening the battery container to the base.

The switch consists of a piece of springy brass 1 in. long × $\frac{3}{16}$ in. wide,

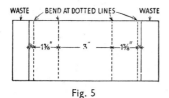

Fig. 5

details of this fitment are shown in Figs. 2 and 3.

A hole to clear a No. 3 $\frac{1}{4}$ in. diameter brass round-headed screw is drilled $\frac{1}{8}$ in. from each end and a screw driven from the back into a small piece of hardwood to form the handle. As the piece of brass forming the switch is small, it will be found easier to do the drilling before cutting to shape. When cut, just snip off the sharp corners to give it a finish.

The clips for fixing the bed light to the head of the bed are cut 2 in. long × $\frac{3}{8}$ in. wide and are not bent to shape until after assembling.

Two more pieces of brass must be cut, one for the contact immediately under the container, upon which the battery contact rests, and the other for keeping the battery in position at the top. The lower one is in the form of a small bracket and is shown clearly in Figs. 2 and 3, while the upper one is merely a strip which presses on the top of the battery.

Concealing the Wires.—In order to eliminate unsightly wires on the front of the base, the connecting wires, consisting of a few inches of 22 gauge double cotton-covered instrument wire, pass through small holes drilled in the wood and are sunk in shallow channels, easily cut with a penknife, at the back. The connections are simple and are indicated by the dotted lines in Fig. 2. The holes may be bored and the channels cut after assembling.

The first step in assembling consists of fixing the battery container to the base by means of half a dozen No. 3 round-headed brass screws $\frac{1}{4}$ in. long. The top edges are kept flush with the top of the base and the edges of the fixing flanges $\frac{1}{8}$ in. from the side edges. The contact bracket is fixed by the same kind of screw immediately underneath the battery container; the lampholder about $\frac{1}{4}$ in. below and the switch underneath the lampholder, as shown.

A brass screw $\frac{1}{2}$ in. long should be used for fixing the switch arm to the base and a couple of small washers inserted between the head of the screw and the wood; the bared end of the connecting wire being inserted between the washers. This also applies to the contact screw on the right-hand side. The opposite screw is used merely for keeping the switch on the "off" position.

Having connected the wires and driven in a short panel pin on each side of the switch arm to prevent it from moving too far, the whole of the back can be covered by pasting on a piece of thick brown paper.

The constructional work is complete when the battery clip at the top has been fixed and the two hooks at the back screwed and bent to suit the shape of the bed rail.

Before inserting the battery into the container the contact consisting of a thin piece of brass between the two cells should be bent forward a trifle to ensure that it presses against and makes good metallic contact with the inside of the container. If this is not done, intermittent light or no light at all is likely to result when the switch is moved to the on position.

The battery is inserted upside down—that is, with the top contact pressing against the angle contact fixed to the base—the clip at the top then being adjusted to keep the battery pressed down.

Where a small accumulator of the wireless type is available, the bed light could be modified to suit, no battery container or bottom contact bracket

being necessary. These parts may be substituted by two terminals for securing the ends of the accumulator connecting leads.

The initial outlay for an accumulator is, of course, greater than an 8d. refill battery. A fully charged one having a capacity of 20 amp. hours and costing about 10s. would give a continuous light for approximately sixty hours, assuming that a 2-volt .3-amp. bulb be used.

The recharging of such an accumulator should not cost more than 6d.

A substantial wooden case should be made for holding the accumulator which could stand underneath the bed.

MAKING AND FITTING A
BURGLAR ALARM

THERE are several types of burglar alarms which are simple to construct and they fall into two classes—the open and the closed circuit. The one described below is an open circuit alarm and the cost of upkeep is negligible.

It can be fitted to almost any type of window, fan-light or door and is very reliable if it is kept in good order.

It consists chiefly of two strips of metal, one thin and springy and the other thicker and stiff.

The action of opening the door or window causes the thin strip to spring into contact with the other.

The best metal is brass, which is not only easy to work but is also less likely than most other metals to corrode with exposure.

First Steps.—Obtain two strips of brass about 4 in. long and $\frac{1}{2}$ in. wide. One should be about $\frac{1}{16}$ in. thick and the other of the type of which the

connecting strips of torch batteries are made—that is, thin and springy.

These two strips should be drilled in the way shown in Fig. 1.

The holes should be large enough to take a $\frac{1}{8}$ in. thick screw and those in the thicker strip should be countersunk, so that, when the alarm contact is constructed, there is a flat surface.

This is important, otherwise it will be

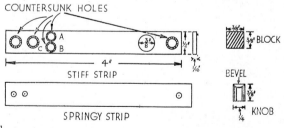

Fig. 1

difficult to fit the alarm and allow the window to be shut.

It will be noticed that in Fig. 1 the thicker strip has a large hole at one end. This should be made at least $\frac{3}{8}$ in. in diameter.

As well as being drilled, the thin strip can, at this stage, also be bent to the shape shown in Fig. 2. It is easy to do this with a pair of pliers.

Then obtain a little cubical block of some insulating material and a little cylindrical-shaped piece of the same material.

The Mounting Block.—A hard fibre material is ideal, as it will not swell with damp. But a hardwood like oak may be used satisfactorily.

The length of each side of the block should be about $\frac{3}{8}$ in.

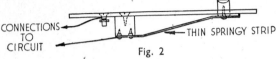

CONNECTIONS TO CIRCUIT

THIN SPRINGY STRIP

Fig. 2

The cylindrical piece will be subject to the opening and shutting movement of the window, and should be bevelled off on one side as shown in Fig. 1. It should be about $\frac{3}{8}$ in. long and not more than a $\frac{1}{4}$ in. in diameter.

The complete contact is illustrated in Fig. 3. The block is first mounted on the thicker strip with two small counter-sunk brass screws ($\frac{3}{8}$ in. by No. 4 will be the size) through holes A and B in Fig. 1. The thin strip is then screwed to the block through the two holes at one end, using round-headed screws. Under one of these screws it will be found advisable to put a small washer, as one of the

connecting wires will be placed here, using the screw as a terminal. The other connecting wire will go under a nut on a countersunk bolt through the hole c in Fig. 1.

The next step is to fit the cylindrical knob to the other end of the thin strip, also by means of a wood screw.

This knob should have its bevelled edge facing the oncoming portion of the window, so that the window, in closing, does not first strike a sharp corner. If this is not done, the knob may be pushed off instead of merely being depressed.

Fixing to the Window.—It is fitted to a window as shown in Fig. 4. It will be noticed that the contact, when assembled, is not at any point thicker or deeper than $\frac{1}{4}$ in. It will not, therefore, be necessary to groove out the window frame to a depth greater than $\frac{5}{8}$ in.

Mark out the size of the front (the thicker strip on the frame) and measure

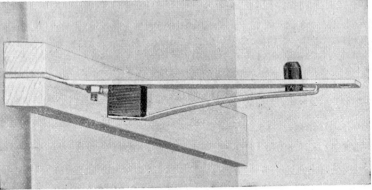

 Fig. 3

in towards the centre of the rectangle so marked to a distance of $\frac{3}{8}$ in. This will give a second rectangle inside the first. The second rectangle, assuming that the first is $4 \times \frac{1}{2}$ in., will be $3\frac{1}{4} \times \frac{1}{2}$ in.

Make a groove in the window frame about $\frac{5}{8}$ in. deep and within the limits of the smaller rectangle.

We now have at each end of the large rectangle a small section $\frac{3}{8} \times \frac{1}{2}$ in. which is so far untouched.

These ends should be grooved out to a depth of exactly $\frac{1}{16}$ in. The complete contact should now fit flush with the face of the frame and, when the wires have been connected, can be screwed in position with countersunk wood screws.

Before finally securing, make a little slot in the window frame from the inside edge of the frame to the edge of the deep groove at the block end of the contact.

This should be deep enough to contain the wires and to allow them to enter under the front strip.

The wiring diagram is shown in Fig. 5. It will be noticed that a switch has been incorporated. This is so that the window can be opened legitimately without the alarm sounding.

Current Supply.—Two low resistance dry bell cells have been used. There are alternative methods of supplying current besides the use of cells, which deteriorate with standing and have to be replaced.

If the premises have an alternating current lighting supply, use a bell transformer, which supplies a current for working an electric bell at a voltage which can be either 4, 6 or 8 volts broken down from the main's supply.

If a transformer is used, it is best to obtain an A.C. bell, although an ordinary bell will work quite well provided magnet coils only be used.

Another method is to use a Leclanche cell, which can be obtained cheaply from an electrical store. For this it it necessary to make in the jar a solution of sal ammoniac in water. Sal ammoniac crystals can generally be bought for a few pence from the same shop where you purchase the cells. Warm the water slightly and dissolve crystals in it until no more will dissolve.

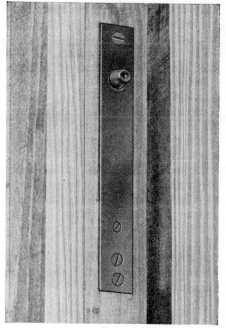

Fig. 4

You will then have a saturated solution in which the rod and porous pot must be immersed. The rod will have a wire for attaching to one wire of the circuit and the pot will have a terminal for the other. It is advisable to use at

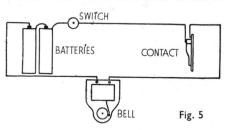

Fig. 5

least three of these cells as their individual voltage is only 1.5 volts.

The Leclanche cell has the advantage of not wearing out when not in use, but it requires periodical attention as the solution evaporates and requires renewing, and the zinc rod corrodes and is gradually eaten away.

Dry cells, on the other hand, are more

easily renewed, and are perhaps preferable to those who do not mind the slight extra cost.

The use of accumulators is not practicable as long periods of idleness are ruinous to them.

Invisible Wiring.—Wiring should be carried out in good rubber insulated bell wire, and should be kept out of sight and reach of the window as much as possible.

The contact itself is inaccessible until the window is actually opened, but if the wire is first cut—say, through a broken pane—the window can be opened without operating the bell.

Keep the wire on the top of the picture rail and bring it down from the window frame in the corner formed by it and the wall.

The switch and battery should also be kept as far from the window as possible —preferably in another room, in a cupboard or some other inaccessible place.

The alarm can be extended to any number of windows or doors by taking a wire from each of the connections on the contact to the next contact.

The alarm should be tested from time to time to ensure that it is ready for infrequent emergency.

The battery should be examined periodically and the terminals kept clean.

It is important to clean the spring contact every now and again. Otherwise it may fail to give alarm at the right moment, even if the complete system has recently been tested.

A PORTABLE ELECTRIC BELL

A PORTABLE electric bell is almost indispensible in the sick-room and the one illustrated in Fig. 1 has the ad-

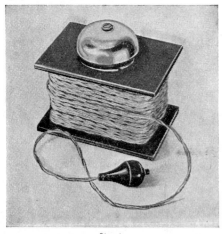

Fig. I

vantage that the flex can be wound round the case when not in use, the top and base forming flanges to keep it in place.

Obtain a 3 in. circular battery-operated bell. Such a bell, mounted on a wooden base, can usually be obtained at the local electricians. The base should be removed and mounted on top of the body of the case, forming the battery container and flex winder after construction.

Procure a piece of plywood or mahogany, finished size, 6 in. long, 4 in. wide and $\frac{3}{16}$ in. thick for the top, and a similar piece, $\frac{1}{4}$ in. thick, for the base. Two pieces are wanted $4\frac{1}{2}$ in. long $\times 3\frac{1}{4}$ in. for the sides and two pieces $2\frac{1}{8} \times 3\frac{1}{4}$ in. for the ends. These four pieces should be $\frac{3}{16}$ in. in thickness, as shown in Fig. 2.

Saw and plane the top and base square, and round the ends as shown.

Mark out the sides and ends and assemble these pieces with tube glue, and reinforce the joints with fine panel pins $\frac{3}{4}$ in. in length.

Round the edges at the ends with a

file and glass-paper to avoid cutting the wound-up flex.

Mark out on the underside of the top piece the position of the body previously assembled and fix the top to the body with glue and panel pins, taking care to fix it squarely.

The base is fixed to the sides and ends with long thin brass countersunk-headed screws driven in from the underside. To find the position of the screw holes in the base, place the assembled car-case squarely on top of the wood and trace the outline with a pencil. Draw lines parallel to these, $\frac{3}{32}$ in. towards the centre. Six screws will be sufficient, one in the centre at each end and two equally spaced in the sides. Drill the holes in the base to clear the screws and drive them in.

Electric Contacts.— The next operation consists of cutting two pieces of springy brass to form contacts with the terminals of the battery, the battery being of the standard three-cell box type with screw terminals on the top.

Remove the base, put some marking material such as blacklead on the terminals of the battery, insert the battery and press it tightly up against the top of the case, keeping the battery to one side. This will mark the position where the contacts are to be fixed.

Cut two pieces of thin springy brass, bend them to the shape shown at A in

Fig. 2, drill two screw holes in each and fix them with small screws over the marked position in the case.

Wiring Up.—Procure 12 yds. of thin twin flexible bell wire, bare the ends at one end and connect one core to one of

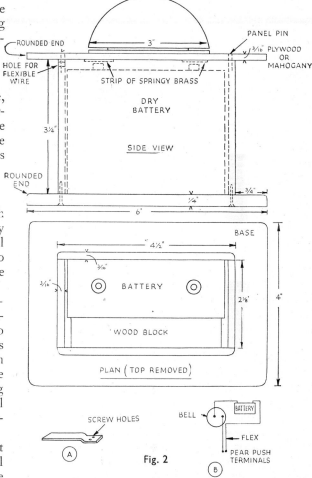

Fig. 2

the brass strips. Drill a hole in the top at some convenient position under where the bell will come, and thread a sufficient length of the other bared piece of flex through the hole so that it may be connected to the bell.

Now drill another hole in the top for one of the wires from the bell to be connected to the other brass strip.

Remove the top of the bell and connect the bared end of the flex to the other bell wire, using a small piece of insulation tape at the joint.

Fix the bell down to the top with screws. At the other end of the flex, connect a small bakelite pear push, taking care that the strands of each wire are fixed securely under their respective terminals and there is no possibility of a short-circuit.

A diagram of connections is shown at B in Fig. 2.

Prepare a block of wood a trifle shorter than the length of the interior of the case and thick enough to keep the battery in position, insert the block and the battery and fix on the base.

If plywood has been used for the case, stain it to the desired colour and polish with a rag moistened with linseed oil.

Mahogany does not need staining. Finish by rubbing with an oily rag.

INSTALLING TUBULAR HEATERS IN A GARAGE

THE problem of heating a garage can be solved by installing one or more electric tubular heaters. This type of heater, as illustrated in Fig. 1, is fitted with a low temperature element supported on suitable insulators and enclosed in a light steel tube 2 in. in diameter. Stock sizes of such heaters are 2, 4, 6 and 8 ft. in length, while intermediate lengths can be obtained to order.

Electric tubular heaters are cheaper to install than hot water or steam heating and have not their complications, and they are safer than oil stoves.

Amount of Heat.—The standard loading of the majority of tubular heaters is 60 watts per foot, so that a 4 ft. length or two 2 ft. lengths would consume 240 watts or just under a quarter of a unit. Two 4 ft. lengths or their equivalent should be sufficient for keeping a garage measuring about 18 ft. long × 9 ft. wide at a normal temperature during winter. If you are on the all-in system whereby a fixed charge is made plus ½d. per unit, the cost of running will be less than ¼d. per hour, excluding the standing charge.

In order to get an equal distribution of heat, it is a good plan to fix, say, two lengths or units on the back wall and a single unit on each side wall. A convenient height to fix them is 2 ft. above the floor or level.

If the garage is not already wired for a power circuit, no difficulty should be experienced in running a pair of power wires back to the house supply. These can be connected through a pair of subsidiary cut-outs to the main-fuses or to the power fuse-board, whichever is the nearer. Diagrams of these connections appear at A and B in Fig. 2.

Assuming that it is necessary to provide a suitable circuit between the house and the garage and that the former is within a few feet of the latter, as most garages are, wires could be run overhead or buried underground.

Twin lead-sheathed cable consisting of two separate cores of insulated copper wire will do for the work provided that it is adequately protected from mechanical injury. Thus, if the cable is run overhead, it could be supported on top of a strong wooden batten, fixed sufficiently high to give ample head room as shown in Fig. 3, or run through a length of ¾ in. diameter heavy gauge screwed galvanised steel conduit. The latter will protect the cable if it is run underground.

Fig. I

Choosing Wire.—The size of the wire is determined by the amount of current flowing through it, and as the amount of current flowing is obtained by dividing the total number of watts by the voltage, the current consumed will be approximately $\frac{500}{200} = 2\frac{1}{2}$ amperes, assuming that the voltage or pressure simply to be 200 volts. A twin 1/18 S.W.G. lead-covered cable would be of ample size safely to carry the current for the heaters but, in order to provide for other electrical apparatus that might be installed later, use a cable of the next larger size, namely, a 3/20.

Running the cable overhead is simple. The cable should be fixed securely by means of buckle clips to the top of the wood spanning the space between the garage and the house, and it may be possible to bore a hole in the top of a convenient window frame to allow it to pass into the house.

A typical example of how to run a cable in steel galvanised conduit underground is shown diagrammatically in Fig. 4. Here it will be seen that the end of the underground tube B is taken

under and a short distance up the wall of the garage, while the tube c is connected to B by means of a screwed coupling. Another screwed coupling connects D, which runs up the wall of the house, to c. The bends near the ends of B and c are made by boring a hole, 1 in. in diameter, in a piece of stout wood, inserting the end of the tube to be bent into the hole and gradually forming the curve by exerting pressure on the other end, bending a little at a time and pushing the tube forward a trifle as the bending proceeds. Fig. 5 shows the process. Don't bend too much of the tube at a time, otherwise it will be flattened.

Screwed bends could be used if desired, but bending the tube is better and saves expense. Sharp elbows should not be employed, as difficulties will be experienced in drawing the lead-covered cable through them. The ends of the tubes must be filed perfectly smooth.

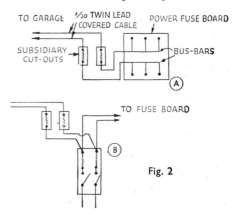

Fig. 2

Wiring the Tube.—Having completed operations on the tubing, a strong draw-wire should be inserted into the tube; the bared ends of the cable anchored to the draw-wire and the cable carefully drawn through. This operation calls for the services of a helper, who will feed the cable into the tube as you pull the draw-wire. To simplify the drawing-in process, the vertical length of tube D could be removed until the cable is in position. The tube could then be threaded over the cable and screwed to the connecting socket. The outlet at the end of D should be sealed by binding insulation tape round tube and cable. The tube

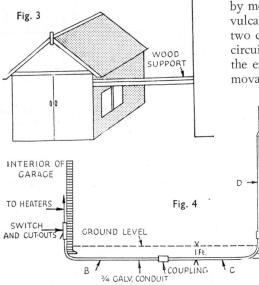

Fig. 3

WOOD SUPPORT

INTERIOR OF GARAGE

TO HEATERS

SWITCH AND CUT-OUTS

GROUND LEVEL

Fig. 4

D →

1 Ft.

B   ¾ GALV. CONDUIT   COUPLING   C

can then be clipped on to the walls and the soil reinstated in the trench.

The next procedure is to wire up to the heaters. This can be done effectively with lead-covered cable of the same size as that used for the outside work. Three-pin combination switch-plugs should be used to control each heater. It is advisable to insert a combined main-switch and cut-out between the outside cable and the inside wires.

Special tinned brass buckle clips for supporting the cable should be nailed to the walls at intervals of not more than 1 ft. apart, and the combination

switch-plugs must be mounted upon hardwood blocks fixed to the walls.

The heaters are mounted upon special brackets designed to keep the tubes from touching the wall, which are supplied with the heaters by the makers. These should be firmly fixed to the walls.

Connecting Up.—Connection between the heater and the plug is made by means of a short length of double-vulcanised triple-cored flexible cable, two cores of which are connected to the circuit terminals, to be found under the end cap of the heater, and the removable plug top of the switch-plug. The other core is connected to the earth terminal of the heater and the earthing-pin of the plug-top.

The lead-covered cable must be effectively earthed by connecting it with a 7/22 stranded copper wire to a cold water main. Suitable clips can be obtained for attaching the earth wire to the lead sheathing of the cable.

A wiring diagram of

Fig. 5

the complete circuit is shown in Fig. 2.

FIXING AND CONNECTING ELECTRIC LIGHT FITTINGS

THE usual method of fitting practically all modern hanging fittings is by means of a plate (on which there are three or more hooks) secured to the ceiling and chains from the plate to the bowl or chandelier or whatever fitting it is desired to hang.

For comparatively light fittings, such as a small bowl, it is generally satisfactory to secure the plate to a wooden block, which is first screwed to the ceiling through the laths, as represented in Fig. 1.

But for anything more than the very lightest of fittings this is not really a safe method.

It is preferable therefore, either to secure the block to a joist, if there is one in the right place in the ceiling, or else to construct a cross member in between two beams as in Fig. 2.

Two small pieces of wood A and B (about $1\frac{1}{2} \times \frac{1}{2}$ to $\frac{3}{4}$ in. thick) are first nailed to the joists as shown, and then a piece C about 6 in. wide is placed across A and B and secured with screws. If a $\frac{1}{2}$ in. thick round block is used, two 3 in. No. 8 countersunk screws will be found most suitable for securing it to a cross member of this description.

For screwing straight in to a joist a shorter screw than this will be required, and for screwing into laths it will be found best to use a fairly thin screw, usually a 2 to $2\frac{1}{2}$ in. No. 6.

Fixing the Block.—Assuming that the point has already been wired ready for the fitting, the first thing to do is to fix the block. This must previously have been drilled to take the wires and the screws.

A fairly large hole—about $\frac{1}{2}$ in. in diameter—should be drilled for the

wires in the centre of the block, and two smaller holes—about $\frac{1}{8}$ in.—for the screws. These small holes should be countersunk, and care must be taken that they will not be in the way of the screws that will secure the hook-plate to the block.

The wires should then be brought

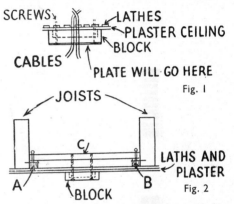

Fig. 1

Fig. 2

through their appropriate holes and the block screwed into position.

The next step will depend largely on the fitting itself, but for the sake of simplicity we will go through the process of fitting and adjusting an ordinary bowl-type fixture.

In this case the first thing to do, before screwing up the block, is to join a piece of good quality flex of double vulcanised class of suitable length on to the wires coming through the block. The method of doing this, again will partly depend on the type of plate to be used, owing to the fact that the space behind different plates varies a good deal. If there is room behind the plate the best method is to use a china connector as illustrated in Fig. 3.

Stripping the Wires.—First strip the wires to a distance of just under

½ in. from the ends and then double back the bared part.

The cable used for house wiring is insulated with vulcanised rubber and this is protected by a layer of tape (in the case of lead cable) or by a layer of tape and a further layer of a thicker braided material (in the case of V.I.R. or vulcanised india-rubber), treated with a waxy compound.

These outer layers are not insulating and if they are allowed to come into contact with the bare wire, when any damp gets to them, they actually become poor conductors and thus cause a slight leakage of current.

In order to avoid this, it is customary to strip these coverings back a little

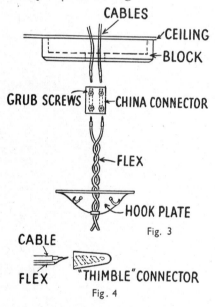

CABLES

CEILING

BLOCK

GRUB SCREWS — CHINA CONNECTOR

FLEX

HOOK PLATE

Fig. 3

CABLE

FLEX — "THIMBLE" CONNECTOR

Fig. 4

further than the rubber, thus preventing their coming into contact with the wire.

Make sure that the grub screws in the connector are as tight as possible and then bind the whole joint round with insulating tape.

If there is not sufficient room behind the plate for a china connector, it may be found possible to use two "thimble"

connectors. These are little thimble-shaped pieces of porcelain inside of which wide screw threads are moulded so that they screw on to the end of the cable.

The method of use is to strip the cable and flex as already explained and twist them together. Then cut the twisted wire off at the tip, leaving about ¼ in. of bare wire neatly twisted together. Now screw the connector on fairly tightly, holding the insulation of the wire in one hand to prevent its becoming twisted. When fixed, it is advisable to bind a layer of insulating tape around the base of the thimble.

Fig. 4 shows the thimble method of making the connections.

If the space behind the ceiling plate is very limited it might be found best to make the old-fashioned tape and rubber joint.

This method is to twist the flex and cable together as before, leaving about ½ in. bare wire, and then double the bare part back. Next bind the joint round with rubber tape, which should be stretched before using, and finally cover with a layer of ordinary insulating tape.

Having made the joint, knot the flex just below it to take the weight of the lamp, and then pass the flex through the plate and screw this in position.

It might be mentioned that rubber tape, which is not often seen except among electricians, is not undesirable on any joint as an added safeguard against leakage.

Hang the bowl on the chains at the approximate height required and then put the lampholder on the flex at sufficient distance from the bottom of the bowl to allow the lamp to swing clear. This clearance is important as the heat from the lamp may cause the bowl to crack if allowed to come in contact.

Final Adjustments.—In nearly all cases of reflected light—the light being, reflected from the ceiling—there is a shadow thrown round the room.

In a room with a picture rail, this can be rendered unnoticeable, and at the same time obtain the maximum amount of reflection by adjusting the length of the flex, until the edge of the shadow is level with the picture rail.

This can be done by moving the flex up and down with the hand until the required height is obtained. The flex can be cut and the holder replaced at the correct level.

There are so many different types of fitting that it would be impossible to deal with them all in detail, but it will be found that the remarks and instructions contained in this article will apply to almost any type at present available.

Chandelier Fittings.— The three or four chains used for suspending a bowl are here replaced, as a rule, by a single chain hung from a central hook in the plate.

These chandeliers are supplied with the three or more lights wired ready for connecting, but if they are not it will be generally found that either the arms which carry the lampholders are removable or else there is a removable part at the centre of the base of the fitting, which conceals a cavity which is used as a junction box.

The arms and the central spine of the fitting are hollow, enabling a piece of twin flex to be passed through each and a joint made in the cavity, using one of the methods already described.

This form of chandelier is illustrated at A in Fig. 5, while the wiring diagram for it is shown at B.

The fitting of a fixture of this type is slightly more complicated than that of a bowl, owing to the fact that there are two joints to be made instead of one.

The branches of the fitting are first wired, with the exception of the piece of flex through the spine.

Next, take a piece of flex long enough to reach from the ceiling plate to the bottom of the chandelier, always remembering that the strain must be taken by the chain and not by the flex. Join this to the cable protruding through

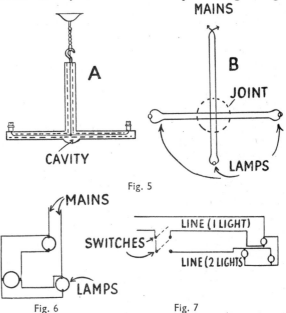

Fig. 5

Fig. 6

Fig. 7

the block on the ceiling and then screw the plate into position.

Next, thread the chain on to the flex, link by link, so that when the chain is extended it is intertwined with the flex.

Now support the chandelier by placing the chain on to the hook and then threading the flex through the central spine. The joint can now be made at the base of the fitting.

There are various types of chandelier, and in some of them it is necessary to join the flexes from the lampholders, somewhere other than at the base of the fitting. If this is the case, the lampholders can be looped together and a pair taken from one of them (Fig. 6).

Occasionally, it is required to have some of the lights of a chandelier separately controlled, so that it is not necessary to have them all on at once. This can only be done if there is an extra wire from the switch to the point. It is usual to loop one side of each lampholder to one side of the next, as shown diagrammatically in Fig. 7, and then take one wire from one of them, through to the return cable (usually the black) in the ceiling.

The other terminals of the lampholders of each set to be separately controlled are then looped together and one wire from each set taken to their respective switch wires in the ceiling.

Converting Gas Fittings.—There are quite a number of gas chandeliers still in existence which the majority of people discard the moment their premises are wired for electricity.

It is possible to obtain an adapter to convert the thread which normally receives the burner fittings, to a thread which will take a screw-on lampholder.

Sometimes a lampholder can be obtained that will screw straight on to the gas thread, but in any case, even if neither of these courses is adopted, it needs but the exercise of a little ingenuity to find a method for achieving the same purpose.

The lampholder can, for instance, be soldered on, or even merely suspended on the flex, coming through the tubes of the fitting, though the latter method is not a really satisfactory one, owing to the fact that the flex is inclined to fray on the end of the tube.

Whatever course is decided upon the chandelier should be wired with flex, using one of the diagrams already described for an ordinary chandelier.

As the apertures of the gas taps are

Fig. 8

usually of insufficient size to allow the flex to pass, they can be enlarged by drilling them. This is a simple matter, as such taps are generally of brass.

If the taps are sufficiently near the ends of the tubes, the drilling can be done without removing them, though it may be necessary to remove them and then, if desired, to replace them after they have been drilled.

It is a good idea to drop some small, though fairly weighty objects attached to a piece of string or wire so that the flex can then be attached to the string and drawn through the tubes with it.

With the aid of a little thought and ingenuity, it is possible to convert many things designed for other purposes, into electric reading lamps, etc.

Adapting Oil Lamps.—Oil lamps can be adapted in a similar way.

The oil container may have a small hole drilled in the side near the bottom for the flex to come through and it may be necessary to remove some of the mechanism which alters the height of the wick, but the modification necessary should not present any great difficulties.

Suitable adapters for converting oil lamps into electric ones are to be obtained quite cheaply at most electrical stores. The advantage of using one of these adapters is that no drilling of the oil reservoir or alteration of the burner is necessary, thus enabling the lamp to be used for oil burning should the necessity arise.

Bottles and jars of an ornamental design sometimes make very attractive reading lamps and can be converted for this purpose very simply.

It is possible to buy a form of patent clip which can be expanded by means of a screw in the body of the jar to hold it firm and which is made to take a lampholder. This is shown in Fig. 8.

It is not difficult, however, to make a simple form of clip as illustrated in Fig. 9 which will generally serve the same purpose. The diameter of the circular part of this clip should be about $1\frac{1}{8}$ in. and the length of the arms

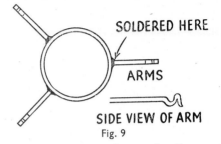

Fig. 9

will of course depend upon the diameter of the mouth of the jar.

The arms are soldered on to the ring and are made so that they clip very tightly on to the mouth of the jar. The lampholder can be of the ordinary switch cord-grip type and secured by means of the shade ring.

ELECTRIC LIGHTING AND EFFECTS FOR PRIVATE THEATRICALS

IT is assumed that readers who want to fit up and operate the electrical equipment of a small stage, such is generally found or can be erected in a private hall, have at least an elementary knowledge of installation work. That is to say, they understand how their homes are wired for electric light.

This knowledge is important, because a breakdown might be fatal to the performance.

Switch Grouping.—It is a good plan to have a self-contained control panel such as is illustrated in Fig. 1. The panel consists of a double-pole fuse-board, combined main switch and cut-outs and sub-circuit switches, all mounted upon a wooden board. This control panel

should be fixed at a convenient height and as near to the front of the stage as possible without being in view of the audience.

The current for feeding the panel should be obtained from a convenient plug connected to a separate circuit of its own sufficiently stout to carry a current in excess of that required. Such a plug is usually found installed for the purpose on the stage. If not, run a pair of leads back to the main switch controlling the lights of the building.

The diagram in Fig. 2 illustrates a convenient position for the control board, while Fig. 3 shows how the various circuit wires radiate from it.

It will be noticed that a separate

sub-circuit is provided for footlights, floods and battens. Each sub-circuit is protected by separate double-pole fuses so that, in the event of a short-circuit, the fault affects only the lamps and apparatus connected to that circuit.

Fig. 1

In wiring the control board, all connecting wires should be run at the back. The fuse-board should be covered with a glazed front so that the risk of a burn from a fuse blowing is reduced to a minimum. It also prevents the operator from coming in contact with live terminals when in use.

One or two spare fuse-carriers already wired should always be to hand so that, in the event of a faulty lamp blowing a fuse, the remaining lamps on that circuit can be put into service again instantly. Wiring up a fuse takes time and partial darkness on any part of the stage, even for a couple of minutes, is irritating to audience and actors.

Switches.—All switches should be distinctly marked with the names of the lights they control. This precaution mini-

mises the risk of operating a wrong switch. Gummed paper answers the purpose and can be removed or replaced easily.

Why is a main switch necessary on a control panel? The answer is that the switch is not only useful for its normal function of cutting off the current when the stage is not in use, but it is also necessary for carrying out a black-out—that is, a short interval of complete darkness which sometimes occurs during a play.

A small 5-watt pilot light should be provided for the operator so that he can see what he is doing, and a small electric torch should be kept near.

Dimming Lights.—In some scenes it may be necessary to reduce the light gradually. This can be arranged by inserting a variable resistance in the

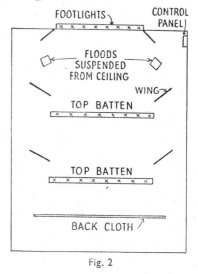

Fig. 2

main circuit. Such a resistance can be liquid and is improvised as follows.

Procure a large glazed earthenware drain pipe and seal up one end with portland cement. Make sure that the joint is watertight. Cast two discs of lead, one about $\frac{1}{2}$ in. thick and $\frac{1}{4}$ in. less in diameter than the bore of the pipe and the other of the same thickness but 1 in. less in diameter. Construct a framework of 2×2 in. planed deal to support the pipe, as shown in Fig. 4. Now make the flanged pulley shown at the top of the illustration. This can be built up of deal, ¾ in. thick by about 12 in. in diameter and faced on each side with ¼ in. plywood, 13 in. across. Bore a number of ⅜ in. holes right through the disc and near the edge as shown. Bore the centre to take a short length of wood of 1½ in. circular section. A piece of broomstick will serve the purpose well. Drive the spindle into the hole, allowing about 3 in. to project on each side. Make a handle of a piece of wood and screw it to the disc.

Now construct two brackets to support the pulley, and bore a hole in each to take the spindle. These holes should be large enough to allow the spindle to revolve easily. Drill a ⅜ in. hole to correspond with the holes round the disc, and screw the brackets down to the top of the frame, in such a position that the inner edge of the pulley is central with the centre of the pipe.

Connect a length of heavy cab-tyre flex to the larger disc and lower the disc into the bottom of the pipe, connecting the other end of the cable to a suitable terminal. The other lead plate is connected to one end of a longer cable which passes over the pulley wheel and ends at another terminal. The cable should be anchored to the pulley in the position shown and it should be sufficiently long to allow the lead plate to rest on the bottom one.

The terminals should be connected in series with the main cable between the

main switch and a bus-bar in the fuse-board as indicated in the diagram Fig. 5, and the pipe filled nearly up to the top with a weak solution of salt and water.

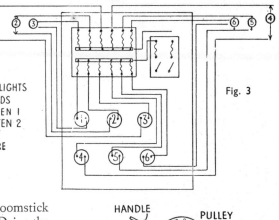

1	FOOT LIGHTS
2	FLOODS
3	BATTEN 1
4	BATTEN 2
5	SPOT
6	SPARE

Fig. 3

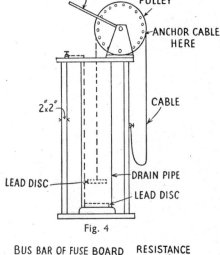

Fig. 4

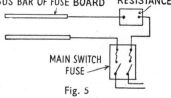

Fig. 5

When the lead plates rest upon each other, the resistance to the current flowing is negligible and the lamps glow normally. As the distance between the plates increases when the pulley is operated, the resistance also increases and gradually dims the lamps.

If the apparatus is operated steadily and slowly, dimming will be perfect.

A ⅜ in. diameter peg inserted through the hole in the bracket and one of the holes in the pulley keeps the latter in the desired position.

As the dimmer is not likely to be used through a whole performance, a short circuiting switch should be incorporated as shown in Fig. 6.

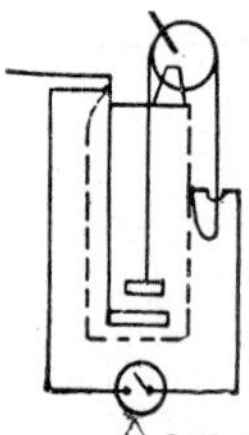

All wiring will be of a temporary nature, but should be done carefully to ensure safety. This can be done by carrying the majority of the circuit wires overhead and securing them with china cleats.

Fig. 6 SHORT CIRCUITING SWITCH

The circuit wires may consist of good vulcanised india-rubber cable, as used for house wiring. It is good practice not to load up a pair of 18 gauge leads india-rubber. Long trailing flexes on the stage should be avoided.

The ends of the circuit wires should terminate in a plug top which will connect to a corresponding socket on the piece apparatus, be it a bank of lamps, top battens, footlights or floods. This arrangement allows individual devices to be disconnected or connected up in the minimum of time, which is important when scene shifting and altering positions of lights. Fig. 7 shows the arrangement as applied to a bank of lamps forming a top batten.

Front-stage Lighting. — Footlights should be arranged in a trough, in such a manner that the lamps are hidden from the audience and the batten upon which the lampholders are mounted should be inclined at an angle as illustrated in Fig. 8.

A guard of galvanised wire netting should be fixed in front of the lamps. Small iron brackets drilled to take wood screws could be used for fixing the footlights to the stage. Make the foot-

Fig. 7

to a greater extent than 3 amps.—or, say, fifteen 40-watt lamps or their equivalent—if the voltage is 240 and a proportionately less number of lamps if the voltage is lower.

Thin twisted flex should not be used for portable lamps and apparatus, but there is no objection to employing the thick flex known as cab-tyre flex, where two insulated cores of wire are further protected with a covering of vulcanised lights in units of about 4 ft. in length to facilitate handling. They can be connected together with plugs and sockets, as suggested for the top battens.

The interior of the troughs should be painted white. A couple of coats of washable distemper will serve admirably, are easier to apply and dry quicker than ordinary paint. Polished tinplate can be fixed behind the lamps to reflect more light, but this will generally be found unnecessary on a small stage.

When fitting ceiling lights or battens, suspend them from pulleys, so that they can be lowered to replace the bulbs by others of different colours.

A Floodlight.—An excellent floodlight, Fig. 9, can be made out of a large square biscuit tin obtained at a small cost from a grocer's shop. Such a tin measures approximately 9 in. square.

Besides the tin, a piece of strip iron 27 in. long ×$\frac{3}{4}$ in. wide and $\frac{1}{8}$ in. thick, a couple of 1×$\frac{1}{4}$ in. diameter bolts fitted with wing nuts, two iron screw-eyes and a cord-grip lampholder fitted with a shade ring are the principal items required.

First remove the paper label from the tin. Then cut a 1$\frac{1}{8}$ in. diameter hole in the centre of one side which forms the top A as indicated in Fig. 9. The lid is the front. The centre can be found by scribing diagonals from opposite corners, the centre being where they cross.

The best way to make the hole which accommodates the lampholder is to punch a centre mark and, from this centre, scratch a circle 1$\frac{1}{8}$ in. in diameter with a pair of dividers. Drill a series of small holes as close together as possible on the inner side of the circle and sever the metal between the holes with a small sharp cold chisel. Smooth the edge with a half-round file. When drilling and chiselling, support the underside of the metal with a block of wood.

Find the centre of each side B and C, centre-pop and drill holes a trifle larger than the bolt.

Drill a series of ventilation holes near the top at the back as shown at A in Fig. 10.

With a pair of old scissors or tinman's snips, make a cut $\frac{3}{8}$ in. deep at the top front corners, bend the metal down and under and hammer it flat. This forms a recess into which a piece of frosted glass

and coloured gelatine screens can be inserted.

Now cut two strips of $\frac{1}{4}$×$\frac{1}{4}$ in. hardwood and fix them to the inside faces of the sides and in line with the edge of the top. The strips can be fixed by driving in short thin brass screws driven through from the outside.

Now cut and bend a piece of tinplate

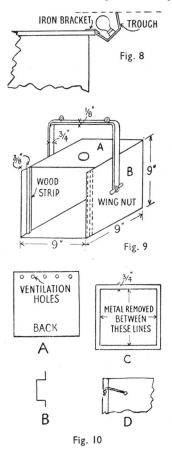

Fig. 8

Fig. 9

Fig. 10

to the shape shown at B in Fig. 10, and solder it to the back to mask the ventilation holes.

This completes the body.

Prepare the iron suspending strip. Drill a hole near each end to clear the bolts and bore similar holes 10 in. away from the ones at the ends. These holes should be bored to the same diameter as the plain upper part of the screw-eye shank. Place the length of iron in the vice and bend to shape.

The next procedure is to cut the shanks of the screw-eyes so that only a trifle over ⅛ in. of the metal remains below the eye. This is done with a hack saw. File the ends square, insert the stub shanks into the holes in the strip and rivet the ends over with a hammer.

Now make the front from the lid of the tin. This takes the form of a frame as shown at C in Fig. 10. Scribe lines round the face of the lid ¾ in. from the edges as shown. The metal within these lines has to be removed. This can be done in the same way as suggested for the hole at the top of the body.

Snip the top corners and bend the flange down flat on the inside.

Procure two thin brass hinges 1 in. long × ½ in. wide and solder them to the bottom flange of the lid and the bottom of the body.

Suitable fastenings for keeping the front closed can be made by soldering a cut-down brass wood screw to each side of the front, near the top, to take a stout wire hook fixed to the body by means of a small bolt, washers and nut as indicated at D in Fig. 10.

Better results will be obtained if a curved reflector is placed at the back of the lamp. This consists of a piece of polished tinplate soldered in position.

To cover the top aperture when the screens are in position, cut a piece of tinplate a trifle longer than the width of the floodlight and about 2 in. wide. Bend one long edge at right-angles at a distance of ½ in. and hinge this to the top of the body in the way described for hinging the front to the bottom. The ½ in. portion of the piece fits over the front.

All that remains to be done is to wire and fit the lampholder and fix the suspending iron by means of bolts and wing-nuts. The wing-nuts are to tilt and lock the floodlight at any desired angle.

The outside should be cleaned and given two coats of Berlin black. This gives a matt finish. Spirit enamel should be avoided as it chips off.

In using the floodlight, place a gelatine screen of the desired colour in front of a piece of frosted glass, cut to fit loosely in the aperture. The glass prevents the heat of the lamp damaging the screen.

If a more powerful light than that obtained from a 150-watt lamp is desired, an Edison screw lampholder should be substituted in place of the bayonet type.

A handy type of adjustable floor standard floodlight suitable for amateur theatrical purposes will be found in the article on home-made photographic apparatus.

It should be noted that these suggestions apply to private performances, carried out in private halls and buildings. If a public performance is to be given in a licenced building the licensing authorities must be approached before carrying out the work as it must conform to regulations.

Effects.—Lightning can be imitated on the stage with a powerful lamp controlled by a bakelite bell-push mounted on the control panel; thunder, by rattling a large piece of thin tinplate suspended by a stout cord from the ceiling.

A good imitation of motor car noise can be produced with a small electric motor driving a spindle to which a couple of leather strips are attached. The leather is made to knock against a large wooden box held in various positions.

Moonlight showing through a window is obtained by a floodlight fitted with a blue lamp, at the back of the window.

Telephone and other bells can be operated from the control board.

ELECTRIC INSET FIRE

THE greatest advantage of the inset electric fire over the ordinary portable type is the comparatively small amount of space which it occupies.

A three-bar (3 kilowatts) portable fire is rather cumbersome and not really a very sightly article of furniture. In a very small room, even a single-bar fire is apt to occupy quite a lot of space.

The inset stove is gradually becoming an almost universal standard fitting in the modern house and one of the many types available is shown in the accompanying illustration Fig. 1.

The power point or source of supply will be discussed later, but at the moment it will be assumed that there is a point already in the vicinity of the position at which the stove is to be fitted.

The stove usually projects at the back to a depth of about 4×6 in. and a space in the wall just over that depth is therefore necessary. The width and height of this aperture should, of course, be less than the face of the stove so that the face of the stove completely covers it when in position.

Fitting.—The method of fitting the stove is usually to make the mouth of the aperture just large enough to take the body of the stove, upon the bottom of which are fitted two spring clips.

At the top of the stove through the front face part is a hole to take a screw. The stove is forced into the aperture and screwed into position through the hole, the clips holding the bottom firm as in Fig. 2.

It is obvious that the mouth of the aperture must be hard and solid. Furthermore, since we have to bring wires in through the bottom of the aperture and since the clips have to slip over something, the aperture must be of greater dimensions inside than at the mouth.

If the stove is to fit flush on to a wall without a surround of any description, the best method is to fit into the mouth of the aperture an iron frame, which can usually be supplied by the makers of the stove.

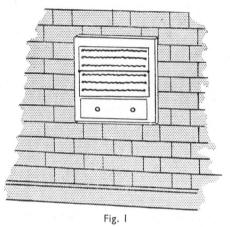

Fig. 1

The frame is generally cemented into position, and has at the top a threaded hole to take a metal screw which passes through a corresponding hole in the face of the stove.

The Surround.—This method can also be used for fitting a stove in a tiled surround and is very convenient where there was originally a coal grate. The front of the grate is bricked up and tiled to match the original surround. The frame is cemented into position as before.

Some times the frame has two threaded fixing holes, one at the top and one at the bottom, the bottom one replacing the metal clips.

This method of using an iron frame is probably the best available, giving a very firm and easily obtained fixture. It is illustrated in Fig. 2.

A very common method which has come into use recently and which gives a very pleasing effect is to use a surround made of a composition very closely resembling slate as in Fig. 3. This material can be obtained in various colours and in such effects as marble,

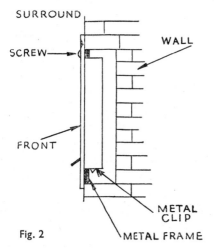

Fig. 2

etc., and can be drilled fairly easily.

The usual type of fixture with a surround of this description is very similar to that using the iron frame. There are the same clips at the bottom of the stove but instead of a threaded hole in the frame, there is just a plain hole drilled in the surround.

If possible it is preferable when cutting out the aperture in the wall or having a space bricked up, to allow the brickwork behind the hole in the surround to remain solid so that it can be plugged to take a wood-screw through the front of the stove.

If this is not done, however, it is generally found not too difficult to plug the actual hole in the surround itself, though the chief disadvantage of this is the fact that each time the stove is removed for examination it necessitates the re-plugging of the hole.

Another method of fitting this type of surround is to plug the brickwork through the surround, using either two or four holes in the face of the stove. The surround itself is usually fixed by means of a wood-screw and plug in each corner.

Screws.—An ordinary wood or metal screw with the slotted head is not very decorative and therefore the screws that are generally used are slightly different.

A hole is drilled in the very centre of the head (the screw being of the flat countersunk type) and this hole is threaded. The usual slot passes right across the hole so that the screw can be inserted by means of a screwdriver in the usual way.

With the screw there is supplied a semi-circular chromium plated knob with a thread projecting from the centre of the flat side. This knob screws into the hole in the screw itself, and when the whole thing is in position, nothing is visible but a neat little plated knob.

The connections to the stove are usually made to terminals underneath a sheet iron cover that encloses the whole of the back of the stove.

These terminals are generally situated at the bottom of the stove, and if it is of the "multi-bar" type a spare terminal will generally be found on the switch controlling one of the bars or 1 kilowatt elements, and another terminal will be found which connects direct to one of the bars.

The Connections to a typical three-bar, two-switch type of stove are shown in Fig. 4. It will be noticed that the positive from the supply goes to the switch and the negative to the element.

An important point which must never be overlooked is the earthing of the stove.

Somewhere near the other two connections will be found a terminal which makes contact with nothing but the case or frame of the stove. This is the earth terminal.

The earth wire which connects here should be of stout copper wire and should be connected at its other end to the conduit or lead casing of the cable supplying the stove. This conduit should be earthed in turn, according to the electric supply company's requirements.

The cable to the elements should somehow be brought into the cavity behind the fire either through the side or at the bottom.

It will be noticed in Fig. 2 that a space has been left for this purpose at the bottom, the cavity continuing a little below the bottom of the stove.

When a surround has been specially built to house an electric stove, the wiring is, of course, quite simple as it can be done before the surround is completed. When the surround has been adapted for this purpose, there will not be any wiring "built in."

It is necessary, therefore, if the wiring is to be concealed, to knock a hole through the side of the cavity as near the bottom as possible to come out somewhere on the side of the chimney breast.

In the case of a tiled surround this is not very difficult as there is generally a fairly thick layer of plaster in between the bricks of the wall and tiles.

It is usual in the case of an adapted coal fire grate to make the hole in the cavity through the fire brick at the side of the grate, pointing the cold chisel slightly towards the front and bottom of the grate so as to come out somewhere at the side of the surround behind the wooden framework of the fireplace.

It is nearly always the practice to install beside the grate (except when the wiring is built in) a 15 amp. switch plug. The wires from the stove are then plugged into this fitting. This method has the advantage even in the case of

built-in wiring of providing a readily accessible switch, by means of which

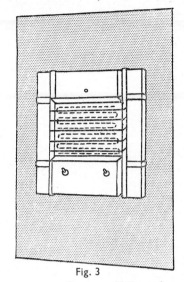

Fig. 3

all current can be cut off from the stove in time of necessity. This plug should

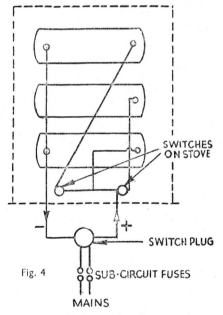

Fig. 4

for preference be of the three-pin type, the earth wire being connected to the third pin.

The wiring of a one-bar fire should be carried out with cable not smaller than 7/.029 (seven-strand wire, each strand of which is .029 in. in diameter).

In the case of two or three elements, the wiring should be at least 7/.036.

The wiring can be carried out in various systems. There is the ordinary vulcanised india-rubber (V.I.R.) in which the cable is taken through steel tubing or conduit. A system which is quite extensively used in the lead wiring system. In this case the insulated wire is enclosed in a casing of lead. In both these systems the metal casing must be efficiently bonded and earthed.

Another system which has become very common recently is the "tough rubber" system. The wire in this case is covered by an extra layer of specially toughened rubber.

In the two latter systems it is advisable to pass the cable through tubing where it goes through the wall or behind the tiles particularly in the case of tough rubber.

In every case the point must be on a separate circuit and protected by a pair of 15 amp. capacity cut-outs.

ELECTRIC MOTOR FOR A SEWING MACHINE

WITH the advent of a supply of electricity in nearly every district in the country, the hand operated sewing machine is rapidly becoming a thing of the past and even the treadle is now being replaced by the small, efficient electric motor.

Most sewing machines are adaptable for use with electricity. Motors, complete with foot-controls, specially made for the purpose of fitting to sewing machines are obtainable at a cost of about £3 to £4 and if one of these units is purchased, the fitting is simple and needs little description.

Fig. 1 shows a commercially constructed unit which can be fitted to any machine.

We are concerned more, however, in this article with the adaption and fitting of a motor not specifically designed for this purpose.

First we must obtain one suitable for the particular supply for which it is intended, and of suitable horse-power, i.e., the voltage must correspond and it must be A.C. or D.C. according to the supply, unless a universal motor, which will work off both direct and alternating current, can be obtained.

The usual horse-power required for driving a sewing machine is about 1/20.

The Control. — It is practically essential to have the resistance or speed-control, foot-operated, as it is obvious that both hands are required to manipulate the work. There are many types available, manufactured by various firms and the type which we require is a series resistance. When ordering the control, do not forget to state the details of the motor and the supply.

The Shaft.—The motor must have a shaft projecting from the armature, to take the pulley wheel, this shaft being either a plain rod or threaded.

If it is plain, the pulley is generally secured by means of a grub-screw. It is as well either to drill a shallow hole in the shaft, or to file a section of it flat, where the grub screw will press upon it, as this will help to prevent any slipping of the pulley wheel which might otherwise occur.

Should the shaft be threaded, the best

way to secure the wheel is by means of a lock-nut at either side of it.

The Wheel in this case should also really be threaded, but this is not really essential providing a good fit is obtained.

These two methods of fitting the wheel are shown in Fig. 2.

The final adjustment of the position of the pulley wheel on the shaft, to bring it in correct alignment with the wheel of the machine, cannot be satisfactorily made until the motor is actually in position, and it is therefore advisable before any filing or drilling of the shaft is proceeded with, to attend to all other details first, then temporarily secure the motor in position and so obtain the exact position of the wheel upon the shaft.

A great number of commercial units fit on to the actual iron frame of the machine, but there are some that are bolted to the wooden table. The latter is the method more convenient for the fitting of an adapted motor.

Belt Tension.—In order to obtain the proper tension of the belt, it is necessary to allow means of adjustment of the distance between the pulley wheel of the motor and the wheel of the machine. Since the shaft of the motor is fixed, the adjustment is generally in the distance of the whole motor from the machine. This can be effected by elongating the holes, through which the fixing-bolts pass, either in the casting of the motor casing or in the table. The latter method is the easier. Thus before finally securing the motor the tension on the belt can be adjusted and the bolts then tightened up.

In Fig. 3 the holes in the table have been lengthened to allow for this adjustment. A good way of making a hole of this shape is first to drill two holes of the desired diameter (according to

the thickness of the bolt employed) and, say, an inch apart, and then saw out the intervening section by means of a pad saw.

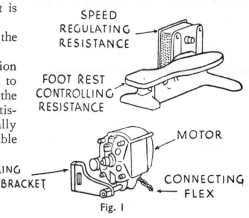

SPEED REGULATING RESISTANCE

FOOT REST CONTROLLING RESISTANCE

MOTOR

FIXING BRACKET

CONNECTING FLEX

Fig. 1

It is advisable to include a metal washer in between the nut and the wood, and also a locking nut, as there will be a considerable whip on the motor, and unless these two details are attended to, it will continually have to be tightened and adjusted.

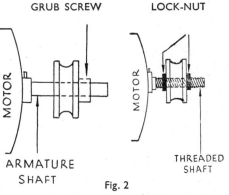

GRUB SCREW   LOCK-NUT

MOTOR   MOTOR

ARMATURE SHAFT

THREADED SHAFT

Fig. 2

For the belt, the usual thick circular rubber band is used. Rubber bands are supplied especially for this purpose, at only a few pence each, by many of the leading stores.

The Foot Control.—This works on practically the same principle as an accelerator pedal of a motor-car, and should, therefore, if possible be secured firmly in position.

This is not always possible, of course, as in the majority of rooms the machine is not kept permanently in the position it occupies when being used. However,

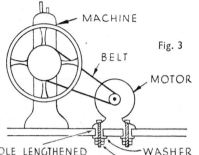

MACHINE

Fig. 3

BELT

MOTOR

HOLE LENGTHENED TO ALLOW ADJUSTMENT

WASHER

TWO NUTS

most of these controls can be used quite well without fixing.

The control can simply be screwed to the floor, or, if the machine is moved

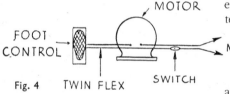

MOTOR

FOOT CONTROL

Fig. 4   TWIN FLEX   SWITCH

about and is of the treadle type, it is quite a good plan to secure the foot control to the treadle by placing strips of wood or metal underneath the control, and then bolting them through the treadle.

The Wiring of the Motor and speed control can be carried out in ordinary lighting flex, provided it is of good quality, as the current consumed by the motor is very small, being generally of a similar value to an electric light bulb of about 60 watts.

The wiring diagram is shown in Fig. 4, and on referring to this, it will be noticed that a switch is included in the circuit.

This item is unnecessary when one is incorporated in the speed control unit. If a switch is not included in the unit, a "torpedo" type of switch provides a very convenient kind for the purpose. It should be inserted in the flex, somewhere in the vicinity of the motor, where it is easily accessible.

One lead of the flex can simply be cut through wherever the switch is to be connected, and the two ends so formed connected to the terminals of the switch. This will save the making of a joint, which should be avoided whenever possible.

MAINS

Earthing.—Like all other electrical appliances, the motor and the foot control should, whenever possible be earthed. This can best be done by installing a three-pin plug, the earth wire being secured under one of the fixing bolts or under one of the bolts in the casing.

A STATIC TRANSFORMER

IT sometimes happens that the available voltage is either too high or too low to suit a piece of electrical apparatus such as a wireless set or a small electric motor designed to work off an alternating current supply of a definite pressure.

In many instances this difficulty can

be overcome by lowering or raising the pressure by means of a simple piece of apparatus known as a static transformer.

As its name implies, a static transformer has no moving parts. In an elementary form it consists of two separate coils of insulated wire wound on an iron core. One coil is known as the primary and the other as the secondary.

A.C. Transformer.—Briefly stated an alternating current transformer functions in the following way. When an alternating current is sent through the windings of the primary coil the alternations of the current cause a correspondingly fluctuating magnetic influence in the iron core, and this in turn induces a current in the secondary coil. The pressure of the current in the secondary coil depends upon the number of turns in it as compared with those of the primary.

The transformer shown in Fig. 1, constructional details of which will be found in the following paragraphs and accompanying illustrations, is designed to work off an alternating current supply whose frequency is 50 cycles, a frequency largely employed in this country.

The apparatus must not be used where the supply is not of that frequency and on no account must an attempt be made to use it on direct current mains.

The output of the transformer is 80-100 watts at a pressure of 100, 105 and 110 volts when supplied with current at one of any of the following voltages: 200, 210, 220, 230, 240 and 250. This is known as a "step down" transformer.

Construction.—The general construction is quite simple. Here is a list of materials:

1¼ in. (thickness) No. 28 Stalloy transformer stampings for the core (Sankey and Co.).

1 bobbin to suit same; this can be made by the constructor.

A sheet of Empire cloth, an insulating material, 10 mils. thick, 18×24 in.

18 ft. varnished paper, 3 in. wide and .001 thick.

2 or 3 yds. single vulcanised rubber insulated flex.

1¼ lb. No. 24 S.W.G. double silk

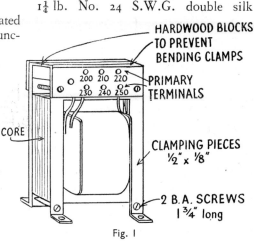

HARDWOOD BLOCKS TO PREVENT BENDING CLAMPS

200 210 220 230 240 250

PRIMARY TERMINALS

CORE

CLAMPING PIECES ½" x ⅛"

2 B.A. SCREWS 1¾" long

Fig. 1

covered copper instrument wire, for the primary coil.

1½ lb. No. 21 ditto, for the secondary coil.

A piece of copper foil, 10 in. long, 2¼ in. wide and .005 thick.

1 set of clamps.

Terminals, ebonite, Chatterton's compound, insulating sleeving and odds and ends.

Start by making the bobbin upon which the primary and secondary coils are wound. This may be made of millboard or a good quality cardboard to the dimensions given in Fig. 2. The two end cheeks are 3⅝ in. square and 3/32 in. thick, with rounded corners, while the core-tunnel is 1¼×1¼ in. (full) and 1/16 in. thick. These parts should first be marked out and then cut to shape, using a sharp penknife guided by a metal straight-edge, and afterwards stuck together with a reliable adhesive such as seccotine. Allow sufficient time for the adhesive to set and then give the bobbin a coat of shellac varnish.

Wind the wire forming the primary on to the bobbin. This is best done with the aid of a simple winder, as illustrated in Fig. 3, unless you happen to possess a lathe.

The winding apparatus consists of a wooden base, supporting two uprights between which is a cranked spindle made of $\frac{3}{16}$ in. diameter mild steel rod. A Meccano spindle 12 in. long will answer the purpose quite well.

A wood block or former is then made to fit tightly in the transformer bobbin, and in order to do this it is a good plan to make the block a trifle tapered. A hole slightly smaller than the diameter of the spindle is then drilled through the block and the latter forced on to the rod. To prevent the block from slipping, a Meccano wheel can be fixed to the spindle and screwed to the block.

Before winding the primary coil,

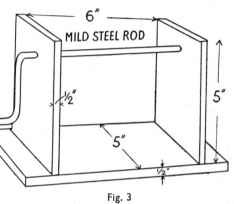

Fig. 3

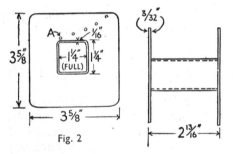

Fig. 2

drill a $\frac{1}{8}$ in. diameter hole in one cheek of the bobbin, as indicated at A in Fig. 2, and wrap two thicknesses of Empire cloth round the tube portion.

Insert through the hole one end of a piece of flex about 9 in. long. Solder the end of the 24 S.W.G. wire to the inner end of the flex, pull the flex through the cheek so that about 2 in. of the flex remains on the inside of the cheek, as indicated in Fig. 4, and wrap a small piece of Empire cloth round the joint.

Now fix the bobbin in the machine, turn the handle and start winding on the

wire, carefully noting the number of turns put on.

One way of checking the number of turns applied is to stick a piece of paper on one corner of the bobbin-supporting block, jotting down on a piece of paper every ten or twenty turns.

When the first layer of wire has been wound, a strip of varnished paper of the appropriate size should be wrapped round before winding the next layer.

This operation should not be omitted as it protects the adjacent layers from insulation breakdown because, while there is slight potential difference between adjacent turns, there is a far greater potential difference between the end turns of adjacent layers.

The varnished paper should fit snugly against the end cheeks, and the next layer started—say, $\frac{1}{16}$ to $\frac{1}{8}$ in.—from the cheek and ended at a similar distance from the opposite one. This also is important, as it tends to make the transformer reliable, for it is at the ends of the layers that trouble is likely to occur.

When 1,067 turns have been wound, a tapping should be made in the wire by either of the following methods:

1. A loop is twisted in the wire as indicated at A in the sketch, Fig. 4, and a short length of insulating sleeving pushed over it. This is then pushed

through a conveniently situated hole, carefully bored in the cheek.

2. A piece of flex may be soldered direct to the winding. In either case the tappings should be wrapped with a piece of Empire cloth. It should be noted that when a tapping has been made the insulation between the tapping and the next layer of wire should be of Empire cloth in place of varnished paper.

Tappings should be made at the turns indicated in the following table.

Primary Voltage	Turns	Secondary Voltage	Turns
200	1,067	100	555
210	1,120	105	583
220	1,174	110	611
230	1,226	..	..
240	1,280	..	..
250	1,334	..	..

One need not, of course, wind on all the turns if the transformer is to be worked at a lower voltage than 250. For instance, if the supply voltage is 230, the total number of primary turns is 1,226.

Having completed winding the primary coil, the end of the wire should be finished in the same manner as that adopted at the start—that is, soldered to a piece of flex.

The next step is to wrap three layers of Empire cloth on top of the primary coil.

The copper foil will now be required. It is used for screening the primary coil from the secondary. This could be omitted, but its inclusion greatly improves the performance of the transformer.

The screen itself should be 2¼ in. wide and sufficiently long to form one complete turn.

Before placing the foil in position it is essential to put it—sandwich-fashion—between two sheets of Empire cloth a

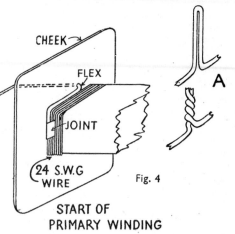

CHEEK

FLEX

JOINT

24 S.W.G WIRE

A

Fig. 4

START OF PRIMARY WINDING

full 2¾ in. wide and 2 in. longer than the screen, as the ends of the screen must not touch each other. Failure to observe this precaution would possibly end in a burnt-out primary, because the metal forms its own electrical circuit which, having a low resistance, puts a large load on the primary coil.

A lead should be taken from the screen to earth—that is, the frame—which incidentally should be connected to earth when the transformer is in use.

Wrap a further three layers of Empire cloth over the screen, and having done this the secondary windings may be wound on in the same manner as the primary. The number of turns for the secondary will be found in the winding table.

To complete the coil and give it a professional finish, wrap three layers of Empire cloth over the secondary coil. The end of the cloth can be fastened down with a little melted Chatterton's compound.

The bobbin may now be removed from the winding device as it is now ready to receive the core.

The Core is in the form of thin stampings of special iron that take the shape of U's and T's, as indicated in Fig. 5.

To assemble the core, place the bobbin

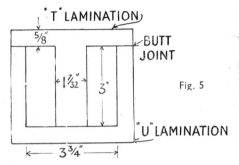

Fig. 5

on two of its long edges and pass the stem of a T lamination through the bobbin tunnel. Then place a U stamping in position from the opposite side. The bottom U lamination will have to

Fig. 6

be fitted when the core is clamped together as there is no support for it at this stage of construction.

The next T should be inserted from the opposite side to the previous one, and likewise the U's, so as to get a satisfactory magnetic circuit.

This staggering of the stampings should be continued until the bobbin tunnel is packed tight.

In Stalloy stampings one side is coated with a special substance resembling thin white paper, and it is important that all the prepared faces should be kept either upwards or downwards when building up the core.

When the core is complete the transformer is workable, but to make a smart

Fig. 7

and permanent job of it the core should be secured by metal clamps, and the wires attached to suitable terminal blocks of ebonite as indicated in Fig. 1.

The clamping pieces can be made of brass strips $\frac{1}{8}$ in. thick and $\frac{1}{2}$ in. wide bent at the lower ends to form feet. They should also be drilled in the positions shown in Fig. 1, to take No. 2 B.A. bolts and nuts by which the clamps are fixed to the core.

The terminal boards are best arranged as shown, while the terminals themselves should be soldered to the various tapping leads, etc., before fitting, care being taken not to cut them off too short.

To enable the tapping leads to be easily identified it is a good plan to label each one during the winding operation. Various coloured cottons are also useful for this.

When testing the transformer, three ampere fuses should be placed in the primary circuit, and a 100 watt lamp of 100 volts connected in the secondary, as a working load.

To make sure that the insulation of the transformer is as it should be, it is a wise plan to let the local electrician make an insulation test, before connecting it to the mains.

As it would be dangerous to work the transformer unprotected, a tinplate case should be made for it. The metal should be provided with a number of holes to allow efficient ventilation, and it should be earthed as well as the copper screen and the transformer frame.

When making the cover and the wooden base it is advisable to make the latter large enough to take a couple of plug sockets to which leads can be connected from the primary and the secondary terminals.

The illustration appearing at Fig. 6 shows the completed winding machine, while the process of winding the coil is pictured in Fig. 7.

BATTERY-OPERATED LAMPS

IT is strange that despite the fact that battery-operated lamps, torches, etc., as represented at Fig. 1, are in common use, very few people seem to know how to maintain them in proper order.

One of the most important things in all torches is to make sure that the voltage of the battery and the bulb nearly correspond. The flat standard type of torch has a three-cell battery, making a total voltage of about 4.5 volts. The bulb for such a lamp must not be of a lower voltage than 3.5.

This type of torch, if it is not properly looked after, is sometimes inclined to give trouble when being switched on.

Very often people are to be seen shaking a torch before it will light. A glance at Fig. 2 will help to make the explanation of this clear. The illustration shows a flat torch with one side cut away; s, the switch knob, and c, the switch contact, are actually joined together through the slot in the side of the torch case; B is the bulb, one contact of which is made to the torch case by means of the metal threaded part of the bulb, and the other contact is made to the long strip of the battery by a small metal projection in the centre base of the bulb.

When the switch is at the " on " position, as can be seen, a complete electrical circuit is produced as follows:

From the side connecting strip of the battery to the switch thence through the switch to the metal case, through the case to the metal thread of the bulb, through the bulb to the little contact at the bottom and so back to the battery.

The two weak points in this circuit are the contact between the switch and the short contact on the battery, and the contact between the bulb and the long battery strip.

When putting a new battery in the torch, make sure that the short strip is bent back at right-angles to press firmly on the switch contact when it is down. Also give the switch contact a rub with fine emery cloth or glass-paper, every now and then.

The other weak defect at the bulb and battery contact may be remedied by adjustment when putting in a new battery. Make sure, of course, that the bulb is screwed right home. The battery strip, instead of being left in a

Fig. 1

vertical position, may require bending slightly as in Fig. 2.

Occasionally, the battery is packed at the bottom of the case by means of pieces of paper or cardboard, etc. This is seldom necessary, but it is worth remembering if you happen to purchase a battery the short contact strip of which is too short.

Cycle Lamp.—An example of this is shown in Fig. 3. The circuit is the same as before, the only difference being in the form of the contacts and the difference in voltage.

This type of lamp generally has a two-cell battery having a voltage of just under 3 volts. The bulb supplied is usually of 2.5 volts.

The position of the contacts on the battery are, as is probably known, one at the top and one in front. The one on the top makes contact with a switch, which instead of sliding up and down as in the ordinary flat torch, screws in and out. The strip in front makes contact with the bulb.

The remarks referring to the switch and contacts for the hand torch, apply equally well for this type, as they do indeed, for almost any torch available.

The Reflector has to make an electrical contact with the metal case, and the edges of it must therefore be occasionally cleaned.

The cover which holds the glass is rather inclined to stick if the thread is allowed to get at all rusty. This can be prevented by giving the thread an occasional thin application of vaseline.

The square, wooden cased type of hand lamp is worth mentioning, as the observations on it will apply to practically any lamp not fitted with a metal case. This type of lamp is shown in Fig. 4.

It generally has a larger battery than those already mentioned and this is of the three cell class and has a voltage of about 4.5 volts. The battery usually has two contacts on one face. These contacts are not of the usual spring type, but are merely two brass strips which lie quite flat against the face of the battery and rely for the pressure that is necessary for making good contact on a spring fixed to the back of the case, or sometimes, just on the tightness of the fit of the battery.

The Switch usually takes the form of a moving arm, which makes contact with a little flat knob, when moved in one direction, and breaks the circuit when moved in the other. The circuit is shown in Fig. 4B. As before, the various contacts must be kept clean.

The usual trouble with this lamp, other than with the contacts, is due to the wiring which occasionally breaks down. Look for the break in places where the battery presses on the wire and where the wire joins the contacts.

A break should be repaired by soldering and not by merely twisting the wires together, which is seldom satisfactory.

In conclusion here is some advice which applies to all torches of every make and description.

Many good torches have been ruined by their owners failing to remember to remove the battery when it is worn out.

Whenever the torch is to lie idle for some considerable time, or when the battery is run down, it must always be removed. This is especially important in hot weather.

If this is not done, the battery will not only corrode the inside of the torch but it will also swell up to such an extent that it will be found almost impossible to remove it.

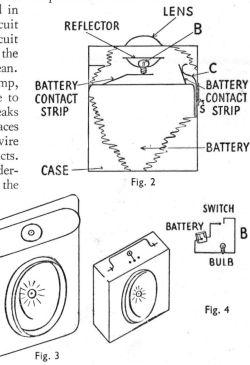

Fig. 2

Fig. 3

Fig. 4

If this should occur the best thing to do is to put the whole torch in a bath of paraffin for about a week. The battery can then possibly be forced out.

ELECTRIC ALARM CLOCK

A N ordinary alarm clock can be made very easily to give a much louder and more prolonged ring than it normally would, by adapting it so that it will switch on an electric bell, which will, of course, continue to ring until switched off again.

The complete alarm, that is the battery bell and clock, etc., can be assembled into one unit as shown in Fig. 1, which can either be hung on the wall or stood on the table.

The switch can be placed anywhere, at a distance from the alarm unit or on the same board, as desired.

Construction.—An alarm clock of which the winding key is of the fixed type and not of the hinged pattern as the older ones were, will be required. Such a clock can be obtained for about, five shillings. Also one or two small pieces of brass; an electric bell costing about two shillings and sixpence, a pair of large dry cells, or if preferred a torch battery (though this will not last so long); and two pieces of wood about $9 \times 7\frac{1}{2} \times \frac{1}{2}$ in. thick.

Fig. I

The automatic contact is the most complicated part to make, so it is best to tackle this first.

Three pieces of brass strip about $\frac{1}{10}$ in. thick and 3 in. long $\times \frac{1}{4}$ in. wide will be required, two of which must have a hole drilled in each end, about a $\frac{1}{4}$ in. from the tip. The third piece only requires a hole in one end.

A fourth piece of brass about $\frac{1}{2}$ in. square with a hole drilled in the centre is also necessary. This acts as a weight. All the holes should be about $\frac{1}{8}$ in. in diameter.

Now take one of the pieces with two holes in it and measure along from one end a distance of $\frac{1}{2}$ in. At this point

make a right-angled bend (which can be done very easily in a vice) and then do the same with the other piece containing two holes.

Now take one of the pieces of board and mount the two pieces of brass, which have just been bent, in the position shown in the plan at Fig. 2. The long part of each piece should, of course, be vertical and a wood screw through the hole in the short piece secures it in position. The distance between the vertical uprights should be just a trifle over $\frac{1}{10}$ in.

Place the end of the remaining long piece of brass with the hole in it in between the uprights, and pass a bolt through the three holes. The bolt must, naturally, have a nut on the end, but this nut should not be tightened very much.

The arm of the contact if held up, should be free to fall down when it is let go. It is as well to put an additional nut on the bolt, which should be tightened down on the first one, so as to form a locking nut.

Now make a mark where the end of the arm rests on the board. Over the mark, screw on the square piece of

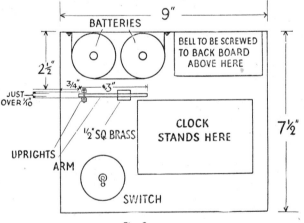

Fig. 2

brass, keeping the screw just a little further back towards the uprights than the mark, so that the arm rests on the brass and not on the screw.

There is just one more thing to do, before securing the other piece of wood (which will form the back) and that is to connect two pieces of wire, one to one of the metal uprights and the other to the square plate on the base. The wire can either be soldered on, or else secured under the fixing screw. If the latter method is adopted it is advisable to put a washer under the head of the screw. Make these wires about a foot long. They can then be cut to the exact length required when the rest of the job is complete.

Now drill two holes in the long side of the other piece of wood, $\frac{1}{4}$ in. from the edge, and 3 in. from each end, and screw this into position at right-angles to the baseboard, thus forming a back.

The bell can next be fitted on to the back board, as near to the top as possible, and a little to one side so as to be clear of all else.

Place the battery or batteries on the baseboard as indicated in the plan in Fig. 2, and secure them in position by placing a thin brass or copper band across the front, and screwing it at the sides to the back board.

Wiring.—The free end of one of the wires already fixed is connected to the bell and the other wire goes to a terminal of the battery.

The other side of the battery and the other side of the bell are both connected to the switch, of which, so far, no mention has been made.

The switch can be of the ordinary tumbler type in which case it is secured to the baseboard, preferably in the position shown in Fig. 2.

Alternatively it can be a pear switch and can then be hung over the head of the bed. If the latter course is adopted, the wires should be fixed firmly to the baseboard, by means of an insulated staple to prevent the connections from being pulled off.

In order to make a neat job of the wiring it is best to staple it down in position. The wiring diagram is shown in Fig. 3.

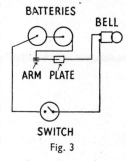

Fig. 3

How to Use the Apparatus.—Wind the alarm clock and set it to go off at the desired time, in the usual way. Place the clock on the board and rest the brass arm just on the alarm winding key. Fig. 4 shows the alarm unit with

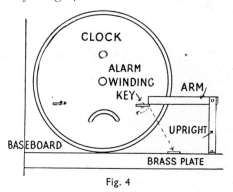

Fig. 4

the back removed to show the clock and the arm in this position.

When the alarm goes off the key will turn round and throw off the arm, which will fall on to the brass plate and so complete the circuit.

The alarm hammer of the clock can of course be removed if required.

HOME-MADE BATTERIES

THE simplest of all cells is the wet Leclanché cell and it is the making of one of these that will be considered first.

Wet Leclanché Cell.—The manufactured cell consists of a jar, in which there is a solution of sal ammoniac; immersed in the liquid are a zinc rod and a porous pot containing a stick of carbon surrounded by a mixture of granulated peroxide of manganese and carbon.

In the home-made cell what is known as the sack Leclanché system is adopted and in this the porous pot is replaced by a canvas bag or sack and the zinc rod by an encircling cylinder of zinc. An old jam jar will serve as a container.

The sack consists of a piece of good quality canvas made into a cylindrical shaped bag, the bottom of which is made of a circular piece of canvas.

All .the seams should be double stitched and the bag should be about 5 in. high × 2 in. in diameter.

Next a carbon rod or plate of about the same length as the depth of the bag must be obtained, and to the top of this carbon it is necessary to fix a terminal. The best way to do this is to make a lead cap for the carbon in which is embedded one end of the screw of the terminal.

Moulding the Cap.—Make a little mould in some plaster-of-paris for the lead head and in the bottom of the mould place the terminal with the end which is to be fixed to the carbon pointing upwards. Rest the carbon on the end of this screw and then pour into the mould some molten lead. The mould must be absolutely dry before pouring the lead. When the lead is cool, it can be cleaned with a file and given a coat of brunswick black. The carbon element is illustrated in Fig. 1.

Having prepared the carbon, place it in the sack and pack it tightly round with a mixture of granulated peroxide of manganese and carbon. The top of the sack can then be sealed off with bitumen, leaving the terminal protruding.

Next make the zinc plate. This consists of a piece of sheet zinc about 3 in. high; its length being the same as the circumference of a circle about ½ in. larger in diameter than that of the sack. It must be bent round in the shape of a cylinder.

When cutting the zinc leave at the centre of the top a projecting strip 2 or 3 in. long × about ½ in. wide to form a clip to go over the side of the jar and to carry the terminal.

Fig. 2 shows the completed cell and the shape to which this zinc strip should be bent can be clearly seen.

Drill a hole in the strip as in Fig. 2 and fix a terminal through the hole.

Coat the top of the jar, inside and out, for about 1 in. in depth, with brunswick black and also the top of the zinc plate.

The cell is now ready for filling with a solution of sal ammoniac and water.

With the sack and plate in position, fill the jar with warm water—not hot— to just under the level of the brunswick black and then add about a handful of sal ammoniac crystals. A cell constructed in this manner is very reliable and gives a voltage of the order of 1.5. Its chief advantages over the dry cell are that it does not run down when standing idle and is very easily refilled with solution.

It will not, however, supply current for very long periods at a time, as the voltage very soon begins to drop, but if allowed to rest for a short time it gradually recovers and will go on indefinitely in this way until the solution requires replacing.

It will be observed from these facts that such a cell is not satisfactory for working anything in the nature of a radio set, which requires a current for long periods at a time, but it is almost ideal for electric bells and other appliances where the current is only momentarily required.

A Dry Battery.—A dry battery consists of a number of dry cells connected together and so it will suffice to describe the making of one dry cell.

For this a zinc cylindrical-shaped container will be needed.

This can be made out of sheet metal and the seams sweated together with solder. The cylinder requires a bottom which can also be soldered on.

On the outside and at the top of the container, solder either a zinc strip to take a terminal or a piece of wire for connecting purposes. Then make a canvas sack to fit into the zinc container. The diameter of this should be about half the diameter of the container.

In this sack place a stick of carbon and all round it tightly pack a paste consisting of manganese dioxide, sal ammoniac, powdered carbon, chloride of zinc glycerine and water in the proportions of $5 : 1 : 5 : 1 : \frac{1}{2} : 1$ parts respectively.

You will thus have a separate cell in a canvas bag which can now be placed in the centre of the zinc container.

The space between the zinc pot and the sack can now be filled wth a paste

made of a solution of sal ammoniac, zinc chloride, glycerine and water in the proportions by weight of approximately $1 : 1 : 1 : 4$ parts respectively, with the addition of a little ordinary household flour.

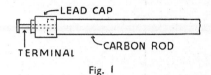

Fig. I

The best way to make this paste is first to prepare a paste of the flour and then stir it into the solution. The solution should be boiled, poured into the cell almost to the top and then allowed to cool.

Melted bitumen can then be poured

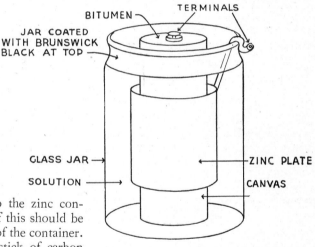

Fig. 2

into the top of the cell to seal it and it is thus complete. It is a good idea, however, to make a cover of cardboard or stout brown paper to fit round the cell and also a disc of the same material to cover the base for the purpose of protection and insulation.

There is just one point to remember in connection with both the wet and dry cells, and that is to make a vent in the top of each container. This can be very easily done by piercing the bitumen with a hot steel knitting needle.

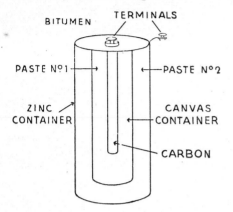

HOME MADE BATTERIES

Fig. 3

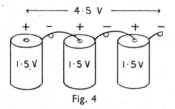

Fig. 4

The dry cell just described has a voltage in the order of 1.5 volts and will not run down to any appreciable

extent when it is allowed to stand idle.

Fig. 3 shows a diagrammatical sketch of the completed cell with the various layers exposed for the sake of clarity.

Wet or Dry Battery.—To make a battery of either wet or dry cells, the zinc of one cell should be connected to the carbon of the next and the zinc of this to the carbon of the following cell, and so on.

Thus in Fig. 4, which shows three dry cells connected together, the resulting battery has a voltage of 1.5 multiplied by 3, or 4.5 volts.

In each case the positive of the cell is the terminal fixed to the carbon and the negative is the terminal attached to the zinc. Therefore in the case of a battery of cells, the end with the free terminal connected to the zinc is the negative end of the battery and the free terminal at the other end is the positive end.

There are many other useful types of primary cells in addition to those described in this article. Enough has been said, however, to show that the making of simple cells is a feat not beyond the powers of the average man. It can, in fact, provide an interesting and also instructive recreation.

RADIOGRAM PICK-UP

T‑O-DAY, gramophone pick-ups can be bought for a very small sum, and, as the following article will show, it is not a matter of very great difficulty to fit them to an existing gramophone in order to be able to use them in conjunction with a wireless set.

It is advisable when buying a pick-up to obtain one that has already a volume control attached, since it is essential to have some form of volume control and to have one incorporated in the pick-

up simplifies matters a great deal. It will therefore be assumed that the pick-up is fitted with a volume control.

The fitting of the pick-up is the same for a portable gramophone as it is for any other type of machine, whether table or pedestal; but in every case the length of the lead to the radio set should be as short as possible.

The first thing to do, in order to ensure the best results from the radiogram and also to lengthen the life of the records, is to obtain the correct tracking of the needle, or in other words, to find the position in which the base of the pick-up is to be screwed to the motor board.

This is when the needle is running as nearly parallel as possible with the tangent of the curves formed by the grooves in the records. It is obviously impossible to obtain this right across the record but a very near approximation can be obtained with care.

Finding the Position.—The necessary appliances comprise a set square and a strip of cardboard. The cardboard should be just a little longer than the radius of a 12 in. record and 1 in. or more wide.

Near one end of this cardboard strip make a hole for the spindle of the turntable to go through. Then draw a line right down the centre of the strip and make a mark on the strip at the points at which an average record starts and another at the point at which it finishes.

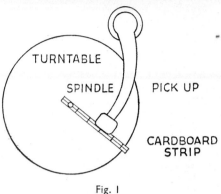

Fig. 1

Next divide the space between these marks into four equal parts. Put the strip on the turntable, at the same time inserting the spindle through the hole and then place the pick-up on the motor board with its base in a similar position to that which it will eventually occupy and with the needle resting on the centre mark of the strip and on the line down the centre. (See Fig. 1.)

Take the set square and place one of its edges along the centre line of the strip and in such a position that the right angle just touches the needle as represented in Fig. 2.

If the position of the pick-up base is correct, the line made by the other edge of the set square and the needle when looking along the edge of the square should be continuous or in other words the needle will not appear to lean over to either side as in Fig. 2.

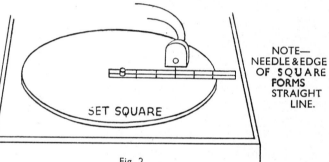

Fig. 2

If this is not so, the position of the pick-up must be moved about until the desired condition is obtained. Then place the needle at point 5 remembering to keep it always on the line down the centre of the strip and adjust the position again to approximately the same condition. If the needle leans over at a very great angle when viewed along the edge of the square or if the angle at which it leans over is only slight, place the needle at point 1 and then point 2 and so on. Continue these adjustments until the position of the needle on the middle mark is vertical with the least deviation at the other points.

With perseverance it is possible to get the position of the pick-up nearly correct, and there is no doubt that a little time and trouble spent on obtaining this position is amply repaid by the results.

Having obtained the position of the pick-up, trace the outline round the edge of the base with a pencil and then drill a hole inside this mark through the motor board for the connections of the pick-up to go through, and if the

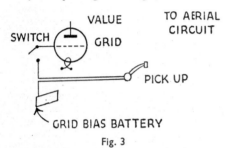

Fig. 3

case of the gramophone has a back to it, a hole through this also.

The wires coming from the pick-up should be passed through these holes and the pick-up screwed in position.

It may be necessary to remove the motor board from the base to do this,

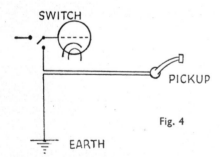

Fig. 4

but this is a very simple business as the board is generally only secured by means of four or six wood screws.

Shielding the Lead.—As previously stated the length of this lead must be as short as possible, but if owing to necessity it is rather long, use a shielded

wire which is wire having an outer cover of plaited wire strands.

Shielded wire can be bought at most radio stores and if it is decided to use it the original lead on the pick-up can be cut off within an inch or two of where it joins the pick-up and a lead of the new wire can be substituted by making a soldered joint, which should be insulated with adhesive tape.

The outer shielding should be earthed at the most convenient point by soldering a piece of wire to it and securing the wire under the earth terminal.

Connecting the Pick-up.—In the majority of modern factory-built sets, two terminals are provided at the back of the set for the pick-up leads—and as a rule a gram switch is also provided.

We will, however, describe the simplest way of connecting a pick-up to an existing set which is not provided with these terminals.

In a battery set, one wire from the pick-up lead should be taken through a switch to the grid of the detector valve, and the other to one of the negative plugs of the grid bias battery, or if preferred a separate plug can be used in the grid bias battery for this purpose alone.

It is usually found best to have this plug in a tapping of about $1\frac{1}{2}$ volts (negative) but the best position can be found most satisfactorily by experiment. This circuit is shown in Fig. 3, which includes a single pole change over switch.

The switch can, however, be of the ordinary single type and merely connected so as to break the pick-up lead, but in this case it may be necessary to detune the set or even unplug the aerial when the gramophone is in use.

There are many different types of switches on the market suitable for this purpose but almost all of them are secured to the panel of the set by mean of a threaded spindle inserted through a hole drilled in the panel with a nut on either side.

Whatever switch is used, however, it should be as near the valve holder as possible.

Fig. 4 shows a diagram of a circuit for connecting a pick-up to a mains-operated receiver and it will be noted that the difference here is that the lead, which in the battery circuit went to the grid bias battery, is now taken to earth. This should either be secured under the earth terminal or soldered at a convenient earth point.

The remarks regarding the switches which were made for the battery receiver apply also for the mains set.

ERECTING EFFICIENT RADIO AERIALS

IN order to obtain the best results from a radio receiver, it is important to have an efficient aerial for "picking up" the wireless waves, for however good the set may be, satisfactory results cannot be expected if this part of the equipment is faulty.

An outside aerial should always be used where possible, in preference to the indoor type.

To get good results with a receiver designed to work on medium and long wavelengths, an outdoor aerial of about 40 ft. in length including the lead in will generally be found satisfactory, although in some cases it may be better to reduce or increase this length.

If possible, the height of the pole should not be less than 25 ft. as the higher the aerial the better the results will be.

In these days an aerial of insulated stranded copper wire is favoured by a good many radio enthusiasts in preference to bare wire. One of its advantages is that the aerial can be taken direct to the aerial terminal of the receiver through a small hole bored in the window frame.

In fitting such an aerial, china insulators should be used for supporting purposes, as indicated in Fig. 1, and a pulley fixed near the top of the pole to allow the wire to be hauled up or down.

A couple of coats of white paint will make wireless aerial poles less unsightly than leaving them in their bare state.

In erecting the pole, dig a hole at least 2 ft. deep to accommodate the base, and set the latter firmly in concrete, allowing the mixture to extend

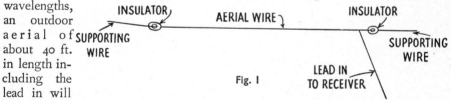

Fig. 1

about 6 in. above the ground level, as indicated in Fig. 2. This will help to prevent the pole from rotting, especially if the concrete is finished to taper upwards to allow the moisture to run off easily.

A better job can be effected by fixing the mast to a separate pedestal, the bottom part of which is concreted into the ground. The pole is supported between two side members by means of stout bolts and nuts. Fig. 3 shows the arrangement.

The advantage of such a fixing is that the pole can be taken down at any time and repainted.

A proper earth is equally as important as an efficient aerial. This should be as short as possible and connected to the earth direct by means of a proper earthing tube (A, Fig. 4) or by attaching one end of the earth lead to a cold water main. The end of the earth wire can be attached to the pipe by soldering or by using a special clip, as shown at B in Fig. 4. Hot water pipes and gas pipes should not be used for earthing purposes.

Before attaching the clip, any paint must be removed from the pipe and the surface scraped bright.

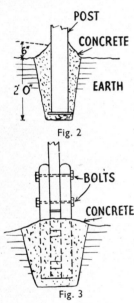

Fig. 2

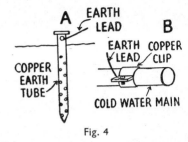

Fig. 3

An aerial fixed in the loft space between the roof and the top floor ceiling solves the difficulty of obtaining an aerial where circumstances do not permit of having an outdoor one.

To get the best results from such an aerial the insulated wire should span the loft and not be attached directly to the beams.

In a good many cases the down lead which connects the aerial to the set can be taken outside the building by boring a small hole in the soffit which covers the space between the roof rafters and the wall.

If this method is adopted better results will be obtained if the wire is not allowed to come in contact with the wall. This also applies to the down lead of an outside aerial.

To keep the wire off the wall, fix one or more wooden distance pipes about 10 in. long and 1 in. square, and drive them into holes made between the mortar joints of the brickwork.

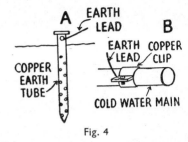

Fig. 4

The wire can be held in position by means of insulated screw hooks fixed at the ends of the wood.

If it is not possible to install a loft aerial, quite good results can be obtained by fitting a "Pix" aerial, illustrated in Fig. 5.

This ingenious aerial is in the form of a narrow tape which encloses a thin

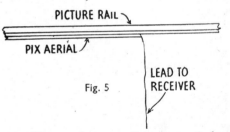

Fig. 5

metallic conductor. One face of the tape is treated with an adhesive compound, which enables it to be held in position without further support.

A good place to fix a "Pix" aerial is just below a picture rail, where it will hardly be seen. A length of flexible wire is attached to the aerial ready for connecting to the radio receiver.

A picture rail can also be used for accommodating a suitable length of flexible insulated wire aerial which can be stapled down at intervals to the wood to keep it in position. In using flexible wire the starting end—that is, the end furthest from the receiver—should be covered with a small piece of electrician's adhesive tape to prevent any stray strands of the wire touching surrounding wood or the wall.

It is advisable to fit a lightning arrester in the circuit of an outside aerial. There are several devices for this purpose to be had and their use is much to be preferred to the old-fashioned method of employing a switch. Fig. 6 shows a sketch of a reliable lightning arrester which is automatic in action.

A great number of modern receivers are provided with means of receiving short-wave transmissions—i.e., between 10 and 100 meters. A suitable aerial for such a set is known as a doublet or di-pole aerial and consists of two separate lengths of wire each about 15 to 20 ft. in length. These lengths are arranged in one straight line and insulated at the middle as shown diagrammatically in Fig. 7. The lead-in consists of heavy twin twisted cable, the top ends of which are connected one to each section of the aerial in the position shown. The lower ends are connected to the primary terminals a special type of H.F. transformer, the secondary terminals being connected to the receiver terminals.

In erecting an aerial of this type it is essential to keep the wires parallel to the ground and also to keep the wires of equal length.

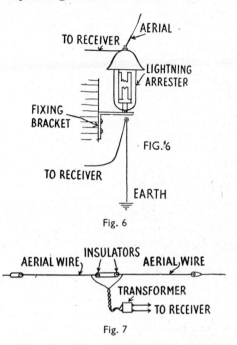

Fig. 6

Fig. 7

As such an aerial is more or less directional, it is advisable to erect it in such a position that the transmitting station is approximately at right-angles.

ELECTRIC LAMPSHADES

MAKING shades provides a most interesting and useful hobby, or even a profitable spare-time occupation. The amateur can tackle the most simple or the most elaborate of designs and there is practically no limit to the variety.

All the materials necessary are obtainable at a large number of the big stores, and they can be purchased in a variety of colours.

The Frame.—The first thing to

obtain is the wire frame. This can either be bought ready made or constructed as described below. It is best to start with a comparatively simple shade, such as the one shown in Fig. 1, the frame of which is indicated in Fig. 2.

As will be seen from the illustration, the shade consists of four sides made up of shaped panels which can be of either parchment or some other suitable material of the maker's own choice.

To construct this frame a length of

Q

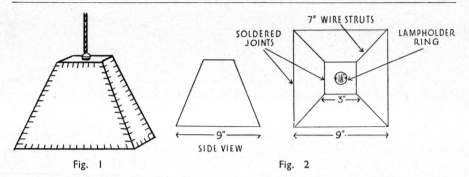

Fig. 1   SIDE VIEW   Fig. 2

stout tinned-iron wire, a soldering iron, solder and flux are necessary.

First cut the wire, with the aid of a pair of cutting pliers, to the correct lengths, namely, one piece 36 in. long and another 12 in. and four pieces each 7 in. long. Mark off on the longest piece a distance of $4\frac{1}{2}$ in. then three points 9 in. apart. Bend the wire at each of these points, to a right-angle, thus forming a square having one side divided at the centre. Do the same with the 12 in. piece; the distances in this case being $1\frac{1}{2}$ in. and 3 in.

Soldering the Frame.—We now have two squares and four straight pieces of wire, and it now remains to solder these parts together. To do this first clean all the ends of the wires with emery cloth or by scraping with a knife. To save time, this operation can be done while the soldering iron is getting hot.

Now tin the ends of the wires by smearing the end to be "tinned" with a thin coating of flux. A semi-solid flux sold in tins is excellent for the purpose as it is clean and easy to use and does not corrode the wire.

Then apply the hot soldering iron (with some solder on it, of course) all round the end of the wire for a distance up from the top of about $\frac{1}{4}$ in. The end of the wire will now be covered with a thin layer of solder.

To make the solder stay on the iron,

the heated iron (not red hot) must also be tinned by cleaning the copper end with a file, then smearing it with flux and rubbing it on the solder. It will be found that a small quantity of solder will remain on the iron until it requires cleaning again.

Place the ends of the wire of one of the squares together, tip to tip, and apply the hot iron loaded with solder under the two of them, thus soldering them together. As it may prove awkward to keep the ends of the wire butted together during the soldering process, the wire can be tacked down lightly to a board in the manner shown in Fig. 3.

Repeat the process with the other square.

Now take the large square and at each corner solder one of the straight pieces of wire and then solder the other square to the free ends of these pieces.

A Ring for Fitting to the Lampholder.—Make a plain circle of wire of $1\frac{1}{8}$ in. internal diameter and on this solder two pieces of wire sufficiently long to go from the ring to the opposite corners. Solder this to the top square and thus complete the frame.

Covering the Frame.—The next step is to cover the frame with tape of similar colour to that of the material of which the panels are to be made. This is quite easy to do, the tape being bound round as illustrated in Fig. 4 and a few stitches being put in at either end to hold it in position.

Now cut out the panels.

First mark out the outlines faintly in pencil and then cut along them. The best method is to lay a metal straight-edge or rule along the line to be cut and run a very sharp penknife along the guide. Even better results can be obtained by using an old type of hollow-ground razor. This method is to be preferred to using scissors, but if great care is taken there is no reason why scissors should not be employed.

Cut out four panels of the same measurement as the sides of the frame.

These panels must now have holes punched along the sides for the tape or cord to pass through which will secure them in position on the frame.

First punch a small hole $\frac{1}{4}$ in. from each corner and $\frac{1}{8}$ in. in from the edge, in the top, bottom and sides. Now down the right-hand side, looking at the panel from the front and starting at a point $\frac{3}{4}$ in. down from the first hole punch a line of holes $\frac{1}{2}$ in. apart. Do the same down the left-hand side, but start from a point $\frac{1}{4}$ in. down from the first hole. Thus when the adjacent panels are bound together the tape will slant towards the right.

The holes along the top and bottom of the panels should be punched at a distance of $\frac{1}{4}$ in. apart.

The panels can now be secured in position by passing the tape through the holes as in Fig. 5.

The material used for securing the panels need not, of course, be the very narrow tape that is generally used. Silk cord, leather thong or any such thing can be used to suit the maker's taste.

The best method of securing the tape is to pass it through the first and last holes twice instead of once and then

stitching it to the binding on the frame.

Other Shapes.—Having made a simple shade on the lines just mentioned the maker will perhaps like to try his hand at making one or two more elabor-

Fig. 3

ate types as suggested and described below. No dimensions, however, will be given as, of course, the maker must

Fig. 4

decide these to suit his own requirements.

Fig. 6 shows an extremely tasteful shade, embodying either parchment or other suitable material and a fringe of silk.

The frame, Fig. 7, consists of two

semi-circular diagonals of wire at right-angles to each other at the centre. These diagonals in reality consist of four pieces of wire, the top of each piece being soldered to a ring for fitting on to

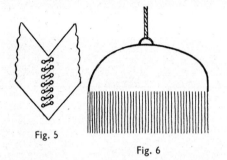

Fig. 5

Fig. 6

a lampholder as already described. The bottom support is simply a length of tinned wire carefully bent to form a circle of the desired size, the ends being fixed together by solder.

This frame may be strengthened if desired by the addition of curved struts from the top ring to the lower one, as indicated by the dotted lines.

The panels should be inserted in the manner already described after the frame has been bound and the fringe added.

A word or two should be mentioned here on the cutting of the panels.

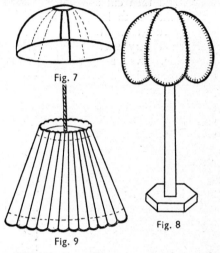

Fig. 7

Fig. 8

Fig. 9

This is not quite such a simple matter as that of the plain flat shade already described as the dimensions cannot be simply measured and then transferred to the materials.

The best way is to obtain a piece of thin paper and place it in the position which the panel will eventually occupy, and then pencil round the frame. The paper can then be cut along these pencil marks, so forming a very convenient pattern.

Fig. 8 shows a very pretty shade which is usually rather small. This shade consists of six panels arranged in a sort of flower-shaped pattern. Such a shade measuring 9 in. in diameter at the bottom would do admirably for a standard lamp for a table or desk.

A good colour arrangement in this type of shade is to have alternate panels of different colours, preferably of pastel hues.

Another very simple shade is shown in Fig. 9. It consists essentially of two rings of wire, the top one being smaller

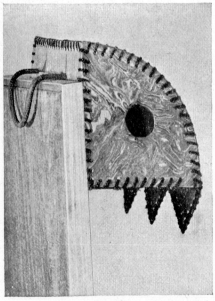

Fig. 10

than the bottom one. The covering material is pleated crepe paper and is stitched to the frames with silk of the same colour as the paper. Vertical supports are unnecessary on a small shade of this description, but if a large one is required it may be an advantage to incorporate five or six such supports. The top ring must, of course, be fitted with a small ring 1⅛ in. in diameter to take a lampholder.

Fig. 10 shows an easily constructed electric lampshade suitable for hanging on the headrail of a bedstead. It will be seen that a 1⅛ in. diameter hole is provided in the side for accommodating a cord grip key-switch lampholder to enable the lamp to be switched off from a convenient position.

The shade consists of six separate panels, three in the front, two forming the sides and one at the back.

A wire bent to form a hook is provided at the back for hanging purposes. The hook can be enclosed in a thin rubber tube or bound round with tape to prevent scratching the surface of the bedrail.

A quarter of an hour spent in studying the designs of electric lampshades in a catalogue of electrical goods will give the amateur some valuable ideas for constructing many more lampshades of pleasing and original pattern.

USEFUL ELECTRICAL DEVICES

ONE of the regulations of most electricity companies is that cookers should be provided with a main-switch which incorporates a pilot light. This pilot light is of very low consumption and gives a dull red glow, and the object of it is to ensure proper warning that the current has not been turned off. But there are many electrical appliances which provide no visible indication of whether they are turned on or off and which are not normally fitted with a pilot light.

Pilot Lamp.—The first of our devices is a pilot lamp, fitted in conjunction with the plug switch from which these appliances are worked.

The first thing to do is to obtain the required materials. These are, a small 5 watt neon lamp, with an ordinary bayonet cap (these lamps are made by all the big lamp manufacturers and can be obtained from any electrical store at a cost of just under 4s.), a batten holder (which is a lampholder made for screwing on to a flat surface) and a "two-way" switch block (which is a block of rectangular shape and is big enough to hold two switches, although in this case it will be required to hold the switch plug and the batten holder).

Having acquired the materials, the original switch plug must now be taken off, not forgetting to turn off the power first.

Now place the switch plug and the batten holder on the new block side by side, and mark their positions and also the positions in which the holes will have to be drilled behind the three terminals of the switch plug.

Practically all switch plugs are provided with three terminals although, except for less usual purposes, such as this, only two of them are used. The use of the third terminal will be explained later.

The arrangement of these three terminals is shown in the illustration of a typical switch plug in Fig. 1. Drill holes at these points and one fairly large one (about $\frac{1}{2}$ in.) in the centre behind the batten holder. Now drill two fixing holes in the block, one behind each fitting, making sure that they will not be in the way of the screws that will secure the fittings to the block. These holes should be countersunk. The arrangement is shown in Fig. 2.

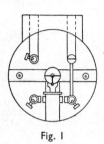

Fig. I

Next take a piece of wire from hole 3 of the plug to the hole of the batten holder and a piece from hole 1 to the batten holder. The wire will only carry a very small current and so it

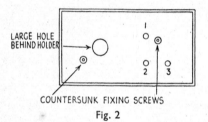

LARGE HOLE BEHIND HOLDER

COUNTERSUNK FIXING SCREWS

Fig. 2

will not have to be of a very heavy gauge, but it is advisable to use V.I.R. (vulcanised india-rubber) or else "tough rubber," in preference to flex, which is not provided with sufficiently hardy insulation.

The position of the fixing holes should now be marked on the wall and the wall plugged if necessary.

Push the positive or feed (red) wire or wires through hole 2 and the return wire (black) through hole 1, and screw the block in position. Push the wires through their appropriate terminals and mount the plug and batten holder.

The neon lamp, of course, fits into the batten holder and it can then be seen that the indication given by it, serves a double purpose, in that it not only indicates when current is passing

through any appliance that is plugged into the switch plug, but also shows whether the plug itself is left switched on when not in use.

If the positions of the terminals of the plug to be used do not coincide with the arrangement in Figs. 1 and 2 the arrangement for any particular plug (which, however, must have three terminals) can be worked out quite easily from the wiring diagram in Fig. 3B.

Fig. 3A shows the complete device.

An Automatic Cupboard Light.— Another very useful device for turning on the light in a cupboard or larder as the door is opened.

A switch for this purpose can be bought ready made, but for anybody of an ingenious frame of mind who is interested in making things for himself, a fairly simple method of adapting an ordinary tumbler switch for this purpose, is described below.

The first thing to do is to remove the switch (which must be situated if it is to be adapted for our purpose, on the wall inside the cupboard near the door post). It should then be turned round and replaced so that the knob works backwards and forwards instead of up and down, as is normal. The knob should be pointing towards the door when the switch is turned on and away from it when turned off.

We shall now require a piece of round brass rod, two or three inches longer than the distance between the face of the back of the door when it is shut and the knob of the switch when it is in the off position. The rod should be of about $\frac{1}{4}$ in. diameter.

We shall also require about a foot of strip brass about $\frac{3}{8}$ in. to $\frac{1}{2}$ in. wide $\times$ $\frac{1}{16}$ in. thick.

Round off the ends of the rod with a file and then bend it so that when one end is touching the door and the rod rests against the door post at the other end it rests against the cover of the switch, or in other words if one end rests on the top of the switch knob the other end will be about $\frac{1}{4}$ in. from the face of the door post.

The manner in which the rod is "set" or bent is made clearer by a glance at Fig. 4 which shows the rod held in this position, looking at it from the top.

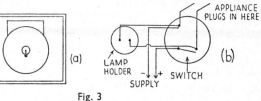

(a)

Fig. 3

(b)

Holding it in this position with the switch off and the end resting against the closed door, make a mark on the rod where it touches the switch knob. Drill a hole in the mark, just a shade larger in diameter than that of the shank of the switch knob and file the spherical part of the knob so that it is of the same diameter as the shank.

Now with the shank fitting in the hole and the straight sections of the rod parallel with the wall, measure the exact distance between the rod and the face of the door post at one end and the face of the wall at the other, taking the measurement from the centre of the diameter of the rod in each case.

Using the strip brass, make two brass staples of the shape shown in Fig. 4B, each having the distance from the base to the centre of the circle, the same as one of the measurements we have just found, thus providing a simple form of guide for each end of the rod. In each of the feet of these guides drill a hole for the fixing screws to pass through.

If the wall has a very soft surface, it may be found best to mount the guide furthermost from the door, on a thin block of wood, and if this is done the height of the guide when it is made must be measured accordingly.

A spring is the only other thing required. Its purpose is to pull the switch into the on position, so that it will have to be fairly strong although the ordinary tumbler switch does not require as much pressure as one might imagine.

The length should be just under the distance of the centre portion of the bent rod, although the actual length can be adjusted afterwards to give the required tension.

A small screw-hook should be screwed into the back of the door post on the same level as the rod and the end of the spring can be bent into the shape of a loop to go over the hook.

A very small hole should now be drilled in the middle of the centre portion of the rod and the other end of the spring should be passed through it, and then doubled back on itself and twisted round, in order to make it perfectly secure.

The whole can now be assembled and should resemble the illustration in Fig. 5 which is a plan viewed from the top.

It will be seen that as the door shuts, it forces the switch to the off position and as it opens the spring pulls the switch on. Thus it is impossible to leave the light turned on in the cupboard and even if the spring becomes loose or breaks (which is the most likely fault to develop), the door cannot be shut without the light being turned off.

A Bureau Light.—A light actually fixed inside the bureau eliminates the necessity for having an ordinary standard lamp balanced precariously on top of a bureau.

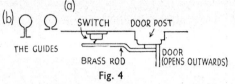

Fig. 4

This can be very easily accomplished by drilling a hole through the back of the bureau and pushing through a good length of flex.

Connect a batten holder on to the

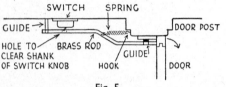

Fig. 5

end of this flex and secure the batten holder inside one of the pigeon holes or at the most convenient place. Staple the flex down at the bottom of the back of the bureau by means of insulated staples and on the other end put the plug, for putting into the switch plug from which the supply is to be taken.

That is the light in its simplest form, but it can be developed and improved upon according to the taste or requirements of the user. For instance, instead of one, two lights can be fitted, one at each side of the bureau, by simply looping another piece of flex from the first batten holder, and connecting and fixing another holder at the other end.

Then again it is usually found more convenient to have a switch within easy reach of the person working at the bureau and this can be fitted inside the bureau on one of the sides or underneath the top.

The connections to the switch can be made by cutting one strand of flex and just making a small groove so that the wires will fit neatly underneath the switch.

The same method can be adopted for fitting a light inside a gramophone cabinet and many other similar places. It can be seen also that the fitting of the automatic switch already described, would not present a very great problem in a position of this sort.

Bedroom Clock Light.—Another useful place to have a light is over a bedroom clock, and here again the best thing to do is to use a batten holder.

If the clock has a wooden case, the holder can be mounted on a little strip of wood, secured to the back of the clock, the wires being brought through holes drilled in the wood.

If the clock has a metal case, it is quite a simple matter to construct a neat stand, consisting merely of a base and a narrow back which can if desired, be patterned with a fretsaw.

A small 5 watt neon lamp forms a very good night-light and the consumption is very small indeed. It will in fact take 200 hours to burn one unit, which at $3\frac{1}{2}$d. per unit is less than $\frac{1}{20}$d. per hour.

REPAIRING ELECTRIC ACCUMULATORS

IT is not intended in this article to give a detailed account of the theory of accumulators, but it may be mentioned here that the lead cell consists of lead plates, contained usually in a glass, celluloid or other container of acid-resisting material.

The lead plates are divided into two

Fig. I

the plates as clearly seen in Fig. 3 so forming a short circuit.

There are several ways of dealing with this. First the cell can be washed out. This is done by emptying out the acid and refilling the cell with distilled water, or rain water.

The use of ordinary tap water should be avoided unless it is absolutely impossible to obtain anything else, as it may contain iron and other impurities, detrimental to the cell.

When almost filled, the stopper is replaced in the cell and then, over a sink, the cell given a good shake, upside down and emptied again. This procedure is repeated several times, until the bottom of the cell is perfectly clear.

It should then be rinsed out with sulphuric acid of about 1.250 specific gravity (Sp. G.), filled with acid of just over 1.200, and recharged slowly.

This method is frequently used in sets. In the case of the two plate type as represented in Fig. 1 the dark coloured one (chocolate) is the positive plate and the other (grey) is the negative.

In the multi-plate type (Fig. 2) there is a set of positive plates, all joined together and a set of negative plates, also joined together. The electrolyte, or liquid in this case, is dilute sulphuric acid.

Short Circuits.—In all accumulators one of the most common sources of trouble is a short circuit across the two sets of plates. This, as a rule, is caused by the active material of the plates dropping out and falling to the bottom of the container, thus forming a layer of conducting material, which gradually gets thicker and thicker until it reaches the level of the bottom of

Fig. 2

wireless shops, and accumulator charging depots of that description, but it has several disadvantages. It does not

Fig. 3

allow the loosened paste to be scraped off the plates. Furthermore the shaking which the cell receives loosens the paste still more, so that before very long the cell requires cleaning again.

A much better method is to withdraw the plates from the jar.

The plates are secured at the top to a small sheet of ebonite, which is held in the top of the jar by bitumen (a form of pitch). This is illustrated in Fig. 4.

To remove the plates the bitumen must be loosened from the jar.

This may be done by inserting and

running a hot knife round the edge between the bitumen and the jar, thus separating one from the other. Then, holding the jar with one hand, pull on the terminal of the cell with the other and it will be found that the plates, complete with the ebonite top, can be withdrawn from the jar.

Another and possibly a better way, if a small gas or spirit blow-pipe is available, is to melt all the bitumen and then quickly withdraw the plates. This method must, however, be used with the greatest of care in order to avoid cracking the jar.

Note here that it is extremely inadvisable to apply heat to any cell without first emptying out the acid, as the gas given off by the electrolyte of a fully charged cell is explosive.

A very gentle flame must be used and the cell must be kept constantly turning round, so that the flame never remains in the same spot for more than a few seconds at a time. The outside of the jar, at the top, should be carefully and gently warmed first, and then the bitumen melted.

The plates can then be thoroughly washed in distilled water and the loose paste gently scraped off with a knife.

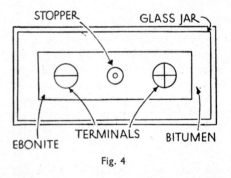

Fig. 4

The jar must also be thoroughly cleaned out and care must be taken to see that it is fairly well dried inside and out afterwards.

To Replace the Plates, first remove by means of a knife or a screwdriver all the bitumen from the ebonite.

Place the plates and the ebonite back in the jar and lay one or two thin, narrow strips of bitumen around the edge of the trough, which will have been formed by the removal of the bitumen. This is to prevent the melted bitumen which will be poured back from running down inside the jar, through the slight gap between the edge of the ebonite and the sides of the jar.

Melt the bitumen in an old tin or some container of a similar description (an old saucepan does very well) over a very low flame. When this is melted it can be carefully poured all round the trough, and when it is hard the cell is ready for refilling with acid and then charging.

Replating.—Sometimes the plates become so poor that they are practically useless, and it is necessary either to procure a new cell or to replate the old one.

In the better types of cell the ebonite is moulded round the post of the plate, and in this case the best thing to do is to procure a set of plates with the ebonite top and put this in a jar in the manner already described.

Where the plate posts are threaded below the terminal thread and the plates are merely held in position by means of tapped nuts or washers, as indicated in Fig. 5, replating is a rather more simple matter.

When replating this type of accumulator, remember always to replace all the original washers, otherwise the acid will creep up and corrode the terminals.

Accumulator Terminals are frequently a source of trouble. In order to

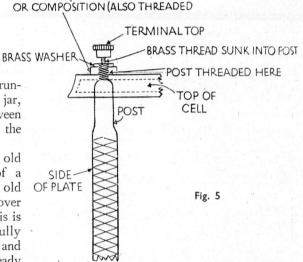

WASHER, USUALLY EBONITE
OR COMPOSITION (ALSO THREADED

TERMINAL TOP

BRASS THREAD SUNK INTO POST

BRASS WASHER

POST THREADED HERE

TOP OF CELL

POST

SIDE OF PLATE

Fig. 5

avoid corrosion they should be kept well coated with vaseline. Should they become so badly corroded that they cannot be loosened by ordinary means, heating or saturating them with paraffin oil will generally have the desired effect.

In some cases the terminals become so corroded that they completely break off. If this occurs the terminal post can be redrilled and tapped.

To do this, file the top of the post flat and then centre punch that portion of the terminal which will still be in the post. Drill a hole of slightly larger diameter than the original one and then thread it with the appropriate tap. This must be done very carefully and gently as, of course, lead is very soft.

Next, screw in a short piece of threaded brass rod (this can be bought in short lengths with a thread to suit the particular tap used) leaving about $\frac{1}{2}$ in. projecting above the terminal post.

Screw on to this a brass washer and tighten it down on to the post. Finally, fit a nut or a terminal top and the terminal is complete, Fig. 6.

The Celluloid Container, though

lighter than a glass one, has the disadvantage of being very easily cracked.

If the plates swell at all, there comes a time when the celluloid cannot stretch

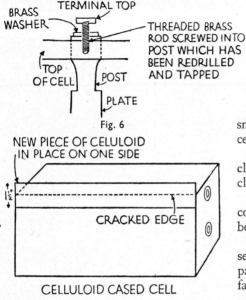

Fig. 6

NEW PIECE OF CELULOID IN PLACE ON ONE SIDE

CRACKED EDGE

CELLULOID CASED CELL

Fig. 7

or distend any more, and it will then crack—usually on the corner.

The best way to repair a crack of this description is to cement another piece of celluloid by means of celluloid cement, which can be obtained at most accumulator charging stations.

First cut a piece of celluloid of the same length as the height of the cell and about $1\frac{1}{2}$ in. wide. Soak this for a short while in the cement to soften it a little. Roughen the sides and corner of the cell where the patch is to be, using a piece of emery cloth or a small file.

Place the piece of celluloid along the side of the cell, having first smeared both thinly with a coat of cement (see Fig. 7).

The patch and the cell should now be clamped together by means of a wooden clamp or in a vice until it is dry.

Then fold the celluloid over the corner smear with cement and clamp as before.

Do not attempt to commence the second part of the job until the first part is quite dry, as this is never satisfactory.

Patching a hole on a flat surface of the cell is comparatively simple, but even in this case it is advisable to roughen the surface as before and to apply slight pressure to the patch until the cement begins to harden.

NOTES AND HINTS ON RADIO

To overhaul a receiving set and its appurtenances is not such a complicated matter as some people imagine it to be.

If the receiver is connected to an outside aerial it is advisable to go over this part of the installation at least once a year, preferably in the summer, so that, provided nothing untowards happens to it in the meantime, it will be ready to function without interruption during the winter when a wireless set is mostly used.

The Aerial.—The best way to overhaul the aerial is first to remove it from its attachments as by so doing the strength of the wire can be tested. Constant swaying may have weakened it to such an extent that it may snap during the usual autumn gales.

To test the strength of the wire, fasten one end round a post or a tree and pull at the other end. If the wire withstands a reasonable tension, all well and good as the wire can be reinstated.

If it breaks, a new one should be provided as it is false economy to effect a repair when the wire may cause further trouble in the near future.

It may be that the top of the aerial post has rotted if it does not possess a metal cap to keep moisture from penetrating the end grain of the wood. To remedy this defect, remove the affected part, saw the end to the shape of an inverted V and fix either a thick zinc or lead plate over the V, as shown in Fig. 1, using galvanised nails for the purpose.

Examine the pulley (if fitted) to see that it is working freely. Remove any rust with emery paper, give it a couple of coats of aluminium paint and when dry smear it over with vaseline or motor grease.

If the pole is painted, apply two coats of lead paint, and if unpainted, give it a couple of coats of creosote.

The majority of wireless poles are fixtures. Therefore, it is wise to examine the condition of the post at ground level, as in Fig. 2. If badly rotted, the safest plan is to take out the pole and remove the faulty section.

It may be that the aerial is of bare wire suspended between porcelain insulators, as indicated in Fig. 3. Clean the insulators, as a deposit of soot and dirt reduces the insulating properties of the china and consequently the efficiency of the aerial.

In reconnecting the aerial wire, make sure that all terminals are clean and bright as well as the ends of the wires.

If "lead in" tubes are used, bind a layer of electrician's adhesive tape round the outside ones to protect them from the weather.

Do not omit to examine the earth connections and wires. Crackling sounds in the receiver are sometimes caused by corroded connections.

It may be mentioned here that brass terminals can be effectively cleaned by dipping them in nitric acid and then rinsing them in water. This is much

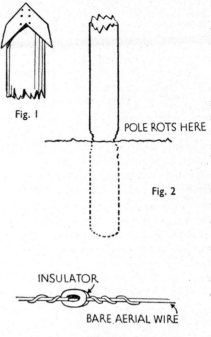

Fig. 1

POLE ROTS HERE

Fig. 2

INSULATOR

BARE AERIAL WIRE

Fig. 3

quicker than scraping. If acid is used, be careful not to allow it to touch the hands. The terminals should be fixed to a wire and then immersed in the acid.

The Receiver.—Assuming that the receiver is of the battery-operated type, proceed as follows: First examine all external connecting wires such as flexibles. Pull the ends of these as they may be hanging only by a few strands of wire. If the insulating covering of rubber is hard and brittle, replace with new wires.

Having dismantled all external wires, remove the back of the receiver and disconnect the accumulator and large dry battery that supplies the high-tension current to the valves. Then take out the valves, noting carefully the position of each. Put distinguishing marks on the valves 1, 2, 3, etc., so that they may be replaced in their proper sockets or holders.

Do not allow the valves to lie about with other accessories on the table, but wrap each one in paper and place them in a box.

Now remove the controlling knobs, usually to be found at the front of the instrument. In the majority of sets these parts are fixed to projecting spindles by means of grub screws, while in some a spring device is employed. Take care not to lose any screws.

If the set being overhauled is of modern design the interior components will generally be found on top as well as beneath the metal chassis, and the loud-speaker fixed either above or below the latter. In order to remove the chassis from the cabinet it may be necessary to unsolder the loud-speaker connections, but some manufacturers provide screw terminals for connecting purposes. In any case the loud-speaker leads as well as the terminals should be labelled or otherwise marked so that they can be replaced in their original position. This is important, as cross connecting may damage some of the components.

The Chassis is usually kept in position in the cabinet by means of metal screws. When these have been taken out, the chassis is free to be withdrawn.

Handle it very carefully. If necessary, support the ends on wooden blocks.

First remove any dust. This is best done by blowing it out with the aid of a vacuum cleaner. If such is not available, use a very soft-haired brush. Go over the whole of the parts systematically, taking every precaution not to apply too much pressure as this may bend a wire, causing it to touch another and thus produce a short circuit. If the tuning condensers are of the open type they should be carefully examined because any specks of dust allowed to remain are liable to get between adjacent plates and give rise to crackling noises.

Removing dust between condenser vanes is a delicate operation and is best done with a clean feather. On no account use a brush.

Having removed all dust, examine carefully all soldered connections. In doing this, try each wire by inserting the blade of a penknife under the wire and exerting a little pressure. If an unsatisfactory joint is found, resolder the part carefully.

Inspect the high tension, low tension and accumulator leads and replace them with new ones if they show signs of wear. Make sure that the ends of the flexible wires are making proper contact with the wander plugs that fit into the high-tension battery and the grid battery and scrape the spade-shaped accumulator connections if corroded.

The Loud-speaker. — It may be worth while to take out the loud-speaker and apply a jet of air in order to remove any particles of dust which may have lodged between the magnet core and the speech coil. A few particles of dust here will cause the loud-speaker to give unsatisfactory reproduction. If the speaker is working well, however, it is advisable not to interfere with it in any way.

The Valves.—Having replaced the chassis into the cabinet, refitted the control knobs and reconnected the loud-speaker, the next step is to get the valves tested, especially if they have been used for over 1,000 hours. It does not necessarily follow that because the heating filaments are intact that the valve is in first-rate condition. In time they gradually lose their electron emission qualities, a symptom of which is lack of volume of sound from the speaker.

Take the radio set with the old valves

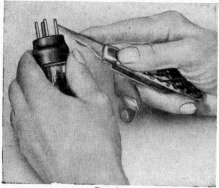

Fig. 4

to your local radio service engineer and he will be able to tell you whether they are functioning normally or not, by either substituting new valves or testing them with an instrument.

If you do not possess a voltmeter it would be as well to get the high tension and grid batteries tested at the same time.

In replacing the valves it is as well to see that the pin contacts are making proper contact with the valve holder sockets. If they appear to be loose, open the pins a trifle by carefully inserting the point of a pen-knife in the slots provided for the purpose. This operation is seen in Fig. 4.

An ill-fitting pin can be made to fit tightly in the socket by wrapping a piece of silver paper taken from a cigarette packet round it, as indicated in Fig. 5.

The Accumulator.—It is advisable

to wash out any deposit which may have formed at the bottom of the cell, with distilled water or have this done next time the accumulator goes to the radio stores for recharging, unless, of course, you recharge your own.

Mains Sets.—The above also applies in the main to radio receivers obtaining their power from the electricity supply, except those remarks referring to the batteries and accumulators.

It is hardly necessary to point out that on no account should any work be carried out on such a set whilst it is connected to the mains.

Particular attention should be given to maintain the mains connecting lead in good condition, and light capacity

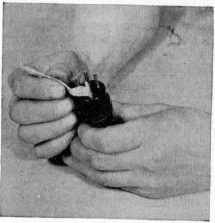

Fig. 5

fuses only should be used for protecting the set.

If the receiver obtains current from a power plug the light fuses previously mentioned should be inserted in the circuit between the plug and the set.

ERECTING A LIGHTNING CONDUCTOR

Practically all tall buildings are protected from lightning damage by lightning conductors. The reason for this is that they stand out above the surrounding buildings and are consequently more liable to be struck. In large towns and suburbs, houses of approximately the same height are grouped closely together and so the chances of any one house receiving damage from this source are greatly reduced.

This does not render them completely immune, however, and as prevention is obviously better than cure, it is quite a wise move and certainly does no harm to take the precaution of fitting a lightning conductor, and for premises that are at all isolated it is almost a necessity.

A lightning conductor consists primarily of a point, or set of points, fixed at a distance above the highest point of the building, and connected to a conductor which in turn is connected to a metal plate buried in the earth.

The air terminal or point gathers the atmospheric electric discharge, and conducts it through the conductor and metal plate to earth, before the building has a chance to be damaged.

The usual conductors are of copper which can be either a strip or in a stranded cable, which should weigh at least 6 oz. to the foot.

Copper should be used in preference to iron, but should strip iron be employed, it should weigh at least $2\frac{1}{4}$ lb. to the foot.

The air terminal should be of copper rod, about $\frac{3}{4}$ in. in diameter and should consist of one central point surrounded by a group of three or more points, at a distance below the central point of about one foot. The points should have a conical shaped top. (See Fig. 1.)

The earth plate should be a large sheet of copper about 2 ft. square $\times$ $\frac{1}{16}$ in. thick. The larger the better.

Having obtained all these materials the first thing to do is to decide where the top of the conductor should be fixed. This, of course, depends largely upon the building which it is desired to protect, but there are three points that should be remembered for all buildings.

The first of these is that it should be taken to the highest point of the building, and the second is that it is best if possible to run the conductor down the dampest side of the building, always providing that this does not interfere with the third point which is, that the straightest possible run down to earth should be chosen.

On the average residential building it is usually found best to secure the points of the conductor to the chimney stack and to run the conductor down the side of the house rather than the front or back.

Construction.—First of all, the wall should have a series of holes punched at regular distances (say about 2 ft.) all down the face.

These holes are to be used for fixing the screws of the clips, or saddles which will secure the conductor in position, and they will therefore probably be in pairs, but that, of course, will depend upon the clips to be used.

The holes will in any case require plugging with wood.

It is a good idea to use either brass

or copper strips for securing the conductor, the method being to place a strip across the cable and screw it down on either said. (See Fig. 2.)

Now climb up to the chimney stack (the best way being to use a ladder lying flat on the roof, though expert advice should be obtained on this point for purposes of safety) carrying a length of rope long enough to reach the ground.

It will be necessary to have an assistant at the bottom, who can now secure the end of the conductor to the rope.

Pull up the conductor while the assistant uncoils it from the ground, and when you have pulled up sufficient, secure the end to the chimney stack.

Next clip the conductor down the side of the house in the manner already described.

The most important thing to remember in running the conductor is to avoid as many bends and projections in the wall as possible and that wherever it is absolutely essential to make a bend in the conductor, such as over a gutter, it should be in the form of a long gradual curve, and there should not be a single sharp bend anywhere in the whole run.

The next thing to do is to secure the rod which carries the points to the chimney stack.

Unless the set of points has a clamp connector already fitted, it is as well at this stage to connect the conductor to the rod.

This can be done by means of copper clips, such as are used by electricians for securing earth wires to water pipes and conduits.

The conductor should be placed along the rod and the clips put round both of them and screwed up, thus clamping both the conductor and the rod firmly together, as illustrated in Fig. 1.

The rod can be secured to the chimney stack by means of saddles, again of the type used by electricians for fixing conduit.

The stack should first be plugged,

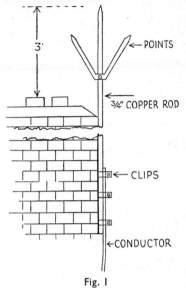

Fig. 1

making fairly large, deep holes to secure a very firm fixing for the points will be subject to a good deal of strain from the wind.

The points fixed and the conductor neatly laid straight and flat down the

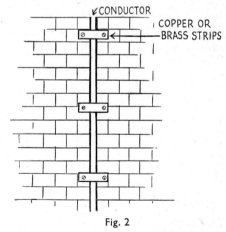

Fig. 2

slant of the roof, the most difficult part of the job is done, and it now only remains to finish off at the bottom.

The conductor should be run to a point at least 3 ft. from the wall and if possible, this last little run should be buried underground. A hole, about

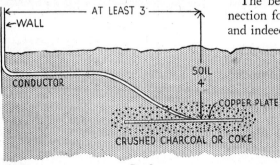

Fig. 3

4 ft. deep and wide enough to take the copper plate should now be dug and the inside lined with either crushed charcoal or coke. This hole should be in fairly damp soil if possible, and so the distance the conductor will have to be run from the house will, obviously,

depend upon the situation at which the plate is to be buried.

The conductor should now be cut to the correct length and connected to the plate. The best way to make a good connection for this purpose is by soldering and indeed there is no other method that can be really relied upon. It is possible, however, to make a much less reliable connection by drilling the plate and securing the conductor by means of bolts, nuts and washers.

Having placed the copper plate in the hole, a good layer of crushed charcoal or coke should be put on top of it and the hole refilled with soil. (See Fig. 3.)

This plate should always be kept damp and should therefore be kept well supplied with water during the dry months of the year.

ELECTRIC FIRESCREEN RADIATOR

A N inexpensively constructed electric radiator is described below. Its current consumption is only 500 w. and it can be made easily with ordinary tools. Fig. 1 shows the suggested design for the radiator.

The materials required are an ordinary 500 w. bowl such as can be bought for about ten shillings, a sheet of copper, some copper strips and rivets. The copper sheet should be about 1 ft. 9 in.× 1 ft. 6 in. and about $\frac{1}{16}$ in. thick.

Construction.—The first thing to do is to cut a hole in the centre of this sheet, just large enough for the bowl to pass through, with the exception of the lip on the reflector of the fire. The fire is later to be clamped at the back of the

screen, so that this lip is pressed hard against the front of the copper sheet.

The relative size of the hole and the fire is illustrated in Fig. 2, which shows the screen cut in half and viewed from one side. The usual size bowl fire is of 11 in. diameter and in this case the size of the hole will be about $10\frac{7}{8}$ in. in diameter.

The best way of cutting a hole as large as this, is to mark out the hole and then drill a series of small holes (say $\frac{1}{8}$ in.) all round just inside the mark.

These small holes should just touch or overlap each other and when the circle is completed, the inside will fall out. The hole can then be filed out with a round or half-round medium file, exactly to the line.

Marking Out.—Some slight difficulty may be experienced in marking out the hole. If a compass large enough for the purpose is not available, a good substitute will be found by using a nail and a piece of string. Tie the string to the nail and knock the nail through the very centre of the copper sheet. Then fasten the pencil on to the other end of the string, so that the mark made by the pencil, when the string is stretched, is exactly the same distance from the nail as the length of the radius of the circle is required.

Drill four holes at equal distances from each other round the circle. They should be about ½ in. from the edge of the aperture and ⅛ in. in diameter.

Next, along the top (which is one of the longer sides) drill five holes; one at each end, at a distance of 1⅜ in. from the side and then three more between them spaced at equal distances apart. Treat the bottom in the same manner.

The sides must also have five holes drilled in them, but this time the distance from the end holes from the top and bottom is to be 1 in. and the distance between the remaining holes 4 in. All these holes should be at a distance of ⅜ in. from the edge of the sheet and ½ in. in diameter. The position of the holes is shown in Fig. 3.

Hammering.—A radiator of this sort looks much better if the screen is "hammered." This effect is obtained by banging the copper all over at an even strength with a rounded hammer.

A special hammer is obtainable for the purpose, but if you have one with one side flat and the other side rounded

to the shape of a ball, such as is used by nearly all workmen, it will serve the purpose equally well.

The copper should be placed on a

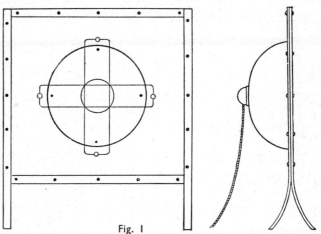

Fig. 1

wooden bench, and no attempt should be made to keep all the hammer marks in straight lines. Hammer the sheet all over, at the same time making the indentations even and equidistant. It is as well to experiment on an odd piece of metal before starting on the actual screen.

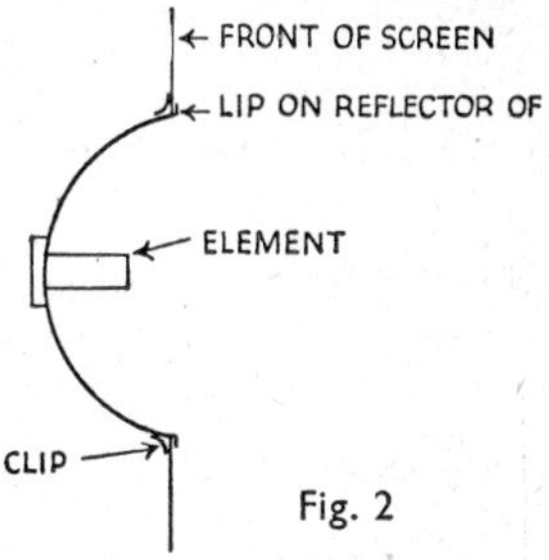

The Strips.—The next job is to cut and drill the copper strips, which are to go round the sides of the screen. These strips should be ¾ in. wide × 3/16 in. thick.

Four strips, each 24 in. long will be required for the front, back side pieces and four similar pieces 1 ft. 9 in. long for the top and bottom. These should be drilled with holes to correspond with those along the edges of the screen and in the exact centres of the width of the strips.

← FRONT OF SCREEN

← LIP ON REFLECTOR OF

← ELEMENT

CLIP →

Fig. 2

The additional length of the strips for the sides allows them to project sufficiently at the bottom so that they can be curved away from the other in the shape of a curved inverted V as shown in Fig. 1.

These side strips can be curved before riveting them in position down the

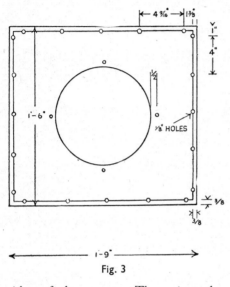

Fig. 3

sides of the screen. Then rivet the strips along the top and bottom.

Use round headed copper rivets ($\frac{1}{8}$ in. thick) and get them slightly longer than the thickness of the complete screen—about $\frac{1}{2}$ in. File these down so that

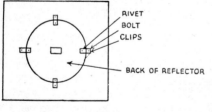

Fig. 4

when they are pushed through the holes in the two strips and the sheet they will project about $\frac{1}{16}$ in.

Now place a rivet through the strips and sheet, rest the head on some hard

metal object like the top of the vice and hammer the end of the rivet until the burr that results holds all three pieces of metal closely together. The head of the rivet should, of course, be in front of the screen.

When all the strips have been riveted on, the next item to claim attention is the fixing of the bowl fire.

The method of doing this is shown in Fig. 4, and the clip is also to be seen in Fig. 2.

The clip is made of the same material as that used for the edges of the screen and the angle at which it must be bent is best found by experiment.

Four holes must now be drilled in the reflector of the bowl fire. These should come opposite the holes around the edge of the aperture in the screen.

Next, holes should be drilled in the clips to correspond one with a hole in the bowl and one with the hole in the screen.

The heavy metal stand which is usually fitted to bowl fires will not be required so this can either be removed at the hinge or sawn off with a hack saw.

The clips should now be riveted to

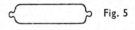

Fig. 5

the back of the bowl secured to the screen by means of bolts passed through the clips and nuts at the back.

The Guard.—It is really not safe to use an electric radiator without some sort of guard.

This guard usually takes the form of thick wire secured across the front of the fire.

The best way to construct a guard is to get two lengths of No. 12 S.W.G. and bend them to the shape shown in Fig. 5.

The complete loop at one end can be formed round a screwdriver or some similar object and the loop at the other end can be made without much difficulty by means of a pair of pliers or in a vice. The distance between the parallel wires of the guard, should be about 3 in. and four loops at the ends of the guards can be secured under the heads of the bolts, which hold the bowl fire.

It will be necessary to put a fairly large washer under each bolt, and these can be made if desired out of the same material as the screen.

When this has been fitted, the whole screen except the bowl should be cleaned and polished with a good metal polisher and given a coat of clear cellulose lacquer which prevents the metal from becoming tarnished.

ELECTRICAL EQUIPMENT OF A CAR

THIS article outlines the principles of some of the electrical equipment used in motoring and give some hints on maintenance.

In a car supplied with coil ignition the source of electric supply is primarily the battery, which is charged by the dynamo. We will, therefore, deal with the battery first.

An electrical accumulator, or battery, consists of two sets of lead plates immersed in sulphuric acid.

Care of Battery.—In order that the composition of the plates may be maintained and the battery work efficiently, it is important that the acid be kept to the correct specific gravity, which is generally about 1.275.

The specific gravity is tested by means of a hydrometer, which usually takes the form of a glass syringe containing a float marked at different levels to indicate the state of the acid. The process of ascertaining the specific gravity of the acid is pictured in Fig. 1.

If the level of acid in the battery is maintained, by adding distilled water when necessary just to cover the plates, it will remain at the correct specific gravity for a considerable time. If neglected and allowed to get very low,

the addition of a lot of distilled water will so far weaken the electrolyte, as the liquid is termed, as to make it constantly wrong. It is advisable in these circumstances to use a little acid as well as the water.

Except in such circumstances, it is bad to add acid as it strengthens the electrolyte and is harmful to the plates.

Keep the terminals clean and covered with vaseline or car grease to prevent corrosion.

Ignition System.—Coil ignition is almost universal again to-day after a lapse of many years.

The main feature is the coil, which is really a sort of transformer used to step up the battery voltage to a high degree.

There is a primary and a secondary winding, the former having a mechanical contact breaker in series with it to provide fluctuations in the current from the battery. The current through the primary winding induces a smaller current at a much larger voltage in the secondary winding, which in turn supplies the sparking plugs, through the distributor.

Fig. 2 shows diagrammatically the

usual circuit arrangement for coil ignition.

The contact breaker and the condenser —whose function is to prevent sparking

Fig. I

at the points of the contact breaker—are generally assembled in the distributor casing.

Any faults in the coil unit are usually found in the leads, except on rare occasions when one of the windings develops a fault and burns out.

The chief point of trouble in the distributor is the contact breaker.

If the contact points are dirty they can be cleaned with a very fine nail file, but if badly pitted they should be replaced.

Trouble is sometimes caused by the contacts not opening and shutting properly and this is generally caused by dirt or grease or lack of tension in the spring. Occasionally, there may have been excessive sparking at the points, causing them to fuse together. If this

happens, it is usually necessary to replace the points.

Sometimes the condenser breaks down —in which case the effect will be excessive sparking at the points of the contact breaker and a poor spark across the gap between the rotating arm of the distributor and the metal segments which are connected to the plug leads. This will cause the engine to run poorly, especially at low speeds, and the only cure is to replace the condenser.

The metal segments which connect the sparking plug leads are found in the top half of the distributor and should be kept clean and free from grease.

Points About Plugs.—A sparking plug, constructional details of which appear in Fig. 3, consists of a central point, separated by a spark gap from one or three other points.

The central point is mounted in a base of porcelain or fibre, which insulates it from the main body of the plug. The other point or points form part of the main body and are thus earthed through the cylinder head, when the plug is in position. The lead from

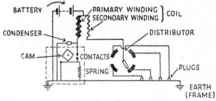

Fig. 2

the distributor connects to the terminal on the top of the plug and so to the central point. The spark leaps across the gap from the central point to the outside points.

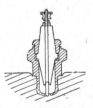

Fig. 3

If an engine is running poorly and a plug is suspected, the best way to find

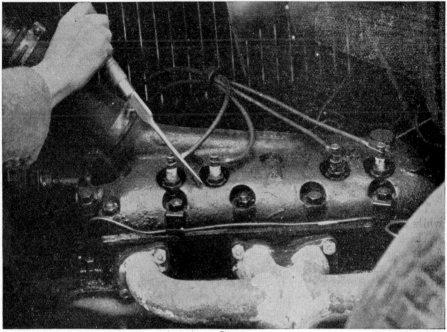

Fig. 4

the offender is to short-circuit each of the terminals in turn by placing a screwdriver across it to the cylinder head shown in Fig. 4, with the engine running slowly. If a plug is firing correctly, the effect on the running of the engine is instantly noticeable. If there is no effect, the plug is not firing. This is not necessarily the fault of the plug. The breakdown may be in the lead or the distributor.

The easiest way to find out if it is the plug is to change it to another cylinder and test again.

When a plug has been used for some time the insulation becomes covered with carbon, and this tends to short-circuit the points.

To clean the insulation by hand, the two octagonal parts, see Fig. 3, should be unscrewed and the central portion can then be withdrawn.

The insulation should be cleaned with a stiff brush until all trace of black

Fig. 5

deposit is removed. Fig. 5 shows the operation.

Some plugs used on modern cars are in one piece—or, rather, the two parts are inseparable—and in this case the best thing is to have them cleaned on a machine at a garage. It only takes a few minutes and the usual charge is threepence per plug.

The width of the spark gap is important. It is usually about 0.4 to 0.5 mm. and can be adjusted by means of a feeler gauge of that size.

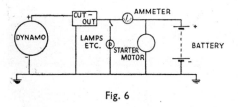

Fig. 6

The battery is charged by the dynamo while the engine is running.

The charging circuit is shown in Fig. 6. It consists principally of a shunt-wound dynamo, an automatic cut-out which prevents the battery from discharging through the dynamo when the engine is at rest, and the battery.

The Dynamo.—The first principles of the dynamo are to have an armature, at one end of which is the commutator

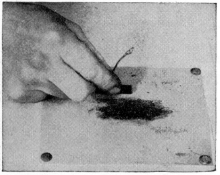

Fig. 7

and, pressing on the commutator, two brushes.

As a plain dynamo would send a larger current through the battery and through the other accessories as the speed of the engine increased, a third brush is incorporated. This automatically regulates the voltage of the output and places a maximum on the current supplied.

This third brush is thinner than the others and easily recognised.

The brushes are the components most requiring attention in the dynamo.

Trouble with the dynamo is generally caused either by brushes worn too low or sticking in their guides. In the latter event, the brushes should be removed and their sides rubbed down a little on fine sandpaper, as illustrated in Fig. 7.

If there is a lot of sparking at the brushes, see that they bed down properly on the commutator.

This is accomplished by wrapping a piece of fine sandpaper around a cylindrical piece of wood of the same

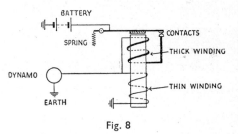

Fig. 8

diameter as the commutator and rubbing the brush gently across it, keeping it in the same position as it occupies on the commutator.

If the commutator is dirty, it may be cleaned also with fine sandpaper.

Fold the sandpaper over the end of a long thing piece of wood of the same width as the commutator and press this gently against the commutator with the engine running or being turned by hand.

The brushes and commutator of the starter motor may be treated in the same way.

The principles of the voltage control, or cut-out, are these. A thin winding is placed on a soft iron core through which the current from the dynamo passes while the cut-out is open. At a predetermined voltage, this current causes the electro-magnet so formed to attract an armature and, in doing so, closes the cut-out contacts.

This brings the charging circuit into operation and the current now passes through another winding on the same core.

Fig. 8 gives the diagram of these windings and shows the action of the cut-out.

The main points for attention on the cut-out are the contacts and the spring for returning the movable one to the open position.

The moving armature, which contains the moving contact on one end, should always be free when the engine is idle, except for the tension of the spring.

If it is pressed against the core of the magnet, however, it will stay there, owing to the discharge through the windings of the current from the battery and should never be allowed to remain in this position for more than a few seconds.

The distance of the armature from the magnet is sometimes adjustable, and the correct space in this case is easily found.

INSPECTING THE NEW HOUSE

THINGS TO DO ABOUT THE HOUSE

SAFETY FIRST IN THE HOME AND WORKSHOP

Most mishaps, the results of which may be of a very serious nature, can be avoided if care is exercised. The examples given are some of the simple steps which differentiate between danger and safety.

The Position of the Kettle.—The illustration appearing at Fig. 1 shows a thoughtless method of placing a kettle on a lighted gas stove. It will be observed that the spout overhangs the front where anyone passing may get badly scalded from steam or, worse still, catch the projecting spout with the clothing, with disastrous results.

The Household Steps. — Fig. 3 shows a method of seeking trouble with a pair of household steps. The assistant is standing on the weakest part and may bring disaster to both himself and his companion.

Never allow anyone to stand on the cross-rail of a pair of steps.

Loose treads, faulty hinges, a loose cross-piece and frayed cords should be remedied at once and, when replacing worn cords, see that they are well stretched and that the knots are so adjusted that the angle formed between the steps and the back is neither too acute nor too obtuse. The treads should be quite horizontal when the steps are in the open position.

Window Sash Lines.—Many accidents are caused by broken window sash lines. The cords should be examined periodically and worn ones replaced.

Remember that there are several qualities of sash cord. Only the best should be used. A little tallow applied to the cords will prolong their life.

Picture Cords. — Heavy picture frames should never be hung at the head of a bed.

Slipping Mats.—Mats slipping on polished lino are another source of

Fig. 1

danger and many an arm has been broken from this cause. The remedy is not to polish the lino under the mats.

A Cracked Hand-basin.—A cracked hand-basin is extremely dangerous and might have serious consequences should an unwary user apply pressure to the faulty part. Fit a new basin sooner than run this risk.

A Loft Ladder.—If you possess a loft ladder of the flimsy type, always get someone to place their feet at the base to prevent it slipping when using the ladder. Never attempt to rear a ladder by yourself but get a helper to stand at the bottom rung when so doing.

Removing Broken Glass. — In removing broken glass from a window sash or other fitment use an old pair of gloves or a duster to protect the hands, and do the job gently to avoid cuts.

Electric Fittings.—Before fixing an electric light bulb into a fitting see that the current is switched off. The fila-

Fig. 3

ment of the lamp may be faulty and cause the lamp to explode.

Never touch any electrical equipment whilst having a bath. Even if the switch operating the light is shock proof, there may be a surface leak which, if touched, may give a bad shock. In the event of a switch being within reach of the bath, have it removed to a safer position even if the switch has to be fixed behind the door.

Fig. 2 shows a safe type of electric radiator for use in a bathroom. It consists of a heating element and a chromium-plated reflector which can be adjusted up or down as desired to focus the heat rays. The heater should be fixed at a height of about 7 ft. on a wall well away from the bath and wash basin, and it should be connected to a 3-pin combination switch-plug at the side to enable it to be efficiently earthed.

An excellent and safe electrical device in the shape of a plug and socket known as an "M.K." has an insulated shutter which covers the sockets when the plug is withdrawn. Such fitments are invaluable in a home where young children may push scissor-points and other metallic objects into unprotected sockets with unpleasant and sometimes dangerous results.

Before effecting any repair or adjustment to the domestic electrical installation, the current should be switched off at the main switch, as this removes any likelihood of shocks and burns, and before making adjustments to a

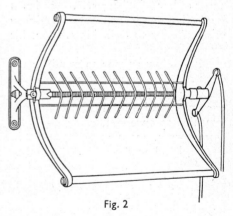

Fig. 2

mains radio receiver always disconnect it from the supply.

The Fire Guard.—Some people responsible for the welfare of children may not know that it is a serious offence not to provide an efficient guard in front of a household fire for the protection of children; so the provision of this safety device should never be overlooked.

Safety Gate.—It is also a wise plan, when an upstairs room is used as a

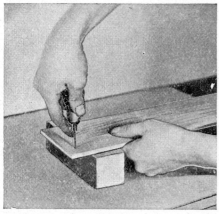

Fig. 4

nursery, to fit a gate at the top of the stairs to prevent youngsters from falling down. Articles on how to construct an efficient fireguard and a gate for the stairs will be found elsewhere in this volume.

Sources of Danger.—Loose slates and tiles, faulty gutters and defective ceilings are a source of danger.

Keep a look out for, and remove, rotten branches of trees and do not let rambler roses project over a public footway. You are responsible for any injury they may cause.

A nail projecting upwards from a piece of wood lying on the floor of the workshop is a menace to the unfortunate individual who happens to tread on it. Always withdraw nails from unwanted wood before casting it on the floor.

Fig. 4 illustrates the wrong way to hold a bradawl when boring a hole in a thin piece of unsupported wood, for unless pressure is relieved when

the blade is nearly through there is every likelihood of the point penetrating quicker than expected, with the result that the forefinger gets a nasty pinch.

When unscrewing the back iron from the cutter of a plane, support it on the

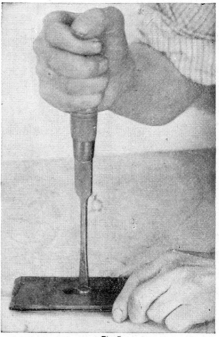

Fig. 5

Fig. 6

bench as shown in Fig. 5. Unscrewing it in the hand is seeking trouble because the cutter may slip and cause a nasty gash.

How to Hold a Chisel.—Carpenters' chisels are useful tools if properly used, but dangerous if incorrectly applied. Fig. 6 shows the safe method of holding a chisel when paring the corner off a piece of wood.

Avoid Loose Hammer-heads. —

Fig. 7

Loose hammer-heads should not be tolerated. Apart from the inconvenience of using a tool in this condition, there is the danger of the head flying off the shaft.

A greasy striking-face of a hammer may cause it to slip off the head of a nail, resulting in bruised fingers. To avoid this, rub the face of the hammer on the ground.

Damaged fingers may also result from using a cold chisel whose head has become flattened and badly burred as Fig. 7 shows. Before a chisel reaches this state, grind off the jagged edge.

Using a file without a handle is a practice to avoid, as is the foolhardy trick of shifting a belt on a machine in motion.

Engine Repairs.—The loss of two fingers, a badly mutilated hand and a couple of months in hospital was the reward of a motor-cyclist who unthinkingly attempted to make an adjustment whilst the engine was running. The driving chain and sprocket wheel was responsible for these injuries.

Cranking a motor-car engine, unless done properly, may cause a broken wrist, should the engine backfire. Grip the handle as shown in Fig. 8; never as indicated in Fig. 9.

Running a motor-car engine in a

Fig. 8

Fig. 9

closed garage should be avoided. If it is necessary to let the engine run in the garage, open the doors and windows so that there is ample ventilation, otherwise deadly carbon monoxide from the exhaust may fatally overpower you.

MAKING AN OLD CYCLE LOOK LIKE NEW

A CYCLE of good make will give years of service provided it is looked after and adjusted in a proper manner. There comes a time, however, when it pays to dismantle the machine and give it a thorough overhaul, when every part can be examined and adjusted and faulty ones replaced.

If the machine is shabby, no better time can be chosen for re-enamelling it than when the parts are dissembled, and if the following instructions are carried out the machine will be given an extra lease of life and will also look like new.

Let us assume that an ordinary cycle of general purpose type is to be over-hauled and enamelled.

Before beginning the operations, obtain a few empty tins in which to place small parts such as bolts and nuts, as small items are easily lost if left about. It is also worth while to make a support for handling the machine when re-enamelling.

A Convenient Support.—Such a device for screwing down to the bench or other suitable fixture may easily be constructed for a few pence and is shown in Fig. 1. It consists of nothing more than an iron backplate having a ¾ in. screwed hole in the centre, a short length of ¾ in. gas pipe screwed at both ends, a ¾ in. screwed tee-piece and a couple of lock-nuts, all of which can usually be obtained at the local ironmongers. A lock-nut is first screwed on the ends of the pipe and then the tee-piece and backplate and the fitment screwed down to the bench by means of stout screws. To complete the job, a round piece of hardwood about 8 in. long is fitted tightly into the tee-piece and the pro-

jecting part made to fit the saddle tube of the cycle. This arrangement allows the frame to be adjusted to any desired angle and locked in position by the lock-nuts.

In order to carry out the work

Fig. 1

methodically, all tools and accessories should be looked out at the beginning as much time will be saved by having things ready to hand.

The necessary tools include a hammer, shifting spanner, cone spanner, pliers, screwdriver, an old knife, a supply of old linen rags, emery paper, paraffin, petrol, vaseline and several old dishes or tins, a small stiff brush besides enamel or other chosen finishing medium and a brush with which to apply it.

The best way of tackling the dis-sembling is to suspend the machine from the ceiling of the workshop in the manner shown in Fig. 2, by means of a couple of stout cords fixed to hooks or screw-eyes, in which case the saddle pillar and saddle can first be removed as well as the brakes and handlebar. The machine may then be slung up as suggested, and the front wheel and mudguard removed. This should be followed by disconnecting the chain, taking off the chain wheel, pedals and cranks and then removing the bottom bracket axle complete with the cups and ball bearings. The front fork is the final item to remove from the frame. This is done by first unscrewing the ring or lock-nut that keeps the lamp bracket in position and then slacking the nut at the side of the head-clip, which should then just lift off. In removing the head-clip, care must be taken to support the fork in position or

Fig. 2

else the ball bearings, both under the fork and at the fork crown, are likely to fall out and be lost.

To prevent loss of the balls when removing them from the bearings, it is a good plan to spread a cloth immediately below the parts being operated upon. It is very important that cloth should be used and not newspaper as the former prevents the balls from rolling about.

Painting the Frame. — Before attempting to clean dissembled parts it is advisable to prepare the frame for finishing as attention to the other components may be given whilst the frame is drying.

To prepare frame for re-enamelling,

the whole of the metal must be scraped perfectly clean, following with the vigorous use of emery cloth of medium grit.

Suitable chemical paint remover is obtainable at moderate cost at most cycle dealers and its use eliminates tedious scraping. All that is necessary is to cover the surface of the old enamel with the medium, leave for a few minutes and then rub off all the old enamel. Paint remover can be used for cellulose lacquer and varnish with equal success, and has the advantage of being non-inflammable; it will not damage metal, as it contains no acids or alkalies, and will not harm the skin.

Having removed every particle of enamel and polished the frame with emery paper the metal should be rubbed over with a clean linen rag damped with a little petrol to remove any grease, which if allowed to remain would spoil the new finish. From this it follows that the subsequent handling of the frame before and when applying the new enamel should be done with a clean rag as bare hands are likely to be greasy.

At this stage the worker must make up his mind as to the kind of finishing medium he intends to use. A quick-drying spirit enamel is not recommended as it easily chips and scratches. Cellulose lacquer is excellent and so is good quality hard-drying enamel. In either case it is necessary to give the frame one or two undercoats before applying the final one.

If cellulose lacquer is the chosen medium it is important that the brushing kind be specified as similar lacquer is supplied for spraying on, which is unsuitable for brush work.

Special cellulose undercoating can be obtained and this is applied with a soft brush. Half a pint of cellulose undercoating and an equal quantity of the finishing medium will be ample for the frame including forks and mudguards.

Apply the undercoats and allow each one to harden before applying the next. In putting on the finishing coat, care must be taken to cover the surface as

Fig. 3

smoothly and quickly as possible as cellulose lacquer sets in a very short time and for this reason it cannot be touched up satisfactorily should any part have been missed.

If ordinary enamel is used, give the frame and forks two good undercoats of flat oil paint, rubbing down each coat when thoroughly dry with fine pumice powder and water before applying the next. The same applies to the outsides of the mudguards, but the insides should receive three undercoats as a preventive of rust.

The enamel should be flowed on carefully with a soft brush. The room in which the painting is done must be free

from dust and at a temperature of anything above about 60 deg. F. Ordinary enamel takes about twenty-four hours

Fig. 4

to set. Fig. 3 shows the process of enamelling.

Assuming that the plating of the handle bar, wheel rims and hubs, cranks and other plated parts is in a good state of preservation it may be cleaned, examined and adjusted. If the surfaces of these parts are in a dilapidated state and it is not considered advisable to have them replated they can be cleaned and finished as in the case of the frame and thus convert the cycle into an all-weather machine.

In making the necessary adjustments, a start can be made on the front wheel.

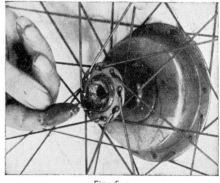

Fig. 5

This is best done by laying it flat on a bench or table, as seen in Fig. 4.

Ball Races.—Unscrew the adjustable

R

cone, remove the balls and place them in a saucer of paraffin to remove dirt and grit. If any of the balls are pitted or misshapen it is wise to replace them with an entirely new set, and this applies to any other sets of ball bearings in the machine. Ball bearings are not expensive. If this is done, and provided that the ball races are in good condition, you are unlikely to experi-

Fig. 6

ence trouble from this source for many hundreds of miles.

If the balls are in perfect condition, they may be replaced into their respective races. This may appear to be a tricky job, but little difficulty will be experienced if a small quantity of vaseline or motor grease is first inserted into the races and the balls placed in position, as the balls adhere to the vaseline, which prevents them from falling out. This process is pictured in Fig. 5. The cone should be tightened up and then slackened off a quarter or half turn so that the wheel turns easily yet without any rock. The same procedure is

followed with the back wheel, bottom bracket and pedal bearings, every part of which should be thoroughly cleaned with paraffin and polished with a clean cloth.

Clean the chain by allowing it to soak in paraffin, replacing the oil from time to time as the dirt soaks out of the chain. Clean the chain wheel with paraffin applied with a stiff brush. Then examine both by placing the chain over the wheel. If the chain does not bed down perfectly it shows that either the chain is stretched or the teeth of the sprocket are very much worn, or both.

The chain should also be applied to the small sprocket on the back wheel and if necessary all of these parts should be replaced. The cost will not be large. A good chromium-plated chain wheel with cranks and cotters can be obtained for about five shillings, a free-wheel sprocket for half a crown and a serviceable chain for five shillings. This money is not wasted, as the proper functioning of chain and sprockets is all important in easy riding.

If the back wheel is fitted with a three-speed hub it is unwise to take it apart as the mechanism is somewhat complicated. If anything is wrong with it, the wheel should be taken to a skilled cycle mechanic. No injury will be done, however, if the gear is thoroughly cleaned by squirting paraffin into the bearings via the lubricator.

The Tyres.—Mention has not yet been made of tyres. It may be that both covers are so worn that little remains of the treads, in which case both tyres should be substituted by new ones, not only because the life of such covers is nearly at an end, but because it is dangerous to use tyres in this condition. The tread is there to grip the road and prevent side-slip.

In the event of the front wheel cover

being in a good condition and the rear one being only slightly worn, the tyres should be reversed—that is, the rear cover should be fixed to the front rim and vice versa.

In these days the majority of tyres are of the wire-edged type, and to remove them from the rims a set of tyre levers, costing a few pence, will be necessary. To remove the cover, deflate the tyre by unscrewing the valve and insert the spoon-shaped end of the lever at one side between the cover and the rim, care being taken not to pinch the inner tube when so doing, lever up the wire edge over the rim and fix the cranked end of the lever to a spoke by means of the slot.

A second lever is then brought into operation a few inches from the first and secured to a convenient spoke, and then the last one, when the remainder of the edge of the cover can be pulled over the edge of the rim with the fingers. Fig. 6 shows the operation. Next remove the remaining parts of the valve and take out the tube. The opposite wire edge of the cover can then be levered off the rim.

An adjustable tape will be found at the bottom of the rim, so placed as to prevent the nipples at the ends of the spokes from chafing the inner tube. If the tape is very much discoloured by rust or is rotten, replace it with a new one, and if the inner tubes are stretched and thin it is wise to replace them.

In the event of a tube being punctured, proceed in the following way: replace the valve and partially inflate the tube and pass it inch by inch through water contained in a convenient bowl. The puncture will be revealed by the issue of numerous bubbles. The position should be marked and the remainder of the tube

tested to make sure that there are no further leakages. Fig. 7 shows the method of locating the puncture.

To repair the puncture all that is necessary is thoroughly to clean the

Fig. 7

Fig. 8

surface round the leak, apply a thin film of rubber solution to it and to a clean rubber patch, allow the solution to become tacky and then stick the patch over the defective part. The patch should be kept pressed to the tube for a few minutes to allow the solution to harden. To save time, this can be done with a spring clothes "peg" (see Fig. 8).

Assuming that the tyres are now all right, new valve rubbers fitted to the valves, all parts perfectly clean and adjusted and the forks, mudguards and other re-enamelled accessories perfectly dry and hard, the machine may be reassembled in the following order.

First fit the bottom bracket cups and balls, using the vaseline method of securing the balls, as already explained. Then fit the chain wheel and cranks. Next fix the rear mudguard and rear wheel, chain and rear brake and follow by fixing the front fork, mudguard and wheel.

Before finally tightening up the wheels, make sure that they are running freely without shake and if necessary make adjustments. In fitting the front wheel be careful to see that the adjustable cone is on the left-hand side of the fork—that is, opposite the chain wheel.

If a three-speed gear is fitted, make sure that the indicator—which can generally be observed on the step side— is flush with the end of the projecting step when the lever is in the neutral position. Adjustment for this can be made by the gear adjuster on the opposite side. Before riding, all moving parts must be well lubricated.

CLEANING AND ADJUSTING A TYPEWRITER

THE mechanism of a typewriter soon collects fluff and dust which mixes with the lubricating oil and makes the working parts stiff. It also clogs the type and becomes spread over the ribbon. Adjustments are not often necessary in the course of ordinary use and any but the simplest should be left to a typewriter mechanic.

Machines obtained from reputable dealers can be accepted as being clean and in working order. It is second-hand machines obtained by private purchase that require the most attention before they are fit to use.

Take as an example a very neglected machine. On trial, most of the letters and figures are found to be clogged, some are out of line and the whole machine coated in dust, eraser dust and sticky oil. The paper carriage has a very sluggish movement and is inclined to jump and thud as the keys are operated.

To put such a specimen in working order we shall require the following items:

A bottle of benzine.

A bottle of lubricating oil for typewriters.

A few fair-sized feathers and pipe cleaners.

Supply of rag that will not leave fluff behind.

An old tooth brush.

First Steps.—Remove the machine from its baseboard and place it on several thicknesses of newspaper. If in fair condition the ribbon need not be removed. Slip the paper carriage off out of the way. The method of securing this may differ with the machine, but in any case do not remove any screws or nuts; and this applies to all parts of the machine.

Carefully wipe off the worst of the dirt, going all over and inside the machine, taking care not to bend any of the levers. Having done this, proceed to a complete clean up, starting at the top.

A small wad of rag wrapped round a pencil or a knitting needle will be required to reach under some of the small parts and into openings. Damp the rag with benzine. Use a large feather or a pipe cleaner in the spaces more crowded with levers and type rods.

For cleaning the type a tooth brush moistened with benzine will prove the most effective, but it is also just as well to make sure of closed letters such as "e," "o," "p," "m," and all figures and fractions, by removing the dirt with the end of a match or a needle. Raise each character in turn by depressing the key and, supporting it underneath with a finger, thoroughly clean each type. This operation is seen in the figure. Clean the eraser dust from all the hinge ends of the type levers, and from the pad on which the type rests.

Testing the Keys.—Test the spring of each key and see that it returns without lagging. Slack ones are generally unsprung underneath, so turn the machine on its side and look for a small spring somewhere along that particular lever. The loose end of the spring can soon be reinserted in its proper fixing hole and the end bent round so that it will not slip out again. All should be examined.

Try the ribbon movement and, when near the end in one direction, replace the paper carriage, insert paper and type a few lines, watching the ribbon to see that it reverses of itself when the end has been reached. The mechanism for operating this differs with the machine, so note should be taken of a double pawl action on toothed wheels connected to the ribbon spools. The points of the pawls wear away with the action of the teeth on the wheel and fail to engage when operated into the change-over position. The only real cure is to obtain new ones.

To regulate the movement of the paper carriage, turn the tension screw a few times and then try it by typing a few words, but do not make the tension too strong or the reverse trouble

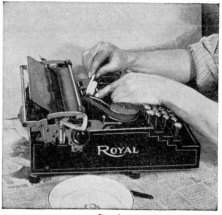

Fig. 1

will be noticed, that is, the carriage will move with a combined jump and thump as each character is used. To slacken the tension, find the pawl lever with a hook at each end engaging with a toothed wheel. Disengage the locked end and the toothed wheel will move round one tooth and become locked again by the other end of the pawl. Work this a few times and try it out. When the right tension has been obtained, do not alter this adjustment again. From the tension driving wheel there may be a band attached to the far end of the paper carriage, by which the latter is pulled along through the tension spring. This band may be worn and, if so, should be replaced by a new one but this is a job for the mechanic and repair shop.

The pawl of the ratchet feed which turns the paper up one, two or three line spacing may require replacement, also the small rubber rollers and guide slips holding the paper close to the roll.

SIMPLE BOOT AND SHOE REPAIRS

THE essential tools for simple boot and shoe repairs include a metal last or foot, shoemaker's hammer, shoemaker's knife, rasp, sharpening tool, pincers, screwdriver and a finishing tool.

A serviceable last, as that shown at A in Fig. 1, can be purchased at most stores for about half a crown, and a hammer B of special shape with a rounded face costs less than a shilling. A half-round rasp, indicated at C, measuring 8 in. long, can be obtained for ninepence and a screwdriver D and knife E for sixpence apiece. A finishing tool of special shape fitted to a handle, as at F, will cost a further shilling, while 7 in. pincers G, which are quite large enough for general purposes, can be obtained for about eighteenpence. The sharpening strop is merely a piece of shaped wood upon the wide faces of which are glued or otherwise fastened strips of emery cloth, medium grade on one face and a finer grade on the other. This accessory is shown at H.

Leather can be bought either in small pieces or in larger quantities. It can be bought in several qualities, but it is false economy to use any but the best. A good piece of leather should be uniform in thickness, smooth on the fleshy side as well as the face, homogeneous in texture and it should not be possible to separate the layers.

There are two methods of re-soleing boots and shoes by hand, known as riveting and hand-sewing respectively. The former is the simpler. It is used principally for boots and shoes that have double soles. Hand-sewing is confined to welted footwear. A welted shoe cannot be riveted successfully as the sole is attached to the uppers by means of a narrow rim of leather or welt, as indicated in the diagram Fig. 2, which has not sufficient width to take rivets.

Rivet Soleing.—To re-sole a pair of riveted shoes, proceed in the following way. First fix one of the shoes upon the last and remove the bottom sole by inserting the blade of a screwdriver between the underside of the worn sole and the middle one at the toe end, and prise it up sufficiently to enable the pincers to be used in the manner indicated in Fig. 3. Do not lift the leather right back to the heel, but cut it across about $\frac{3}{4}$ in. from the instep. Remove any nails and skive or bevel the edge of the remaining piece so that it is flush with the middle sole, as in Fig. 4. Then smooth the face level with the rasp. If the middle sole is worn, place a piece or pieces of felt in the recess to bring it up level with the remainder.

The next step is to cut leather for the new sole. Use the old piece as a pattern, or make a paper pattern by placing the paper over the sole of the shoe and rubbing round the edges with the screwdriver so that it marks the outline of the shoe and then cutting round the outline with a pair of scissors. Another way is to use the fine side of the rasp which will automatically cut out the outline. Place the pattern on the face (dark) side of the leather, and with a sharp lead pencil trace a similar outline about $\frac{1}{8}$ in. larger all round to allow for trimming after the new sole has been fitted in position.

Bevel the edge at the waist—that is, the end towards the heel—on the fleshy side of the new leather. This needs to be done with a sharp knife and finished off neatly with the rasp. Fig. 5 shows the first part of the operation.

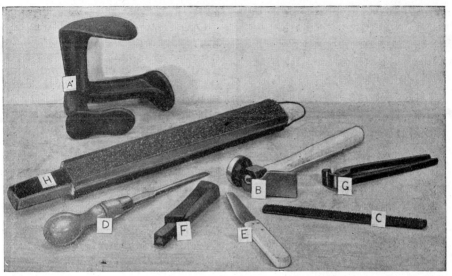

Fig. I

Now place the roughly shaped sole into a bowl of water and allow it to soak for about ten minutes. Then place it on a flat piece of iron, fleshy face up, and hammer it well. Soaking the leather makes it pliable and easy to work, while the hammering closes the pores and increases the durability of the leather.

Replace the shoe on the last, put the new sole in position and fix it down by driving in a couple of rivets near each end. Now trim the leather to shape, as shown in Fig. 6. Keep the knife very keen and, if dull, give it a few rubs on the emery stick.

The sole is now ready to receive the rivets. The length of these is important. They should be long enough to go just through the leather of the sole and the shoe and to clinch the inner sole when driven well home upon the last.

The rivets should be spaced about $\frac{1}{4}$ in. apart at a distance of $\frac{1}{4}$ in. from the edge. It is a good plan for a novice to mark a guide line round the shoe before riveting. A little practice will enable you to judge the spacing of the rivets and so dispense with the guide line. Do not drive in the rivets vertically, but slope them slightly towards the centre of the shoe. Bent and defective rivets should be withdrawn.

Now hammer the heads of the rivets level with the leather and finish the edge, first with a rasp and then with a

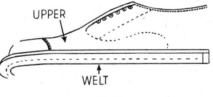

Fig. 2

scraper. The latter can consist of the rounded end of an old table knife blade.

Resole the other shoe and, if necessary, repair the heels. To accomplish this, remove the old leather and cut new top pieces slightly larger than the heel.

If necessary, insert thin slips of leather to bring the heel level. Rivet and trim as in soleing.

The final process consists of finishing.

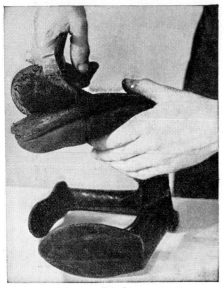

Fig. 3

Apply a coat of burnishing ink, sold in sixpenny bottles for the purpose, and allow it to dry. Then rub some heel-ball along the edges. Heel-ball is a black, waxy substance and needs to be slightly melted before use. Warm the finishing tool and rub it vigorously round the edges and then polish them with a rag.

Hand-stitched Soles.—In resoleing a pair of welted boots by hand stitching, remove the upper sole by carefully cutting away the stitches between the bottom sole and the welt and skive the end of the sole about 1 in. from the waist. Prepare the new soles as already explained.

Place the new sole on the shoe and secure it by partially driving in two or three rivets as indicated at A and B in Fig. 7. Shape the leather to the welt.

Now mark a line about $\frac{1}{8}$ in. from the edge all round and then cut a shallow channel with the knife held at an angle of about 30 deg. to the sole so that the bottom of the channel is further away from the edge than the top.

Open the top of the channel by raising the leather with the aid of either the screwdriver or knife, thus leaving a small ridge or lip of leather projecting above the face of the sole, as indicated in Fig. 8.

Next, with the blade of the screwdriver, make a very small groove at the bottom of the channel. This recess allows the thread to lie flush with the bottom of the channel and enables the leather lip to be hammered down flat after stitching.

The next operation consists of preparing a special strong, waterproof thread. Cotton thread is useless.

The thread comprises five strands of No. 17 hemp. Two such threads will be required, one for each sole. To make a thread, break off five lengths of hemp each about 5 ft. long and twist them together by first placing the middle of them over a nail in the bench and then rolling the strands down the knee with the palm of the hand. The ends of the thread should be tapered before twisting,

Fig. 4

and this is accomplished by placing the end of each strand about 1 in. or so from the next in the manner shown diagrammatically at A in Fig. 9.

The thread is then rendered waterproof by rubbing it thoroughly with cobbler's wax, previously softened by

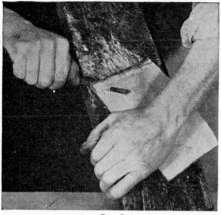

Fig. 5

rubbing it in the hands in the same way as one would soften putty.

Special bristles, obtainable for the purpose, are used in place of metal needles for sewing, four of these will be required, two for each thread. The bristles are pointed at one end and fibrous at the other, and they are attached to the thread in a special

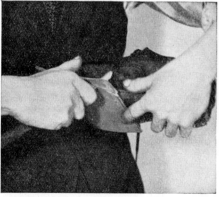

Fig. 6

manner by first rubbing the fibrous end with cobbler's wax and then twisting the thread round the end as shown at B in Fig. 9. To prevent the thread unwinding, make a small hole in the thread, push the bristle through the hole and pull the thread tight. Fix another

bristle at the other end, and repeat the process with the second thread.

Stitching.—The shoe is now ready for stitching. This operation calls for a shoemaker's awl, having a curved blade. Sit on a low chair and grip the shoe between the knees in the manner shown in Fig. 10. With the awl, make a hole large enough to pass the bristle and thread. The first hole should be made about $\frac{1}{4}$ in. away from the waist end of the new sole and the point of the

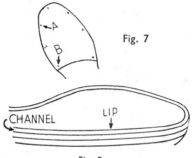

Fig. 7

Fig. 8

awl driven in from the top of the welt into the groove in the channel.

Pass the thread through so that half the length of thread appears at each side. At a distance of about $\frac{1}{4}$ in. from the first hole, pierce another hole and push one length through the top to the bottom and the other thread in the reverse direction, that is, from the bottom to the top. This is shown at c in Fig. 9. Proceed in this manner round the sole, drawing the threads extremely tight at each stitch. At the end of the stitching, tie the threads together and cut off the remainder.

Place the shoe on the last and apply a thin film of rubber solution to the inside of the channel, allow it to get tacky, then seal the channel by running the back of the hammer over the projecting leather and finally hammer it down flat.

Withdraw the partially driven rivets except those at the waist. These are driven home, together with several others right across to form the joint.

Trim the edges of the sole and finish

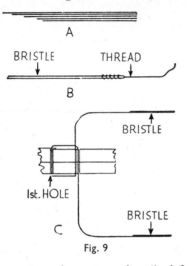

Fig. 9

the work in the manner described for a riveted shoe.

Another satisfactory method of resoleing a welted boot or shoe is to weld or stick on the new sole.

Welded Repairs.—To weld a new sole to a welted shoe, first strip off the old sole as already explained, and cut the leather roughly to shape, not forgetting to bevel the waist end. With a rasp, hack saw blade, or wire brush, thoroughly roughen that portion of the face of the sole exposed after the removal of the old sole leather.

Roughen the fleshy side of the new leather and then apply a thin film of powerful rubber adhesive to the roughened surface of the new leather and the shoe. Such rubber adhesive can be obtained for about ninepence at most stores.

Allow the work to stand in a dry, dustless atmosphere for about twenty minutes, or until the white adhesive turns brown. Now place the two prepared surfaces together. This must be done accurately as the new

sole cannot be removed once it is in position.

With a hammer, first gently tap down the centre in order to drive out the air, then treat the remainder in the same manner, especially at the edges.

Remove the boot from the last, place the edge of the welt downwards on to the edge of the iron foot and tap round again to ensure that the

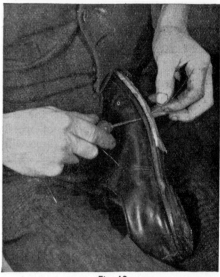

Fig. 10

sole adheres closely to the welt, thus sealing the joint and making it watertight.

Rivet across the waist in the usual manner and anchor the sole at several places by driving in a rivet here and there at a distance of about $\frac{3}{8}$ in. from the edge.

The shoes can be worn immediately after resoleing.

The best way to fix a rubber sole to leather is to roughen the old leather with a rasp, apply a film of rubber solution and put the shoe aside for an hour or two to allow the solution to soak in and get dry. Then place the shoe over the last and tap the prepared surface. Apply another thin coat of rubber solution to the shoe and also apply a film of solution to the new rubber sole. Allow sufficient time for both to get tacky; carefully place the new sole in position and allow the work to dry. If a rubber sole is needed on a new leather sole, roughen the leather first and proceed as above. Rubber heels are fixed by special nails.

HOW TO FRAME PICTURES

To make a simple picture frame, a light hammer, rule, thin bradawl, small backed fine-toothed saw and a small metal plane are the principal tools required; accessories include a mitre-block, a mitre shooting-board for smoothing the ends after sawing and cramps for cramping the frame after gluing. These can be bought or made at home and all three are depicted at A, B and C respectively in Fig. 1.

In addition, a supply of picture-frame moulding will be required, glue, panel pins, a sheet of thin plywood for backing, a piece of good quality glass, a sheet of brown paper and a couple of screw-in picture rings.

The Moulding.—Picture moulding is inexpensive and can be bought in convenient lengths already rebated or recessed at the back for supporting the picture, glass and backing. The moulding can be obtained in various sections and finishes, some in plain hardwood, such as oak, others of more elaborate design.

Before purchasing the moulding, one should, of course, consider the type of picture it is intended to frame. Some pictures, especially water colours, etchings or photographs, look particularly well in narrow frames, while pictures of

a bolder type may be better suited in a frame of wider material. But these are just suggestions. Your moulding is determined by your personal taste.

Having obtained the moulding, the preliminary operation is to mark it to size. The marking should be made on

Fig. I

the rebated side of the wood, as indicated in Fig. 2, which shows the picture laid on the rebate. Note that an extra $\frac{1}{8}$ in. should be added to the length and width to enable the picture to fit easily into the frame and also for trimming up the mitred ends with the plane.

Sawing the Mitres. — The next operation calls for the use of a mitre block. Saw the right-hand end of a long piece first, by placing the moulding, rebated edge downwards and facing you, and in a position so that the mark coincides—that is, is in line—with the saw-slot in the mitre block.

Press the work tightly against the block with the left hand, insert the saw into the slot and saw downwards very carefully and squarely, otherwise the teeth of the saw will possibly cut into the block. This process is pictured in Fig. 3. Now cut the other end of the moulding, using the opposite slot in the mitre block. Make sure that the saw is sharp. Then trim the ends true to length by means of the plane and mitre shooting board, as illustrated in Fig. 4. Before planing the mitred ends, however, give the cutting iron of the plane a rub on an oilstone, as it must be very keen and finely set. Do not remove too much wood. The object of the planing is to smooth the ends and remove any small inequalities left by the saw.

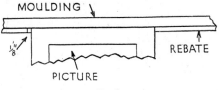

Fig. 2

At this stage it will be as well to verify the correctness of the length of the piece—which may be the top or bottom member of the frame—by placing the edge of the picture into the rebate. If correct, the corresponding long member may be marked from the prepared one, and then sawn and planed as before.

Treat the side pieces in precisely the same manner.

Each piece and its fellow member can now be tested for squareness, as it is essential that the corners be absolutely square.

If they are a trifle out of truth, they may be rectified with the aid of a plane.

Joining the Frame.—The members are now ready for fixing together. If the frame happens to be narrow tube glue may be used instead of ordinary glue which takes some time to prepare. But if several frames are to be made up at the same time, it will be more economical to use ordinary glue or one of

Fig. 3

the proprietory cold glues, that is, a liquid glue applied cold.

In using tube glue, all that is necessary is to apply a thin film on each face to be joined, press the pieces firmly together and then cramp the frame in a home-made cramp. Ordinary Scotch glue needs to be applied extremely hot and if this is used for joining the ends of the moulding, it is an advantage to warm them prior to applying the glue.

When dealing with a comparatively large frame it will be necessary to reinforce the glued joints by means of nails driven in at the corners as indicated in Fig. 5, and in order to prevent the nails splitting the wood, small holes should be bored with a fine bradawl to receive them. The nail-holes should, of course, be made before applying the glue. If the moulding is wide, use two nails at each joint, instead of one.

The frame must not be handled until

the glue has set hard, which usually takes at least a day.

When dry, cut the glass a trifle less in length and width than that between the rebates, as it should be an easy fit. The glass can be cut to size where it is purchased, or it may be that a piece of glass taken from an old picture frame, when cut, would answer the purpose.

A good quality glass-cutter of the wheel type will serve for cutting the glass, unless a glazier's diamond tool is available. When using a wheel cutter, lubricate the cutting-edge of the wheel with a spot or two of paraffin, support

Fig. 5

Fig. 4

the glass on a truly flat surface such as a drawing board, covering this with a thickish cloth.

Clean the glass thoroughly, insert the picture and cut a piece of thin plywood to fit the back. Fix this by thin panel pins, or square-cut tapered sprigs, sold for the purpose. Old gramophone needles are also good.

To keep dust out of the frame, cut a stout piece of brown paper which will cover the back entirely and slightly damp the surface and then glue the paper down. In drying, the damp surface contracts and stretches the paper taut.

The final item is to fix the hanging rings at the back.

Using Mounts.—Some pictures look better if a mount is added. This can be placed either between the picture and the glass or in close contact with the glass. Such mounts should not be too thin and should consist of good quality card. The surface of mounts of poor quality will soon deteriorate and become spotty and discoloured.

Fig. 6 shows how a horizontal picture should be arranged. Note that there is

Fig. 6

a wider margin at the bottom than at the top of the mount. This method of arranging the mount is far preferable to having margins of equal width all round. This applies more especially to pictures which are mounted vertically; an example of such is illustrated at Fig. 7.

Before cutting the mount, it is a good plan to cut one or two paper models of different sizes so that an idea can be gained of how the picture will appear when completed.

In cutting out the interior of a mount, a proper mount-cutting knife should be employed. This instrument has a blade of special shape. A knife of this type can be purchased for about half a crown at most tool shops, and is a good invest-

Fig. 7

ment when a number of mounts have to be cut.

The interior edge of the opening should be bevelled and Fig. 8 shows how the knife is held when cutting the bevel, while Fig. 9 indicates the position of the knife when trimming edges.

For photographs a frame made on similar lines to that shown in Fig. 10 is excellent. Ordinary picture frame

moulding is not employed in its construction, but the frame members A, B, C and D are built up of oak or other

Fig. 8

suitable hardwood, $1\frac{1}{4}$ in. wide $\times \frac{3}{4}$ in. thick, the front inner edges being slightly bevelled, while the backs are rebated $\frac{3}{8}$ in. wide and $\frac{1}{2}$ in. deep. These parts are fixed together by means of single dowels and glue.

The two vertical pieces E and F are $\frac{3}{4}$ in. wide and $\frac{1}{4}$ in. thick and are glued and dowelled by means of headless nails to the top and bottom members A and B. To give the frame a pleasing appearance, a shaped pediment G is fixed to the top and a plinth H at the bottom. A strip of oak, I, 1 in. wide $\times \frac{1}{4}$ in. thick with rounded front edges is fixed between the top of the frame and the lower edge of the pediment, and a similar strip at the bottom. These strips are fixed flush with the back of the frame so that they project $\frac{1}{4}$ in. in the front. The pediment and plinth are both fixed by $\frac{1}{4}$ in. diameter dowels glued in holes bored to receive them. A piece of glass and a suitable mount of either white or tinted card completes the job.

Passe-partout Frames.—Framing pictures with narrow adhesive binding, familiarly known as passe-partout, is very simple, and very effective. All that is required is the binding, obtainable in sixpenny rolls, and in various colours, a piece of glass, a backing of thick cardboard and possibly a mount, and one, or perhaps two hangers. A pair of scissors, penknife, glass-cutter and straight-edge are all that is required so far as tools are concerned.

Two types of hangers are obtainable. One is simply stuck on to the back of the frame and is only suitable for small light frames while the other is fastened to the back by means of metal clips and is suitable for a somewhat heavier frame. It is fitted to the back after the cardboard has been cut to size and before fitting the glass.

After having procured a piece of glass of the required dimensions, cut the backing to size by using either a mount-cutting knife or a sharp, strong pen-knife using preferably a metal straight-edge as a guide. Then cut from the spool two lengths of binding $\frac{1}{2}$ in. longer than the long edges of the glass and two pieces for the shorter ones.

Slightly moisten the face of one of the short lengths of binding with a piece of clean rag or wadding dipped in water, and then turn it over and wet the adhesive side. Allow enough time for the gum to become tacky and then lay the glass, picture and backing complete, face downwards on the binding, making sure that the edge of the binding is parallel to the edge of the glass. The margin on the face of the glass should be about $\frac{1}{4}$ in. wide, depending upon the size of the picture. This operation is indicated at A in Fig. 11. Next, turn the wet binding tightly on the cardboard at the back as illustrated at B and smooth it down evenly, taking care that the picture does not slip out of posi-

tion. Treat the opposite edge in exactly the same manner and turn the work face upwards in order to mitre the corners

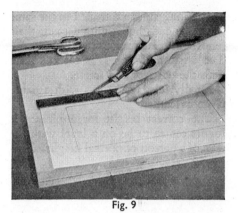

Fig. 9

of the binding. These should be at an angle of 45 deg., as in wooden picture frames. Use either a draughtsman's set square, or a piece of square cardboard

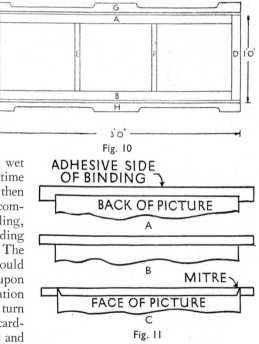

Fig. 10

Fig. 11

cut across diagonally and use one of them as a guide for the knife. The diagram at c in Fig. 10 shows the mitred corners. Remove the surplus binding at the ends, leaving about ⅛ in. so that the binding will come to the edge of the glass.

The long sides are treated in the same way; the ends being mitred to fit their fellow members exactly at the corners. The waste at the ends is cut off flush with the edge of the frame.

Finally, clean the glass with a damp chamois leather.

The correct height for a picture is for its centre to be on a level with the eyes of a person of normal height. This obviates the necessity of tilting the picture. Oil paintings look better if slightly tilted. The tops of the frames should form a straight line and not the bottoms.

Copper wire should be used for hanging pictures in preference to brass wire as the latter soon corrodes, sometimes with disastrous results. A very heavy picture should be suspended by two separate vertical chains.

Avoid, if possible, hanging glazed pictures directly opposite a window. The glass reflects and spoils the effect.

HOW TO MAKE AND FIX AWNINGS

COOLNESS inside the house, and a shady retreat outside, necessitate two different types of blind. There are many varieties of each, but the making and fixing of two kinds which are described here are both simple and cheap.

First we will deal with the awning type of blind, the kind which can be erected outside the house, against any sunny wall, window or door to form a shady arbour, as illustrated in Fig. 1.

The size of the awning naturally depends on the needs of the user, but for most purposes a spread of some 9 × 7 ft. will be found convenient. Striped canvas of any kind will serve, preferably waterproof. Heavy, unbleached calico may be used and is quite cheap.

Assembling Materials. — All the edges of the canvas or calico should be trimmed and hemmed and, if desired, a valance can be cut along one of the long edges to form an ornamental finish for the front.

In addition to the cloth there will be required a length of stout board, preferably beech, 4 in. wide × 1 in. thick and 1 ft. longer than the longest edge of the material (in this case the board would be 10 ft.); two poles about 6 ft. 6 in. high and of 1 in. diameter, fitted with metal ferrules and spikes at each end, and a pole also 1 in. in diameter and the length of the proposed awning, fitted with metal ferrules and metal eyes at each end; two pegs, guy ropes and toggles and four brass hooks and corresponding eyelets.

Fixing the Top.—The board or batten is fixed to the wall at the chosen spot at a height of about 8 ft., by means of plugs and screws. Do not use nails. The brass hooks are screwed into the board at regular intervals, the outer hooks being 7 in. from the ends of the board respectively, as shown at A in Fig. 2. The four eyelet holes are then attached to the material on the longest length (previously hemmed) to correspond.

An alternative method of fixing the top of the awning would be to use a further pole the length of the awning, of about 1 in. diameter and fitted with metal ferrules and metal spikes. A screw-eye at one end and a hook at the other are substituted for the four hooks

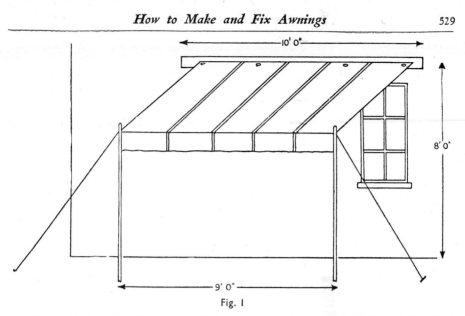

Fig. 1

on the wall board. The material is then glued round this roller and nailed, and the roller is slipped into its bearings. This method of fixing provides a more finished job. The arrangement is depicted at B in Fig. 2.

For the front fitting the other corresponding roller is used. This roller, it will be remembered, is fitted with metal eyes, which are meant to slip over the spikes on the upright supporting poles, as indicated at C in Fig. 2. The material may be fixed to the front roller or not, but for ease of fixing and rolling the blind after use it is better to have the material fixed.

This may be best done for a pole of 1 in. diameter by scoring two lines $3\frac{1}{7}$ in. apart on the upper surface of the cloth about 9 in. from the valance in the manner indicated at D in Fig. 2. The cloth is then strongly gathered together, folding it so that the lines meet on the upper side, thus making a tunnel on the underside into which the pole may be slipped and secured with galvanised tacks.

It is possible to dispense with the bottom roller (especially if a roller is used on the wall fitting) and the cloth may be fastened by means of eyelet holes which are slipped over spikes on the supports. But without the bottom roller there is bound to be some sagging and flapping.

The upright supports are merely fixed in the ground at the required distance and the loops of the guy ropes slipped over the spikes. If desired, these spikes can be finished off with a shaped finial. The toggles are slipped over the two pegs, and the awning should be perfectly steady and stable.

If poles and guy ropes do not appeal, a more ambitious awning can be made as illustrated in Fig. 3. Instead of the upright poles, wooden struts about 1 in. square and fitted with ferrules and metal eyes at both ends are used.

Supposing the height of the top batten has been fixed at 8 ft., then fix to the wall directly below each of the outermost metal hooks on the batten two blocks of beechwood, 8 in. long × 4 in. wide and $1\frac{1}{2}$ in. thick. To the exact centre of each block, screw a metal eye the same size as those on the struts.

When you want to fix the awning in position, the metal eyes on the base of the struts and on the boards are placed in juxtaposition and a wooden peg, fitting tightly, is knocked through both as at A in Fig. 3. The struts are then pulled down horizontally and the front

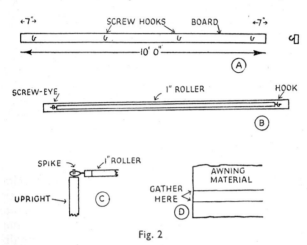

Fig. 2

roller, which has been fitted with spikes instead of eyes, is slipped in. The ends of the spikes on this roller must be fitted with finials or some sort of caps after they have been slipped through the eyes in the struts, or the roller will tend to fall out (Fig. 3, B). For this awning, too, the cloth must be fixed to the roller, so that the whole construction is mechanically knit together.

Sunblinds.—So much for the outside awning. The sunblind for shading the interior of a room is different, and one of the simplest, lightest and most compact is the Japanese reed blind, represented in Fig. 4.

Materials are two battens as long as the blind will be wide (and the width will, of course, vary for different purposes), about 1½ in. wide and ½ in. deep; a number of screw hooks and metal eyes; some small brass pulleys and an amount of thin cord and a considerable quantity of thin bamboo shoots or stout reed stems. Thin wood will, of course, do, but it is more expensive.

Take one of the battens and fix in it, on one of the ½ in. edges, two metal eyes, each about 4 in. from the ends. Fix one of the pulleys at right-angles to the length, as at A in Fig. 4.

Now take a quantity of bamboo or reed, cut to the length of the batten. Cut a piece of adhesive tape, such as that used by electricians, of the length you require the blind to be, place it flat on the bench or table, and carefully spread along its length the pieces of reed or bamboo at not more than $\frac{3}{8}$ in. apart. Now take some broad white tape or webbing about three times the length of the blind, and at one edge, about 4 in., start to bind the lengths together with a basket weave. When you reach the end, carry on back so that the slats are held together tightly. Repeat this at the other edge, fastening off the tape by gluing it round itself. Now take a further piece of 1½ in. batten for the base, fix in the centre another pulley B, Fig. 4, and attach the completed screen of reeds to the laths. This can be done by nailing or binding with waterproof tape.

Rolling Up the Blind.—The only remaining operation is to fix the cord. One end of the cord is first nailed to the back of the upper batten, and it is then brought round through the lower pulley, up the front of the blind and through the pulley at the top, threading through from the front to the back. Now if the cord is pulled the blind will roll up into a compact cylinder. The arrangement of the cord is shown at C in Fig. 4.

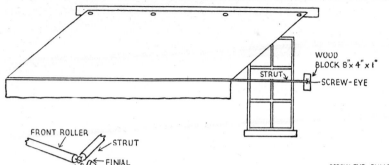

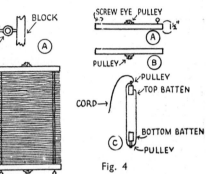

Fig. 3

FRONT ROLLER
STRUT
FINIAL
SPIKE
SCREW EYE

BLOCK
STRUT
PEG DRIVEN IN
(A)

SCREW EYE PULLEY
(A)
PULLEY (B)
PULLEY
TOP BATTEN
CORD→
BOTTOM BATTEN
(C) PULLEY

Fig. 4

The whole screen is attached by means of the metal eyes to brass hooks inserted at the top of the window or door it is desired to cover.

The making of this screen may seem laborious, but the result is worth the trouble. Painted once a year, screens made in this way will last a considerable time, and they do not split or warp, are very light and simple to fix and handle. The cost is small, especially if you happen to live in a district in which you can gather your own reeds. Dried and painted river reeds are quite satisfactory.

A useful sun curtain for protecting the front door consists of striped material as used for the awning cut to fit the doorway. The edges are machine stitched and the top hem is provided with brass curtain rings. These slide along a piece of electric light tubing, suspended between two adjustable brackets or screw-hooks above the door.

CLEANING AND REPAIRING LOCKS

It is not hard to understand the working of lock mechanism, for in the main the locks with which we are familiar are of simple types. Inside the house, for instance, two types are generally fitted: two bolt mortice locks on the main doors and two bolt rim locks where appearance is not important. In either type there is a latch bolt operated by a handle from either side and a dead bolt operated by a key.

Mortice Locks.—The usual type of latch bolt (which is the bolt operated by the handle) is made to slide and is bevelled. This bevel is carefully computed to strike the plate fixed to the door frame easily and efficiently whether the handle is operated or not. Careful adjustment of the bevel has its disadvantage, however, in that if anything becomes slightly misplaced owing to warping the bolt will not act.

When this happens it will usually be found that the striking plate has shifted owing to warping of the wood or loosening of the screws. When the wood has warped the plate must be taken off, the original screw-holes plugged with wood, the correct position carefully computed, and the new fixing made. With the plate in position again it will be an easy matter to adjust the striking hollow with the aid of a sharp chisel.

This, of course, applies to mortice locks only. It will rarely be found that

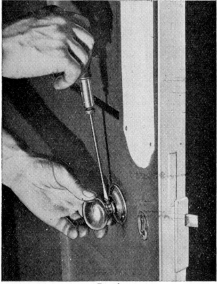

Fig. 1

the iron angle plate of a rim lock manages to slip out of position sufficiently to hinder easy working. If it does happen, usually all that is required is to tighten up the screws that have worked loose.

Loose Handles.—The only other fault which can arise on the outside of an ordinary lock is the annoying tendency of handles to work loose. Here again the cure is simple. Tighten the screws which hold the handle to the shaft, as indicated in Fig. 1. In chronic cases of handle rattle, it will sometimes be found efficacious to change the handles round, pressing them as tightly

as possible against the boss plate whilst rescrewing.

Before we proceed to the interior of the lock it may be remarked that, as a general rule, oil should be used very sparingly. A drop on the spindle holding the handles and another on the latch bolt (applied when it is fully extended) is occasionally beneficial, whilst the dead bolt should be wiped with an oily rag, but not plastered with grease.

Inside the Lock.—The same rule applies to the interior. If a bolt acts stiffly or harshly it does not need oil but cleaning. To clean a mortice lock, the screws on the door edge must be loosened and the lock drawn out of the door as a whole, as shown in Fig. 2, when it will generally be found that one side is easily removed, as in Fig. 3.

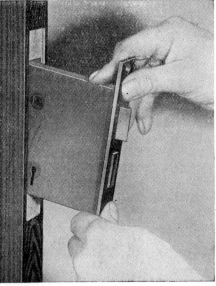

Fig. 2

A rim lock is easily unscrewed, after first removing the handles.

It will be found that the mechanism of the lock consists in the main of the following parts: a crank operated by

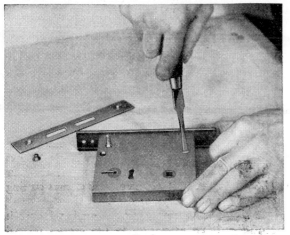

Fig. 3

Rust.—One of the greatest enemies of lock mechanism is rust, which is introduced to the inside of a lock through the key. The only cure for this is to take the lock to pieces, carefully noting the various positions and interlocking connections of the crank and spring, and take the rust off the affected parts with emery cloth. Then it is advisable to soak all the working parts in petrol for two or three hours, afterwards drying them thoroughly before they are replaced. The spring can be thoroughly soaked in a good light oil.

the door handle, a follower that imparts the thrust to the latch itself and a spring usually of the helical or coil compression type. In some old locks a V-spring may be found. In most cases of stiffness it will be found that the follower is choked with dirt. This is best cleaned out with a hard hair brush of suitable size dipped in petrol.

It is rarely that the spring is damaged, but if it is a locksmith had better be consulted. As a temporary measure, it may be found possible to fit the spring on to the stem of the latch bolt. A makeshift spring can easily be made from a section of an old clock spring.

When the key refuses to turn in a lock, or when the dead bolt is stiff or jammed, dirt will probably be found to be the cause again. Dirt reaches the key wards easily, and also tends to jam the slotted arm which controls the dead bolt. If the wards are bent it should be possible to straighten them by tapping very lightly and carefully with a hammer.

In most modern houses the lock fitted to the front door is of the cylinder type, Fig. 4, working through tumblers connected with the key plug. If any fault develops in a lock of this kind the key itself should be examined first to

Fig. 4

see if it is bent or cut, as the lock depends for its operation on the key being perfectly true. If the fault is in the lock itself it should be handed to an expert, for cylinder locks are very delicately adjusted. Rub the key of a cylinder lock occasionally with a paraffin rag, and it will be found that trouble rarely occurs. In any event, if the key sticks, do not try to force it, as this will damage the lock itself. The safe course is to keep both keys and locks clean and firmly fixed. An inspection of all locks in the house might be made once every six months when any slight fault that has appeared can be remedied.

HOW TO BIND A BOOK

S IMPLE bookbinding does not call for expensive tools and the materials are inexpensive.

For binding magazines, or books issued in parts, the tools required include a fine-toothed tenon saw, mallet or bookmaker's hammer, foot-rule, carpenter's try square, glue pot and brush, wide wood chisel, scissors and a needle for thread. The materials con-

Fig. 1

sist of a sheet or two of strong white paper, a sheet of tough brown paper, a few yards of 1 in. wide linen tape, a reel of strong white thread, two pieces of thick strawboard and some bookbinder's cloth and glue.

In addition to these items a sewing frame will be required and an improvised press. The sewing frame can be easily made by fixing three pieces of deal about 1¼ in. wide and ⅜ in. to ½ in. thick on to a base-board about 1 in. thick, as illustrated in Fig. 1, and the

press, Fig. 2, may consist of nothing more elaborate than a couple of pieces of plywood about ½ in. thick, and four 4 in. steel woodworker's cramps costing about sixpence each.

In constructing the sewing frame, it is an advantage to use screws instead of nails for fastening the parts together as it can then be taken to pieces when not in use.

Magazines.—Assuming that it is desired to bind a dozen magazines together, the first step is to place the magazines in their correct order and then remove the wire staples holding the leaves together. This can be done by opening the section at the middle, inserting the blade of a penknife under the ends of the wire, bending them up straight and withdrawing them from the

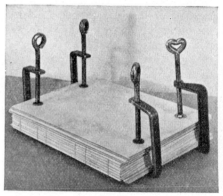

Fig. 2

back. Care should be taken not to damage the paper.

If the covers and insets in the magazines are not required, remove them but do not get the sections mixed up in so doing. Next make them into a neat pile, keeping the backs as well as the heads (as the top edges of books are called), flush, and place them between the press, allowing the backs to project just a trifle above the long edges of the work, and cramp them together.

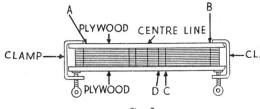

Fig. 3

Now mark the backs prior to sewing. A sharp soft pencil and a carpenter's try square should be used for this as it is essential that the lines at the back be truly at right angles to the sides. Scribe a line across the back, 1 in. from the top edge as at A in Fig. 3, and another B, at the same distance from the bottom edge. Then make a faint centre line and to the right of this line make two more lines C and D, one $1\frac{1}{2}$ in. from it and the other 1 in. farther away. Repeat the process on the left-hand side of the centre.

Now place the whole between the jaws of a bench vice and mark a series of shallow cuts, with a very fine saw, across the marked lines. The cuts are made simply to produce holes sufficiently large to allow the needle to pass through easily. On no account must the cuts be made deeper than to pass the middle sheet of paper. This is shown in Fig. 4.

The Sewing Frame. — The next operation calls for the use of the sewing frame as the parts have now to be sewn together. Place the first copy face downwards on the top of the base, keeping its back flush with the front edge of the wood, and cut off two

lengths of linen tape long enough to span the distance between the bottom edge of the base and the top of the frame, plus about 2 in. Fasten the linen strips vertically with the aid of four drawing pins, allowing 2 in. to overlap at the bottom. The strips should be so spaced that they coincide with the 1 in. spaced guide lines on the back of the section.

Having threaded the needle push it through the first hole on the left, marked No. 1 in the diagram, Fig. 5, then back again via hole No. 2, then over the tape A through 3 and so on to the last hole.

Now place the next section face downwards on top of the first, pass the needle and thread through the corresponding hole and work back in the

Fig. 4

same way towards the original position. Keep the thread taut and lock the stitch when the row is completed by passing the thread beneath the stitch of the previous section and looping it.

Carry on in this way until all the sections have been stitched together, making sure that the thread passes over the tapes in each instance and that there is no slackness of thread.

Remove the drawing pins and cut the

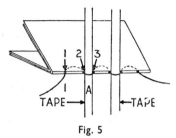

Fig. 5

tapes to length allowing about $1\frac{1}{2}$ in. to project beyond the sides.

Place the partly-made volume in the press so that the back projects a fraction of an inch beyond the edges, brush on a small quantity of hot glue to the back and allow it to dry.

Trimming. — The next operation calls for the use of a sharp wide wood chisel as the edges have to be trimmed. Pencil guide lines on the top sheet, making sure that the lines are square to each other as otherwise the book will not be square when finished. First trim the head or top edge of the book. To do this, place the volume in the press, allowing the bottom board to project an inch or so beyond the edge to be trimmed. Insert a piece of stout cardboard between the underside of the book and the bottom board to protect the latter when cutting. The edge of the upper board should line up with the guide line and then the whole should be cramped together.

Make a number of cuts with the chisel, taking off a little at a time right across the paper, drawing the tool towards you and keeping the fore part of the cutting-edge lifted a trifle, as indicated in Fig. 6.

If the cutting-edge of the chisel appears to drag when cutting, give it

a few rubs on an oilstone, as it is essential that the tool be keen. A blunt chisel will tear the paper instead of cutting it.

Next treat the tail, or bottom edge, and finally the fore edge, as the front edge is called.

Rounding and Backing.—Having accomplished the most difficult part of the process, the back should be rounded. Plane a bevel on a long edge of each board and place the book between the boards allowing the back to project about $\frac{1}{8}$ in. beyond the bevelled edges. Apply the cramps, making sure that the screws are screwed up very tightly and then round the back with a mallet as indicated in Fig. 7.

Cut three or four pieces of stout brown paper of the same length and width as the back and glue them on, one after the other, to the back.

From a sheet of strong white paper cut a couple of double fly-leaves of the same length and width as the book and

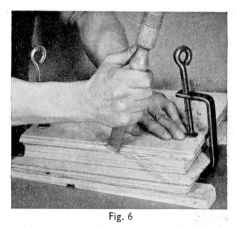

Fig. 6

apply a little glue to the back of the fly-leaf along a narrow margin of not more than $\frac{1}{8}$ in. wide from the folded edge. Stick this in position, glue the undersides of the tapes and fasten them down securely to the outer fly-leaf. Repeat the operation on the other side of the book and cut off the outer leaves about ¼ in. beyond the tape.

The cover consists of two pieces of thick strawboard cut to overlap the three outer edges of the book, by ⅛ in. Mark guide lines on the pieces and cut them with a sharp penknife, using a straight-edge. Do not attempt to cut through the strawboard in one stroke, but make a series of light cuts, keeping the blade square to the straight-edge.

Insert a piece of waste paper under the narrow fly-leaf and give the latter a coat of glue. Carefully place the strawboard in position, stick it down and fix the bottom one similarly.

Now cut a couple of strips of tape about 2 in. long. Apply a coat of glue to one face of each, fold them lengthwise so that they now form two strips of double the thickness and half the width of the original strips. Glue the folded strips to the top and bottom respectively at the back. These strips, or head bands as they are called, reinforce the top and bottom of the back.

Cloth Covering.—The book is now ready to receive the cloth. Special care is needed in cutting this, and it should be sufficiently large to cover the volume in one piece, plus ½ in. for turning over the six edges of the strawboards and about ³⁄₁₆ in. at the top and bottom of the back. Before cutting the cloth, it is a good plan to make a paper pattern as a guide.

Fig. 7

Having cut the cloth to shape, brush some glue on the outer faces of the covers and also on the back, place the covering material carefully in position and smooth it firmly with a clean cloth to exclude air bubbles.

Apply the glue to the narrow margins left for turning in and stick them down securely to the edges and inside faces of the strawboards.

The final operation consists of preparing two double fly-leaves of the same size as the trimmed book, gluing one leaf of each and sticking them firmly to the inner faces of the strawboards.

PHOTOGRAPHIC APPLIANCES

AMATEUR photographers will find the developing bench represented in Fig. 1 and working drawings, Figs. 2, 3 and 4, quite easy to construct.

The bench is built in the form of a table, at the back of which are three shelves for accommodating items such as bottles of chemicals, clock, measuring glass, thermometer and the usual items that comprise the developing equipment.

All parts are screwed together for two reasons. First, the use of screws reduces the amount of constructional work to a minimum without sacrificing strength and, secondly, screws enable the bench

Fig. I

to be taken apart and stored in a small space.

In order to save the table top from liquid stains it should be protected by a suitable material. Linoleum answers the purpose, but white glazed tiles make an excellent surface.

For the former, the bench top should be planed on both sides, but it will be better, with tiles, to leave the upper face unplaned as the comparatively rough surface will give a more satisfactory key to the glue with which the tiles are fixed.

The bench top measures 3 ft. long × 1 ft. 6 in. wide and may be constructed by fastening one or more boards together by means of cross-battens $1\frac{1}{2}$ in. wide × $\frac{3}{4}$ in. thick, screwed from the underside, to obtain the width, unless a single piece of $\frac{3}{4}$ in. thick whitewood is used, which eliminates the use of battens. The top member is fixed to the top rails that

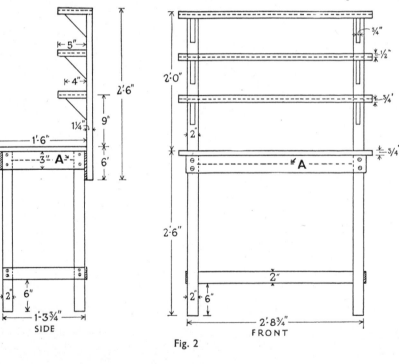

SIDE

FRONT

Fig. 2

support the legs by means of $1\frac{1}{2} \times 1$ in. battens, as indicated by the dotted lines at A in Fig. 2.

A Tiled Top.—If glazed tiles are used, those measuring $6 \times 6 \times \frac{1}{4}$ in. thick,

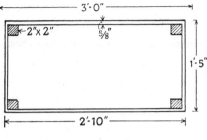

ARRANGEMENT OF LEGS

Fig. 3

costing about twopence each and obtainable at most cheap stores, will answer the purpose admirably. Eighteen tiles involving an outlay of three shillings will be required.

The tiles are simply glued into a shallow tray formed by screwing narrow fillets of wood to the edges of the bench top, details of which are clearly shown in Fig. 4.

As the edges of the tiles should butt together as closely as possible, it is a good plan to place them temporarily in position on the bench top before trimming the latter to size, marking the top and then finishing it to size, after which the fillets can be screwed to the edges.

The fillets are $\frac{3}{8}$ in. thick and 1 in. wide and project $\frac{1}{4}$ in. above the wooden face of the bench top so that the top edges of the fillets are flush with the tiled surface.

To fix the tiles, prepare some Scotch glue and soak the tiles in warm water so that they do not chill the glue when lain on.

Brush some glue on the underside of a tile and also on the table top at the position where the first tile is to be

fixed. Stick the tile down and proceed with the next and so on until the whole of the tiles are fixed, tapping each one down on its bed of glue as the work advances so that they are quite even. Allow the glue to harden for a day and then fill the interstices with plaster-of-Paris and water mixed to the constituency of cream.

The Bench.—The legs and rails which support the bench top are sawn and trimmed to length, care being taken to see that the ends are square. Screw-holes are bored in the rails and the rails screwed to the legs by means of $1\frac{1}{2}$ in. No. 8 iron screws having countersunk heads. Fig. 3 shows the arrangement of the legs and rails.

Having assembled the legs and rails, fix the table top by driving screws through the projecting battens on the underside into the inside faces of the top rails.

Now prepare and fix the back sup-

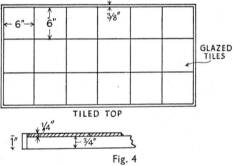

TILED TOP

GLAZED TILES

Fig. 4

ports. These are 2 ft. 6 in. long $\times 2$ in. wide and $1\frac{1}{4}$ in. thick and are screwed to the back rail and legs as shown, a small block of wood $\frac{5}{8}$ in. thick being inserted between the supports and legs to give extra stability.

If the top is tiled, the front of the supports will have to be recessed $\frac{3}{8}$ in. deep to clear the back fillets of the tray.

The top shelf is screwed into the top of the back uprights and is supported on a pair of $4 \times \frac{3}{4}$ in. triangular wooden brackets, as shown. The other two shelves are also supported on similar brackets, all of which are fixed to the

Fig. 5

uprights by screws driven in from the back.

In order to prevent bottles and other equipment from slipping off the shelves, wood fillets $\frac{1}{4}$ in. thick are bradded to the edges all round.

Lighting Details. — The illustration shown at Fig. 5 represents a useful darkroom electric-light fixture suitable for use with the developing bench previously dealt with.

As will be seen, the fixture is provided with two lampholders—one for accommodating a ruby or dark green lamp bulb for use when developing, changing plates or films, and other processes demanding such lights, and the other for taking an ordinary lamp for general lighting purposes.

The lamps are so arranged that they operate from a single two-way switch which is fixed in front of the fitting, as shown in the constructional drawing Fig. 6.

The holders are of the batten type and are mounted upon hardwood or deal

6 in. long $\times \frac{1}{2}$ in. thick which is screwed at right-angles to an arm consisting of a piece of wood $9\frac{1}{2}$ in. long and $\frac{1}{2}$ in. thick. At the other end is screwed a light metal woodworker's cramp, costing a few pence.

The method of wiring up the lampholders and switch is shown at A in Fig. 6. One end of a twin flexible cable is connected to a lampholder adaptor, while one wire is connected to the common terminal of the switch. The end of the other wire is connected to one terminal of each lampholder, the connection between the two holders being carried out in a short single piece of flex. Pieces of single flex connect the remaining unoccupied terminals of the switch to the corresponding terminals of each lampholder.

Before attaching the fitting to the top shelf of the developing bench, it will be

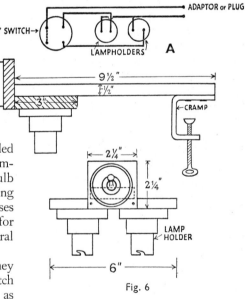

Fig. 6

necessary to make a recess in the front fillet to enable the arm to lie flat on the top of the shelf.

A Floodlight.—The adjustable floodlight fitting illustrated in Fig. 7 will appeal to those who do photography by artificial light.

The top portion, A in Fig. 8, carrying the lampholder and reflector slides into the lower part B, the former being kept at any desired position within

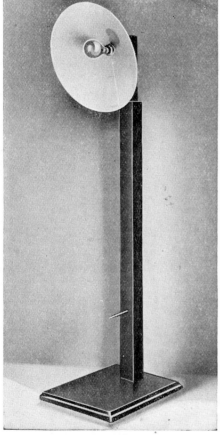

Fig. 7

its limits by means of a peg inserted into one of a series of holes in the latter.

The lower member is 3 ft. long and is built up of strips of hardwood $\frac{3}{8}$ in. thick, in the manner indicated at C in Fig. 8. The strips are simply screwed together and fixed to a deal base measur-

ing 15 in. long × 12 in. wide and 1 in. thick.

When planing the strips, make sure that the edges are quite square with the faces or trouble will be experienced when fitting the upper sliding member A. The latter must also be square, and should be planed so that it is a good sliding fit in the tube.

Before assembling the tube, bore a series of holes $\frac{1}{4}$ in. diameter at convenient distances apart in either the front or back strip. These holes are for accommodating a 4 in. length of $\frac{1}{4}$ in. in diameter dowel or a piece of hardwood shaped to these dimensions. The lower end of A rests on the peg and keeps it at the desired height.

The sliding member is morticed on the front face at a distance of about 1 in. from the top, to receive the end of a piece of hardwood 1 in. wide × $\frac{1}{2}$ in. thick. This piece of hardwood is glued into the mortice and is attached to the lampholder base by means of a bolt and wing-nut which allows the lampholder to be tilted up or down and locked in position.

The mounting or base for the lampholder is merely a piece of wood 3 in. square × $\frac{3}{8}$ in. thick at the back of which is fixed a slotted piece of hardwood 1 × 1 in. and about $1\frac{1}{2}$ in. in length, as shown at D in Fig. 8.

A suitable reflector, shown dotted, can be cut from a piece of plain white cardboard and the edges fastened together with paper fasteners or glue.

The base is a piece of deal 15 in. long × 12 in. wide and 1 in. thick. The upright is set back from the front edge, as shown to prevent the standard from tilting forward due to the weight at the top.

There are several methods of attaching the standard to the base. One way is to glue a block of wood into the bottom of the tube and fix the base to it by

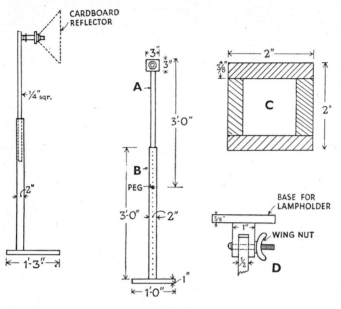

Fig. 8

means of long screws driven in from the underside. Another method is to mortice the base and glue the end of the standard into it. Yet another way is to use plain iron brackets.

One end of a suitable length of twin flexible wire is connected to the lamp-holder and the other to either a plug-top or lamp-holder.

ADHESIVES AND PLASTICS

WATERPROOF GLUE.—An excellent waterproof glue for repairing leather, upholstery and wood can be made with orange shellac, clean india-rubber and ether. Dissolve three parts by weight of shellac in an earthenware vessel and one part by weight of pure india-rubber in another. Add a small quantity of ether to each and place them in a bowl of hot water. Allow the jars to remain in the bowl until the ingredients have dissolved, adding more hot water if necessary. When ready, mix equal parts together and apply with a brush. If the adhesive should be too thick, a small quantity of ether may be added.

Cellulose Cement.—This cement is made by dissolving pure celluloid cuttings in amylacetate, a chemical smelling of pear drops, and is used for joining and repairing celluloid.

As amylacetate is extremely volatile and inflammable, it must be kept away from naked lights. The cuttings should be as small as possible to dissolve quickly. Put the cuttings in an earthenware jar, add a small quantity of amylacetate and place the lid on the jar to prevent evaporation. When ready, it can be thinned with the chemical.

In using celluloid cement, it is essential that the pieces to be joined be clean. This should be done by scraping or by means of fine glass-paper. The adhesive should be applied with a small clean brush to the surfaces to be joined and allowed to get tacky. If possible, cramp the treated parts together or place weights on them until perfectly dry.

Photographic Mountant.—Ordinary flour paste should not be used for mounting photographs as it may discolour the prints. An adhesive which will not have detrimental effects can be made by placing $\frac{1}{4}$ oz. gelatine in a pint of water, allowing it to swell and then dissolving it by heating. To this add a thin cream consisting of arrowroot and water and allow the mixture to boil for a few minutes. When cold, add 2 oz. methylated spirits, mix well and add one or two drops of oil of cloves.

This adhesive will keep sweet for a long time if tightly corked up.

plaster-of-paris makes a good cement for mending broken china ornaments and similar objects which do not have to withstand heat.

Putty for Steel-framed Windows.—Ordinary glazier's putty, consisting of whiting and linseed oil, is unsuitable for fixing glass in steel frame windows. A quick-setting putty for this purpose is prepared by making a thick paste of lithage and glycerine. The glycerine should be heated before use to expel any water. This putty will be found useful

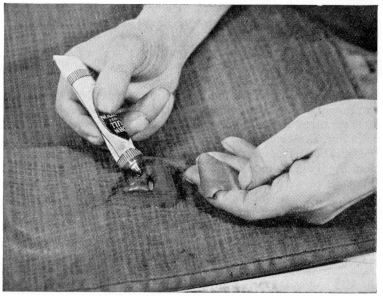

Fig. I

Cement for Refixing Knife Handles.—Ordinary powdered resin makes a good cement for refixing knife handles. Place the resin in a tin container and melt it slowly over a gas stove. Scrape out the old cement from the handle and warm the latter by standing it upright in hot water. Prevent water entering the hole. Heat the tang of the knife, fill the hole with melted resin, insert the tang and allow the resin to harden.

Adhesives for Mending Broken China.—The white of an egg added to

for aquaria and for attaching iron to wood and glass.

Plastic Wood.—Plastic wood is a pliable material similar to putty and can be moulded to any shape. It is a cellulose product and can be obtained in tubes and tins in various wood colours. Plastic wood is ideal for filling in joints, cracks and holes in woodwork.

When set, it can be planed, chiselled and stained, polished or painted in the same way as ordinary wood.

As plastic wood shrinks a little during drying, it is advisable when dealing with comparatively large holes, etc., to apply a little more than is necessary to fill the cavity and, when set, to remove the surplus with a plane or sharp chisel. Replace the lid of the container as soon as the required amount has been withdrawn. The preparation soon loses pliability if exposed for long to the air.

Plastic wood that has become too hard for easy use can be softened with a special fluid.

Rubber Solution.—Rubber solution can be obtained ready prepared in tubes and tins. It can be made at home by dissolving pure rubber in benzine.

It is used for joining and repairing rubber articles such as inner tubes of cycle tyres and rubber mackintoshes. Before applying the solution, clean the surfaces and apply a thin film of solution to the patch as well as the defective part, as shown in Fig. 1. Allow the solution to become tacky and then place the patch in position. Apply pressure to the parts with weights or clips and allow to set.

Paste for Hanging Wallpaper.— Paste for hanging wallpaper is made in the following way. In a clean bucket or large bowl, place $\frac{1}{2}$ quart of ordinary wheaten flour, not the self raising, and add sufficient cold water to make it into a thickish paste. Dissolve a small piece of glue in boiling water and add this to the mixture. Place the receptacle containing the paste on a stove and bring it gently to the boil, stirring it all the time to prevent burning. Allow the paste to cool and strain it through muslin to remove lumps. Add a pinch or two of powdered alum. This will prevent the paste turning bad on paper.

When using paste for wallpaper, do not hang the piece immediately after pasting, but allow it to get tacky; tenacity will thereby be increased.

Another good adhesive for use with wallpaper is a preparation made from rye flour. This is obtained in small bags and cartons under various trade names. Place some cold water into a bucket, add sufficient powder to the water, not vice versa, until the correct consistency is obtained. The mixture must be stirred while being made.

Keene's Cement.—This is a medium for stopping up cracks in plastered ceilings and walls which produces a hard and durable surface. As it sets quickly after having been mixed with water, only a little should be made at a time.

Before preparing the cement, which is a light pink powder, it is advisable to make a hawk for mixing and handling it. This is a flat piece of wood, planed on the face, nailed to a short piece of wood underneath to form a handle. As a makeshift, the cement could be mixed on a roofing slate, but this is not so convenient as the hawk.

Hold the hawk in the left hand, place a small quantity of powder in the centre so that it forms a mound. Make a crater and pour in a small amount of water. Work the cement from the sides of the crater into the water with the pointed end of a small plasterer's trowel. The mixture should not be sloppy.

Before applying the cement, wet the work. This is important as cement will not adhere properly to a dry surface and will fall away when set. The cement is applied with a plasterer's trowel or an old table knife.

BUILDING A GRAMOPHONE

A PORTABLE gramophone is illustrated in Fig. 1, with the overall dimensions in Fig. 2. As the fittings are not of a standard size, it is advisable to have every part to hand before beginning constructional work so that items which do not tally with the accompanying drawings may be allowed for.

Below is a list of parts required for the construction of the case.

Necessary Purchases.—Mechanical parts needed are one double spring-driven gramophone motor, such as a

Start with the lower part of the case. This is a simple plywood box, the constructional details and dimensions of which are shown in Fig. 3. Glued butt-joints are used for fixing the sides and ends together, and the bottom is fixed to these parts by means of screws. A ½ in. square fillet is glued and screwed to the sides and bottom as shown, to give additional strength, while similar fillets are screwed and glued 1 in. below the upper edges of the case to support the motor board.

No.	Size in in.	Material	For
2	$16 \times 11\frac{3}{4} \times \frac{3}{16}$ ..	3 ply wood	Top of lid and bottom of case
2	$16 \times 4\frac{9}{16} \times \frac{1}{4}$ ..	5 ,, ,, ...	Sides of lower part of case
2	$11\frac{1}{4} \times 4\frac{9}{16} \times \frac{1}{4}$ ..	5 ,, ,, ...	Ends of lower part of case
2	$16 \times 2\frac{5}{16} \times \frac{3}{8}$ ..	5 ,, ,, ...	Sides of lid
2	$11 \times 2\frac{5}{16} \times \frac{3}{8}$ ..	5 ,, ,, ...	Ends of lid
1	$15\frac{1}{2} \times 11\frac{1}{4} \times \frac{3}{8}$ ..	5 ,, ,, ...	Motor-board
10 ft.	$\frac{1}{2} \times \frac{1}{2}$	Hardwood	Fillets
1	24×19 (approx.)	Rexine or leather-cloth	Lower part of case
1	22×17 ,,	,, ,,	Lid
1	12×16 ,,	,, ,,	Motor-board
1	12×16 ,,	,, ,,	Lid lining
1	$2\frac{1}{4} \times 46$,,	,, ,,	Lid lining, sides and ends
1	18×11 ,,	Sheet zinc	Internal horn
1	$42 \times 3\frac{1}{2}$,,	,, ...	,,
1	17×11 ,,	,, ...	,,
1	$2\frac{1}{4} \times 2\frac{1}{8} \times \frac{3}{8}$ ..	Soft sponge rubber ..	Horn mounting

Garrard, with 10 in. turntable, speed regulator, a winding handle and escutcheon for same ; a swan-neck tone arm, sound box to fit same, and the following minor accessories: a brake, needle bowl, tone-arm clip, two winding-handle clips, two strap hinges and leather carrying handle, two spring-catch fasteners, screws, nuts and bolts for fixing the hinges and carrying handle, and a small quantity of glue.

The illustration shows how the ends of two of these fillets are cut away to clear the mouth of the horn, while a shaped vertical piece A (Fig. 3) takes the place of a longer vertical fillet as fitted in the other corners.

All the fixing screws with the exception of four above the level of the motor board fillets, are driven through the plywood into the fillets and not into the edges of the plywood. A

S

couple of dozen $\frac{3}{4}$ in. No. 6 counter-sunk-headed wood screws and four $\frac{5}{8}$ in. No. 2 screws will be required for fixing the ends to the sides. This part of the work should be done before attempting to fix the bottom. The operations for making the box are as follows.

1. Cut wood to size. 2. Mark positions where fillets are to come. 3. Fix fillets to sides and ends. 4. Assemble sides to ends. 5. Fit bottom with $\frac{1}{2}$ in. No. 2 screws.

Making the Lid.—The construction

Fig. I

of the lid is slightly more involved as three of the five plys of the side and end pieces are cut away as shown at A in Fig. 4, thus leaving a projection $\frac{1}{4}$ in. deep for keeping the lid in position when closed.

The easiest way of forming the projection is to mark the positions at each end of the side and end pieces and clamp the work between two strips of wood about 18 in. long and $1\frac{1}{2}$ in.

wide and $\frac{1}{2}$ in. thick. Fix the upper edge of the top strip so that it coincides with the marks on the work and use the edge for guiding a fine-toothed tenon saw. Saw very carefully to a depth of 1 ply and remove the waste with a chisel. Treat the second and then the third plys in the same way, taking care not to damage the fourth and fifth laminations.

The sides and ends may now be fastened together by means of $\frac{3}{4}$ in. No. 3 countersunk-headed screws, and then the top fixed in position by the use of $\frac{1}{2}$ in. No. 2 screws.

Placing the Motor.—In making the motor board, Fig. 5, the hole A above which the tone-arm is fixed, should not be bored until the motor and turn-table have been temporarily attached to the board, as the needle in the sound-box has to be correctly tracked. To do this, first fix the sound-box to the tone-arm and insert a needle. Place the point of the needle $\frac{1}{16}$ in. in front of the turn-table spindle, swinging the opposite end of the tone-arm round until it is central to the line B. This gives the distance X. The sound-box and tone-arm will now be in their normal positions. The outline of the base of the tone-arm can now be marked on the wood and the wood bored to suit.

As gramophone motors vary in shape and size, only the position of the spindle is shown in the drawing. The winding handle must be square to either the right-hand side or the front, as the case may be. Some idea of how the motor is fixed will be gathered from Fig. 6 which shows the motor fixed to the mounting board.

Fig. 7 shows an illustration of the lower case with the motor board removed, revealing the horn. Details of this are given in Fig. 8, but the dimensions indicated may have to be varied to suit the measurements x in Fig. 5, and to clear the motor. There should be ample clearance between the narrow part of the horn A, Fig. 8, and the winding shaft.

The Horn.—Make a full-sized model of the horn with thin cardboard and

the narrow end over the rectangular-shaped ring, as shown at B in Fig. 8, and solder these parts together.

A wood plug and wire may now be used to hold the four sides in place. Run a fillet of solder down each seam, remove the plug and repeat the operation until the whole horn is completed. Before applying solder, see that the

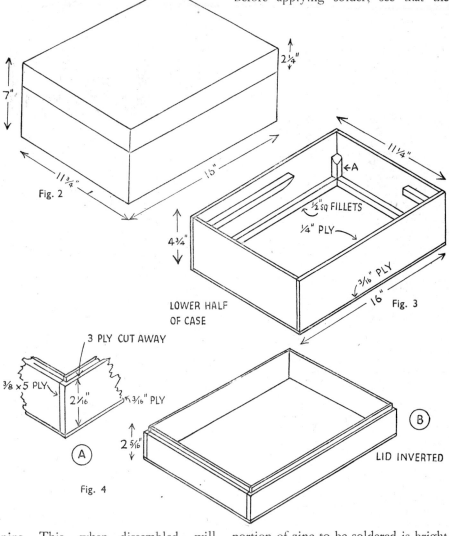

Fig. 2

2¼"

7"

11¾"

15"

4¾"

11¼"

←A

½" sq FILLETS

¼" PLY

3/16" PLY

16"

Fig. 3

LOWER HALF
OF CASE

3 PLY CUT AWAY

⅜ x 5 PLY

2⅛"

3/16" PLY

2 5/16"

A

Fig. 4

B

LID INVERTED

pins. This, when dissembled, will serve as templates for cutting the zinc. Cut the zinc to size, bend the flanges at

portion of zinc to be soldered is bright and clean. Scrape the parts if necessary and use a soldering flux.

Remove all grease, and paint the horn dull black on the outside and as far into the mouth as possible.

The narrow end of the horn is wedged between the motor board and flanged ring by means of a sponge-rubber washer. If rigidity cannot be secured by this method, pack some folded rag between the bottom of the horn and the bottom of the case.

Now mark where the winding crank spindle will pass through the side of the case and drill the hole.

Covering the Case.—Leather-cloth can be used for covering the case. First cut out the material to size, apply glue to the bottom of the lower section of the case and place it in the centre of the piece measuring 24 × 24 in. Allow the glue to set, and turn up the leather-cloth at the ends of the case. Carefully cut the cloth perpendicularly close to

Fig. 6

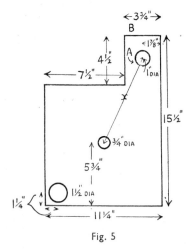

Fig. 5

the case and stick the cloth to the sides. There will now remain a square of cloth in extension to the sides. This should be cut off 1 in. from the end of the case. Turn the remaining pieces round the ends and stick them down. Each end piece may now be glued in position.

The next procedure is to glue the remaining portions of the cloth, turn them over the top edge of the case and

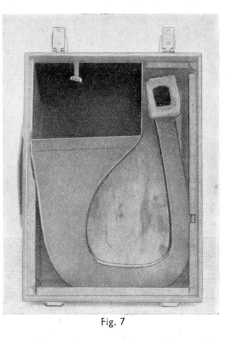

Fig. 7

stick them down inside as far as the fillets.

It should be noted that if a thick covering material is employed it may be necessary to pare down the thickness at the joints. This can be done with a razor blade.

The lid is covered in the same way except that the cloth is turned in only as far as the shoulder. The piece for the underside of the lid is then glued in position, and this is followed by fixing a suitable lining strip at the sides and ends.

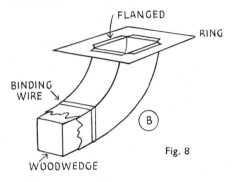

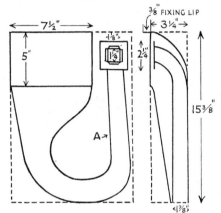

Fig. 8

After sticking the covering on top of the motor board, cut out the holes for the tone-arm and the motor spindle, and drill a hole for a needle bowl, which should be of the unspillable type.

Drill small holes in the back of the lower case and the lid, and fix the hinges with small bolts and nuts.

The position of the carrying handle is in the centre of a whole side including the lid. It is fixed in the same way as the hinges, that is, by small bolts and nuts. To give additional strength between the case and the handle, a piece of zinc, with suitable holes to allow the bolts to pass, can be used under the nuts.

The fasteners and hinges should be fitted when the lid is closed.

The motor board can now be screwed down to the supporting fillets, the tone-arm properly mounted and the sound-box fitted. A clip must be fixed to the back of the case to keep the tone-arm in position when not in use, and a pair of clips screwed to the back of the lid to house the winding crank. The final operation consists of fitting the escutcheon over the winding spindle hole.

OIL-BURNING APPLIANCES

THE old form of oil lamp still found in country districts burns paraffin direct from a wick and costs as much as electricity at fourpence per unit. This lamp is used for lighting because of its low initial cost, and for heating because of its simplicity. The important thing is to keep it clean.

Trimming the Wick.—Even with the little paraffin lamps used for night lights and lofts, consistent attention to the wick is necessary. After every twelve hours of burning the wick should be trimmed, and the trimming should be done so that the wick is convex, as indicated at A in Fig. 1. At least 3 in. of the wick should be immersed in the oil chamber, which should be kept fairly full.

If the lamp smokes, it is probably

because the wick is too high or has burned unevenly. With an oil lamp using a double wick, the two wicks should be trimmed together and turned to the same height for use. If a glass chimney is used, it should be kept clean and should never be put on the lamp when cold. This is liable to crack the glass. To avoid this, warm the glass slightly in the hands before placing over the flame.

If a circular wick is used the trimming of the wick should be level. It is difficult to trim a circular wick accurately with only the eye as guide, and it will be found convenient to keep a piece of cardboard with a circular hole cut in it which will fit just over the wick. It is then easy to trim off the jagged edges, leaving a level surface. Never turn wicks up before lighting; always afterwards. When the lamp has not been

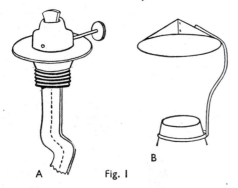

Fig. I

used for some time, drop a little paraffin on the burning surface of the wick before lighting. This will prevent the wick being charred through dryness.

Incandescent Lamps.—The modern oil lamp is incandescent, working on the same principle as the incandescent gas burner. In all types of incandescent oil lamps there is a passage admitting air in the central tube in which the wick is mounted, and the wick is capped by a fitting of varying shape and size which diverts the air to the circumference of

the wick. The air is then spread radially by means of a perforated disc or tube, and when the chimney is in position a non-luminous flame is pro-

Fig. 2

duced which will make a mantle incandescent. Fig. 2 shows the arrangement.

An important item is to keep the perforations of the air-distributing fittings free from oil and dirt. If they are clogged, a flame may be produced on lighting which will destroy the mantle or the efficiency of the lamp will be reduced. Clean the perforated air chamber periodically by removing it from the lamp and saturating in petrol. Dry it thoroughly afterwards.

The wick is raised by a handle acting through cog wheels direct on the disc. If anything goes wrong in this mechanism, and if it is possible to get at it, it will probably be found that one of the wheels has slipped or that the teeth are worn. In the first case, gentle pressure should be applied to the cog wheel, when it will probably lock itself into place again. In the second case, it should be possible to fix in a cog out of a clock mechanism. Should the milled

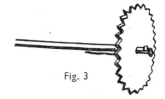

Fig. 3

knob controlling the wick hoist be broken, a further cog wheel from the clock can be used. It is unlikely that the clock wheel will fit the spindle at once, but brass is easily bored. If the fit is too big, a pin makes an excellent wedge, Fig. 3.

Frequent trimming of the wick of an incandescent lamp is not so necessary.

Primus Lamps.—The well-known primus lamp has no wick, and is therefore simpler in use. The oil is vaporised by the heat of the flame and burned as a fine jet, giving a non-luminous flame. Air pressure is supplied by a pump to start the jet. Here again the flame impinges on a mantle. The commonest form of trouble with a Primus is the stoppage of the jet by dirt or oil clogging. The jet should be removed and cleared by blowing through it.

Should the jet be broken or clogged so badly that it will not function, a fitting can be improvised from an old carburetter if you have one handy. If this is not possible, take a brass tube of the correct size, plug it with hardwood and make a small hole in the end. This will serve for a short time until a fitting can be bought.

The familiar type of oil stove illustrated in Fig. 4, acts on the direct-burning principle, and the wick is usually kept in position by a tubular plug mushroomed out at the top to cover the whole of the wick, Fig. 5. Frequent trimming of the wick is necessary to avoid smell and smoking. The cap should never be closer than $\frac{1}{4}$ in. from the wick, and the wick should not be turned higher than is necessary to obtain an even flame. The cap should be kept very clean.

The Oil Level.—Fumes are given off by these stoves and they should never be used without adequate ventilation. Most stoves of this type are fitted with oil indicators of the float type, and these sometimes register inaccurately. The most reliable way to find out how much oil there is in the tank is to have a graduated rod of iron. Punch a hole in

the filler cap and fix the rod so that the end touches the bottom of the tank when the cap is screwed on. Whenever the level of the oil is required, all you have to do is to unscrew the filler cap and consult the rod, as indicated in Fig. 6. A safety mark can be made below which it is unwise to let the level fall.

Another type of heater is the bowl

Fig. 4

radiator, in which a non-luminous flame impinges on a metal mantle placed in the focal area of a concave metallic reflector. The metal mantle should be taken off and cleaned by soaking in petrol, afterwards drying thoroughly, every three months, depending on how much the heater has been used. The mantle is marked at A in Fig. 7.

Oil cookers fall into two classes:

those which burn oil fuel by means of a wick, and which need a surround to render them smokeless, and the wickless type.

In the first type the burners are enclosed and protected against dirt. Nevertheless, it is important to keep them free from surplus oil and to keep the wicks trimmed to prevent smell.

Fig. 5

The flame should be used at full height only when first lit. Afterwards, it should be reduced to suit the needs of the work.

Wickless stoves in their simplest form are used for heating kettles and saucepans. When used for an oven, they should never be used to heat a surface direct as this will cause local overheating and oxidisation. The type of stove for use with a wickless cooker is therefore provided with a special chamber for containing the heater. This chamber should be kept clean and ventilation must be adequate.

The secret of success with oil lighting or heating is to keep the apparatus clean, in the case of the wick lamp to

keep the wick evenly trimmed, and in the case of the wickless type to keep the air perforations free.

A new lamp or a new stove or one

Fig. 6

which has been repainted should always be burned for a few hours outside the house to allow the smell to clear away.

Always provide ventilation where oil apparatus is used.

With the direct-burning type of lamp, always have a surface suspended over the chimney to catch the smoke and take stains that would otherwise be transferred to the ceiling. A satisfactory smoke trap is shown at B in Fig. 1. The materials are stout wire bent to shape and soldered to a tinplate cone.

Fig. 7

MAKING A TORCH BLOW-LAMP FROM AN OLD GARDEN SYRINGE

A WORN-OUT garden syringe can be made into a torch blow-lamp by anyone who can use a soldering iron and a file.

Syringes are usually made of brass and measure about 18 in. in length and $1\frac{1}{2}$ in. in diameter. The spray and piston-rod ends are screwed to the barrel.

Preparation.—Withdraw the piston and place the screw end in the vice and cut the barrel to a length of $4\frac{1}{2}$ in. Do not place the tube between the jaws of the vice before fitting a circular-shaped holder as indicated in Fig. 1 or the metal may be distorted and the thread damaged. To make the clamps, procure a piece of wood not less than $1\frac{1}{2}$ in. thick, bore a $1\frac{1}{2}$ in. hole through it and then cut it across as shown.

Mark a guide line where the metal has to be severed and saw it through with a fine-bladed hack saw.

File the end smooth and square, and prepare a circular piece of brass $\frac{1}{10}$ in. thick. File the edge circular so it fits tightly into the plain end of the tube.

Clean the edge and the internal and external surfaces for a distance of about $\frac{1}{4}$ in. from the end of the barrel, heat the end, apply a suitable flux such as Fluxite and tin these surfaces with soft solder. Clean and flux the disc and then solder the disc into the end of the tube.

The screwed end now requires attention, as a burner consisting of a $\frac{5}{8}$ in. screwed brass nipple, as used by gas fitters and electricians, has to be fixed into the hole. The hole in all prob-

ability will not be larger than $\frac{5}{16}$ in. diameter, so it will be necessary to enlarge it with a small half-round file. Take care not to file it oversize. Before actually enlarging the hole, however, file off the threads from one end of the nipple, slightly tapered as indicated in Fig. 2, as the plain end of the nipple

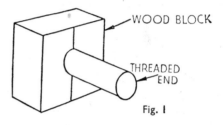

WOOD BLOCK

THREADED END

Fig. 1

has to be riveted over. Solder must not be used here as it will melt when the blow-lamp is in use.

The Burner End.—Force the nipple into the hole and rivet the inside end by tapping it with the ball-pane of the hammer-head.

Now procure a piece of brass tubing $\frac{3}{16}$ in. external diameter and $4\frac{1}{2}$ in. long and gently hammer one end to reduce the size of the hole to about $\frac{1}{32}$ in. or less, to form a jet, and bend it to shape as indicated in the illustration showing the completed article, Fig. 3.

Cut a piece of brass strip $4\frac{3}{4}$ in. long and $\frac{1}{2}$ in. wide, and bend it to form a recess in the centre to accommodate the tube. File off the sharp edges and bend the strip so that it forms a sliding clip on the barrel. Solder the tube into the recess in the clip. The position for this is about 2 in. from the jet end of the tube. Get a piece of $\frac{3}{16}$ in. rubber tubing and slip one end over the lower end of the tube. Shape and bore a hardwood mouthpiece and connect it to the other end of the rubber tube. The next item is to make a suitable cap for the burner. The screwed top of an old metal cord grip electric lampholder will do well for this, provided the screw thread is of $\frac{5}{8}$ in. internal diameter and that a disc of brass be soldered to it to cover the hole. The object of the cap is to prevent evaporation of the methylated spirit and it should always be screwed on after the lamp has been in use.

This completes the construction of the blow-lamp. Loosely fill the con-

Fig. 2

tainer with cotton wool and bring the end through the burner to form a wick. Saturate the cotton wool with methylated spirit. The lamp is then ready

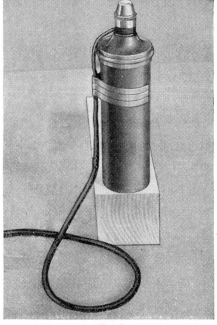

Fig. 3

for use. Light the wick, adjust the height of the jet and use the apparatus in the usual way.

A NEW LEASE OF LIFE FOR THE CARPET

DAILY brushing keeps the pile free from grit and dirt. Places which are in continual use wear quicker than the rest of the carpet. To avoid uneven wear as much as possible, a carpet should be taken up and relaid in a different position, or the furniture should be shifted, about once a year. Even then a hard-wearing rug should be laid where the door opens and another before the fireplace. It will then be found that patchy wear will be greatly checked.

When a carpet has worn in patches,

treatment must be given. If the carpet is a cheap one, it may have faded, but usually this faded look is due to dirt. Test this by cleaning a small patch with benzine and comparing it with a part which has been covered by furniture.

Beating and Brushing.—Faded or not, the carpet must be taken up to make a thorough job of its rejuvenation. If you have a lawn, spread the carpet out. If not, hang it over a stout cord and leave it for a few hours in the sun. Beat it thoroughly with a broad, flat object until the dust which rises is so fine that it can hardly be seen. Then brush thoroughly, first of all with a hard brush, and then finishing with a softer one.

A lot of hair may come away. This is a sign of a good carpet and is usually only loose strands of wool. If the beating has been done well, the carpet is now clean, but still has not the fresh, new appearance which is to be desired. The best way to obtain this is to brush the pile thoroughly with a soft brush dipped in petrol, as shown in Fig. 1. Benzine is better if you have enough. The smell will disappear if the carpet is left out in the air for a few hours.

Obstinate spots should be sponged with a solution of ammonia, three parts to ten of water. Do not use a strong solution, as ammonia has a bleaching action. The use of ordinary carpet soap is not advised, at least for thorough cleaning, as it contains alkali

the selvedges right back before commencing the operation.

Patching.—Bare patches worn in a carpet can be treated in two ways.

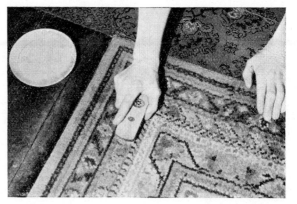

Fig. 1

With a self-coloured carpet, it is possible to pick up remnants of rugs of the same colour very cheaply. In this case, cut out the bare patch, canvas and all, with a sharp pair of tailors' shears, to an even shape and convenient size. Cut a piece from the remnant exactly the same size, and sew the piece into the original carpet from the back, using a lock-

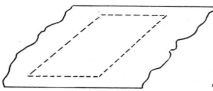

DOTTED LINE SHOWS HOW REGULAR
CUT SHOULD BE MADE IN CARPET.

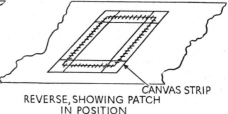

CANVAS STRIP
REVERSE, SHOWING PATCH
IN POSITION

Fig. 2

and is apt to shorten the life of the carpet.

The next step is to go over the carpet and see if repair is needed anywhere. If the carpet is a seamed one, signs of wear may have appeared along the line of the seam. The best way to remedy this is to cut the manufacturers' seam and resew with carpet thread, drawing

stitch. Stitch a broad strip of stout canvas over the seam at the back, fastening the patch securely into position.

It is imperative, when making a repair of this kind, to cut the worn patch into a convenient shape and large enough to take away the whole of the worn portion, Fig. 2.

When it is impossible to obtain

pieces of matched material, a more tedious repair is necessary. The repair will be of two types, depending upon the kind of carpet. In Fig. 3 there is shown roughly, the construction of three main types of carpet: Brussels, Wilton and Axminster. It will be seen

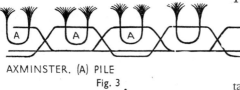

BRUSSELS. (A) PILE (B) STIFFER WARP (C) CHAIN

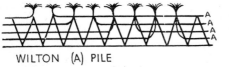

WILTON (A) PILE

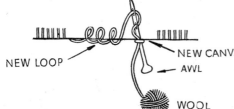

AXMINSTER. (A) PILE

Fig. 3

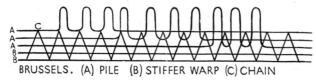

NEW LOOP
NEW CANVAS
AWL
WOOL

REPAIRING BRUSSELS

Fig. 4

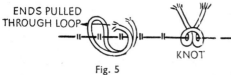

ENDS PULLED THROUGH LOOP
KNOT

Fig. 5

that the first pile is looped and that the other two are tufted.

If the original canvas remains good, this can be used in repairing a Brussels carpet. If it is badly worn, a piece of harn, hessian, burlap or packsheet must be stitched into position to form the backing. Obtain wool of the required shade and consistency and, as in rug-making, prod the wool through the canvas from the back, catching each loop as it is made with the left hand Fig. 4. No tying or knotting is necessary, and although it is not possible to reproduce the original structure of the carpet with its chain, warp and backing a neat repair can be effected.

Special Repairs.—In the case of Wilton and Axminster carpets, the procedure is different. The original canvas backing of the carpet cannot be used, as rug canvas, of the net type, is required. The wool, too, is not used from the ball, but is cut into lengths of about 3 in., this length depending on the thickness of the carpet pile. Rug canvas is sewn across the hole in the carpet. A length of wool is then taken and doubled. The loop is pushed through one of the holes in the canvas and held with the finger or a knitting needle. The two free ends are then brought through the adjacent hole, passed through the loop, and the knot pulled tight Fig. 5.

When the hole is covered, the surface is clipped down to the level of the original carpet. If the hole is a small one, and in an out-of-the-way position, it will generally be sufficient to use wool of the predominant colour of the carpet for filling, without attempting to reproduce the design.

If all gritty substance is cleaned out frequently the life of the carpet will be much greater. Tobacco ash is more beneficial than harmful. Never use a hard soap, or powder cleaner.

When a carpet smells, it is usually due to damp. Apply an antiseptic to the canvas backing and dry thoroughly in the air.

A stair carpet wears on the nose of the stair very quickly. Shift the carpet up or down a few inches now and then. Make sure the felt underneath still covers the nose.

Black spots and black lines sometimes appear across the width of a carpet, especially with Wiltons, probably due to internal oil. Apply benzine frequently until eradicated.

CLEANING AND PRESSING CLOTHES

THE premier cause of shabby clothes is lack of pressing or improper pressing. Let us take as an example a suit which requires pressing and cleaning. Make sure that the iron is clean; even an electric iron can gather dirt on its surface and do damage to an article.

A level and clean surface must be obtained by covering a table or board with cloth. An old sheet over an old blanket can be used and kept especially for the purpose.

Sponging and Spotting.—The garment is laid flat on this cloth. If it is the trousers, see that the legs are lying along the proper creases as indicated in Fig. 1. Make sure there is no dirt or dust on the garment, brushing the cloth vigorously with a hard brush. This operation is depicted in Fig. 2.

Then take a sponge, dipped in lukewarm water and squeezed until just moist, and sponge the garment thoroughly.

If there are grease spots, they will need separate treatment. Apply petrol or benzine with a clean rag. Rub it well in, and let it dry. Turpentine can be used if quite pure. Another method of removing grease spots is to place a piece of unglazed brown paper over the spot and press with a hot iron. If the spot remains, treat as follows. Drop on to it a little oil of tartar, and immediately wash with lukewarm water and then with cold water. Salt of wormwood which has been left in a damp place until liquid, and used in the same way, is also good. If both methods fail, it generally indicates that the spot is indelible, although treatment will cause it to fade considerably.

The results of careless wear of the trousers must be attended to before the pressing is done, or the garment will have to be pressed again.

A seam which has begun to split should be resewn carefully. If left it will extend until a tailor will be necessary. Do not just sew the seam from the front, but examine the underside of it, see how the tailor has done the work and follow this as closely as possible.

Invisible Mending.—A tear is more serious, especially if the edges are ragged or threadbare from neglect. If the edges are strong and clean, the tear can be neatly darned to make the join as invisible as possible.

The method shown in Fig. 3 should be used for a ragged tear. A piece of material of similar colour and texture is placed beneath the tear. The ragged edges of the tear are then cut away, and the clean edges left are turned in and sewn on to the material underneath. Surplus cloth is then cut away and the repair is complete.

Frayed trouser edges and turn-ups can be temporarily repaired with a needle and thread, the frayed edges being drawn together and sewn over. A cross-stitch should be used.

When all spots have been cleaned, tears renovated and all frayed edges trimmed, pressing may be done.

Fig. 1

Make sure the iron is the correct temperature. If it is not hot enough, it will be ineffective; if it is too hot, it may scorch the material. Test the iron by dropping a spot of water on to the surface. If the bead of water slides off easily and rapidly, the iron is at the right temperature. If it sticks, it is not hot enough; if it disappears in steam, the heat is too great.

Take a clean cloth and place it into lukewarm water. Any cotton or linen square will do, or an old shirt can be used. Leave the cloth to soak for a few minutes. Then wring it out and lay it upon the garment as indicated in Fig. 4. Make sure that the garment lies perfectly flat beneath the cloth.

Never put an iron into direct contact with worsted, tweed or flannel or similar fabrics. Ladies' garments of light texture can be ironed and pressed this way, but not men's clothing.

Pressing.—The correct way to press is to lay the iron on the part required and lean heavily on it. Never bang the iron downwards with the idea that

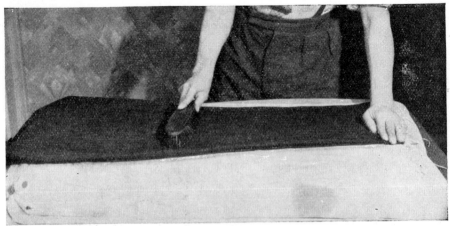

Fig. 2

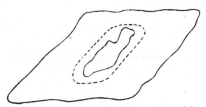

RAGGED TEAR – CUT WHERE DOTTED

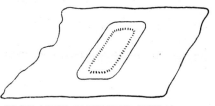

BACK VIEW SHOWING PATCH

Fig. 3

you are applying weight by so doing. It is pressure that counts. Any creases to be made should be attended to first, the material pulled taut while it is being pressed. The covering cloth should be just damp enough to produce a sizzling noise when the iron is applied.

When the clothes have been thoroughly pressed, change the damp cloth for a dry one and iron the garment again with a smooth sliding motion.

If you omit the second iron and dry cloth the garment will ruckle and pull out of shape quickly.

When pressing light - coloured materials, never let the iron linger long in one place. It may be too hot and then a scorch will result, even through a covering cloth.

Shine on dark-coloured cloth of close weave can be removed temporarily in the following way. Sponge the shiny area with a weak solution of vinegar, and allow to dry. Apply the vinegar again, and then press lightly with a very hot iron and a dry cloth.

Never press a garment with anything in the pockets. Ridges and marks will result, which are very hard to remove.

For removing ink stains and liquid marks, a dilute solution of ammonia is useful. Warm the affected part before applying the ammonia, and let it dry thoroughly before ironing.

Unless a garment is very light in colour, do not use soap and water to remove a stain. The mark will certainly be partially removed, but a light patch will be left where the soap and water were applied.

Fig. 4

Button Sewing.—A button is simple to fix. Buttons are provided with eyes, and a needle carrying cotton is passed through the cloth and these holes alternately. When the button has been

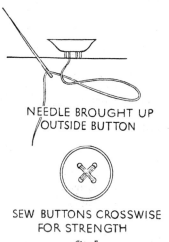

NEEDLE BROUGHT UP
OUTSIDE BUTTON

SEW BUTTONS CROSSWISE
FOR STRENGTH

Fig. 5

firmly fixed, the needle should be brought through the cloth without being passed through the button and the cotton wound round and round between button and cloth. The needle is then passed back, another stitch or two made, and the cotton cut as illustrated in Fig. 5.

If possible, a suit should always be kept in shape by laying the trousers in a press, Fig. 6, when not being worn and hanging the coat on a hanger. If a

Fig. 6

suit smells musty after some time of disuse, clean it with petrol and dry in the open air. Paint can also be removed with petrol and turpentine.

Never use a dirty brush on clothes. The dirt in the brush will be forced into the material, and it will be practically impossible to remove it. It is a good idea to damp a brush slightly before using it for clothes.

CLEANING, OXIDISING AND COLOURING METALWORK

THE secret of cleaning lies in a knowledge of the correct cleanser to use for each metal. Many people polish lacquered brasswork, for instance, destroy the lacquer and wonder why stains appear. The only cleaning agent for lacquered articles is a soft, dry duster.

Ordinary metal polishes can, and do, keep metals bright under ordinary circumstances, but where dirt and grease are present in large quantities, or the article is badly stained, the following methods should be used.

Brass.—Apply a dilute solution of sulphuric acid with a soft cloth or brush. This will remove all dirt and grease very quickly. Take care not to get any acid on surrounding wood. A piece of cardboard cut to cover all except the article to be cleaned, as illustrated in Fig. 1, is useful, or the article can be removed and cleaned in the open air.

If brass is scratched, it can be rubbed with pumice-stone and subsequently treated with fine emery cloth and olive oil.

A badly stained article should be boiled in a solution of potash ($\frac{3}{4}$ lb. to 1 gal. of water) in an enamel pan, taking care to keep all iron out of the solution. Rinse and use a fine wire scratch brush previously dipped in size and water. Articles can then be lacquered or oxidized as directed later.

Steel.—Grease or blacking can be cleaned off steel articles such as kitchen ranges with petrol. If rusty, use a smooth file, afterwards scouring with whetstone or pumice. Follow with emery cloth. A bright polish can be achieved by applying slaked lime, or rottenstone and paraffin, with a leather.

Silver and Gold.—Mix one part rouge and two parts whiting into a paste with ammonia and apply with a soft cloth. The more ammonia the stronger the solution. Keep in a stoppered bottle. Unusual stains can be taken off with ammonia and bone-dust plate powder mixed to a thin paste.

Gilt.—Mix rouge and methylated spirits together with a little water and apply as for silver and gold. Cyanide of potassium, well diluted, is an excellent cleaning agent, but very dangerous to use on table articles as it is a deadly poison. If used, rinse well with cold water and wipe thoroughly.

Plate.—Use a mixture of two parts chalk, one part cream of tartar and one part alum, mixed to a thick cream with water. A liquid cleanser is made by dissolving $\frac{1}{2}$ pint of oleic acid in 1 pint

Fig. 1

of benzole, adding 8 oz. of finest kieselguhr.

Sheffield and silver plate can both be cleaned with the following solutions:

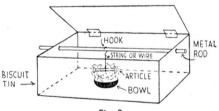

Fig. 2

(*a*) dissolve as much photographer's hypo as possible in 8 oz. water, adding 1 oz. strongest ammonia and 4 oz. powdered chalk, or (*b*) mix 1 oz. ammonia, 60 oz. methylated spirits and 4 oz. chalk.

Aluminium.—Soda water, so often used for cleaning aluminium kitchen utensils, oxidizes the metal. It is harmless, but makes the metal dull. There is no ideal cleaner for aluminium. The best method of keeping it bright is to add a small amount of waterglass to the soda water used for washing up. Medium or hard water should be used for aluminium, as soft water contains potash, ammonia, sodium and other salts and will discolour it.

Lead and Pewter.—Where hot soda water has no effect, use dilute hydrochloric acid, one part acid to ten parts water. Wash thoroughly afterwards with clean, warm water.

Brass can be oxidized by immersing in a solution composed of 4 oz. of sulphide of potassium dissolved in boiling water, to which is added 1 oz. of liquid ammonia. The solution should be kept at a temperature of about 150 deg. F., while the article is immersed. The longer the immersion, the blacker the colour. When black

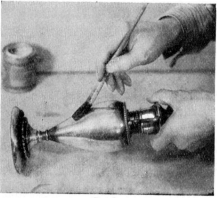

Fig. 3

enough, take out, rinse in warm water and dry.

Another method is to dip the article in a weak nitric acid bath until bright, rinse and place in a solution of one part sulphide of iron, one part white arsenic and twelve parts hydrochloric acid. Dry in sawdust and polish with blacklead. A further solution consists of one part nitrate of tin, two parts chloride of potassium dissolved in water and hydrochloric acid. The more acid the darker the result will be.

An excellent method is to clean the article and give it a deposit of electro silver plate. Then prepare the following. In a little acetic acid, dissolve 2 dwt. of sulphate of copper, 1 dwt. of nitrate of potash and 2 dwt. muriate of ammonia. After warming, apply the solution with a camel hair brush, or immerse the article if possible, and expose to the fumes of sulphur.

This can best be done with a bowl of sulphur placed in a biscuit tin, through the sides of which a rod of metal has been passed, as shown in Fig. 2. A string with a hook should be prepared, and the article is tied to the string and hooked to the rod. The lid of the tin should be closed, as the fumes of sulphur are obnoxious.

Brass can be coloured as follows:

For blue, dissolve 12 oz. of hyposulphite of soda in half a gallon of boiling water. In another vessel prepare 12 oz. acetate of lead in the same quantity of hot water. Pour the latter into the former, stirring all the time, and bring the whole to boiling point. Dip the article when boiling.

For other colours, clean the article of dirt and grease, dip in cyanide of potassium and rinse. Dissolve 1½ oz. of hyposulphite of soda in one pint of boiling water. In another pint of water pour very gently 1½ oz. of sulphuric acid. Pour the second into the first, mix thoroughly and bring to a temperature of 200 deg. F. When immersed, the article goes steel blue, then brown, then red, green and bronzy brown, the last being shot with iridescent colours. The article can be removed at any stage.

When cleaned thoroughly, oxidized or coloured metals should be lacquered both to prevent dirt and to save cleaning. A cold, commercial lacquer can be used and applied with a soft brush, as shown in Fig. 3. Take care to cover in one coat if possible and do not leave marks through hard brushing. Work the brush in one direction only. Put the article in a warm oven for a short while.

A good lacquer can be made by mixing 1 lb. powdered resin in a little less than a pint of turpentine. Let the solution stand for two days. Then add 1½ qts. of boiled oil, shake and leave to stand in a warm room. Pour off the clear portion and add spirits of turpentine to the required consistency.

A hard spirit lacquer can be made by mixing 2 oz. gum mastic, 8 oz. gum sandarac, 1 oz. gum elemi with 4 oz. turps, adding one quart of rectified spirit, 65 over proof.

MAKING LOOSE CHAIR COVERS

LET us deal first with covers designed for the small chairs, such as those in the dining-room. It is usually best to have a self-colour toning in with the general furnishing scheme. The cover should be fine and closely woven, or of tapestry. Do not use velvet. It harbours dirt and is difficult to make up.

The best way to cut the cloth is illustrated in Fig. 1. Lay the material on the seat of the chair to be covered, pin it firmly and mark the size of the seat with tailor's chalk. Then cut, allowing ½ in. all round for seaming. Then cut the box strip (marked B in the illustration) allowing ½ in. again. Three sides of the box piece can be cut in one, but the back edge must be cut separately, and have ½ in. overlap at each end.

Cut pieces from the seat square to fit around the uprights of the chair back, and stitch the three sides of the box edge to the seat piece, taking in the ½ in. turning allowed. The seams can be piped if desired, using stout string for piping. Cut a mitre, as shown by the dotted lines on the front corners in Fig. 1, after stitching, and sew on a button and a button eye at each corner. Hem the outer edge.

Fit the cover to the seat of the chair, wrapping the cut front corners over themselves and securing the studs as shown in Fig. 2. Now sew studs and button eyes (two or three at each end) on the back box edge, about ¼ in. from each end. Secure the back box edge, Fig. 2, by this means and the cover is complete.

If desired, the whole cover can be cut in one piece except the back box edge,

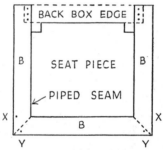

CHAIR COVER LAID (X) BUTTON-EYES (Y) STUDS

Fig. 1

but the piped seam around the seat gives a better finish. Hooks and eyes can be used instead of buttons and studs, but should be neat. If you want a frill, pipe it on to the box edge before stitching to the seat.

Larger Covers.—Easy chair and divan covers are also simple to make. The material should be cretonne, printed linen or chintz. Linen is hard-wearing and can be had in very attractive designs and colours.

The chair or chairs must be measured

to arrive at the quantity of material required. Using material of the standard 31 in. width, the method shown in Fig. 3 will be found satisfactory.

Four inches must be allowed at every inside seam for tucking in. A cover which just fits will be found uncomfortable and unsightly. At least 2 in. must be allowed on all edges of material forming the bottom of the cover, and on the outside measurements ½ in. for turnings. The standard width of material is about right, except with very large or very small chairs. In the diagram, Fig. 3, the measurements of the back and arm rests are taken over the roll of the scroll to the join, so that the seam will come on the line of the join and will thus be hidden as much as possible.

The 2 in. allowed on the bottom edges allow 1 in. for hemming or piping and an inch of overhang to give a finish.

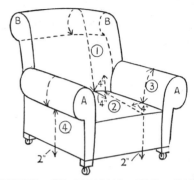

METHOD OF MAKING EASY CHAIR
A ON MEASUREMENTS 1, 2 & 3 ALLOW
4″ INSIDE AND 2″ BEYOND JOIN OF ROLL
B ON MEASUREMENTS 2 & 4 ALLOW 2″
AT BOTTOM.

Fig. 3

and the seat first, then the arms and sides. Have a list before you of the extra amounts required on the various pieces for turnings and tucking so that no mistake is made.

Next, pin the material to the chair, fitting it as centrally as possible. If the full width of the material is not required, remember, in cutting, to leave the 4 in. for tucking on either side.

Cut the scroll faces from the templates, remembering to leave ½ in. all round for turning.

When all material is cut and pinned, it will be found that on the rolls of the back and arms there is a good deal of slack. This is not due to faulty cutting, but to the shape, and the surplus will disappear when the cover is completed.

When the cover is completed, lift it carefully from the chair and tack the seams together strongly. The seams should be cut or notched every few inches, to allow corners and curves to sit properly. When tacking is completed, fit the cover to the chair again, when any alterations necessary to a good fit can be made.

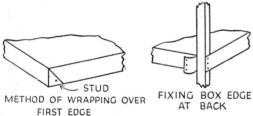

STUD
METHOD OF WRAPPING OVER FIRST EDGE

FIXING BOX EDGE AT BACK

Fig. 2

Avoiding Mistakes. — The scroll faces on the front of the arms A and on the sides of the back B will usually be found to take a lot of material, especially if they are elaborate in shape. It will be helpful to cut out paper templates of these surfaces and to lay them out as shown in Fig. 4. If you estimate the amount of material needed from the measurements of these surfaces, you will generally be wrong.

Cut the cloth on the chair itself, and if there is a design make sure that the motif is centrally placed on the back and on the seat. Cut the two back parts

Stitching.—After this final fitting, the cover is ready for stitching. If piping is being used, shrink the cord before fitting it. Cut strips of cloth against the weave and cover the piping cord, stretch the seams and insert the cord between them. Then stitch everything firmly. It is usual to insert piping cord into the hem to get the bottom of the cover to hang nicely. The front box edge can be pleated or left full as desired, or it can be made separately and attached, as described for the small chair cover.

The cover for a Chesterfield or divan is made on the same lines, measurements being taken as directed to find the quantity of material. In the case of a Chesterfield, however, it will be best to leave at least 6 in. for tucking in. Remember too, that if the Chesterfield has a drop-end, a lot of material must be allowed for the extra face.

Reversible covers are economical, but there are certain objections to them. For instance, desirable as it is to be able to turn the cover inside out, and put it back looking fresh and new, dirt

METHOD OF LAYING PAPER TEMPLATES TO ECONOMISE MATERIAL

Fig. 4

is hidden there. This dirt is capable of working out of the cover and into the fabric of the chair.

A better material can be had for the same price if it is printed only on one side.

Frills at the bottom and sides of covers catch the dirt, never look neat after the newness has worn off and are a trouble to make.

CONSTRUCTING SIMPLE CAMPING EQUIPMENT

THE tent described here can be made for about twenty shillings; it is extremely light and fool-proof. The sleeping-bag is comfortable, light, and draught-proof. The weight of the tent complete is about $5\frac{1}{2}$ lbs. It measures 7 ft. long × about 4 ft. high and 4 ft. wide, which is an adequate size to sleep two people. The size can be modified to suit individual needs but neither height nor width should be reduced.

Any light, strong and waterproof material will do, such as light sailcloth, feather-weight canvas or balloon fabric. The material should be 60 in. wide. About 10 yd. should be purchased, as the sleeping-bag can be made of the same stuff.

Two sections are cut from the cloth as illustrated in Fig. 1. A flap 2 in. wide should be left at B-C on section 1, the remaining 4 in. being left for tuck-in around the bottom of the tent. The whole section should be hemmed. On section 2, the flaps at the ends, G-I and H-K, should be at least 4 in. wide. This piece should also be hemmed.

I-K in the section 2 is then stitched strongly to section 1 by means of the flap at B-C. Four stout eyes are then stitched strongly on the flap B-C, Fig. 2, and corresponding hooks on the side A-B. The hooks are stitched on the underside of A-B so that they can be fastened from the outside. Four eyes are then sewn on in a similar manner to F-E and four hooks on to the flap E-D, so that the fastening can be done from the inside.

Now stitch stout pieces of canvas over all corners on the inside of the

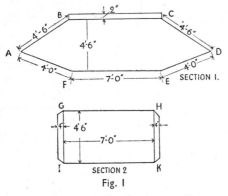

SECTION I.

SECTION 2

Fig. I

tent as shown by the shading in Fig. 2. This will prevent undue wear.

The Poles.—Next take four poles 1½ in. in diameter, each piece being 4 ft. 6 in. long.

Cut each piece in half and fit on one end of each half-section a tubular

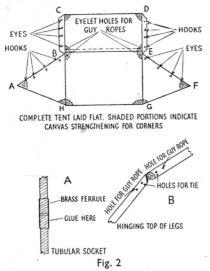

EYELET HOLES FOR GUY ROPES

EYES

HOOKS

HOOKS

EYES

COMPLETE TENT LAID FLAT. SHADED PORTIONS INDICATE CANVAS STRENGTHENING FOR CORNERS

HOLE FOR GUY ROPE

HOLE FOR GUY ROPE

HOLES FOR GUY ROPE

A

HOLES FOR TIE

B

BRASS FERRULE

GLUE HERE

HINGING TOP OF LEGS

TUBULAR SOCKET

Fig. 2

ferrule, which can be glued on. The best ferrules can be obtained from fishing tackle dealers, and are inexpensive. The method of fixing these is

shown at A in Fig. 2. Cut one end of the other four sections at an angle of about 30 degs. and join the sloping surfaces with a brass hinge as shown at B in Fig. 2. The hinge is supposed to be completely closed when the ends of the joined poles are 4 ft. apart, and the exact angle for the particular length being used can be obtained by trial.

Now stand the A pieces thus made with their legs 4 ft. apart, cut the bottom ends to stand flat on the ground and fit 3 in. iron spikes. Bore two holes in the top of each leg as shown in Fig. 2 at B. Take two pieces of stout cord 7 ft. long and insert one end of each piece into each of the upper holes on the legs, knotting on the outside. Do the same with each A piece, and the frame of the tent is complete as shown at A in Fig. 3.

The lower holes are for guy ropes, and for these two eyed holes should be made in the tent fabric at B and E as shown in Fig. 2 (top).

To erect the tent, set up the two legs of each A piece 4 ft. apart and 7 ft. from each other, so that the cord between them is taut. Cover the frame with the fabric as you would slip a cover over a bicycle, bringing up the guy ropes through the holes provided.

Now hook up the flap designed for the back of the tent, H.A.B. in Fig. 2. Peg the guy ropes out equidistantly, about 2 ft. apart, tighten up and the tent is ready for occupation.

It will be found that the whole of the front of the tent is open, which greatly facilitates entry. To fasten the front, bring the large flap over and hook on the small flap by means of the hooks and eyes provided, from the inside.

The complete tent is shown at B in Fig. 3.

Alternative Methods. — Various modifications can be made. For instance, eyed-holes can be provided round the base through which prepared wooden wedges can be driven to anchor the tent in high wind.

If additional bracing is found necessary the ropes under the ridge can be replaced with two ¾ in. poles cut in half and jointed as the main frame.

If it is desired to use square legs for the frame instead of round ones, a little more trouble must be taken to make the frame steady. Instead of ferrule joints, hinges must be used, and the cut should slope at an angle of about 20 deg. It is also necessary to fix brass plates about 3 in. long and screwed at one end only, on each side of the hinge to take up any side play. The complete joint is shown at c in Fig. 3.

Single jointed poles can be used instead of the A supports, but it is then necessary to make provision for four extra guy ropes as a frame for the sloping sides. It will be found that this method is less satisfactory in steadiness and ease of setting up.

It may be found necessary to tie the legs together in rough weather. For this purpose, two pieces of stout cord about 3 ft. 6 in. long should be kept.

The sleeping bag, illustrated in Fig. 4, should be made in the following way. Cut one length 5 ft. 10 in. and another 6 ft. 10 in. and about 3 ft. 6 in. wide. Hem all edges.

To make sure that the sleeping bag will be waterproof, the material, even if sold as waterproof, should be treated as follows:

Soak a quantity of gelatine in water until it swells and then pour on enough warm water to make a strong solution. Soak the material thoroughly. Dry off in the sun and prepare a solution of chrome alum, using the same quantity as gelatine. Soak the material again and expose to sun and air for a few days.

Lining the Bag.—The sleeping bag should have a warm lining, and this can

be made by cutting two pieces from a thick fleecy blanket the same sizes as the pieces of material and stitching the two

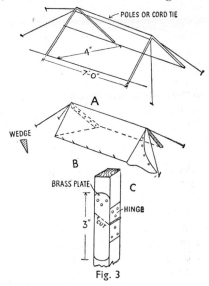

Fig. 3

together strongly. Cross stitching should be made every 2 ft. to hold the lining and prevent it from rucking,

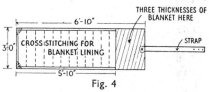

Fig. 4

Fig. 4. Before stitching the lining, sew a strap about 3 ft. long to the longer piece as shown in Fig. 4.

The two pieces of the bag should now be sewn tightly together, lapping over about 3 in. of each piece at the sides and bottom and using best tailor's thread. To make the bag draughtproof, the first line of stitching should be made ¼ in. from the edges. Stout cord should then be inserted in the open seam and the whole stitched in, enclosing the cord between the two lines of stitching.

Now take two pieces of blanket and cut to the same size as the overlapping flap of the longer length, and stitch strongly to the flap so that three thicknesses of blanket are provided. Use linen tape as an underlay to prevent the blanket being cut or torn from the stitches. This flap will serve as a pillow.

The outside edges of the bottom of the bag should be reinforced with adhesive tape, and the corners covered with canvas squares.

If an additional head rest is required, a small pillow can be made by filling a linen pillow-slip with the remaining pieces of blanket. When not in use, the pillow can be inserted in the bag and rolled up with it.

NOTES AND HINTS ON PURCHASING A SECOND-HAND CAR

IT is assumed that the purchaser knows how to drive a car and that he has decided on such matters as size, type of body, horse-power, cost of running and the amount of cash available.

The best car to look for is one which has been driven by one owner and is about a year or so old, as the repair bill for such a car is not likely to be large. The initial cost of a year-old car will be larger than one of longer service. It is to cars in the latter category that the following observations refer.

The first thing is to make arrangements for a general inspection to ascertain the condition of the paintwork, upholstery, tyres, wings and windows.

Doors and Windows.—If this proves satisfactory, ask for a closer inspection. Open and close the doors, noting if they have to be sprung or pushed shut at the last one or two inches. If so, it indicates that the door, or the pillar on which the door is mounted, has received a blow which has upset the hinges. While dealing with doors, note if they are loose when closed or loose on their hinges.

When closing the door the last two inches, see if it rises a trifle. If so, the door has dropped.

Now test the windows for easy working. Some windows may work quite easily for part of their travel, but are stiff for the remainder, showing the guides or the mechanism to be defective. Lower each window and look along the top edge of the glass, noting if it has been splintered. Safety glass with defective edges allows damp to enter between the layers to cause brownish patches. Do not buy a car with windows or screen of ordinary glass for the law will now compel you to substitute safety glass.

If the body has a sunshine roof, see that it operates easily. Look round the runway of the sliding roof inside the car for discoloured or dark patches on the roof covering which indicate penetration of rainwater.

Check the opening of the windscreen and verify whether the glass or frame fits snugly against the rubber cushion when closed.

Most saloon cars are fitted with a blind to the rear window, controlled by a cord which the driver can operate when it is required to stop the glare from the headlights of following cars. See that this is in working order.

Suspension and Steering.—The law requires all cars to be fitted with driving mirrors, to be effective at all times. This requirement is not complied with in the case of an inside mirror and a blind over the rear window, so your purchase must have an outside mirror.

Open the bonnet on one side and rock the car by pushing the body from side to

Fig. I

side and note if the frame and body at the rear of the engine move together or not. If not, the body is loose and faulty. Do this from both sides. Close the bonnet and open a front door. Rock the body and note if both sides of it on either side of the foot opening move together. If they do not, the body is faulty and may prove expensive to rectify.

Turn the steering wheel lightly backwards and forwards to detect wear in the steering box and rods. A 1 in. or 2 in. movement would be in order, as some play has to be allowed, but more than this indicates wear, and a 4 in. movement shows excessive wear. A loose or badly worn ball joint or broken shock spring would also give this movement. Now get the salesman to turn the steering wheel backwards and forwards with the wheels on the ground while you look at the front end of the front spring and note if there is any side movement of the springs. If there is, this movement will be general on all the springs and will give a rolling effect

on the road. It can be overcome by fitting washers to take up the wear.

Jack up the front axle. Take hold of the top and bottom of one wheel and push and pull as shown in Fig. 1 to see if the king, or swivel, pin is worn. If no movement is found here and there is still motion in the wheel, the bearings in the hub are at fault.

If excessive, this defect must be adjusted by fitting new races. Repeat on the other wheel. Now let one wheel down to the ground. Hold the other wheel as indicated in Fig. 2, pull backwards and forwards to ascertain whether the track rod has received excessive wear.

Springs and Transmission.— Inspect the outsides of the springs for broken leaves, observing at the same time if the springs are rusty or well greased. Broken leaves generally occur between points as shown at c in Fig. 3. If the spring at its centre is very close to the frame, it indicates a weak or tired spring.

Jack up one rear wheel, Fig. 4, put in top gear and take the brake off. Now turn this wheel backwards and forwards to find out how much back-lash or play there is in the transmission between this wheel and gearbox. About one-eighth of a turn of the wheel is more or less permissible, but one quarter or more denotes heavy wear in the axle or propeller shaft couplings. The next thing to do is to jack up both rear wheels and test for end play by pushing and pulling each wheel. If in good order, there should be no end movement at all.

If the foregoing inspection is satis-

Fig. 2

factory, start up the engine, and note whether the crank requires a lot of turning or whether it starts easily. Also start the engine with the starter and notice whether the noise is continuous or whether there is a clanking sound. If the latter occurs, it points to badly worn teeth at one spot of the flywheel, an expensive item to put right. Even if the noise is continuous, note if there is any falling off in intensity. This generally indicates that the accumulator is in poor condition and would soon require renewing.

When the engine has started, listen for a tapping noise, which practically disappears when the engine warms up. This indicates worn pistons and cylinder bores and is known as piston-slap. Excessive smoke from the exhaust pipe,

oil filler or engine breather points to badly worn piston and bores. This is another expensive item for, run with these defects, the car would have excessive oil consumption and lack of power.

Points of a Trial Run.—If the engine seems to be satisfactory, arrange for a trial run of fifteen or twenty miles, sitting beside the driver for part of the run and in the back for the remainder.

While seated beside the driver, observe whether he has trouble getting into gear before starting. If he makes several attempts to engage the gear or there is a harsh grating noise, a spinning clutch is indicated. This must be either adjusted, cleared out, or have new clutch plates fitted.

Observe also whether the car glides or starts away with a jerk. If there is a jerk (providing the demonstrator is a good driver), a fierce clutch is the trouble. Adjustment may get over this fault, but new plates may be wanted.

When the car has started, listen for howling noises from the different gears as the driver changes through them up to top. The gear before top gear (third

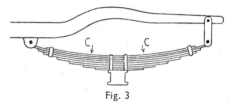

Fig. 3

in a four-speed box and second in a three-speed box) should receive most attention, as this and the top are the most used gears. This noise, if present, can only be cured by new pinions or other parts.

On approaching a steep hill, ask the driver to keep in top gear until the engine nearly stops, and while this is happening, listen for noises such as a dull thumping sound, which indicates worn bearings, a general rattle pointing

Fig. 4

to worn end bearings or a light tapping noise showing a worn gudgeon pin. Worn pistons also give this light tapping noise. A high metallic pinking noise indicates a carboned engine. As the speed of the car falls off, note if the engine gets slower as well, because, if it does not, a slipping clutch is indicated. This can generally be overcome by adjustment, but it might mean fitting new clutch parts.

Brakes and Front Axle.—Ask the driver to apply his foot brake, first gently, for general brake work, and secondly very hard, bringing the car to a standstill to check the maximum efficiency. If a tyre screams on a dry road, if the car swings to one side or a severe shuddering occurs, it may mean defective drums, shoes, brakes or linings. These faults will demand attention.

On a bumpy piece of road, note if the steering wheel moves violently in the driver's hands, or the front part of the car wobbles. If so, it is dangerous.

The driver may repeatedly have to correct his steering on a straight road to overcome wandering. This is a front axle fault, due probably to faulty alignment.

Ask the driver to slow down to fifteen miles per hour, take his foot off the accelerator and then accelerate again, repeating this once or twice. A jerky pick-up indicates wear in the transmission.

Glance at the instruments on the dashboard, and see if they are in working order. The ammeter should show a maximum charging rate of 10 amps. at high speed. More points to a defective dynamo, accumulator or accumulator connections.

If vibration is felt at about thirty-five m.p.h., worn propellor shaft joints, loose engine, worn rear main bearings or unbalanced fan will probably be the cause.

Change over to the rear seat and note if growling noises can be heard from the rear axle while (*a*) running on the level or uphill, but not when running downhill; (*b*) running downhill and not when on the level or uphill.

If the noise occurs all the time, uphill or downhill, a faulty axle part is indicated.

Should the noise consistently vary, a broken tooth or crown wheel out of truth may be the cause.

Body noises, rattlings and window squeaks can be listened for, while sitting beside the driver, and also when behind him. Smooth running over fairly rough roads can be observed. Check over the lights, headlamp dipper, indicators and inside light. Direction indicators and headlamp dipping are now compulsory.

After the run, drive the car again yourself, noting the various points once more.

COMMON HOUSEHOLD APPLIANCES : THEIR CARE AND ADJUSTMENT

DOMESTIC appliances are, on the whole, strongly and simply made, but they do wear out and go wrong, especially if they are neglected or ill-treated.

The Mangle.—Although it is seldom that any parts of a mangle get broken, quite often the rollers or the gears or the turning wheel become stiff and troublesome.

This is due to many causes, but mainly to excessive damp or dirt. If it can be avoided, never keep a mangle where clothes are boiled or where quantities of steam or condensed moisture are generated. Rub the rollers of a mangle after use with a dry cloth, and oil the gears with thick lubricant, periodically.

If the mangle does give trouble, it is best to take it to pieces and clean it thoroughly. This can be done quite easily if the following directions are observed.

First of all loosen the tension spring by means of the pressure handle seen at the top of the illustration Fig. 1. Next release the upper holding-down bolts, lift off the stretcher (which is a loose casting) unscrew the wheel-guard, lift off the sliding bar and then the upper roller.

Next remove the driving wheel and withdraw the washer and split-pin holding the intermediate gears in place and take off the lower roller. Be careful not to lose the split pins.

Take off the wooden trays, unfasten the nuts of the tie rod and the bottom casting, and only the iron side frames remain. Clean the frames thoroughly with an oily rag, brushing out all dirt from the bearing notches. If it is decided to paint the frame do this now. Scrape off all the old paint and then use a good pigment ground in oil thinned with a mixture of japanncr's gold size and turpentine. Let the frame dry thoroughly.

Give all metal parts a thorough cleaning, paying particular attention to the oil holes in the bosses of the wheels, etc., provided by the manufacturer. Use a hairpin or a piece of stiff wire for this. Wipe all gears and the bores of wheels with an oily rag. Clean any rusty parts with emery cloth and wipe over with oil.

The Rollers.—If the rollers are badly worn, they should be replaced by a professional as the average amateur cannot tackle this job.

If the rollers are only slightly roughened by wear they can be smoothed by vigorously rubbing them down with glass-paper Nos. 1 and 0.

The most satisfactory way to do this is to replace the rollers in their bearings and revolve them, meanwhile pressing the glass-paper against the roughened surfaces after assembly.

When reassembling the mangle, oil all bearings immediately the spindles have been slipped in. Rotate the rollers several times after oiling. When bolting up the machine tighten all nuts gradually and equally.

The teeth of the gears can be lubricated with a little animal fat, but use only a small amount and wipe off any surplus immediately. When refitted go over the whole machine, dropping oil into the holes provided and paying special attention to the pressure pads and spring.

The rollers can be rubbed with a little linseed oil to give them a finish, but the mangle must not be used for several days afterwards.

If possible, keep the mangle covered when not in use, and oil it once at least every two months.

The Washing Machine.—The same general remarks apply to its care. Oil, however, should not be used as it may seep into the machine with consequent damage to the clothes.

When a washing machine begins to run stiffly, the following procedure may be adopted. Remove the operating handle by unscrewing the collar. Then unscrew the top cover which, in the case of most machines will reveal the gearing. If the gearing is situated in a metal chamber surrounding the handle stem, it will usually be possible to unscrew the whole box. The gears should be taken out carefully, and wiped with petrol.

A slight amount of vegetable fat (never any mineral lubricant) should be applied before returning the gears.

A ball-race is found on the spindle of many modern washers and this should be handled very carefully.

Fig. 1

It is important to keep the agitator of a washing machine free from the slightest trace of dirt. If through any cause the agitator becomes roughened

Fig. 2

this must be attended to at once, and if it is enamelled and any chip or break occurs the whole bar should be flaked and re-enamelled.

A Wringer is usually fitted to a washing machine, or this may be installed separately. Rubber rollers are usually fitted. The machine shown in Fig. 2 illustrates this. These are apt to become spotted or blotched, and they can be cleaned with a little petrol. After cleaning a rubber roller with petrol, wipe with a cloth moistened

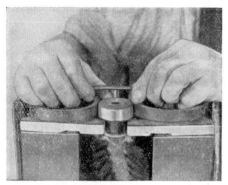

Fig. 3

with dilute solution of ammonia to make certain that no grease or dirt still adheres.

If the rubber rollers of a wringer need replacing it is often found that the old shafts can be used. The wisest course is to send them to the manufacturer who can generally be relied upon to effect the repair.

A Carpet Sweeper should always be emptied of dirt immediately after use, and should it be used several times without emptying a bicycle pump can be employed to blow it clean inside.

One of the frequent causes of trouble with a carpet sweeper is the clogging of the brush and brush bearings, with strands of cotton, carpet hairs, etc. To clean these parts thoroughly the brush should be taken out of its bearings.

To clean the brush use a piece of damp rag, wiping the hairs of the brush from the base outwards.

It will usually be found that the brush spindle is held in position by pegs fixed to two metal bands which span the sides of the sweeper, and is rotated by the rubber-shod wheels which transmit the driving force. Force out the metal bands in the manner shown in Fig. 3. The brush can then be quite easily lifted out of its chamber.

If you find that insufficient power is being transmitted to the brush to pick up dirt properly, the defect is probably caused by the driving wheels having become loose. These wheels are not attached to the body directly but revolve on spindles running through the machine. The spindles are suspended from springs situated at the sides as indicated in Fig. 4, as well as by internal springs. The best plan is to unscrew the springs and bend the ends slightly more together.

If the release mechanism jambs, it is probably due to the screw of the lever having rusted slightly. This screw should be taken out, cleaned, oiled and

Fig. 4

replaced. The elbow joint of the release mechanism should also be oiled.

A carpet sweeper cannot, of course, be kept free from dust. The very nature of its job is a dusty one. To obtain the best results from the carpet sweeper, however, it should be cleaned inside periodically, all choking material removed from the brush spindle and a spot of oil dropped on the spindle itself.

The Non-electric Vacuum Cleaner.—Two types are in use, one which the compression and expansion of a bellows is used to suck up the air, the other in which a revolving fan is used, driven by the sweeper when being pushed along the floor.

The former kind is practically obsolete, and the latter is a well-made mechanical apparatus requiring very little attention. The main points are to keep the fan clean and well oiled, as well as the gears. If you possess the type in which a revolving brush is incorporated as well, see that the brush is kept clean.

Should there be any loss of efficiency in one of these sweepers due to a worn or badly fitted bag nozzle, cut a circle of thin rubber of the same size as the nozzle and screw or clamp this on with the rest of the fitting. A hole in the bag should be mended from inside, using a cycle-type patch or by sticking and sewing on some stout, finely woven canvas using small regular stitches.

SHARPENING AND REPAIRING DOMESTIC EDGED TOOLS

THREE general methods are used to sharpen an edged tool, such as scissors, knives, shears, sythes, etc. In each case the tool is rubbed at a proper angle on one of three substances—stone, emery or steel.

The main requirement for successful sharpening lies in the use of the correct angle for the tool concerned. It is obvious that if the edge of a piece of metal is rubbed against any of these substances, at varying angles, the edge will be alternately sharpened and blunted, the net result being only to wear the metal away. Whereas if the correct angle is used all the time, the sharpening process will be cumulative.

It is usually possible to judge the correct angle at which to sharpen a tool by the angle already ground upon it by the makers.

Grinding is only resorted to when the tool has a badly serrated or dented edge which it is necessary to cut away. Grinding is accomplished by either a revolving wheel with a circumference composed of carborundum or emery, or a wheel consisting of a natural softish stone.

Small hand-driven emery wheels, such as the one illustrated in Fig. 1 are sufficient for the amateur needs and can be bought very cheaply.

When grinding a tool with an ordinary grindstone make a point of having sufficient water, but if using an emery wheel do not use any lubricant, and follow as closely as possible the original angle of the bevel.

Remember that whatever tool is being ground or sharpened, one direction only must be used for each side of the edge. Rubbing a pen-knife backwards and forwards upon an oil stone so that one side of the edge is alternately pushed and pulled will not sharpen it—indeed will tend to blunt it.

Sharpening a Carving Knife.—The best method is undoubtedly by the use of a steel—either plain or ribbed. The edge of such a knife is continually being blunted by contact with hard tableware, etc., and constant use of the steel should be made in order to keep the edge keen. The correct method is shown in Figs. 2, 3 and 4.

A practical demonstration can be had by watching any butcher sharpen a knife. Butchers always use a steel and it is

Fig. i

noticeable that their knives are always keen. It will be seen from the illustrations that two directions are used in moving the knife along the steel.

First the heel of the blade of the knife is pressed against and near the point of the steel, as indicated in Fig. 2, and drawn towards the handle of the latter, the tip of the blade being gradually pulled towards the operator as the stroke proceeds until it comes to rest in the position shown in Fig. 3, thus making contact with the whole of the cutting edge.

Again following the butcher's practice, the next stroke is made by placing the knife at the back of the steel as demonstrated in Fig. 4 and repeating the manœuvre. By this means both edges of the knife are stropped once alternately, and this method is superior to

stropping the knife several times on one side, then turning it over and doing the other side.

Table Knives may be sharpened in the same way. A common fault is for the blade to come away from the handle, the tang, as it is called, having become loose in the cement through continual immersion in hot water. The handles of knives should not be put into hot water when being washed. If necessary the tang can be recemented into the handle as follows: Mix four parts resin, one part beeswax and one part plaster-of-paris. Resin and white sand—or resin, beeswax and silica—will serve (powdered glass can be used for silica). Introduce the powder into the hole in the knife handle, heat the tang over a flame and press. Bind the blade to the

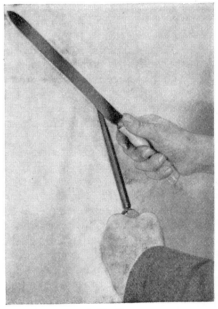

Fig. 2

handle with electrician's tape and leave to harden.

Scissors.—Keen edges are useless unless the two edges of the blades co-operate properly. It will be noticed that if a pair of scissors is held up sideways, the blades are bent in a curve towards each other and that in the operation of cutting the blades actually cross, the cutting part being the joint of contact which moves outwards as they are pushed together. Scissor-blades must be sharpened equally on one side only. If the scissors do not cut properly, examine the blades to see if they have been bent straight or away from each other. To bend back, heat with a flame and use pliers and a vice.

The angle of sharpening should be about 40 deg. from the horizontal. Sharpen each blade equally along the edge all the way. Unscrew the pivot screw and treat each blade

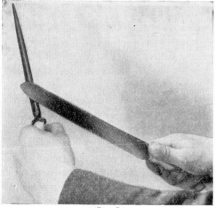

Fig. 3

separately on an oilstone, or if the blades are riveted together hold the scissors as shown in Fig. 5.

The scissors' joint should be oiled

frequently. If the joint becomes loose, tap the rivet with a hammer. If the scissors are screwed, tighten the screw.

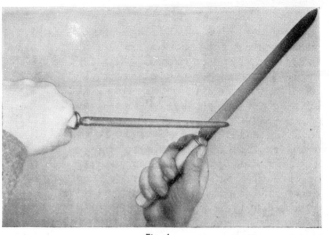

Fig. 4

Shears, Scythes, etc., should be sharpened with a dry honing stone, sold for the purpose, the stone being run along the edge of the tool instead of the tool being moved.

Fig. 5

A loose locking nut of shears can be remedied by placing a small leather or rubber washer between the nuts and then tightening it.

A SIMPLE HEATER FOR A SMALL GREENHOUSE

FOR the purposes of this article, heating the greenhouse is confined to one method, by pipes circulating hot water. The circulation of steam needs complicated apparatus and electric heating is not yet widespread.

Supposing the greenhouse is about 8 ft. long and 6 ft. wide, it will be desirable to heat the whole of one side. Therefore, two lengths of piping should be obtained about 7 ft. long and at least 3 in. diameter. This allows an extra foot to take the pipes through a wall of the greenhouse to the heater. The heating element must be outside as fumes are given off which would kill the plants.

Use for Old Oil Drums.—Now obtain two 2-gall. oil drums. The drums are bored to receive the pipes, the holes in each being made 5 in. from the top and 5 in. from the bottom respectively. A hole is also bored in the top of the drum intended for the inside of the house, to receive the air escape, as shown in Fig. 1.

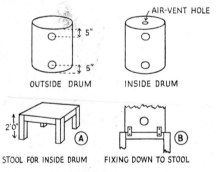

OUTSIDE DRUM   INSIDE DRUM

AIR-VENT HOLE

STOOL FOR INSIDE DRUM   FIXING DOWN TO STOOL

Fig. I

A wooden stand is now constructed, as shown at A in Fig. 1, on which to place the inside drum. The drum can be bolted to the stand if desired by means of metal strips seen at B.

The two pipes are now fitted to the inside drum, being inserted into the greenhouse through holes made in the wall.

It is important that the upper pipe should fall towards the heater element, and that the lower pipe should be parallel. If the upper pipe is level the convection currents caused by the hot water rising will not start, and if it is sloped the wrong way only a small part of the upper tube will be heated. The proper arrangement is illustrated in Fig. 2.

Supposing the wooden stand of the inside drum is made 2 ft. high, allowing the 5 in. from the bottom of the drum to the lower pipe inlet, the lower hole in the greenhouse wall should be 2 ft. 3 in. from the ground, allowing a fall of about 2 in. The pipes should be fixed in position with fireproof clay covered with cement.

The Heater.—The pipes are inserted into the outer drum in the same way. The method by which the outer drum will be supported depends upon the heater employed. If this is an oil lamp the outer drum can be fixed to a wooden stand, over three sides of which are nailed asbestos sheets. Three-ply will do if asbestos cannot be obtained. The fourth side must be left open to allow air to enter and fumes to be expelled, Fig. 3.

If coke is to be burnt, or garden refuse, a small brick chamber should be built as at A in Fig. 3. On one side, a small opening is left by omitting a half brick, and the opening for the firing is about 8 in. wide.

The latter method of heating is

preferable to oil, not only because greater heat can be obtained but because the burning of refuse avoids bills for fuel.

At this stage the whole installation, including the two pipes, is filled with water through the hole bored on the inner drum for the air vent. When the drums are full, a small pipe to which a simple tap has been fitted is inserted and fixed into place. Both pipe and tap can be obtained cheaply from any ironmonger.

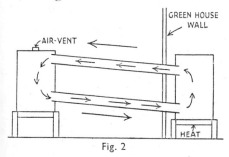

Fig. 2

The heater is lighted, the tap on the air vent being left open. If there is air left in the system it will be blown out,

and the tap is then closed. Air left in the pipes would stop the convection currents.

If desired, the inside drum can be

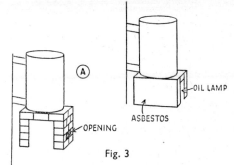

Fig. 3

omitted and a curved pipe used instead, being fixed to the side of the greenhouse by a bracket. But a U-bend pipe will cost more than the oil drum and will not save much trouble.

This apparatus will keep the air in a greenhouse of the size mentioned at an even temperature of 60 deg. F. If an ordinary domestic oil heater is used it will burn about 1 gall. per week.

REPAIRS AND ADJUSTMENTS TO MUSICAL INSTRUMENTS

THE superfine polish of piano cases is easily impaired. Unless it is finished in cellulose lacquer, ordinary furniture creams are not suitable. Should the surface become dull, or inclined to show a bloom, a polish reviver is necessary. This may be bought or made from equal quantities of paraffin, methylated spirits, vinegar and turpentine. This should be sparingly applied with pad of clean, soft material, free from grit or dust, and polished off with a clean duster, preferably of silk. Sunshine bleaches and clouds the polish; keep your piano shaded.

The tops of pianos often become scratched by photograph-frames or vases stood on them. The practice should be avoided as a cure may involve repolishing by an expert.

Piano Keys.—The ivory, or celluloid, keys become stained from the accumulation of dust, moistened by the contact of the fingers. They may also discolour from keeping the keyboard lid closed. The stains may be removed by moistening a soft rag with methylated spirits. This actually dissolves celluloid, so use very little and do not touch the woodwork with it.

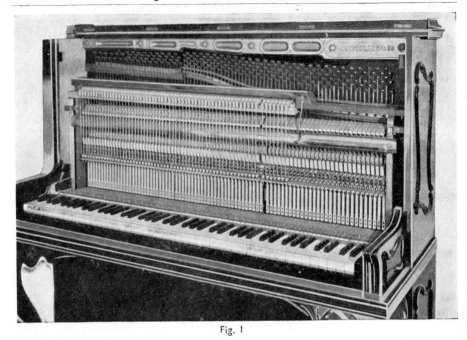

Fig. 1

Rub gently over the surfaces and fronts of the keys. Rub lengthways, never sideways, as this tends to loosen the keys on their pins, and risks catching and perhaps chipping the overhanging edges.

Should the discoloration prove stubborn, a little of one of the household cleansers (provided it is not gritty), or some gilder's whiting, may be mixed to a paste with the spirits and rubbed on the keys. If this is necessary, it will be best to remove the keys one by one to make sure that none of the dried paste is left adhering to their sides. It must not touch the adjacent woodwork.

The Action.—To remove the keys, the action, Fig. 1, must be withdrawn. On opening the half-lid of an upright piano, the front casing, with music stand attached, will probably be seen held in place by sliding cleats or butterfly screws. Disengage these and remove the casing. This will reveal the action

and also the cross blocks of wood to which the keyboard lid is hinged. The second must be lifted out bodily, perhaps after moving similar cleats or thumbscrews, before access is gained to the action. In some pianos a crossbar immediately above the keys has still to be withdrawn.

Removal of the action, which is in one piece and of considerable weight and awkward size, again involves moving cleats or screws. Clear a spare space on the table or floor, on which the action can be stood upright, as illustrated in Fig. 2. In taking hold of the action be careful not to grasp the wires or hammers.

You are now free to attend to the keys. On gently raising the forward end of each, as shown in Fig. 3, it may be coaxed off its metal pins and lifted out. Note the exact position of each key, so as to replace it where it belongs. It is preferable to finish with one and put it back before taking out another

Now that the instrument is dismantled, it will be well to remove dust which, with moth, is the piano's chief enemy. If a vacuum cleaner is at hand, fit the softest suction nozzle available and run it over the parts as indicated in Fig. 4. Otherwise reliance must be placed upon hand brushing and dusting. Be careful not to bend or place strain upon the frail mechanism.

Scrutinise the felts, not only of the hammers, but of the dampers and pads elsewhere. If there are signs of moth, every part throughout the action must be carefully picked over by hand; even if a single grub is left, it will probably mean ruin.

A weekly re-examination of a suspected action is recommended. Insect powder is not advised owing to its dusty nature, but moth-balls may be tied on in muslin bags, where they will not impede moving parts when the instrument is reassembled.

Renovating Felts.—Hammer felts

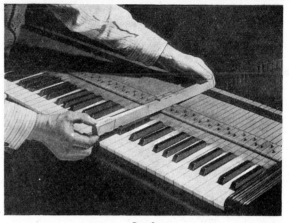

Fig. 3

may be applied from time to time is to prick up the hardened felt. Four or five ordinary sewing needles may be used, inserted side by side, $\frac{1}{16}$ in. apart, in a convenient wooden handle, about 1 in. of the points showing. They are driven well under the surface of the felt parallel to the piano strings when the hammer is in a working position, and the body of the felt is gently levered up. The treatment of all hammers must be uniform or an uneven tone will be produced. Fig. 5 shows the operation.

There is not much more that an amateur can do. Replacing a broken string, or a broken hammer stick is a ticklish business. Such breakages are rare and better left to an expert. It is easy for untrained hands to cause worse damage.

New Strings.—If a string replacement is attempted, the new string must be an exact match of the old in every dimension, as the strings are graded throughout the instrument. The makers will need to know the serial number of the piano and the note concerned before

Fig. 2

usually become hardened from repeated impact on the string. This tends to make the tone hard. A remedy that

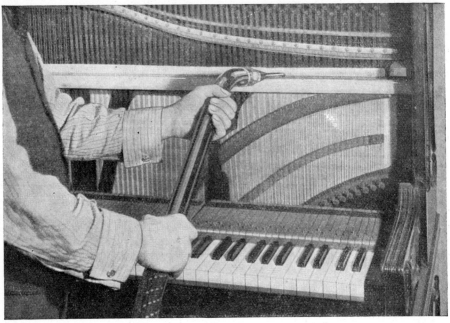

Fig. 4

they can supply it. The new string will come already bent up. Place the loop squarely over the peg. Then thread the

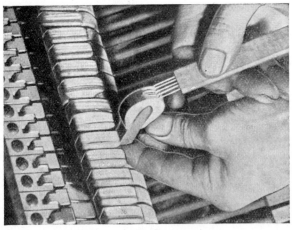

Fig. 5

wire in correct position through its various pins and grooves over bridges. The free end is to be inserted in the

hole in the wrest pin and great care is necessary at this point.

The wrest pins, Fig. 6, are not removable but made to hold friction tight in the wrest plank, and it is essential not to loosen them. With a pair of pliers, the broken end of the wire must be cut and untwisted sufficiently to extricate it. The end of the new wire is then threaded through and the pin wound up with a piano tuning key which will later be necessary to bring the new string into tune.

The front casing of the piano below the keyboard will have been removed, as this is the only means of getting at the lower peg for the string. This removal exposes the mechanism of the

Fig. 6

pedals, the only part ever likely to require lubrication. The remedy for stiffness or squeaks is to track them down and apply black lead to the complaining surfaces, powder if it is free of grit, or a soft lead pencil (say 5B) rubbed on. It will be seen that the two pedals transfer movement to the action by pivoted upright rods and the moving parts of this may also require an occasional application of black lead. Never apply oil to any part of a piano.

Replacing the action is more tricky than taking it out. There will be stops, grooves or dowels into which it fits quite snugly if handled correctly. Never use force. Do not forget to replace the thumbscrews or cleats.

Violin Repairs. — Expert service should be called in for almost all faults in the delicate violin. Even so simple a matter as the sound post which sup-

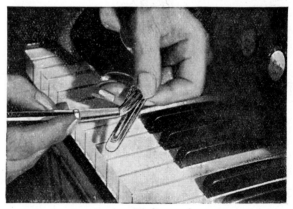

Fig. 7

ports the bridge from beneath the belly becoming unglued or broken is a job that should be done only by a specialist.

Apart from broken strings, however, defects are rare. One that can be remedied is a broken bridge. Procure an exact match of the old one and fit it in exactly in the previous position. The same applies to a damaged tuning peg. Should the new one be an over-tight fit (a slack one is useless), a few turns between a rag sprinkled with fine emery flour held tightly by finger and thumb may be tried. Do not grind too much as the peg must not be slack. Remove all trace of emery with a rag moistened with spirits or petrol before every trial for fit.

The gut loop that attaches the tail piece to the tail pin occasion-ally perishes. It is quite easy to make and fit a new one by using a length of sound D string for the purpose.

Other Instruments.—All this advice applies, generally speaking, to the banjo, mandoline and guitar. A punc-tured banjo tympanium is a case for the expert. Wind instruments are not common among amateurs, who, in any case, usually learn their own running repairs in the course of instruction.

There remain bellows instruments: harmoniums, American organs and the accordion family. The bellows are the most likely part to give trouble through perishing or accident. Such faults may be temporarily repaired by sticking on a patch of leather of the same kind and thickness as the original which a working saddler could probably supply. Use liquid glue which, when dry, retains a certain pliability. If possible, apply the patch inside a harmonium bellows and outside an American organ.

The return springs of the pumping pedals (if fitted) and the webbing that in some designs connects pedals and feeder bellows sometimes give trouble. Replacement is not difficult.

Graphite is again the standard lubri-cant, and dust is an enemy, especially if it lodges in the reeds. These need careful handling when cleaning. Use a brush with long, soft bristles and draw it from the root of the reed towards the tip, as shown in Fig. 7, never the other way. To bend it is fatal.

MANY USES FOR ELECTRIC CONDUIT TUBING

ELECTRIC conduit tube can be used for many purposes other than the protection of electric wires.

This material can be had in several grades. That known as light gauge close-joint conduit is composed of thin steel rolled cylindrically, the long edges of which butt together so tightly that the seam is almost invisible. The exterior and interior of the tube, which are both smooth, are finished with special black enamel.

As it costs less than a penny per foot if purchased in 100 ft. quantities, it can often be used instead of wood, particu-larly where strong but thin rods are wanted.

Household Shelf.—Fig. 1 shows a shelf which could be used for house-hold utensils. The lengths of tube can be removed from their supports and easily cleaned.

The two end supports consist of planed deal battens 2 in. wide and 1 in.

thick, the tops of which are recessed or slotted to take the ends of tubes. If desired the tubes can be painted to match the surroundings.

It is unnecessary to use a hack saw for cutting close joint conduit. A triangular file is better. File a V groove

Fig. 1

round the tube at the desired position, cut at the seam, place the tube, seam outwards, across the knee at the nicked position, and break it by pulling it sharply on the ends.

Curtain Rods.—Curtain rods can also be fashioned out of conduit. After cutting the tube to length, file

The ends of the rod may be given a finish by screwing in small bakelite drawer-knobs which are obtainable for a few pence. Fig. 2 shows the completed curtain rod.

When one is fitting curtain rods of a much longer length than 3 ft., it is advisable to have an extra support at the centre.

Tent Framework.—Fig. 3 shows in diagrammatic form the framework of a garden tent constructed with close-joint conduit $\frac{5}{8}$ in. in diameter. It measures approximately 6 ft. square and 6 ft. high and takes four standard lengths of tube, a standard length measuring a few inches over 12 ft.

In addition to the tube, four elbows and four tee pieces of the lug-grip type will be required. Also, four pieces of 3 in. square × 1 in. thick hardwood for the lower ends of the uprights to rest upon. The upper face of each piece of wood should be bored with a $\frac{3}{4}$ in. diameter bit, to a depth of $\frac{1}{4}$ in.

Cut all eight pieces of tube to length and also cut four nipples 1 in. long. The nipples are for joining the tee pieces to the elbows.

A suitable cover should then be made to fit the frame, a small hole being

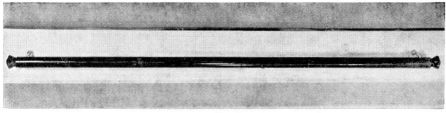

Fig. 2

the ends smooth and plug them with hardwood. Drill a hole right through the tube at a distance of about $\frac{3}{4}$ in. from each end to clear the end of a brass right-angled dresser hook as the latter makes an excellent support for holding the rod.

provided at each top corner for fixing the guy wires. The free ends of these cords can be anchored to the ground with metal skewers.

Wireless Aerial.—A couple of standard lengths of heavy gauge galvanised screwed conduit, $\frac{3}{4}$ in. in diameter, will make an excellent radio aerial mast if suitably stayed. Fig. 4 shows the arrangement.

When purchasing the tube, procure four 4 in. diameter rear entry galvanised back-plates threaded for ¾ in. screwed

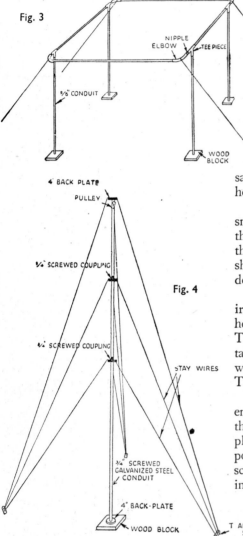

Fig. 3

NIPPLE
ELBOW
TEE PIECE

⅝" CONDUIT

WOOD
BLOCK

4" BACK PLATE

PULLEY

¾" SCREWED COUPLING

Fig. 4

¾" SCREWED COUPLING

STAY WIRES

¾" SCREWED
GALVANIZED STEEL
CONDUIT

4" BACK-PLATE

WOOD BLOCK

STAY WIRE

conduit and two screwed connectors or couplings for joining the tubes together.

At the same time get one length of tube cut in half, and have a thread 1 in. long cut on the plain end of one piece and a similar thread 2 in. in length on the other.

A 2 in. thread will also be required on one end of the single long length.

The back plates may have three holes equally spaced already made in them for fixing purposes; on the other hand, they may have four holes. If they are of the former type only three holes are required for fixing the supporting stays. Should they have four holes it will be necessary to drill a couple of equally spaced holes in addition to one already there.

Drill a hole large enough to take a small ring bolt, 3 in. below the top of the upper tube section. To the ring of the bolt, attach a small galvanised iron sheaf pulley for hauling the aerial up and down.

Prepare three 2 ft. lengths of T-angle iron for fixing stakes, and drill three holes in line near the top in each piece. These holes should be large enough to take a seven-strand 22-gauge galvanised wire of which the guys are composed. The mast is now ready for erection.

Screw a backplate to the short threaded end of the long lower section and at the other end also fix a plate. Screw this plate down to the bottom of the threaded position and, on the projecting thread, screw a coupling. Into this coupling insert the short threaded end of the second section and at the top end of this screw a back plate as before. Then a coupling, T ANGLE IRON STAKE and into this the top section. Finish the top end with a back plate. All these parts should be screwed tightly together and any threads showing should be painted, preferably with aluminium paint.

Now attach the guy wires to the plates through the holes provided.

Place a flat piece of wood at least 1 in. thick under the bottom back plate in the position required and get a helper to hold the mast in a vertical position while you drive in the iron stakes and attach the wires.

Thread a long piece of cord round the pulley before erecting or you will have to take down the mast to hoist the aerial. The aerial wire is attached to one end of the cord and is hauled up by pulling on the other.

Electrical conduit tubing can be used for many other purposes such as the bars in dog kennels, nursery fire guards, and children's play pens.

MAKING USE OF ODDS AND ENDS

IT is astonishing what can be done with many odds and ends that usually end in the dustbin. For instance, rectangular cigarette and tobacco tins serve for the storage of screws, nails, drills and many other small articles, especially if grouped in a cabinet.

Cigarette Tins.—Fig. 1 shows a simple cabinet for such tins. It consists

Fig. I

of a top and base of yellow deal, $\frac{3}{8}$ in. thick, with sides, back and upright divisions of $\frac{3}{16}$ in. plywood. The top and base are purposely made thicker so that the remaining parts can be attached with screws, which, in this case, are better than nails. It is advisable to

house the ends of the vertical divisions into the inner faces of the top and base.

To facilitate withdrawal of the tins, fix a small handle on each. This can be done by drilling the fronts and fitting

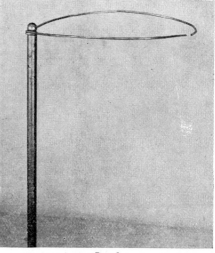

Fig. 2

$\frac{1}{2}$ in. No. 4 B.A. brass bolts and nuts, or small template strips could be soldered to the fronts. Soldering, however, necessitates the removal of the lacquer or paint on the tins.

Each tin should be carefully painted. Cellulose lacquer is advisable for this purpose. The time expended will be repaid in prevention of rust.

Syrup Tins.—Empty syrup tins with lever lids make excellent containers for paint. A handle can easily be added by boring holes in the side and bending a piece of thick galvanised iron wire to the desired shape.

Round brass stair rods are useful as supports for plants, especially if a piece of thin wire is fixed round the top, to hold the plant in position, as in Fig. 2. They will last indefinitely if given an annual coat of paint, preferably of green.

Bottle Vases.—Wide-mouthed glass bottles of artistic shape can be made into excellent flower vases. Cellulose lacquer

Fig. 3

can be used to colour them to suit any room.

An electric table-lamp as illustrated in Fig. 3 can be made with a preserved ginger jar for the body. Shape a piece of wood about 1 in. thick to fit tightly into the mouth and, on this wood, mount a key-switch electric lampholder of the shade-ring type, costing about one

shilling. Connect a length of insulated twin flex to the lampholder. Partially fill the jar with sand and fit the top in position. The sand weights the jar and prevents it from falling over when a shade is fitted. A piece of baize or felt should be glued to the bottom of the jar to prevent it scratching the table.

Cotton Reels.—A serviceable wood-worker's marking gauge can be made

Fig. 4

from a cotton reel by inserting a length of circular hardwood in the centre hole. A small hole should be drilled near the business end of the spindle through which the pointed end of a headless wire nail is forced to form the marker. The spindle should be sufficiently tight in the hole to keep it from slipping when in use.

Cotton reels are also useful for making drawer handles and cupboard knobs. One flange is sawn off and the remainder painted or stained to match the drawer. The handle is fixed to the drawer with a wood screw and washer, as indicated in Fig. 4.

Buttons can be made from cotton reels by cutting them into sections of the desired thickness and shape, drilling holes to take the thread, rounding the edges with glass-paper and painting them with cellulose lacquer.

Old photographic plates, especially those of half-plate size and over, can

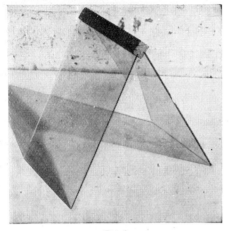

Fig. 5

be used as plant propagators, as illustrated in Fig. 5. The film is removed by soaking the plates in hot water. Groove two adjacent faces of a piece of wood of square section to take the top edges of the glass. Another use for photographic plates is the making of picture frames with a passe-partout binding.

Newspapers.—These are handy for stopping up cracks between floor-boards, and spread evenly on the floor, they make an excellent underlay for a carpet or linoleum. In laying linoleum over a concrete floor never omit a thick underlay of newspapers.

Besides providing patches for puncture repairs, old inner tubes can be used for making rubber bands. Simply cut across the tube with a pair of sharp scissors, which should be dipped in water. Suitable lengths of inner tube also make effective grips for such things as cricket bats and canoe paddles. A strip cut from an old outer cover and tacked round a broom-head prevents damage to

furniture and paint on the skirting boards.

Vulcanite knobs from disused wireless sets make heat-proof knobs for

Fig. 6

kettle lids, as illustrated in Fig. 6.

Sheets of strawboard can be made into loose covers for holding drawings, maps, and music. The boards should

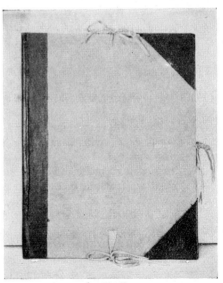

Fig. 7

be covered with stout brown paper or leather paper as used by book-binders. Holes punched near the edges through which tape is threaded provide a simple fastening, as shown in Fig. 7.

Old lino may be used to cover dog kennels and rabbit hutches, while small pieces can be used as packing under the legs of unsteady furniture.

Pieces of Carpet.—Portions of an old carpet can be used for making small mats. These are useful in such places as the scullery and workshop where the floor may chill the feet. Cut out pieces to the desired size and bind the edges with strong carpet binding which can be obtained in a variety of colours for a few pence a yard.

Pitch taken from worn-out high tension batteries is useful. When melted, it can be applied to the ends of wooden posts that have to be buried in the ground. Pitch is also handy for repairing felt roofing material on sheds and poultry houses.

Campers will find that metal meat skewers are useful for pegging small tents.

Seasoned Wood.—It is often possible to obtain well seasoned and expensive hardwoods in the shape of old furniture by paying a visit to a jumble sale. Solid mahogany tables may sometimes be picked up for a fraction of the cost of new wood.

Venetian blinds provide the wood-worker with strips of pine. The paint is easily removed with a chemical paint remover. A razor blade fitted to a wooden handle is excellent for cutting rubber, cardboard, leather and paper, and mounted on a wooden stand makes a good string cutter.

Electricians can use pieces of gramophone records for insulating, while complete discs can be employed for the plates of a Wimshurst's machine for experiments with static electricity.

SWITCHBACK FOR CHILDREN

THE children's switchback shown in Fig. 1 is 8 ft. 6 in. long × 4 ft. high to the entrance of the track, and 2 ft. 2 in. wide.

The following paragraphs describe how to make a switchback to the dimensions shown.

It is important to make the sides out of American whitewood, or other close grained wood that will not splinter and crack under the influence of the weather.

Begin by squaring up two boards each 10 ft. 3 in. × 1 ft. 4 in. × 1 in. American whitewood can be bought any width up to about 2 ft.

Also plane and square up to 3 × 3 in. sufficient lengths of deal to make the six legs, allowing ¾ in. extra length on each one for waste.

Then mark out carefully one of the long side boards as shown in Fig. 2, by squaring pencil lines across it, adopting the following method. From the left-hand end measure a distance of 9 in. then 3 ft. 9 in., 3 ft. 3 in. and 2 ft. 6 in. as shown.

From the ends of the lines, that is, where they meet the near edge of the board, mark three lines across at an angle of 60 deg.

Then measure across to the right of these lines and at right-angles to them, 3 in. and draw parallel lines.

These six lines give the positions, angles and widths of the legs.

Mark out the curves very carefully and measure from the edges of the plank, as shown in Fig. 2.

Next screw the two boards together,

putting the screws into the waste wood marked x.

Put the boards upside down in the vice and bow-saw out the lower curves D only. Spokeshave and finish square, keeping the line flat just where it comes under the legs, as this will be better for fitting the skew shoulders of the legs and boards underneath.

Take the two long legs (6 ft. long),

(length 2 ft. 6 in.), measure down 8 in. and mark out in the same way as the middle legs.

Set the gauge to 1 in. and gauge from the outside of the legs all round the sides and ends as far as the first line you marked round.

Saw all these down and take out the inside pieces as shown in the detail in Fig. 1. Keep the hand-saw on the waste side of the lines.

Screwing on the Legs.—Take apart the two side boards and fit and screw on the six legs whilst the 60 deg. lines are still right across them.

To do this, place an odd piece of

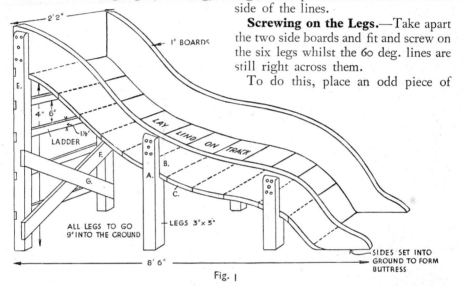

Fig. 1

measure down from the top ends 1 ft. 2 in. and square pencil lines round. Mark all the legs outside and inside as you go.

Then measure down 4 ft. and square round. This indicates the ground line.

Take the next pair of legs (length 4 ft. 6 in.) and measure 9 in. down from the top (square) end from this point on the left-hand edge, mark a line across at an angle of 60 deg. and also at the top.

The bevel should be held in the left hand with its shoulder on the left-hand edge. Take these two lines square across the sides of the leg and at an angle of 60 deg. on the back of it.

Now take the two shortest legs

$\frac{3}{4}$ in. stuff on the under shaped edge of the long board, just where the leg goes, place the leg in position and screw it on, take out the odd piece and apply it to the other legs, because at this stage, the shoulder is not up against anything.

Compare the two boards—see that all the legs coincide. Stand them up and view them. If all is correct, take out the screws from the legs and proceed to lay the track by cutting off a number of $7 \times \frac{3}{4}$ in. deal boards, each 2 ft. 2 in. long.

Note where the curve sharpens these boards must be sawn narrower, say $3\frac{1}{2}$ in. The rest of the track may be laid with the 7 in. boards.

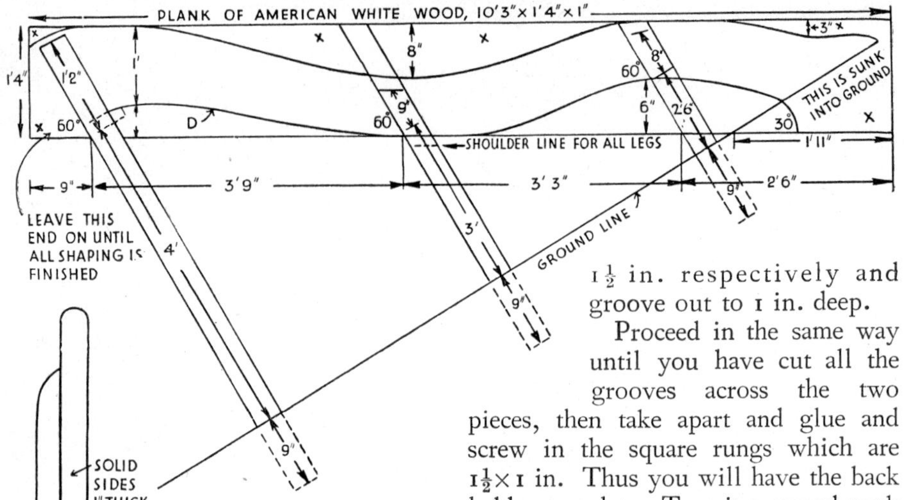

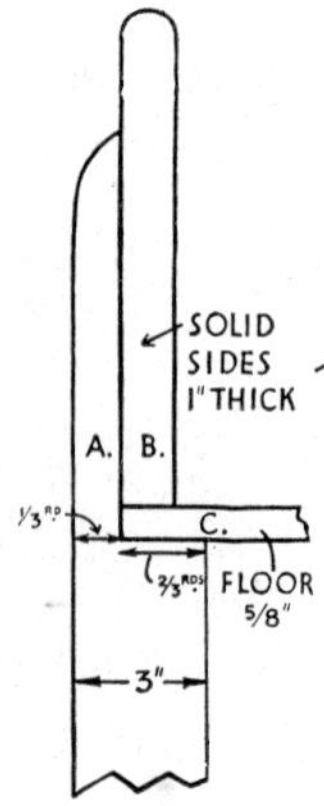

PLANK OF AMERICAN WHITE WOOD, 10'3" x 1'4" x 1"

THIS IS SUNK INTO GROUND

SHOULDER LINE FOR ALL LEGS

GROUND LINE

LEAVE THIS END ON UNTIL ALL SHAPING IS FINISHED

SOLID SIDES 1" THICK

FLOOR 5/8"

Fig. 2

Fix the two long side boards upside down on the bench, with nails or screws at the ends.

Then bore and countersink the track (transverse) boards and screw them on. Use about three screws at each end of the 7 in. boards and two screws for the narrower pieces. It should be noted that by putting boiling water on the side you wish to be round you can warp the boards and so avoid planing smooth the inside surface of the track. This operation must be done before screwing down. If this method is adopted, be sure to allow at least twelve hours for the track to dry thoroughly.

Take again the two longest legs and pin these together. With the back surfaces as "face sides," measure down $1\frac{1}{2}$ in. from the 1 ft. 2 in. line you drew before (this is the top of the track). Square two lines across and cut a groove $1\frac{1}{2}$ in. wide × 1 in. deep and fit and screw in the top rung of the ladder, as shown at E in Fig. 1.

Then measure downwards 6 in. and

$1\frac{1}{2}$ in. respectively and groove out to 1 in. deep.

Proceed in the same way until you have cut all the grooves across the two pieces, then take apart and glue and screw in the square rungs which are $1\frac{1}{2}$ × 1 in. Thus you will have the back ladder complete. Turn it over and mark across the positions of the two brace (cross) pieces by pinning on the piece F first and pin the centre of G in position on top of it.

It will now be possible to mark off the side grooves and the centre lapped halving joint—half out of each piece.

Take this apart and gauge along the edges to $\frac{7}{8}$ in. on the inside of the legs, and along the edges of the centre part of the cross pieces for the halving joint.

Cut out the halving joint recesses first and fit this carefully together, then glue and screw up.

You can now apply the cross brace with certainty to the marked slot positions on the insides of the legs. Correct any faults, cut out the grooves and screw and glue in the brace.

Leave this piece of the work to dry.

Shaping the Top Edge.—Now take the track again, remove all the treads (cross pieces) and shape the top of the side boards with a bow-saw and spokeshave.

This top edge must now be very carefully rounded, first with a spokeshave and finished with fine Nos. 2, $1\frac{1}{2}$, 1 and 0 glass-paper.

It is quite possible, with careful sawing, to shape these top edges without unscrewing the track. Proceed in this way: fix the track on the bench by screws put in the ends (waste pieces) then pin a couple of 1 in. strips across the top—one at each end—to hold the sides firm when sawing. The positions of these supports may be altered as the work proceeds.

When this is all finished put a few reinforcing strips consisting of 2×1 in. battens, across the inside of the tracks—so as not to strain the sides when screwing.

Turn the track upside down and glue and screw on the legs.

Oxidising the Screws.—Use long stout screws and oxidise them to prevent rusting. To do this, put the screws in an old, deep tin and only just cover them with olive oil. Put the tin on the gas-stove with the gas jet high and when they have bronzed take them out.

Making the Foundation.—Now that the construction is complete, stand the switchback up in the garden and prepare the holes for the legs and lower end, which also goes into the ground and forms a buttress. The holes should be dug about 7 in. square ×9 in. deep. In the bottom of each hole put an old tile or thick piece of slate.

When these holes are ready, turn the switchback over and paint the ends of the legs as far as they go into the ground, with Burgundy pitch. To prepare the pitch put it in an old saucepan, make it hot (be careful) with the gas jet low, then apply it with an old brush.

After having allowed about twelve hours for the pitch to dry, lower the switchback into the holes and pack well round the legs a quantity of small stones mixed with earth, and ram well down. Test the structure for squareness and rigidity in all directions.

When quite firm, saw off and round the top ends. Also round off every part of the structure. Glass-paper every part smoothly, taking every precaution not to leave any splinters.

The whole work may now be painted, and when quite dry, the top of the sides should again be glass-papered smooth.

Finally, firmly tack on the face of the top rung, with big tacks, a sufficiently long piece of stair lino 2 ft. wide to cover the entire track. This will bed down without further fastenings.

Thoroughly oil it with raw linseed oil and allow three days to dry. Then wax polish it with any of the well-known wax polishes.

The children should be given an old mat to sit on.

SEE-SAW AND MODEL SHOP

MOST children appreciate a see-saw and the one illustrated in the working drawings Figs. 1, 2 and 3, and described below is quite easy to construct.

Procure a piece of sound timber 8 ft. long ×8 in. wide and 1½ in. thick, smooth with a sharp jack plane and remove all sharp edges.

Scribe a line across the centre of one wide face and fix centrally with this mark a piece of iron 1¼ in. wide × $\frac{3}{16}$ in. thick, bent at right-angles at the ends and drilled to clear a ½ in. diameter bolt, as at A in Fig. 4.

The length of the iron is 12 in. and is bent 2 in. from either end, the holes being drilled 1 in. from the ends. Clean

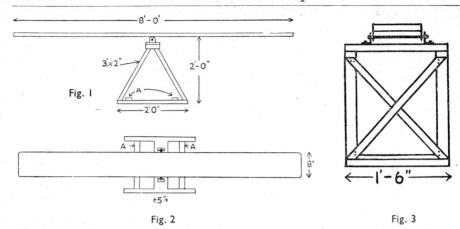

Fig. 1

Fig. 2

Fig. 3

and trim the ends of the iron with a file. Drill three holes in the centre of the width of the strip to clear No. 10 wood screws. The arrangement of this is shown in Fig. 4.

Now construct a pair of supporting frames as indicated in Fig. 1, and screw on the tops a piece of planed wood 18 in. long × 5 in. wide and 1 in. thick.

Saw and plane a couple of battens 18 in. long, 3 in. wide × 1 in. thick and secure these to the bottom of the frames in the position shown at A in Figs. 1 and 2. Also fix a couple of cross braces at the ends of the two frames as indicated in Fig. 3.

Draw a line down the centre of the width of the top board and scribe a line across it at a distance of 9 in. from one end. From this line mark another on the left-hand side and a shade over 4 in. away from it and a similar line at the same distance on the right of the centre line. These give the positions of the two right-angled brackets, through which a central hole is drilled in each to clear the ½ in. bolt.

Make these brackets of the same material as that used under the plank, drill the bolt holes and the holes for taking the fixing down screws.

Place the brackets at the marked position on the top board and fix them down

with No. 10 round-headed wood screws.

In fixing the brackets allow about ⅛ in. play between their working faces and the faces of the bracket on the long plank. Place the long plank in position and pass a 10×½ in. diameter bolt through the holes and screw on a nut, thus joining the plank and its support together. Iron washers should be inserted under the head of the bolt before passing it through the holes in the brackets and another washer should be placed under the nut.

This completes the see-saw. If it is to be used by very young children, it is advisable to make and fix backed seats across the ends to prevent their falling off backwards. Straps should also be provided to prevent their falling forward.

The see-saw should be finished in bright colours, say blue for the support, half the length of the plank yellow and the other half red. A spot of oil should be applied to the bearings.

A Model Shop.—A model shop is a toy that will keep children amused for hours. The one described here and illustrated by the dimensioned drawings Figs. 5 and 6, has a glazed detachable front and doorway and a removable roof, which adds greatly to its appearance. It can be made in a few spare evenings with the aid of a few simple tools.

Start work by constructing the base which is best made out of plywood ¾ in. thick. The finished size of this is 19 in. long and 13 in. wide. Make sure that this member is cut and trimmed perfectly square and is quite flat.

Then prepare the parts for the detachable front. This is built up of corner posts of ½ in. square yellow deal, planed true to size and plywood ¼ in. thick.

Cut two front end posts, A in Fig. 5, each 10¾ in. long and two intermediate posts 9 in. in length as indicated at B, also the horizontal pieces of the following lengths: One 17 in. for the top cross piece C, two 6 in. for the bottom of the windows D, one 4 in. for the top of the doorway E. Four uprights each 9 in. long will also be required at the back, as well as two horizontals to correspond with those at D.

Also cut and square up some pieces of plywood ¼ in. thick to the following sizes: Two pieces each 9 in. long × 3 in. wide for the sides, two pieces of the same size for the sides of the doorway, four pieces 6×3 in. for the lower front and back panels, one piece 1 ft. 6 in. × 4 in. for the roof strip, one piece 1 ft. 5¼ in. × 1½ in. for the facia board, two pieces 6¼×3 in. to cover in the spaces between the rails D, and the corresponding ones at the back, a piece 4¼×4 in. for the floor of the doorway and one piece 4×1 in. for the panel at the top of the door. The corners of the floor for the doorway will have to be recessed to clear the posts.

Before starting to assemble these parts make a groove ⅛ in. deep and ⅛ in. wide in the centre of the inner faces of four

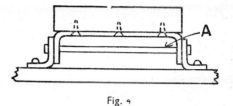

Fig. 4

front uprights. These grooves accommodate the ends of the glass windows and the ends of the facia board which should be trimmed off to ⅛ in. thick.

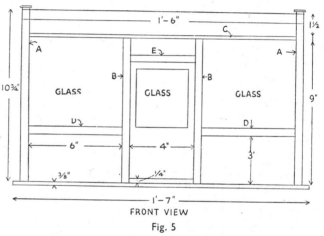

FRONT VIEW

Fig. 5

Then assemble the parts by means of tube glue and 1¼ in. panel pins. The edges of the plywood will lie back ⅛ in. from the faces of the posts. First build up the front by fixing the four front uprights to the two plywood pieces forming the panels underneath the window, then fix the two side pieces and the upright pieces between the doorway. Cut and slide the glass into the grooves, fix the roof and then the four back posts and the roof strip.

Next fit the two lower panels at the back, the floor of the doorway, the head panel and finally the facia board.

Make a door 4 in. wide and 7¼ in.

long of ¼ in. plywood. Cut out the upper part to take a piece of glass and round the long edges. Hang the door

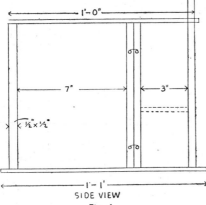

SIDE VIEW

Fig. 6

by means of pivots formed by driving in panel pins. To do this insert a headless pin ⅛ in. from the right hand top corner, into the wood and make a corresponding hole under the door head, using a very fine bradawl for the purpose. Drill a hole through the doorway floor in line with the hole above, place the door in position and press a panel through the hole in the bottom into the lower edge of the door. This completes the front.

For the main structure, cut four lengths of ½ × ½ in. stuff each 9 in. long for the corner posts, two pieces of ¼ in. plywood for the sides and another piece for the back. The sizes are 7 in. long and 9 in. wide and 11 × 9 in. respectively. Assemble these three parts to the posts as already explained and cut a piece of plywood for the roof, size 18 in. long × 8 in. wide.

Do not proceed with any further constructional work at this stage as the next operation consists of painting the parts. It is worth remembering when finishing off toys of this description, including model railway stations, and dolls houses, always to use a high grade oil-bound

water paint in preference to oil paint as the appearance of a completed article so treated is greatly enhanced. First size the wood to stop absorption of the paint, and when dry apply two coats of the colours desired.

In this instance a dark grey colour may be employed for the baseboard and the top of the roof, mid-stone for the interior and exterior of the walls of the shop, white for the ½ in. square vertical and horizontal posts, the underside of the roof and facia board.

Use a soft brush to apply the paint. Do not have the paint too thick and be careful to keep all lines well defined and sharp as nothing looks worse than one colour running over another. Each coat must be allowed to dry thoroughly before applying the next.

Then fix the back and sides to the base by driving in screws from the underside into the corner posts and strengthening the joints by hammering in 1 in. panel pins, spaced at a distance of about every 2 in.

Next fix the front section to the back part by means of small hooks and eyes. The roof of the back section can be kept in place by tacking on strips of ¼ in. square wood on the underside so that they butt against the sides and back inside, like the lever lid of a tin box.

Then fit shelves and drawers to accommodate the "goods" and to make a suitable counter.

The shelves may consist of strips of plywood 3/16 in. thick and an inch or so wide, while the drawers can be constructed by sticking a number of match boxes together and fitting them with miniature handles.

The counter also can be made of plywood, to any shape desired.

Such a structure would answer well as a confectioner's shop; imitation cakes, tarts and the like could be made in coloured plasticine or modelling wax

MAKING A REFLECTORSCOPE

THIS simply constructed apparatus, illustrated in Fig. 1, will give endless pleasure to the younger members of the family. It is similar to an optical or magic lantern as it is commonly called, the main difference being that in the reflectorscope the image of any opaque object or picture is thrown on to a screen direct, whereas if you wish to show a photograph through a magic lantern it is necessary to have a special transparent glass slide made of it.

Nor is this the only advantage gained by using a reflectorscope, for picture postcards, illustrations taken from magazines, flowers, etc., can be projected in actual colours on to a screen, giving pictures up to about 4 ft. in diameter.

As its name suggests, the reflectorscope is worked by reflected light thrown on to the surface of the object by an electric or other lamp and then again reflected through the lens which enlarges the image and projects it on to the screen.

To construct the apparatus as illustrated in Fig. 1, you will require the following material.

Four pieces of wood—deal will do quite well, although plywood is to be preferred—each 9×6×⅜ in. for the top, base, front and back, and two pieces 5¼×6×⅜ in. for the sides. These parts when assembled will form the box.

A circular disc of wood, 2¾ in. in diameter and ⅜ in. thick. This piece is afterwards cut in half to form the feet or base of the reflectors.

A double-convex lens—that is, a lens whose surface curves outwards on both sides. A reading glass lens will do well for the purpose. It should be about 3 in. in diameter.

A cardboard or ebonite tube, whose internal diameter will allow the lens to fit tightly inside.

Four pieces of tinplate to form the fixed tube or housing for the lens tube, fixing ring and the two reflectors respectively.

Two electric lampholders fitted with cord grips and shade carriers, a standard

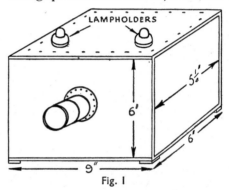

Fig. 1

fitting which can be obtained at almost any electrician's shop.

A suitable length of flexible wire and

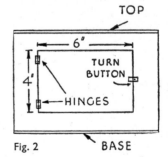

Fig. 2

an adapter for attaching to the electric light circuit.

A pair of small brass hinges.

A few screws, glue, solder, etc.

Start by making the box, and when you have sawn and squared up the parts to the sizes given above and as indicated in Fig. 1, make a hole 3¼ in. in diameter in the front.   This hole must be in the centre and can be cut with the aid of a fret-saw.

Next, cut a doorway in the back, Fig. 2. If you fret-saw this piece carefully, the portion removed will serve as the door, otherwise you will have to make one to fit the aperture.

Make two holes a shade over $1\frac{1}{8}$ in. in diameter in the top piece to take the lampholders, as shown in Fig. 1.   Wire according to the diagram, Fig. 3, taking care not to cross-connect the wires or results may be obtained contrary to those expected. Fit the lampholders into their respective holes in the box and then turn your attention to the reflectors illustrated in Fig. 4.

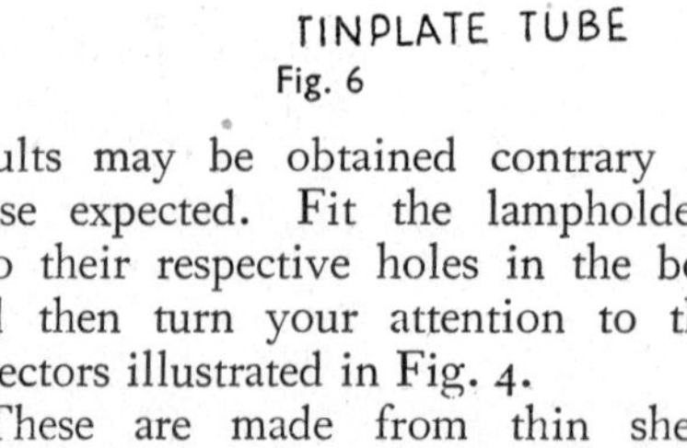

These are made from thin sheet tinplate, the size of each being 5 in. high and about $4\frac{1}{2}$ in. in the flat.

Bend these pieces to shape and fit them to the semi-circular base-pieces. Screw the reflectors down to the bottom of the box in the positions shown in Fig. 5, using one screw only for each. By so doing the reflectors may be swivelled round and adjusted to the most suitable angle.

The lens should be fixed tightly in the cardboard tube at a distance of about $\frac{1}{2}$ in. from one end.   A ring of thin cardboard should be glued on each side of the lens to keep it in position.

A tinplate tube, about 3 in. long and of suitable diameter to allow the card board cylinder to slide in and out, should now be prepared.

Cut a piece of tinplate to size and solder up the seam, taking care to see that the inside bore is perfectly smooth and true. Also, cut a tinplate ring $\frac{1}{2}$ in. wide to fit tightly over this tube to form a flange and solder it on securely at a distance of about $\frac{1}{2}$ in. from the back end of the tube.   Details are shown in Fig. 6.

The lens and its components are now ready to be placed over the hole in the front of the box and fixed in position with small screws.

Now carefully assemble the box together, using 1 in. countersunk-headed screws, brass ones for preference.

Fix two strips of tinplate to the inside surface of the door to grip the pictures, etc., you intend to show, and fix a little wooden or metal button on the door to keep it shut.

The door may be hung with a pair of $1 \times \frac{3}{8}$ in. brass butts.

See that the interior is perfectly light-tight, except, of course, where the lens projects. If you find that the light leaks through any cracks or crevices you must stop them up.

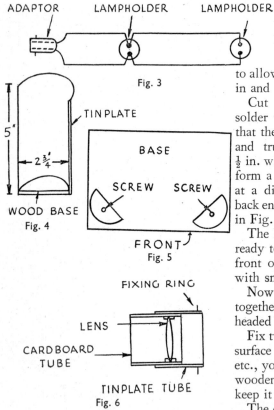

Fig. 3

Fig. 4

Fig. 5

Fig. 6

Before the apparatus is ready for use the interior should be painted a dead matt black. Lamp black mixed with turpentine is an excellent pigment to use.

To give the exterior a good finish it should be stained and varnished, and if a small square of wood about $1\frac{1}{2} \times 1\frac{1}{2} \times \frac{1}{2}$ in. is screwed on to each corner at the bottom the general appearance of the apparatus will be greatly improved.

Projection.—Hang a white sheet, about 5 ft. square, to a wall and place the reflectorscope on a table a few feet from the screen.

Place two 40 watt gas-filled electric lamps of the correct voltage—the pearl or frosted lamps should be used in preference to the clear ones—in the lampholders provided. Remove the electric light bulb from the nearest lighting point and insert the adapter.

Put a picture postcard in the clips and shut the little door at the back. Turn off all lights in the room and then adjust the lens to obtain the correct focus.

This is done by pushing or pulling out the lens tube until the picture on the screen appears perfectly sharp and clear.

If electric light is not available you need not be disheartened for it is quite possible to use oil lamps for the purpose of illuminating the picture. In this case, the body of the reflectorscope should be made of metal—tinplate will answer very well—but proper ventilation must be provided and proper arrangements made to prevent light escaping anywhere except through the proper place—namely, the lens.

MECHANICAL DOOR BELL

THERE are two common types of mechanical bells. That shown at A in Fig. 1 is operated by a bell push as the push is pressed or until the spring has run down. From this it will be observed that it is essential to keep the

Fig. I

like an electric bell. When the button is pushed it releases a spring driven hammer and continues to ring as long spring wound up as in a clock. This is effected by turning the dome in a clockwise direction. An excellent bell of this type can be had for about 5s.

The other type is illustrated at B in Fig. 1. The hammer of this bell is operated by turning a knob, and as it is not fitted with a main spring, does not need to be wound up. Such a bell is slightly cheaper than the spring-driven type.

Both bells are fitted to the door in practically the same manner, the only difference being in the fixing of the controls.

To fit the push-operated spring-driven bell, proceed in the following manner:

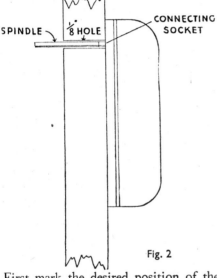

Fig. 2

First mark the desired position of the push. The latter is usually mounted at a convenient height in the centre of the mounting of the door or on the centre rail.

Having marked the centre position of the push button, examine the other side of the door to see that there is nothing to obstruct the fitting of the bell, because the centre of the bell does not come in line with the centre of the bell push. The spindle socket which accom-modates the end of the spindle and connects the press to the bell is situated near the rim of the frame that supports the gong, as indicated in Fig. 2.

At the marked point bore a hole $\frac{1}{8}$ in. in diameter through the door, using a sharp twist-bit for the purpose, taking care to see that the hole is square with the flat surface of the door. Remove the dome and insert the end of the wire firmly into the connecting bush at the back of the bell, push the spindle through the hole and fix the bell with $\frac{1}{2}$ in. brass screws. Next cut off the projecting end of the wire $\frac{3}{4}$ in. full from the face of the woodwork, place the button on the end of the wire and press the button case into place.

If the bell rings when placed in position it follows that the spindle is too long, so a small piece can be cut off with the aid of a pair of cutting pliers or a file. When this adjustment has been made, fix the button plate with small round-headed screws. These are generally provided with the bell.

In replacing the dome make sure that the spring is fully wound or damage may be done to the mechanism.

Rotary Knob Type.—Much the same procedure is followed when fitting a bell of this type. Here the spindle connecting the knob to the bell is in line with the centre of the bell and is rectangular in section. To obtain sufficient clearance for the spindle, bore the hole with a $\frac{5}{16}$ in. twist-bit. Having bored the wood, fit the shank and fix the bell, make adjustments to the spindle and fix the knob.

Bells of this description do not require cleaning as they are generally bronze finished. An occasional drop or two of oil is all that is necessary to keep them in serviceable condition.

REPAINTING A MOTOR CAR

BEFORE going into details of how to repaint a motor car one or two points should be observed.

First it is useless to expect to obtain a good finish if the garage in which the painting is to be done is full of dust and dirt. All unwanted articles should be removed and the walls and floor swept and washed thoroughly. Before the actual painting proceeds, hang clean dust sheets over the doors to prevent ingress of dust. Cleanliness is of the utmost importance.

Brushes.—Good work cannot be done with unsuitable brushes. This does not mean that old brushes must be discarded, but if used they should be cleaned thoroughly by placing them in boiling vinegar and water. They should then be rinsed in clean water and rubbed dry on a clean piece of wood.

Before use new brushes should be washed and dried on a board as this will remove any loose hairs.

Three brushes will be required and the best kind to use are those with good quality bristles, not too stiff, and set in rubber. Two of these brushes, one measuring $2\frac{1}{2}$ in. across and the other $1\frac{1}{2}$ in., will be needed for painting the body, while another brush—$1\frac{1}{2}$ in. wide will do—should be kept for painting these parts of the chassis such as the springs, etc.

Temperature.—If the work is to be carried out in the winter, some means of warming the garage must be installed as it is essential that the temperature should not be below about 65 deg. F., especially if enamel or varnish is to be employed.

A reliable oil stove of the type that is not liable to smoke, will be of service if an electric heater is not available.

Before applying any finishing medium the old surface of the car body should be examined to see whether it was previously finished with cellulose lacquer, paint and varnish or paint and enamel. The condition of this should be noted.

If the car is not very old the chances are that it was finished with cellulose lacquer, sprayed on and polished. If this surface is in a fairly good condition and has only lost its lustre, the brightness can be restored by applying a coat of coach varnish. This, however, should only be used if the original finish is at least twelve months old as varnish is likely to flake off. It can be applied over a lacquer surface provided the latter is not too new.

If the lacquer is only slightly faded and discoloured it can be brought into condition by carefully repolishing it with rottenstone mixed with oil. This treatment, however, should only be attempted if the lacquer coat is sufficiently thick to withstand the polishing.

If the lacquer is thin it is better to give the body a couple of coats of brushing lacquer.

In treating a car finished in stove enamel or paint and varnish and the undercoats of which have not faded to any appreciable degree, a coat of high-grade coach varnish will restore its brilliance. It may be that the undercoats have become very much faded in which case it will be better to use enamel. One coat of enamel may suffice but better results will be obtained by giving two coats. The second coat must not be applied before at least three days after the first one has been done, in order to give the latter time to become perfectly hard.

Before starting to apply paint to the car, the body should be washed thoroughly with soap and water applied with a softish brush to remove all dirt, and the same treatment must be given to the axles and springs if it is desired to repaint these parts.

Having washed the car it is as well to wipe the surface with a clean soft rag moistened with petrol. Then to rub it down with a very fine grade of glass-paper, and remove the dust thus formed with a cloth slightly damped with petrol. This work is best done out of doors, and every precaution must be taken not to allow a naked light to ignite the petrol vapour. The rest of the work should be carried out in the garage.

Preparing the Paint.—Strain the finishing medium through several thicknesses of muslin. The receptacle into which the liquid is to be poured must, of course, be perfectly clean and entirely free from dust. This container should only be used for accommodating the bulk of the paint and effectively sealed when not in use. A small container such as a china pudding-basin can be employed for holding the varnish or enamel during the painting.

Painting.—As a rule it is best to start from the top and work down. If it is decided to paint the roof, this should be done first. In order to carry out this part of the work in comfort, it is advisable to work from a plank placed about a foot above and across the roof, each end of the plank being supported by a pair of household steps. A short scaffold board could no doubt be hired for a few pence from the local builder. Before using such a board,

however, do not forget to clean it thoroughly as such boards are usually dirty and dusty.

Having treated the roof the next item is to paint the windscreen frame and engine cover, then the doors, treating the upper part of the door just before the lower half. Next proceed with the body panels, leaving the mudguards until last, as these may be of a different colour than that of the body.

The springs, axles, etc., should then receive attention and lastly the wheels.

One of the most frequent troubles experienced by the amateur is the formation of runs and blobs of the finishing medium due to improper application and overloading the brush.

A professional painter never allows too much paint on his brush.

To get the best results, one panel should be completed at a time. The enamel or varnish is flowed on until the whole surface under treatment is covered and then the surface is brushed out with a brush in order to remove the excess material.

To brush out the surface, proceed in the following manner: First wipe the brush on the edge of the paint container and apply it to the top of the panel, working it back and forth, horizontally towards the bottom, and wiping the brush on the edge of the container from time to time. Then repeat the operation by drawing the brush vertically and then again horizontally. On the first brushing-out put a little pressure on the brush; on the second, not quite so much pressure, and very little on the third. If this method is carried out to the latter, an excellent surface without brush marks will result.

REPAIRING CHINA

WHEN a mishap occurs to a china article of sentimental value—be it ornament, crockery or other similar object—an attempt should be made to repair it, unless the article in question is so shattered that it is rendered useless.

There are numerous proprietary adhesives which can be had for repairing broken china. Some of these have to be melted before use. Such cement always be perfectly clean and free from every trace of grease.

When making the repair a thin film of adhesive should be applied to both edges of the broken parts and the latter pressed firmly together as illustrated in Fig. 1. In many cases it will be found an advantage to bind the parts securely with electrician's adhesive tape. Do not use the repaired article

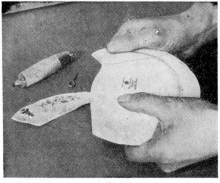

Fig. 1

should not be employed for repairing articles that have to withstand heat. In using this kind of adhesive the parts to be joined should be warmed, otherwise it will be chilled before it has had time to stick properly, and the resulting joint will be weak.

Liquid glue is also suitable for joining china that does not have to withstand heat.

Remember, when applying any kind of adhesive—and this applies equally when joining wooden articles—to use as little as possible. It is a mistake to think that the greater the amount of fixing medium used, the stronger the joint will be. Cement too thickly applied also causes an ugly and obtrusive joint. The parts to be joined must

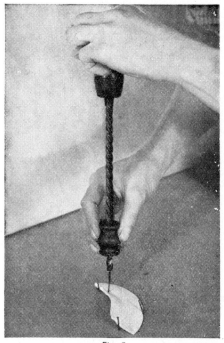

Fig. 2

for at least a week, in order to allow the cement to set.

A simple and effective home-made adhesive for joining china is made by mixing some plaster-of-paris to a paste with the white of an egg. This preparation should not be made up until it is actually required, as it sets and becomes hard very quickly.

Good results can also be obtained from white lead and linseed oil. In preparing this it is essential that the white lead be ground very fine, free from small lumps and mixed with the oil to form a stiff paste.

Riveting.—To repair a plate or other article that has to withstand heat and be extremely strong it is best to rivet the parts together. The chief requirements are a suitable drill, properly applied, and one or two sundry tools such as pliers, light hammer, etc.

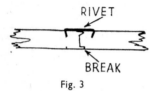

Fig. 3

A special drill having a diamond point is used by professional china riveters, but as such a tool is not likely to be in the possession of an amateur, an ordinary hard steel V-pointed drill, driven by an archemedian drill-stock as shown in Fig. 2 will suffice, provided that any hard glaze is first removed. This can be effected by a glass-cutter.

The rivets generally used for china repairs are made of tinned brass wire, $\frac{1}{16}$ in. thick and the holes to receive them should be a trifle larger—say $\frac{3}{32}$ in. Therefore it is advisable that a drill bit of this size should be used.

It is best to make the holes $\frac{1}{4}$ in. from the edge of the break and slant them slightly inwards as shown in Fig. 3, as the springiness of the rivets draws the parts closely together. The holes should be drilled to a depth of not more than $\frac{2}{3}$ in. of the thickness of the parts to be joined, and when boring the holes, lubricate the drill with turpentine.

The length of the rivets should be about $\frac{5}{8}$ to $\frac{3}{4}$ in. and the ends bent to coincide with the sloping holes in the work.

To make a rivet, hold the wire between the jaws of flat nosed pliers and gently tap the ends with a light hammer. Then bend the ends of the wire slightly inwards and flatten the middle portion by placing it on a piece of hard metal and tapping the rivet gently with a hammer. The flat surface so made allows the rivet to lie close to the surface of the china. The rivet is then sprung into the hole and tapped home by striking it very lightly with a hammer.

Three rivets are generally necessary to join each separate part of the broken china.

Plasticine or putty can be used to advantage for supporting broken parts while springing the rivet in place. To finish, fill up the hole with liquid plaster-of-paris.

GLASS-CUTTING, FROSTING AND DRILLING

GLASS can be cut in two ways, with a glazier's diamond or with a steel wheel which revolves as the cut is made. In each case a shallow mark is produced and the crystalline quality of glass is then used to break it at the cut.

The diamond is a better tool, but it is expensive and requires expert handling. It is best to get some old pieces of glass of different thicknesses and make trial cuts on these before undertaking serious work.

Technique of Cutting.—The glass must be laid on a perfectly flat surface. Any undulation may cause a crack. A cushioned surface of two or three thicknesses of soft cloth is excellent.

Fig. 1.

For guiding the line of the cut, use a draughtsman's T-square, as shown in Fig. 1. A number of right-angled triangles can be cut from five-ply wood, ranging in length of side from about

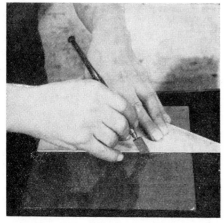

Fig. 2

6 in. to 3 ft. These triangles must be accurately cut, but they will be useful for work involving measurements and angles. The method is to place one of the sides of the right-angle along a straight side of the material cut and the

other side of the right-angle will form a guide both as to line and angle, as shown in the illustration Fig. 2.

Make sure there is adequate support on either side of the line to be cut.

Fig. 3

Then draw the diamond along the glass following the rule, holding the handle almost upright and using only a slight pressure. The operation is shown in Fig. 3. The diamond should emit a clear, singing note whilst cutting, and the angle of inclination of the handle should be altered until this is obtained.

Breaking Off.—The cleaner and

Fig. 4

finer the groove, the easier the glass will break. To break the glass, shift the groove on the table side, take hold of the projecting end with a piece of cloth and with a firm, steady pressure break off the unwanted piece. Fig. 4

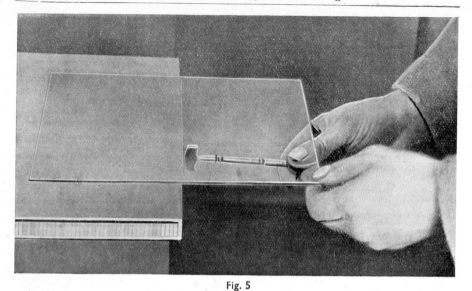

Fig. 5

shows how this is done. The cloth is necessary in case of a jagged break.

Another method is illustrated in Fig. 5. The glass is moved to the end of the table until its edge coincides with the groove. Holding the unwanted piece with the left hand, tap the underside gently with the glass cutter from left to right.

The wheel glass cutter requires more pressure, but the method of cutting and breaking is the same. If the wheel does not cut properly, moisten it with paraffin. A little abrasive powder of water and carborundum, or water and sand, should be spread along the line of the cut. The steel wheel is better than the diamond for cutting curved lines. When not in use, keep the end of the tool in light machine oil. This prevents the wheel from becoming rusted.

Thick Glass.—For cutting thick pieces of glass, or shapes which cannot be attempted with wheel or diamond, a disc of iron or steel whose edge has been dipped in an abrasive mixture is used. The disc should be about $\frac{1}{8}$ in. thick, notched slightly at the edge with a file, and of good diameter. Hold the disc between thumb and bent forefinger, dip the edge into the abrasive mixture and use the disc like a plane, sawing back and forth along the **required** line.

Fig. 6

To cut curved lines, a template of the desired contour should be made from stout cardboard or plywood. This is laid on the glass. A steel wheel is used. Do not cut too sharp a curve as the glass may split across the line of cut when breaking. If a sharp curve is necessary, make the groove deeper and cut radiating lines to the edge of the glass. The breaking is done with pliers wrapped in cloth, a small piece at a time being broken off.

Drilling Glass.—Methods depend on the size of the holes to be drilled. If under ⅛ in., procure a steel rod of the requisite diameter. Silver or nickel-steel is best. Heat about 1 in. of the end dull-red, cool off by plunging in clean cold water, and break off a fraction of the treated end. This forms a jagged cutting edge. Test the hardness of the end with pliers, which should not make a mark.

Take a piece of sheet metal in which a hole of the correct size has been drilled and clamp glass and metal between two thick boards, in one of which an aperture large enough to allow operations has been made. Drill the hole with a drilling machine or handstock, using the steel rod as a drill. Do not use much pressure. Break off pieces of the tempered end to sharpen the drill. This process is illustrated in Fig. 6.

For a larger hole a tube of copper or brass is required, notches being made in the end of the tube to hold the cutting abrasive. The abrasive consists of emery powder and water and the abrasive should be dropped frequently into the deepening hole.

To frost glass, make a solution of full strength fluoric acid, one part, to water, two parts, mixing in a lead vessel out of doors. Add carbonate of ammonia gradually until effervescence ceases. Dip the glass in this solution. Tests should be made to find out the length of time necessary as glass varies in composition.

Artificial Frosting. — This effect may be produced by adding hot water to ½ lb. of gum arabic, letting the gum soak for several hours. When quite dissolved, add ½ lb. of Epsom salts and dissolve thoroughly by standing the vessel in hot water. Paint the glass quickly and evenly with this solution.

Another solution can be made from finely powdered whiting, two-thirds raw linseed oil and one-third japan, mixed to a stiff paste and thinned with turpentine. The glass is painted with this and dabbed with a clean cloth until a frosted appearance is obtained.

Glass can be made translucent by grinding on a level surface with fine emery powder and water, or knife powder. The motion should be circular, and with a regular pressure.

CLOCK CLEANING

THE untrained amateur with some knowledge of mechanics, good sight, patience and light fingers can be successful with the cleaning and adjustment of clocks. Watches are best left to those who have specialised training. Watchmakers' screwdrivers of two or three sizes, fine pliers, camel hair brushes and forceps are the necessary tools. An eyepiece is an advantage. A saucer of petrol is used for cleaning metal slime off the bearings, the dirt being dislodged with one of the brushes. For wiping, a piece of soft silk or cambric will serve provided it does not shed fluff. Work under a good light on a firm

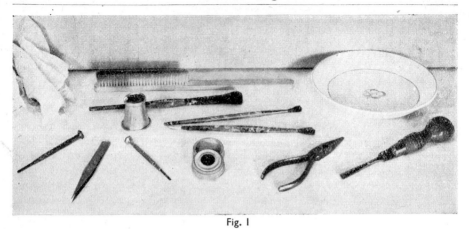

Fig. I

table covered with white paper so that small parts may be easily seen. Fig. 1 shows the necessary tools and accessories.

Careful Oiling.—Use nothing but clock-oil. Ordinary machine-oil is quite unsuitable. Leave no vestige of petrol on the working surfaces, and be very moderate in applying the clock-oil. It is wanted only in the bearings: excess does no good and merely collects dust. Clock-makers sometimes dip the tip of a small screwdriver into the oil and just touch the parts concerned with it, as illustrated in Fig. 2.

A rough cleaning and re-oiling can be undertaken without dismantling the works themselves. Take the clock out of its case. First disengage the pendulum (being careful not to bend or damage the fine steel ribbon or suspension spring on which it hangs, or touch the screw regulator) and withdraw it, (Fig. 3). Next, unless the striking bells or gongs are part of the movement, remove the standard supporting them. This should leave the way clear for withdrawing the clock movement as a whole, probably after slacking off or

Fig. 2

removing a couple of screws. Most movements come away from the back. The retaining screws of one coming away from the front will probably be disclosed on opening the front glass.

When you have taken out the movement, set it down without resting it on any working part, especially the striking hammers, which can easily be bent.

Removing Dust.—Dust the case thoroughly inside and out. Dust will have collected in difficult places, inside the bezel or frame holding the glass. A camel-hair brush will dislodge it, but will not carry it away easily. A jet of compressed air from a motor-tyre pump will dispose of it.

A thin, pointed adapter nozzle about 5 in. long, screwed at one end to fit the thread of the pump and drilled at the other with an orifice about the size of a pin's head, would be useful for this and other purposes. It must be home-made or specially ordered. Slow strokes will produce a blast of surprising efficacy. Fig. 4 shows the operation.

Having brushed and blown, allow time to settle and wipe as clean as possible. Clean and polish the glass, inside and out, with warm soapy water.

Cleaning the Movement. — The greatest care must be taken not to bend any of the mechanism. Handle it only by the framework and be careful when you introduce cleaning implements into the works. The air jet, if directed to the bearings of the various spindles, will blow out some at least of the metal slime resulting from wear. This can be wiped away with clean pipe cleaners of the wire and wool variety. If there is old oil which has become sticky and hard, moisten the pipe cleaner with petrol. It can be bent up into any shape necessary to reach awkward corners. The illustration shown at Fig. 5. shows the cleaning process. If the air pump is

U

not available, brush and pipe cleaner will between them accomplish a good deal. If the face is begrimed, it may be

Fig. 3

washed with a soft, clean, soapy rag and dried and polished, taking care to avoid the hands.

Oil can be applied with the tip of a

Fig. 4

pliable wire such as a wire paper clip. Give special attention to the escapement wheel and to the second wheel which

Fig. 5

carries the minute hand, as these do much of the work. Confine your oiling to the bearings. Oil on the pinions and cogs does more harm than good. Wipe away any excess.

If the clock is fitted with a balance wheel, as in Fig. 6, instead of a pendulum, lock-nuts are sometimes provided for taking up wear. You may have to fashion a small plate spanner to fit them out of stout sheet iron, making the hole with a drill and small square file. The adjustment is a case of trial and error. Do not screw up the bearings too tightly. Whatever you do, do not touch the hair-spring, and be careful not to get oil on it. Time keeping depends upon its shape and weight and interference is bound to impair it.

Striking Clocks.—In clocks with striking movements, Fig. 7, the spindles of the striking mechanism should have attention and also the pivots (often three) on which the striking rack and levers swing, together with the bearings of the striker arms. Sometimes the clamps or screw securing the bells wear loose owing to vibration so that they give a deadened buzzing note. If this is the case, tighten them up. A brightly polished bell emits a clearer tone than a dull one. Bells should, therefore, be polished; gongs are usually of blued-steel wire and require nothing more than dusting.

When the movement has been put back in the case, it is probable that, in the case of gongs, adjustment for position will be necessary. Adjustment is correct when the felt striker stands appreciably clear of its gong. If actually touching, the second will be damped in striking; if nearer still, the hammer may strike a series of diminishing blows instead of one clear one. The correct position is ultimately found after testing patiently until successful.

There is usually more than one way to make the adjustment. The spindle of the gong-standard is probably screwed at its lower end, and provided with a stop inside the base of the case, and a nut and washer outside. It is therefore simple to raise or lower it as a whole. Furthermore, the felt striker is usually attached to its lever by a set screw, allowing fine regulation. Cases may occur, however, where the lever itself (usually of brass wire) must be bent. This requires care and judgment. Be careful to support the lever during the process and never bend it against the unaided resistance of the mechanism.

Regulating.—Now start the clock going and see what sort of time it is keeping. In pendulum clocks the beat should be perfectly even; if it is not the movement should be slightly skewed in the case or any levelling set screws manipulated. As a last resort, the case itself may be packed with strips of cardboard or paper under the feet until the beat is even.

However careful you may have been, it is likely that the clock will require regulating anew. In pendulum clocks, time keeping depends on the length of the pendulum, which is shortened to accelerate. Two adjustments are commonly provided, a coarse one by a screw on or below the bob, and a fine one by a michrometer at the point of suspension of the pendulum, its spindle being brought through to the face of the clock, and operated by a small subsidiary key. In balance wheel clocks, in common with watches, the only adjustment is by means of an indicator lever, moving over a graduated scale, which regulates the length of the hairspring left free to oscillate.

A word on setting the clock to the correct time when starting it. In nonstriking clocks, the minute-hand may be turned either way without risk.

But, in striking clocks, it should never be turned backwards. Moreover, when turning it forward, make a pause just after each hour or part hour striking-point is reached, to allow the mechanism to complete striking. If the number struck

Fig. 6

does not tally with the hour shown, the hour-hand, which is merely a friction fit, may be moved to correct the error.

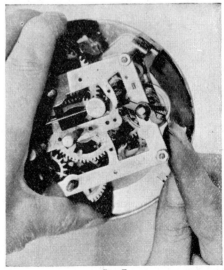

Fig. 7

Some standard time keeper is necessary. Wireless time signals afford an efficient check on the fast or slow running of the piece under observation. Make a comparison every twenty-four hours and touch the regulator accordingly. It is a tedious process sometimes extending over weeks and one calling for great delicacy of touch near to correct time keeping.

Repairs are Risky.—There is little the amateur can do in the way of repairs to clocks, and nothing to watches. Spring breakages are chiefly concerned and to do anything with springs involves drilling, filing, annealing and retempering, processes requiring special appliances and great experience.

The amateur, however, may at least remove the glass-holder, in the case of a broken glass, or the whole movement, in the case of an internal defect, to avoid transporting the weight of the case when taking the clock for repair. In weight-driven clocks, gut is sometimes used to support the weight and it should not be beyond the amateur's capacity to effect replacement.

Electric clocks are increasing in vogue. These require oil like others. But they call for greater care in its application as the wiring is very fine and easily broken. Those depending on a battery will require new cells from time to time, a simple replacement. Those working on the telechron system, off alternating current mains are infallible time-keepers and give very little trouble.

Watches are best left alone. Even to oil them is impossible for most amateurs. The fact of their stopping is proof that they need attention. Nevertheless, a watch that has stopped through a particle of dust in its works may sometimes be induced to go again if the case is opened and the dust blown out with the air-jet, but keep the blast away from the hair-spring, and take the watch to the watchmaker as soon as possible.

SIMPLE CONSTRUCTIONS USING WORKING DRAWINGS

THE working drawings presented with this volume include fifteen useful articles all of which are very easily constructed with the aid of a few "everyday" tools.

Here is a list of the items:

A SUMMER HOUSE

THE summer house illustrated in working drawing No. 1 is of the semi-open type, that is, the upper portions of the front, sides and back are not protected from the weather.

As will be seen from the drawings, the structure is 9 ft. long, 7 ft. wide, 6 ft. 8 in. to eaves and 8 ft. 6 in. to ridge.

Construction.—In constructing the summer house, start by making the floor. This is composed of tongued and grooved boards 1 in. thick (7/8 in. finished) laid on five 3×2 in. joists, narrow faces up. The joists should be kept off the ground and this can be done by using bricks placed with their wide faces up.

Before placing the bricks in position, make sure that the ground is perfectly level and well rammed down, and do not space the bricks too far apart; the more supporting bricks there are the less likely is the structure to cause trouble later.

To prevent damp from penetrating the joists, cut some pieces of roofing felt and put them on the top of the bricks before placing the joists across.

When these preliminaries have been attended to, cut the joists to length and fix the first floor-board after having removed the tongue. The plain edge of the floor-board should be flush with the front ends of the joists.

Then fix a floor-board temporarily at the back, square up the framework and finish laying the floor, using 2 in. floor-brads for fixing purposes.

The next item is to cut the bottom plates (shown by the dotted lines in the drawings of the front view and the side view). All plates are of 2×2 in. section. Two such plates will be required at the front, two at the sides and one at the back.

Saw the four uprights, each 6 ft. 5 in. long, taking care to keep the ends perfectly square and follow by cutting the front, and back top horizontal members. The length of these is 10 ft.

Now fit the bottom plates to the floor, using 3 in. screws for the purpose. These plates must be kept flush with the outer edges of the floor-boards, as they form a substantial fixing for the lower ends of the tongued and grooved matching. The ends of the plates are also employed as a fixing for the uprights as indicated in the illustration of a bottom corner joint. The verticals are simply nailed through to the ends of the plates as shown. Two iron brackets should be fixed at each corner to reinforce the joint.

Mark accurately the positions where the top ends of the uprights meet the front and back horizontal members and nail the latter to the former using 6 in. wire nails. Drill holes through the horizontals before driving in the nails, otherwise the wood will probably split. One nail at each joint is sufficient.

Now get a companion to hold the front frame, while you fix the lower ends of the posts to the plates, and nail a temporary strut between both posts and the floor to keep the frame in position while the same operations are proceeded with at the back.

Then saw the side cross-pieces to length and fix them with nails. Make sure that the whole of the framework is square and fix temporary braces to keep it in a square and staple position. The bottom corner brackets can now be fixed. Cut eight top corner braces and fix them in position as shown. These will add greatly to the strength of the framework.

At this stage it will be better to prepare the front posts and the rails and then to fasten the matching and when this is completed to proceed with the roof.

Saw the two short vertical pieces which support the ridge board, cut the latter to length and fix. Then follow by cutting the two 2×2 in. rafters and nail them to the ridge board and front and back horizontal members. Do not forget to notch the undersides of the lower ends of the rafters and be sure to make the angles at the top accurately.

The next procedure is to fill in the gable ends with matching, after which the 1 in. thick rafters can be fixed.

Cover the roof in with $\frac{3}{4}$ in. ($\frac{5}{8}$ in. finished) tongued and grooved matched boards. Use V edge type of matching in preference to that having a beaded edge.

Saw a couple of lengths of 1 in. stuff to cover the lower ends of the rafters and finish the structural work by sawing, planing and fixing the strips to cover the top edges of the matching and the rails at the front, sides and back.

The Roof should be covered with a reliable roofing felt. The covering should extend from the bottom edges of the facia boards up to the ridge. It should also overlap the end rafters. To ensure a watertight joint at the ridge a strip of roofing felt should be cut sufficiently wide to cover the ridge and extend for a distance of about 4 in. down each side of the roof. Use $\frac{1}{2}$ in. galvanised clout nails for fixing the roofing material and further secure it by fastening five $1\frac{1}{2} \times \frac{1}{2}$ in. planed battens between the ridge board and the eaves both at the back and front.

To give the summer house a professional finish, cut two finials of $1\frac{1}{4}$ in. square stuff and nail them to the ends of the ridge board.

The structure can either be creosoted or painted according to taste. If paint is desired give it three coats of the best quality lead paint. In the event of a closed back being required, the framework can be carried out on the lines shown in the diagram.

A TABLE DESK

THE table desk represented in working drawing No. 2 is one of those useful combination pieces of furniture which can be used to advantage where floor space is limited.

Such a fitment can be made of oak, mahogany or any other suitable hardwood, including American whitewood.

Reference to the drawings show that a space is provided under the table top for the desk portion, the latter being supported by two cross pieces fixed between the front and back rails.

Construction.—To construct, proceed as follows: First prepare the legs which are $1\frac{3}{4}$ in. square. Cut these to length, namely 2 ft. 5 in. and then mark them out for the taper. The faces of the legs are parallel for a distance of 6 in. from the top and then taper down to $1\frac{1}{8}$ in. square at the bottom.

Next prepare the front, back and side rails. The length of the longer ones is 2 ft. 8 in. and that of the shorter, 1 ft. 1 in. Take care to see that these pieces are "dead" square so carefully shoot the ends with a sharp plane.

Now mark out the position of the recess on the front rail and then cut out the piece with a fine toothed pad-saw. If this is done carefully the waste portion can be used to make part of the desk flaps.

Mark and cut out the trenches in the front and back rails for housing the ends of the cross rails A and B indicated in the detail of the frame. Make the channels $\frac{1}{4}$ in. deep and $\frac{3}{4}$ in. wide.

Dowel joints are used for housing the rails to the legs so the positions of these should now be marked out and then bored with a $\frac{3}{8}$ in. twist bit. Bore three holes at each joint and make them $\frac{3}{4}$ in. deep. The holes should come in the centre of the joining faces of the legs as the front faces of the rails lie back $\frac{1}{4}$ in.

Having cut the cross-pieces to length the parts should be assembled to see that everything fits correctly. If all is as it should be, glue the parts together, square, cramp up and allow at least twenty-four hours for the glue to dry.

Now cut out a piece of $\frac{3}{16}$ in. good quality birch faced plywood to form the bottom of the desk. The length of this is 1 ft. $7\frac{1}{2}$ in. and the width $\frac{1}{2}$ in. less than that of the distance between the outer edges of the long rails of the frame.

Fix the plywood in position by driving in $\frac{1}{2}$ in. screws through the bottom and into the bottom faces of the cross rails and front and back rails.

Cut a strip of wood 18 in. long $\times$ 3 in. wide and two smaller pieces for the ink and pen compartments as shown, and fix these in position with glue and panel pins. Then cut two pieces of $\frac{1}{4}$ in. plywood for the lid of the desk and the flap. Make sure that the desk lid is an easy fit. Fasten a strip of $\frac{1}{4} \times \frac{1}{4}$ in. to each cross member, keeping the top edge $2\frac{3}{4}$ in. above the bottom of the desk. The strips form a support to the flap which is hinged flush to the front rail as shown.

Now construct the desk flap, utilising the waste piece removed from the front rail. A detail of this is shown in the drawing. Hinge the flap to the front rail using brass butts for the purpose. The next item consists of making the table top. If any difficulty is experienced in obtaining a single board sufficiently wide for this, the top will have to be made of two or more narrow boards joined together.

There are several methods by which the boards may be joined together. Glued dowel joints can be used to advantage as they are simple to make. Another method is to groove the joining edges of the boards and use loose tongues, the whole being glued together afterwards. If dowel joints are employed be careful to see that they do not come in line where the table top is divided into three sections. Having made the joints, cramp the table top and allow the glue to dry, after which the edges can be trimmed up to size and the faces smoothed with a keen smoothing plane.

The table top can then be marked and sawn across carefully into three sections. Use a sharp finely-set saw for this and cut squarely.

Fix the two end sections of the top to the framework by means of screws driven through holes bored slantwise in the inner faces of the framework and into the underside of the top sections.

Hinge the intermediate portion to the back rail. Fix a couple of struts between the cross rails and the underside of the centre portion of the table top to keep it open when in use.

Finish by making a stationery rack to the sizes shown in the drawing, and fix it to the underside of the hinged portion of the table top flap.

A NEWSPAPER HOLDER

NEWSPAPER holder.—A couple of evenings can be profitably spent by constructing the newspaper holder illustrated in working drawing No. 3.

The frames may be made of oak, the front and back and side panels of oak faced plywood $\frac{3}{16}$ in. thick, the centre division of solid oak and the bottom of birch or alder ply.

First prepare the parts of the framework which consist of 1 in. square section material. Cut to length and plough grooves for the panels, a trifle over $\frac{3}{16}$ in. wide and $\frac{1}{4}$ in. deep.

Make the front and back frames, glue the parts together and allow the glue to dry. Then cut the partition piece to shape, recessing the ends to enable them to clear the end frames.

Make the rectangular hole for the handle and carefully remove the edges with a sharp chisel. Also slightly round the long edges at the top.

Cut the end panels to size and glue them into the grooves of the top and bottom end rails. Fix one end to the front and back panels by means of screws driven through the uprights into the ends of the top and bottom end rails. Then fix the partition to the completed end by screws and then repeat the operation with the remaining end. Finally fix the plywood bottom using $\frac{1}{2}$ in. gimp pins for the purpose.

Stop the top of the screw-holes with plastic wood, smooth all parts with fine glass-paper, remove the dust and finish with good quality wax polish.

BOOKSHELVES FOR A RECESS

A SET of bookshelves for a recess is an inexpensive article to construct. Full details are given in working drawing No. 4.

This fitting is 3 ft. 6 in. high, 2 ft. wide and 1 ft. 2 in. from back to front. The sides are constructed of $\frac{5}{8}$ in. V jointed matching, the chief advantage of using this material being its comparative cheapness. Plain tongued and grooved boards may be used if desired.

Three shelves are provided and these are supported on $\frac{1}{2}$ in. square pieces screwed into the sides.

The top overlies the front and sides by $\frac{3}{4}$ in. while the back edge is flush with the back. Four pieces $1\frac{1}{2} \times \frac{3}{4}$ in. batten are screwed to the underside of the top, to which the top ends of the matching and the plywood back are fixed. The arrangement of the battens is indicated in the plan.

A pleasing finish is obtained by mounting the fitment on a plinth. The one shown is 4 in. high, the front, back and sides of which are cut away to form feet as shown.

The Plinth is of straightforward construction and is made of $\frac{3}{4}$ in. stuff. The ends should be mitred, glued and pinned together, while fixing battens 1 in. wide and $\frac{3}{4}$ in. thick should be screwed to the inner faces at the top so that the bottom board of the carcase can be screwed down to them.

The back consists of a sheet of $\frac{3}{16}$ in. plywood bradded on to the back edges of the sides, the shelves and the top and bottom boards. Strips of $1 \times \frac{1}{2}$ in. wood are fastened to the front edges of the bookcase. The ends of these pieces should be neatly mitred as shown.

The fitment can be either stained and varnished or painted, as desired.

A UTILITY CUPBOARD

A UTILITY cupboard — Working drawing No. 5 shows a utility cupboard constructed on the framework system. Such a cupboard is convenient for the storage of light articles, and would look well if painted and enamelled.

The carcase consists of three plywood panelled frames, one at the front and two side ones. The back as well as the bottom is of plywood, the former being $\frac{3}{16}$ in. thick and the latter $\frac{1}{4}$ in. The top of 1 in. thick deal has a backboard 3 in. high and $\frac{3}{4}$ in. thick, as shown.

Construction.—Start work by constructing the two side frames. These consist of planed battens $1\frac{1}{2}$ in. wide × $\frac{3}{4}$ in. thick. The corner joints should be morticed and tenoned, the uprights being morticed and the rails tenoned. Square up these parts and glue them together, cramp and set aside for the glue to dry. The same procedure is adopted with the foot frame.

Now make the door frame in a similar manner, but note that the stiles or vertical members are only $1\frac{1}{4}$ in. wide while the rails are $1\frac{1}{2}$ in. in width.

The top piece can be constructed of two 9 in. prepared boards to obtain the width. An ordinary glued butt joint may be used for uniting the two pieces. In making the top piece, cut off the front corners. This can be done by either chiselling or sawing. Mark, saw and plane the backboard to the dimensions and shape shown.

It will be noted that no mention has been made as to the forming of grooves for housing the edges of the plywood panels. False grooves can be utilised by making them of stripwood of $\frac{1}{4}$ in. square section. This material can be bought ready planed at most dealers who cater for amateur woodworkers' requirements.

Fix the stripwood by means of 1 in. panel pins, spaced at a distance of about 4 in. apart. Fasten the back strips first then fit the panel, glue the edges and then fix the front strip.

Having completed fitting and fixing the panels the parts can be assembled.

Assembling the Parts. — No difficulty should be experienced in joining the parts as they are simply fixed by wood screws.

Start by fastening the front frame to the sides. To do this first bore holes 2 in. from the ends and $\frac{3}{8}$ in. from the outer long edge, and then drill two similar holes between these into the front edges of the side members, taking care to see that the edge of the front frame is flush with the face of the side batten.

Next cut three pieces of batten to fit accurately between the inner faces of the vertical side pieces at the back and fix two of these pieces in line with the top and bottom side rails. The remaining length should be fixed across at the centre. Screws, of course, should be used for fastening the parts. The cross battens are shown at A, B and C in the side view.

Now fix the top board to the carcase by means of screws driven in from the top and into the top edges of the frames.

Cut a piece of $\frac{3}{16}$ in. plywood to cover the back and nail it to the back edges of the frames, top board and horizontal battens.

Prepare another piece of plywood $\frac{1}{4}$ in. thick and fix it to the undersides of the bottom rails. This forms the bottom. Make the backboard of $3 \times \frac{3}{4}$ in. deal and trim the corners off neatly as shown. Fix the backboard to the top of the cupboard by using dowel pins and glue. Hinge the door and hang it whichever side is the more convenient and lastly fix a lock and key or other suitable door fastener.

The arrangement of the shelves in the interior is left to the discretion of the constructor, but these should not be less than $\frac{5}{8}$ in. thick and supported on cross-pieces screwed to the inner faces of the side frames.

A CABINET OF DRAWERS

A CABINET of Drawers of simple design for accommodating stationery, etc., is illustrated in working drawing No. 6.

The overall dimensions are 1 ft. 9 in. high, 1 ft. $1\frac{1}{2}$ in. wide and $10\frac{1}{2}$ in. back to front, excluding the $\frac{3}{16}$ in. plywood back.

The top and bottom marked A and B in the front view are $\frac{5}{8}$ in. thick and consist of yellow deal, or, better still, whitewood, while the sides are of the same material $\frac{1}{4}$ in. thick. Plywood could be used for the sides, unless the look of the laminated edges are objected to.

Five drawers of equal size are provided but these could be made more shallow or deeper as the case may be.

Each drawer except the bottom one slides upon runners consisting of a frame made up of $\frac{1}{4}$ in. thick strip-wood to the dimensions shown in the plan.

Construction.—To make the cabinet, cut the top and bottom pieces and then the sides. Prepare sufficient material for making four drawer supporting frames. Take particular care to keep them perfectly square. Then glue the parts together with tube glue as this adhesive does not take so long to dry as ordinary hot glue.

Next construct the five drawers, details of which appear in the drawing. The ends of the front of each drawer should be rebated to accommodate the ends of the sides. Panel pins and glue are used for fastening the parts together. The bottom is of plywood and is simply pinned and glued to the underside of the drawer frame.

Small bakelite handles with screw shanks, obtainable at most cheap stores, should be fixed to the drawer fronts as shown.

Before attempting to assemble the carcase, mark the position the drawer supporting frames are to occupy on the inner faces of the side pieces. This operation needs to be done with precision otherwise difficulty will be experienced in fitting the drawers.

Fix the sides to the top and bottom members by means of brass counter-sunk headed screws and slide the first drawer division into place after having applied a little glue to the ends. Then fix them by driving in 1 in. panel pins through the sides. Continue in this way until all frames have been fitted and then square up the carcase, cut the plywood back and fix it also by panel pins.

The back plywood covering must be absolutely square as the squareness of the cabinet depends upon the accuracy with which the back has been prepared.

Now fit the drawers into their respective compartments and if they fit tightly ease them with a sharp plane and glass-paper.

Use an oil stain for finishing, rub the surface lightly with fine grade glass-paper and give the cabinet a coat of varnish. Do not use a spirit varnish stain as a finishing medium as it shows every scratch.

A CORNER CUPBOARD

A SPACE can generally be found in a room for a corner cupboad and the one shown in working drawing No. 7 can be used for many purposes.

Procure two pieces of wood each 1 ft. $0\frac{1}{2}$ in. long, $8\frac{5}{8}$ in. wide and $\frac{3}{8}$ in. thick. Reduce the width of one piece to $8\frac{1}{4}$ in. and fasten them together to form a right angle as shown in the plan. These two pieces form the back of the fitment. Saw and plane off the top corners as shown in the front view.

Now prepare two pieces of wood of the same thickness as that of the back for the top and bottom of the cupboard. These two members are identical in shape and size, the dimensions of which are shown in the plan.

Next prepare the side pieces A and B shown in the front view and plain and bevel the front edges to an angle of 45 deg.

Assemble all these parts together by means of screws driven in from the back, top and bottom members.

Lastly, cut a piece of $\frac{3}{8}$ in. plywood to fit accurately between the side members and the top and bottom of the cupboard.

Fix a couple of brass hinges to the right-hand edge of the door and hang it neatly to the side member. The edges of both the door and side piece should be recessed to take the leaves of the hinges. Finish off the job by fitting a small brass lock and key and bore a $\frac{1}{4}$ in. hole in each of the members forming the back. These holes should be drilled in the positions indicated in the front view. They are for fixing purposes only.

AN ADJUSTABLE MIRROR

A HANDY adjustable mirror, suitable for placing on a chest of drawers, is shown in working drawing No. 8.

The mirror is of the frameless type having a bevelled edge and is supported by means of small metal clips fixed to the edges of a $\frac{1}{4}$ in. plywood back. The glass swings between two tapered uprights, the latter being fixed to the base which contains a useful drawer.

The dimensions given in the drawing need not be strictly adhered to as the mirror can be a larger one than that shown.

To construct this fitment as shown in the drawing, procure a mirror having a bevelled edge, 1 ft. 2 in. long × 11 in. wide. Such a mirror is generally about $\frac{1}{4}$ in. thick. Cut a piece of $\frac{1}{4}$ in. birch-faced plywood to the exact size of the glass and make eight small brass clips about $\frac{1}{2}$ in. wide out of thin sheet material. At a distance of $\frac{1}{8}$ in. from one end of each clip, drill a small hole to clear a $\frac{3}{8}$ in. No. 2 round headed wood screw. Cut off the sharp corners at the opposite ends of the clips and screw them to the edges of the plywood backing. Place the mirror in position on the plywood and bend the clips over the bevelled edge of the glass. The positions of the clips are shown in the front view of the drawing.

Put the mirror in a safe place for the time being and carry on with the construction of the woodwork.

Cut and square up two pieces of hardwood—oak is excellent in this case—each $11\frac{1}{2}$ in. long, 7 in. wide and $\frac{1}{4}$ in. thick for the top and bottom of the base and two pieces 7 in. long × $2\frac{1}{2}$ in. wide and $\frac{3}{8}$ in. thick for the sides. Glue and pin these parts together and add a $\frac{3}{16}$ in. plywood back. Bevel the edges of the plywood before fixing, to render them less conspicuous.

Make the two upright supports of $\frac{3}{8}$ in. stuff. The length of these is 1 ft. $1\frac{1}{2}$ in. and the width, 2 in. at one end, tapering to 1 in. at the other. Bore a $\frac{1}{4}$ in. diameter hole in the centre and at a distance of 11 in. from the bottom in both pieces and fix the latter by countersunk-headed screws to the sides of the base as shown.

Now make a drawer to fit easily into the base. The front of the drawer should be of the same material as the base, but the sides, back and bottom can be made of commoner wood. When completed make a small horizontal handle about 2 in. long and $\frac{3}{4}$ in. square and fix it in the position indicated by screws driven in from the back of the drawer front.

The next operation consists of making a suitable pivot to enable the glass to be adjusted. This can be done in the following manner.

Procure a 13 in. length of $\frac{1}{4}$ in. diameter iron rod, cut a screw-thread for a distance of about an inch on one end. Heat the rod up to a cherry red colour and hammer three flats, all in the same plane, in the iron. Drill the centre of each flat and fix the rod by screws to the back of the mirror.

Cut a couple of hardwood washers $\frac{1}{4}$ in. thick and remove one vertical sup-port. Slip the washers over the projecting ends of the spindle and insert one end into the fixed upright and the other end in the opposite one and refix the vertical support.

Place a metal washer over the projecting threaded end of the rod and screw on a wing-nut.

Smooth the wood with fine glass-paper and wax polish it.

MAGAZINE AND BOOK STAND

IN working drawing No. 9 is seen a stand of pleasing design for accommodating books and magazines, periodicals, etc.

This useful article should be made of the same class of wood as that of the furniture in the room it is intended to occupy.

Procure four pieces of wood each 2 ft. 10 in. long, $7\frac{1}{2}$ in. wide and $\frac{3}{4}$ in. thick. These pieces when joined together in pairs will form the sides.

Pair the boards so that the grain matches as near as possible and plane the long edges to be joined. Mark the pieces Nos. 1, 2, 3 and 4 and proceed with the gluing. Place one board of a pair, prepared edge upwards, in the vice, apply very hot, thin glue to the edge and also to the corresponding edge of its fellow member. Rub the two edges together lengthwise to exclude as much glue as possible, cramp tightly and allow the glue to dry. Repeat the process with the other pair of boards, not forgetting to wipe off surplus glue with a moistened rag.

Allow sufficient time for the glue to harden thoroughly. This will take about twenty-four hours if the members are placed in a warm dry room.

Square up the ends with a plane. The finished length is 2 ft. $9\frac{7}{8}$ in. Skim over each wide face with a keen smoothing plane and plane a face edge on both members.

Now mark out the positions of the trenches that will house the ends of the shelves and the book trough. The width of the grooves is $\frac{5}{8}$ in. Then draw guide lines for the taper. The finished width at the bottom is 1 ft. 2 in. and that at the top 9 in. Also mark out the curved position at the bottom.

With a handsaw, cut on the outside of the lines representing the taper and finish the edges with a plane. Remove the waste at the bottom with the aid of a pad saw and smooth the curve with a spokeshave.

Put the two end members aside for the time being and proceed with the shelves. The shelves should be finished to a length of 1 ft. 11 in. which allows $\frac{1}{4}$ in. at the ends for housing.

The exact width of the shelves can be ascertained from the finished sizes.

Make notches in the ends of the shelves $\frac{1}{2}$ in. long and $\frac{1}{4}$ in. wide as the housing is stopped $\frac{1}{2}$ in. from the long edges of the side members. This forms a neat joint.

Now place the end of each shelf on the grooved marks on the side pieces and mark the lengths of the grooves.

Cut the wood for the book trough

and notch the ends in the same manner as that of the shelves.

Chisel out the grooves and be sure not to make them too wide. The ends of the shelves, etc., should fit hand tight.

Assemble the parts to verify that they fit correctly. Make adjustments if necessary then glue and screw the parts together, taking care to see that the fitment is square.

There is no need to use cramps as the screws will draw the parts together. Clearing holes for the screws should, of course, be bored in the sides.

Fill the screw holes with a suitable wood filler, such as plastic wood, smooth with glass-paper and apply a suitable finish.

If oak is employed, a black overlay 1 ft. 11 in. long ×2 in. wide as shown will greatly enhance the appearance of the stand. The wood should be stained black before fixing.

A FOLDING CARD TABLE

THE folding card table (working drawing No. 10) is of very light construction and can be used equally well for other purposes than that for which it is intended.

Start work by making a flat frame 2 ft. square of $1\frac{1}{4} \times 1$ in. planed batten. Dowel the ends together and glue and pin an accurately-cut sheet of $\frac{3}{16}$ in. plywood on the top.

Then make the two pairs of legs marked A and B in the drawing. These are constructed of the same material and of the same size as the table top frame, namely $1\frac{1}{4} \times 1$ in. planed batten.

The width between the outer faces of the pair of legs A is 1 ft. $9\frac{1}{2}$ in. and the upper ends are hinged to the table top by means of a pair of right-angle brackets made of thick sheet brass. The brackets are shown clearly in the drawings. The width between the outer faces of the inner pair is slightly less than the distance between the inner faces of the outer one, while a $\frac{5}{8}$ in. dowel rod is fixed 3 in. from the upper ends of the legs B to keep them at the correct distance apart. The top ends of this pair simply butt against the inner edge of the table top batten.

Holes are bored through the centres of the legs through which $\frac{1}{4}$ in. diameter bolts are inserted, as shown and cross braces consisting of stripwood 1 in. wide and $\frac{3}{8}$ in. thick are fixed by screws at the lower ends of both pairs of legs in the positions indicated.

A piece of thick baize 25 in. square should be cut to cover the top, the covering material being kept in place by bradding strips of wood 1 in. wide and $\frac{1}{4}$ in. thick round the edges.

SHOE-BRUSH HOLDER

THE shoe-brush holder illustrated in working drawing No. 11 serves two purposes, that of housing the brushes and cleaning material and a stool for supporting the foot of the person who cleans his shoes when being worn.

No object is served by using an expensive wood for an article of this description; indeed it can very well be made from wood procured from a box, provided the thickness of the wood is not less than $\frac{1}{2}$ in.

If advantage is taken in using box wood, the wood should be skimmed over with a plane, but before doing this first make sure that the wood is quite free from grit otherwise the plane iron will suffer.

The Sides.—Make these first. These are 8 in. wide and a little under 1 ft. long at the back and 10 in. at the front. Then construct the back. This may take two pieces of wood to obtain the width. The long edges of the boards where they meet need not be glued together as a satisfactory joint can be obtained when joining the parts to the sides, provided, of course, that care has been taken in planing the edges straight and square.

Saw and plane the base to size, namely 1 ft. $1\frac{1}{2}$ in. $\times 8\frac{1}{2}$ in. The edges of this overlap the body $\frac{1}{4}$ in. all round.

Mark on the face side of the base the position the body is to occupy and also mark guide lines on the underside for centreing the nails by which the base is fixed to the carcase.

Now prepare the top, the top front rail and the front bottom rail, and assemble all the parts using $1\frac{1}{2}$ in. oval brads. Lastly, saw and plane and fit a piece of wood for the door. This is hinged at the lower edge as shown and is kept closed by means of a small hardwood turnbutton screwed to the top rail. A small screw knob should be fixed to the door as shown.

Having completed the structural work, smooth the wood with glass-paper, apply knotting to the knots and give the holder two or three coats of oil paint. If care has been taken with the wood the tidy will last indefinitely.

A CUTLERY BOX

A CUTLERY box (working drawing No. 12) is another example of a useful piece of woodwork for everyday use. It is much to be preferred, hygenically and in other respects to the old fashioned open rectangular basket.

The wood used in the construction of the article is American whitewood $\frac{3}{8}$ in. thick and the following pieces will be required.

Base 1 ft. $2\frac{1}{2}$ in. $\times 8\frac{1}{2}$ in.

Front and back each 1 ft. 2 in. $\times 2\frac{1}{2}$ in.

Two ends each $7\frac{1}{4}$ in. $\times 2\frac{1}{2}$ in.

One partition 1 ft. 2 in. $\times 4\frac{7}{8}$ in.

Two lids each 1 ft. 2 in. $\times 3\frac{13}{16}$ in.

There is nothing of a complicated nature in marking out and cutting and squaring the base sides and lids, as they are merely rectangular pieces of wood. The centre division, however, requires slightly different treatment. Cut and

square this piece, saw and plane the slope at the top and recess the ends so that they fit tightly between the end pieces of the box. Cut the hole for the handle with a fretsaw, if such a tool is available, if not use a pad saw, having a fine-toothed blade. Slightly round the edges with the aid of a sharp chisel and smooth with glass-paper.

Assemble the parts with glue and screws—not brads—use small brass butt hinges for fixing the lids and line the compartments with green baize.

Four rubber-headed tacks should be fixed to the underside of the base. These can be bought for about two-pence per set and they prevent scratching a polished table.

The cutlery box will look well if sized, stained and finished with two coats of french polish, applied with a soft-haired mop.

A TRESTLE TABLE

A TRESTLE table as shown in working drawing No. 13 can be put to many uses. For instance, it could be used for cutting dressmaking material, making working drawings or by the amateur decorator for pasting wallpaper.

The table top is made on the same lines as that described for the folding card table, but the supporting battens are 1¾ in. wide × 1 in. thick, and the plywood is ¼ in. thick. If the table is to be used for draughting purposes, it is absolutely essential that the top be perfectly square.

As will be seen from the drawings the length is 5 ft. and the width 2 ft. 3 in. while it stands 3 ft. above the floor level.

These measurements could be modified but it would be a mistake to have such a table too small.

Make both pairs of legs 1 ft. 11 in. wide (bare) at the top and mortice and tenon the joints, cutting the tenons on the rails and the mortices on the legs. The tenons should go right through the mortices and be secured by glue.

Slightly round the outer long edges of the top rails and fasten each pair of legs by 2 in. steel butt hinges at the top. Drill holes in the centres of the bottom rails to take the cords as shown, and use a good quality stretched sash cord to prevent the legs spreading outwards.

A TIER OF TRAYS

A TIER of trays as illustrated in working drawing No. 14 is an excellent device for workshop use for the storage of small tools, electrical accessories, wireless parts, etc., or it could be used for accommodating many small articles in and about the home.

As will be seen from the drawing of the general arrangement, the fixture consists of five trays all joined together by strips of wood. To avoid confusion these strips are not shown in the front, end and plan views.

The bottom tray forming the base is double the size of the smaller ones and is divided into two compartments. The bottom of the tray extends ¼ in. beyond the sides and ends, while those of the others are all flush.

The four small trays are all of the same size, but the two upper ones are provided with lids.

Start operations by constructing the

bottom tray. The base and sides are ¼ in. thick and the end pieces ⅜ in. thick. The front and back strips of all the trays overlap the end pieces. This is the orthodox method of treating such parts as no joints are seen at the front.

Make up all the frames first and use tube glue and panel pins at the joints. Then saw and square up the bottoms and attach them to their respective frames, also with glue and pins.

It matters little whether the parts are cut out of plywood or ordinary solid hardwood but the latter is better if the trays are to be used in a living-room or a bedroom, as the laminated edges of plywood do not add to its appearance.

Having constructed the trays, prepare the lids and back pieces for the two upper ones. The back part of each of these trays has a strip of ¼ in. wood 2¾ in. wide, as shown in the plan, fastened to the top edges of the back and sides, to which the lids are hinged.

When all the units are complete, cut eight strips of wood $5\frac{1}{4}$ in. long, $\frac{3}{4}$ in. wide $\times \frac{1}{4}$ in. thick and four similar strips $9\frac{1}{2}$ in. long. Round the ends as shown in the drawing of the general arrangement, and drill holes to clear No. 6 gauge wood screws, at a distance of $\frac{1}{2}$ in. from the ends. Also drill screw-holes in the centres of the longer pieces.

Smooth these parts with glass-paper, and fix them to the trays in the position shown. Insert small metal washers between the sides of the trays and the strips and also place a washer under each head of a screw. Use $\frac{5}{8}$ in. brass screws of the round headed type. Do not drive them in too tightly.

Prepare two handles of $\frac{3}{4}$ in. square wood, 2 in. long and fasten them to the sides of the top trays as shown. Fix them by screws driven from the insides of the trays.

Finish with stain and varnish.

UNDER-BED WARDROBE

THE under-bed wardrobe (working drawing No. 15) is useful for storing sheets, blankets and bed linen in general. Those readers whose bedrooms are small will find that such a commodity is of great convenience.

The wardrobe consists of five panel units; namely the front and back, the two ends and lid.

Saw and plane up sufficient $1\frac{1}{2} \times \frac{3}{8}$ in. yellow deal batten for making the frames. Trim the parts to size and plough $\frac{3}{16}$ in. (full) grooves, $\frac{1}{4}$ in. deep, to take the panels, which consist of $\frac{3}{16}$ in. alder or birch plywood.

Simple joints such as dowel joints can be used at the corners and for joining the cross-pieces across the front, back and lid.

If a grooving plane is not available, the plywood panels can be glued and pinned directly to the back of each frame member, in which case the overall dimensions will be slightly larger than those shown in the drawings.

Make the two end frames first. These are identical in size, as are the front and back members. Bore the necessary dowel holes (if this method of joining the parts is adopted) in the vertical and horizontal members, using a $\frac{3}{8}$ in. diameter twist-bit for the purpose. Make the holes $\frac{3}{4}$ in. deep and cut and fit the pins, not forgetting to round the ends of the pegs and to make a shallow, longitudinal groove in each to allow the air to escape when applying the glue.

Fit together the members of both frames to ascertain that they fit correctly and then cut the plywood to correspond with the grooves. Make sure that the panels are square. Use a fine-toothed tenon saw for cutting the plywood. If the marking out is done carefully and the sawing accurate there will be no need to trim the edges except to smooth them with glass-paper.

Apply hot glue to the grooves and joints of the frames and the edges of the panels and cramp up in the usual way, using either improvised cramps or the usual tools as the case may be.

Follow on by making the front and back members in exactly the same way as that adopted for the ends. These members are of the same size but do not forget to include the centre uprights.

The same method of construction is employed for the lid.

The back edge of this member is flush with the faces of the back battens, and the sides and front overlap the faces of the ends and front of the carcase.

The next operation consists of assembling the front and back panels of the carcase to the end ones. These are simply screwed together by first boring holes to clear No. 8 countersunk-headed screws, 2 in. long.

The positions of the screws are shown clearly in the front view in the working drawing. Countersink the tops of the holes and drive the screws into the narrow faces of the end members, using a sharp bradawl for piercing the wood before actually driving in the screws. Now prepare two lengths of $\frac{3}{4}$ in. square stuff and nail it to the inside faces of the bottom rails of the front and back panels as indicated in the sectional drawing.

This forms a support for the bottom of the fitment which consists of tongued and grooved matching either $\frac{1}{2}$ in. or $\frac{5}{8}$ in. thick, as preferred.

Keep the lower faces of the supporting strips flush with the bottom edges of the panels.

Cut a sufficient number of lengths of matching to fill in the bottom and fasten them down with oval brads.

Before actually fixing the boards, square up the carcase and fix a brace diagonally across each corner, for the time being, to keep it square.

The Lid.—The fitment is now ready to receive the lid. Fix three strong butt hinges to the back edge of the lid and to the face of the top batten of the back panel. The two outer hinges should be fixed about a couple of inches from the ends and the intermediate one equidistant between the two.

Fit a substantial hook and eye in the position indicated, for keeping the lid closed. It is advisable to fit a couple of hinged stays to the underside of the lid and the inside faces of the end top battens to keep it open when in use.

Line the interior with sateen or other suitable material and finally fix four ball castors as shown.

HOUSEHOLD HINTS FOR THE HANDYMAN

If you want to colour an electric lamp bulb, switch on the current and immerse the lamp in a bowl of lacquer as illustrated. Withdraw the bulb from the lacquer, shake it gently to remove the surplus and allow it to dry while the current is still flowing and the bulb is warm.

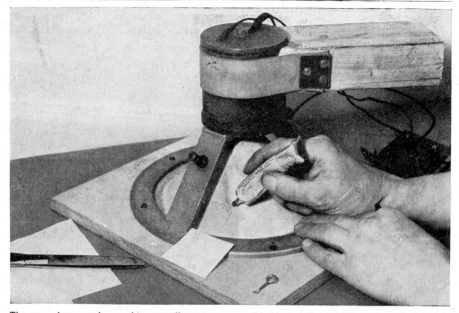

The two photographs on this page illustrate an excellent but quite simple method of repairing a damaged loud-speaker cone. You should first stick a patch of thick cartridge paper over the defective part of the loud-speaker, as shown in the photograph above.

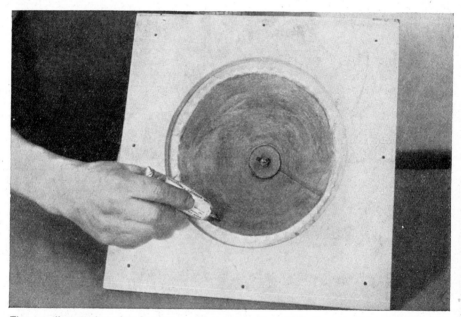

Then, as illustrated in the photograph above, a thin film of adhesive should be applied to the edges of the break at the front. Do not omit the second operation, otherwise an objectionable buzzing noise may be caused by the vibrations of the loose edges of the tear.

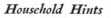

The back rails of the chair shown in this photograph have just been re-glued, and the picture shows a simple method of cramping the parts. Note the pieces of waste wood at the sides. These pieces of wood prevent the cords bruising the edges of the chair, causing marks that are almost impossible to remove.

An exhausted dry cell can sometimes be given a new life by pouring in a little saturated solution of sal-ammoniac through a hole in the bottom, using a paper funnel as shown.

A well-known device for supplying a hen's drinking vessel. Suspend an inverted bottle filled with fresh water so that its neck is below the surface of the water in the dish.

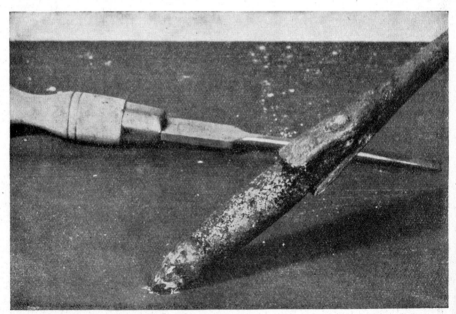

It sometimes happens that a screw will prove obstinate and refuse to yield to ordinary treatment with a screwdriver. In such a case, apply a hot soldering bit to the head of the screw, as shown in the illustration above, and very often the screw can then be easily withdrawn.

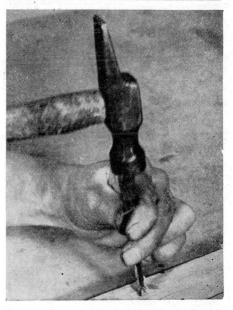

When planing always set the back-iron close to the cutting-edge of the cutting-iron (see A), for finishing work, and further away (see B) for roughing out.

Here is a neat method of hiding a nail-head. With a sharp chisel lift a small section of wood, drive in the nail with the aid of a punch, and glue the wood back into position.

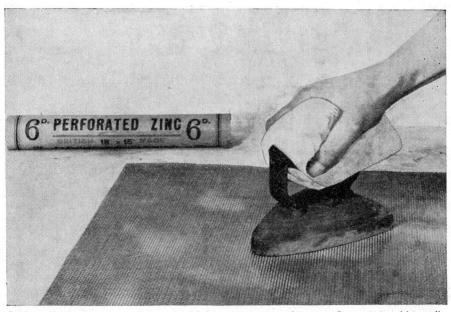

Perforated zinc is a very useful material for covering meat safes, etc. But as it is sold in rolls, it is not easy to work with until it has been flattened out. This can be done with an ordinary heated domestic iron as shown in the photograph just as though it were heavy cloth.

If you fear that a crack in the wall is widening, stick a piece of paper over it as shown. If the fissure widens it will break the paper.

The handle of the screwdriver illustrated here contains a lamp, bulb and battery which projects a light through holes at the base of the blade.

The jaws of a spanner should fit the nut accurately and exactly. In cases where the distance between the jaws does not permit of this, insert a piece of metal of the proper thickness as shown, and tighten or slacken the nut in the usual way.

Searching for keys is merely a waste of time. With a piece of ⅜ in. thick plywood, a few dresser hooks, and some pieces of gummed paper, the handy key-board which is illustrated here can be made in a few minutes. It will be found to be well worth the small effort involved.

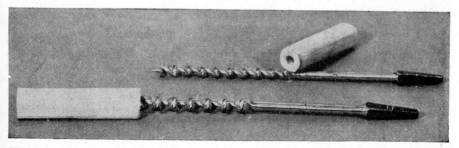

Twist-bits are not easy to re-sharpen and therefore their cutting edges should not be allowed to be blunted by coming into contact with other metal tools. It is only a matter of a few minutes to make sheaths of soft wood such as those illustrated here.

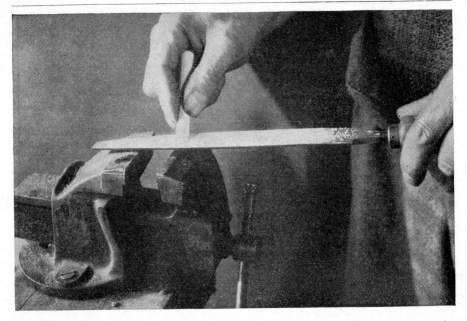

It is a very good plan to rub chalk on a second-cut and on the smoothing file as is shown in the photograph above. This greatly reduces the tendency of the metal to stick between the teeth, and as a lubricant, in addition. The chalk should be rubbed well in between the serrations.

If you have paint brushes which are hard with paint, this is a useful method for cleaning them. First put them into boiling vinegar as shown here, then rinse them in water; clean them next with turpentine, and then with soap and warm water before giving them a final rinse in cold.

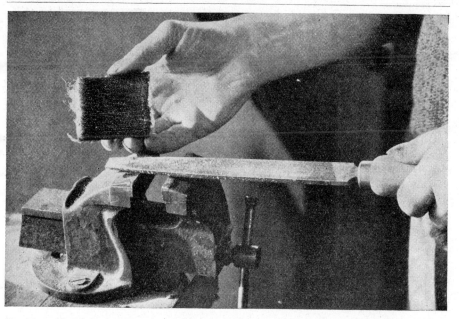

Here is another hint for those who cherish their files. A piece of file-card should find a home in every workshop, and should be used regularly as shown here. It is rubbed over the surface and is invaluable for keeping the files in good condition.

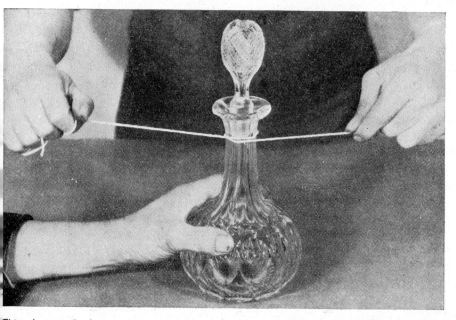

This photograph shows a simple method of withdrawing a glass stopper which has become obstinate. Wind a cord round the neck of the article and draw the cord rapidly to and fro. The heat generated expands the glass and lessens the grip on the stopper.

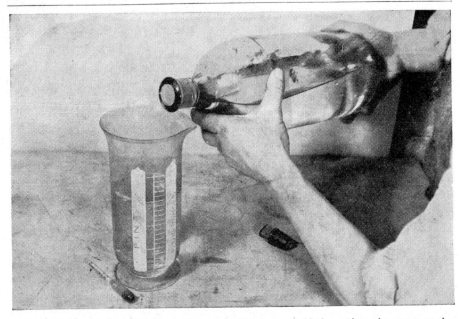

When you are diluting sulphuric acid always remember to add the acid to the water as the illustration shows. *Never* add the water to the acid. If you fail to observe this simple precaution a mild explosion may take place resulting in serious injury to yourself.

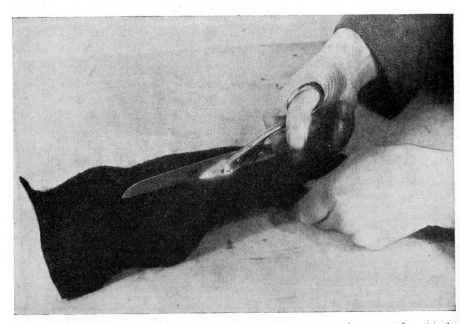

The photograph above shows the correct method of handling a pair of scissors. Surprisingly few people understand how to use them with the proper force and direction. Note that the thumb is placed in the smaller hole while the first and second fingers pass through the larger.

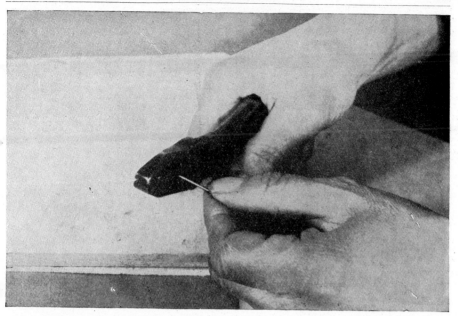

When you are nailing very thin wood there is a danger that you may split it. To prevent this it is a good plan first to cut off the point of the nail or panel pin with a pair of pincers as shown here before driving it into the wood. The blunted point will penetrate quite easily.

If all the electric bells in the house fail, first examine the batteries. The electrolyte may have evaporated as this picture shows. Remove the porous pots, clean out the containers and recharge by filling with a saturated solution of sal ammoniac and water mixed in a jug.

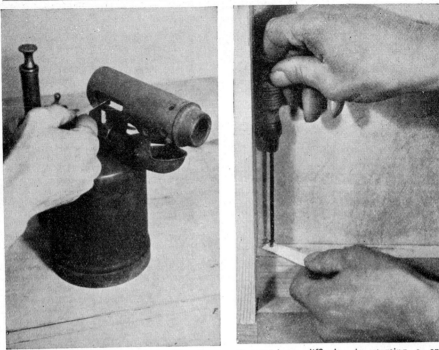

Always keep the tiny nipple of a blow-lamp free from obstruction. You should use the pricker every time you use the lamp.

If you have difficulty in starting a small screw insert the end in a slip of paper and use it as a holder as illustrated here.

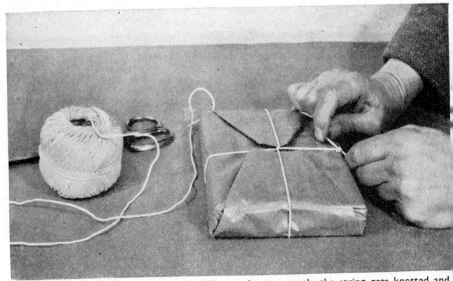

Balls of string are liable to unwind themselves and consequently the string gets knotted and has to be wasted. This difficulty will not arise if you withdraw the string from the centre of the ball as illustrated, retaining the other end in its original coils on the outside.

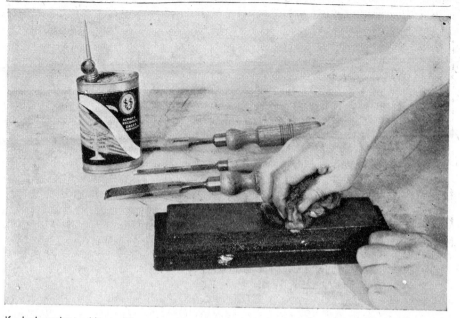

If a bad workman blames his tools, a good workman will look after them. It is a good thing to make a point of cleaning your oilstone with a piece of rag every time you have finished using it. This takes only a few seconds and prevents the formation of clots of stale oil and dust.

Dust between the plates of a radio wireless condenser very often causes crackles in the loud-peaker. The best way to get rid of the dust is to push a feather between the plates as shown here. A turkey feather is best because it is larger, but it must be clean and dry.

This photograph shows a very simple but excellent gadget that can be used to ascertain accurate depth when drilling. It is simply a Meccano collar with its grub screw which makes a very good depth gauge for small drills, and greatly facilitates quick measurements.

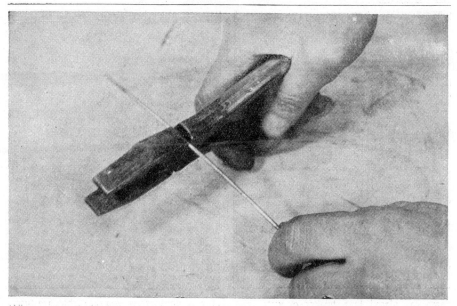

When cutting thick wire, never place it between the jaws of the pliers. Use the slots provided at the side. This shears the wire neatly and prevents the pliers from becoming strained.

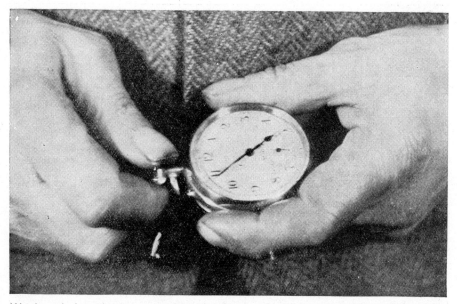

Watches, clocks and other spring-driven mechanisms should never be wound to their fullest extent. If you have ascertained by experiment that a watch or clock requires twenty turns to wind it completely, then only nineteen should be given. To maintain a watch in good condition form the habit of always winding it at the same time every day.

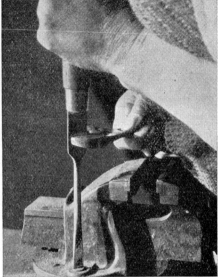

Some hay placed in a bucket of water and stood in a newly-painted room will help to remove the smell of the paint.

In this photograph you are shown a useful method of obtaining extra leverage when you are dealing with large screws.

A loose hammer head may be the cause of a very unpleasant accident if it suddenly flies off while being used. As soon as the hammer shows sings of working loose from the handle, refix the head, and insert a new wedge in the top, hammering it well down as shown in the illustration.

If your files are worn down, and you think you will have to discard them, here is a useful hint. Immerse them in diluted sulphuric acid as shown in this photograph. If this treatment is carried out it will restore them to a workable condition by eating into the worn surface of the files and sharpening the edges.

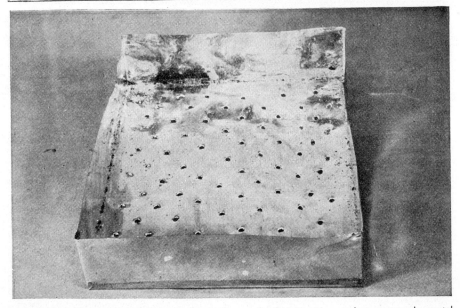

A useful sink-basket can easily be improvised out of a biscuit tin or other rectangular metal box, by punching a series of holes at intervals all over the bottom. Remember to make the holes from the interior so that the rough edges project downwards.

When you are fitting new shafts to gardening tools such as the one shown here, always leave a short projection at the end, and drive in the wedge. The inlayed wood will cause the shaft to splay out above the head and prevent the tool head from slipping off.

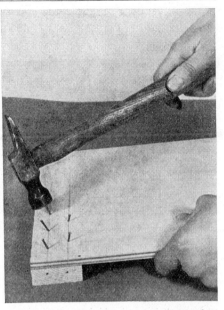

Remember to use metal washers beneath the heads of screws as well as between the surfaces of moving joints. Lubricate with graphite.

When nailing a butt-joint, greater strength is obtained by slanting the nails to form dovetails than by hammering them in vertically.

When sawing a number of pieces of wood of the same length, fix a fence to the end of the bench to act as a stop, and mark guide-lines on the bench top to correspond with the working edge of the bench hook, as shown. This will save a great deal of time and trouble.

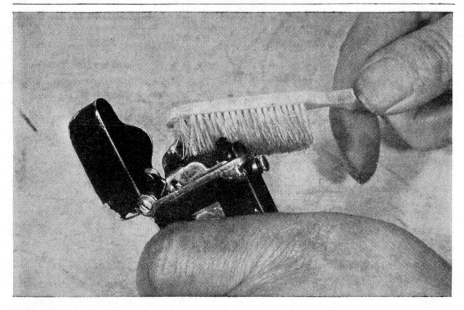

Cigarette lighters should be periodically freed from soot and kept in good condition by scrubbing carefully with an old, dry tooth-brush as shown in the illustration above.

This photograph illustrates a useful hint for amateur photographers. Pieces of cork fixed to the ends of the camera legs will prevent them from slipping on a polished surface. In addition, when engaged in indoor photography the corks will give a firm grip on carpeted floors without damaging the fabric in any way.

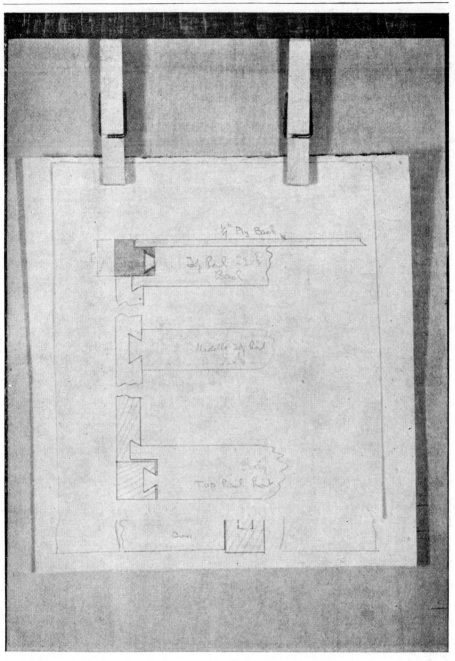

A couple of spring clothes-pegs fixed to a piece of plywood three-eights of an inch thick makes a useful holder for working diagrams, notes, etc.   One side of the clothes-peg should be screwed to the surface of the boards, or strong glue may be used instead, although this last method is neither so strong nor so lasting.

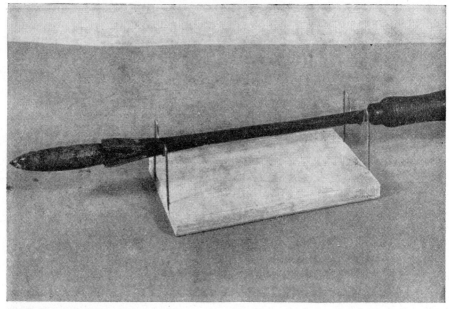

This picture illustrates a useful holder for a soldering iron. It consists of a small piece of flat wood for a base, and two pieces of thick wire, bent to shape, the ends driven into the wood.

Amusing " relief " pictures may be built up out of photographs in the following manner. The background—a land or seascape—is pasted on thick card and a sheet of clear glass laid over it. On this is mounted the cut-out figures, with another sheet of glass on top of that. Next comes the foreground. A third sheet is placed on top and the whole bound with passe-partout.

Above is shown an infallible test whether the bellows of a camera is light-proof. Attach an electric light bulb to a length of flex and lower the light into the extended bellows of the camera. Scrutinise carefully for pin-holes. The appearance of any particle of light inside will make these instantly visible.

When straightening wire, fix a few screws at intervals along the edge of a piece of wood in line. Straighten the wire by drawing it through them, as indicated in the photograph, holding the end of the wire in one hand while pulling strongly with a pair of pliers.

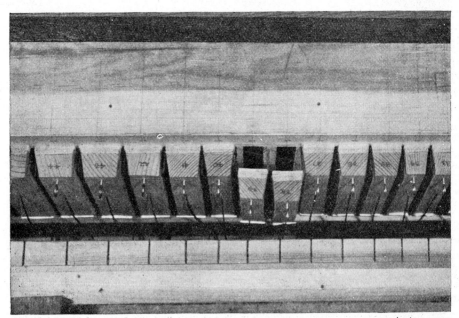

The illustration shows part of the interior of the sound-box of a home-constructed pipe organ and emphasises the importance of accurate marking out. The simplest work, to be efficient and workmanlike, must fit exactly and everything depends on careful measurements.

To clean the interior of an old, encrusted bottle, half fill with warm water and add a small quantity of sand or crushed cinders. Shake vigorously. A little vinegar added to the water is useful for removing chalky deposits. The mixture should be fairly strong and nearly boiling.

The naked jaws of a metal vice should never be permitted to come in contact with the surfaces of an important piece of work, as they will cause permanent scratches on the surface and may damage the edges. If a metal clamp is not available use shields made of pieces of old linoleum.

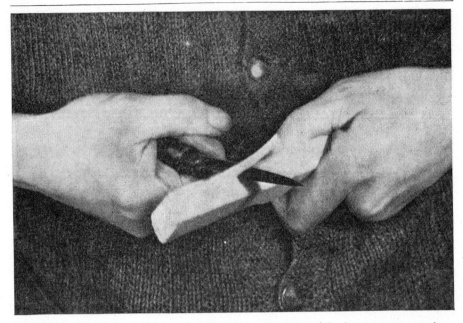

A small but important point to remember when whittling wood is always to cut away from you—never towards you. Neglect of this simple precaution may cause a dangerous cut.

When driving a screw-tap, a tap wrench is the proper tool that should be used. If this is not available, however, a lathe carrier makes an efficient substitute, as the illustration above indicates.

HANDICRAFTS FOR THE HANDY MAN

POTTERY

MANY people who are now recognised professional potters began their work in the craft in a casual sort of way, circumstances being such that what was a hobby has now become a life's work. Some of these "amateur professional" potters have undoubtedly added a good deal to the quality of the production in clay and at the same time have been the means of keeping alive the old traditional hand-methods of making pots.

Interest in the craft and a practical acquaintance with it always lead to a keener desire to increase the facilities at one's disposal and to improve the quality of one's output. A steady approach to a craft like pottery, with a minimum of equipment at the outset, is more certain to be productive of a successful connexion with the work than ability to purchase at the outset an up-to-date kiln, wheel and all the other paraphernalia of a well-equipped studio. There is always a good deal to learn about clay and it is best learned by the beginner adopting handcraft methods of making pots.

The Materials.—Clay may be either white, buff or red, white being the colour most commonly used. It should fire at a temperature of from 1,000 to 1,200 deg. C. If the clay can be purchased locally, so much the better. The interest of the local works is always a valuable asset to the beginner and a great deal can be quickly learned of the preparation of the clay. It must be realised that the clay as used for making pots is not the same mixture as it is when dug. It has probably been weathered, washed, ground, mixed with various alkalies, etc., sieved, settled in tanks or tubs and passed through a pugmill to get it into its final condition. It is worth while for every amateur to try his or her hand at preparing clay.

If the clay cannot be obtained locally, it should be purchased from any reliable works. A quarter or half a hundredweight will do for a beginning. It will arrive in a damp condition and should be stored in a zinc dustbin, with damp cloths to cover it inside the bin. If it does arrive in a hard state—perhaps the weather is hot and the journey long—place it in the bin with a few inches of water, sprinkle it with water, cover with wet rags or sacking and leave it for a few days. Much of the outside of the lump will then be found in good condition and ready to be worked. Every precaution must be taken to keep the clay clean.

Equipment.—The following will form a satisfactory equipment at the beginning of your work: A bowl for containing water for moistening the hands, a sponge of fine texture for removing superfluous moisture from pots, a few tools for using on the clay when it is soft and plastic, some cutting tools for finishing when the clay is tough and a short length of thin wire, twisted round small pieces of wood at each end to make handles, for use in cutting the clay.

With the aid of the above tools and

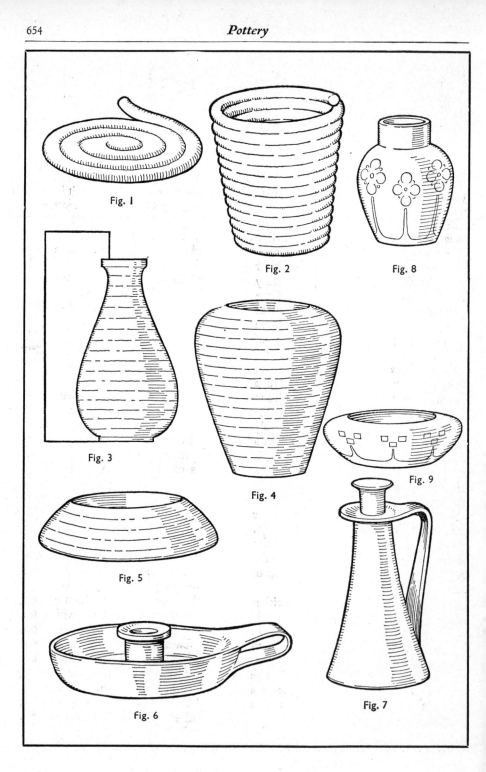

Fig. 1

Fig. 2

Fig. 8

Fig. 3

Fig. 4

Fig. 9

Fig. 5

Fig. 6

Fig. 7

the fingers quite a large variety of pots can be modelled.

Methods of firing are discussed later on.

Making a Coiled Pot.—Knead a double handful of clay until thoroughly mixed, form it into a ball, and roll it on a flat wet surface to form a short stumpy cylinder. Now roll it with both hands into a long cylinder about $\frac{1}{2}$ in. diameter. You will find it necessary to adjust the pressure of the hands so that the roll is gradually and evenly elongated without any ridges. Make several of these. Now coil one roll to form a circular base of a pot, say 5 in. diameter, press it flat and weld the coils together to make a solid mass, see Fig. 1. Take another roll and coil it on the edge of the base, round and up, each ring being pressed firmly on the one below to press out air cavities which might blow out on firing, see Fig. 2. Level off the top and use the finger ends of one hand to stroke and weld the coils together on the outside while the fingers of the other hand are being used inside the pot to support the clay against the pressure from outside. Figs. 4 to 9 show the kind of useful article which can be made by coiling. The shape develops from a simple cylinder to more difficult curves as the skill in coiling is developed. A template of tin or zinc plate can be used to control the shape, as in Fig. 3.

Decoration can be added by means of incised lines either left as traced or filled in with a clay of another colour, pressed in when the shape is rather dry and tough. Clayslip—liquid clay—of another colour can also be used as a paint and decoration painted on with a brush.

Making Pots from Slabs of Clay.— Square or any rectangular shapes can be built up by using flat slabs of clay, about $\frac{1}{4}$ to $\frac{3}{8}$ in. thick according to the size of the article. The slabs are easily and quickly made by nailing two laths $\frac{1}{4}$ to $\frac{3}{8}$ in. thick 10 or 12 in. apart to a table top. Wet the surface and beat or roll out a layer of clay in the hollow, filling it completely. Scrape off the superfluous clay with a straight edge and use a rolling-pin to flatten the top surface. Mark out through a paper pattern on the surface, the shapes and sizes of the parts of the pot to be built (see Fig. 10). Run a thin knife round each shape but do not cut quite down to the table. Cut along the inside edge of each strip to allow the whole slab to contract evenly and leave it to toughen slightly. This makes it easier to handle the slabs without fear of spoiling the shape.

To assemble the parts, prepare a roll of clay, hold one of the sides against one side of the base and work a piece of coil firmly into the angle between the two parts, pressing the edges well together (see Fig. 11). Each side is dealt with in this way and the vertical angles well filled in with the roll of clay. It may be necessary to use the wooden tools instead of the fingers on the tall shapes. Suggestions for shapes are given in Figs. 12 to 15.

Drying.—Pots should be very carefully and thoroughly dried before they are fired. Slow drying is always safe. It is not wise to attempt to hasten the drying process by placing the pot in front of the fire or in the sun or in any place where one side may dry more quickly than the other, unless it is certain that the pot can be turned very frequently. A cupboard over a radiator is useful, a small gas ring or bunsen burner under the bottom of a biscuit tin, with the pots supported so that they are not in contact with the warm metal, or a long period in a warm room may each prove an efficient means of drying. The gas oven may also be used. It must be realised that a good deal depends upon the amount of care

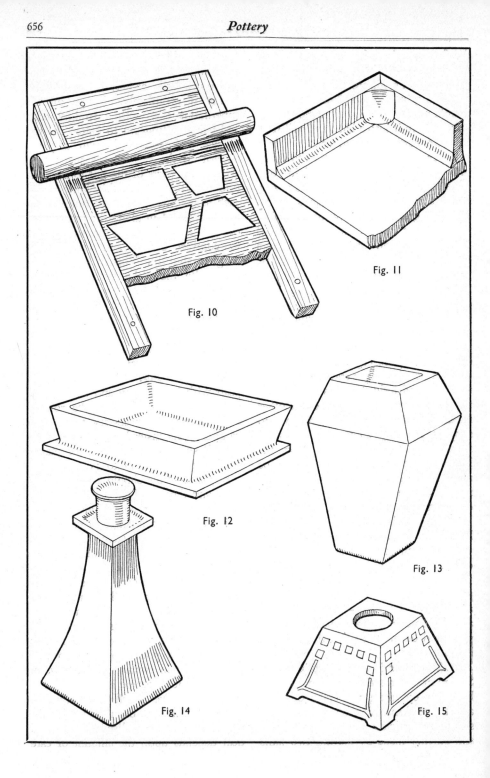

Fig. 10

Fig. 11

Fig. 12

Fig. 13

Fig. 14

Fig. 15

and thoughtfulness put into this work and many little dodges may be adopted by the thoughtful worker which in the hands of someone else would spoil a job.

Firing.—Gas, oil or electrically-fired kilns can be purchased from the manufacturers at prices varying according to size. Those who wish to acquire that kind of equipment are advised to write for quotations and advice, but most beginners take a simpler line of experiment for themselves. The real joy and excitement of work in our hobbies lies to a great extent in the opportunity provided for using our own ideas regarding any craft in which we may be interested.

Firing pots can be just as exciting. Small trials can be fired in crucibles in an open fire, on a gas ring, on a primus stove or in a gas oven. Flower pots can be used as crucibles. Where space permits a small kiln of brick can be built over a large inverted flower pot in which the dried pots are placed. The fire is built inside the brick work, and the latter is plastered over with clay leaving a hole at the top for feeding the fire. A hole is made in the pot and through the brickwork to allow inspection of the interior during firing.

If there is a brickworks in the locality it will be worth while to cultivate the acquaintance of the management with a view to obtaining permission to fire in their kilns; also to obtain their advice as to the design of a simple form. There is, however, no doubt that the gas, oil or electrically-fired furnaces are much the best for the potter in a small way. Three or four hours at top heat is sufficient to produce a pot tough enough for most purposes but to fire a pot so that when it is taken out it rings with a good clear note from twelve to twenty-four hours firing is necessary.

The Next Stages. — After your experience with hand methods of build-ing a pot you will probably be keen to work on a wheel and "throw" a pot. Simple and effective potters' wheels can be purchased for a few pounds or you can build one for yourself. If you do attempt to make your own wheel it should above all be strong and steady so that no pushing of the treadle can affect the evenness of the running.

Throwing a pot is an operation not quickly learned and should therefore be practised by trying to throw simple low shapes. Later, the height and the form of the pot might be increased and made a little more complex.

Casting.—Casting is a very common commercial method of producing pots. The method is useful to the amateur who requires to repeat a design a number of times. The shape is designed and carefully drawn on paper, care being taken that there are no undercut members in the outline as these might prevent the withdrawing of the shape from the mould. Allowance must be made for shrinkage; this can be best judged from experiments with the particular clay. The original is then modelled in the solid clay and trued up carefully to shape. If a lathe is available, this original can be turned to shape out of a block of plaster-of-paris which has been cast on to a tapered wooden mandrel. The clay positive is laid on a bed of clay, in a wooden box a little larger than itself, the surface of the clay bed being exactly along the central line of the shape. Half of the latter is now projecting above the surface of the clay bed. Liquid plaster-of-paris is poured over this projecting half and left to set for half an hour or so. Take away the sides of the box, carefully remove the clay bed from the other half of the positive, place the sides of the box again in position round the plaster block now holding the positive, cut a few holes in the surface of the plaster. Paint the latter with oil to prevent adhesion and cast liquid plaster on to the other half of the positive to a depth of $1\frac{1}{2}$ or 2 in. above the highest point. When the plaster is set, remove the sides of the box, divide the two halves of the mould, and take out the clay positive. The holes which were cut in the lower half of the mould will now be seen to have formed corresponding projections on the upper half. These act as guides to the perfect fitting of the two halves of the mould. Cut a large hole in the top of the shape to provide a channel through which liquid clay-slip can be poured.

Paint the inside of the mould and the adjacent surfaces with a mixture of soft soap, water and paraffin oil until they are no longer absorbent, when they should be rubbed with a piece of soft rag. Paint the surfaces with oil.

Tie the two halves tightly together. Mix clay with water to a thick creamy consistence by rubbing small pieces of clay in water through a fine sieve. Leave to mature, stirring frequently. Pour the slip into the mould till full; as the slip subsides, fill up again. When a sufficient thickness has been deposited—this can be tested by scraping round the top of the hole—empty out the slip into a bucket. Leave to dry for a few hours, ease off the mould, trim the edges and joint line of the casting and leave to dry. Clean up with fine glass-paper, if necessary, wipe over with a damp sponge and proceed as previously described for "Drying" and "Firing."

Glazing.—Glazing the biscuit ware, as the fired pottery is called, is by far the most exciting part of the craft. It may also be the most disappointing. Glazes can be purchased from merchants at the potteries and full instructions regarding their melting points, etc., can be obtained.

To carry out good glazing you will need a clean form of heat. A properly-built kiln is really necessary. The biscuit ware is coated inside and outside with glaze of a creamy consistency either by spraying, dipping and pouring or painting, and refired until the glaze runs freely. The heat of the kiln should be raised quite slowly and after completion of the firing cooled down very slowly to avoid cracking in the glaze.

Tilemaking.—Tiles may be made of various kinds and sizes. A box or frame of similar arrangement to Fig. 10 and of a size to give the tile required in length, breadth and thickness is necessary. The length and breadth can be varied in the frame by having adjustable cross-bars. The depth necessary for small tiles is about $\frac{5}{8}$ in. Dust the mould with french chalk or dry clay dust to prevent sticking and press a slab of clay into it. True up and toughen the surface by rolling and scraping with a straight iron edge. The tile is removed by running a knife round the edges and tapping the back of the frame. Leave the tiles to dry and toughen before firing.

Tiles with raised pattern require a frame about $1\frac{1}{4}$ in. deep. Cast a layer of plaster $\frac{5}{8}$ in. thick into the frame, take out and smooth off a level top surface. Draw the design of the tile on this surface by transferring it from the paper. Then incise it with a firm point, such as a hard pencil, to give finally a rectangular depression about $\frac{1}{24}$ in. deep. Place this plaster mould back in the wood frame and press the clay tile on to this negative to obtain the positive projection of the design.

Simple, strong designs are preferable to thinner and weaker ones.

The production of pattern on the surface can also be carried out by squeezing slip clay from a tube or tracer in the same manner that icing is put on to iced cakes. Glaze should be applied very liberally in this work.

CARDBOARD WORK

So many of the things around us which are made from paper and cardboard can be so easily and profitably made at home that we give in this section a number of variations on some well-known ideas.

Materials.—The equipment required is small and inexpensive. An ordinary pen-knife, a non-slip rule, a 6 in. 45 deg. set-square, paste, paste brushes, glue-pot, tool for fixing press studs, bookbinder's awl, leather punch, scissors, a light hammer and a piece of wood covered with rather fine emery cloth for use in sharpening the knife. A small guillotine will be useful for cutting cardboard, and one or two presses would be useful though not absolutely essential.

Greeting Cards.—This is an idea which will enable you to send cards of distinction, unlike any others your friends are likely to receive. On page 667 are several suggested designs for greeting cards. These are made from thin coloured cards or stiff paper which may be purchased in large sheets from the stationer or art dealer. The sheets with a rough surface make up very attractively; for the inside leaves use a coloured paper to match. The ribbon or cord which ties the cover and leaves together as well as the ink in which the greeting is written should also tone in with the general scheme. For example, if you use a warm dark brown colour for the cover, take a fawn coloured paper for the inside, a fawn ribbon or cord, and write the greeting inside in a dark brown ink and outside in a fawn coloured ink. The latter can be purchased ready for use, but they are easily made up from ordinary poster colour,

another scheme could be dark grey cover, light grey inside, light grey ribbon and black indian ink. Still another attractive scheme would be light grey card, pale orange colour for the ribbon and the inside, and dark brown ink.

Once you begin making cards along these lines you will find that ideas come along fairly easily, and you will be able to devise new shapes and work out your own colour schemes.

Envelopes.—How many times have you wished you had an envelope of a special shape and been unable to buy one? On page 660 are a few suggestions for making envelopes of various shapes and sizes for a variety of uses. For strong work use manila paper, or strong brown paper of any kind; for lighter work ordinary cheap cartridge paper serves quite well. Fig. 7 shows an envelope with a gussetted side and bottom. This is a useful container. If three or four more of these are made without the flap they can be stuck firmly to the front of this one and so make a very useful folio for papers, see Fig. 8.

Filing Covers and Albums. — Covers to contain papers of any kind, for use as holders for your writing pad, and also an album for photographs, films, cigarette cards are easy to make, cost very little indeed and may be just as useful and attractive as anything of the kind that you can buy. Fig. 9 is a simple cover which is made of manila or other strong paper. The holder for the papers is a large envelope made as previously described. The two are held together by a piece of cord or narrow tape passed through a hole punched in both cover and envelope. The cover

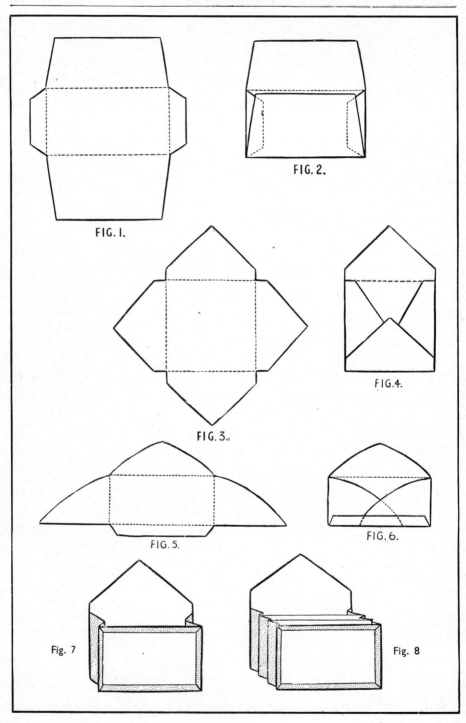

FIG. 1.

FIG. 2.

FIG. 3.

FIG. 4.

FIG. 5.

FIG. 6.

Fig. 7

Fig. 8

illustrated in Fig. 10 is also made from strong paper, or thin cardboard, with a double fold in the back. To fix the papers in this cover holes are punched through them and the cover so that they register with one another. A cord is used as a fastener, or two hinged rings may be used instead.

Fig. 11 also illustrates a cover made from strong paper. The flaps are useful for holding the contents in place. Tapes are passed through the slits in the outer cover and the ends pasted down on the inside for a length of about 2 in.

Pieces of thick card are used on the top and bottom of the packet of papers tied up in Fig. 12. The cardboard should be covered inside and out with coloured paper. Fig. 13 shows the layout for the piece to cover the outer surface. The paper is cut at the corners so that it will mitre on the inside. A piece of paper is then cut to make a panel with $\frac{1}{8}$ in. margin to cover the inner surface.

Fig. 14 shows a file which can be hung up. The back and top are all in one, made up from three pieces of cardboard set out on a large piece of paper with margins as shown. The margins are turned over and pasted down. The layout is shown in Fig. 15. The front board is a plain covered piece of cardboard made as in the previous example.

In all this work of covering cardboard with paper or cloth it is essential that you should apply paste to the whole of the surface of the paper so that solid contact is made all over the cardboard. Spread the paste evenly and not thickly. Ordinary home-made flour paste will do quite well for the purpose. It should be fairly thick and free from lumps.

Fig. 16 shows a very useful cover for a telephone or writing pad. It is made from two pieces of thick cardboard, a piece of book cloth, covering paper and two elastic bands. The size depends upon the size of the pad. Allow $\frac{1}{4}$ to $\frac{1}{2}$ in. all round the pad for the size of the bottom and top pieces of cardboard. These are laid out as in Fig. 17, AAA being the margins of paper and B a piece of bookbinder's cloth about 4 in. wide with a margin of $\frac{3}{4}$ in. at top and bottom. The pieces of cardboard are stuck down to the paper and cloth and the margins turned in. Two pieces of elastic are now fixed by folding in the ends for about 2 in. and sticking these firmly in position with some kind of liquid glue such as seccotine, croid, etc. Leave these to set before covering the inside of the boards with panels of paper. Also face up the cloth hinge with another piece of cloth, leaving a margin of about $\frac{1}{8}$ in. at each end. The cardboard back of the pad of notepaper is slipped in underneath the bands of elastic and the folio is ready for use.

An Album Cover can be made as shown in Fig. 18. The sizes will depend upon the use to which the album is to be put. The sizes given below are for cigarette cards or small snap photographs. Cut two pieces of thick cardboard 6×4 in. and three pieces 4×1 in. Lay these out, as shown, on a piece of bookcloth $5\frac{1}{2} \times 6$ in. with $\frac{1}{4}$ in. spaces between the pieces of cardboard. Remove the latter, lay paste on the cloth and replace them. Turn in the edges of the cloth and cut another piece to face up the inside, leaving a margin of $\frac{1}{8}$ in. top and bottom. Now cover the outside of each large piece of cardboard with suitable coloured paper as described for Fig. 17, overlapping the cloth edges only about $\frac{1}{8}$ in. Face up the uncovered part of the inside of the covers with panels of paper, leaving $\frac{1}{8}$ in. margin on the three outer edges. Put the cover under flat pressure to dry and set and prepare the leaves of paper which are to

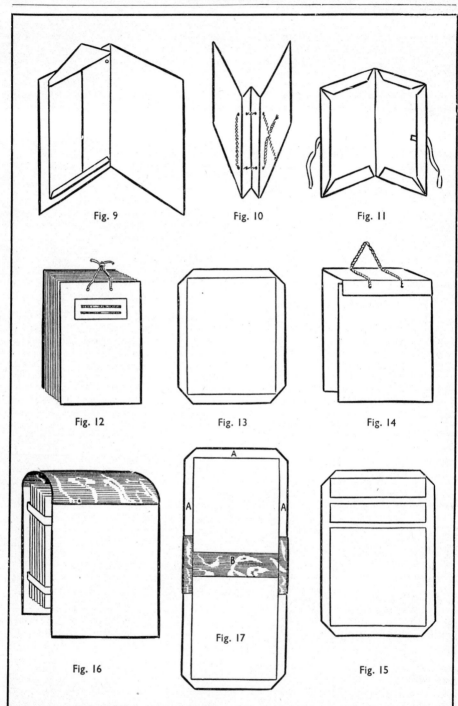

Fig. 9　　　　　Fig. 10　　　　　Fig. 11

Fig. 12　　　　　Fig. 13　　　　　Fig. 14

Fig. 16　　　　　Fig. 17　　　　　Fig. 15

form the inside of the album. These should measure in length from xx to $\frac{1}{4}$ in. from the front edge and $\frac{1}{2}$ in. narrower than the cardboard covers, i.e., in this case $3\frac{1}{2}$ in. Punch holes through these sheets and through the cover as shown and fix all together with a piece of cord. Do not fill the cover to capacity with leaves of paper, or there will be no room for the pictures when they are put in.

The method of fixing the latter is either by means of slits in the leaves through which the corners of the picture are slipped or by means of small adhesive paper discs which can be purchased very cheaply at the stores. They are decidedly less troublesome to use than any system of slits in the leaves.

A much larger example of this album can be used as a cover for any papers it is desired to file or for large pictures. This idea is quite useful for storing the pictorial records of various holidays, an album for each holiday. It should be borne in mind that the larger the size the thicker the board should be. For very large work it is necessary to use cardboard about $\frac{1}{4}$ in. thick. Do not think that it is necessary to purchase cardboard of this thickness; it can be made up by pasting or gluing together sheets of smaller thickness. It is much easier to cut the thin sheets to size and then stick them accurately together than it is to attempt to cut a board of $\frac{1}{4}$ in. thickness, i.e., unless a guillotine is available. Another point to remember is that cardboard from old boxes, advertisement cards and so on will serve just as well as any new material for all this kind of work.

Calendars.—Here is another idea which can be profitably made up in a great variety of ways at once attractive and saleable. For much of this work what is known as pastel board is necessary. This is a thin cardboard with a pleasant soft coloured surface. Both sides are almost alike. Browns, greys, blues, orange colour, soft greens, and similar shades and tints can be purchased in good variety from a good stationer's shop or art stores. A suitable picture can be used as the main decorative feature, or the manuscript pen might be used to work out a simple border design.

The Colour Schemes are very important in all this kind of work. The pictures must tone with the background. If the large piece of cardboard or thick paper used for the back is anything from cream to brown in colour, a picture in shades of brown will be safe to put on it. It is generally advisable to cover the front of the small calendar with a piece of the same paper or thin card, or a paper in a lighter or darker shade or tint. Another point which is helpful is this; if the background is dark in colour, let the picture and cover to the calendar be in a lighter shade; if it is light in colour, put on a picture and calendar cover which is darker. In this way simple contrast is obtained which adds quality to the whole. Further, if ink is to be used, make it from ordinary poster colour and make it to tone or contrast with the paper. Cream coloured ink on a brown background, orange colour on blue, greenish yellow on purple, brown on cream, green on red and so on are all good to use.

When you have mounted a picture on a background you may feel that you have not quite secured the result you wanted. Try the effect of a line drawn about $\frac{1}{4}$ in. away all round the picture. The ink should be of a colour to contrast with the background. It will generally sharpen up the whole composition and give you a far finer result.

Blotters, Writing Pads and Cases. —There is a great variety of forms into which these useful cases, etc., can be made up. The main consideration in all of them is that they should be strong enough to stand hard wear. They are made in thick cardboard, paper, bookbinder's cloth of various qualities, or leather, and may be either quite inexpensive or fairly costly and valuable and fit for any desk. Where leather is used, tooled decoration on the surface adds to the value.

As in any other section of this type of work it is important that the finished article should be pleasant in colour. Blue cloth and grey paper, green cloth and light brown or grey paper, fawn cloth and brown paper or vice versa, are all safe and enjoyable, but the reader will no doubt his own ideas for colour combinations.

Fig. 19 shows a simple straightforward blotter which can be made in any size to suit requirements. Use cardboard about $\frac{1}{8}$ in. in thickness. Cover the top surface of the cardboard with paper and fold the paper over the edges on to the underside about 1 in. all round. Now cut out four 4 in. squares of cloth, paste each one on the underside, fold in two as shown and then cut off the corner about 1 in. each way as shown in the small sketches. Paste these in position on each corner of the covered cardboard, allowing about $\frac{3}{4}$ in. overlap on the underside of the latter. Paste only on that part of the cloth which is in contact underneath and leave a space between the triangular shaped piece of cloth on the top surface and the latter so as to allow room for the blotting paper to be inserted. Cover the underside with a panel of paper, insert blotting paper to match the cloth corners, place under flat pressure and leave to set.

Fig. 20 shows a large piece of thick cardboard covered with paper, on which is fixed, on the left-hand side, a blotter made as in Fig. 19 and, on the right, a calendar and a note pad or diary. The two latter are covered with paper or cloth to match the blotter.

Fig. 21 is made from three pieces of fairly thick cardboard, bound by a piece of book cloth to form a folding cover, the remainder of the outside covered with paper and the inside lined with cloth and paper. A blotter is made and stuck down on one side and a pad of paper covered and stuck down on the other side. It should be remembered that the thickness of the blotter and pad together must not exceed the width of the piece of cardboard in the middle of the back cover or the case will not close properly.

Fig. 22 is a similar case so far as the cover and the blotter on one side are concerned. On the right-hand side a small gussetted envelope to contain paper and envelopes is made and stuck in position.

Fig. 23 shows a much larger writing case which is just as simple in construction as the previous examples. This should be made of cardboard up to $\frac{3}{16}$ in. thick.

Writing Pads.—It is not a difficult matter to make up your own pads of paper for use in all this kind of work. Fix together a number of sheets of paper, perfectly flat at the top edge. Cut a piece of muslin about 2 in. wider than the thickness of the pad and the same length as the width of the latter. Place the pad of paper under pressure, with the true edge projecting to keep all the leaves tightly together, and paint the projecting edge with seccotine or liquid glue. Leave it for a few minutes until it dries a little and then place the muslin centrally on the tacky edge and rub it well so that the mesh is engaged with the glue. Leave to dry and set. Now fold the $\frac{3}{4}$ in. pieces of muslin which project over on to the sides. Cut a piece of cardboard for the top and one for the bottom and stick them down,

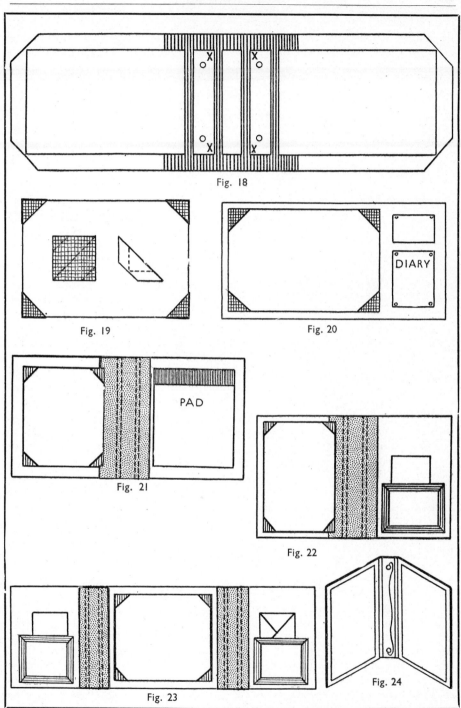

Fig. 18

Fig. 19

Fig. 20

DIARY

PAD

Fig. 21

Fig. 22

Fig. 23

Fig. 24

one on each side to the end papers and the muslin. Cover the top piece with coloured paper, folding over the edges on to the inside and then paste back another sheet of the pad to cover the folded edges.

Magazine Cover.—Fig. 24 shows the details of the cover which can be used to protect any kind of weekly magazine which may come into the house. It is made from three pieces of thick cardboard. The centre back piece is only about $\frac{1}{2}$ in. wide. It may be omitted and the same space allowed between the large pieces of cardboard. When the outer piece of cloth is fixed, two holes are punched in the position shown, a piece of cord or a narrow tape threaded through and the ends either knotted outside each hole or they are continued outside the back and tied together. The paper or magazine is opened at the centre and threaded underneath the cord.

Coloured-cover Papers.—In all this work it is very interesting to make your own coloured papers for use in covering. Distinctive colours and patterns can be obtained in a variety of ways.

Paste-coloured Papers.—A very simple method is as follows: Take a sheet of plain paper, not too large, either coloured or white, paint it with water and then with thin paste. A thin flour paste does quite well. Now mix some water colour, rather thick, and put dabs of it all over in any sort of way. Work the paint so that it covers the whole of the surface. Begin to work pattern into this film of colour by dabbing it with the brush or making zig-zag lines with it. Or, take a small sponge and dab the surface regularly. Or again, cut teeth in the edge of a piece of stiff cardboard and comb pattern into the colour. Even the finger ends may be used to make pattern, or a screwed-up piece of paper. You will find that you can obtain quite distinctive patterns in some odd way which no one else has thought of. If you use coloured paper as your background, you can increase the colour interest of the work. Mix the separate water colours on the paper and obtain a variety in the surface itself.

These papers are useful both as cover and as lining papers and they can be used with the best class of work.

Oil-coloured Marbled Paper.—papers made by the following process can be used on the very best work in cardboard or bookbinding. Any one can obtain really first-class results if a little thought is applied while carrying out the operations.

The Materials (Paper). — Any plain-coloured clean paper will do— e.g., white drawing paper, coloured pastel paper, rough or smooth (unglazed) brown or other packing paper, or the back of suitable wallpaper.

Oil Colours.—Half-pound or pound tins of oil colour as sold by the iron-monger or colourman. The small tins of oil colour sold by artists' colourmen are cheap and give very good results.

Paraffin or Turpentine.—One of these (not both together at any time) to be used as a thinner for the oil colour. Paraffin is cheaper than turpentine and generally more easily obtained, but not quite so effective.

Brushes.—For use in mixing the colours and splashing them on the size. Any small paste or paint brushes will do.

Combs.—Any hard-pointed instrument will serve as a comb—e.g., a metal meat skewer, an old comb, a pencil point or a fork—or a comb may be made by driving nails, say 2 in. long, at intervals through a piece of wood $\frac{3}{4}$ or 1 in. thick × about 2 in. wide, or smaller nails through a thinner piece of wood.

Tray.—A tin tray may be made from

SUGGESTIONS FOR GREETING CARDS   Fig. 26

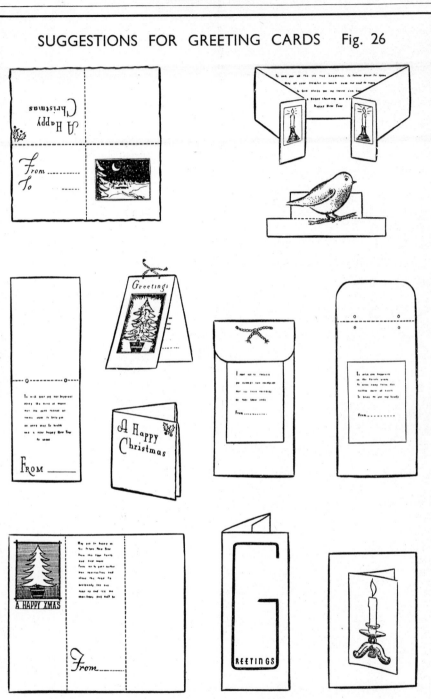

a biscuit-tin lid, but this is rather small. A good useful one is made from tin plate 19×15 in., turned up 1 in. all round and the corner joints soldered so that they are watertight. This gives a tray 17×13×1 in. deep, large enough for paper 15×11 in.

Method.—Dissolve 2 oz. of paper-hangers' size in 1 pint of boiling water. When completely dissolved, add water to make up to about 2 quarts. Pour into the tray and leave until cold. To test the size in order to ascertain the right state of fluidity, slightly lift one corner of the tray. The size it contains should run freely and not show any part of the surface which is "jellied" and does not run. If any part of the surface is like jelly, stir in a little more hot water to reduce the stickiness.

The Colours.—Put a brush full of oil colour in a jar and add about the same quantity of turpentine and stir well. Mix up the necessary variety of colours.

Preparation of Colour and Pattern on the Size.—With a brush for each colour, splash spots of colour on to the surface of the size. If the colour thins out quickly on the size and loses practically all its strength it is too thin; add more colour to the mixture. If the colour sinks to the bottom of the size, it is too thick; add a little more turps or paraffin to the mixture. Having applied the various colours which are required in the scheme—two or at most three colours are sufficient—begin to work up the pattern with the combing tool. When satisfied with the effect, take a sheet of paper, hold it by two opposite edges, allow it to dip in the

middle and lower it gently on to the surface of the size. Tap the sheet all over to ensure that the whole of the surface is in contact with the size and to exclude all air bubbles. Take hold of opposite corners of the sheet and lift carefully. Allow the superfluous size to run off into the tray.

To Dry the Print. — Place the printed sheet in front of a fire or on a radiator. A second print may be taken off. It will be thinner than the first and will serve for end papers for books, while the first print is used for cover papers.

Ironing the Paper. — When the printed sheet is dry, it may be perfectly flattened by ironing with a hot iron, applied on either the marbled or the blank side of the paper.

Hints.—The size "goes off" in about twelve days and should be thrown away and a new lot made.

Clear the size after each print, or two prints, by drawing through the size a folded piece of newspaper. This will lift off any spots or bits of colour.

In working the pattern draw the tool slowly through the surface of the size and so avoid breaking up the colour too much. More definite pattern can be obtained in this way and the colour is not driven to the bottom of the size. Avoid large unbroken patches of any one colour. If smaller quantities are to be dealt with, tubes of ivory black, Prussian blue, emerald green, raw sienna and scarlet oil colours will be found to give a wide range of colour effects.

Any shades of colour it is required to print must be mixed in the jars before applying to the size.

PAPIER MÂCHÉ AND CEMENT WORK

SERVICEABLE bowls for use in winter when putting the bulbs into fibre for spring flowering can be made out of waste newspaper or any other soft paper.

Materials for Papier Mâché.— You will need two or three basins or clean aluminium pans, a quantity of ordinary flour paste and plenty of waste paper.

Tear the paper into small shreds not more than 3 or 4 in. in area and soak it well in water. Take the basin or pan, place it upside down on the table and put a layer of damp strips of paper all over the outside, see Fig. 1. Work quickly so as to preserve an even thickness.

Having covered the basin with one layer paint it all over with paste. Now put on another layer of paper. Paint this with paste and carry on until about ¼ in. of paper has been laid evenly and firmly all over the basin. Leave this to dry and set. The paper casting can now be removed.

Trim the edges true with a sharp knife and glass-paper. Rub down the unevenness of the outside and the inside with glass-paper so as to form as smooth and even a surface as possible. Decide now what colour the finished bowl is to be. Paint it with oil or water colour and leave it to dry. Now paint it with thin paperhanger's size and leave again to set. Finally paint the outside and inside with clear varnish.

Another method of colouring which gives good solid effects is to paint the bowl with size when it is dry, leave it for several hours to set and then paint with enamel of the required colour.

The above method of putting the paper on to the outside of a bowl gives a smooth inside to the papier mâché bowl. If it is desired to have the outside of the bowl as true as possible in shape, then the pieces of paper must be laid on the *inside* of the bowl or pan being used as a mould, as in Fig. 2.

At all times when laying this kind of papier mâché good pressure should be applied in order to squeeze out all superfluous water and air pockets, so making the thickness of the sides as solid as possible.

Another method of making papier mâché is as follows: Tear up into strips any old newspaper or a coarse brown paper. Put it to soak in water until thoroughly saturated. Now place it in a saucepan with a little water on the fire or gas ring and bring to the boil. Add about a pint of flour paste to a gallon of paper pulp and stir well. This mixture which is quite pulpy can be modelled on to the outside or the inside of a basin or pan. When being laid it should be welded together by overlapping and pressure. Care must be taken to obtain an even thickness throughout. Leave to set as before, and smooth the surfaces with glass-paper.

If about 1 lb. of whiting is added to this mixture the result is most useful for modelling of all kinds. Relief maps, fruit and animal shapes, beads, toys, marbles and almost any form can be modelled in it. When dry and set the result is very hard and tough. It can be glass-papered to a fine surface, painted to any scheme and varnished or enamelled to a good finish.

It is also possible to press this mixture into moulds cut in wood or made in plaster-of-paris.

Cement Work.—A good deal of profitable occupation can be obtained by making tiles for the scullery or bath room, garden paths, teapot and dish stands, door stops, etc. Cement can be purchased at about 2s. 9d. per hundredweight, and when mixed in the right proportion with sand and gravel and allowed to set, a hard-wearing substance is obtained. Decorative effects can be obtained by the use of colours and/or modelled form.

Garden-path Tiles.—Paving tiles for the garden paths can be made by fixing together four strips $2 \times \frac{3}{4}$ in. wood as shown in Fig. 3. These can be fixed at each corner by means of a piece of dowel rod slipped into holes in each piece at a corner. These fit fairly loosely so that they can be easily withdrawn when necessary. Small pointed irons bent and used as in Fig. 3 can also be used. This framework acts as a mould into which the mixed cement is placed. Make about a dozen of these frames so that you can get on with the work more quickly.

Garden tiles do not need to be made of a very fine texture so the mixture of cement, sand and gravel will be fairly coarse. Take one measure—say one shovel or one bucketful—of cement, two measures of sand and three of gravel, and pour them out on to a flat board. Mix them thoroughly together with a shovel while dry. Then add water through the rose of a watering-can and mix thoroughly until a good plastic mass is obtained. Now shovel some of the mixture into each mould or frame until they are all filled level with the top edge. Leave these to set for two days and then remove the frames by pulling out the pegs or iron dogs and tapping the pieces of wood with a hammer to remove them from the edge of the tile. While the tiles are setting, you should prepare the bed of the path which is to be tiled.

Laying the Tiles.—The tiles can be laid dry on a bed of ashes. The joints can be filled in with cement and sand mortar or they may be filled with soil and small flower seeds sown in them. The size of the tiles may be made to suit the width of the path. The larger the tile, the thicker it should be, from 1 to 2 in. being a useful thickness.

Various colours may be introduced if required by mixing powdered colours such as yellow ochre, various reds, burnt sienna, burnt umber, lamp black, and so on, with sand and cement and water, so making a coloured cement. A thin layer of this is put into each mould before the bulk of the natural-coloured mixture is put in.

Small Tiles. — Small tiles with patterned surfaces can be made quite simply. These tiles make quite distinctive presents for your friends as well as being quite saleable.

If you wish to make tiles which are quite plain in colour, proceed as above described, using a mould which is only $\frac{3}{8}$ in. deep. Make up a mixture of one part of cement to one of fine sand, with colour as desired.

These small tiles are quite easily made in the house, care being taken not to stir up the cement so much that it is scattered in the air. Patterned tiles are far more interesting to make. The pattern may be in colour, incised or raised ornament. A pattern which can be worked out by anyone of these methods is given in Fig. 4.

Coloured Tiles.—To carry out this idea in colour, prepare the mould as before to the size of the tile; 6 in. square is the usual size. Draw the pattern on a piece of stiff paper. Mix neat cement with colour and sufficient water to make it plastic. Take a small brush and paint this mixture on to the pattern to a thickness of about $\frac{1}{8}$ in. Place this while wet into the bottom of the mould with the cement pattern upwards, see Fig. 5. Mix one part each of cement and fine

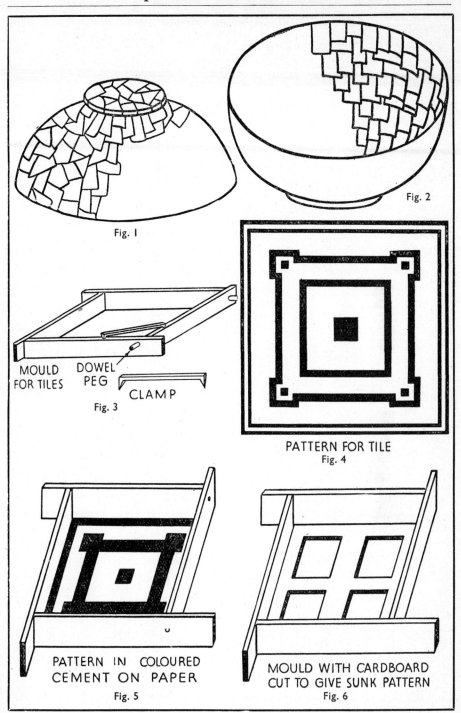

Fig. 1

Fig. 2

MOULD FOR TILES   DOWEL PEG   CLAMP

Fig. 3

PATTERN FOR TILE
Fig. 4

PATTERN IN COLOURED CEMENT ON PAPER
Fig. 5

MOULD WITH CARDBOARD CUT TO GIVE SUNK PATTERN
Fig. 6

sand with water and fill the mould. If a number of moulds are made, the production will be increased. Leave the mixture to set for two days. Knock away the moulds and remove the paper. The pattern will be found to be in colour on the surface.

Sunk Pattern.—The pattern in Fig. 6 can be sunk in the surface by cutting out the squares and so leaving the cross and border in a piece of cardboard which fits into the mould as shown in the illustration. Place this cut out pattern on the bottom of the mould and fill in the cement mixture as before. Leave to set for two days, take away the mould, tear off the cardboard, and so obtain a recessed pattern. This is carefully filled with a coloured cement mixture and left to set for a few days.